American Pedagogy.

# EDUCATION,

# THE SCHOOL, AND THE TEACHER,

IN

# AMERICAN LITERATURE.

REPUBLISHED FROM
Barnard's American Journal of Education.

SECOND EDITION.

HARTFORD:
BROWN & GROSS.
1876.

# CONTENTS.

# EARLY TRAINING.

## APHORISMS AND SUGGESTIONS—ANCIENT AND MODERN.

---

We are physiologically connected and set forth in our beginnings, and it is a matter of immense consequence to our character, what the connection is. In our birth we not only begin to breathe and circulate blood, but it is a question hugely significant whose the blood may be. For in this we have whole rivers of predispositions, good or bad, set running in us—as much more powerful to shape our future than all tuitional and regulative influences that come after, as they are earlier in their beginning, deeper in their insertion, and more constant in their operation.

Here, then, is the real and true beginning of a godly nurture. The child is not to have the sad entail of any sensuality, or excess, or distempered passion upon him. The heritage of love, peace, order, continence and holy courage is to be his. He is not to be morally weakened beforehand, in the womb of folly, by the frivolous, worldly, ambitious, expectations of parents-to-be, concentrating all their nonsense in him. His affinities are to be raised by the godly expectations, rather, and prayers that go before; by the steady and good aims of their industry, by the great impulse of their faith, by the brightness of their hope, by the sweet continence of their religiously pure love in Christ. Born, thus, of a parentage that is ordered in all righteousness, and maintains the right use of every thing, especially the right use of nature and marriage, the child will have just so much of heaven's life and order in him beforehand, as have become fixed properties in the type of his parentage.

Observe how very quick the child's eye is, in the passive age of infancy, to catch impressions, and receive the meaning of looks, voices, and motions. It peruses all faces, and colors, and sounds. Every sentiment that looks into its eyes, looks back out of its eyes, and plays in miniature on its countenance. The tear that steals down the cheek of a mother's suppressed grief, gathers the little infantile face into a responsive sob. With a kind of wondering silence, which is next thing to adoration, it studies the mother in her prayer, and looks up piously with her, in that exploring watch, that signifies unspoken prayer. If the child is handled fretfully, scolded, jerked, or simply laid aside unaffectionately, in no warmth of motherly gentleness, it feels the sting of just that which is felt towards it; and so it is angered by anger, irritated by irritation, fretted by fretfulness; having thus impressed, just that kind of impatience or ill-nature, which is felt towards it, and growing faithfully into the bad mold offered, as by a fixed law. There is great importance, in this manner, even in the handling of infancy. If it is unchristian, it will beget unchristian states, or impressions. If it is gentle, ever patient and loving, it prepares a mood and temper like its own. There is scarcely room to doubt, that all most crabbed, hateful, resentful, passionate, ill-natured characters; all most even, lovely, firm and true, are prepared, in a great degree, by the handling of the nursery. To these and all such modes of feeling and treatment as make up the element of the infant's life, it is passive as wax to the seal. So that if we consider how small a speck, falling into the nucleus of a crystal, may disturb its form; or, how even a mote of foreign matter present in the quickening egg, will suffice to produce a deformity; considering, also, on the other hand, what nice conditions of repose, in one case, and what accurately modulated supplies of heat in the other, are necessary to a perfect product; then only do we begin to imagine what work is going on, in the soul of a child, in this first chapter of life, the age of impressions.

I have no scales to measure quantities of effect in this matter of early training, but I may be allowed to express my solemn conviction, that more, as a general fact, is done, or lost by neglect of doing, on a child's immortality, in the first three years of his life, than in all his years of discipline afterwards. And I name this particular time, or date, that I may not be supposed to lay the chief stress of duty and care on the latter part of what I have called the age of impressions; which, as it is a matter somewhat indefinite, may be taken to cover the space of three or four times this number of years; the development of language, and of moral ideas being only partially accomplished, in most cases, for so long a time. Let every Christian father and mother understand, when their child is three years old, that they have done more than half of all they will ever do for his character. What can be more strangely wide of all just apprehension, than the immense efficacy, imputed by most parents to the Christian ministry, compared with what they take to be the almost insignificant power conferred on them in their parental charge and duties. Why, if all preachers of Christ could have their hearers, for whole months and years, in their own will, as parents do their children, so as to move them by a look, a motion, a smile, a frown, and act their own sentiments and emotions over in them at pleasure; if, also, a little farther on, they had them in authority to command, direct, tell them whither to go, what to learn, what to do, regulate their hours, their books, their pleasures, their company, and call them to prayer over their own knees every night and morning, who would think it impossible, in the use of such a power, to produce almost any result? Should not such a ministry be expected to fashion all who come under it to newness of life? Let no parent, shifting off his duties to his children, in this manner, think to have his defects made up, and the consequent damages mended afterwards, when they have come to their maturity, by the comparatively slender, always doubtful, efficacy of preaching and pulpit harangue.

Dr. Bushnell. *Christian Nurture.*

"A virtuous and noble education" is whatever tends to train up to a healthy and graceful activity our mental and bodily powers, our affections, manners, and habits. It is the business, of course, of all our lives, or, more properly, of the whole duration of our being. But since impressions made early are the deepest and most lasting, that is, above all, education which tends in childhood and youth to form a manly, upright, and generous character, and thus to lay the foundation for a course of liberal and virtuous self-culture.

ALONZO POTTER. *The School and Schoolmaster.*

Costly apparatus and splendid cabinets have no magical power to make scholars. As a man is, in all circumstances under God, the master of his own fortune, so is he the maker of his own mind. The Creator has so constituted the human intellect, that it can only grow by its own action; and it will certainly and necessarily grow. Every man must therefore educate himself. His books and his teachers are but his helps; the work is his. A man is not educated until he has the ability to summon, on an emergency, his mental powers in vigorous exercise to affect his proposed object. It is not the man who has seen the most, or read the most who can do this; such an one is in danger of being borne down, like a beast of burden, by an overloaded mass of other men's thoughts. Nor is it the man who can boast merely of native vigor and capacity. The greatest of all the warriors who went to the siege of Troy, had not the preëminence because nature had given him strength, and he carried the largest bow; but because self-discipline had taught him how to bend it.

DANIEL WEBSTER.

Education is development, not instruction merely—not knowledge, facts, rules—communicated by the teacher, but it is discipline, it is a waking up of the mind, a growth of the mind—growth by a healthy assimilation of wholesome aliment. It is an inspiring of the mind with a thirst for knowledge, growth, enlargement—and then a disciplining of its powers so far that it can go on to educate itself. It is the arousing of the child's mind to think, without thinking for it; it is the awakening of its powers to observe, to remember, to reflect, to combine. It is not a cultivation of the memory to the neglect of every thing else; but is a calling forth of all the faculties into harmonious action.

DAVID PAGE. *Theory and Practice.*

Oh, woe to those who trample on the mind,
That deathless thing! They know not what they do,
Nor what they deal with. Man, perchance, may bind
The flower his step hath bruised; or light anew
The torch he quenches; or to music wind
Again the lyre-string from his touch that flew;—
But for the soul, oh, tremble, and beware
To lay rude hands upon God's mysteries there!

*Anonymous.*

We regard education as the formation of the character, physical, intellectual, and moral; as the process by which our faculties are developed, cultivated, and directed, and by which we are prepared for our station and employment, for usefulness and happiness, for time and eternity. W. C. WOODBRIDGE.

All intelligent thinkers upon the subject now utterly discard and repudiate the idea that reading and writing, with a knowledge of accounts, constitute education. The lowest claim which any intelligent man now prefers in its behalf is, that its domain extends over the threefold nature of man; over his body, training it by the systematic and intelligent observance of those benign laws which secure health, impart strength and prolong life; over his intellect, invigorating the mind, replenishing it with knowledge, and cultivating all these tastes, which are allied to virtue; and over his moral and religious susceptibilities also, dethroning selfishness, enthroning conscience, leading the affections outwardly in good-will towards man, and upward in gratitude, and reverence to God.

Far above and beyond all special qualifications for special pursuits, is the importance of forming to usefulness and honor the capacities which are common to all mankind. The endowments that belong to all, are of far greater consequences than the peculiarities of any. The practical farmer, the ingenious mechanic, the talented artist, the upright legislator or judge, the accomplished teacher, are only modifications or varieties of the original *man*. The man is the trunk; occupations and professions are only different qualities of the fruit it yields. The development of the common nature; the cultivation of the germs of intelligence, uprightness, benevolence, truth that belong to all; these are the principal, the aim, the end,—while special preparations for the field or the shop, for the forum or the desk, for the land or the sea, are but incidents.

The great necessities of a race like ours, in a world like ours, are: a Body, grown from its elemental beginning, in health; compacted with strength and vital with activity in every part; impassive to heat and cold, and victorious over the vicissitudes of seasons and zones; not crippled by disease nor stricken down by early death; not shrinking from bravest effort, but panting, like fleetest runner, less for the prize than for the joy of the race; and rejuvenant amid the frosts of age. A Mind, as strong for the immortal as is the body for the mortal life; alike enlightened by the wisdom and beaconed by the errors of the past; through intelligence of the laws of nature, guiding her elemental forces, as it directs the limbs of its own body through the nerves of motion, thus making alliance with the exhaustless forces of nature for its strength and clothing itself with her endless charms for its beauty, and, wherever it goes, carrying a sun in its hand with which to explore the realms of nature, and reveal her yet hidden truths. And then a Moral Nature, presiding like a divinity over the whole, banishing sorrow and pain, gathering in earthly joys and immortal hopes, and transfigured and rapt by the sovereign and sublime aspiration TO KNOW AND DO THE WILL OF GOD.

HORACE MANN.

# PREFATORY REMARKS.

THE series of lectures, of which the following are a part, was addressed, originally, to students pursuing a course of professional study, under the author's direction, in the Merrimack (N. H.) Normal Institute, and in the New England Normal Institute, Lancaster, Massachusetts. The course, as delivered, extended to the subjects of physical, moral, and æsthetic culture; including, under the latter heads, remarks on principle as the foundation of character, and suggestions on the cultivation of taste.

In the delivery of the lectures, it was deemed important to avoid the unfavorable influence of formal didactic exposition, in a course of professional lectures to a youthful audience. Equal importance, however, was attached to a strict observance of the systematic connection of topics, and the theoretic unity of the whole subject. The method adopted, therefore, in the routine of the lecture-room, was to treat a given point daily, in a brief oral address on one prominent topic, selected from the notes embodying the plan of the whole course.

At the suggestion of Dr. Henry Barnard, the notes, in their connected form, were transcribed for insertion in his Journal; and the lectures on Intellectual Education were selected for this purpose, rather as an experiment, on the part of the author, in his uncertainty how far it might be advisable to present the whole series. But the unexpectedly favorable reception which the course on intellectual education has met from teachers, both at home and abroad, would have induced the writer to transcribe the other portions of the series, had health and time permitted. The subjects here referred to, however, will be introduced, from time to time, as may be practicable, in future numbers of Dr. Barnard's Journal.

The thoughts presented in the following pages, the author hopes, may serve to attract the attention of teachers who are so situated as to occupy the ground not merely of instructors but of educators, who have it in their power to control, to some extent, the plan and progress of education; and all teachers of the requisite zeal and thoughtfulness, even in the most limited sphere of responsibility, can do much in this way, by their personal endeavors in instruction. It is not in one department only, or in one stage, that the field of education needs resurveying.

The whole subject, notwithstanding our many valuable recent improvements in processes and methods, physical and moral, as well as intellectual, needs a careful reconsideration as to its true requirements, and a thorough revision of our plan of procedure and modes of culture.

It is true that, in seminaries of education of every grade, we are ceasing from a blind following of prescription imposed by the past. Mental discipline, rather than intellectual acquisition, is now more generally recognized as the true aim of education; and liberal changes and generous allowances, as regards the adaptation of text-books and plans of instruction, have accordingly been made. But, as yet, the point of view selected by most even of our most considerate and genial counselors on the great theme of education, has been far from a commanding one. It has been that of subjects and sciences and departments of knowledge, with their respective demands upon the mind, instead of that of the mind itself, and its divine laws of action and progress, as prescribed by its own constitution and wants, its appetites and instinctive preferences. To attract attention to these, as the true principles of education, is the chief aim of the suggestions embodied in the following pages.

## PART I.

# INTELLECTUAL EDUCATION.

# CONTENTS.

# CULTIVATION OF THE PERCEPTIVE FACULTIES.

INTRODUCTORY OBSERVATIONS.—The circumstances in which the following lectures were delivered, will, it is thought, account for the prominence given in them to many things merely elementary, as regards the science of mind and the philosophy of education. An audience favored with the advantages of high intellectual culture, or of long experience in instruction, would, doubtless, have required a different treatment of many topics discussed in such a course of lectures as the present. But a long series of years occupied in the training of teachers, has proved to the author of the present communication, that the greater number of candidates for the office of instruction, and of those to whom its duties are comparatively new, need nothing so much as an elementary knowledge of intellectual philosophy, and of logic, in their connection with education, as the science which teaches the appropriate development and discipline of the mind.

*The Teacher's Aim in Instruction.*—Few teachers, at the present day, regard knowledge as the great end even of intellectual education. Few are now unwilling to admit that the chief aim of their daily endeavors, as instructors and educators, should be to train, develop, and discipline the powers by which knowledge is acquired, rather than tc attempt the immediate accumulation of knowledge itself. In practice, however, and, more particularly, in the case of young teachers, and of those who follow the occupation as a transient one, and not as the vocation of a life-time, the eagerness for definite and apparent results, or even showy acquirements, too often induces the instructor to confine his attention to the mere mechanism of specific processes, —to the committing to memory, and the repetition of a set task, with or without the aid of explanation. This course he knows will nominally secure a single point in practice or effect. He thinks, perhaps, that, although not fully understood or appreciated now, it will certainly benefit the mind of his pupil at some future day, when his

*The series of lectures of which the present forms a part, extended to the departments of physical and moral training. But those on the progress of intellectual culture. are selected as more easily presented in the form of a series of articles for an educational Journal.

mind is more mature. Hence, we still have, in our school routine, too much of mere rule and repetition, detached fact and specific direction, the lesson of the hour and the business of the day, and too little of the searching interrogation, close observation, reflective thought, and penetrating investigation, by which alone the mind can be trained to the acquisition of useful knowledge, or the attainment of valuable truth.

*Necessity of Plan and Method.*—The master builder, when he goes to oversee his workmen, and watch their progress in the work of raising the edifice, for the construction of which he has entered into contract, never fails to carry with him his plan of erection, and with that in his hand, for constant reference, gives directions for even the minutest details in working. He does nothing but in execution of his plan, and in strict accordance with it. The master builder thus reads a lesson to the master instructor, (inward builder,) who, although he needs not plan in hand, for his peculiar work, needs it no less, ever present to his mind, if he wishes to become "a workman that needeth not to be ashamed;" if, in a word, he would enjoy the conscious pleasure of referring every day's labor to its destined end of building up the mental fabric in strength, and symmetry, and enduring beauty.

The young teacher, as he reviews the business of the day with his pupils,—and would that this were a daily practice in every school!—should ever refer, in his own mind, at least, to the general effect of every exercise, as tending to the great results of education,—to the expansion of the mind, to the formation of habits of observation and inquiry, to control over attention, to the clearing and sharpening of the percipient faculties, to the strengthening of the mind's retentive power, to securing, in a word, intellectual tendency and character, as the basis of moral development and habit. The teacher, not less than the builder, should ever have, in his mind's eye, the plan of his edifice; and while, during the whole process of erection, he wastes no time on fanciful theory or fantastic ornament, every operation which he conducts should be, to his own consciousness, part of a great whole, tending to a grand consummation. Text-books, processes, exercises, apparatus of every description, are properly, but the pliant tools, or the subject material, in the hands of the skillful teacher, by means of which he does his great work of "building up the being that we are;" and all these aids he arranges, selects, modifies, and applies, according to the system suggested by his plan and purpose.

As the overseer and artificer of the mental fabric of character, the teacher who is worthy of the name, must necessarily possess a knowledge of the material on which he works. It would be well, were this knowledge always profound and philosophical; and, among the happy anticipations suggested by the establishment of normal schools, none is more cheering than the hope that, ere long, society will be furnished with a numerous class of teachers, competent to understand and guide the young mind through all its stages of growth and development, and furnished with all the requisite means of securing the noblest results of human culture.

Meanwhile, the laborers who are already in the field, and who have not enjoyed, perhaps, extensive opportunities of acquiring a scientific knowledge of the chemistry of mental culture, must be content with such aids as their own observation, reading, reflection, or experience, may furnish.

As a slight contribution to the common stock of professional facilities, the author of the present article would submit the following outline to the consideration of his fellow teachers, as an intended aid to the systematizing of their efforts for the mental advancement of their pupils.

The analysis which follows, extends, it will be perceived, no farther than to the limits of intellectual education. The physical and the moral departments of culture, may be discussed at another opportunity, and must be dismissed for the present, with the single remark, that the natural unity of the human being, demands a ceaseless attention to these, in strict conjunction with that more immediately under consideration.

Preliminary Analysis.—Contemplating man's intellectual constitution as subjected to the processes of education, we may conveniently group his mental powers and faculties under the following denominations:—*perceptive*, *reflective*, and *expressive*. In expression, as a function of man at the period of his maturity, the order, in the preceding classification, may be termed the normal or usual one. Man perceives, reflects, speaks. But in education, whether regarded as a natural process or an artificial one, the order of classification suggested by the experience and the history of the human being, in his early and comparatively immature condition, would present the *expressive* powers as in exercise long before the *reflective*, and, subsequently, as the appointed means of developing these, through the medium of language.

Outline of Intellectual Culture.—An outline map, or plan of intellectual culture, as aided by the processes of education, may be carried into practical detail, as suggested by the following prominent points of analysis.

1. Classification of the intellectual faculties, by the different modes, or forms of mental action.

2. Statement of the actuating principle, or impelling power of each class or group of faculties.

3. The tendency, or habit of action in each class.

4. The result, or issue of such action.

5. The educational processes adapted to each class of faculties with a view to aid its natural tendency, and secure its results.

From the imperfection of our language, in relation to topics strictly mental, or purely philosophical, the word *faculties* is unavoidably employed to represent the diversities in modes of action of the mind, which, in itself, is, properly speaking, one and indivisible. But if we keep fully before us the etymological signification of the term *faculties*, (resources, means, powers,) we shall regard it but as a figurative expression, suggestive of the indefinitely diversified states, acts, operations, processes, powers, or modes of action, attributable to the mind, —itself a unit.

Adopting the general classification before referred to, we may commence the partial filling up of our outline with

## I. THE PERCEPTIVE FACULTIES.

1. Their *modes* or forms of action :

*a*, sensation ; *b*, perception ; *c*, attention : *d*, observation.

2. *Actuating principle*, or impelling force, *curiosity*,—or the desire of knowledge.

3. *Tendency*, or habit of action,—*observation*.

4. *Result*, or issue of action,—*knowledge*.

5. *Educational process*, forms of exercise, or modes of culture, development, and discipline suggested by the four preceding considerations,—*examination*, *analysis*, *inspection*, *interrogation*, *direction*, *information*, *comparison*, *classification*, *induction*. In other words, the appropriate *presentation of objects to the senses*, accompanied by mutual question and answer by teacher and pupil ;—with a view to quicken sensation, awaken perception, give power of prompt and sustained attention, confirm the habit of careful observation, stimulate curiosity, and insure the extensive acquisition of knowledge.

### (1.) CLASSIFICATION OF THE PERCEPTIVE FACULTIES, BY THEIR MODES OF ACTION.

(*a*,) *Sensation*,—the *organic* action by which objects, facts, and relations are presented to the mind, through the media of the *senses*, and which form the conditions of perception.

(*b*,) *Perception*, or cognition,—the *intellectual* action by which the mind *perceives*, (takes notice, or cognizance of,) data presented by the senses.

(c,) *Attention*,—the *mental* action by which, under the incitation of *desire* or *volition*, the percipient intellect *tends*, for the purposes of distinct cognizance, towards the object, fact, or relation presented to it.

(d,) *Observation,—the voluntary, sustained, or continuous exercise of attention*, with which the mind directs itself toward the object of its contemplation, for the purpose of complete intuition and perfect recognition.

All the terms now defined, are but different designations for the various forms in which the intuitive action of the intellectual principle is solicited by objects external to itself. The English language, as the product of mind working chiefly in practical directions, posses- ses little of the clearness and distinctness in nomenclature which the topics of intellectual analysis so peculiarly require. But the four terms used above are sufficient to comprise the prominent forms of perceptive action, in the various processes of intellection. They all refer significantly enough, to the first efforts of intelligence, when, previous to any introversive or reflective act, of comparatively subtile or intricate character, it obeys the instinct of its appetite, and finds its sustentation by feeding on the aliment tendered to it by its Author, in the objects which environ it. To watch and guide, and coöperate with this instructive principle, is the true office of education, as a process of nurture and development, working not in arbitrary or artificial, but in salutary and successful forms,—forms not devised by the fallible ingenuity of man, but by the unerring wisdom of Supreme intelligence.

*Prevalent error in the order of cultivation.*—Contrary, however, to the obvious suggestions of fact, education is still too generally regarded as consisting, during its earlier stages, in arbitrary exercises of memory on combinations of printed characters, abstract numbers, or even the metaphysical relations involved in the science of grammar. The excuse offered for a blind following of precedent in this direction. usually is the peculiar susceptibility of memory, during the period of childhood, and the comparative difficulty experienced in attempts to cultivate it at a later stage. Were the educational cultivation of memory directed to the retaining and treasuring up of those stores of knowledge which are naturally accessible to the mind of childhood. within the range of its daily observation, the plea would be justifiable; man's endeavors would be in harmony with the obvious instincts and endowments of the mind, and would tend to its natural expansion and development. But directed to the mechanical and arbitrary results at which these endeavors so generally aim, their influence is detrimental. Their immediate effect is to quench the natural thirst for knowledge, to create a distaste for intellectual activity, and thus to defeat the best purposes of education.

The law of true culture lies in the primary craving of the young mind for material on which the understanding may operate; digesting it, in due season, into the regular form of knowledge which memory loves to retain, and which judgment ultimately builds up into the systematic arrangements of science.

### (2.) CURIOSITY, THE ACTUATING PRINCIPLE OF THE PERCEPTIVE FACULTIES.

*The Teacher's proper place.*—The teacher who enters intelligently upon his work of cultivating the minds entrusted to his care, knows that his chief duty is to cherish the spontaneous action of their powers, and to make them intelligent and voluntary co-workers in their own development. He observes, therefore, with careful attention, the natural tendencies and action of the intellectual system, as the physiologist does those of the corporeal, so as to become competent to trace the law of development, and adapt his measures to its requirements. He thus becomes qualified to take his proper place, as an humble but efficient co-worker with the Author of the mind, recognizing and following His plan, in modes suggested by a wisdom higher than human.

The attentive study and observation of the natural workings of the mind, in the successive stages of its progress, from incipient intelligence to maturity of reason, imply, however, not merely a careful analysis of the facts and modes of mental action, but a watchful observation, with a view to detect, in all cases, the moving power or *impelling principle* of action, to aid and regulate which is the educator's chief work. The ceaseless intellectual activity of childhood, maintained through the various media of perception, furnished by the organs of sense, is obviously stimulated by the constitutional principle of *curiosity*, an eager *desire to know* and *understand*, and therefore, *to observe* and *examine*. Hence the irrepressible and searching questions with which children, in the instinct of faith, appeal to whomsoever they think can satisfy their craving for information.

To feed this mental appetite, to select and prepare its proper nutriment, to keep it in healthy and healthful activity, to quicken and strengthen it, to direct and guide it, as a divine instinct, leading to the noblest ends, should be the teacher's constant endeavor. To awaken curiosity is to secure a penetrating and fixed attention,—the prime condition of human knowledge; and even when it leads no further than to wonder, it is preparing the advancing mind for the awe and the reverence with which, in later stages of its progress, it looks up to the knowledge which is "too high for it."

*The emotion of wonder analogous to the instinct of curiosity.*—Curiosity, like the kindred element of wonder, finds its sustenance in whatever is new to sensation or perception; *wonder*, in turn, leads the mind to dwell on whatever is *strange*, *intricate*, or *remote; astonishment*, arrests it by whatever is *sudden* and *powerful; awe* commands it by whatever is *vast;* and *amazement* overwhelms it by whatever is *incomprehensible* or *inscrutable.* Yet all of these effects,—even those which, for the moment, act on the perceptive intellect with a repulsive force that makes it recoil in conscious weakness from the object of contemplation,—are but various forms of stimulating, impelling, or attracting force, acting on the irrepressible vitality of the mind; and no incitements are ultimately more powerful in maintaining the most resolute and persevering activity of its powers.

*Mental effects of novelty and variety.*—In the great primary school of nature, as established and furnished by the Author of all, we observe, accordingly, that in the multiform variety of objects with which the young human being is surrounded, at the first dawning of intelligence within him, the novelty of the whole scene around him, and of every class of objects which it presents, is forever tempting his susceptible spirit to observe and examine, and explore, by the conscious delight which every new step affords him.

*Evils of monotony, and advantages of variety.*—Nor is the obvious design of the great Instructor less conspicuous in the feeling of satiety and weariness which is always superinduced by continued sameness of mental action, whether prolonged in the same mode of exercise, or on the same class of objects. The observant teacher thus learns his own lesson of duty,—to avoid undue limitation in the objects and forms of intellectual action, to shun sameness and monotony of routine, and protracted exertions of attention, as all tending to exhaust and enfeeble the mental powers. His endeavors, on the contrary, are all directed to a due diversity in the presentation of objects, and in the mode of mental activity which they call forth; and, in whatever instances frequent repetition is indispensable to exact perception, he is particularly careful to exert his ingenuity to the utmost, in devising new modes of presentation, so as to secure fresh and earnest attention to the same objects or facts, by the renovating effect of the new lights and new aspects in which he causes them to be viewed.

*Faults in former modes of education.*—It is unnecessary, in our day, to dwell on the obvious faults of the obsolete practice of confining young children within doors at all seasons, compelling them to remain long in one attitude or posture without relief, condemning them to long periods of silence and constraint, and forcing them to con unmeaning and irksome tasks. These injurious practices are now, for the most part renounced; and more genial and rational modes of early education are beginning to prevail. As yet, however, we have only made a beginning. We have reformed our modes of school architecture, and have allowed children the unspeakable benefits of space and air, and more frequent change of place, and posture, and exercise. Objects and pictures are now employed, to some extent, as instruments of mental culture; and the wisdom of all these changes is proved in the greater happiness and better health of our little pupils, and, more particularly, in their greater docility, and their superior intellectual progress, as contrasted with the state of things under the former *regime* of irksome monotony, restraint, weariness, and stupidity. We are very far, yet, however, from approaching the bountiful variety and delightful novelty furnished in the great model school of infancy and childhood, as established by the Divine founder.

*Intellectual furniture of school-rooms.*—Our primary school-rooms should be so many cabinets of nature and art. Every inch of wall not indispensably required for blackboard exercises, should be secured for educational purposes, by specimens of plants, minerals, shells, birds, and whatever else can be appropriately placed before the eye. The arranging, classifiying, and describing of these, should precede any analysis or study of letters or syllables. Pictures representing such objects, should form a second stage of exercises in attention, observation, and description, before any alphabetic drilling whatever. The examination of objects and of pictures, should, in a word, form the natural preparatory training of the perceptive faculties for the more arbitrary and more difficult exercise of studying and recognizing the unmeaning, uninteresting forms of alphabetic characters with their phonetic combinations.

*Injurious effects of mere alphabetic drilling.*—Curiosity, the natural incitement of intellect, is easily awakened when we obey the law of the Creator, and direct it to His works,—the natural and appropriate stimulants of the perceptive powers of infancy; but when, leaving our proper sphere, and restricting our educational efforts to the mechanical training of eye and ear, we use these organs, and the informing mind, for the limited purpose of recognizing the complicated and irregular geometrical combinations of line and angle, presented in alphabetic characters, and repeating the sounds so arbitrarily associated with these, we take the mind out of its native element; we consequently force and distort its growth, dwarf its stature, and enfeeble its powers.

*Effects of the salutary excitement of the feeling of wonder.*—But it is not in the first stages only of mental culture, that the influence of novelty and variety is required as an incitement to observation, by the frequent presentation of new and fresh objects of attention, by the agreeable surprises occasioned by new forms and new stages of animal and vegetable life,—all tending to excite a lively curiosity, which leads, in turn, to careful attention, close examination, and successful study. Curiosity should often be awakened by the yet more powerful influence of *wonder.* Objects rare and strange, combinations intricate and even puzzling, should sometimes be called in, to excite a yet more energetic action of the perceptive intellect, in its endeavors to grasp the objects of its contemplation.

Whatever in nature is wonderful,—whether we employ the microscope, in revealing the intricate structure of plant or insect, in the minuter and closer examination of the works of the Creator; or the telescope, in the contemplation of the starry heavens, and the study of the magnitudes and motions of the bodies which people the depths of space,—all should be brought to bear on the young mind, to call forth that sense of wonder which so delights and inspires it, and prepares it, at the same time, for the influence of those sentiments of awe and reverence with which the advancing intellect learns to trace the signatures of Deity.

### (3.) OBSERVATION, AS THE TENDENCY OF MENTAL HABIT, UNDER THE INCITING INFLUENCE OF CURIOSITY.

*The natural effect of intellectual instinct.*—The motive power, or impelling force, by which, in the ordinations of the mind's omniscient Author, its perceptive faculties are incited to activity, and induced to render their tribute to the resources of intelligence, consists in that restless desire to observe, to examine, and to know, which constitutes man a progressively intelligent being. Impelled by this insatiable mental thirst, he is led instinctively to those streams of knowledge which constitute the waters of intellectual life. His perceptive powers thus stimulated, acquire a tendency to ceaseless activity,—a trait which forms the peculiar characteristic of the early stages of his mental progress, and which is greatly quickened by the vividness of sensation in the constitution of childhood. Hence the promptness and versatility of attention at that period, and its remarkable susceptibility to the influences of cultivation and discipline.

These aids, it is true, are, as yet, too scantily furnished in the processes of education; and, even without them, the human being, as he advances under the promptings of instinct, and the guidance of self-intelligence, attains, as in the case even of the savage, to a high degree of perceptive power. The keen, quick, and penetrating glance of his eye, the acuteness and certainty of his ear, the readiness and exactness of his observation of every object within the range of his vision, the searching closeness of inspection with which he examines everything new or uncertain, often furnish an impressive lesson on the value of training, to those whose means and opportunities of intellectual culture are so superior to his own.

*Effects of cherishing the habit of observation.*—The habit of observation, duly cherished in early years, by the judicious care of the parent and teacher, becomes the security for ample acquisitions in the field of knowledge, and for the daily accumulation of mental resources and of intellectual power. The observant mind, like the close-knit net of the skillful fisherman, encloses and retains the living treasures within its sweep, and deposits them, for use, in their appropriate place. The undisciplined, inattentive, unobservant spectator seizes and retains nothing in his slack and ineffectual grasp.

*Suggestive significance of terms in intellectual and educational relations.*—The etymology of the word *apprehension*, (seizing, grasping, laying hold of,) suggests an important lesson regarding the value of intellectual training, as dependent on the habit of attentive and close observation. The word *attention*, (tending, reaching, or stretching toward,) is not less instructive in its signification, implying the *tendency*, or the gravitating of the mind's perceptive power toward the object of notice, for the purpose of cognizance, as the first stage of intelligence. The term *observation*, (watching, with a view to obey or follow,) is yet more monitory to the teacher; as it intimates that the true study of external nature demands vigilance, docility, and fidelity; in one word, the devotion of the whole mind to the business of intellectual acquisition. *Perception*, (taking, through a medium,) refers us back to the humble office of sensation, as indispensable to the process of *taking into* the mind the treasures of knowledge offered to the grasp of sense, for the purpose of transmission to the percipient power, the inner principle of intelligence. All of these terms, in the nomenclature of mental science, tend to the same important end, in the uses of practical education: they all point to the appropriate discipline of the perceptive faculties, by means of objects addressed to the senses, as the primary stage of intellectual culture.

*Educational errors.*—Former modes of education rendered the use of terms such as the preceding, a nullity, or an absurdity. The child shut up within the naked walls of a school-room, seated on his uncomfortable bench, and mechanically conning by rote, the ill-fitting names of alphabetic elements, or trying to piece them into syllables, had little use of the precious gift of *sense*, but a few lines and angles to *perceive*,—unless a friendly fly should happen to alight upon the page of his primer,—no inducement to *attention* but the fear of Solomon's prescription for "minds diseased," nothing half so interesting to *observe* as the little winged being accidentally crawling on the page before him, displaying the curiously constructed mechanism of its form, its gauzy wings, and many-feathered little limbs, or stopping now and then, to dry-rub instead of washing them, and its tiny head, and flexible bit of neck, almost too diminutive to be seen. But woe to the little student of nature, in the genuine act of *observation*, if he should lift his eye from his book, and follow his brisk little visitant flying off to perform the visible miracle of walking up the perpendicular plane of the window pane, or the yet more puzzling feat of walking the ceiling with his head downward.

*Rational method.*—The child, in the case supposed, indicates the real want of his nature, and mutely, but most eloquently, pleads for a lesson on insect life, (entomology,) before one on the alphabet. Furnished with the data which the lesson on insect life and form, character and motion, would present to his eye, he would be receiving a rational preparatory discipline of attention and observation, in the close and careful examination of all the details of shape and configuration, exhibited in the living and attractive object before him. His recognition of figure and outline, thus secured, he would, in due season, transfer, easily and willingly, to the artificial display of them in the forms of printed characters.

*Benefits resulting from the early formation of habits of attentive observation.*—The early training of the perceptive faculties, by a varied and genial discipline of the power of attention, so as to render the habit of observation an unfailing characteristic of the man, becomes doubly valuable, as a result of education, when we regard its effects on the intellectual tastes and pursuits of individuals. A taste for the study of nature, early formed, leads to the practice of collecting specimens, and thus furnishing the means of successful study to the person himself, who collects them, and at the same time to all whom he is disposed to aid in such pursuits. Were even the elements of botany, geology, mineralogy, and zoölogy, generally adopted, as they ought to be, as subjects of attention in primary education, a knowledge of natural science, would, ere long, be diffused throughout our community; a taste for the study of nature would become an intellectual trait of our people; the pursuit of agriculture, abroriculture, and horticulture, would be more intelligently and more advantageously followed; the citizen would doubly relish his season of respite in the country; taste and intelligence would extend their influence over all modes of life; and science would be unspeakably a gainer, in its noble purposes and offices, by the multitude of active minds and busy hands called in to collect, and contribute materials for its various forms of investigation. The field of human knowledge might thus be indefinitely enlarged, and its advantages and enjoyments be more extensively diffused.

But it is not merely as a matter of scientific progress, or of taste and enjoyment, that the proper training of the perceptive faculties, by means of objects and observation, rather than by the materials furnished in books, becomes an important consideration in the planning of modes of education, and methods of instruction. Practical utility, also, has its claim to urge in this relation. The larger number of persons, even in the most advanced communities, as regards civilization and refinement, are occupied in some form of active exertion, as the daily vocation of individuals; and while no generous mind can ever look on education as a benefit or a blessing, if it is to be used as a means of training for the occupation of a given caste, it is not less true, that every individual, in whatever class of society, would be vastly benefited by an early course of cultivation on all subjects akin to those which are to form the staple of his mode of life. Botany, geology, chemistry, entomology, for instance, all have their relations to agriculture; and a few hours devoted weekly to the elements of these sciences, will, by their inspiring influence on the young mind, expedite rather than retard the ordinary processes of school education.

*Importance of commencing early the study of Nature.*—But while no formal or extensive study of these branches can be rationally attempted in primary education, it is most emphatically true, that, in the study of nature, more than in other forms of intellectual action, nothing can be advantageously done but on condition of an early beginning, and the judicious improvement of the opportunity afforded during the period of leisure and susceptibility which occurs to all human beings but once in life. Childhood and youth are, by the Creator's appointment, the period for forming taste and acquiring habits. The most resolute struggles in after years, seldom succeed in effecting a change of mental occupation, or in lending attractive interest to new pursuits. The "pliant hour" must be taken for all processes of mental budding, grafting, or pruning, as well as in those of the orchard. An early dip into the study of nature, will serve to saturate the whole soul with a love for it so strong as to insure the prosecution of such subjects for life. The season is auspicious; the senses are fresh and susceptible; the mind is awake; the heart is alive; the memory is retentive; nature is yet a scene of novelty and delight; and application is a pleasure. The twig may now be bent in the direction in which the tree is to be inclined.

*Universal susceptibility to instruction, drawn from Nature.*—In a diversified experience of nearly forty years in the field of education, one teacher, at least, can testify that he has not yet found the mind so dull, or the heart so callous, as to resist the attractive intellectual influence of the analysis of even one plant or one mineral. The mysteries of beauty and awe which hang over such objects, as an investing celestial glory, entrancing the imagination and the heart, and all but translating the intellect itself, have a power of attraction which the dullest, coarsest, and most brutalized boy in a ragged school, cannot resist. But of the moral influence of early education, when directed to the aspects of nature, it will be more appropriate to speak in that special connection.

*Effects produced on mental character, by the study of Nature.*—*The solidity and the firmness of mental character*, which are acquired by the study of *things*, preceding and accompanying that of words and books, are a natural effect of the early and seasonable cultivation of the habit of observing, analyzing, comparing, and classifying, which even the slight examination of any natural object induces.—A clear, decisive, and discriminating judgment, and a retentive memory, are among the other fruits of that mental training which commences with definite objects, capable of being analyzed and reconstructed by the natural and appropriate action of the young mind, in virtue of its own powers and native tendencies. But these considerations, also belong properly to another and more advanced stage of intellectual discipline, at which *the reflective faculties*, and maturing reason, are beginning to put forth their claims for culture and development, in addition to the preparatory training which they may have received in the blended exercises of sense and intellect, in the action of the perceptive faculties.

### (4.) KNOWLEDGE, THE INTELLECTUAL RESULT OF THE ACTION OF THE PERCEPTIVE FACULTIES.

Impelled by the instinct of curiosity, and guided by the habit of observation, the young mind,—whether more or less assisted by education,—advances to the goal designated by creative Wisdom,—*the acquisition of knowledge*, the appointed means for erecting the fabric of character on the scale outlined by the Great Architect, but left to man's industry and intelligence, for the filling up and the symmetry of detail.

The part of education which lies more immediately before us, as the object of our attention, being the cultivation of the intellect, the acquisition of knowledge becomes, in this view, a consideration of primary importance, as, at once, a source of intellectual wealth and power, and a most effective means of mental development. Knowledge, as a result of culture, is undoubtedly of inferior value to discipline. But the efforts put forth in the acquisition of genuine knowledge, are, in themselves, a disciplinary process, and the indispensable instruments of further cultivation. Yet more,—intellectual acquirements are true and durable riches,—valuable for their own sake, not merely from the resources which the accumulation of them places at the mind's command, but from their own intrinsic value, as imperishable because intellectual things, and as the successive steps of mental elevation in the scale of being. In reference to intellect, knowledge is, in one most important sense, an end, not less than a means and a measure of progress. Profound, extensive, and varied knowledge, is one of the crowning glories of man, as an intellectual and progressive being, capable of ceaseless development and acquisition. Most emphatically is this true of him, the soundness, and exactness, and completeness, of whose knowledge, are the assurance that he shall be a safe and competent guide along the path of education.

*Actual knowledge.*—But what is knowledge? How is it acquired?—not by the repetition of the words or the processes of others, not by the transfer from one mind to another of the verbal statements of fact or of abstract principles, not by the formation of vague and partial notions, formed on superficial data, and floating loosely in the mind, not by a half perception or half consciousness of something indefinite or supposititious, not by an assent to rash assumptions or confident assertions, not by the recollections of extensive reading, or perhaps, of attentive listening, retailed in fluent expression, not by accumulating the amplest furniture of second-hand theories and systems, whether plausible or absurd, or even logically consistent. *Knowledge is what we have experienced in our own intellect*, by means of our own observation or reflection, the fruit of personal perception, or of conscious reason, acting on the positive data of sensation. So narrowly must the term be limited, when we refer to the action of the perceptive faculties, or to their appropriate training and discipline. Knowledge, in these relations, is *the accurate interpretation of the facts of sense*, in matters, usually, of color, form, number, weight, or sound, and the relations which these bear to one another in the processes of induction and classification. With the other sense of the term, in which it refers whether to truth or to theory, and implies the deductions of reflective *reason*, we have not, at present, to do. It belongs to a subsequent stage of the analysis of the modes of mental action, as subjected to the processes of intellectual cultivation, and occurs in connection with the discipline of the "reflective" faculties.

*Literal accuracy of verbal statement, a false test of knowledge.*— The acquisition of knowledge, however, is, notwithstanding all our advances, of late years, in the philosophy of education, too generally confounded with the repetition of the verbal statements of definitions, rules, and systems, as contained in books, even in relations so palpable as those of form and numbers. The test of knowledge, accordingly, with some teachers, to this day, is, even in the exact sciences, the fluency with which a definition or a rule is orally repeated, verbatim, from a text-book, and the mechanical accuracy or despatch with which a correspondent problem is solved, or a proposition demonstrated.

*True knowledge experimental and personal.* — True perceptive knowledge, on the other hand, or that which is actual and personal, implies, in all relations of form and number, that the individual who possesses it, has seen the object in question, or its representative, in palpable shape, in surface or in outline, that he has subjected it to actual measurement and comparison, or has an exact image of its form and configuration before his mind, that he has actually counted or grouped objects in numbers presented to the eye or to the mind, or that he has compared these with one another, and traced their relations, by strict and exact observation; and the proper office of the text-book is but to confirm and embody the result, and classify it in the exact language and systematic arrangement of formal science, as the specimens are labelled and shelved in a collector's cabinet. The use of scientific method, in the statements of text-books, is but to give logical arrangement to mental acquisitions, not to induce mere assent, whether silent or oral, and not to facilitate the mere repetition or verbal enunciation of propositions.

*The proper business of the teacher, as a superintendent of mind.*— The true office of the teacher is to see that the pupil is led by his own conscious experience and observation, through the process of perception prescribed in every exercise which he attempts; that the operation is intelligently performed at every step, and the result rendered certain, as far as the limitations of human faculties permit. By frequently repeated performance of the requisite process, the principle in question thus becomes an integral part of personal knowledge with the individual; and his faculties receive, at the same time, a discipline which gives them facility and force in all analogous procedure in which expertness and skill are desirable attainments. In due season, also, he is able to sum up his acquirements in knowledge, in the clear and definite and precise language which science demands, and of which his text-book furnishes a perfect specimen on which he can rely.

At first, however, the young operator may need even the palpable aid of actual objects; and the judicious teacher knows well when to give, and when to withhold such help, when to appeal to the blackboard, and when to have his pupil rely on the mind's eye, during the successive stages of intellectual training. He is careful, however, not to slight or hurry over the business of the rudimental course, in which the reference to actual objects is the main reliance for a sure personal knowledge of the facts of form and number. The collateral discipline, also, arising from the attentive observation and careful study of plants, minerals, leaves, insects, and other natural objects, the intelligent teacher values highly, from the power of attention, and the habit of exact observation, which it tends to secure, by the definiteness which it gives to the action of the mind, and the certainty which it stamps on knowledge.

*Contrasted examples of neglect and culture.*—True education has no more striking proof of its good effect than may be observed, when the apathy and ignorance of young persons who have been allowed to neglect the observation and study of nature in childhood, and afterwards to go through a class-drill on a given branch, by means of a text-book, are contrasted with the intelligent personal interest and intimate knowledge of those who have been wisely induced to turn an early attention on the productions of nature, and thus to acquire an early love for such studies, and a life-long enjoyment of the pleasures which they afford. Adults of the former class take little interest in the "floral apostles" of the poet, who are ceaselessly preaching the perfection of their Source, or in the pebble at their feet, which, to the intelligent eye, is the medallion struck by the Creator's hand, in commemoration of one of the epochs in His reign. These eloquent monitions of a perpetual Divine presence, are, to such minds, the dead letter of a handwriting which they have not been accustomed to trace, and on which their listless eye falls, as does that of the sceptic, on the page of written revelation. The mind, on the other hand, which has been early trained to an intelligent personal interest in the productions of Creative wisdom and power, enjoys a personal property, and a personal reference, in every object in nature, finds, in "the meanest flower that blows, thoughts that do often lie too deep for tears;" and ultimately to it,

"The delicate forest flower,
With fragrant breath, and look so like a smile,
Seems, as it issues from the shapeless mould,
An emanation of the indwelling Life,
A visible token of the upholding Love,
Which are the soul of this wide universe."

The definiteness and the certainty, however, which give conscious life and power to all such knowledge, depend, to a great extent, on the faithful training which the perceptive power has undergone in the nurturing stage of education. The poet whose words of truth and love convince us that he has attained to the rank of an inspired seer, set out on his career from the common starting place of infancy, in blank ignorance of every object and of every fact around him; and his brother bard whose office it is to announce, in the language of astronomy, the harmony of the spheres, and read to mankind the legislation of the heavens, had no vantage ground at his outset on those excursions which ultimately extend beyond Orion and the Pleiades. Nor was there any special dispensation antecedent to the slow but sure processes of culture, in favor of the electrician who, in the maturity of his acquirements, became competent to transmit and diffuse intelligence with the literal rapidity of lightning; and what shall we say of the barefooted mason's boy, who commences his career of "glory and of joy," plodding over the stone which he has broken with his unpracticed apprentice hammer, and, at length, reads, from that same fragment, to the delight and astonishment of mankind, the facts of an antediluvian world? All the treasures which such minds have brought from their various explorations, as tributes to the treasury of science, and to man's dominion in the sphere of knowledge, are but the varied fruits of unwearied, progressive observation, accumulating fact upon fact by the patient process of attentive examination of objects, and by the skillful exercise of well disciplined perceptive faculties. Such noble efforts of mental power we contemplate with a delight mingled with reverence and gratitude to their authors, as benefactors of the race. The worship which human ignorance, in its wondering admiration, extended, of old, to the mythic demi-god and hero, might, we think, have been pardoned had it been offered to our venerated contemporary Humboldt, who, at an age rarely attained by modern man, withdraws, at intervals, from the onerous duties of a councilor of state, to record the acquisitions of a mind which, from early years, has been exploring the wonders of nature, and now, year after year, pours forth another and another book of the great epic of creation, to which he has so appropriately given the sublime title, "Cosmos."

The written life of this truly great man, however, only enables us to trace the progress of another watchful observer of nature, as, step by step, he observes, examines, compares, classifies, aggregates, and accumulates, till he stands before us an intellectual Atlas, upholding the sphere of human knowledge. Liberal education, favorable opportunities faithfully improved, an insatiable thirst for knowledge, and devoted application to the acquisition of it, explain the wonder. Let us inquire then, for a moment, into the processes by which human culture achieves the miracle of such results.

(5.) THE APPROPRIATE EDUCATIONAL PROCESSES FOR THE EXERCISE, DEVELOPMENT, AND DISCIPLINE, OF THE PERCEPTIVE FACULTIES.

*The law of progressive intellection.*—Watching the successive steps of man's intellectual development, as he advances, consciously or unconsciously, in pliancy and power of mind, we see him first incited by an irrepressible principle of *curiosity*, stimulating him to watchful attention, *close observation*, and *minute inspection*, for the purpose of acquiring a satisfactory *knowledge* of things around him; that he may, in due season, be prepared to enter upon a new and higher cycle of his ceaseless progress, and from the materials of *perception*, feed the *reflective* faculties of *judgment* and *reason*, which lead to the higher goal of *truth*, where alone the cravings of intellect can find rest and satisfaction.

*Provision of educational apparatus.*—The first care of the watchful and intelligent teacher, as the guide and director of the intellect, is obviously, in compliance with the law of intellectual progress, as traced above, to make liberal provision of the palpable material of *perception*, by which the instinctive appetite of curiosity is at once fed and stimulated, attention awakened, observation secured, and knowledge attained. Objects abundant in number, and varied in character, form and aspect, but chiefly those furnished by nature, and, more particularly, those which occur most frequently within the range of the child's actual observation, are the true and appropriate apparatus of his education. To the examination and inspection of these his mind naturally tends; to the process of extracting knowledge from these, his perceptive powers are expressly adapted; in such occupation he takes delight; working on such material, he is inspired by the consciousness of progress and of perpetually augmenting vigor; and thus he becomes a willing and efficient, because an intelligent agent in his own development.

DISCIPLINE OF THE SENSES.—*Sight; color.*—Sensation, though the humblest form of mental action, being the first in the natural order of intellectual development, suggests to the parent and teacher the great importance of a due attention to the early cultivation of the senses, especially of those whose action is so distinctly intellectual in character and result as is that of *sight* and *hearing.* The proper organic training of the eye implies, what is too often overlooked, an attentive regard to *color*, as well as *form;* the former of these being very early developed, and evidently, in all normal cases, a source of peculiar delight in infancy, not less than of high æsthetic gratification in subsequent appreciation of beauty, both in nature and art. Long before the infant shows any distinctive recognition or appreciation of form, it manifests a keen perception and intense pleasure in the observation of all objects of brilliant color.

Under the management of the judicious mother, balls of the three grand primary colors of the painter,—blue, red, and yellow,—form an inexhaustible source of pleasure to the infant eye; while they give an unconscious exercise and discipline to the perceptive faculty, and prepare the way for the subsequent, definite, and intelligent recognition of the great lines of distinction drawn on the field of vision by the Hand which has blended color with light. Field or garden flowers, or even wayside weeds, placed within the range of the eye, serve a similar purpose. Subsequently, the principal intermediate *gradations* of color, as they occur in objects of nature or of art, in varied tints and hues, may be presented to the sight, in due succession, as a pleasing exercise for the faculties of childhood, in its progress. For this purpose, flowers, the prism, the tints and half tints of the clouds, the glow, or the hue of evening and morning skies, throughout the year; the ever-varying colors of autumn, from their fullest flush to their gradual waning and decay; all are admirable materials for the intellectual and æsthetic cultivation of the human being, along the successive stages of his development. The mind early trained to a sense of the beauty of color, can hardly be withheld, in after years, from the profoundest application to the study of light, as "a feast of nectared sweets, where no crude surfeit reigns." Purity and perfection of taste in art, are another sure result of early cultivation, in this respect. How much intelligence, and how much intensity of pure and even sacred gratification, may thus be superadded to the sentiment of reverential delight in the works of the Creator, it would be difficult for even the most skillful master of expression to say.

*Form.*—The early cultivation of a discriminating perception of the distinctive characters of *form*, through a carefully conducted, progressive discipline on objects submitted to the eye, is one of the most purely intellectual processes to which the mind of childhood can be subjected. The cube, the sphere, the cylinder, the cone, the pyramid, when judiciously introduced among the playthings of early childhood, as was strikingly exemplified in the schools of Pestalozzi, become unconsciously, but most surely, a basis and standard in all the relations of form; and, under the guiding suggestions of the teacher, they tend to give the mind definiteness and certainty in its action, on whatever relates to geometrical details of figure in nature, art, or mechanism. The primary truths of solid, superficial, and linear geometry, are thus imbedded in the mind, identified with its action on all visible objects, and help to constitute the observer an intelligent spectator, through life, of the grand elemental forms of the universe.

*Measure.*—Convenience and utility, too, have their claims to urge in favor of an early discipline of the eye on all details of *measurement.* An exact appreciation of measure, for in-door purposes, should be laid in permanent inch, and half and quarter inch marks, on the school-room wall; and to these should be added those of the foot and the yard. A mile, with its subdivision into halves, and quarters, should be measured off, as a permanent standard for the young eye, as it approaches or leaves the threshold of the school-room. The acre and the rod, and all other details of land measure, should be made familiar to the eye of boyhood, by express measurement, in the nearest accessible field or square.

*Number.*—Veritable ideas of number belong, also, to the early discipline of the eye, and are greatly dependent on the actual presentation of objects, for this special purpose. We read, in the accounts of one English exploring voyage, that the inhabitants of one group of islands in the Pacific, had do definite ideas of any number over five; and experienced teachers are well aware that, in the case of pupils accustomed to depend on the mere verbal memory of the words which represent numbers, and unprovided with a firm basis of actual observation of palpable objects, and the personal knowledge which such experience gives, there is an obstinate difficulty in forming definite and distinct conceptions of numbers, which resembles, too nearly, the confusion and helplessness of mind felt by those unfortunate islanders, in their attempts to transcend the limits of their terminal number, five.

Most of the early arithmetical operations of very young pupils, should consist in handling and counting visible objects, in enumerating marks, in grouping objects and marks, in numbers gradually progressive, from the smallest to the largest in amount; so as to secure expertness and promptness in the process of addition, in varied forms. Successive exercises should follow in multiplication, in subtraction, and division, all performed, day after day, on visible objects handled, and on marks expressly made for such purposes of training, before the purely mental processes of arithmetic are attempted on abstract numbers, even of the smallest groups. A prevalent error with teachers still continues to be that of merely exemplifying true teaching in such forms as have been mentioned, for a limited period, too limited to tell upon the habits of the mind. Long continued training alone, is adequate to the proper purposes of discipline, certainty and skill, namely, in forming combinations which must sometimes be both extensive and complicated. It is unreasonable to expect rapidity and expertness in the processes of mental arithmetic, without the preparatory discipline which results from the actual observation of the facts of number and combination, in objects presented to the senses. Such discipline alone, can yield that personal knowledge, and that conscious grasp of mind, which give clearness and certainty to the action of the intellect in arithmetical operations.

*Natural objects: animated forms.*—But it is not merely the contemplation of inanimate objects which the mind, in childhood, requires as a foundation for true perception and exact observation, or as a means of securing prompt and sustained attention. The liberal training of the senses, as a primary step in intellectual cultivation, extends the study of color, form, number, and sound, to the rich domain of animated nature, in the animal as well as the vegetable kingdom, and thus brings the vivid sympathy of the young heart with kindred life and motion to the aid of the opening intellect. From the *pebble*, the *shell*, the *flower*, and the *leaf*, the judicious mother and teacher will pass to the *insect*, the *bird*, the *quadruped*, and the *fish*; and as their individualities and diversities are successively enumerated and dwelt upon, the details of color, form, and number, arrest and fix the volatile attention of the child, and win him to habits of close, minute, and exact observation.

*Analysis* and *classification*, the two great master powers for the acquisition of knowledge, in whatever direction, are also thus called in to aid the progress of the young observer in his study of nature.

The tendency of the mind to *observe*, *compare*, *examine*, and *classify* whatever is submitted to its action, thus early encouraged and stimulated, becomes an habitual trait of the mental character, and tells, with powerful effect, on the intellectual progress of the individual, in the more abstract relations of *language* and of *mathematics*. It is a great error to suppose that, because of the intense pleasure which attends the study of natural objects, there is not a profound and rigorous discipline of mind attending the equally intense intellectual action which accompanies the pleasure. *Analytic examination* is one and the same process, whether it is directed to the component parts of a *plant* or of a *word*. Keen and penetrating attention, close, minute, and thoughtful observation, exhaustive analysis, systematic arrangement, and methodical classification, are equally indispensable in the one case as in the other. But in giving precedence to the study of the object, and postponing that of the word, we are obeying the ordination of the Creator, who has furnished the apparatus of the first stages of human development, in the natural objects which first solicit the attention of the child, by the attractions of beauty and pleasure.

*Pictorial art.*—Nor is it only by means of natural objects that the sense of sight contributes to the exercise and discipline of the perceptive intellect. Art, too, renders here a rich tribute to the resources of education. Models and pictures, and the humblest attempts to produce these, as repetitions of the mental impressions received from nature, give inexpressible delight to the susceptible and imitative spirit of childhood. Their effect is invaluable, in training the perceptive faculties to the keenest, closest, long-sustained action, without the sense of weariness or fatigue; and their inspiring and refreshing influence gives vivacity and force to the whole mind. The clear perception, fixed attention, watchful observation, and active exertion, which they both require and cherish, particularly when the child is permitted to attempt to produce imitative efforts of his own, in drawing or modelling, meet so successfully the craving of the young spirit for action and endeavor, that they become powerful aids to mental development. The working hand is thus brought to the aid of the active eye, as a test, at the same time, of its correctness of vision, which is proved by the degree of truthfulness in the delineation. This productive method of exercising the perceptive and executive faculties, yields to the child the peculiar delight of having achieved something palpable, as a proof of power, and is, meanwhile, working in his mind the silent effect which is to appear, in due season, in the symmetry and gracefulness of his handwriting, and the neatness of whatever he attempts, whether in plan or execution.

*The ear: music.*—The varied world of sound, comprising *music* and *speech*, is another wide field of culture to the intelligent mother and the elementary teacher. The extent to which the sense of sight may be cultivated, as regards precision and certainty and truth of action, is indicated in the perfection which is attained by the sculptor and the painter, whose copies of nature are, in some instances, so faithful, and so beautifully perfect, as to confer an immortality of fame upon their authors. But little notice, comparatively, is taken of the delicate susceptibility of the *ear*, in relation to the offices of culture. Yet no sense, not even that of sight itself, is capable of attaining to so high perfection by the aids of training and discipline. The innumerable minute distinctions of sound, which the performance of even a single piece of music, by a single performer, often requires; but, still more, the multitude which the composer of one of the master-pieces of harmony must be capable of recognizing, discriminating, and combining, with a measured exactness transcending all other efforts of perceptive intellect: these remind us, most impressively, of the extent and value of cultivation, when we recall the fact, that the performer and the composer commenced their artistic training on the common footing of all human beings, a percipient mind, and an organ capable of telegraphing to it the notes of the singing bird, the song of the mother or the nurse, or the artless strains of some juvenile performer on pipe or flute.

*Speech.*—We have yet another proof of the susceptibility of the ear to the influences of cultivation, when "the well trod stage," in the exhibition of a play of the 'myriad-minded' Shakspeare, displays in the voice of the skillful actor, the whole world of human passion, with its ever-varying tones, uttered in the language of poetic inspiration, now moulded by the serene influence of heavenly contemplation, as when Lorenzo speaks to Jessica, while they sit on the moon-lit bank, of the "smallest orb which she beholds, still quiring to the young-eyed cherubim;" now breathing the deep tones of Hamlet, solemnly musing on the mysteries of life, and death, and destiny; now the hollow mutterings of conscious guilt from Macbeth, while meditating the murder from which he yet recoils; now the hoarse accents of remorse wrung from the bosom of him whose "offence is rank" with the blood of "a brother's murder;" now the scarce articulate horror of "false, fleeting, purjured Clarence;" the maddened scream of mingling grief and rage from the injured mother, Constance; the love raptures of the empassioned Romeo; the ringing laughter of Mercutio; or the torture of Othello, as he fluctuates from the ecstacies of overflowing love and joy, to the curses of hatred, the outbursts of grief, and the agonies of despair.

In all these forms the well trained actor, by the mastery of his artistic skill, exerts a power over the sympathies of his audience which far transcends the highest achievements of representative art in any other form. The arduous training to which the histrionic artist subjects his voice, in order to produce such effects, shows to what extent the cultivation of the ear may be carried. It is by the indications of this faithful, prompting monitor, that he guides every step of his vocal efforts, till he attains to those consummate effects of genius which, in some instances, have conferred on the individual a fame coëxtensive with the civilized world. Yet he who is, perhaps, thus renowned, commenced his early efforts, with the usual stumbling utterance of a school-boy.

*Enunciation.*—Passing from the higher sphere of music and poetry, in their influence on the cultivation of the intellect, through the medium of sense, we come to one of the most important stages of education, in the discipline of the voice for the useful purposes of speech, as dependent on accuracy of ear,—the only reliable guide to correct results. The unconscious freedom with which we utter thoughts in our native tongue, leaves all persons who are not advantageously trained by precept or example, exposed to the evils of incorrect habit, in utterance. The extensive prevalence, also, of corrupted usage, in the negligent practice of general society, increases the liability to error in the style of the individual. There was wisdom in the Roman maxim, that the nurses of children ought to be persons of correct habit, in enunciation. The influence of early example, is the most binding rule of speech, as the baffled and disappointed teacher, after all his endeavors, is often made to feel.

One early begun and long continued daily practice, in primary training, should consist in the careful, correct, and distinct *articulation* of the component elements of speech, as accomplished in our own language. These should, at first, be practiced with reference to *the exact sound of every letter of the alphabet*, singly and separately; afterwards they should be enunciated in the groups which constitute *syllables*, on a graduated progressive scale of difficulty, till every variety of combination can be uttered with perfect distinctness and perfect fluency; finally, *the pronunciation of words* should be practiced in a similar manner, till the style of the young learner is freed from all corrupt and local mannerism, and he is prepared to take his place among the cultivated in speech as well as thought, and, by his personal manner of expression, to evince the style of educated habit as preferable to that of vulgar negligence.

*Elocution.*—In the secondary and in the more advanced stages of education, the discipline of the ear should be extended, so as to embrace all the refining and highly intellectual influences of music and poetry, as combined in *elocution.*

Intellect, feeling, and imagination, are all inseparably united in the appropriate expression of sentiment, as embodied in the language of *oratory* and *poetry;* and their finest effects in utterance depend on a nice susceptibility of ear, which culture only can secure to full extent. Music and elocution, the most humanizing of all arts, prescribe the apparatus and the forms of training to which the ear should be subjected, through the whole course of education. In the analysis and the discrimination which vocal discipline demands, in the recognition which it secures of the almost infinitely diversified and ever varying character of tones, in their expression of intelligence or of emotion, there is an admirable discipline of intellect implied, which, though less formally displayed than in other modes of exercise, is not, on that account, the less effectual. Of the high *moral* value of the susceptibility which such training tends to cherish, it is not now the appropriate time to speak. We may advert to it under a subsequent head.

The subject of *healthful physical training* is not now under consideration; yet sensation, and consequent perception, are dependent on the condition of the organs of sense, and therefore of the whole corporeal frame, which must be in a healthy condition to secure the natural and true action of nerve and brain,—the apparatus of perceptive action in the intellect. The attentive and efficient cultivation of health should be regarded, not merely as a condition of intellectual life, but as the first step in the formation of intellectual character. The clear eye and the quick ear of health are highly intellectual in their tendencies, and are for ever detecting and offering material for the intellect to examine or explore. The dull organs of a morbid frame, on the contrary, are too torpid to respond to the awakening touch or beckoning invitation of nature, and leave the clouded intellect to sleep or to dream.

## PROGRESSIVE CHARACTER OF THE PROPER DISCIPLINE OF THE PERCEPTIVE FACULTIES.

The varied exercises of eye and ear, as organs of sentient mind, should always, under the guiding management of the teacher, advance in intellectual character from stage to stage, so as to secure the benefits of a progressive discipline, commencing, indeed, at the threshold of sense, but ever tending more and more inward, till they become nearly inseparable from the action and character of pure intellect. They thus render the keen eye and the quick ear prompters to clear perception, fixed attention, penetrating observation, careful comparison, and discriminating judgment, and so conduct to consummate intelligence.

The teacher who works in intelligent coöperation with the constitution of the beings whose character it is his office to mould, is content to labor patiently in the field of *sensation*, as, at first, forming the sole ground on which he can rationally meet the dawning mind, with the hope to exert a genial and effectual influence on its development. He dwells long, accordingly, on the prominent outward characteristics of objects, as most accessible to the unpracticed faculties of infancy, as best adapted to elicit their activity, and tempt them forth to more and more energetic effort. He furnishes, with no sparing hand, the opportunities of intuition, in the abundance and variety of the objects which he presents to the senses. He selects these, however, with such judgment and skill that the young mind shall be incapable of regarding them with a mere vacant aspection or listless intuition, but, on the contrary, shall be made to feel that there is within them a soliciting power, a magnetic attraction, to which its own nature responds, and by which it is led on, from stage to stage, till it finds itself in possession of the mental treasures of clear perception and definite knowledge.

## VOLUNTARY EXERCISE OF THE PERCEPTIVE FACULTIES, A CONDITION OF INTELLECTUAL DEVELOPMENT.

*Attention as a voluntary act.*—The teacher who recognizes the law of intellectual growth, is aware that, in adopting measures to aid the progressive unfolding of the perceptive faculties, he may trust largely to the mind's own instinctive and spontaneous tendencies to action, if only due provision is made for mental activity, by supplying the objects of sense which naturally invite and stimulate perception. But regarding the mind as a voluntary and self-directing agent, he knows that unless its own efficient coöperation is secured in the processes on which its energies are exerted, its activity will be ever tending to subside, or to degenerate into mechanical and unmeaning routine. The result, he is aware, must, in such circumstances, be a morbid intellectual inertness of habit, or a deceptive show of forced organic action, instead of the movements of mental life. His great endeavor, therefore, will be to succeed in evoking ATTENTION,—that power of the mind which brings into vigorous and efficient activity the percipient intellect,—that power which, by its own innate force, impels and sustains perception, in whatever direction it is called to act, or in whatever process it is employed.

The customary definition of this power, or faculty, as *voluntary per-*

*ception*, suggests to the educator his true office in cultivating and developing it. It implies that he no longer restricts his efforts to presenting such objects as solicit and secure the mind's notice, by the law of natural instinct, but that, addressing himself to the principle of *volition*, he calls it forth, as a moving force, impelling the mental machinery from within, and enabling it to arrive at knowledge, by its own action. The true teacher never commits the error of resorting to the exercise of his own will, instead of that of his pupil, as the propelling power. He is aware that his success, as an educator, is to be measured, not by the force with which he can bring his own power of compulsion to bear on the faculties of his pupils, but by the intensity with which he can bring their mental energies into voluntary play, in processes which leave a *residuum* of living force, as a result on mental character. He knows well that no degree of exertion can command attention, by a mere act of will, at the moment; that, by the law of the mental constitution, a train of circumstances must be laid before the desired result can be ensured; that an exercise of will is not, in the natural analogies of mental action, a merely arbitrary act of self-determination; but that, on the contrary, *will* is solicited by *desire*; a feeling or affection of the mind being the natural and necessary preliminary to volition; and that the intelligent guide of the intellectual powers must, therefore, appeal to *feeling*, as the natural and reliable prompter of the will. In other words, the educational process, rightly conducted, is so contrived as to create a desire to arrive at the given result, and proceeds upon that security for the action of will in determining the direction of the mind, and sustaining the exertion of its powers.

Trained under such influences, a disciplined attention is the sure fruit of culture; and power of attention is not unjustly termed the key which unlocks all the gates of knowledge, and secures an entrance to its innermost secrets of intelligence.

Attention, as a power or mode of intellectual action, regarded in connection with the cultivation of the perceptive faculties, requires the application of the various expedients by which it may be rendered *prompt*, *earnest*, *close*, and *continuous*, as the exigencies of subjects and of the mind may demand.

*Promptness of attention.*—Such results imply that the educator, as a skillful gymnasiarch in the arena of mind, trains it through every variety of evolution by which it may be rendered *quick* in movement, ever ready for instantaneous action, so as to secure that pliancy and versatility by which it can at once direct itself to its object, or relinquish one object or train of thought for another, when the moment for change has arrived, and pursue the object of its aim with whatever velocity of motion may be requisite to reach it, in due season.

Speed and despatch, however, not haste and hurry, should be the ends at which the teacher aims in all drilling processes. A wakeful and lively attention, ever on the alert for action, implies sound and healthful and invigorating training. A harassed and exhausted mind, dragged or driven along the path of exercise too arduous, or too long continued, can never yield the results of genuine discipline.

With very young pupils, especially, the obvious indication of nature is, make free use of *striking* and *attractive* objects, illustrations, and remarks. One object at a time; words few and well chosen; no lagging or drawling on the part of either pupil or teacher, yet no hurry, no impatience, no impetuosity; proceeding smoothly and swiftly, but quietly and gently in all movements; yet sometimes, for the purpose of arresting attention, adopting the grateful surprise of a sudden change, briskly executed:—these are the characteristics of skillful and genial training, such as quickens the life power of intellect.

*Earnestness of attention.*—The power of *earnest* attention is another trait of mental habit to which the successful teacher directs his endeavors, as an invaluable attainment to be secured, through his agency, by his pupils. To this end, he avoids carefully all exercises not interesting or inviting to the young mind. *Objects, pictures, penetrating questions, vigorous exertion*, in varied forms, for mind and body,—strenuous endeavor called forth, at intervals, to cope with *difficulties, interesting facts* stated, or stories told,—the wonders of nature and of art exhibited, *interesting conversation* maintained, in which the pupils interchange thoughts with the teacher, *word-pictures* of peculiar power and beauty, selected from the poets, early attempts at *drawing*, exercises in *planning* and *building*, tangible illustrations in architecture, masonry, carpentry, or joiner-work, in juvenile style, for hours of recreation, the *analysis of plants*, the tracing of the *anatomy* of animal forms, in specimens of *insect* organization, in the osseous construction of *birds, fishes, reptiles*, &c.; all lessons made, as far as practicable, matter of *active work*, rather than merely passive attention; the ceaseless use of the *slate*, the *pencil*, and the *blackboard*, in recording, repeating, and illustrating every thing which admits of such forms of expression; these, and every other resort which ingenuity can invent, are all required in the exigencies of actual teaching.

Earnest attention and strenuous application, on the part of pupils, are the natural result and unfailing reward of the teacher's own facility and skill in devising and executing inspiring models of whatever he would have his pupils execute. The efficacy of his own ear, eye, and hand, secured by his own self-culture, is the only guaranty of his success, as a faithful trainer of the perceptive faculties. The general introduction of music and drawing, now in progress in all well-taught schools, together with the increasing attention given to elementary lessons in botany and mineralogy, is opening a highly beneficial course of discipline for the young mind, in whatever concerns the power of earnest and effective attention, as an attribute of intellectual character.

*Closeness of attention.*—The thorough discipline of attention, however, as the directing force of the perceptive faculties, implies that it is not only rendered prompt and earnest in action, but *close* and *minute* in its application. A faithful *analysis* is conditioned, in all departments of study, on a clear and distinct perception of *every particular.* Nothing must be suffered to escape notice. No analysis can be complete that is not exhaustive, to the extent of its object. Close and minute inspection is indispensable for the exact observation of many of the most instructive and the most beautiful of the details of nature, in the forms of animal and vegetable life,—for the successful watching of the processes of chemistry,—for forming exact estimations of quantity and number,—for tracing the diversities of even inanimate form, the delicate gradations of color, the minutest difference of sound and form, in the details of language, together with all the nicer distinctions, and discriminations of thought, when embodied in words, for the purposes of communication.

To secure these results, we are again directed to the early and effectual training of the perceptive faculties on the objects of nature, as the first step in the true education of the mind. The minutest point of form in the structure of leaf or blossom, the child traces with delight; and this native tendency of mental action, extended in its range of objects, and confirmed by the law of habit, becomes not only a source of intellectual enjoyment, but of conscious power and ultimate success, in all investigations, not merely of nature and external objects, but, by the inevitable law of analogy, in every department of research on which the intellect is competent to enter. The power of close attention, sharpened by judicious early training of the perceptive faculties, attains in due season, to consummate certainty and success in those processes of minute analysis which are, in many instances, the crowning glories of science.

No contrast can be more striking than that exhibited in the two cases of neglect and culture, in this relation of mental action. On the one hand, we have the loose, superficial, imperfect attention, which glides listlessly over the surface of things, without note, and consequently without knowledge; on the other we see an acute, keen, penetrating, searching inspection, which nothing escapes,—a mind whose knowledge is exact and complete, whose information is the result of narrowly examined and well ascertained particulars.

The intelligent teacher, knowing that the keenest exercises of discriminating judgment are, by the law of mental constitution and habit, not unfrequently dependent on the close examination of details, on the power of tracing and detecting the minutest shades of difference in objects and their component parts, leads his pupils, by the closeness of his questioning, to follow the minutest ramifications of diversity, amid apparent similarity, in the objects which he uses as instruments for sharpening their perceptions to the keenest inspection of every feature which is accessible to the discernment of sense. Beyond this point he passes to the use of the microscope, one of the most valuable implements ever devised as an aid to the processes of human culture. A cheap instrument of this description, in the hands of an attentive teacher, has a power which no degree of mental inertia can resist. It has been known to convert, in a few days, a whole school of uncultivated, thoughtless, turbulent children into an attentive, thoughtful, inquiring, docile, and orderly company of little students of nature.

A few minutes occupied daily in observing and tracing the forms of objects, in detail, is, in addition to its ultimate effects on mental habit, of the greatest service in the humble relations of alphabetic teaching. A ground work is thus laid for the accurate recognition of the elements of form combined in the visible shapes of printed and written characters, and a surer and more rapid, because a more intelligent, progress secured, as regards the accuracy of the eye in recognizing, or of the hand in repeating the lines, angles, and curves, which constitute the complex forms of letters. Accustomed to the close and minute analysis of form on visible objects of different sorts, the child, if permitted to treat his alphabetic characters in a similar way, takes delight in detecting and naming their constituent parts; and, particularly, when he is permitted to try to delineate them for himself, and thus, as it were, bring them under a kind of ideal subjection to his power.

The discipline of particular observation and searching attention, early secured, becomes, in due season, a complete guaranty for the correct and successful performance of the various gradations of mathematical problems in which a well trained and exact attention is required, whether for the relations of form or those of numbers; and throughout the successive stages of education, in all its departments.

The well trained mind becomes ultimately like the thoroughly magnetized instrument, which leaves no stray particles of the steel-filings scattered abroad, but agglomerates them every one to itself; with a certainty which renders the act no unfitting analogy for illustrating the universal law of gravitation.

*Tenacity of attention.*—Having used his best endeavors to render the faculty of attention prompt, earnest, and close, in its action, as the guide of the perceptive faculties, the teacher has yet another character to stamp upon it. He would have it not only quick and vivid, and searching, but *tenacious* and *persistent.* From an element volatile, fluctuating, and superficial, in its first manifestations, he would have it become, at length, a power fixed, and steadfast, and unfailing. Patiently training it through its incipient stage of short, feeble flights, he inures it to lengthened excursions and sustained exertions, such as all valuable mental attainments demand. Here, again, Nature comes to his aid, furnishing him liberally not only with numerous instruments of discipline in her manifold forms, as objects, individually, attractive and interesting, but with those *complexities* of shape, and color, and number, those *organic relations*, and *organic contrivances*, those *compound bodies*, those *intricate combinations of elements and processes*, which all require not only an earnest and close, but a long-sustained, unflagging attention, as the only condition of faithful and exact observation and accurate knowledge.

The intelligent teacher watches carefully the progressive development of his pupil's power of attention, and exercises it according to the increasing force and firmness of its grasp, so as to secure a perpetually *growing power of retention*, through all the successive exercises which he contrives for its discipline, on *natural and artificial forms*, their various *combinations, numbers, powers, and characteristics*, of whatever denomination in the vocabularies of science and art.

Regarding attention as the master power in the grasp of the perceptive faculties, he values, most of all, its strength and retentiveness, its ability to maintain an unbroken sequence of activity, such as not unfrequently demands the incitement of the most earnest desire to arrive at the wished for result, and produce, in turn, the most resolute determination of the will to persevere in action till the result is mastered.

Here, again, the teacher finds his best resort in the objects and processes of nature; unwearied attention is in no way so effectually secured, without undue or fatiguing exertion, as in analyzing and inspecting the various *parts* of *plants*, or the *anatomical mechanism* of animal forms, and, more particularly, of insects. While no humane or enlightened teacher would ever propose even one half hour of unbroken attention, on the part of very young pupils, twice that time may safely and advantageously pass in the suggestive questions of the teacher, and the ready answers of the pupils, during the examination of a single specimen of the productions of nature. In such circumstances, instruction takes its best form,—that of interesting *conversation;* and time flies only too fast for both parties in the exercise. Another sustained effort of attention may, by a judicious change in the form of mental action, be as easily secured by permitting the pupil to make such attempt as he can at *delineating*, in detail, the parts of the object which he has been contemplating; still another may be obtained by permitting him to describe in *words*, and at full length, what he has observed; and even the giant Despair of "composition" may be conquered by allowing the pupil to write his description.

Such processes prepare the young student in due season, for those arduous and unflagging exertions of attention by which he ultimately succeeds in solving lengthened and complicated problems in mathematics, disentangling long and inverted sentences by tracing the grammatical relations of their parts, and following, with patient assiduity, every step in extended and abstruse processes of reasoning on subjects more purely mental in their character.

The teacher who would merit the rank of an educator, and who would render all his processes of instruction not merely didactic but disciplinary, can never be too careful to accustom himself to survey the whole field of human culture in its completeness; to keep ever before his own mind the strict unity of the principle of intelligence, the analogy and cotendency of its various modes of action, and the identity of their results in the enlarging and quickening of its powers, and the strengthening of its grasp, on whatever subject it may be called to fasten. Philosophical writers, of high repute, have, sometimes, in their zealous advocacy of the value of their special studies, as instruments of mental discipline, been led greatly to underrate the disciplinary influence of all intellectual training connected with the observation and study of nature. They seem to have overlooked the fact that quick, acute, penetrating, close, persevering attention is one and the same priceless attainment, whether exhibited in the examination of an external object or in the investigation of the most abstruse of subjects that can be submitted to the action of human intellect.

The experienced and observing teacher knows well that his students who excel in the exercises prescribed in the departments of logic and metaphysics are those whose faculties have been most thoroughly disciplined in the processes of analysis, comparison, and classification, of induction and deduction, applied to the study of natural objects, under the guidance of mathematical and physical science. The materials on which the mind works in each of these great groups of subjects are undoubtedly wholly different; but its action is virtually the same in both—attention leading to discernment, discernment to fact or to truth.

The student who is thus trained in the true unity of his intellectual being, issues from the preparatory sphere of education well prepared to meet the exigences of actual life, whether these present themselves in the form of intelligent and prompt activity, or in that of rigid investigation and profound research.

### NATURAL CONNECTION OF THE PERCEPTIVE AND THE REFLECTIVE FACULTIES.

To enable his pupils to extend the exercise of *attention* into that of continued *observation*, is the great aim of the teacher, who works intelligently on the material of mind, with a view to elicit power of thought. As far as the discipline of the perceptive faculties extends, the end of culture is to create an *observing* mind; from which, in the beautifully perfect arrangements of the great Author of intelligence, spring, in succession, a *reasoning* and a *reflecting* mind. The latter, however, can never be obtained without due obedience to the Creator's law of succession, in the development of intellect. The materials of reason and reflection lie, to a great extent, though not exclusively, in the field of observation; and, a regard to the law of natural and healthy development, therefore, induces the teacher to look carefully to the first steps of his procedure in the processes of cultivation. Having used his best endeavors to vivify and invigorate the power of attention, by all appropriate means and appliances, he proceeds to the use of every genial method of confirming the tendency of the mind to maintain that faculty in *habitual action;* to stamp on the intellect, as a characteristic trait, an inquisitive and appropriating spirit, which examines and searches into all things within its sphere, aggregates their riches to itself, and ever comes home laden with results for the exercise of powers and faculties yet greater than itself; and, to which it is ordained to minister. It is thus that the mind becomes the delighted and conscious agent in its own advancement.

### PROCESSES BY WHICH THE HABIT OF OBSERVATION IS SECURED.

The frequent solicitation of attention, by the presentation of attractive objects, would, of itself, as we see in Nature's unaided training of the savage, provoke a tendency to observe and to inquire. But, the action of the intelligent teacher, in aid of Nature, and in obedience to her dictation, is founded on a law of moral certainty, derived from the study of the laws of mental action. Understanding and relying on the susceptibility of the mind to the influence of the objects by which it is surrounded, and the perfect adaptation of these objects to that end; and, aided, no less effectually, by that inward thirst for knowledge, that burning desire to observe and understand, which actuates the young mind itself, the enlightened teacher knows he has but to attract *attention* to the object which he wishes to employ as a material in the fabric of knowledge. Attention gained, secures *perception;* if the object is properly selected, and skillfully handled.

The volatility of attention in the immature mind, which, if unguarded, tends to mental dissipation and superficial observation, the teacher counteracts by genial measures, adapted to arrest and fix this subtle element of mental power, and carry it successfully forward, from step to step in observation, till the end in view in investigation is attained. The successive steps of the mind's progress, under the guidance of a skillful instructor, in endeavoring to arrive at the result of true perception, exact observation, and complete knowledge, are suggestively indicated in the process of investigating the structure of any visible object, and naturally present themselves in the following order: *examination, analysis, inspection;* aided by *interrogation, direction,* and *information,* and extended successively to the more complex processes of *comparison* and *classification.*

*Examination, as a Process in Intellectual Training.*—In the absence of the prompting and directing power of genial culture, it is true, perhaps, that most of our race are permitted to fill the measure of their days without one definite or quickening thought of the objects by which they are surrounded for a life-time. The peasant boy, who, of all human beings, is the most favorably situated for the contemplation and intelligent study of nature, seldom experiences the friendly aid of a suggestive question, that might lead him to appreciate the elements of intellectual wealth, in which the field of his daily labor abounds. Education has given him the ability to compute his wages, to read, or to sign a receipt; and, thus to meet the humble demands of his animal subsistence. It may even have afforded him some formal instruction in grammar or geography. But, it has not even hinted to him that, in "herb, tree, fruit, flower, glistering with dew," there are wonders of skill, and beauty, and power, fitted to fill his soul with delight, and to exalt him to a higher intelligence; that, in the bud, as it opens in spring, in the expanded blossom of summer, in the tinted leaf of autumn, in the shell which he picks up from the sand of the brook, in the very pebble which he "turns with his share, and treads upon," there are offered to his mind whole volumes of the richest knowledge, which the study of a life-time cannot exhaust.

An eloquent American writer, speaking of the advancement of education, says: "The time may come when the teacher will take his pupil by the hand, and lead him by the running streams, and teach him all the principles of Science, as she comes from her Maker." The teacher is here rightfully represented as fulfilling, in his humble sphere of duty, the highest offices of philanthropy and of religion. Such is the teacher's noble and beneficent function, in favoring circumstances; yet, not less when, yielding to the exigencies of life, he is confined within the walls of his school-room, but brings in Nature's apparatus from without, to give life, and meaning, and efficacy to his instructions, and win the young mind to the earnest and devoted study of the works of the Creator.

*Intellectual Effects Resulting from the Examination of Objects.*— The zealous teacher, working with such light shed upon his labors, knows that, in presenting a product of Nature to the eye, he is presenting a germ of thought to the mind, which, under his skillful management, shall duly unfold, in leaf, and blossom, and ultimate fruit. He knows that, in the absence of a guiding suggestion, his young pupil may have looked a thousand times on that leaf, as a thing which did not concern him; on the shell, as only something queer; on the pebble, as an unintelligible intruder, perhaps, on his personal comfort; on the flower, as something pretty, that his sisters are fond of; on the fruit, as a sufficiently satisfactory morsel for his palate; and, that thus, in the great universal hall of learning, stored with library and apparatus, the orphaned mind may have sauntered away the precious hours of early life, without having been induced to study a single lesson, or engage in a single exercise. All this the teacher is well aware of; but, he knows, too, the hidden life and power that lie wrapped up in the little object with which, as a specimen from Nature's cabinet, he proceeds to magnetize the sentient intellects before him. He knows that, as surely as these susceptible beings are brought near enough to come within the range of action, they fall under the spell of its power, are charmed to rapt attention, and carried on, in wondering and delighted observation, till they are finally arrested by the grateful surprise of conscious knowledge, and advanced intelligence.

Is it a plant which forms the subject of the lesson he would give? He has but, by a striking question, to break the crust of habituation, which has blunted the perception of his pupils, and hinders their mental vision. He has but to ask them to *describe* its parts, in detail, as he holds it up before them, and he has gained the grand preliminary condition of effective perception,—attentive *examination.* As the description extends its ramifications, the weed, which had been a thousand times trodden under foot, without a thought of its nature or construction, becomes an eloquent expositor of Creative mechanism and life; its parts become organs and channels of vitality,—a wondrous laboratory of chemical elements and action; the individual object becomes a member of a family, each of whom has his life and his history, his birth, growth, maturity, and decay; leaving, as the moral of his story, the parting suggestive question, riveted in the wondering mind, "Am I not wonderfully made?"

One such result,—and the more common the object which secures it the better,—one such result is sufficient to ensure a repetition of itself, in a thousand other instances. The ice of indifference is broken; and the observer may now see clearly, through the transparant water, the many-formed beautiful pebbles on the sandy bed of the stream. The time and trouble of examination, it is now found, are amply repaid in the conscious pleasure of intelligent observation; and, they are no longer begrudged. The mind has now become desirous to observe, examine, and explore. It has already set out on a career which, were all educators intelligent agents, would be ceaseless to all to whose advancement it is their part to minister.

*Example of a Successful Teacher.*—A most striking exemplification, in this respect, of successful instruction, was often exhibited in the devoted labors of the late Josiah Holbrook, who, although the very extent of some of his plans for the advancement of popular education may have rendered their execution difficult for the endeavors of an individual, yet was uniformly successful in his attempts to introduce the study of natural objects, as a part of early education in all schools. Trusting to the power of attraction and development latent within a stone, picked up by the wayside, he would enter a school, with no other apparatus of instruction provided; and, holding up the familiar object, would succeed, by means of a few simple but skillfully-put questions, in creating an earnest desire in his young audience to be permitted to look more closely at the object. He would then hand it to them, and have it passed from one to another.

Having thus secured the preliminary advantage of *earnest attention*, his next step would be, by a few more brief questions, to lead his little class to a close and *careful examination* of the specimen submitted to their notice; and, to their surprise and delight, to enable them to see that the bit of granite in their hands,—although but one stone to the eye, at first sight,—actually contained portions of three different kinds of rock. He would then give his pupils an unpretending but thoroughly effective exercise in *analysis*, by inducing them to point out distinctly each component element, apart, and to describe, at the moment of doing so, its points of difference from the others, by which the eye might recognize and the mind distinguish it.

Another stage, in the well-planned lessons of this true teacher, would lead to a yet closer *inspection* of the component elements in the object of observation, by the presentation of separate specimens of each, in *comparison* with the smaller portions of them perceptible in the stone. The transparency of the *mica*, its laminated form, its beauty to the eye, would all come up in turn, for due notice and remark; nor would its peculiar adaptation to several of the uses and conveniences of life be overlooked. The *quartz* element, with its beautiful crystalline aspect and forms, its value as a gem, its wide diffusion in the granular condition, its presence and its effects in the composition of rocks and soils,—all briefly exemplified and enumerated,—would form a copious subject of instruction and delight. The *feldspar*, too, with its creamy tint and block-like configuration, and its valuable uses in the hands of the potter and the dentist, would come in for its share of delighted attention and studious observation.

Here was the true office of instruction faithfully exemplified. Here was genuine mental activity, on the part of the pupil; and, here were its natural effects,—vigorous, healthy expansion and development, together with the pure, natural, and salutary pleasure of intellectual exercise,—more dear to the child than even his favorite play. Here, too, were effectually secured the moral influences of culture, docility, order, regularity, voluntary attention and application, gratitude to the instructor for personal favor and benefit consciously received, an earnest desire implanted for the true and enduring pleasures which spring from knowledge, and the first steps taken in the life-long pursuit of science. The teacher, having put himself into a true living relation to the mental constitution of his pupils, could, without delaying for formal calls to order or attention, proceed; at once, to the benign office of his vocation, as the guide of the young mind. By a wise preventive method,—not by authority, rule, or penalty,—he secured the devoted attention and good order of his pupils, and, not less, their own happiness, their sympathy with him, at the moment, and their habitual reverence for him, as the living source of knowledge.

After one lesson, such as has been described, the substantial and durable effect resulting from it was usually perceptible in the fact that, on the dismission of the school, the juvenile members of Mr. Holbrook's audience would be found resorting to whatever place they thought likely to furnish them with specimens such as he had exhibited in his lesson. This was almost universally the case when the lesson happened to be given in a rural region, where objects of the kind in question were easily obtained. But, not less zeal for collecting specimens for juvenile cabinets, would sometimes be manifested in the more confined sphere of city life, an instance of which it would be difficult for the writer to forget.

An eager group of little collectors were scrambling for specimens around the temporary shed of the stone-masons occupied in the erection of a public building. They were busily replenishing their pockets with such pieces as struck their fancy, and stopping now and then to compare specimens, or each to examine his own more closely. Drawing near to the juvenile company of geologists, as their heads were clubbed together in earnest inspection of a specimen, the observer heard one exclaim, "Well, I do not think it is the right kind. For, you know, Mr. Holbrook said the way to spell granite was not *g-r-a-n-i-t-e*, but '*mica, quartz,* and *feldspar*.' Now, there is not a bit of mica in any of these stones." The observer happened to know of Mr. Holbrook's visits to the school to which the boys belonged; and, as he saw that the little students had just found their way to the exact spot in investigation where Mr. H. would be glad to meet them, so as, by means of a little closer analysis, to enable them to detect the difference between granite and "sienite," he relieved their anxiety by telling them that they had better not throw away the pieces they had picked up, but carry them to the school-room, next morning, and ask Mr. Holbrook to tell them why there was no mica in their specimens, and what those black specks were. One of the little explorers returned to his home, on the following day, to tell, with a face all radiant with intelligence, about the quarries of Syene, in Egypt, the quarries of Quincy, and those of the "Granite" State, and even to go into some details, in which neither of his parents was sufficiently versed in science to follow him satisfactorily.

*Analysis, in its Connection with the Discipline of the Perceptive Faculties.*—An eminent writer has truly said that a dwarf, behind his steam-engine, may remove mountains. Analysis is the correspondent power of the intellect. It is the grand instrument in all the operations of the perceptive faculties. It is observation working scientifically; and, of all the implements of science, it is the keenest in its edge, the truest in its action, and the surest in the results which it attains. It is the key to knowledge, in all departments of intelligence; and, perfection in its processes is the crown of glory on the head of him who stands foremost in the field of scientific research. Education, as the power which trains and forms the mental habits, has no higher boon which it can confer, as the result of years of practice and discipline.

Valuable, however, as this process is, education, in the history of the past, could lay but slight claims to the merit of having formed the mental habits which it implies; since the means and opportunities of analytic intellection were withheld or neglected, to a very great extent, in consequence of the omission to provide the requisite objects and exercises for the discipline of the perceptive faculties. Education, while it consisted chiefly in arbitrary forms of exercise on abstract principles, connected with formulas in language and in number, drawn from the sciences of grammar and arithmetic, precluded the exercise of perception, by causing the learner to assume, instead of investigating, the primary facts of language and of number. At the present day, we obey the law of inductive procedure, and substitute personal observation and distinct perception for wide assumption and broad assertion. This is true of, at least, the modes and methods of all who profess to teach philosophically, as not mere instructors, but educators of the mind. Still, there remains much to be done with reference to the early direction and training of the intellectual faculties, so as to ensure the selection and presentation of the proper materials on which the intellect should be exercised in the first stages of its course of discipline.

Analysis, as a process of observant mind, implies the presence of objects which, by its solvent power, it is to reduce to component elements; and, as the real object, the fact, the actual relation, precede, in the order of nature and development, the ideal image, the intellectual abstraction, the logical deduction, early education in its primary operations, should conform to this law of order and of progress, and, in prescribing its first forms of exercise and discipline, should obviously draw its materials from the external universe of palpable realities, and not from the internal world of pure thought, in which the young mind possesses so little conscious power. Nor is it well for the mind that the habit of analytical observation and study, so indispensable to its successful action, in all forms of acquisitive exercise, should be deferred to the later stages of intellectual culture. Facility in analysis, acquired by practice on the accessible forms and relations of external objects, is easily transferred, by analogy, to the arithmetical exercise of resolving complicated numbers into their simpler constituent groups; or, the grammatical one of reducing a perplexing period to its primary elements, and these, in turn, to their component parts.

Progress in mathematical science and linguistic study, would be much surer and more rapid, if, instead of being demanded of the earlier stages of mental progress, it were postponed to a period subsequent to that of analytical exercise, practised, for years, on objects perceptible to the senses.

Analysis, as the systematic process of examination, is one and the same thing, in whatever direction it is applied; its power as an instrument of discipline, is as fully felt in investigating the structure of a plant as that of a sentence; and, the intelligent teacher, while superintending such a process, will feel the same weight of obligation resting on him in the one case as in the other. He will, accordingly, be watchful over the manner in which the process is conducted, that it be not superficial, or hasty, or partial, but thorough-going, deliberate, and exhaustive, as far as it ought to extend; and, that it be furnished with faithful expression, or record, at every step of its progress. It is thus only that the indispensable broad line of distinction can be drawn, which gives certainty to knowledge, by separating what has been examined from what has not been, and measures what is known by what has been done.

*Inspection, as a Disciplinary Process for the Perceptive Faculties.*—When analysis has faithfully performed its peculiar task, and singled out for observation the very last component element in the object of investigation, there remains yet, to the attentive teacher, another stage of perceptive progress to be accomplished by his pupil, under the suggestive direction of a mind which has already traveled the path of knowledge. The searching *inspection of the individual elements* which compose a complex whole,—an inspection so minute, that each element may be described and defined in its distinctive unity of constitution and character, and, in the clearly traced relation which it bears to the whole, as well as in each of its own chief characteristics, or prominent features,—becomes, perhaps, in turn, an element in some wide-sweeping induction, for purposes of comparison and classification.

Elementary botany,—that which a young child is perfectly competent to study, and which requires but the seeing eye and the attentive mind, to examine and describe the different parts of a plant, or even a root, a stem, a bud, or a leaf,—abounds in the best of materials for exercise in close and minute examination of details. To render this process a tendency and a habit of his pupil's mind, is here the office of the educator. Yet, this is but one of the numerous resources of nature on which he may draw for the cultivation of the highest traits of intellectual skill and expertness, as attributes of the young minds, which it is his business to train to the highest pitch of mental power to which he can raise them.

In the examination of a plant, for example, he does not limit the attention of his pupils to the mere analysis of the whole into its parts. Every part, separately, he makes an object of distinct inspection and investigation, in every light in which observation or science enables him to hold it up. No feature of individual character is suffered to escape notice,—no detail, how minute soever it may be, in which it differs from, or resembles, a correspondent point of form or function, in another specimen of kindred character.

In lessons on animal life,—to use another example,—the juvenile student, under the charge of the watchful teacher, is directed to observe the fact, which minute inspection discloses, that, in one instance, where he would naturally, at first glance, think that he has seen two *feet;* he will actually discover, on closer inspection, two *hands;* that, in observing the figure of the chimpanzee, he has been contemplating neither biped nor quadruped, but a quadrumanous (four-handed) animal; and, that this distinction is founded chiefly on the careful examination of the member which he had been accustomed to call a *toe*, but which is, in reality, a *thumb*, designed to aid in the actions of grasping and climbing, which are so important to the animal's mode of life. The close inspection of one member thus becomes, for the time, the turning point on which the young student depends for the recognition of a grand distinction in nature, and for the true understanding and proper appreciation of the scientific term in which this distinction is recorded.

*Interrogation, as an Instrument of Intellectual Discipline.*—In the language of general writers on subjects connected with the experimental and tentative processes of science, man is said to *interrogate* nature. The figure is a most suggestive one to the teacher, with reference to his business and duties. It presents man in his appropriate attitude of an attentive and docile child of Nature, inquiring trustfully of her concerning the causes which lie too deep for mere intuition, but which her maternal spirit is ever ready to reveal to earnest desire and faithful endeavor. The human parent and the teacher stand, to the young mind, in the same oracular relation, as expounders and interpreters of the great volume of creation. But, how seldom is the inquiring spirit of childhood encouraged to avail itself of its lawful provision for the furnishing of that knowledge which it consciously craves, as the sustenance of its life! How seldom does the teacher feel the full force of the obligation which the inquisitive habits of childhood lay upon him, to encourage the spirit of curiosity which prompts the many questions of the child! How seldom does he feel that his business is to incite, and stimulate, and prompt, and enliven, in every way possible to him, this primary instinct, which impels the mind toward the goal of knowledge! How seldom does he enter into the spirit of the wise suggestion of the poet; and, even when in the very act of feeding the intellectual appetite, so contrive as "by giving" to "make it ask!"

*Book Questions.*—The teacher is not usually so remiss in regard to the importance of interrogation, as a stimulus to intelligence, so far as concerns his own resort to that process. Far from it! He knows its value, as a pointer or guide-post, to definite results. Nor are there wanting instructors so reliant on interrogatory forms, and so distrustful of their own power to devise them, that they conduct the whole business of a lesson, following literally the numerous questions printed on the page of the text-book. Such questions, it is true, are not to be despised and rejected in the wholesale style in which they are sometimes disposed of by the young and sanguine teacher, who has just begun to see their inadequacy to the purposes and wants of personal instruction. The printed question, even when extended to minutiæ, may be rendered very serviceable to the formation of habits of faithful application and close study, as well as accurate recapitulation; if the young student is directed to make use of it as a test, in regard to the exactness of his preparation for a personal examination on the subject of his lesson; if he is duly trained not to regard the printed question as merely the teacher's part in a verbatim mechanical dialogue between the master and himself, in which the last word in the sentence of the one speaker forms the literal "cue" to the first word in that of the other, but, as a criterion of his knowledge of the subjects, as a friendly intimation that, if he can not furnish an answer to the question before him, he is so far deficient in his preparation to give intelligently an account of the part of the subject to which the question refers.

*Children's Questions.*—But, it would be more to the purpose of the young teacher's business, if,—instead of the printed aid offered to him in what should be his own part of a lesson, and which, if he respects his own mind, he will draw only from his own resources, according to the needs of the pupil,—the page of the text-book abounded, rather, in the questions which *children* would like to ask, for their personal information. The judicious instructor will always make free use of interrogation, as a means of ascertaining or aiding the degree of his pupil's intelligence. But, he will not overlook the fact that this process, like that of the printer, in taking his proof impression, is to certify a result,—not to create it. The questions which the child is permitted or encouraged to put to his teacher, are, often, the sole means by which the former is enabled to "set up" accurately in his mind the facts of the lesson required. The number and the closeness of these questions become, further, the expression and evidence of the interest which the pupil takes in the lesson. To the teacher who possesses the patient and sympathizing spirit of his office, these questionings come gratefully to his ear, even when they betray the "blank misgivings of a creature wandering in worlds not realized." It is then that he is most impressively reminded of the true nature of his work, as an intellectual guide and conductor. He is ever careful, therefore, to provoke, rather than repress, interrogation; and, even so to frame his own questions that they shall serve to call forth fresh inquiries from his pupils.

The appropriate discipline of the perceptive faculties, depending, as it does, on the frequent presentation of objects of sense, with a view to win attention, and secure exact observation, implies that the teacher resorts, on all occasions, to close questioning, as the suggestive process by which the pupil is induced to use his own perceptive power, to rely on the fidelity of his own observation, and thus to acquire a knowledge which is substantial and thorough-going. But, it is not less true that, in proportion to the pupil's interest in the efforts which he makes, and the progressive steps which he takes in every process, his very attainments will be suggesting and prompting further inquiries, for his future guidance. The spirit and intelligence, as well as the pleasure, therefore, with which he proceeds in his work, will depend, to a great extent, on the consciousness that he is not working in the dark.

*Mode of Answering Questions.*—The answer to the pupil's questions, however, the true teacher is well aware, is not always to come from the lips of the instructor. It is often left intentionally to be the fruit of the learner's further efforts and closer examination. To withhold an answer to the most eager question, is sometimes a truer kindness than to give it. The ripe and perfect fruit of knowledge must sometimes, like that of the tree, be patiently waited for, and wrought for.

*Leading Questions.*—The wise teacher, however, will know as well when to put the skillful leading question, which does not supersede, but rather calls forth the activity of the pupil's mind. The leading question, though unlawful at the bar, is, under the management of the prudent teacher, the very turning point, in some cases, which decides whether he is "apt to teach," as an intelligent guide to the results of actual knowledge and true discipline.

*Direction and Information, as Didactic Processes Connected with the Exercise and Discipline of the Perceptive Faculties.*—The answers given by a judicious teacher to the questions of his pupils will often consist in references to the sources of information, rather than in direct replies. In the study of natural objects, it is peculiarly important that the pupil should see, and think, and judge, and discover, for himself. To such training in self-reliance and self-help, the exercise of the perceptive faculties on the details of form in animal, plant, and mineral, is preëminently adapted. The embarrassing complexity and intricacy, and the baffling abstruseness, and the perplexing obscurity, which sometimes characterize other subjects of investigation, and which call so loudly for the teacher's frequent aid to his pupil, do not exist here. The simplicity and the beauty of nature's products, invite and attract attention; and, every successive stage of examination leads unconsciously to another. The teacher has but to indicate and to prompt, and thus leave the mind the rich satisfaction of achieving its own progress. He is not tempted to fall into the besetting sin of instruction,—that of anticipating, and assuming, and asserting, and so quenching the mind's healthful thirst by the lukewarm distillations of precept and rule, instead of leaving it to refresh itself by drinking at the cool, vivifying fountain-head of original observation.

An eminent naturalist once gave a very impressive lesson in the art of teaching to one who is himself, professionally, an instructor. The question proposed to the savant was, "How may we distinguish snakes which are venomous from those which are not?" "Come into my study," was the answer, "and I will place before you some of each kind; and, then, by examining, you can see for yourself." It is thus the true teacher proceeds with his pupils: it is thus he gives certainty to knowledge, and clearness and vigor to the mental faculties.

As a guide and director of the mind, the intelligent instructor points his pupils to the sources from which he himself obtained information, and thus admits them to the honor of partnership with him in investigation and accumulation. Teacher and student thus become allied by friendly participation in the same pursuits; and, a high, though unostentatious, moral effect is blended with the cultivation and enjoyment of intellect.

The teacher, however, who thus wisely throws his pupils, as far as practicable on their own resources, does not thereby preclude the ample furnishing of all needed information, which intelligent appreciation and successful application may require. He will, on the contrary, take pleasure in disclosing facts, in tracing analogies, and furnishing explanations, when these serve to give additional value and attraction to the theme of his instructions. He will thus contrive, at once, to satisfy and to stimulate the mind's natural craving for knowledge, and make every step of progress the foothold and the impulse to yet another. He will still be careful, however, even when imparting direct information, to confine it within those limits which shall leave a wide and inviting field for the pupil's own investigations, and secure his personal interest in future explorations, which may subserve the important purposes of acquisition, as connected with attainments in the various departments of education, or with those advances in science which may form a large part of his own conscious happiness, and contribute, ultimately, to the general diffusion of knowledge.

*Comparison, as a Disciplinary Exercise of the Perceptive Faculties.*—The unity of the intellect, as a principle in the human constitution, forbids any attempt at literal or exhaustive analysis, in the study of its diversified character and modes of action. In educational relations, more particularly, all attempts at the analytic observation of mental phenomena, for purposes of intelligent and healthful culture, must ever be regarded as merely analogical presentations and figurative expositions. The successive stages of mental development and discipline, in like manner, are incapable of being cut apart and separated by any dividing line of demarcation. On the contrary, they naturally blend into one another, with a closeness of connection, and a delicacy of shading, which does not admit of precise distinctions, or marked discriminations.

When we group, therefore, the various modes in which intellect manifests itself in action, and designate one of these groups by the term "perceptive," and another by the term "reflective," we recognize a distinction, with regard to which, even a superficial observer of the mind's activity, would not venture to say that it is not founded on an actual difference. Still, we should find it extremely difficult to lay down a precise line of demarcation, and say with certainty, in every instance, here terminates the perceptive, and here commences the reflective action of intellect. Thus, in assigning its place to the master faculty of intelligence, we should feel no hesitation in ranking *reason* among the reflective faculties. But, when this noble power descends, as has been so happily expressed, to the humble office of "judging according to sense," it necessarily partakes of the character of the class of faculties with which it mingles in action. It constitutes, thus, an element and a condition in *perception* itself; as is verified by the consequences of its absence, in the intellectual action of the insane person, who distinctly enough *perceives* the form of his friend, but, in the inexplicable aberration of reason, salutes him as a foreign ambassador, come to do him the honor of a visit, in consideration of his world-renowned skill in disentangling complicated questions in state policy.

Comparison combines, usually, an act of volition with the process of observation, directed to two or more objects, for the purpose of recognizing their unity or diversity of character; and, hence, is properly regarded as but the preliminary or introductory step to the act of *judgment*, which pronounces the case one of analogy or anomaly. It is not unusual, therefore, to class comparison as purely an act of judgment, or decisive reason; and, by its office, a *reflective* faculty. As a process of intellection, however, it obviously commences with the perceptive act of attentive *observation;* and, as a disciplinary and developing operation in mental culture, it falls under the special care of the educator, as an exercise in the early training and forming of intellectual habit.

*Proper Rank of Comparison, as an Intellectual Process.*—Regarded in connection with the study of natural objects, the act of comparison, is an exercise of the perceptive faculties, which, in the order of intelligence, is the immediate sequel to the processes of examination, analysis, and inspection. These, indeed, are but the legitimate preparatory stages for its wider mode of action, and higher offices in the sphere of intelligence. Yet, in its turn, it is but the humble ministration of intellect to the yet higher offices of *classification*, under the guidance of the master function of *induction*, which presides over all the varied forms of intellectual activity, connected with the observation and study of nature.

*Intellectual Effects of the Discipline Resulting from the Exercise of Comparison.*—Comparison, as a process of intelligence, commenced under the watchful eye of the teacher, on the objects of perception,—the only sure and firm ground of early mental development,—gives a certainty and a skill to the perceptive action of the mind, which tell, with sure effect, on all analogous operations of a more purely intellectual or even an abstract character, in later stages of education. The influence of the habit of careful and exact comparison, extends, with full effect, to the highest efforts of mature mind, in the most complicated and intricate relations of thought, in mathematics, in logic, and in language. Comparison, as the first step in the higher progress of the mind, when making its transition from the study of single objects to that of numbers, and grouping them, by their *analogies*, in *classes*, brings the intellect under the dominion of *order*, introduces it to the discipline of *method*, and ultimately rewards it by the recognition of *law*. *Principle* and *rule* then take charge of the intelligent mind; and, as "strong siding champions," beat down every barrier to its progress toward consummate knowledge.

*Natural Objects peculiarly adapted to the purposes of Comparison, as a Disciplinary Exercise.*—As means of discipline for the perceptive faculties, in various modes of comparison, the materials for practice, furnished in the different departments of nature, are peculiarly adapted to the great ends of education. Their mutual resemblances and contrasts, the prominent features of their correspondent forms, seem to solicit comparison and classification, as destined results of man's mental adaptation to the scene in which he moves, and which so abounds in objects of attractive interest,—the germs of intelligence, enveloped in consummate beauty, that they may lead to the conscious delights of knowledge.

By the introductory discipline resulting from the humble exercise of carefully comparing objects and their characteristic parts, the young mind receives its preparation for the scientific intelligence and the conscious pleasure with which it subsequently enters on the wide range of action afforded by the inviting analogies revealed in the study of comparative physiology and anatomy, and in all investigations to which science conducts, wherever exact classification and consummate knowledge are dependent on attentive and faithful comparison,—a condition equally indispensable, whether in collating the vestiges of past eras in the physical history of our globe, or those of language and of intellect, as revealed in the investigations of philology.

*Classification, as an Exercise for the Discipline of the Perceptive Faculties.*—This form of intellectual action,—which, in its various aspects, may be said to constitute and to consummate human knowledge, in whatever department we contemplate,—is the immediate sequel of the preceding act of mind, in collating the objects of observation, or their peculiar features and characteristics. The resemblances which comparison recognizes in objects, become the leading titles and significant designations of groups and classes. Intellect is thus freed from the burden of the endless and unsatisfactory task of wandering from object to object, in detail, without any conscious thread of connection or guidance, and without any suggestion of a definite end in view, in its wearisome mode of action. By the aid of classification, the chaos of disconnected individualities is converted into an orderly creation, where everything, as of old, is seen to exist "after his kind." Knowledge thus becomes a series of aggregated accumulations, arranged and labelled to the intellectual eye; and, investigation is rendered a rational and inviting pursuit,—directed by definite aims, and leading to satisfactory results.

*Benefits of Classification, as an Intellectual Exercise.*—By the process of classification, man is enabled to trace the successive footsteps of the Creator in the outward world, to recognize the grand law of universal order, and yield obedience to its dictates in his modes of mental action. The student of nature, pursuing his investigations in this spirit, is prepared, by successive illustrations of fact, to amplify his classifications into those wide inductions which are the glory of science, and which aid the intellect in accomplishing the vast generalizations for which its powers of comprehension and its ceaseless aspirations seem equally adapted.

The exercise of classification tends to create in the young mind the love of order and method. It is, in fact, a strictly logical discipline, resulting in the highest mental benefits, and preparing the heart for the influence of the most exalted moral principle. It belongs, however, as a process of mental culture, to a very early stage of intellectual progress, and begins appropriately with the first conscious steps of advancement in the observation and study of nature. The child, in Nature's great school, finds himself placed in a vast cabinet of specimens, which he takes a peculiar pleasure in examining, and from which, even when little aided by formal education, he draws, with delight, stores of personal knowledge, and the pure pleasure of the conscious activity which his spirit craves.

The objects of nature, as the results of a designing Mind, seem peculiarly adapted to the end of drawing forth the action of intellect and building up intellectual character in the human being. In no respect is this more true than with reference to the facilities furnished in the three great kingdoms of nature, for the purely intellectual processes of arranging and classifying the objects of observation. The young mind here finds itself placed in a sphere of order, in which every thing is arranged for the correspondent action of thought; in which every object invites to observation, and every group solicits a recognition of the principle of classification.

*Early Training in Classification.*—Furnished with such an apparatus for the purposes of instruction, the teacher has but to point suggestively to the successive classes of objects most easily accessible to the young learner in the great classified receptacles of earth, air, and water. He has but to encourage his pupil to collect, compare, and classify the various forms of mineral, plant, and animal, which lie within the range of his daily walks; or, even to deposit, in any convenient and suitable receptacle, groups of leaves of similar form, and to define the shape or the feature which, in his distribution of them, is made the ground of classification. The learner thus obtains a measure and a record of his progress in knowledge; and, the knowledge which he acquires, possesses a true and substantial character, which, in turn, affects that of his mind, giving it a taste for solid acquirements and genuine pleasures.

## CULTIVATION OF THE EXPRESSIVE FACULTIES.

INTRODUCTORY OBSERVATIONS.—The classification of the mental faculties under the designations of "perceptive," "expressive," and "reflective," was adopted in the preceding lecture of this series, as a convenient one for a survey of the human mind, with reference to the purposes of education. This classification, it was mentioned, could not be regarded as founded on lines of distinction which could be assumed as rigorously or literally exact; since its terms are properly but so many names for various states, acts, or operations of the mind,—itself one and the same in all.

Imperfect as such a classification must necessarily be, however, it enables us, by its distinctions, to trace more clearly and definitely the forms of mental action, and the power which the mind possesses of exerting itself in different modes; and it affords to the educator, when contemplating the intellectual capabilities of man with reference to the processes and effects of culture, the advantages of analysis and systematic examination, as aids to the prosecution of his inquiries.

Following the order of nature and of fact, when we trace the succession of action in the exercise of man's intellectual powers, as these are designated in the classification which we have adopted, we observe that, in the mature and deliberate use of the mental faculties, the habitual and normal succession is, (1.) *Observation*, (2.) *Reflection*, (3.) *Expression*. In the immature and susceptible condition of childhood and youth, however, the spontaneous activity and development of the communicative tendencies of the mind cause the action of the expressive faculties to precede that of the reflective; and to this law the order of education will properly correspond.

The perfect action and discipline of the power of expression, require, no doubt, all the aid derived from the maturity of reason and reflection, and, consequently, an advanced stage of intellectual culture. But, in the history of man's mental progress, under the guidance of natural laws, the educator perceives and recognizes in the young mind, an early necessity of utterance, or of expression in some form, as one of the divinely implanted instincts by which it is actuated, and which therefore becomes an indication to be obeyed in the plan and progress of culture.

The phenomena of the external world irresistibly impel the child to utter the emotions which they excite; and the judicious educator will always encourage the young observer to record them, long before the era of experience in which they become subjects of reflective thought or profound cogitation. To give consistency and effect, however, to the forms of expression,—whether for purposes of record or of discipline,—a certain degree of progress must have been attained in the exercise and development not only of the perceptive, but also of the reflective faculties;—a result inseparable, indeed,—as was mentioned in the preceding lecture,—from the right direction of the perceptive powers themselves. In this and in every other attempt to trace the order of mental development, we are always brought back to the grand primal truth that the mind is properly *one*, in all its action; we are reminded that this great fact is the basis of all true culture, and that the different intellectual *faculties*, as we term them, are but the varied phases or modes of action of the same subtle power.

As an introduction, accordingly, to the discussion of the principles which regulate the cultivation of the expressive faculties, as a department of intellectual education, our last lecture followed, to some extent, the necessary connection existing between the discipline of the perceptive faculties and the primary action of the reflective. With this preliminary preparation, we will now proceed, on the plan indicated in the first lecture of this series, to the study of the various forms of mental action which, in the figurative language unavoidable in all intellectual analysis and classification, may be termed the *expressive* faculties.

The plan proposed embraced, it will be recollected, the following prominent features:—(1.) an *enumeration* of each group of faculties, by its *modes*, or forms, *of action;* (2.) *the actuating principle*, or impelling force, of each group; (3.) the *tendency*, or habit, of action in each; (4.) the *result*, or issue, of such action; (5.) the *educational processes*, forms of exercise, or modes of culture, suggested by the four preceding considerations.

Following the order here mentioned, we commence with the

### (I.) Enumeration of the Expressive Faculties.

These may be grouped under the following designations:—Emotion, Imagination, Fancy, Imitation, Personation, Representation, Language, Taste.

*Explanatory Remark.*—To ascertain, with precision, what powers or attributes of the human being should be regarded as properly comprehended under the above denomination, the educator would do well, here as elsewhere, to advert to the primitive signification of the term which is employed to designate the class of faculties to which it is applied. At every step of his progress in the study of man as a being capable of systematic development, the teacher finds a guiding light perpetually emanating from the primary sense of the terms which constitute the nomenclature of intellectual philosophy, in its nalysis of the human faculties. These terms are often highly figurative, and hence peculiarly suggestive with reference whether to distinctness of classification, or to purposes of culture and development. In no case does this remark apply more forcibly than in the present. The term "expression," (*pressing out*,) implies, in the first instance, the existence of something *within*, which, under the action of a force, working whether from within or from without, is *pressed out*, and thus rendered external, palpable, or perceptible.

Referring this term to the phenomena of human experience, we derive, from its primary and figurative sense, the inference, or implication, that man is endued with the power of giving an external manifestation to his internal conditions of thought or feeling. The form of this manifestation may be that of attitudes and actions of the body, changes in the aspect of the countenance, effects on the tones of the voice, or efforts in the organs of articulation, and modifications of the accents of speech; it may appear in imitative acts, in suggestive graphic delineations, or in intelligible written characters. But in all cases, it is the *re*presentative *ex*pression (pressing *out*,) of what has been *im*pressed, or is *present*, *within*.—The inward working may be that of a feeling, an affection, an emotion, or a passion: it may be that of an impressive idea, or of a thought, an opinion, or a sentiment. But the result is invariably an outward effect, audible or visible.

Whatever power or faculty, therefore, has an agency in the process of thus giving an external manifestation to an internal mental condition, will be appropriately comprehended under the designation "expressive;" and the classification will be exhaustive and complete, if it include all those mental states, acts, or operations which give *form* to thought or feeling. The preceding enumeration of the expressive faculties, however, is intended to present only those which are prominently active in the ordinary conditions of humanity, and which are the principal subjects of disciplinary training, in the processes of education.

1. Emotion: *its Offices in Expression.*—Emotion is the natural language of that *sensibility* which tends to render man conscious of

himself, which serves to unite him, by a law of sympathy, with other beings as well as with those of his own race, and which, as a stimulus to his power of will, impels him to the various forms of salutary and pleasurable, or injurious and destructive action. Without this power, ("emotion,"—*moving outward,*) man might, indeed, possess the profoundest capacity of feeling, the utmost depth of thought, the grandest or the most beautiful forms of imagination. His whole inner world might be consciously a scene of ideal glory. But, to his fellow man, he would be mute and unintelligible. Self-contained and solitary, the individual would be as destitute of sympathy as of expression, and live unappreciated and uninterpreted, because incommunicative and unintelligible.

Emotion, therefore, we find is not left wholly at the discretion or the control of man, as a purely voluntary power. Its first and all its strongest manifestations are spontaneous and involuntary. It is the natural and irrepressible language of that wondrous capacity of pleasure and pain with which the human being is invested, in consequence of the susceptive sensibility with which his Creator has seen fit to enliven and to protect his nature.

Emotion, as the natural expression of sympathy, renders feeling legible and audible, and thus enables man instinctively to utter or to interpret the language of the heart; as an intimation of the will, it enables him to read the disposition and intentions, friendly or hostile, of his fellow beings. It is an early instrument of power to the helplessness or the sufferings of infancy, while it proclaims the presence of pain, and brings to the little patient the ready sympathy and remedial aid of the mother. It expresses and attracts the sympathetic affections of childhood and youth. It gives eloquence to the speech of man, warmth to the cordial welcome of friendship, or fire to the hostility of hatred. It melts in pity and compassion for suffering; it glows with indignation at oppression and wrong; it bends in humility and adoration before Infinite majesty, and in reverence to human worth; or it looks haughtily down on the lowly, spurns the petitioner for mercy, and tramples on the weak and the unresisting. Its power for good or evil is unspeakable in all that involves the moral or the intellectual character of human utterance.

*The Forms of Emotion.*—These are as various as the mental relations of man. It is Love, in the instincts of *affection;* Wonder, in those of the *intellect;* Awe, in those of the *spirit;* Admiration, in those of *sentiment;* Joy and Grief, to the *heart;* Hatred and Revenge, in the *malignant* passions; Ardor and Enthusiasm, in the aspirations of the *soul;* Courage and Exultation, in *conflict;* Fear and

Terror, in *danger ;* Embarrassment, Confusion, and Shame, in *failure* or *defeat ;* Anguish, in *pain ;* Contrition or Remorse, in conscious *guilt ;* Agony and Despair, in utter *ruin ;* Serenity, Tranquillity, and Peace, in conscious *rectitude ;* Calmness and Composure, in *self-control ;* Sorrow and Gladness, in *sympathy ;* Laughter, in *mirth ;* Caricature, in *humor ;* Gloom, in *melancholy.*

*Effects of Emotion.*—Its aspects and its traits are as numerous as the ever-changing moods of the "many-sided mind;" and its power of expression ranges through all degrees of force, from the gentle half-whisper of confiding love, or the accents of a mother's tenderness, to the scream of madness and the burst of rage. It moves to deeds of gentleness and mercy, as consciously pleasing acts dictated by the principle of duty; and it prompts to the perpetration of crimes at the thought of which humanity shudders. In all circumstances it becomes an expressive language of indescribable power,—a power for the exercise of which man is laid under responsibleness the most appalling. Its genial effects carry man beyond the limits of his nature, and enable him to approximate to the benignity of an angel; and its malignant workings invest him with the character of a fiend.

*Emotion, the Inspiration of Language.*—Emotion, as the natural, involuntary, or irrepressible manifestation of feeling, is, in itself, the primary form as well as cause of expression. The writhings and the outcries of pain, the tears and the wailings of sorrow, the smiles and the sweet tones of pleasure, the leaping and the laughter of exuberant joy, the exultant attitudes and shouts of triumph, the frown, the harsh tone, and the blow of anger, are all a universally intelligible language. But emotion is also the power which gives life, and force, and effect to *voluntary* and *deliberate* utterance, not only in the tones of spoken language but in the burning words which the glowing heart prompts to the pen of the eloquent writer, and which, when read from the mouldering parchment or the crumbling tablet, ages after they were written, have still the power to stir men's blood, "as with the sound of a trumpet." It inspires the modern youth with the eloquence of Demosthenes, in the words with which he "fulmined over Greece;" it kindles the heart of the student in his "still removed place," with the fire and the shout and the fierceness of the battle scenes of Homer; it appalls him with the spectacle of the victims of inexorable fate, in the defiant appeals of the suffering Prometheus, as he writhes on his rock of torture,—in the superhuman agonies of the doomed Orestes,—in the wailings of the guiltless Œdipus, when he is awakened to the complicated horrors which he has unwittingly drawn down upon himself and upon the very authors of his being.

It is the same expressive power, in its more genial forms, which lulls the youthful reader into the dreamy repose of the pastoral scenes of the eclogue, where

> "Every shepherd tells his tale
> Under the hawthorn in the dale."

It is the same power, in its ecstatic moods, which lights up the soul with the brilliant fire of the lyric ode, whose burning words have immortalized equally the bard and the hero of the antique world of gods and godlike men; and it is still the same magic power over sympathy which holds us entranced over "what, though rare, of later age," we feel to possess the same sway over the heart as that which was written of old for all time.

2. Imagination: *its Office in Expression.*—Emotion endows man with the *power* of expression: his ability to give force and effect to expression, is as his capability of emotion; and the vividness of emotion is dependent on his susceptibility of feeling. But the utmost intensity of feeling might exist in internal consciousness merely; the most vehement excitement of emotion might find no definite or intelligible manifestation; it might be but the idiot's "sound and fury, signifying nothing;" the noblest sentiments of the human soul might find no adequate expression; were it not for the action of another faculty,—that whose office it is to give *form* to the vague effects of feeling, to embody the evanescent phenomena of emotion, and to give to the abstractions of thought and the generalizations of sentiment a definite shape and the durability of a permanent record.

Consciousness and introversion might enable the individual man to hold communion with his own inner conditions of thought and feeling; and memory might enable him to recall them. But, as it is not given to man, by any act of mere direct introspection, to read the heart or mind of his fellow man, sympathetic and intelligent human intercommunication requires, as a condition, the aid of some power or faculty by which feeling may be distinctly manifested, not merely in its stronger and involuntary excitements, but also in its quietest moods, in its gentlest movements and most delicate effects. The communication of pure thought, apart entirely from excited emotion, is also a necessity of man's mental character and relations. Intellect, not less than feeling, has its claims on utterance, that the individual may become consciously a progressive being, and that mutual intelligence and benefit may be ensured to society. Some means, in a word, are needed to *re*present what is present to the mind, to suggest the idea or the thought which, by a law of his nature impelling him, man desires to communicate to his fellow being.

*Analogy, the Medium of Expression.*—Taught by a wisdom above his own, man finds, in the analogies of the outward universe, correspondences to his own inward states of thought and feeling. These analogous forms he refers to as interpreters, in his acts of expression; he transfers them, by a heaven-taught instinct, from their original places in the visible outward sphere to his own inner and invisible world of thought and feeling. These borrowed forms, addressing themselves to a common nature in common circumstances, become the suggestive language of emotion and intelligence between man and man; and, as intellectual skill and expertness are developed, these forms are at length multiplied and complicated so as to assume all the varied shapes of the current coin of speech, even in its most arbitrary modes;—just as, in the history of human intercourse, traffic, which commenced with the interchange and barter of commodities, gradually becomes a process of purchase and sale, by the adoption of convenient forms representing value and price.

*Significance of the term "Imagination."*—The power by which man recognizes the analogies of form presented in the external world, the power by which he *re*presents these, the power by which he transfers these to his own internal world, and thus *images*, by analogy, his invisible, impalpable, feelings and conceptions; the power which thus embodies sentiment, and gives shape to language and all other modes of expression, is suggestively named "Imagination,"—the *imaging* faculty.

*The Sphere of Imagination.*—The office of this faculty, as an expressive power, is one of vast extent and of immense value; and its domain, like that of emotion, is indefinite. Intellect, in its widest excursions and its highest aims, is definite and limited. Its outward sphere is that of sense, as comprehended by the understanding, and measured by the rule of judgment; its inner sphere is that of reason acting on data of definite thought, even in its purest abstractions and widest generalizations. Intellect, in its judicial and critical capacity, may justly assume the authority of deciding on the symmetry and proportion of expression as the form of thought. But it has no creative, no inventive power by which to call up form; it may interpret or explain feeling; but it can not, without the aid of imagination, embody it. Imagination extends its dominion alike over feeling and intellect: it possesses, exclusively, the power of investing them with form. As a sovereign in the vast world of analogy, it reaches, in one direction, to the farthest limits of the outward universe, wherever form exists, in conditions known or unknown; in another direction, it penetrates the deepest secrets of human feeling, and brings them up from their darkest regions of half-unconscious being to the world of form and light, endues them with conscious life and speech, and sends them abroad as ministering angels of good or evil; in still another direction, it explores the ethereal world of thought, and, by its creative energy, gives imagery, and form, and recognized character to impalpable ideas, clothes the naked conceptions of intellect with the garb of symmetrical expression, forges the golden links of language for the continuous processes of reason, invests sentiment with the living majesty and power of utterance, and crowns the inspired productions of the artist and the poet with the consummate beauty of form and the music of immortal verse.

3. FANCY: *its Effects on Expression.*—This faculty, although it possesses a character so peculiarly marked by external tendencies, and proneness to a lower sphere of action than that of imagination, can hardly claim, with justice, the dignity of a separate and independent existence. The term "Fancy," (*fantasy*,) is, strictly speaking, but another name for *imagination*, when that faculty, as an expressive power, assumes, occasionally, a lower than its wonted office, and, not content with the creation of *form*, descends to the addition of minute detail, in the shape, or figure, or color of its embodiments. Fancy, considered as a separate faculty, may be regarded as the servant and laborer of imagination, employed to take charge of all the merely outward effects of expressive art, but whose ambition sometimes leads it to aim at higher offices than it is, in itself, competent to fill. Attempting the creation of visible beauty, it assumes the office of a presiding deity over the fleeting, fluctuating phenomena of fashion and other manifestations of arbitrary taste. Uniting itself with humor and burlesque, it displays the whole world of fantastic oddity, drollery, and grotesque effects, of every species. It handles, with peculiar skill, the pencil of the caricaturist, and delights, sometimes, in the most hideous exaggerations. It contrives, occasionally, to lay mischievous hands on Taste, and with perverting influence to make her play all manner of antics, quite unconscious, all the while, how infinitely absurd and ridiculous she is making herself appear. Hence the whole world of absurd form and combinations in modes of dress and decoration, in incongruous architecture, deformed sculpture, distorted drawing, tawdry coloring, paltry novel-writing, fugitive (and vagabond) verses, agonistic orations, and nondescript lectures.

Fancy, however, has also her own becoming and proper part to play, when, in strictest unison with true Taste, and in filial obedience to her parent, Imagination, she gives symmetry to our dwellings and to our garments, genuine grace to manners, true beauty to our gardens, happy touches to the details of artistic execution, chaste style to writing, and manly plainness to speech.

4. Imitation: *its Tendencies.*—The faculty of Imitation and the tendency to its exercise, which,—in the earlier stages of life, more particularly,—man possesses in common with many other of the animal tribes, form, in whatever regards expression, a peculiar source of power. It ensures, when judiciously developed, as a salutary instinct, all the advantages arising from native facility, as contrasted with the comparatively slow acquirements and laborious endeavors of mere artificial or mechanical training. The long non-age required for the comparatively slow development and maturing of the human being, implies a large dependence on the fostering care of parental guardianship and example; and the innate propensity to imitation, on the part of the child, coincides, in the effect of rendering more ample the opportunity of a long course of model training and practical lessons in the appropriate accomplishments of humanity. Among these, Speech, as the consummation of the expressive faculties, thus becomes the inheritance which one generation transmits to another,—a possession unconsciously acquired, although actually the result of long-continued training, and sometimes, of painful efforts in detail.

*Drawing, as an Imitative Art.*—The imitative tendency of the young, leading, as it does, to the perfecting of utterance, as an exercise in which practice begets skill, extends its influence, by the law of analogy, far and wide, over every branch of art which involves expression as a result. Nor is there one of all these branches which does not, by the habitual practice of it, under the same law, serve to discipline and perfect the power of expression in every other.

The feelings, the imagination, the conceptive power, the taste, and even the critical judgment of the young mind, are all called into as active exercise, in every earnest attempt to draw in outline, to shade, or to color the form of any external object, as in any endeavor to describe it by tongue or pen. Indeed, the extreme fixedness of attention demanded for exact and faithful delineation by the pencil, ensures a yet higher degree of mental activity, than does any other form of descriptive execution, and contributes more effectually to the development of graphic power of expression in language, than can any direct exercise in speech or writing; because the same powers are exerted in the one case as in the other, but with much more care and closeness of application.

*Music, as an Imitative Art.*—Another of the poetic and purely beneficent forms of the divinely implanted faculty of imitation, by which man attains the development of his powers of expression and communication, is that of Music, in the form of *song*. The young ear drinks in, instinctively and intuitively, the beauty of sound, as the eye takes in that of form and color. The laws of melodic variation of tone seem to be inscribed on the human ear, with few exceptions, as the laws of graceful form and expansion are stamped on the plant. But the musical sense is not a merely dry perception or recognition, or a mechanical obedience to law. It is one of the most delightful forms in which man becomes conscious of the pleasure of feeling or the power of emotion; and, as his culture extends, he recognizes it as the intelligent utterance of sentiment, in the noblest expressions of social sympathy, or even of devotional aspiration.

The imitative practice of music, accordingly, in all its forms, from the humblest lullaby of the nursery to the most exalted strains of the perfect vocalist, becomes a powerful discipline of the ear, because of the heart, the intellect, and the imagination. It prepares them to receive more fully the impressions of the melody of speech, and, in due season, to give forth their effects in appropriate expression. The child imbibes from the mother's song the theme of its own imitative efforts, and from the simple beauty of the natural model, catches, at the same time, unconsciously, the emotion of which it is the utterance, and thus early learns to unite expression with feeling. At a later stage of his musical culture and development, he acquires more consciously and more distinctly, a perception of the inspiration which marks the tones of the empassioned eloquence of the orator and the poet, and learns to appreciate the delicious melody of the "numerous verse" which "clothes the poet's thought in fitting sound."

The great masters in musical science and art, abundantly prove, by the transcendent delight which their efforts yield to universal man, the power and value of music as an expressive art, independently of its relation to the cultivation of the power of language. But the intensity of pleasure derived from the perfection of musical composition and execution combined, suggests instructively to the educator the power which even the elementary practice of this imitative art exerts on the character of expression, when embodied in the forms of language,—the ability which it gives to touch the heart, or to kindle emotion, and to throw the whole soul of the speaker and the writer into the mould of utterance.

5. PERSONATION: *its Tendency and Effects, as a Mode of Expression.*—The faculty of *imitation* with which man is endowed, as a form of expressive power, leading him to the acquisition of language, is early manifested in the passion of childhood for Personation; the living, actual representation of what he sees going on in the human

world around him. The lively feelings of the child are not satisfied with the mere verbal presentation of thought and feeling in the arbitrary and conventional forms of language. He has an instinctive desire to impersonate the being of others in himself, and thus to enter more fully into their feelings, and acquire a truer power of expressing them. To his fresh sympathies and ever active imagination, life around him is a drama: "all the world's a stage, and all the men and women are but players," each performing his part.

The child, the primitive man, the poet, all tend to dramatize human life, and to present it in living impersonation. The boy struts the mimic soldier, to his own mimic music; he drags his little wagon as an imaginary fire-engine, or mounts a chair and plays the orator to his little mates. In his puerile sports, he enacts a character or an incident, in dumb show, and requires that his juvenile companions shall express it in words. He personates a hero in history, or makes one in a group in a tableau, in which, as an Indian brave, he is about to dash out the brains of Captain Smith with his war-club, when his sister, as the compassionate princess Pocahontas, rushes in, and rescues the hero. At the academy exhibition, he personifies Mark Antony weeping over the murdered Cæsar, and with words of fire rousing the Romans to mutiny, "crying havoc! and letting slip the dogs of war;" or he resorts, in preference, to the pen, and dramatizes a scene from his country's history, which he and his class-mates enact to the life, according to their power. In the maturity of his intellect, and amid the grave duties of professional life, he pauses, perhaps, to recreate himself, and delight the world with the production of a Comus or a Hamlet, in which, besides furnishing the composition, he still takes an active part in the business of representation, and, true to the dramatic instinct of his nature, sustains a character himself. It is thus that he completes the educational training by which he attains to the height of eloquence and expressive power in word and action; and this dramatic faculty of personation, while it gives vividness and intensity to his utterance, proclaims the meaning and intention of the self-discipline to which he was early impelled, by unconscious instinct.

6. Representation: *The Language of Signs.*—In addition to the more imaginative and, sometimes, physical or corporeal manifestations of expressive power, which the human being exhibits in imitative acts, he possesses, as his special attribute, in virtue of his intellectual endowments, working in unison with the instinctive elements of his nature, that peculiar faculty of Representation, by which he is enabled to suggest his thoughts or feelings to the mind of his fellow man, by substituting for graphic or mimetic, or other forms of delineation, con-

ventional *signs*, audible or visible, devised by his imaginative faculties of invention and combination. These signs are recognized and defined by his conceptive intellect; they are interpreted by the understanding, acting on a law of arbitrary association, established by mutual agreement or common consent, and ultimately sanctioned by prevalent usage. Furnished with this primitive telegraphic apparatus of audible and visible signs, man is enabled to put himself in communication with his sympathetic, intelligent, and rational fellow-beings,—to reveal to them the workings of his mind, and disclose the inmost secrets of his heart.

*Speech and Writing.*—Disciplined and perfected by art and skill, and aided by ingenious and asiduous educational cultivation, man's primitive power of utterance and expression, ultimately manifests itself in the consummated forms of *spoken* and *written language*, regulated by the laws of thought, as dictated by the sciences of *logic* and *grammar*, and adorned by the graces of *rhetoric.*

*Language, a measure of Power.*—The feeble but persevering endeavors of childhood to conquer the difficulties of articulation, and to compass the power of oral expression, indicate, by the successive years which the task demands, how arduous is its accomplishment, and how thoroughly it puts to proof the ability which the young human being possesses to direct and develop his own powers of execution. Yet more striking is the magnitude of the task and the triumph, in the progress achieved by the student of written language, from the date of his first attempt, in boyhood, to pen a letter or compose a theme, to the time when, in the maturity of his intellectual manhood, he rises to address assembled multitudes of his fellow men, and to sway them by the potency of triumphant eloquence; or when he issues from his poetic privacy a work which shall live for ages, as an object of wonder and admiration.

*Pictured and Written Characters.*—Somewhat similar, indeed, have been the difficulty and the progress in the attainment of a mastery over the merely external part of written language; as we perceive when tracing the process from its primal rude attempts in the form of graphic delineations, through its advancement to symbolic representation, and, ultimately, to phonetic characters and alphabetic letters. Of the width of this vast field of human labor, and of the toil which its cultivation has cost, we have no adequate conception, till we look at the graphic delineations which form the historical records of Nineveh, or at the symbolic hieroglyphics and the clumsy phonetic characters inscribed on the temples of Egypt, and then contrast with these the simple and symmetrical letters of the Greek or

Roman alphabet, known and read alike throughout the ancient and modern world of civilization.

*The Value of Language.*—Man's expressive power seems to have consummated itself in the representative phenomena of language. In this form his whole nature, animal, intellectual, and moral, finds effectual utterance; and by this instrumentality, does he become preëminently a progressive being. Language is the channel in which the ceaseless stream of mental action flows onward to its great results. Without this outlet, his soul, imprisoned within itself, would stagnate, and all its wondrous powers perish from inaction. As the medium of communication between mind and mind, language renders education practicable, and brings to the aid of the individual the accumulated thoughts of all times and of all men. Language is the peculiar and chosen province of education. Every process of human culture is conducted through its agency; every result attained in human progress is recorded in its terms; and in every civilized and cultivated community language is justly taken as the measure of individual and social attainment.

7. TASTE: *The Signification of the Term.*—The word "Taste," employed to designate one of the expressive faculties, might seem, from its primary signification, (*relish,*) to be one appropriately applied rather to a passive and receptive condition of mind, than to one so active or energetic as are all those which are properly termed "expressive." But, in the affairs of the mental world, not less than in those of the political, *influence* is often more efficient than *power.* So it is with Taste.—The office of this faculty in relation to expression, is to retain, in the selection and use of language, the *relish* for appropriateness, symmetry, and grace, which the soul has imbibed from the primitive beauty of the forms and the effects—in other words, the language—of nature,—that other name for life and truth.

*Character of True Taste.*—As true taste secures genuine beauty of effect, it is not a merely passive power. It rejects every false savor; for it relishes only the true. It refuses to inhale the flavor of the artificial perfume; because it prefers the aroma of nature. It detests the ugly, and shuns the ungraceful; but it loves the truly beautiful, and builds the fabric of noble thought "after the pattern shown it on the mount," as a chaste harmonious whole, conceived in pure ideal perfection, and executed with faultless skill, like that structure which

"Rose like an exhalation, with the sound
Of dulcet symphonies and voices sweet;
Built like a temple, where pilasters round
Were set, and Doric pillars overlaid
With golden architrave; nor did there want
Cornice or frieze with bossy sculpture graven;
The roof was fretted gold."

Taste is not a quality merely negative in its influence: it is, in language, a positive power. It suggests and prescribes beauty; and, in all expression, beauty is power. Taste virtually decides and ordains the forms of language. It is therefore justly classed as an expressive faculty. It blends its effects, undoubtedly, with those of imagination and fancy, and with those of sentiment and emotion; controlling and directing and modifying these by its intuitive recognition of the eternal laws of beauty and proportion, and instinctively rejecting every blemish. If it is sometimes lost, to appearance, in the effects produced by the more obvious working of other expressive forces; its actual presence and power are not less deeply felt in the pervading harmony which, in such circumstances, it has established, and the genuine beauty which it has diffused. Its influence extends over every form of expressive art; and its results are equally legible in all. It guides the pencil of the painter, the chisel of the sculptor, the tool of the artizan, the hand of the musician, the pen of the poet, the voice and action of the speaker. It reigns over every form of language; and it moulds alike habit, character, and manners; for all of these are but varied modes of expression.

*Taste, under the Influence of Culture.*—Of all the faculties with which man is endued, none, perhaps, is more susceptible of cultivation than taste; and none yields larger results to the process. Trained under the fresh aspects of nature, and the strict discipline of truth, it becomes one of the most healthful influences that a liberal culture infuses into the human soul. It leads to the true, the pure, and the beautiful, in every relation of thought and feeling. Next to the hallowing influence of religious principle, it elevates and refines the whole being, and confers pure and lasting enjoyment on its possessor. It forms one of the most attractive graces of character, and breathes a genuine charm over the aspect of social life. But neglected, corrupted, or perverted, deprived of the healthful air of nature, abandoned to coarse and low association, vitiated by the influence of false custom, distorted by conventional regulations, or tainted by the impure atmosphere of vice, taste becomes depraved, and morbidly craves deformity instead of beauty, and prefers falsehood to truth.

### (II.) The Actuating Principle, or Impelling Force, of the Expressive Faculties.

Feeling: *its Office in Expression.*—The Sensibility with which the constitution of man, as a sentient animal and as a self-conscious moral being, is invested, and by which he is stimulated to action and to utterance, may, for our present purpose, be defined as that element in his nature, which,—whether manifesting itself in temporary *sympathy*, in permanent *affections*,—in vivid *emotion*, or intense *passion* has, for its office, the excitation of his being. As the stimulus of his constitution, it impels man to the function of expression, as a result indispensable to sympathy and communication,—the necessary condition of his social and moral life. It originates in that sensibility to pleasure and pain by which the Creator has enhanced to man the enjoyment and the value of his organized and conscious existence, and secured it, at the same time, by a law of instinctive dread, from exposure to peril and to destruction.

*Feeling, as an Incitement to Sympathy.*—The effect of sensibility, in this relation, is three-fold; producing in man, (1.) a sympathy with the conditions and aspects of the surrounding external world, whether pleasurable or painful, attractive or repulsive; (2.) the mutual sympathy, conscious correlation, and consentaneous action of the two component elements of his constitution,—body and mind; (3.) a sympathy with his fellow men, which makes him a partaker of their pleasures and pains, causes him to desire a return of their sympathies to himself, and consequently leads him to expression and communication, as the means of exciting and attracting it.

*Feeling, as an Involuntary or Empassioned Instigation.*—The sentient and susceptible nature of man, his capacity and his experience of pleasure and pain, affected by causes whether external or internal in their operation, render him liable to unconscious and involuntary excitement, rising, sometimes, to the height of passion. This excitement manifesting itself in emotion,—the main spring of expression,—becomes, in some circumstances, itself a language sufficiently definite, intelligible, and expressive; as may be observed in the laughter and the crying of the infant, in the sympathizing countenance of the compassionate mother, in the ruffled features and angry temper of impatient youth, in the ghastly face of the terrified child, in the glare of the hostile savage, or in the glad smiles of the emancipated schoolboy at his holiday sport.

*Feeling, influenced by Imagination and Volition.*—The beings and forms of his own ideal world of imagination and fancy, or of creative thought, have also their exciting power over the internal sense of pleasure or of pain, and impel man, more or less voluntarily, to exhibit emotion, and to find its natural or customary form of expression in the articulate words of speech,—in the simpler eloquence of mere vocal tone, uttered or suppressed,—or in the silent but more enduring form of the written word.

*Influence of Feeling on the Artist.*—Even language itself, however, in its most distinct and definite forms, is not always sufficiently expressive for empassioned emotion. The admiration of grandeur or beauty may be strong enough and deep enough to demand some more palpable and durable shape in which to express itself. The intense delight in beauty impels the Artist to devote himself to days and nights of toil over the image which alone can satisfy the longing of his soul, for the visible presence of the loveliness which his fancy has conceived in his inner world of life and form.

*On the Actions of the Child and of the Adult.*—It is the untaught, unconscious working of the emotion of love which makes the child find expression for his sympathy in the act of imitating the gait and actions, and the characteristic expressions of those whom he admires. Nor does adult man always escape the effects of this tendency, when maturity of mind and habits of grave research seem sometimes to render the result ridiculous.

*On the Actor and his Audience.*—The natural delight in sympathy and communication, is the incitement which impels the actor on the stage to assume and exhibit, in his plastic frame and features, the agonies of dramatic passion, in all their terrific extremes, while he personates the ravings of Lear, the frenzy of Othello, or the remorse of Macbeth ; and it is the same cause which attracts, night after night, to the crowded theatre, the audience who thus acknowledge the force of the great element of sympathy in human nature, and the power which vivid expression exercises over the heart, when it has even the well sustained semblance of coming from the heart.

*On the Eloquence of the Orator.*—It is from sympathy with the very passions which he delights to excite, that the orator devotes his days of seclusion and nights of application to the study of every art by which expression may be heightened and emotion aroused, when the decisive moment is come, and the interests of the state are at hazard, and men are to feel that their welfare or their safety is to depend on adopting the views of an eloquent and competent leader.

*On the soul of the Poet.*—It is sympathy with the highest sentiments and emotions of his race, and the conscious delight in giving these a noble utterance, that inspires the poet with the assurance of immortality, while he meditates his great theme, and touches and retouches his artistic work, till it stands forth complete in the majestic beauty and perfection after which his soul has, for years, aspired.

*Universality of Feeling, as the Actuating Principle of Expression.*—In all the above and similar instances, the sympathetic feeling which thirsts for expression, and impels to the utterance or the recording of sentiment, is one and the same. It may assume the definiteness and the depth of a personal affection, or the intensity and the comparative excess of a passion, to whatever extent the instigation of feeling may excite the sentient agent. But it is still the same element of sensibility, only working in deeper channels, and with a stronger tide, and therefore doing its work more effectually and impressively. In whatever form, it is still but an act of obedience to the law of his constitution, by which man, as a sympathetic being, is impelled to expression, that he may attain to the power and the habit of communication; and thus fulfill the conditions of his social and moral nature.

*Influence of Feeling on Moral Character, as a Form of Expression.*— The extent to which the element of feeling exerts its power over expression, and the degree to which its development in this relation may be carried, under the influence of educational culture, can be appropriately measured only when we trace it to its effects on the tendencies, the character, and the will of human beings individually, or in their aggregations in society. In either case, we see it in the gentle, the peaceful, and affectionate spirit of the genuine disciple of Him whom we reverence as the "meek and the lowly," and in the genial intercourse of communities governed by the influence of His law of universal love; or we read it in the arrogance, the violence, and the hatred, of which perverted humanity is so fatally capable. As "out of the abundance of the heart the mouth speaketh," the prevalent emotions and expression, the manners, and the habitual language of man, in these opposite conditions of individual and social life, will depict themselves on character and action.

*Influence of Feeling on the Character of Art.*—In the visible language of graphic art, we read the same lesson of the power of feeling as an element of expression. We see it in the appalling force with which the sculptor has presented the agony of pain and struggle, in the writhing frame and contorted features of Laocoon, or the perfect placidity and repose with which he has invested the face and form of Antinöus. Nor is the lesson less impressive when we turn from the superhuman fierceness of expression in attitude and features, which characterizes the delineations of passion and penal torture, in some of the figures depicted by the hand of Angelo, to the serenity, the sanctity, and the unutterable loveliness, beaming from the half-divine forms in which innocence or holiness is pictured by the pencil of Raphael.

*Its power in Music.*—The ear drinks in the same lesson of the power of empassioned expression, while it listens to the great masters of musical art, and feels the majesty of its utterance, as conceived in the soul of Handel, and worthily executed by the skillful hand of the accomplished performer. From such effects of sublimity and force and solemn grandeur, down to the breathings of tenderness in a plaintive strain of pastoral melody, the thrill, responding to the stirring air of the soldier's march, or the wild gayety of the peasant's dance, we have but the varied forms in which emotion evinces its sway over this most expressive of arts, by the inspiration which it breathes into its numberless moods.

*Its Effect on Language.*—To the emotive force of feeling, Language owes all its sublimest and most beautiful forms of cultivated utterance, whether in expressing the depth of affection or the intensity of passion; and the remark is equally true of the literature of the elder world and that of modern times. In no record of humanity is the fact more strikingly exhibited than in the pages of the Sacred volume, where the heart of man is laid open in all its workings, in the primitive language of poetic imagination and Divine truth combined, and where the human soul pours itself forth in every mood; now wondering at the vastness of the creation, or adoring the infinite majesty of the Creator; now humbled to the dust, under the sense of man's insignificance, or, in the tones of contrition and penitence, imploring the boon of pardon; uttering thanks for boundless goodness and mercy; rejoicing in the conscious favor of God; sympathizing in the gladness and beauty of nature; touched by the paternal tenderness and compassion of Jehovah, or joining in the denunciations of "indignation and wrath, tribulation and anguish," threatened to his enemies.

In all the uninspired delineations of thought which have come down to us from ancient times, it is the same pervading element of feeling which has given them their lasting life and their sway over the mind. To some prominent passages of this character we have already alluded; and, for the present, the allusion must suffice. Nor have we time now to dwell on corresponding examples drawn from modern literature, the peculiar charm of which, in one word, is the power with which it calls forth the natural emotions of the heart. In every form which literature assumes, as a power or an influence over the soul, exerted through the medium of expressive language, the main spring of effect, the grand motive power, is feeling. The life of expression, in all its cultivated forms of language or of art, is emotion.

*Feeling, under the Guidance of Education.*—Recognizing the fact last mentioned, the intelligent superintendent of education will direct his endeavors to the due cherishing, strengthening, and developing, as well as to the moulding, guiding, and governing of this great element of intellectual and moral power. With his eye fixed on this momentous issue, he will watch the natural tendency and direction of the instinct whose action he is to guide, so as intelligently to coöperate with its spontaneous working, and aid in the accomplishments of its peculiar office.

The teacher is, to a certain extent, or, at least, so far as he is a teacher of language, bound to furnish his pupil with the invaluable advantage resulting from a ready command of correct expression, one of the surest passports to usefulness and success in life. But the life-spark of expression can not be struck from a dull mind. The latent fire of feeling must be kindled, must be brought to the surface, that it may glow in the living look and audible tone of emotion, or beam forth in the burning words of eloquence, whether flowing from tongue or pen. The judicious instructor will resort to every expedient suggested by the life and beauty of nature and of art, as sources of inspiration, whence corresponding life, and beauty, and expressive power may be breathed into the soul of his pupil, and live in his utterance.

### III. The Tendency or Habit of Action, in the Expressive faculties, as it is Manifested in Utterance.

*Utterance an Instinct.*—When we contemplate man as a being capable of education, he may, for our immediate purpose, be regarded as furnished by his Creator, with what may be termed the *apparatus* of expression, in the gift of the various faculties which we have been hitherto considering. We perceive him further provided with an adequate *motive power*, by which this apparatus is propelled, in the involuntary or voluntary action of feeling. The indication next to be observed by the educator, as the suggestion for his guidance, in his endeavors to coöperate with Nature's tendency to development, is, In what direction does the action of the expressive faculties naturally tend? What, in this instance, is the instinct of spontaneity? What, under the guidance of his own inward promptings, does the child incline to do or to become? What habit or attribute of character does he thus acquire? The answer furnished by observation, in this case, plainly is,—Man, as a sentient, intellectual, and sympathizing being, acting under the primary impulse of instinct, and without any interference of human culture, obviously inclines to Utterance, (throwing himself *out*,) or, in other words, to *self-revelation*, as an ordained function of his nature, verifying and crowning his intelligence, and constituting him a social and moral being, capable of progress and of culture. He craves and finds expression, accordingly, in many and various forms: he makes himself felt and understood, in some way or other, by his fellows. Under the guidance of education, he but learns to do this more definitely and successfully, through language and expressive art. From a sentient and intelligent, he develops thus into a communicative being,—the result, so far, of the combination of unconscious and voluntary education, and, at the same time, the condition and the pledge of subsequent intellectual and moral progress.

*Repression a Common Error of Educational Training.*—The attentive observation—not to say the systematic study—of man, to which the educator and teacher should ever feel himself bound, as the only security for the intelligent and successful discharge of his duties, suggests, at this stage of our subject, the fact, that a prominent feature of error, in the too prevalent arbitrary modes of education, has been the *repression* rather than the development of the natural desire of utterance in childhood.

From the very first steps of his mental and moral progress, man is not a merely selfish and receptive being. He longs to impart his feelings, and to communicate his observations: he wishes to give, as well as to receive: he feels impelled to utter himself that he may impart and confer, not less than receive. His impulse, as a sympathetic one, is unselfish, generous, noble. When the child exclaims to his playmate on the beauty of the flower which they see, he does not merely call for sympathy in the delight which he feels: he would, by his instinctive expression of pleasure, suggest and impart that delight.

Utterance, under the benign guardianship of Nature, as its Author's interpreter, is thus, essentially and substantially, a moral process, not less than a merely sympathetic and intellectual one. Nor, in education, should it ever be forgotten that, by the Creator's ordination, every utterance of a feeling or an emotion, gives it additional strength and life; and that, obeying the divinely instituted law of speech and communication, we are aiding in the process of building up, day by day, and hour by hour, the fabric of human character.

Arbitrary education, however, is, in no feature of its meddling mismanagement more conspicuous than in the *restriction*, the *reserve*, and the *silence*, which it is ever so prone to impose, and on which it is so apt to plume itself, with reference even to the very first stages of its repellent sway.

The five years' probationary and preparatory silence which Pythagoras is said to have exacted of his disciples, might be an excellent discipline for mature minds, as an introduction to the "metaphysic bog profound," into which he meant thereafter to plunge them. But one of the first and most urgent wants of childhood is utterance. The innocent little human being is ever thus holding out his petty link in the golden chain which binds heart to heart, mind to mind, and man to God: he is ever ready to join his link to that of his neighbor. But the mechanical educationist, with his "look at your book, and not at me!" frowns the infant volunteer back to his seat, to his individuality, and his isolation; and the chain by which the little petitioner for sympathy and knowledge, might have been lifted with the conjoined force of the mental world, is of no avail to him. his link of connection with it is yet detached. His turn has not yet come, in the great game of opportunity; and he must bide his time as best he may.

*Appropriate Training.*—Under the unerring and genial guidance of the mother, the child is not perpetually immured within doors, or confined to one spot, or fixed in one posture: he is allowed, occasionally, at least, to behold the outward world, to range the fields, to walk on the road, to observe the objects around him, to feel their attractive force, to admire their beauty, to wonder and to inquire about what is new to him, to utter his exclamations of pleasure, to examine, and to name whatever strikes his attention. He thus enjoys his own nature in the free exercise of his faculties; he is consciously progressive in intelligence and in speech, as in feeling, and, so far, is effectually and successfully preparing to become, in due season, eloquently expressive.

*Disadvantages of City Education.*—The worst, perhaps, of all the many evils attending the supposed necessity of congregating in cities, and adopting artificial modes of life, is one but little thought of. The parent who relinquishes his rural home in the open village street or in the field, flatters himself, perhaps, that he is securing better educational advantages for his children, when he takes up his abode in one of the confined dwellings of the close-crowded city. He may find, by the exchange, a teacher more expert in turning the machinery of instruction, and a more ample supply of the learning to be had from books. But the nobler, the truly liberal part of his childrens' education, he has foregone forever. The free scope, the pure, bracing air, the rich variety of nature,—the healthful influence of these on the growing frame and the expanding mind, on the susceptible heart, on the plastic imagination, on the whole soul and character; these are sacrificed, and with them, the best capabilities of culture.

*Educational Benefits of Rural Life.*—In no respect are the losses just mentioned greater than in regard to the part of education which we are now contemplating. To the child reared in the freedom and the beauty of nature, everything around him becomes a language, expressing the happiness which he unconsciously enjoys. His vocabulary is furnished in the forms, the colors, the life, the sounds and motion, amid which he finds himself. The half-conscious awe which he feels, under the deep shade and the sweeping boughs of the great elm, through which he looks up, with a pleasing dread and wonder to the over-arching sky, the beautiful wild-flower which waves and nods to him as he passes, the brook which runs bubbling and gurgling through the meadow, the majesty of the flowing river, the roaring of the winter wind through the bare trees, the whirling of the snow-flakes, the glittering garment of the ice-storm, the opening of the spring buds, the fluttering of the summer leaves, and the sailing of the falling leaf in autumn, the enlivening voices of the domestic animals, the entrancing music of the birds;—these, and a thousand other unpaid teachers, have all been training him in a language true, copious, perfect, and inspiring,—compared to which, book-learning is but as the dry husk to the rich nutritious grain.

*Genial Culture.*—To favor and cherish, not to check, utterance—to elicit, not to repress expression,—to multiply, and deepen, and expand, and fill, not to dry up, the sources and reservoirs of language;—these are the true offices of education. The cultivation of the young mind, taking a suggestive hint from the cultivation of the young tree, should allow a liberal scope of nutrition, of growth and expansion, before calling in the aid of the pruning knife. A large part of early education should consist in conversation, in which the pupil should freely partake, as the natural means of acquiring accuracy and expertness, as well as freedom, in expression. The tendency to write and to draw, should have full scope and ample encouragement. Care should be taken to render interesting and attractive every form of exercise by which the student may ultimately attain to the free, forcible, and correct expression of thought. To the various modes of securing such fruits of culture, in detail, we shall have occasion to advert in the sequel.

## IV. Result of the Action of the Expressive Faculties:—Communication.

*The Power of Communication.*—In the previous stages of our present inquiries, we have been occupied with the *classification* of the powers of expression, their *springs of action*, and the *habitual tendency* and direction of their current, under the guidance of unassisted nature and of education. The next step in the progress of investigation preliminary and introductory to the actual work of express culture, is the consideration of the Results at which, whether by the law of natural development or that of educational cultivation, the human being arrives, in consequence of the exercise of his powers of expression.

The immediate result of utterance is Communication,—the impartation and interchange of sympathy or sentiment, by which man inspires his fellow man with the same feeling, affection, emotion, passion, thought, or sentiment, which actuates himself; and which, as the circle of kindred minds is enlarged by the aggregation of numbers, extends his personal mood or mental condition throughout the sphere of the community of which he is a member.

*Intellectual and Moral Effects of Communication.*—The views, the will, and the power of an individual, acquire, through communication, an ascendency, it may be, over a nation, or even over the whole civilized race, for successive ages; while, on the other hand, the intellectual acquisitions, the moral and spiritual attainments, the sympathies and the accumulated resources of nations and of ages, may be brought to the aid of the individual, through the magic power of language.

For good or for evil, man's power of communication with his fellows, gives to the aggregated multitudes of a whole people, or even of the race, the unity of purpose, the singleness of aim, the directness, the personal efficiency, the ease and the certainty of action of a single agent; while it equally arms the individual with the intellectual, the physical, and the moral force of millions. The sage, the orator, the poet, the artist, the statesman, the warrior, thus become the recognized representatives of a people or of mankind, to whom communities and nations bow in submission or in homage, and to whose ascendant genius they render the tribute of heart and hand, of treasure, or of life. Thus, too, the youth, in his studious endeavors to advance his intellectual and moral condition, has the aid arising from the experience, the counsels, the guidance, and the sympathies of the intelligent and the virtuous of every age and nation which possesses an accessible record of its progress; and the student whose days have been spent in strictest seclusion and unremitting investigation, enjoys the assurance that the fruits of his solitary research and strenuous application shall be gathered not by himself alone, but by whatever enlightened and sympathizing minds, throughout the world, and in all subsequent time, shall come within his sphere of communication by living voice or written word.

*Value of Communication.*—Communication, as the boon of language, is not to be measured by its immediate results merely, as a telegraphic convenience for the impartation of feeling or the conveyance of thought,—great as its uses, in this relation, are to the whole race. Language is the vehicle of all knowledge. Like the noble ship, costly and valuable in itself, but yet more valuable in the treasure with which it is fraught, it comes laden with the accumulations of countless minds and boundless wealth. To measure its full value, we should have to compute the number and the worth of every acquisition which the mind has garnered up in the records of every department of science and literature, and thus rendered capable of conveyance from man to man, and from generation to generation, throughout the world.

V. Educational Processes for the Cultivation of the Expressive Faculties.

These may be classed under the following heads: The Attentive Observation and the Love of Nature; the Study and the Practice of Art; the Study of Language; the Practice of Exercises in Oral and Written Expression.

Omissions and Defects in Modes of Culture.—*Language.*—The plan of education generally adopted for the exercise and discipline of the expressive faculties, indicates little philosophical design, logical consistency, generous spirit, or liberal scope, in the course which it prescribes. It is founded on views too narrow and exclusive; and its execution has been too mechanical. The mother's and the teacher's eye has been fastened too exclusively on the facts of *language* alone, as so many detached points to be mastered in detail. Hence the injury sometimes done to the organs of speech, by premature attempts to conquer some of the difficulties of articulation, in the mother's zeal for the precocious development of the faculties of her child; and hence, also, the mechanical and arbitrary processes of alphabetic training, in its customary forms. The eager desire for immediate definite results, has caused the teacher, too generally, to overlook the great facts that language is but one of the forms in which the expressive faculties are exerted, or in which expressive power is to be developed, and that the successful cultivation of language is inseparable from due exercise in all the kindred forms of expression to which the mind naturally tends.

The general plan of education is limited to instruction and practice in the oral and written forms of language, in the school routine of *reading* and *grammar*, and what is termed *composition.* The forms of exercise and the methods of training, also, in these departments of education, have too generally been literal and mechanical; and the poverty and imperfection of the results have betrayed the defects of the plan which prescribed them.

*Methods too exclusively Passive and Receptive.*—The great importance of a full and generous development of the whole mental constitution, as indispensable to the right action of any of its elements, having been overlooked in the plan of education, due allowance has too seldom been made, in the training of the mind, for the adequate exercise and discipline of the active nature and of the expressive powers of the human being. The general prescription of the processes of instruction, has evidently been directed to the *receptive* action of the *understanding* and the *impleting* of the *memory.* The mind of the pupil has been too uniformly kept in a comparatively *passive* condition. He has not been permitted and invited to use sufficiently even those materials of expression which he has, from the earliest steps of his progress, in the routine of education, been so laboriously employed in accumulating. Expression, neglected in early training, becomes difficult in later stages; and conscious failure incurred in attempting it, renders it distasteful. Effort, under such circumstances, is reluctantly made, frequently intermitted, and ere long discontinued.

*Neglect of our own Language.*—No remark is more common or more true, than that even our highest and best courses of culture do not result in furnishing accomplished men, as regards the actual use, in speech or writing, of our own language. Ample time, comparatively, is usually allowed for the study of the ancient languages, and even for that of some of the modern; but little is expressly assigned for the thorough acquisition of our own, which, to ensure to the student a perfect command of it, should be the groundwork of daily exercises, thoughtfully planned and carefully executed, from the first steps in education onward to the last day of professional preparation for the business of life.

*Faults of Unconscious Teaching.*—Some of the many causes of imperfect teaching, in the department of language, may be found in the fact, that the true nature and actual character of early training are not recognized by those whose office it is to superintend the first steps of childhood in the path of development. The mother and the primary teacher too often overlook the vast influence of *example*, which, to the imitative nature of childhood, always becomes a model. Hence the imperfect articulation, incorrect pronunciation, mechanical monotony, and lifeless tone, which are so generally prevalent in school reading. These faults are, too often, faithful copies of the style which the ear of the young learner has unconsciously caught from his mother, his teacher, or his class-mates, and which habit rivets on his voice, for life.

*Error in Alphabetic Instruction.*—The mechanical manner in which the child's first lessons in reading are sometimes conducted, is another cause of failure, in the department of instruction to which we now refer. In many schools, the young pupil never has his attention called, definitely or consciously, to the fact that the letters of the alphabet are *phonetic* characters, the whole value of which consists in the *sounds* which they represent: in many, he may pass through the whole course of instruction without being once called to practice the constituent elementary sounds of his own language: in very many, there is no attempt made to exercise and develop, modify, or cultivate, in any form, the voice itself. Hence the prevalence of the errors which have been already mentioned as fruits of unconscious imitation, and which careful, early cultivation can alone prevent.

*Neglect of the Meaning of Words.*—An obvious defect in prevalent modes of education, as regards adequate preparation for the free and correct use of our native language, is the yet too common neglect of early and progressive *etymological training* in the analysis of words, and the tracing of the significant value of their component syllables, so as to ascertain and fix in the mind their exact meaning and full power, and to follow their transitions from a primary to a secondary sense, or from one which is figurative and imaginative to one which is purely intellectual or merely practical. It is such intimate knowledge, and such only,—the fruit of daily exercise and careful training,—that can give, at length, to the mature scholar, or the professional speaker, that mastery of words, which now so often, when almost too late, he feels that he needs for the full and perfect expression of his thoughts.

*Defective Forms of Reading Exercises.*—A common and marked failure of education, as regards the course of instruction in reading, is partly attributable to the cause last mentioned,—the unintelligent enunciation of words,—but largely, also, to the mechanical perusal and unmeaning pronunciation of sentences, as merely so many successions of audible sounds. Such exercises deaden rather than enliven the powers of expression, as they blunt rather than sharpen the understanding, for the intelligent conception of meaning. Yet, in not a few schools is it the fact, that even quite young pupils are never asked, in performing a reading exercise, to point out, previous to the pronouncing of a sentence, those words in it which are most significant or expressive, and accordingly require that special force or turn of utterance, which alone can render them *emphatic*, so as to convey their full sense, or bring out the whole sentiment which the sentence was framed to express. A similar neglect is too prevalent as regards the effect of proper *pauses* in reading, which should always suggest to the ear an intelligent analysis of a sentence into its constituent portions of sense, not, as is very frequently the case, a mechanical analysis, servilely following the grammatical punctuation with measured uniformity of utterance, whatever be the depth of thought, or the force of feeling, implied in the language of the composition. As the syntactical punctuation, although it may often coincide with the expressive and significant rhetorical pausing, does not necessarily do so, but, on the contrary, is sometimes directly at variance with it, the effect of uniformly following the points, must, in such cases, be a positive hindrance rather than a help to intelligible or appropriate reading, as an exercise of voice. The utterance of the common phrases, "Yes, sir," or "No, sir," will furnish sufficient illustration here. The comma preceding the word "sir," is due to the eye, on the score of syntax, but not to the ear or the voice, on that of sense.

It is in the audible reading of *poetry*, however, that the defects of current education are most strikingly exhibited, as regards the discipline of the expressive faculties. Poetry, as the language of imagination and feeling, speaking to the heart, properly requires a mode of reading obviously quite different from that of the usual forms of plain didactic prose, addressed to the understanding merely. The word-pictures of the poet paint their imagery on the imagination; the intellect interprets their forms; the heart beats in response to the graphic delineation; and the voice gives expression to a correspondent melody of tone, while it utters the words of the verse. To read poetry aright, therefore, implies the poet's inspiration, imparted to the soul and voice of the reader,—an exalted state of imagination, a sympathetic vividness of feeling, unconscious quickness and acuteness of intellectual conception, a plastic voice and expressive tone. An appropriate course of preparatory discipline of feeling and imagination, is obviously, then, as indispensable to poetic utterance, as the right understanding of the intellectual sense of a sentence, is to the ordinary reading of prose. For this purpose, every grand or beautiful form of nature or of expressive art to which he can resort, with a view to give susceptibility to feeling and imagination or pleasure to taste, now becomes, in the hands of the intelligent teacher, an instrument of power, to aid him in the processes of culture. Now is the time when he feels how deeply he must ever be indebted to the vivifying influence of music, painting, and sculpture, and every chaste form of decorative art, as the effective means of opening the eye of the soul to the vision of grandeur or of beauty, firing the heart with the ardor of inspiration, touching it with the sense of tenderness and love, and refining the taste by the display of true elegance and grace.

The dry, prosaic, lifeless style in which poetry is too generally read in our schools, is more injurious than beneficial, not merely to the faculties more immediately concerned in the conception or utterance of poetic composition, but to the action and influence of all those powers, mental and moral, which tend to elevate and refine the soul, and mould the character to the highest forms of excellence. There is something akin to the barrenness of spirit with which the sceptic peruses a page of sacred scripture, in the utterly mechanical manner in which the well-drilled pupil in mathematics or in grammar, is sometimes permitted to read strains of the purest poetry, embodying the sublimest sentiments, and calling for tones of the deepest and most vivid emotion, or even of the most exalted passion.

The general neglect of appropriate means for cherishing sensibility and cultivating taste, in the relation now referred to, is the more to be regretted that it prevails most in that form of education and in that class of schools in which it tells with the deepest effect :—I refer to our common modes of mental cultivation, and to those seminaries in which the mass of our people are trained. The recuperative influences of classical culture, in our higher literary institutions, does something to redeem, in this respect, the omissions and the defects of earlier training. But it is much to be feared that, even in our boasted New England education, as generally conducted, the young who are to receive no such remedial aid for disproportioned and defective cultivation, close their school course without the benefit of a single effort, on the part of instructors, to render their pupils capable of appreciating or expressing the sentiments embodied in the best passages of our own literature and that of the parent land,—a literature which contains confessedly more of the inspiring elements of pure morality and noble character, as well as genuine beauty, than any that has yet appeared on earth; not excepting even the model languages of classic antiquity.

*Instruction in Grammar.*—It is but of late that those who prescribe the forms of education or the modes of instruction, have furnished the working teacher with the means of rational and philosophic training for his pupils, in another department of culture professedly occupied with the discipline of the expressive faculties, but, in past years, so formally conducted, for the most part, as to embarrass and retard rather than aid the progress of development. A great change, unquestionably, has taken place in the character of text-books on Grammar; and in this branch of instruction we have recently been provided with valuable facilities for improvement, in several excellent treatises, well suited to the true uses of a text-book,—not a synthetic synopsis of the science as it lies in the mind of the consummate grammarian, but a gradually progressive and practical presentation of the subject, from its simplest elements upward, in a course, at the same time, so strictly logical, that every step leads, by a law of thought, to another, and so thoroughly practical, that,—to use the not inapt expression of a German instructor visiting one of our American schools,—the pupil is made, at every step, to "*experience* grammar."

*Defective Methods.*—Still, too many of our teachers cling to the narrow practice of following, in every grammar lesson, the order of a *synthetic* text-book, in which the subject is admirably arranged for a systematic and philosophic review of the science, but by no means for the successive steps of progress to the young mind commencing the study of it. The method of such text-books is precisely that which must be *inverted* in all true, living, oral instruction, or in any rational attempt to introduce a learner to a knowledge of the subject, and to guide him in his first endeavors to reduce it to practice in illustrative forms of exercise. The logic of instruction requires that the whole science of grammar should be first subjected to a rigorous *analysis* in the teacher's own mind, that its elements may be exhibited individually and successively to that of the pupil, and so become the groundwork of his *inductive* and intelligent progress from the recognition of facts to that of principles and laws. The practical part of the instructor's business, requires, in this, as in all other branches, a strict compliance with the rule of presenting one element only at a time, but in such succession as to develop the whole subject in easy steps of connected progress,—each perfectly understood and thoroughly exemplified; nothing assumed, but everything proved; nothing merely defined without being reduced to practice.

*The Practice of Composition.*—Till very recently, in comparison, no branch of education connected so immediately with the discipline of the expressive faculties, has been more faultily conducted than this. Without waiting for the development and efficient action of the reflective faculties, or the power of abstract conception and general thought, the teacher, when he has conducted his pupils through a very imperfect course of grammar and mechanical "parsing," and, perhaps, a little technical rhetoric, proceeds to prescribe a task in composition, on some *general* theme requiring the thoughts of a mature and capacious mind, besides the command of a skillful pen, for its proper treatment.

*Results of Defective Methods of Teaching.*—Called thus, without means, to perform a task which leads him entirely away from the region in which his mind naturally and habitually works,—the *concrete* world of actual observation and of clear conception or conscious feeling,—the pupil finds himself unable to do what is required of him as a personal effort. In these circumstances, if he does not actually shirk the task imposed on him, he has no resort but to repeat the commonplace thoughts and sayings of others, in which he feels no interest, and which, to his consciousness, have no truth. The precious moments of youth are thus worse than wasted; the expressive faculties are withered and dried up; and education, thus misdirected, destroys the powers which it was employed to cherish.

*Advantages of Seasonable Training.*—Teachers who take the pains to observe well, know that there is a stage in the life of childhood, when expression is a spontaneous tendency and a delight,—when to construct a sentence on his slate, or pencil a little note on paper, is to the miniature "ambitious student," a conscious achievement and a triumph of power. Then is the happy moment for beginning the work of practice, which, if neglected at that stage, will never be easily, naturally, or effectively done afterward. The attempt may be made at a later period, under the influence of a sense of duty, or a feeling of shame, or the consciousness of compulsion. But, by this time, the plastic suppleness and pliancy of the mind is gone; and the whole endeavor proves an affair of difficulty and dislike. The teacher's policy is never to let the moment come when composition, whether in the form of note or letter, or narrative, or description, is felt to be anything else than a pleasure and a privilege. The expression of sentiment, and the argument for an opinion, will then, become as easy, as natural, and as pleasurable employment, as the first steps of conscious progress, in the penning of a juvenile note or letter.

*Rhetoric.*—The great defect in conducting this branch of education,—a defect which is still very prevalent,—consists in the fact that the study of it is so much a matter of theoretic speculation on principles of taste, or is limited to the mere committing of rules to memory. Rhetoric, to become a useful branch of modern education, should embrace a gradually progressive course of exercises, embodying successively the facts of language, in the use of words and the construction of sentences; it should include the practice of daily writing, for successive years; frequent exercises in the logical arranging of thought for the purposes of expression, and the adapting of the forms and character of expression to thought; and it should be accompanied by the close study and critical analysis of the works of distinguished writers, with a view to acquire a perfect mastery over every form of style.

*Elocution: Errors in Modes of Instruction.*—Few branches of education are so little understood or rightly practiced as this. We have, in our current modes of instruction, little choice between the faults of style arising from what the indolent incline to term "a generous neglect," through fear of "spoiling" what they claim as "nature," and those faults, on the other hand, which are attributable to literal and mechanical modes of cultivation, and consist in the obtrusion of arbitrary details and artificial forms. Hence the results which characterize the one, in the gross errors of slovenly and low habit, coarse and disgusting manner, uncouth effect, bawling vehemence, and gesticulating violence, of what is sometimes dignified with the name of "popular oratory;" and hence the opposite traits of finical taste, affected elegance, false refinement, and studied contrivances of effect, which belong to perverted culture.

*Errors in Theory.*—With the advocates of neglect, the true teacher, as a believer in the value of cultivation, can have little sympathy, further than in the condemnation of false and artificial manner. Neglect of culture, he knows well, produces, in regard to all expressive art, the same obvious faults of rawness and inappropriateness, awkwardness and error. It is much to be regretted, however, that the language of some eminent writers, in their anxiety to protest against the errors of mechanical and literal training, gives countenance to the claims of ignorance on this subject, and seems to sanction the utter neglect of cultivation. Prominent among these it is to be regretted that we find an authority otherwise so justly eminent as Dr. Whately, whose own brilliant talents and ready power of expression, while they tend to give him an ascendency over the minds of students and teachers, are perhaps the very circumstances which disqualify him to form a true judgment on the modes of cultivation best adapted to the great majority of minds which fall under the care of the teacher, in the common routine of education. The error,—if one may be pardoned the term,—by which ingenious minds are, on this subject sometimes entirely misled by superficial observation and hasty conclusions, is that of overlooking the great fact that, in the cultivation of any branch of expressive art, education is properly charged with a double duty,—that of aiding, by every favoring influence, the inward power of conception, and that of watching over the outward form of expression. In the former function, education is spiritual, genial, inspiring, intellectual, in its suggestions: in the latter, its office is formative and exterior; it watches, with the nicety of a musician's ear and a painter's eye, over every point of detail, and assiduously trains every organ of the pupil to exactness, as the law of truth, extending to the minutest effect of vocal utterance and visible action. True culture, in this relation, aims at a perfect result, and descends, therefore, to the moulding of every detail.

*The necessary Union of Theory and Practice in Teaching.*—It is a great error to suppose that, in doing its practical work, education must do it in a narrow and servile spirit, or in a merely mechanical form. Genuine instruction, in its minutest direction, recognizes and impresses a principle which prompts the preference of one form of expression to another; and it takes care to deepen the impression of the principle by means of the associated art in practice. Faithful teaching must always extend to details. There is no slighting or slovening in its work. The difference between true and false instruction, in all art, is simply this: the former in prescribing a rule, refers to the parent principle from which it is derived, and thus makes instruction *logical*; the latter lays down the rule as a detached and arbitrary fact of mere inculcation, and thus renders instruction *empirical* and *mechanical*. The skillful teacher knows how, in inculcating the closest application to detail, to keep the mind intent on the principle which suggests it. No error in educational training can be greater than that of shrinking from or shunning particulars, under the plea of generalizing. In all matters of expressive art, principle must be developed and applied in practice.

*Necessity of Detail.*—The right expression of a sentiment by voice and action, like every other external act of mind and organ, has necessarily a mode and a form, coëxtensive with the words in which it is embodied; and neither teacher nor student can afford to dispense with one element of the true effect. The attention, therefore, must be directed to the study and observation, "analytically, of the emphasis, tones, pauses, &c.," unless we are willing to neglect the proper effect of these on speech. If we can not communicate sentiment without a due observance of these, they must evidently be studied, more or less, according to their value and importance; and the very office of instruction is, in all such cases, patiently to descend to the study and practice of detail.

Yet Dr. Whately, in his Elements of Rhetoric, asserts that the analytic study of detail, in such matters, "must vitiate every system of instruction founded upon it." For this conclusion, fortunately, however, he gives no reason but what is contained in the brief phrase, "according to my views," and adds, further, the saving clause, "if those views be correct." A true and efficient friend of education, in other respects, thus sides with the opponents of culture, by speaking from the preferences of personal taste and arbitrary opinion, instead of the laws of analogy and universal truth.

In most Anglo-Saxon communities, the teacher of elocution receives his pupils encrusted,—one might say,—with the errors of neglected or corrupted habit, unconsciously contracted from the current faults of his home, his early school, the street, the local style of his vicinity, or that of some popular public speaker. The eradication of these errors is obviously the first duty of an instructor. But, according to the views of Dr. Whately, the instructor must not put forth his hand to touch such faults; for this could not be done without incurring the evil of entering into "analytic details of emphasis, tones, pauses, &c." The fabric of education, in this as in all other departments, resembles the well constructed edifice, liberally and scientifically planned, symmetrically proportioned, and thoroughly finished in detail. The outside observers of the processes of instruction,—among whom Dr. Whately, for the time, takes his position,—are quite willing that the intellectual structure should be a goodly mansion, on the whole, but insist on the notion that it shall be built without any detail of wood, stone, or brick, in particular.

"*Natural Advantages.*"—In the act of utterance, the glance of genius may suffice, at times, for the intuitive recognition of a principle; and the empassioned impulse of artistic temperament, may prompt to instantaneous and perfect expression. The possessor of such attributes may, on exciting occasions, dispense with reflective thought and studious application as securities for success in utterance. But the majority of mankind, whether in youth or maturity, consciously and habitually need all the aids of analysis and study, and are successful in proportion to the closeness of their application and the thoroughness of their practice. The aid, in such circumstances, to be rendered by the intelligent and faithful teacher, is precisely that work of detail to which Dr. Whately objects. The student, through inadvertency, overlooks, for example, the true and appropriate manner of expression in solemn emotion; and, in the utterance of a passage of that character, runs on, through the influence of neglected habit, in a *high*, *loud*, and *rapid* voice. Here, the mechanical teacher will, of course, rectify the error, for the moment, by merely exemplifying the proper style, and making the pupil repeat in imitation of the model, but with no explanation, and with no reference of any point to a fixed principle which might be a guide in future practice. The true teacher, —who never can rest satisfied with anything merely mimetic or parrot-like,—when he indicates errors, endeavors to correct them by referring his pupil to the principle from which they deviate. He interrogates him in this case as to the true and natural style of voice in which solemn emotion is uttered, and directs his attention successively to the facts that it is characterized by tones which are comparatively *low*, *soft*, and *slow*,—as heard in the natural and appropriate utterance of devotional feeling. Teacher and pupil have thus a defi nite aim and an intelligent course before them in the reiterated practice which may be required for the correction of error, and a guiding light to direct them in all similar difficulties which may occur in subsequent exercises. In this department of education, as well as in others, true instruction is nothing else than the exposition of a *principle* along with an *analytical application* of it. Yet this is the very mode of procedure which Dr. Whately condemns, when he objects so decidedly to that method of elocutionary training which calls the attention of the student first to the prominent vocal effects of an emotion, and then descends to the particulars of expression in "emphasis, pauses, &c."

The errors of theory, regarding this department of education, have been dwelt on longer than might have otherwise been necessary, were it not for the proneness of those who superintend and control the forms of instruction, to defer to the authority of distinguished names, and to discourage the well directed efforts of the teacher. The mode in which reading is taught, or elocution practiced, in the successive stages of education, has a greater effect on mental and moral development, than any other branch of instruction: it affects not only the intelligence, but the taste, the habits, and the whole character of the mind. To the young teacher, therefore, it is exceedingly important that his views on the subject be clear and correct.

*The practice of Gesture.*—The visible part of elocution,—expressive action,—is another subject on which the errors of theory and practice are numerous and great. They consist chiefly, however, in intentional or unconscious *neglect*, on the one hand, and *mechanical cultivation*, on the other. The former cause of faulty habit appears in inexpressive, unmeaning, and inappropriate forms of bodily action, in insignificant tricks of personal habit, or in excessive and violent gesticulation, accompanied by awkward and uncouth attitudes: the latter shows itself in unnatural, affected, or fantastic gestures and positions. The expressive actions which naturally and properly belong to public address on subjects which call forth emotion, being larger and more forcible than those which belong to the habitual style of private conversation, it is of great service, in the training of youth, that, in addition to all the healthful aids arising from manly exercises and enlivening sports, there should be a daily course of training on the principal forms of oratorical action, with a view to ensure force, and freedom, and propriety of manner, as regards the natural language of attitude and action. This language has its principles for the guidance of the teacher and the student as well as the artist. The attentive investigation of these principles is the only source of true and liberal instruction or useful study. From these principles rules for application necessarily flow; and it depends on the teacher and the student whether the latter shall be well and skillfully trained, neglected, or superficially taught.

*Artistic Cultivation of Taste.*—Provision is formally made, in many seminaries, for a more liberal allowance of cultivation for the expressive faculties, than is afforded in the mere learning to read, in the study of grammar and rhetoric, or in the practice of composition and elocution. The demands of Taste are recognized and complied with, so far as regards a certain measure of instruction in *music* and *drawing*. But, in very many seminaries, the little arbitrary and imperfect instruction which is given in these branches, is too frequently much worse than none; unless we are willing to recognize the forming of bad taste in either art as an admissible service of education.

*Lessons in Drawing: Common Mistake.*—Many parents and teachers never bestow a thought on the true character or proper uses of art, as a means of mental culture, or as a practical accomplishment, but labor under the false notion that a little dabbling in it, under a very ordinary instructor, is at least something gained toward refinement of taste and graceful habit. There can not be a greater error committed in education than this. Every attempt to copy an imperfect model, brings down the tone of taste, and does something to hinder the attainment of excellence. Neglect is wholesome, when compared with perversion or with false instruction.

"My daughter," says an affectionate mother, "wishes to learn drawing; and Mr. Blank is getting up a class; and I think I shall let her join. Mr. Blank's drawing is no great things, to be sure. But a little notion of drawing can do my daughter no harm, at least; and, perhaps, she may take a liking for it; and then she can find a better teacher, when it will be worth while to have one." Here are the common errors,—that there is any benefit in a little *poor* or *bad* art, or that any speck of it is not a positive blemish; that the elements of art can be taught by an incompetent teacher; and that, after having taste thus perverted, the pupil can rally, acquire new principles, and form new habits. The actual experience of most pupils thus misdirected, is the painful conviction that, without a perfect command of elements, nothing whatever can be done in art, and that every neglected false line or touch, in rudimental lessons, is sure to injure the habits of eye and hand, in all subsequent execution, besides lowering the standard of excellence, and degrading the taste of the student.

*Music: Singing.*—An error similar to that just mentioned, prevails with regard to instruction and practice in *music*,—more particularly, in instrumental music. The vocal department, however, is not without its many evils of erroneous conception and faulty instruction. Singing, by the formal manner in which it is sometimes taught, becomes one of the listless tasks which the juvenile pupil is compelled to perform in the routine of school duty, instead of being one of the natural enjoyments and welcome recreations of daily life, in which intellectual activity is accompanied by pleasing emotion and free expression. The young learner, who should be permitted to enter at once on the pleasure of listening to pure and perfect strains of actual music, and then to join in the attempt to execute them, in the natural training of ear and voice, is commonly detained for a long course of drilling on technical terms and arbitrary rules. Music is thus rendered a tasteless, irksome, artificial exercise to the pupil, and fails of accomplishing its main objects of quickening the ear, enlivening the feelings, moulding the voice, and cultivating the taste, by the influence of pure and beautiful examples of vocal sound, in the expression of feeling and sentiment.

*Demoralizing Influence of Low Taste.*—The result is still more injurious when low taste is permitted to obtrude its degrading influences on the sacred sphere of music; when song is treated as merely a form of amusement or of sport, and when the corrupting effects of gross humor and ridiculous caricature, are intentionally introduced in the lessons of an art designed to purify and elevate the soul. When to such influences there is added the express utterance of degrading and demoralizing sentiment, in the words of a piece of music selected for a school exercise, the work of the enemy who sows tares in the field, is fully accomplished; and education lends its hand to the act of helping the young mind not upward but positively downward.

*Deficient and Faulty Instruction.*—When the grosser evils which have been mentioned, are avoided, there are not unfrequently others, quite serious in effect, arising from the influence of imperfect cultivation and false taste in the teacher, or in the community of which the pupil is a member. Inaccurate, slovenly, and heedless execution defeats all the purposes of musical cultivation, and renders the absence of culture preferable to the possession of it. Every repetition of a fault confirms an error of perception, a perversion of feeling, or a corruption of taste, and deepens it into a vice of habit and a defect in mental character.

*Instrumental Music.*—The more laborious forms of culture which are indispensable to success in the performance of *instrumental* music, strike yet deeper into the taste and tendencies of the mind, as regards the character and effects of expression. Faults in this department of musical instruction, are, it is true, not so widely diffused as those which are so often displayed in the teaching of vocal music. But they are not less prejudicial to the pupil individually. The incessant and arduous application which is required of all who wish to perform successfully on any instrument, exhausts and discourages pupils who have not a true and deep love of music, together with the enduring physical vigor and muscular power which consummate execution demands. The attempt to continue practice, under such disadvantages, is more injurious than beneficial; and when the pupil is dragged through the daily infliction, the whole course ends in that miserable failure over whose multitude of sins the false charity of society is so often called to throw its mantle. In music, as in every other form of expressive art, no culture is greatly to be preferred to that which entails error and imperfection.

*False Models.*—The evils of defective cultivation are not less conspicuous when the pupil possesses both taste and diligence and good ability, but is misled in style, by the influence of a false model in instruction. Of late years, the facility of obtaining instruction of the best order, is greatly increased. But a fatal error is still quite current among parents, that elementary lessons do not require a high standard of perfection in the teacher, and that therefore the rudiments of music may be acquired under any supervision. In this way, vast numbers of pupils are rendered imperfect performers, for life, by wrong habits acquired in the earliest stages of instruction and practice,—habits which no subsequent reformatory training is capable of correcting.

## Means of correcting prevalent Errors in the Cultivation of the Expressive Faculties.

*Remedial Effects of Good Instruction.*—The remedy for existing evils in this as in other departments of education, lies partly, it must be acknowledged, with parents and the official guardians of public instruction; and some of the evils adverted to are confessedly beyond the sphere of the teacher's action. Still, in the actual business of teaching, even under all the impediments arising from false views of education and false plans of established procedure in instruction, much may be effected in the way of beneficial reformation, by intelligent and judicious measures on the part of the teacher, in his mode of conducting the daily lessons and exercises in those branches of instruction which are recognized and demanded by general opinion or by legislative enactment.

*Examples.*—Referring to the utterly deficient provision which the general plan of current education makes for the cultivation and devel opment of the *perceptive* faculties, an enterprising and vigilant teacher will find no difficulty in inducing his pupils to take a short walk with him, for a few minutes daily, at a suitable season of the year, with a view to a little familiar conversation with them about the form and character of a *plant*,—even though but a weed on the road-side. The conversation can be easily so managed as to lead to the attentive observation and close examination of every part of the plant, as designated, first, by the name in ordinary use, and, afterward, if convenient, by the more exact term of scientific nomenclature. A microscope, such as may be easily obtained for a few dollars, will be an infallible attraction to observation and inspection, in such excursions, and will prove a most efficient assistant teacher. Curiosity, and wonder, and inquiry, once excited in this way, will cause the young mind to drink in, with delight, every item of information which falls from the lips of the teacher. Actual knowledge will thus be obtained, and its pleasure consciously felt. Feeling and emotion, the main springs of expression, are now brought into play; imagination is awakened, and, under the guidance of intelligence, will recognize the traces of beauty and skill in the handiwork of Nature. To record, in writing, what the eye has seen, and the ear heard, and the mind conceived, during such a lesson, will be no hardship of Egyptian task-work, but a pleasure and a privilege. Many a faithful teacher in our New England States, has, in this way,—without waiting for an educational millennium, in which *botany*, *composition*, and *natural theology* shall all be introduced into our common schools, by legislative authority,—"taken the responsibility," personally, and given an excellent elementary lesson in all three.

*First Lessons in Spelling and Reading.*—The unphilosophical and arbitrary manner in which many branches of education are actually taught, admits obviously of a remedy at the teacher's will. There is no necessity of blindly following the practice of making the child commit to memory the names of all the letters of the alphabet before he is asked to join the sounds of two, so as to read the words *he* or *me*. There is abundance of rhyme, but very little reason, in making the child read a whole column of rarely occurring and even of unintelligible words, because they all happen to have the same or similar combination of letters; while his bright eyes would sparkle with intelligence and delight, to see, in the column, a single word whose familiar sound would soon render its face as familiar. To the young learner in *the primer*, *the spelling-book*, or *the school dictionary*, the whole volume arranges itself in three classes of words: (1,) those which children of his age *understand and use*; (2,) those which they *understand*, when they hear them from the lips of older children or of adults, but which they do *not use* themselves; (3,) those which they *neither use nor understand*, but which with the aid of teacher and book, they are, in due season, to learn to understand and use aright. To follow the true order of teaching, in such circumstances, will cost the teacher no more trouble than the simple act of dotting with the pencil point, on the column of the given page of the pupil's book, those words which he finds adapted to the class-lesson of the hour, according to the intelligence and advancement of his scholars.

*Phonetic and Empirical Methods.*—Another expedient for the removal of impediments to successful elementary instruction, and one which the teacher can easily adopt, after having made the selection of words, as suggested above, would consist in the subdivision of each of the classes mentioned into analogous and anomalous sub-classes. All the words of the first class, for example,—those which are familiar to the child's ear and mind, by daily personal use,—are either regular or irregular, as to the combination of their letters in name and sound. The former of these sub-classes may be easily learned by the process of spelling them by the *sounds* of the letters which compose the words. Thus, in the word "page," the names of the first three letters very readily suggest their sounds, the combination of which constitutes the reading of the word. But not so with the word "gag," in which not one of all the letters suggests its own sound by the name given to it. By the principle of analogy, therefore, all words in which the name of the letter prompts the sound to the ear, may be advantageously taught by the *phonetic* method of merely articulating the sounds of the letters successively. The simplicity of this method enables children to make rapid progress in syllabication and in reading; and on the principle of allowing children the pleasure of helping themselves forward in an intelligent, conscious progress, this part of early training should never be neglected. But, even in those words which are familiar, in sense and in use, to the ears and minds of young children, there are very many in which there is little or no analogy between the names of the letters and the sounds which they receive in the pronunciation of a word or the enunciation of a syllable. The *orthography* of such words is no reliable guide to their *orthoëpy.* To name their component letters, therefore, can effect nothing further than to satisfy the teacher that the eye of the child has taken in every letter of the word before him. So far well. But, after all, the child's eye actually learns to take in such words by the letters in mass, and depends on an arbitrary effort of memory, in pronouncing them. The sooner, therefore, that the little learner acquires the habit of reading such words at sight, without puzzling himself with the confusion arising from the discrepancy between the names and the sounds of their component letters, the more easy and the more sure will be his progress.

Each of these methods of teaching, in the elementary processes of spelling and reading, is good for its own purpose;—the phonetic for the analogies of orthoëpy, and the empirical, as it may be called, for its anomalies. But the error in teaching has been the indiscriminate and exclusive use of the one or the other; in consequence of which, the learner's progress has been rendered unnecessarily difficult and tedious. The inherent difficulties of a language so irregular as the English, render the closest attention, on the part of the teacher, to every means of overcoming them, doubly important in early training.

*Orthoëpy.*—In this branch of instruction everything depends on the living teacher,—on the correctness of his own exemplifications and the diligence of his endeavors. Indeed, there is, commonly, no reason, but neglect on the part of the instructor, why every child at school is not daily and thoroughly trained in the exact articulation of all the elementary sounds of the English language, and in the distinct enunciation of their principal radical combinations; nor any other reason why an obsolete, awkward, or inappropriate manner of pronouncing common words should be tolerated in any stage of education.

"*School Reading.*"—A similar remark may be made, as regards the unmeaning and inexpressive style of reading, which is so current, not only in schools, but in higher seminaries and professional exercises. This fault, so commonly remarked, would not exist at any stage of education, or in any form of life, private or public, if our primary teachers were only attentive to accustom their pupils, in their very first exercises in the reading of sentences, to repeat them carefully, with a view to *the expression of sense* and not the mere pronouncing of words.

*Academic Elocution.*—This department of instruction is another in which the appropriate cultivation of the expressive faculties is not dependent on any change in the prescribed forms of education, so much as on the personal endeavors of the teacher. Our public speakers would not so generally utter their words in the formal tones of arbitrary pulpit style, were teachers duly attentive to point out to young *academic declaimers* the natural and appropriate vocal expression of feeling and sentiment; nor should we ever see those frenzied extravagances of passion and grotesque gesticulation, which so frequently degrade the style of popular oratory, were teachers careful to cultivate, in academic declamation, purity of taste, and true force of effect, in the utterance of emotion.

*Grammatical Instruction.*—Even in the teaching of *grammar*, where less scope, perhaps, is given to the discretion of the teacher, it still depends on himself whether he shall follow the precise order of topics in an ill-arranged text-book, or use his own judgment, and present the subject to the minds of his pupils in the order which he feels that an intelligent and practical study of the subject, and a rational progress in its application, demand. Nothing lies more properly within the province of the teacher, than the duty of seeing to it that his pupils thoroughly understand every word of their various lessons, and thus reap the benefit of grammar, in the perfect interpretation and right use of the current words of their own communications by speech and writing, and in the perusal of the useful productions of the press. The faithful use of an etymological spelling-book, and of the dictionary, is all the cost of an aid so valuable to the teacher, and of an attainment so valuable to the pupil.

*Practical Rhetoric: School Exercises.*—Training in the appropriate use of the English language, ought not to be limited to the mere grammatical exercise of composing sentences. Even in our common schools, it should extend to that cultivation of taste by which neat as well as correct expression is acquired as a habit. To cultivate, in his pupils, the power of appreciating excellence in language, it is not necessary that the teacher should refer them to a systematic treatise on rhetoric. The school reading book usually furnishes abundance of the best materials for culture, in the presentation of the best modes of composition, as exemplified in the language of the pieces prescribed as reading lessons. The very best training for the acquisition of sound judgment and good taste in expression, may easily be had, if the teacher will but secure the intelligent and voluntary action of his pupils, in frequently *analysing* portions of some of the best of such passages, in occasionally *transcribing* them, and even *committing them to memory.* The exercise of careful transcription, is, perhaps, the best practical expedient that can be found for securing that literal and mechanical correctness in the details of the written forms of language, as to orthography and punctuation, which though, indeed, but minor matters, are yet so important, as indispensable to the decencies and proprieties of style. How ineffectual, for such purposes, the common routine of education proves, none can know but persons whose business brings them into extensive observation of such particulars.

*Rhetorical Exercises in higher Seminaries.*—To remedy the evils arising from the narrow and artificial character of our higher forms of rhetorical culture, we need a wider scope of discipline not only in rhetoric itself, but in logic, and in the principles of taste as embodied in the æsthetics of every form of expressive art. We need, yet more, however, a special course of practical training, for which the rhetorical teacher ought justly to be held responsible,—a course which should consist in the careful and close analysis of distinguished models of successful composition, so as to trace their order and method in the arrangement of thought, the artistic character of their æsthetic light and shade and coloring, the mechanism of their sentential structure, and the aptness of their verbal expression in detail. A long and rigorous course of disciplinary exercise in such forms, would not only furnish the pen of the ready writer for the varied demands of actual life, but the requisite preparatory training for the office of public speaking, in which a ready command of well digested thought and fit expression is so important to successful effort. The student would, by such training, effectually learn the value of clear consecutive thinking, of genuine taste, of manly plainness of diction and simplicity of expression: he would be thoroughly secured from falling into the "bald, disjointed chat," the pompous harangue, the insane extravagance of emotion, and the fantastic verbiage, which are so often palmed on our popular assemblies, and lauded in our transient vehicles of criticism, as wonderful displays of original genius or oratorical power.

*The Study of Language.*—One very important aid to the generous culture and full development of the expressive faculties, is, as yet, very imperfectly furnished by our higher forms of liberal education. While the study of the ancient languages is formally acknowledged as one of the most efficacious methods of training the mind to a distinct perception of whatever constitutes power or perfection of expression; and while liberal provision of time and means is carefully made, with a view to secure the full benefit to be derived from the contemplation and analytical examination of these faultless models; too little attention is paid to the invaluable advantages which might be gained from a corresponding rigor of study and analysis, directed to the great authors who constitute the classics of modern literature, in foreign languages, and in our own.

The perfunctory perusal and verbal recitation of a few passages from such authors, which usually form a part of academic exercises, in this department of education, can never be seriously proposed as effecting the purposes of critical appreciation and thorough discipline.

In our highest seminaries, little is attempted beyond the processes of grammatical analysis and interpretation, in a course of literal and mechanical routine, even with regard to the ancient classics; a mere modicum of the same species of attention is usually given to the very noblest writers of Germany, France or Italy. The Spanish and the Portuguese languages are given up, for the most part, to those persons who happen to have occasion for the use of them, as a convenience in mercantile operations. The languages of the North of Europe, whose ancestral affinities with the English render them so richly instructive, as regards the full and true understanding and expert use of the most significant and expressive part of our own native language;—these, as yet, are left to an adventurous few, comparatively,—the solitary explorers and pioneers in the study of modern literature.

America, in its peculiar national position, which brings to its open homes men of all countries and of every tongue, possesses unequaled facilities for the extensive acquisition of all the benefits resulting from the study of language in its various forms; and a wide range of advantages, in this relation of culture, should be justly held as the birthright of our children, and as the characteristic distinction of our educated youth and mature scholars. Not that we would have American teachers pursue the course, which is unfortunately yet too common, of giving a superficial attention, for a few months, or a few weeks, perhaps, to one or more of the languages of modern Europe, and then attempting the task of teaching them. But, generally speaking, American teachers who wish to enjoy the advantage of teaching more intelligently and effectually their native language, in consequence of the opportunity of better understanding its character, by their ability to compare it with others,—an advantage beyond price;—most, if not all, of such teachers have easy resort to a living instructor in whatever language they desire to study, and may, in due time, become possessed in this way, of a vast amount of intellectual wealth, the benefit of which is sure to be felt, not only in their own mental action, but in the attainments of their pupils.

In the department of language, however, there is no acquirement of which teachers and pupils stand in more urgent need than that of a perfect command of correct, clear, strong, expressive English. The attention paid to this most important attainment is, as yet, utterly inadequate to the demands of a generous cultivation or those of actual life and its daily duties. Nothing is more common than this humiliating admission. Yet little is done to do away with the necessity for it. We have, it is true, of late years, made some advances toward a better state of things, in our educational provision of better modes of teaching grammar, synthetically as well as analytically; and, in some schools, the practical study of etymology receives a commendable degree of attention. Yet it is rare to find in any seminary that thorough analytical investigation of the words of our language which every student is expected to exemplify in his exercises on a page of the ancient classics.

The study of English words, if faithfully pursued in the daily lessons of our schools, with any thing like the application exhibited in the examination, and classifying, and arranging, and labeling of the specimens of even a very ordinary cabinet, would enrich the intellectual stores of the young and even of the mature mind, to an extent of which we can, at present, hardly form a conception. Nothing, however, short of such diligence will serve any effectual purpose. The student of his own vernacular tongue must be content to employ the same close, minute inspection, the same careful examination, the same correct designation, the same exact location and scrupulous conservation of every word that he would intelligently appreciate or skillfully use, as the mineralogist adopts in the selection and arrangement of his specimens.

Our prevalent modes of education have been so defective, as regards the means or opportunities of acquiring a proper knowledge of the English language, that the humble attainment of perfect orthography is comparatively rare, even among the "liberally" educated. Few students, even in our higher seminaries of learning, are trained to recognize and appreciate the value of an English root or primitive word, to trace a secondary to a primary sense, or a primary to its secondary, to translate a passage of Latinized English into its Saxon equivalent words of the mother-tongue, to draw the line of discrimination between present and obsolete usage in expression, to detect the nice shades of meaning in words regarded as synonymous,—to use, in fact, their own language expertly.

It is universally admitted that no language needs such processes to be applied to it so much as our own. Its vast copiousness, in consequence of its many sources, the conflicting character of these themselves, the comparatively small number of English writers who have been willing to take the pains to write correctly, so far as to merit the name of models, the contradictory usage which has, from this cause, prevailed, even among distinguished authors—all have conspired to render careful study and extensive practice indispensable to the student who would do justice to the great language which it is his birthright to inherit, for all of life's best purposes.

# CULTIVATION OF THE REFLECTIVE FACULTIES.

---

Introductory Observations.—In the preceding lectures of this series, we were occupied with the consideration of the *perceptive* and the *expressive* faculties, with a view to the plan and purposes of education. Following the historical order of development in the different classes in which the mental powers may, for such purposes, be grouped, we enter now on the study of the various modes of intellectual action which may be classed under the denomination of

Reflective Faculties.

Here we are met anew by a difficulty inherent in our native language, in the paucity and indefiniteness of the terms which it employs to designate the phenomena of mind. The vagueness of the phrase "reflective faculties," is a serious impediment to clearness and distinctness of conception, as regards any attempt at exact definition or satisfactory classification of intellectual acts or conditions. The term "reflective," however, if we resort once more to the serviceable aid of etymology, as a key to the interpretation of language, will prove strikingly suggestive of meaning; and, by its figurative force and peculiar significance, will atone, to some extent, for its deficiency in philosophic precision.

The term "perceptive," (literally, *taking through*,) suggests the intellectual condition in which the mind is in the act of *taking*, receiving, or forming, ideas *through* the medium of the senses. The term "expression" implies a state in which the mind is undergoing a process of *pressing*, or *being pressed*, *from within outward*. But the term "reflection," (*bending back*,) suggests, figuratively, that state or act of the mind in which it reflects, repeats, or *gives back*, *inwardly*, the images impressed upon itself,—the effects of which it is conscious,—whether produced from without or from within, whether occasioned by perception, imagination, conception, or emotion. In this condition is is implied that attention turns inward, and dwells, more or less consciously, on its internal subjects, rather than on the objects by which they may have been occasioned.

The history,—so to term it,—of intellectual action implied in the application of the word "reflective," represents the mind, as in the act of going forth from its inner self, meeting the forms of the external world, and, by the impression which these produce upon it, "reflecting," (turning back or inward,) upon itself, to contemplate and deliberately consider what it there consciously beholds. Nor does the term lose aught of its significance, when it is applied to the inward action of the mind on the phenomena of its own consciousness, when the forms of imagination, or even of pure thought itself, become so forcible as to attract and absorb the attention. The figurative word then represents the mind as turning back upon itself, to look inward, so as to ascertain and define, or consider more fully, the objects of its own creation, and to follow the trains of thought which these suggest. In either of the supposed cases,—whether the objective or the subjective world furnish the data of thought,—the result is an ultimate inward movement, which, although it may, in given instances, lead to the anticipation of external action, as a consequence, is, so far, a purely mental condition, sanctioning the popular usage which applies the term "reflection" to all modes of intellectual action which are of a strictly internal character.

Recognizing this fact of language, and pursuing our analysis of the human faculties as subjects of disciplinary culture, we now, therefore, change our field of observation, and pass from the outward spheres of perceptive observation and expressive communication to the silent, inner, invisible, spiritual, and purely intellectual region of *Thought.* We now contemplate man as made in the image of his Maker, as an intelligent and rational being; and we trace the working of those powers which ally him to "things unseen and eternal."

Following, as before, the method of observing (1,) the *forms* of mental action grouped under a given classification; (2,) their *actuating principle*, or motive force; (3,) their natural and habitual *tendency;* (4,) the *results* of their action; and (5,) the *educational processes* consequently required for their development and discipline, we proceed to a summary

### (I.) Enumeration of the Reflective Faculties.

Memory, Conception, Consciousness, Reason, Understanding, Judgment.

*Explanatory Remark.*—This classification is presented not as one philosophically complete or exhaustive, but merely as a suggestive outline, for educational purposes. It is intentionally limited to the chief of those forms of mental action which may be regarded as acts or powers not only strictly interior, but *purely intellectual*, as contradistinguished from those which are concerned with the external objects and facts of *perception*, from those which consist in inward or outward movements of *feeling*, and from those which are conversant with the ideal forms and creations of the *imagination*. A more extensive classification, including the subdivisions and subordinate details of reflective intellection, will necessarily present itself at a later stage of our analysis, when we come to the consideration of the various forms of exercise to which this group of faculties is subjected in the processes of education.

(1.) Memory: *the Basis of Reflective Power.*—This faculty naturally claims our first attention, when we contemplate man as a being endowed with the power of reflective intelligence. It is this faculty which enables him to take the first step from the exterior and objective world into the interior and subjective. Its exercise empowers him, even in the absence of the objects of sense, to retain or to recall, for indefinite periods, and at indefinite intervals, the ideas which he derived from them. He can thus, at pleasure, dispense with the actual presence of external objects, and yet, by dwelling on them mentally, after he has withdrawn from them outwardly, pursue the trains of thought to which they give rise. As a result, he thus acquires a more intimate knowledge of their relations to his own interior being, and converts the pabulum of intelligence, furnished in the data of the outward world, into the pure elements of intellectual sustenance. The activity of this power is, in fact, the measure of his growth in mental stature and strength. It is the condition of all intelligent progress, whether we regard memory as the grand receptacle and depository of all those elements of knowledge which are at once the rudiments of intellectual life, the springs mental of action, and the material of thought, or as the chain which links the past to the present, and retains every acquisition as a foothold for the next step forward in the processes of reason and the investigation of truth.

*Remembrance.*—The faculty of memory, even in its comparatively passive and quiescent form of mere retention, or *remembrance*, gives man the power of holding with a firm grasp all the treasures which observation enables him to accumulate from without, and to carry them with him into that internal region of thought where they are to be assimilated to his own mental being, and become component parts of it, in transfigured forms of living power and beauty. Not only so: but even the involuntary susceptibility of this vast capacity preserves in the mind the imprint of every passing thought, every form of imagination, and every mood of feeling, which has character enough to excite his attention and recall him to himself, in the exercise of consciousness and reflection.

*Intellectual and Moral Offices of Memory.*—This benign retentive power gives unity to man's intellectual and moral life. It is the sure and steadfast anchor by which he grapples the present to the past, and is saved from the fluctuation and fragmentary tossing of "the ignorant present." In the wide field of culture, memory makes the mind the seed plot and garden ground of all the knowledge which human care and kindness have the skill or the power to drop into it. Fertilized by the genial influences of well directed education, the retentive capacity of memory becomes rich in every precious and noble product of mind by which the intellectual life of the world is nourished and sustained.

But it is as an element of intellectual and moral power in human *character*, that this faculty reveals its chief value. Its very nature and tendency is to constitute man a *reflective* being, by withdrawing him from the influence of a too exclusive regard to the present and the external; by soliciting his attention to the profoundest verities of his own intelligent and immortal being; and by balancing the stern realities of experience against the sometimes fallacious solicitations of hope, or the grave actualities of the past against the doubtful promises of the future. It prompts to *thought*, and leads to security amidst uncertainty and distraction. It invites to reflective *meditation*, by the suggestive materials in which it abounds. It cherishes *contemplation*, by opening to the mind's eye the long vista of the past with its fast-linked trains of scene and incident and action, and the ineffaceable impressions which all these have graven upon the heart. It tends to make man a considerate and thoughtful being, by the faithful monitions which it furnishes to the lips of wisdom warning against the errors of judgment or of will, by reminding of their penalties formerly incurred.

Remembrance saves from the domineering ascendency and absorbing attractions of the sensuous and the transient, by intermingling with the fluidity and evanescence of the present the solidity and permanence of the past. It thus tends to give gravity and weight to character; and if its influence is sometimes a shade too sombre for gayety, it contributes a not undesirable element to the sternness of manhood, as a safeguard to the firmness of will. Its office is, in this respect, a preventive one,—to save man from the instability which the exclusive influence of things present and things outward might induce; and, by attracting him inward to himself, it favors the acquisition of that self-knowledge which is the anchor of his safety.

*Recollection.*—This term is but another name for the faculty of memory, and merely intimates that the impressions made on the mind by a given object, scene, or event, may have been, for a time, effaced, or its elements dispersed, by the intervention of other agencies; and that, with or without an effort of the will to that effect, but by the operation of some law of mental association, the idea recurs or returns, as it were, and, perhaps, unexpectedly and suddenly, to the mind. We are then said to "recollect," (*gather again*,) or recall what had, for a season, escaped the retentive hold of memory.

The very abruptness and suddenness of the transition of thought, in such instances, exerts a peculiar power on the reflective action of the mind, and makes it more striking, more impressive, and more effectual. Recollection may thus light up the soul with the instantaneous gleam of a rekindled thought, or plunge it into the depths of a past grief; or it may arrest the will on the very brink of remembered evil. A long train of profound reflections may thus be suggested, which may exert an influence on the character of a whole life.

A mere flash of reflection has sometimes sufficed, by the instant recalling of scenes of childhood's innocent enjoyment, or the injunctions of parental wisdom and love to reinstate conscience on its rightful throne, and bring back the tempted to himself, or to restrain him from the first steps of a career of ruin. A remembered promise, pledging honor and truth, has sometimes risen up as a barrier against an approaching tide of overwhelming guilt. A verse of sacred Scripture, darting across the mind, has checked the hand already stretched out to do the deed of wickedness which no after tears of penitence could have sufficed to wash out.

But not as a *preventive* only does memory thus subserve man's highest interests: its recurring suggestions are not less frequently inspiring *prompters* to every form of virtue. To the dispirited traveler on the pathway of life, it comes, sometimes, as an inspiring angel, with messages of cheering and encouragement drawn from the remembered virtues of the struggling great and good who have gone before. It points him to "their footprints on the sands of time," and bids him "take heart again." It reminds him that his great reliance is not on the outward and the material, but on that "hidden strength" of which our greatest poet speaks so eloquently. The maxim or the motto which the guardian care of the mother or the teacher had engraven as a watchword on the tablet of the heart, in early years, recurs, sometimes, to incite to noble deeds or noble enduring, the man encompassed by difficulties and dangers before which he would otherwise have staggered. The "one, last, best effort, more," which wins the crown of victory, is that, not unfrequently, which follows the backward glance of memory to the parting scene, and farewell words of a parent's blessing.

*Memory as a Subject of Cultivation.*—In either form, whether that of retentive remembrance or momentary recollection, memory furnishes the material, and solicits the action, of the whole class of reflective faculties. To the educator, therefore, the judicious cultivation and development of this capacity, in the minds committed to his care, becomes a matter of vital moment, that the impressible memory of the young may be rich in valuable resources, and strong for the aid of every good purpose, sound and healthy in its action, firm in its grasp, and prompt to yield up its acquisitions when in demand for intellectual emergencies.

The true teacher will be careful that this indispensable servant of the mind be not exhausted by overwork, that its strength be not expended on worthless material, that its receptive capacity be not crammed to unhealthful and unprofitable repletion, at the expense of inaction and inanity to all the other capacities of the mind. But of the appropriate modes of exercise for the cultivation of this faculty, we shall have occasion to speak more fully under the head of educational processes.

(2.) CONCEPTION: *Etymological Sense of the Word.*—The primitive signification of this term, implies that the mind has the power of "taking" (*receiving*, or *forming*,) ideas "with," (*within*,) itself, whether on data furnished from without, and by the alchemy of mind, transmuted into intellectual forms, or on materials found within itself, originating in feeling or in thought, partaking of its own character, and wearing forms purely ideal. In the process of intelligence, *conception* presents itself as the counterpart of *perception*, performing, in the interior world of thought, an office similar to that of the latter in the domain of exterior observation.

*Its Proper Acceptation.*—The term "conception," in its full and proper acceptation, comprehends the action of the mind in the intelligent contemplation or cognition of any object or subject in the whole range of the ideal world. It applies to the recognition or creation of the forms of imagination and the figures of fancy, not less than to the ideas of pure intellection. In the former relation, it stands connected with the action of the expressive faculties, as discussed in a previous lecture; but it is in the latter sense, as a contemplative and reflective faculty, that we now regard it. In this connection, it approaches, sometimes to the sphere of memory, and draws from that source the materials on which it acts,—whether these were originally external or internal in their origin.

*Different Views of this Faculty.*—Contemplated in the light last mentioned, the faculty of conception has, by some eminent writers on intellectual philosophy, been considered as identical with *memory;* while, by others, its definite action on forms furnished by *imagination*, has been regarded as identifying it with that faculty. Hence, we read of the "conceptions of memory," and the "conceptions of imagination." A third class of authors treating of intellectual topics, evidently regard conception as simply an act of the understanding.

The unsatisfactory character of popular usage in our own tongue, as regards the application of language to mental phenomena, is strikingly exhibited in the several arbitrary senses in which the term "conception" is used, as suggesting imperfection, dimness, or remoteness in the objects or subjects of contemplation. We can not, therefore, rely on any consentaneous use of nomenclature as a guide to the character or action of the faculty in question. Adverting, however, to the highly suggestive etymological sense of the term "conception," as it has been employed in the metaphysical vocabulary of all nations, for successive ages, we find the susceptive intellect figuratively represented by it as—when in the act of forming ideas—*impregnated*, or fertilized, not only from the various sources of intelligence furnished by the external world of perception and the interior spheres of feeling and imagination, but as possessing a *self-vivifying* power of creating and contemplating an inner world of its own, more or less analogous to that without, though formed of materials purely intellectual and spiritual;—a condition which is exemplified in the exercises of its own conscious intuition, in the sequences of thought, and in the processes of reasoning. Nor is the independent power of this faculty in any case more distinctly perceptible than when, borrowing the congenial aid of reason, it inspires with intelligence, and moulds into symmetry the fluctuating forms of imagination which hover in the ideal atmosphere.

This strictly interior power of the mind may be regarded as the first step in its consciously reflective action, in which,—not as in the partly involuntary condition of mere remembrance or recollection, it is comparatively passive, or works under a law of necessity,—but voluntarily and deliberately coöperates with impressions received from without, with a consciousness of their tendencies and of its own action. It is this power which virtually confers on man a world of his own, —an intelligent sphere of activity, independent, for the time, of the external universe in which he moves,—a sphere in which his higher intellectual and moral nature has its appropriate scope. The strength, the clearness, and the precision with which this faculty acts, determine his rank in the scale of intelligence and moral power.

*Its Susceptibility of Cultivation.*—In the relations of educational culture, the exercise of this faculty becomes a subject of deepest interest to those whose office it is to train the mind to true and effective habits of action. Nothing, indeed, can give a more impressive view of the benefits of proper cultivation, or of the susceptibility of this faculty to the influence of culture, than the contrast between the feeble and futile efforts of the child to form an adequate conception of the causes of the most ordinary phenomena of daily life, and the comprehensive grasp of conceptive intelligence with which the mature mind of man reads the great volume of facts and their relations, and interprets their most hidden laws. A similar contrast is exhibited to us in the wondering ignorance of the savage, contemplating the varying aspects of nature, and the man of science, to whom they present themselves as necessary results, thoroughly understood, and as verifications of philosophic theory.

The mere perceptions of the child or of the savage may often be more exact than those of the philosopher, because these depend on the freshness and vividness of sensation. But the *conceptive* power of the mind is, to a great extent, the result of the force of processes purely mental, and the skill and exactness with which these are conducted. In such operations, practice and discipline alone can yield perfection as a result; and for success in them the candidate must look to the sustaining aid and the crowning hand of education.

If we would form even the humblest idea of the mental value of the power of conception, we must refer to all that man has achieved in the acquisition of knowledge or the attainment of truth; we must advert to all the relations which he sustains to things lying beyond the sphere of sense, in the wide regions of opinion, of theory, and of sentiment; we must include his views of his own position in the universe, his views of the character of Deity, of the immortality of the soul, of the obligations of duty, of his social and civil life, and of all the institutions to which his conceptions of these various relations have given origin.

It is in these wider and higher references that conception, as a power of reflective intelligence, indicates its peculiar rank and office. Working by the blended lights of reason and of consciousness, it enables man to construct the fabrics of science and of character, by a consecutive progress of attainments in which every deposit becomes but a substratum for another in the series of an indefinite succession.

(3.) Consciousness: *Etymology of the Term.*—The etymological signification of this term invites our attention for a moment, to the peculiar suggestive value of the first element in the composition of the word. Primitively, the meaning of this element is fully given by the equivalent term *together*, always implying a reference to *duality* or *plurality*. It ranges, accordingly, over the whole class of synonyms which may be grouped under the terms, "collation," "apposition," "union." In the use, therefore, of the term "consciousness,"—since the *root* of the word signifies *knowledge*, or intelligence,—the mind is represented as acting *together* with, or in *union* with, itself—that is, with *self-intelligence*. The prefix of the term, in this instance, accordingly, as in that of the word "conception," has the virtual significance of *inner*, *inward*, or *interior*, and suggests the idea of the mind acting on itself, on the objects of its own creation, or on the subjects of its own reflective conceptions.

*Fitness of its Application*.—There is a striking appropriateness, in this view, of the term "consciousness" as a designation for that power by which the mind becomes capable of momentarily detaching, as it were, from itself the idea of its contemplation, and working as a two-fold power; one effort of which is to hold up the ideal object, and the other to direct a wakeful and conscious attention to it, for some purpose of examination or reflective inquiry. The intelligent principle thus works—according to the interpretation of the term—*together* with, or in union with itself, in the compound or two-fold action of *conception*, and *attention*; the latter being introverted, so that the mind is aware of its own condition.

The peculiar fitness of the term in question becomes yet more distinctly apparent, when we advert to the common fact of experience, that, in the outward tendencies of the faculty of perception, the attraction of external objects is often so powerful and absorbing as to cause the mind to "lose its consciousness" in the contemplation of what it beholds, and to forget, for a time, its own existence, in the force of the attraction by which it is evoked, or the intensity of the excitement to which it is subjected, and which it temporarily identifies with the object of its attention. In the state of consciousness, on the other hand, the mind is *self-possessed*; it is *aware* of its own state of thought or feeling, and *voluntarily* dwells on the fact of introversion.

*Different Opinions on the Nature of this Faculty*.—Consciousness, as a term applied to the designation of a mental faculty of the reflective class, is, like many other terms in the nomenclature of intellectual analysis, a confessedly imperfect yet significant attempt to suggest a perfect recoginition of an act or state purely internal. The imperfection here felt, attends more or less obviously, yet unavoidably, every attempt to define the action of mind,—that transcendent power whose subtle agency often proves too fine for the grasp of its human representative, language, an interpreter whose terms are all, in consequence of the limitations of humanity, "of the earth, earthy."

The diversity of opinion among intellectual philosophers, therefore, on the nature of this power, is not surprising. Some would ignore its existence as a cognizable faculty, and identify it with the mere reflex act of attention; others elaborate its action in detail, so as to identify it with voluntary and prolonged reflection. Both these classes of observers evidently take the ground that it is dependent on the exercise, more or less active, of the will. But the painful act of consciousness in the experience of corporal or mental suffering, is often altogether involuntary, and resists, sometimes, the strongest efforts of the will, even in the loftiest moods of heroism itself; and the intellectual attraction of a mathematical problem, or a metaphysical question, will fascinate the conscious thinker, and draw him on involuntarily, from stage to stage of its processes, till, in the poet's language, he "forgets himself to marble."

Other authorities on topics of intellectual philosophy, have deemed it more rational to assume that consciousness is an inseparable attribute of intelligence,—necessary to its very existence. They represent it as the element which constitutes the dividing line between thought and mere reverie, between judgment and imagination, or, sometimes, between reason and insanity.

*Educational View of this Faculty.*—For the preliminary analysis which the intelligent conductor of education requires as his guide in the planning of his procedure, it is sufficient, perhaps, to take the acknowledged ground that consciousness is that state, act, or operation of the mind in which it is aware of its own activity. He will, from this view of the subject, derive two most important conclusions: (1,) that the vividness and distinctness of consciousness must always be in proportion to the clearness, exactness, and force of the ideas which are, so to speak, impressed on the mind from without, and solicit its conscious action as subjects of thought; and (2,) that the definiteness, the fullness, and the depth of consciousness, must always be in proportion to the power of directing and controlling the attention of the mind with reference to its own inward acts and conditions.

*Intellectual and Moral Offices of Consciousness.*—It is thus that consciousness assumes its true place as a reflective faculty, in the relations of intellect, as the power by which the mind learns to see clearly with its own inner eye, to define with accuracy the ideas which conception creates, to interpret nature's innermost secrets of causation, to follow the lengthening processes of reason, in the profoundest depths of investigation, and so to construct the magnificent fabrics of pure science. The reflective power of consciousness becomes yet more impressive to us, when we regard its vast influence on the moral relations of mental action. It then reveals itself as an agent but a little lower than the divine element of *conscience*, and as the very condition of the paramount influence of that power over heart, will, action, and character. In the unconscious condition of childhood, and in the immaturity of experience, conscience moves with the light step, and the gentle hand and the soft accents of the guiding angel of Innocence. But it watches with a jealous eye, restrains with a firm hand, controls with the tone of command, or rebukes with the voice of reproach, the conscious agent who, in maturity of years, departs from the path of rectitude. But not in the stern monitions or the agonizing inflictions of remorse alone, does conscience act on consciousness. The sting and the lash are not its only implements of discipline. Conscience appeals to man's conscious power for good, when it uses "the spur which the clear spirit doth raise," and reminds him of his position "but a little lower than the angels," his resources of intellect, his moral ability, his relations of duty, his capacity of ceaseless progress, his desire to win the crown of excellence, his obligations to the Author of his being, and his aspirations after an immortality of glory.

*Educational Culture of this Faculty.*—The educator, therefore, while he would guard his pupils against that selfish and morbid consciousness which dwells exclusively on the condition of the individual, and keeps him forever in the abstracted mood of introspection and introversion, shut up in the cell of self, and withdrawn from usefulness to others, will use all salutary measures to give vigor and life and full activity to this powerful element of mental action and character.

(4.) REASON: *Explanatory Remark.*—The successive changes which, in the progress of time, are produced on the original meanings of words, will sometimes render a literal adoption of the primitive sense of any term an uncertain guide in metaphysical investigations connected with the action and phenomena of mind. A due regard, however, to the etymological structure of terms employed to designate the intellectual faculties, will always serve to suggest useful ideas for the guidance and direction of education. Such terms, it is not to be forgotten, had their origin in simple and primitive states of human life and character, and are therefore exempt from the uncertainty and ambiguity resulting from the mental condition of more advanced stages of society, in which opinion is refined, by false as well as true culture, into more subtle and more sceptical forms, and sometimes falls into the entangling web of sophistry and false judgment. The primitive uses of language betray, it must be acknowledged, the historical childhood of man; but they possess, also, the truthfulness, the simplicity, and the directness of that stage; and their vivacious and figurative character always render them strikingly suggestive. In philosophic investigations connected with the analytic study of mind and the adaptation of modes of culture to mental discipline and development, the primitive signification of terms, whether it be literal or figurative, becomes, at least, an index to analysis, which, if faithfully traced, may lead to true and satisfactory conclusions on topics otherwise obscure and uncertain.

*Etymology of the Term.*—To apply this remark to the instance before us. Clearer conceptions and juster views of the faculty which we designate by the term "reason," would generally prevail, and would exert a corresponding influence on modes of mental culture, were the original meaning of the word adverted to in discussions connected with these subjects. The word "reason" is but the Latin scientific term "*ratio*," so familiar to the ear and mind of every teacher and every student of mathematics. It has merely undergone some slight modifications in passing from the Latin language, through the French, into our own. Its original sense, therefore, suggests the idea of *rate*, *measure*, or computation, as a conscious application, or act, of intelligence; and if we would trace the simplest and purest form of reason, we thus find it in the act of recognizing or constituting *rate*, or *ratio*, which in complicated processes, becomes *proportion*, or *symmetry*.

*Reason characterized by the Definiteness and Certainty of its Action.*—The idea suggested by the primary application of the term "reason," is that of *definiteness* and *exactness* of observation, carried even to the extent of examination by actual *measurement* or computation. No certainty of knowledge can be greater than what is thus intimated, when the inner action of intellect is verified by a direct appeal to objective reality attested by sense; and, in the legitimate uses of language, the measured exactness of verified observation is figuratively transferred to the decisions of judgment and the deductions of reason, in the comparison and examination of ideas and conceptions begun, continued, and ended, within the mind itself.

The processes of thought conducted on this firm ground, possess a definiteness which places the conclusions of reason in striking contrast with the comparatively vague and indefinite intimations of *feeling*, around which the boundary line of distinction can not with certainty be drawn, even in the most vivid states of consciousness. The ideas of reason stand thus contrasted, also, with those of *imagination*, which are often shadowy and indefinite, inexact, or inadequate, and always comparatively fleeting and uncertain;—sometimes, unreal and false, the mere flitting phantoms of fancy. The purely intellectual conceptions of reason, as subjects of the mind's own inner *consciousness*, are, yet further, distinguished from the merely *perceptive* action of sense and understanding, in the relations of intelligence directed to the *external* world. Reason, working on data strictly mental, ever partakes of the *certainty of personal knowledge* and *conviction*, which, to the individual,—whatever it may be to others,—is, in its proper relations, the surest of all the grounds of mental action. Our senses, we are aware, may misinform us: our conscious experience can not.

*Offices of Reason in Definition and Discrimination.*—This faculty, by the measured accuracy of its action, becomes the means of *defining* our ideas and *discriminating* them in differential detail. It groups them in the *genera* and *species* of orderly *classification*, and *analyses* the complex into the simple, even to the minutest individual element of the compound. It thus enables the mind to search and scrutinize the obscure or the uncertain, till every object is brought out into the light of certainty and conscious knowledege. In these, as in all other forms in which this faculty is exerted, the appropriateness of the primary application of the term by which it is designated, is distinctly perceived. In all its operations, it is stable, sure, exact, to absolute certainty. It was in virtue of its authority that the great modern philosopher "carried," as has been happily said, "the measuring line to the boundary of creation;" and all its inward and conscious exercises partake of the same exactitude.

*Reason, an Authoritative Power.*—When this faculty condescends to its humbler offices of recognizing the intimations of sense, and accumulating the deposits of knowledge, and maintains a comparatively quiescent, receptive, or passive condition, it bears the unassuming designation of "understanding;" as it is then regarded as merely furnishing the *groundwork*, or under stratum, of intelligence. But when it assumes the higher office of deciding on and determining the exact relations of thought, it is honored by the highly figurative appellation of "judgment"—a term the etymology of which implies the enunciation of *right*, or *justice*, and hence, whatever, also, is implied in its synonyms, *decree*, *sentence*, or *decision*. Reason, when thus occupied in comparing, measuring, or exactly estimating things or their relations, is, by the use of language, personified as the *judge*, whose office it is to *scrutinize*, *compare*, and *balance evidence*, so as ultimately to *decide* or *determine*, and give *judgment*, *sentence*, or *decree*, according to the usage of ancient times, when it was that officer's prerogative to discharge the office assigned to our modern juries, as well as that still recognized as proper to him who presides in the court of justice.

When this master faculty of human intelligence soars to a yet higher pitch, and its action, whether "intuitive or discursive," embraces great and *general principles*, sees or traces the relations of *necessary* and *universal truths*, and announces the majesty of *causation* and of *law*, it resumes its wonted designation of *reason*,—a term too limited for the scope and grandeur of its action, and the dignity of its office, as man's highest functions, in the relations of intellect.

True, it fails whenever it would usurp the appointed place of *conscience*, and *reason* man into perfect rectitude, or when it presumes to supersede the guardian office of *faith*, and offers man the guidance of mere intellection to the recognition of a paternal God. But, limited as it is, by the conditions of humanity, it still is, within the sphere of pure intelligence, that which reflects in man the image of God, and to which, in healthy and normal conditions, all his other intellectual powers pay homage.

*Reason as cognizant of Relations.*—Reverting to the primitive sense of the term "reason," as recognized in the application of the word "ratio" to processes of measurement connected with time and space, and figuratively transferred to operations purely intellectual, we are reminded that, in all such processes, one object or subject is *referred* to another, with a view to determine or define a *connection* of some sort or other between them. This fact accounts for the usage in language by which reason is represented as the faculty which takes cognizance of, or traces, *relations* in general, or, in other words, refers one thing to another, for purposes of *examination*, *comparison*, or *investigation*, with a view to ascertain their *connection*, or their *independence* of each other, as an element of thought essential to the acquisition of knowledge or to the discovery of truth. The mind is thus introduced into a sphere of action coëxtensive with all the outward objects and inward subjects of thought, and expatiates, with the delight of conscious freedom and power, in the two great domains with which it is endowed as its heritage and birth-right; for reason, not less than imagination is an *excursive* faculty, designed to give amplitude and expansion to the being of man; and many of the grandest creations of the latter, are those which it achieves when following the sure and firm steps of the former, in its excursions into the unexplored.

*Reason as an Inventive Faculty.*—The reference of one object or idea to another, the comparison of one with another, or the discovered relation of one to another, yields within the mind itself, as a result, a *third* idea, or conception, a creation of its own. Reason thus becomes a combining, creative, and inventive, (*finding*,) faculty, not less than imagination is, in its peculiar sphere; and, by following its well ascertained discoveries through their long and complicated successions of ever fresh-springing truth, attains, at length, the conscious power to move in new spheres of knowledge, created by its own activity, and in which it furnishes its own material, and erects its own structures. It is thus that it empowers man to fulfill the poet's condition of "erecting himself above himself." Reason, not less than its noble kindred powers, Faith and Imagination, is then justly said to "soar."

In the processes of investigation in which the mind pursues its quest of knowledge as the guide to truth, reason becomes the master key of intelligence, the paramount authority of intellect, the law which gives order and unity to man's intellectual being, the crown and glory of humanity in its distinctive supremacy over the lower tribes of partially intelligent nature.

*Aberration of Reason.*—When disease or passion has beclouded, or disturbed, or deranged this power, which heaven has ordained as the *executive* of its own first law of *order*, in the gradations of intelligence, man is then dethroned and discrowned; and, with the eye of his mind extinguished, wanders, like the blind champion of old, seeking some one to lead him by the hand.

*Reason in the processes of Analysis and Abstraction.*—When this faculty is occupied with the processes of collating and comparing, for purposes of discrimination, its action assumes the form of "analysis," (*loosening*, *detaching*, or *resolving*,) so as to simplify the objects or subjects of contemplation, and scan their utmost details of individuality, in character, that the component elements of the concrete may be distinctly recognized, in all their differential relations. Subjected to this process, the *genus*, or general class, is reduced to its component *species*, and these, in turn, to the *varieties* or the *individuals* of which they consist. Last of all, the scrutiny must be extended to the difference between individual and individual, or where still more minute examination is required, to the distinctive elements which may be found comprised within the unity of the individual.

Such, in our previous discussion of subjects involved in the theory of education, we found to be the requisite action of the mind in the exercise of the *perceptive* faculties, when observation descends to the minutiæ of difference on which true distinctions are founded. A similar operation goes on in the interior world of conception, when the *reflective* faculties are called into their peculiar province, when the com plex ideas or thoughts of the mind are subjected to the processes of scrutiny and analysis, and the qualities of objects, or of ideas, are, by an act of *abstraction*, (*taking away*, *withdrawing*,) considered separately, as if they had for the moment, an independent existence. One quality of an object, one attribute of a subject, is, by this concentrated and exclusive act of attention, "abstracted," (*drawn away*,) or detached, mentally, from the object itself, and from all the other qualities of which it is possessed. The mind is, in consequence of this act of "abstraction," enabled to contemplate more distinctly, or to examine more closely and discriminate more exactly, the given quality. The quality so discriminated may, in turn, become the groundwork of classification, or the commencement of a train of abstract reasoning on broad and general principles connected with the laws of nature and the truths of science.

*Intuition.*—The immediate action of reason by which it assents to self-evident and necessary truths, on mere "intuition," (*inspection or sight*,) without the aid of any intermediate or intervening thought for the discovery of sameness or difference, might, at first view, seem to be improperly introduced in a survey of the reflective faculties or of educational processes for development. But, the *intuitive* exercise of reason is, not unfrequently, the basis of its *reflective* action, and, sometimes, is the *authority* to which it appeals, when prosecuting examination and inquiry to the profoundest depths of research.

*Processes of Inference and Deduction.*—Reason, as the faculty by which one object or idea is referred to another, in virtue of some real or supposed connection existing between them, takes cognizance of *antecedence* and *consequence*; and, when this relation is, in given circumstances, observed to be uniform, reason, working by the great law of *analogy*, "infers," (*brings in*,) the *continuance* of this uniformity as a necessary principle or law of *order*. In such instances, this "inference," supported by the undeviating testimony of personal or accredited experience, becomes a firm *belief*, which identifies uniformity of antecedence with the power of *causation*, and uniformity of sequence with the character of *effect*. *Sequence* thus becomes the law of rational *connection*, and a security for the attainment of *truth* in matters of *theory* referring to the *external* universe.

In the consecutive *internal* acts of mind, reason gives "sequence" to the relations of *thought*, in exercises purely *discursive* and *intellectual*, by recognizing the dependence of one idea or conception on another, in the relation of *effect* to *cause*. From one defined antecedent idea the mind is authorized to "infer" another, as a *consequence*; from "premises," (*thoughts antecedent*,) to "deduce," (*draw down*, *derive*,) "conclusions," (*closes*,) results, or final consequences; and thus, by giving *certainty* to *opinion* and *assurance* to *belief*, in relations purely *mental*, it forges the successive links of that golden chain of *intellectual necessity* which binds together the elements of the *moral* world.

*Reason, in its processes of Generalization and Induction.*—In the wider action of this sovereign power, it takes that highest course of which human intellect is capable; and, in tracing the relations of *causation*, aspires, by its power of *generalization* and its processes of *induction*, to announce and interpret the *laws* of the universe, and to read the evidences of a First ordaining Cause.

In these excursions, reason gathers in, from the vast field of analogy, *corresponding* facts and relations; and, in virtue of that pervading *unity* which comparison has enabled it to discover as existing among them, recognizes that spacious principle of *generality* coëxtensive with its own capacities of thought, by which it rises above the limits of the concrete and the particular to the contemplation of those abstract ideas and comprehensive principles which constitute the prime elements of intellectual and moral truth, and which bear the stamp of supremacy and the inscription of Law, human or Divine.

Not less impressive or sublime is the action of this august faculty of the human soul, when it puts forth its *constructive* power, and, aided by the scrutiny of patient experiment, it verifies the analogies of phenomena and of fact, "inducts" them, (*leads* them,) into their appropriate groups of *affinity* and *correlation*, plies them with its tentative, magnetic, aggregating power of "hypothesis," (*theoretic, interrogative assumption*,) and, by careful *induction*, at last consummates the vast fabric of "theory," (*intellectual vision*,) whose foundations are laid in the certainty of *knowledge*, and whose walls rise, in the symmetry of *truth*, to heights which inspire the mind with awe.

*Ratiocination.*—In the dimness of abstract conceptions, in the obscurity of abstruse relations of thought, or in the apparent conflict of contrasted truths, when the eviction of hidden causes, or when the detection of intermediate and reconciling principles, becomes essential to the conscious recognition of ideas, to the distinct conception of relations, or to the firm conviction of truth, reason comes to the mind laboring under *uncertainty*, and brings the aid of its *discursive* processes of *ratiocination*, in the form of *dissertation, argument, discussion*, and *debate*. Assuming the seat of *judgment*, it thus institutes *inquiry*, conducts *examination*, prosecutes *investigation, discriminates terms, scrutinizes allegations, compares* conflicting *arguments, weighs* opposing *evidence, judges* of *facts, rejects assumptions, exposes error, detects truth* or *falsehood*, and pronounces its authoritive and final *decision*, as the inevitable *law* of intellection.

*Reason, as cognizant of Truth.*—Reason, in its judicial capacity, traces, or recognizes and announces, the correspondence or the discrepance of idea with object, thought with fact, conception with conception, principle with principle, proposition with proposition, sentiment with sentiment, opinion and statement with fact, language with thought, argument with argument, effect with cause. It thus, by the eviction of *truth*, produces in the mind the result of *conviction;* and *truth*, as the consummated and perfect result of the action of *reason*, in its cognizance of the ascertained relations of *knowledge*, demands, in virtue of the supremacy and authority of the faculty by whose agency it is discovered, the assent of the mind, in the form which we term *belief*,—not a bare comprehension or merely passive reception by the *understanding*, not the mere negative acquiescence or silent admission of the *judgment*, but the consentaneous recognition and adoption which come from the *voluntary* action of *reason*, uniting itself with the subject of its contemplation, and identifying with it all its own consequent action. Reason, therefore, has to do with all the preliminary processes by which truth is established; and in the moral not less than in the intellectual relations of thought, has, for its office, the sifting of *evidence*, the scrutiny of *testimony*, the weighing of *proof;* on the validity of all which, *belief*, as the normal and healthy tendency of the mind, is conditioned. In the yet higher sphere of Sacred truth, belief becomes subsidiary to the Faith which *trusts.*

*Reason, as susceptible of Cultivation.*—As the subject of disciplinary culture, this faculty presents itself to the educator as that to which his chief attention is due, in the relations of intellect, not only from its supremacy in the class of faculties to which it belongs, and the fact of its being the very constituent of intelligence, but from its peculiar susceptibility of development and training, and the extent to which it may be rendered clear, decisive, vigorous, and comprehensive, by appropriate exercise. No faculty reveals more distinctly than this the progressive character of man, as an intelligent agent, if we advert to its dim, uncertain, and feeble action in childhood, and its ceaseless growth in soundness, clearness, and vigor, as life advances to its maturity. But when we contrast the reasoning powers of such individuals as Newton, Locke, Butler, or Edwards, in manhood, with the mere germ of latent capability which they possessed in infancy, we perceive yet more distinctly what education may accomplish for the eduction and strengthening of this powerful element in the mental constitution of man.

The cultivation of this faculty becomes yet more important in its results, when we advert to its value in the relation of morals. Reason is naturally the firm ally of *conscience*, in discriminating between *right* and *wrong*, and in instituting those reflective trains of thought by which man is arrested in the pursuit of sensual gratification, and called home to himself, in the conscious exercise of higher faculties, in the enjoyment of truer satisfactions, and in obedience to the rectitude which he feels to be the great law of his being. Reason, in coöperation with conscience, then becomes the regulating principle of his actions; raising them from mere obedience to *prudence* and *judgment*, and conservative *propriety*, to the higher influences of *self-intelligence*, *consentaneous action*, and *rational conformity* with the *laws* and *conditions* of *his own nature*, and of the Power by which those laws were ordained. Reason is the eye by which he learns to read the volume of revelation,—whether that written in the language of the "elder Scripture," which speaks of the "eternal power and godhead of the Creator," or that of the recorded Word which makes man "wise unto salvation."

(5. and 6.) Judgment and Understanding: *their Identity with Reason.*—It has been justly remarked by an eminent writer on intellectual philosophy, that, in arbitrarily multiplying the number of faculties attributed to the mind, we confuse our own views of mental action, and lose rather than gain by such uses of analysis. In the prosecution of our present inquiries, it will be recollected, that it has been uniformly our endeavor to keep in mind the absolute *unity* of intellection, under whatever apparent diversity of processes it conducts its action; and the preceding observations on *reason*, as a reflective faculty, have, it may have been perceived, presented the operations of *judgment* and *understanding* as virtually but different functions of *reason*. To venture on a figure drawn from the sciences of observation: *Reason* may be regarded as bearing the relation of "genus" to *judgment* and *understanding* as "species." Reason surveys the whole ground of intellection, whether directed outward or inward; it works in the great field of *analogy*, and on the common ground of *correlation*, *cotendency* and *consistency*, in the universal sphere of thought. In its comprehensive action, it proclaims the *harmonies* of the universe. It has the power, therefore, of *investigating* and *proving analogies*, and, consequently, of *rejecting discordant elements*. Descending to this task, reason becomes, in the vocabulary of intellection, "judgment." Stooping yet lower, to *trace* and *verify relations* of *humbler value*, or of *exterior character*, or processes of *passive reception* of *knowledge* or of *truth*, it assumes the lower office and familiar name of "understanding."

Maintaining the justness of this definition of the faculty of reason, we would not, however, overlook the fact, so important to the right management of education, that the more closely we watch the operations of intellect, the more searching the investigation, and the more minute our analysis, we shall be the better prepared to minister to the manifold wants of the mind, and to its healthful development. The subdivision of *reason* into "judgment" and "understanding," if taken as merely a temporary assumption of *theory*, with a view to fuller provision for mental action and discipline, can not be objected to; and, indeed, the common branches of useful knowledge and of scientific acquirement which constitute the material and media of intellectual education, address themselves distinctively to that classification of the mental faculties which is commonly adopted or recognized. Of these we shall have occasion to speak, when discussing the modes and processes of culture. Nor can any detriment to a just view of mind as subjected to invigorating discipline, arise from adopting, for the time, that more comprehensive classification of the forms of mental action, which is now proposed.

An extensive course of study in every department of mental philosophy, can not be too earnestly urged on the attention of all teachers who are so situated as to exert a controlling or directing influence on the plan of education, or to enjoy adequate opportunities of pursuing a full course of professional reading. No serious evil will in this way be incurred, even if the teacher become, in consequence of his studies, the disciple of a particular school of metaphysics or psychology; provided he do not lose sight of the great fact that, as a teacher, he is called to work as a personal and original observer of the actual workings and tendencies of the young mind itself, and, as its guide and director, to proceed according to his own personal observation and convictions, independently of all theories and speculations of a merely abstract character.

One of the greatest metaphysicians of modern times*—who, more than any writer or teacher on his class of subjects, is entitled to the rank of an authority—who, to a depth of research and a profoundness of learning which man has seldom attained, adds the simplicity, the docility, and the candor of a child in the attitude of inquiry—has most justly said to the student of mental philosophy: "If he only effectively pursue the method of observation and analysis, he may even dispense with the study of philosophical systems. This is, at best, only useful as a mean toward a deeper and more varied study of himself, and is often only a tribute paid by philosophy to erudi-

* Sir William Hamilton.

tion." With the same characteristic frankness he remarks, in another connection, that psychology (the direct study of mind) is yet incomplete as a science; since the phenomena of which it takes cognizance have not yet been exhaustively enumerated or defined, and speaks, at the same time, of the service which, in this respect, might be rendered to philosophy by adequate investigation and faithful reporting.

To so noble an office no candidate can more justly aspire than the intelligent teacher. His occupation renders him conversant with mind in its purest and truest states, its primal tendencies and aspirations, its incipient endeavors, and forming habits.

## II. The Actuating Principle of the Reflective Faculties: Inquiry.

*Its analogy to Curiosity.*—When we trace the natural development of the human faculties, in their first stage of *perceptive* action, we observe them working by a law of incitement manifesting itself in the restless principle of *curiosity*,—the desire of knowledge. It is this feeling which prompts the child's appealing question, as he points to a new object that has attracted his attention,—"What is this?" But, as his reflective power developes, and his capacity of knowledge enlarges, his desire of information pierces deeper; and his interrogation takes a shape which indicates a more profound exercise of thought. He now inquires not "*What* is this?"—but "*How*," or "*Why* is this?"

Reason, as the principle of intelligence which gleans and assorts the contributions of knowledge, has helped him to *understand* the exterior character of the object of his attention, and by the due exercise of *judgment*, in analytic observation, to distinguish, and classify, and denominate it accordingly. But a deeper thirst than mere curiosity as to external phenomena and characteristics, now actuates him: a more powerful instinct is at work within him. Reason has reached a maturer stage of development, and, prompted by inquiry, sets out the young explorer in quest not of mere facts, but of *relations* and *causes*. He thus learns to trace the successive links of *connected* phenomena and facts,—to investigate the *connection* itself, and determine its character, to search for interior and hidden springs of *sequence*, to arrive at *principles* and *causes*, to read and interpret *laws*, and, ultimately, to reach the certainty and the completeness of *science*.

The appetite of *curiosity* is satisfied with the knowledge of phenomena and of facts *individually*, or even as *detached* matters of observation: *inquiry* is restless till it arrives at their *connections* and *dependencies*, and the mind is thus put in possession of those relations of knowledge which constitute *principles* and establish *truth*. As an impelling and actuating force, *inquiry*, or inquisition, performs for the intellectual powers, in their comparative maturity, the same genial office which was discharged by the awakening influence of *curiosity* at an earlier stage of mental activity. It is, in fact, but the same instinctive law of the irrepressible desire to *know*, only working in a higher sphere, and for a higher end. *Curiosity*, working on the *perceptive* faculties, induces a tendency to *observation*, and forms the habit of wakeful attention to external *phenomena*, as the elements of KNOWLEDGE: *inquiry*, as the expressed desire to ascertain *relations*, *principles*, and *laws*, awakens the *reflective* faculties, and impels to *investigation*, with a view to the discovery of TRUTH. In the development and formation of mental character, *curiosity*, as the desire of *knowledge*, tends to create an *attentive* and *observing* mind, characterized by *intelligence: inquiry*, as the quest of *truth*, produces a *contemplative*, *thoughtful*, *reflective*, *reasoning* mind, addicted to *exploration* and *research*, and delighting in the attainments of *science*.

But in this higher sphere of intellectual activity, the human being is still acting under the guidance of an implanted *instinct*;—no longer, indeed, a mere unconscious stimulus, but a conscious and recognized impulse of progression toward a definite end and a satisfying consummation. The tendency, however, proves itself equally irresistible in the one form as in the other. For, while the child is sometimes so absorbed in the contemplation of the visible attractions of objects of beauty or of curiosity, as to forego even the calls of appetite for the sustenance of his body, in obedience to the more imperious claims of the wants of his intellectual nature ; the adult man may lose himself yet more profoundly, when inquiry compels him to investigation, and plunges him into depths of thought in which he becomes lost to all surrounding objects and relations, and, like Newton, meditates on the fall of an apple, with an intensity and concentration of reflective attention which beguile him of needed sleep, and render him unaware of the presence of food or of the fact of his having omitted its use.

### III. The Tendency of Action in the Reflective Faculties: Investigation.

*Its manifold directions.*—Inquiry, as the grand prompter of the reflective faculties, impels to habits of investigation and research. It not only leads to the scrutiny of the present, in quest of causes and of truth, but ransacks the records of the past, and penetrates into the probabilities of the future. It impels reason to explore the inmost recesses of nature, in pursuit of latent causes. It prompts man to conduct the experiments by which he interrogates nature of her processes, and wins, as the reward of his faithful inquest, the answers which he records in the archives of science. In the relations of moral truth, it compels the investigation of evidence, the verifying of proofs, the sifting of testimony, for the attaining of certainty and the confirmation of belief. But for its influence, the world would be to man a mass of unconnected objects or facts : he would be to himself a mere embodiment of inconsistent elements, unintelligible and destitute of purpose.

*Examples of the spirit of Investigation.*—Incited by this principle, the *naturalist* explores the remotest regions of earth, to contemplate the productions of nature, to survey the great features of the globe, its various aspects of scenery, its mountains and rivers, its atmospheric phenomena, its mineral, vegetable, and animal products, and the mutual relations of cause and effect which all these bear to each other.

The *scientific voyager* and *traveler*, impelled by the irrepressible desire to prosecute his favorite researches, patiently endures fatigue, and sickness, and exhaustion, through every extreme of heat or cold; he exiles himself from society, for months and years, to pursue his solitary investigations ; regardless of danger and difficulty, he bravely encounters every obstacle, and patiently endures every form of pain and privation. He goes forth with the spirit and hardihood of an invader, to extend the domain of science, and returns laden with the trophies of victory, in discoveries which enlighten and enrich the human race.

In the same spirit of investigation, the *astronomer* secludes himself, for successive months and years, to contemplate and record the phenomena of the heavens, and to immure himself in those labyrinths of computation by which the sublime truths of his noble science are investigated and revealed.

Actuated by the same principle, the *historian* pursues his laborious researches in the records of remotest time, in the half-effaced carving on the crumbling monument, or the dim characters on the decaying parchment,—in the obscure tradition or superstitious myth,—wherever a gleam or a spark of truth is to be found regarding the past life of man on earth. From his devotion to such investigations, no fresh charm of nature, or invitation of social delight, can induce him to withdraw, till he has sifted every alledged fact, verified every event, dispersed the clouds of fable, and let in the pure light of *truth* upon the historic page.

The *philologist*, in quest of a particle of meaning or significant value in the component elements of a word, is another impressive example of the spirit of inquiry leading to profoundest research. Whole years, nay, a long life, are joyfully devoted by him to such pursuits. Language after language, by his slow but sure processes of mining and sapping, is forced to give way to his irresistible energy and persevering toil. Nothing can divert his attention, or turn him from his course of persistent indagation. A syllable or a letter, he feels assured, contains a secreted gem of meaning, the investigation of which will put him in possession of wealth untold; and that element he will trace, at whatever cost of persevering investigation, through libraries and through languages, till the lustre of the intellectual diamond beams full upon his mind. His personal acquisition, purchased at such a price, becomes, in due season, through the instrumentality of his devoted labors, the common property of the intellectual world.

The investigations of the *mechanician* into the laws and forces of nature, again exemplify the power which the spirit of inquiry exerts over the human mind, and the value of the results to which it leads. The long and complicated processes of computation by which the devoted servant of science pursues his study of its principles, when occupied with the intricate combinations involved in the invention of some device of mechanism, by which the well-being of mankind may be promoted for ages; the unabating ardor with which, in spite of every discouragement, he continues to consume fortune and life in the prosecution of his purpose;—all indicate the moving force of the mental principle by which his own interior world of invention and contrivance is actuated; and the results ultimately obtained reveal the value of the intellectual habits which are concerned in the processes of investigation.

The *chemist*, interrogating nature, as he investigates the constitution of her elements, is yet another forcible example of the same spirit. At the risk, sometimes, of life itself, he pursues his inquest of hidden relations, perplexing facts, and hitherto undiscovered elements and undeveloped forces, till he is enabled to enlighten the world by the revelation of a new material in the construction of the physical universe, and an invaluable aid to the welfare of man.

Investigation, in all the relations of mental action, is, in brief, the just price of labor, which man is doomed to pay for value received. The noblest of all intellectual acquirements, the grandest discoveries and most useful inventions, are due alike to this process by which the mind is enabled to read, whether in the world of matter or that of spirit, the laws instituted by the Creator; coöperating with which, man becomes possessed of a portion of divine power, and unaided by which, every attempt of human force or skill must be baffled. The tendency and the ability to penetrate into the depths of causation, constitute the mental prerogatives of man; they lift him up to the rank of nobility, in the orders of intelligence, and make his mind the well-spring of a stream which is destined to flow on forever,—not with the mere casual or limited contributions of *observation*, but ever enlarging itself by the broad and deep affluents of profoundest thought and reflective reason, and richly laden with all the treasures of discovery, which have been accumulated by laborious and successful *investigation.*

## IV. THE RESULT OF THE ACTION OF THE REFLECTIVE FACULTIES: TRUTH.

*The successive stages of intellectual progress.*—Furnished with the interior principle of *intelligence*, invested with the organized apparatus of *sensation*, and provided with the physical *material* for the exercise of his powers, the child, under the guidance of Creative wisdom, sets out on the career of intellectual progress, actuated by the impulse of *curiosity*, whose tendency is to insure the habit of *observation* and that discipline of his perceptive faculties by which he is ultimately enabled to win the prize of KNOWLEDGE. He thus accomplishes his first *curriculum* in the great school established by the benignant universal Providence which careth for humanity, and under whose discipline the law of progressive intellection secures, to a given extent, the welfare of man, whether more or less favored by intelligent human culture. To this first stage of development gradually succeeds that other, in which, through the inward action of the divinely-implanted principle of intelligence, man's own inner, mental world of conscious condition, act, cause, effects, tendency, and power,—of memory, reason, imagination, feeling, and will, is revealed and explored, as a theatre of comparatively unlimited expansion and ceaseless action. Within himself, he finds, at once, the power, the springs, the scope, the materials of this new career of activity, in which he is impelled by the same earnest irrepressible desire to discover and to know, as before, but now working in a higher sphere, and with a higher aim. Prompted by *inquiry*, and impelled to *investigation*, he is thus led onward to that higher goal of intellectual progress, where, by the disciplined action of the *reflective faculties*, *knowledge* is consummated in TRUTH, and where man discovers, and learns to reverence and obey, the highest law of his being,—subordination to the sway of the Reason which reigns supreme in the universe of thought.

*Appropriate application of the term Truth.*—The sense in which the word "truth" is properly used in general discussions connected with mental processes, is, of course, wider than that in which it is employed in relations strictly or exclusively pertaining to the science of logic. In the latter case, it implies no more than the exact conformity of the terms of a proposition to the fact which it is obviously meant to announce. But, in well-sanctioned forms of expression on general topics, *truth* is, with equal justice, predicated of the correspondence of language to thought, of art to nature, of action to intention, of antitype to type,—in any relation whatever.

In the working of the mind, the term applies, with not less propriety, to the correspondence of perception to object, of conception to idea, of word to thing, of language to relation, of action to conscience, of habit to character, of aim to end, of opinion to sentiment or statement to fact, of expression or representation to reality or actuality. The word "truth," in brief, covers, properly, the whole ground of intellectual, æsthetic, or moral conformity of thought, expression, or action, to an exact and recognized standard, sanctioned by the canons of criticism or of conscience. It stands opposed, therefore, equally to falsity of conception, of expression, or of action. As a quality, it characterizes alike the habits of the correct thinker, of the exact artist, whether in the use of pencil, pen, or tongue, and those of the sincere and honest man. It secures the individual from the unintentional defects of error, and guards him against the voluntary deviations of design.

In relation, however, to the subject of human culture, and, in particular, to the discipline of the mental powers, truth is regarded as a result of voluntary and studious application,—as a product of the exercise of the reflective faculties, in the quest of ultimate principles in science, physical, intellectual, or moral. Examples in point are furnished in the process of tracing the great laws of physics, in the demonstrations of geometry, in the verification of history, in logical ratiocination, in the discussion of moral obligations, in the scrutiny of evidence. In such investigations, the quest of truth, conducted by well-disciplined reflective faculties, is steadily, skillfully, and successfully pushed onward to the grand crowning result of *certainty* and *conviction*. Unaided by the skill which culture and discipline insure, the mind has no security against the involuntary illusions of error, or the intentional misrepresentations of deceit; it discovers no stability in the outward universe, has no confidence in its own conclusions, no just reliance on itself, no firm conviction of duty, no enlightened faith in testimony; but blown about by every plausible assumption of theory, and every shifting phase of circumstance,—a prey to every reigning delusion, unsettled on any sure foundation of moral principle,—skeptical as to every vital truth, plunging into every approaching fog-bank of error, and drifting, without chart or compass, on the great ocean of uncertainty,—suffers, at length, an intellectual and moral wreck.

Most justly, as well as beautifully, has Bacon said, "truth, which only doth judge itself, teacheth that the inquiry of truth, which is the love-making, or wooing, of it,—the knowledge of truth, which is the presence of it,—and the belief of truth, which is the enjoying of it,—is the sovereign good of human nature."

Guided by his own unassisted reflective reason, man does unquestionably attain to great results, both intellectual and moral. But, enlightened by the knowledge which science and education shed on every relation of his being, what a vast expansion, what a wondrous elevation is he capable of attaining;—all resulting from the faithful application and skillful exercise of the reason with which his Creator has crowned his intellectual faculties! How noble, in this view, becomes the office of the educator, whose daily endeavor it is to cherish, and strengthen, and vivify this master principle of all intelligence!

## V. Educational Processes for the Development and Discipline of the Reflective Faculties.

*Defective Methods.*—If we look at what is professedly and formally done, in our common modes of education, for the exercise and discipline of the reflective faculties; and if we found our estimate on the number of branches of knowledge or of science, and the number and variety of books nominally employed for the purpose, we might be inclined to suppose that, in this important part of culture, much is effected. But, on examining the actual state of things, errors and oversights, in this respect, are found to be numerous, and methods comparatively ineffectual.

*Exclusive reliance on exactness of recollection.*—*Memory*, the appointed servant of the reflective faculties, whose office it is to collect and keep and furnish the materials for their action, is, indeed, amply laden with the semblance and show of matter;—but most of it in the form of Hamlet's book of "words, words, words." The too exclusive use of *manuals*, the mere records of knowledge, instead of the actual study of *objects*, *facts* and *relations*, the observation and the understanding of which constitute knowledge *itself*, leads to the cultivation of a verbal and mechanical memory, instead of a living and intelligent one. The fact is still too generally overlooked, that memory is not so much a separate faculty, which can be trained and disciplined by itself, as the mind,—in virtue of its spiritual nature and exemption from limits of time and space,—retaining or recalling what it has once observed or conceived; that the vigor of this retention, or the force of this recurrence, must always be as that of the original impression, and that the only rational reliance for the healthy and effective action of *memory*, must therefore be the freshness, the force, and the depth of *attention*. But, obviously, no impression made on the mind through the medium of language,—no matter how exact may be the definition, or how true the description,—can ever be so complete or so effectual as that of direct observation through the senses, personal experience, or distinct conciousness. Here, again, we are referred to two great educational principles: that the study of things should precede the study of words, and should always be resorted to, in preference, whereever there is a choice of modes of instruction; and that, to awaken and develope the reflective faculties, the true course is, in obedience to the Creator's appointment, to use the objects of nature as the apparatus which His wisdom has provided, not only for the exercise and training of the mind's perceptive faculties, with a view to the acquisition of *knowledge*, but for the expanding and deepening of its capacities of discovering *truth*. Observation naturally prompts to thought and reflection. There is, in such circumstances, a conscious, living transition from one sphere of intelligence to another,—from one comparatively lower and more limited to one higher and more spacious. But in the mere contemplation or repetition of the words which describe an object, record a fact, or state a principle, the condition of mind is that of abstraction; and the mental associations, in such conditions, are always less vivid, forcible and distinct, than in the observation of concrete realities; and, when the former of these conditions is recalled, its impress is necessarily dim and obscure, compared to that of the latter, which, by the experience of actual perception, has become a comparatively inseparable part of the mental life and history of the agent.

The difference in these two cases will be rendered yet more strikingly apparent, if we suppose,—what is commonly true in verbatim processes of committing to memory,—that the mind of the learner, in his anxiety to retain and repeat with exactness the phraseology of the book which he studies, often glances aside from the contemplation of the *fact* or the principle which he is enunciating, to the literal succession of the *words* in which it is expressed. The mind's power of abstraction becomes, in this way, the very means of its deterioration; and the memory, abused by this arbitrary and mechanical mode of exercise, loses its healthy power of retention and recollection; and unfortunately, most of all, in those reflective processes of earnest thought which demand its most vigorous exertion.

The prevalent methods of teaching, moreover, are still too exclusively directed to the exercise of memory, at the expense of neglecting the other faculties,—an evil inseparable from the false views which still usurp the seats of instruction, and make education consist in processes of passive reception, on the part of the pupil; as if his mind were a capacity to be filled, rather than a capability to be developed, or a life-power to be awakened.

*Reading.*—The greater number of the subjects which are introduced in early education, as means of exercise and discipline for the mind, are still too commonly treated under the influence of these erroneous views of the character and objects of mental culture. Hence the wearisome experience of the child, when compelled to drudge through the task of committing to memory the *names* of all the alphabetic characters of the language, before, or perhaps without ever, acquiring a knowledge of the *power*, or actual *sound*, of any one of the whole group. Every day, he is giving two or three of these sounds in every one of the short and easy words which he uses in conversation. But he is not allowed the satisfaction of recognizing the fact, that these troublesome and perplexing marks before his eye, are little graphic characters to suggest, phonetically to eye and ear, the very words which he is constantly uttering. When the alphabetic task is accomplished, there follows, usually, in the child's experience, that of hewing his way through whole columns of words, to him unmeaning, because lying out of his sphere in the understanding and use of language; and to this useless toil too often succeeds that of reading multitudes of unintelligible sentences of a character corresponding to the words which baffled him. But we need not dwell on this topic now, having entered into it at length, in former connections of this part of our subject.

*Arithmetic.*—In arithmetical instruction, which might be so effective an aid to the development of the mind's reflective power, the same evil still too generally prevails, as in the rudimental stages of spelling and reading. The very first step taken, in some instances, is to prescribe and enforce the committing to memory of elementary tables of numbers, by arbitrary repetition of the words in which these are expressed. Were the child allowed the fair opportunity of first *seeing*, in concrete form, the facts which he is made to assume and communicate in parrot-like form; and were he allowed to *create* them for himself, in visible or tangible shape, in copious instances, and thus to generalize the facts from his own observation, memory would have an intelligent, living office to perform, would work with freshness and strength, and long retain, or easily recall, what attention had proved. Were it required of the pupil thus to *construct* the given table, instead of merely repeating the words in which it is expressed, the exercise of memory would be as pleasing as it would be invigorating. It would thus be aided by the deepening and strengthening effect of the not less delightful processes of *combining* and *constructing*, in the actua work of practical operations. The busy hand would thus help the thinking head to clearer views and deeper impressions; and the true and proper work of memory would be done in accordance with the law of mental action.—"AS IS THE EARNESTNESS OF ATTENTION, SO IS THE DURATION OF REMEMBRANCE, OR THE DISTINCTNESS AND READINESS OF RECOLLECTION."

*Geography.*—The subject of *geography* furnishes very frequently another example of memoriter lessons, exacted, perhaps, with a well-meaning rigorous fidelity to the language of a text-book, but sacrificing the useful knowledge, the pleasing information, and the invaluable mental training and discipline, which this instructive branch of science might be made to furnish. Detached facts, comparative numerical tables, and assumed definitions, are yet too uniformly imposed as a burden on the memory; while the actual survey of even a limited portion of the earth's surface, within daily view, perhaps, of the learner, would furnish him with the best materials on which to build up the noble and majestic structure of geographical science.

Fortunately, through the labors of Professor Arnold Guyot, in his luminous exposition of the philosophy of instruction in this department of science, a new and better era is begun in American schools; and this branch of education is now, in many seminaries, taught on methods strictly logical. The study of geography thus becomes an admirable intellectual discipline, in addition to the systematic forms in which it embodies the great facts and pervading laws of nature, which are its peculiar province as a science. The student, who is trained on this admirable method, has the great features of the globe, and all their relations of consequent fact, imprinted forever on his memory. The very inequalities of the earth's surface, become to him an intelligible language, by which he reads the laws of design, and traces effects to causes, with the certainty of distinct recognition. Taught in this manner, few sciences are more adapted to the development of the reflective faculties, in their first steps of advancement from the field of perceptive observation to that of contemplative survey and rational inquiry, or to that of profound scientific investigation. The methods which Professor Guyot has transferred from the lessons of his own distinguished instructor, Carl Ritter, and the views of the patriarch of geographical science, Baron Alexander Von Humboldt, will, it is to be hoped, soon find their way not only into our text-books, in which they are beginning to appear, but into all our seminaries in which the young mind is undergoing the formative processes of education.

*History.*—Of all the sciences which are naturally fitted to invite the mind to the full exercise of its reflective tendencies, none would seem so happily adapted to this end as *history*. Its records, while they are, in one sense, but forms of memory, are still the records of man moving on his amplest stage of action, as a human being, intelligent, rational, and moral; blending the relations of individual character and social life with those of the national and political sphere,—with the founding the government, or the fall of states and empires.

History, as it necessarily exhibits man in his moral relations, ought to be one of the most instructive and suggestive of studies. If any subject can excite reflective thought, it is this. Its analysis and scrutiny of human character; its investigation into the motives of action, in every form and condition of life; the research, to which it invites, into the manners and customs of by-gone ages; the careful examination which it induces of the testimony of conflicting records; the views which it discloses of national character and institutions; the insight which it gives into the policy of nations, and the influence of different forms of government; all bespeak the tendency of historical studies to evoke the most earnest and profound reflection. The study of history should be, in itself, an effective discipline of the mind, in all the noblest relations of its action. But, here, too, the mere imprinting on the memory a naked record of detached facts, of single events, or striking incidents, or of the items of a chronological table, is the too prevalent law of custom in the requisitions of educational establishments. The life of history, its suggestive power, as a reflective and moral instructor, is thus killed; and, instead of the living form, in its natural lineaments and beauty, we have but a meagre outline of the dry bones of what, in the technical language of historic compilation, is most aptly denominated a "skeleton."

To the mature mind, willing to encounter fatiguing effort, and patiently to add stone to stone of the intellectual fabric, the plan too commonly adopted in the instruction of young learners, of beginning the study of history with a mere outline of dates and events and eras, may prove practicable, though not easy or pleasant. But, to the youthful spirit, the great attraction of this study lies in its pictures of life and action, and in the sympathies which these evoke. To the juvenile reader all history is biography. The policy of nations, the intrigues of state, the strategics of war, are unintelligible and uninteresting to him; and he ignores them, if they intrude upon the narrative. But the feeling and the character and actions of individuals, he understands, and admires or hates, according to the promptings of his unperverted heart. He follows the steps of the historic hero, through all his scenes of struggle and trial, of effort and of triumph; imbibing unconsciously, in the successive stages of this ideal progress, inspiring lessons of wisdom and virtue from all, or listening to the warnings which recorded experience gives on the evils of folly or of vice.

A course of judiciously selected *biography*, should be the educational introduction to the study of history. The interest attached to the personal narrative, accompanies the young student into his reading on the broader scale of national movements and their various consequences; and the life breathed into the study from the character of its earliest stage, gives warmth and attraction to all its more extensive views and complicated relations.

*Language*, as the product of the expressive faculties, and as a discipline for their development, we had occasion to discuss under that head, in a former lecture. But we have still to do with it as a part of education adapted to the strengthening of the mind's power of reflective investigation. Our common error in this department, as in others, is a too exclusive attention to the acquisition of a certain amount of knowledge of the etymological and syntactical forms of words and phrases,—a knowledge depending entirely on the exercise of memory in retaining or recalling these forms. Through the various stages of education, the attention is too exclusively fixed on these minutiæ of language; and, neither in the study of ancient or of modern languages, nor even in that of our own, is the mind duly attracted to the character of the sentiments embodied in the works of the authors which are read in the progress of education, nor to the broad distinctive traits which form the character of the given language,—to the individuality which a successful writer stamps on it, or to the mental value of the forms of expression which he adopts. *Philology*, a pursuit so peculiarly adapted to the cultivation of the mind's reflective and investigating powers, is cut off from the student till the strong bias of personal taste or inclination induces him to open this mental vista for himself. *Criticism*, too, the art which demands the closest application of reflective judgment, in addition to perfect purity of taste, is handed over to the lessons of some meagre text-book, which does not contain matter enough within its boards for the proper discussion or fitting elucidation of a single principle of æsthetics.

*Logic* is another science belonging to the more advanced stages of education,—the study of which ought to exert a powerful influence on the tendencies and habits of the reflective faculties, but which is sometimes very inadequately taught even in our higher seminaries of learning. In some of these institutions, it is customary to restrict the study of logic to the ancient Aristotelian form of it, and without the advantage of the scholastic, syllogistic disputations, which, although always formal in character, and sometimes frivolous in result, were yet designed to be rigorously exact exemplifications of pure logical reasoning; and which, with all their faults and failures, secured, at least, one great practical object of education, by giving the mind active exercise in applying principles, instead of leaving it merely to listen, and remember, and record. It is true that, in some educational establishments, a more liberal view of logic is entertained, and that, in these seminaries, the science is regarded not merely as one which teaches the art of reasoning, but as that which investigates and enunciates the laws of thought, and involves, therefore, a knowledge of the elements of intellectual philosophy, together with the application of all the principles of mental science which affect the exercise of any class of the various powers and faculties of the mind.

An instructive exposition of this view of logic, as the first stage of purely intellectual discipline, is given in the "Outlines of Philosophic Education," by the late Professor Jardine, of Glasgow University, who, for fifty years, conducted, with distinguished success, his course of instruction, on the plan delineated in his work. That eminently skillful teacher,—for he regarded the duties of a professor in his department as consisting quite as much in conducting the practical processes of training exercises, as in the didactic routine of lecturing,—regarded the study of the Aristotelian logic but as a very limited part of intellectual discipline, and, while he allowed it its distinct place and full value, justly maintained that, for the purposes of modern education, which imply so wide and varied applications of thought,—in directions so different from those pursued in ancient times,—the sphere of study must be greatly enlarged beyond the narrow limits of the scholastic discipline, and a course of training prescribed which shall prepare the mind for the new demands made upon its powers, in the new modes of action with which modern science is conversant.

This broader view of logical discipline is fortunately taken by several of our own recent writers on the subject; and the course of instruction is, accordingly, in some seminaries, enlarged so as to embrace the elements of intellectual philosophy, as indispensable to clear and satisfactory views of logic itself, and to the purposes for which the study of logic was originally constituted a department of education. But even in such instances, the young student is not trained to apply the principles embodied in his text-book to an extensive course of practical exemplifications and personal discipline. He is not called to perform any series of practical exercises bearing the same relation to the science of logic that analytic parsing and written composition bear to grammar. He is not trained to trace the logic of great arguments exemplified in the productions of eminent metaphysical writers. He is not disciplined in the digesting and methodizing of his own conceptions on prescribed subjects, so as to give sequence or soundness to argument, and certainty to his own conclusions.

In the study of *intellectual philosophy* we see, too often, another instance of the imperfect learning by book, without the contemplation of the thing itself of which the book treats. Our current instruction, in this department, consists in little more than the assigning of so many pages of a text-book to be committed to memory; and the progress made in the study of the science is judged of by the correctness or the fluency with which the terms employed in the nomenclature of a favorite system can be repeated, rather than by any actual knowledge or personal opinions on the subject itself. The student is not invited to put forth his own mind, in actual investigations on the topics which he studies: he is not permitted to enjoy the benefit of those conversational discussions with his instructor, which might create a living interest in the subject prescribed, and induce the student to prosecute with effect those unaided researches of individual application, without which knowledge is not to be acquired, or truth ascertained.

In the department of *moral philosophy*, a subject so peculiarly adapted to the development and discipline of the reflective faculties, we find, usually, the same mechanical routine of book-study and recitation adopted. In this highest relation of human instruction, the mind is still left passive and receptive merely; while there is no subject on which original, vigorous, and personal thought is so important to the acquisition of principle or the formation of character. Here, more than anywhere else, living, eloquent instruction from the man, rather than the book, is indispensable to the production of deep and enduring impressions of truth, and the exciting of hearty sympathy with its applications. Here, too, more than elsewhere, is the active use of the student's own mind necessary to the results of true culture on personal habit and character. His own investigations, and his own record of these, ought to be required of him, as the only rational benefit of the guidance afforded by a text-book or a teacher. Conversation and writing would throw life into these subjects, and make them matters of personal interest and personal conviction to the individual; and the fruits of education would thus be more extensively reaped in the experience of society.

Appropriate Methods of Discipline.—We will now turn from the consideration of the subjects which form the usual material for the education and development of the reflective faculties, to the more immediate contemplation of those faculties themselves, with regard to their natural wants and appropriate aids; and, first, as regards the faculty of

*Memory.*—In the fact of *muscular* action, the power to retain depends on the firmness of the original *grasp*. The analogy holds in the exercise of memory: the retentive or repeating power depends on the depth of the impression: concentrated and sustained attention is the condition of remembrance. If we would strengthen the memory, we must cultivate force of attention. The indication of nature to the teacher, in this case, obviously is, Select for the mind's first exercises, striking or attractive objects of attention, or interesting subjects of thought. For more advanced stages of mental progress, when accuracy demands comparative minuteness and multiplicity of uninteresting detail, rely on the moral force of the will and disciplined habit, to give closeness and persistency to attention. In all cases, keep fully in mind the great value of mere *repetition* and frequent *review*, without which all ordinary subjects of past thought are ever tending to sink into dimness and obscurity, and, ultimately, into utter forgetfulness.

Mechanical aids to memory may sometimes appear very plausible; and they often are very amusing temporary expedients. But they actually destroy memory, by setting it aside, and usurping its place. The physiologist tells us that if we omit the due use of the teeth, we forfeit the possession of them. The fact is strictly so of memory. The juggling tricks of perverted ingenuity may seem to conjure up a substitute for the sound and healthy exercise of this faculty. But the subject of the experiment, in this as in all other forms of charlatanry, finds himself, in the end, the victim of deception.

Memory, when employed on subjects comparatively complex, or intricate in their relations, finds its surest reliance,—next to close and fixed attention,—to consist in the grand universal law of *order*. *Arrangement*, *classification*, *system*, *method*, are powerful auxiliaries to memory, as they all tend, more or less, to give sequence to thought, by the law of causation, in the closest connection of antecedent and consequent. One stage of thought thus suggests another; and the machinery of memory, so to speak, works smoothly and well. The security for remembrance or for recollection, in such circumstances, lies, of course, in the clearness with which connections and relations are perceived, and the fidelity with which they are observed. A treacherous memory is often but the report of unfaithful observation or dim conception.

*Habits of Conception dependent on those of Perception.*—*Conception*, as a primary power of reflective intelligence, performing for the relations of pure intellection, the same office with that of *perception*, in the exercise of the understanding on the objects of *sensation*, depends, to a great extent, on the character and habits of the *perceptive* faculty. The *relations* which the *conceptive* power discerns between the objects and facts, presented to it by the ministrations of sense, constitute the condition of *intelligent observation*, as differing from mere *ocular aspection*. But these relations necessarily derive much of their reality and force from the vividness of the sensation and the clearness of the understanding, which have attracted *attention* to the external phenomena, and thus have elicited the conceptive acts of mind by which the relations perceived and understood become the ground-work of *reflection* and *meditation*, leading in turn to farther processes of thought, inductive or deductive, as investigation may require.

Clear, forcible and true *perceptions*, therefore, are requisite antecedents of corresponding qualities in *conception*; and a sound and active condition of the latter depends on similar conditions and habits of the former;—just as healthy *sensation* is, in turn, the pre-requisite of distinct *perception*. We are thus again referred, in adopting educational measures for strengthening and developing the mind's conceptive power, to the attentive observation of external nature, as the proper commencement of early mental training; as the only security, also, for the vigor of all those faculties which aid the mind in digesting and assimilating to itself, by purely internal operations, the materials of knowledge acquired through the action of sense, for the purpose of being incorporated into the mental fabric. We are, at the same time, reminded of the great fact, of which education should never lose sight, that, whatever be the number of faculties into which the intellectual philosopher may, in his scientific analysis, subdivide the action of the mind, or whatever may be the personified individuality which the figurative language of popular usage may arbitrarily confer on any one mode of mental action,—to distinguish it from others,—the principle of intelligence is strictly a *unit*; that it is the *same* agent, whether contemplating the external world through the windows of sense, or looking inward upon itself, and interpreting its own action. In both circumstances, we recognize a voluntary act of attention, followed by an apprehensive or a comprehensive act of understanding. In either case, *intelligence* is the power at work; *knowledge* is the *immediate*, and *truth* the *final* result.

*Conception as dependent on Memory and Imagination.*—Under the term "conception," however, in the vague usage to which the English language is unfortunately prone, in all subjects purely intellectual, we usually include states or acts of *memory* and of *imagination*. Nor is it to be denied that the conceptive faculty is often called into action on data furnished by *memory*, as well as on those presented by *sense* or by *reason*. To vivify and invigorate the power of conception, therefore, in such relations, we are admonished to pursue the same course of exercise and discipline by which that faculty is rendered prompt and retentive. Whatever we succeed in doing to improve the *memory*, becomes thus a gain to the power of *conception*.

Again, the prevalent use of language refers many of our conceptive acts to forms of *imagination*. The astronomer, speaking of the sun, tells us of its dark, central body,—of its first layer or substratum of cloudy atmosphere,—of its photosphere, or luminous atmosphere, and of yet a third rarer element, ethereal and slightly colored,—as to the character of which, science is somewhat perplexed with uncertainty. The conceptive power of the mind enables us, in this case, to follow the entrancing description as the scientific observer, aided by the many appliances which modern instruments provide, proceeds with his verified observations; and, with wondering attention, we draw on the tablet of imagination the successive images which his graphic but exact expressions suggest: we see, with the mind's eye, the sun-world, and its enfolding atmospheres, as distinctly in our consciousness as if we surveyed them with eye or "optic tube."

*Correctness of Conception.*—Even in such cases, however, the truthfulness and the distinctness of the mental picture depend, to a great extent, on the exactness of its correspondence to fact, as regards not only the forms but the character of objects, and the relations existing between them. Here, again, we are referred to the working of the intelligent principle in the modes which we denominate *understanding* and *judgment*, without which the whole structure erected in the mind would be as the poet's "baseless fabric of a vision."

In educational training, therefore, while every endeavor should be used to vivify and incite *imagination*, and to awaken it to its utmost activity by appropriate exercise, with a view to the vast power which that faculty confers on conception, as a creative energy of mind; and while all the aids which nature, art, and poetry, offer to this end, should be fully employed; there remains yet a task for education to perform, in inuring the conceptive faculty to the discipline of *reason* and *judgment*, so as to render it exact, and truthful, and symmetrical, in all its work.

The means by which the mind is to be formed to such habits in its conceptive action, are evidently the same which we would employ for developing and strengthening the reasoning powers: first, *the interesting presentation* of the objects and facts of the *natural* world,—so as to elicit thought and reflection on their character and relations; secondly, the *teacher's* skillful *suggestion*, designed to aid the observer in tracing those relations to principles and laws of logical science; and, thirdly, the careful training of the mind to *the contemplation of its own action*, to the critical inspection and exact *discrimination of the results* of its action, and to the thorough *investigation of the laws of thought*, applied to the quest of truth.

CONSCIOUSNESS:—*as an aid to Reflective Reason.*—Of the reflective conditions of mind which tend to give accuracy to knowledge, or certainty to truth, none is more conducive to such results than that of *consciousness.* Not that it necessarily constitutes a separate power or faculty; (since it is plainly but an act of introverted attention, by which the mind becomes aware of its existing states, acts, or processes;) but rather that it is a mental condition distinctly recognized in all the languages of civilized man, and implies the power which the intelligent principle possesses of holding up, in distinct vision to itself, its own acts and operations;—whether these refer to the external world of perception or the interior world of thought. This power of self-observation, when the attention is directed to relations purely intellectual, is necessarily the condition and the measure of force with which the mind pursues its trains of reflection, traces the invisible relations of sequence, or follows the continuous processes of meditation, in the prosecution of those profound researches which the depth and intricacy of scientific or moral truth not unfrequently require.

*Its Susceptibility of Culture.*—In the relations of moral culture, this faculty,—so to term it,—works in so close and intimate union with the great master principle of *conscience*, that its importance as a fact of mind demanding the earnest attention of the educator, in his capacity of moral guardian, is, at once, apparent. On that department of our subject we do not, at present, dwell, as it will invite our attention hereafter, in its proper place. But, as an intellectual condition, subject, to some extent, to the action of the will, and to the influence of disciplinary exercise, it is obvious that conciousness or self-observation, may, like any other power which the mind possesses, be rendered vivid, prompt, and operative, by repeated action.

Man commences his intellectual and moral life an *unconscious* agent, in the unknown and wonderful world around him, in childhood. He is as utterly unconscious of the influences exerted on himself as he is ignorant of the true character and relations of the objects by which he is surrounded. Absorbed in the contemplation of the broad field of the external world, or in the observation of its objects individually, he is lost alike to the consciousness of his own being, and to that of the effects which are wrought within him by these very objects. Drawn onward by an unconscious power of attraction, he follows the study of nature, in obedience to an instinct of which he is not yet aware, but which, by leading him out of himself, conducts him to the school of *observation*, where knowledge commences, and from which he, in due season, returns, empowered by the instruction he has received to *observe* and *understand himself.*

As his nobler powers mature, they begin to work on the data which observation has furnished; and, as he examines, he thinks, he compares, he reflects, he reasons; he becomes aware of a more powerful influence and a deeper satisfaction than that of mere observation, while he consciously follows his successive conceptions, and meditates not only on the relations of object to object, and of effect to cause, in the outward universe, but on the yet more wonderful and mysterious action of his own inward being, to the conciousness of which he is now fully awakened. This newly-discovered world attracts his attention with a yet greater force and intensity of interest than that of the external sphere, in which he has hitherto moved; and the growing strength of his intellect, he finds, is more fully exerted and more decidedly proved in this inner region of its action, than in the outer field of sense and perception. He delights, accordingly, in this conscious exercise of a higher power, and recognizes the nobility of reason.

Such is man's progress, even when little assisted by the formal aids of education. But we see thus more clearly how judicious and skillful training may render conciousness comparatively *vivid*, *definite*, and *distinct*, by aiding, with appropriate appliances of exercise and discipline, this capability of reflective contemplation, of self-intelligence, and of self-development, which grows with the growth, and strengthens with the strength of the maturing mind. If this power is permitted to lie neglected and undeveloped, the result is uniformly a characteristic dullness, obscurity, and vagueness in the mind's habitual action. This fact we recognize, in full exemplification, when we contrast the uncultivated, half-conscious child, youth, or man, with the well-educated and the self-intelligent.

*Mode of Culture.*—Subjected to processes of cultivation, however, this faculty, like memory, can not be brought under the law of direct action. *Memory* is to be reached through *attention;* to enliven and strengthen the former, we must work upon the latter. We have no more power over it, separately, than we have over the reflection of an object in a mirror. Memory is the reflection of attention. We can not render the image distinct, unless the object is so. The same is true of *consciousness.* It has no separate or independent existence

It is, so to speak, the mind's reflection of itself; it is but an act of attention directed inward. The vividness, the definiteness, and the distinctness of consciousness, are,—as the corresponding properties in the act of attention,—blended with the consentaneous force of will coöperating in the act. In this latter circumstance, its action differs from that of memory, which is often, even in its most vivid delineations, wholly involuntary. But the depth and fullness of consciousness are always dependent, more or less, on the force of the will which directs the act of attention inward. It is thus rendered more perceptibly a subject of culture by educational training.

*Morbid Unconsciousness.*—To some minds the intellectual and moral value of habits of wakeful consciousness, is very great from, perhaps, some defect of organization or fault of habit, inclining the individual to a half dreamy condition of *reverie*, in which the mind loses power over its own action, and becomes lost amid the scenes of memory or of imagination. To the artist and the poet, an intensity of abstracted attention is, in some relations, the condition of imaginative power of conception and of living expression. But, in such cases, the mind is healthy, vigorous, and voluntary, in its action: it is obeying one of its own highest laws, which demands this almost superhuman power of abstracted and concentrated attention, for the contemplation and embodiment of ideal images of perfection. The abstractedness and "absence of mind," on the other hand, which become habitual from neglect, are nothing else than a *morbid unconsciousness* indulged,—a result of organic or mental *weakness*, and a habit utterly destructive of voluntary power of attention or depth of thought. In some mournful instances, it is the sure precursor of insanity.

In all circumstances, the tendency of such habits is to cherish a morbid preponderance of imagination over reason and judgment, and to create a dreamy twilight of thought, in preference to the clear light of intellectual day. Listlessness of attention, and dullness of understanding, and every other evil of mental torpor, are thus entailed on the intellectual character.

*Cultivation of the Reasoning Faculty.*—The principle of reflective intelligence assumes, in the language of recognized usage, the various forms of action implied in the terms *understanding*, *judgment*, *reason*; and this triple denomination suggests also the progressive measures adopted in education, for the cultivation of this master power of intellect.

*Understanding*, as the primary act and condition of intelligence, is involved in every instance of *perception*, even in the cognizance of the mere form and character of outward objects; in the contemplation of facts, its aid is indispensable to the *apprehension* of their connections and relations; and, in the tracing of these, its assistance is requisite to enable the mind to arrive at the *comprehension* of principles and causes. When the mind is unable to put forth this prehensile, (*seizing, grasping, holding,*) power, we say, in current phrase, the connection, the principle, the cause, or the relation, is "not understood." Reverting to the etymological signification of the term, by which this faculty is designated, we observed that the action of the "understanding" was represented as a necessary *ground*, or *foundation*, without which, of course, there could be no superstructure of thought or knowledge. In the terms now introduced, which denote the two chief forms of action in the process of understanding, the figurative suggestion is not less forcible or appropriate, than in the former instance. The uninformed understanding, is, in the latter case, represented as the *powerless hand*, which is not put forth, which does not lay hold on its object, or which lets it slip.

*Natural Development of the Understanding.*—The appropriate training of this fundamental faculty of the mind is distinctly indicated to the educator in the first natural workings of intellect in childhood. The inciting principle of curiosity impels the child to observe and to learn. But he is not satisfied with the mere knowledge of the external character of objects; he is eagerly desirous to understand their internal construction, and hence he tears open, and pulls to pieces, even the flower which delights him; and the indulgent father knows that it needs a sharp eye to keep the little investigator from practicing a similar experiment on a gold watch.

*Educational Development.*—That spirit of inquisition which is implanted in the mind, to secure its progressive development, renders the examination and inspection of objects, for the discovery of their internal structure and character, an exercise still more attractive and inviting to a child than that of the perception even of beauty in form or color; and the investigation of the connection and relations of phenomena and of facts, yields him a deeper gratification than the delight arising from the recognition of any merely exterior trait of character in outward objects. Here, then, is the proper place where to commence the training of the understanding to the exercise of true apprehension and full comprehension, in the acqusition of a thorough knowledge of the objects by which the child is naturally surrounded, and of their relations to one another, in mutual adaptation, or in cause and effect. Perception is thus transmuted into knowledge; without which transition there is no intellectual progress. The understanding of relations is the mediating process by which object is linked to object, fact to fact, and relation to relation ; till knowledge, in its turn, becomes the completed chain of principle and truth, in the relations of system and science.

*Practical Exercises.*—One of the most hopeful indications of the general progress of opinion on the subject of education, is afforded in the comparatively recent introduction into primary schools of lessons on *objects*,—not merely the productions of nature in animal and vegetable and mineral form, but the common objects of observation in the child's daily notice at home and in school, in the street, and in the workshop. The young mind is thus strengthened, while it is gratified, by the exercise of tracing design and adaptation in the various contrivances of mechanical ingenuity. The conscious understanding of relations and processes, becomes to the mind what the expanding and enlivening influence of light is to the plant; while the self-intelligent agent enjoys the double pleasure of growth and the consciousness of it. Understanding, as the mind's prehensile and digestive power, appropriates to itself the material of its own life and strength, and quickens and expands with every acquisition, till it reaches the culminating point of the full maturity and vigor of a well-developed capacity.

*Observation of the processes of Nature.*—Next to the study of the elementary principles and application of mechanics, as a means of enlightening and invigorating the understanding by disciplinary exercises in tracing combination and operations to their causes, should come appropriate exercises in watching and tracing *the great processes of nature, daily* passing before the learner's observation, and inviting him to the study of those larger displays of power and intelligence, which are exhibited in the mechanism of the worlds moving in space, and obeying the laws of time.

The *chemistry* of nature, too, should be made to furnish ample employment for the exercise of the understanding, in tracing the curious relations which that vast department of knowledge discloses. No science has more power than chemistry to stimulate curiosity, and provoke inquiry, and thus invite the mind to penetrate the mysteries of nature, and evolve the hidden causes and secret influences at work in phenomena, which the mind can not contemplate without the feeling of wonder, and which, at first, seem to baffle the power of intelligence; but through which the prying eye of the understanding learns, ere long, to penetrate, in the inquest of relations by which mystery is solved and difficulty explained. A simple elementary course of experiments, in this department of science, by the light which it sheds on common phenomena, exerts a great power over the young mind;—suggesting inquiries and leading to investigations which call the understanding into wakeful and vigorous action on all facts accessible to observation. The teacher, who is true to his office, as guardian of the young mind, and who takes pleasure in aiding the formation of habits of intelligence and inquiry, will spare neither time, nor trouble, nor expense, in his endeavors to secure to his pupils the benefit of such aids to their intellectual culture.

*Combined Exercises of Understanding and Judgment: Arithmetic.* In the department of mathematical science, there is no lack of attention to the study of *arithmetic*, as an important branch of exercise and discipline for the reflective faculties, in the relations of the understanding operating on numbers. In this branch of culture, the purely mental processes first introduced by Pestalozzi, and transferred to American schools by the late Warren Colburn, have let in a flood of light not only on the subject of arithmetic, as an instrument of intellectual discipline, but on the whole field of education, and on all the details of methods of instruction, as regards the principles of rational and genial development applied to the human mind. Whatever may be the case elsewhere, there are few schools, in New England at least, in which arithmetic is not philosophically and successfully taught; and the vast improvement, or rather the entire renovation of the character of our primary schools, since the introduction of Colburn's method, may well suggest to the thoughtful teacher the immense amount of benefit which would certainly follow corresponding changes in other departments of education.

*Geometry.*—Another branch of mathematics admirably adapted to the cultivation of the mind's reflective and reasoning powers, when applied to external relations, and one which forms, by its very nature, the vestibule to all the other apartments of the great temple of knowledge, has not commonly met with that attention or that place which its importance requires. Geometry is too commonly deferred till a late stage, comparatively, in the progress of education; and it is, for the most part, taught abstractly, commencing with its *linear* forms. But the few teachers who have ventured to break away from the trammels of routine and prescription, and who have taken their suggestion from the obvious fact that, even in early childhood, the mind is delighted with the observation of definite forms in all their simple varieties, and that, at this stage of progress, form exists only in the visible and tangible concrete, and not in the abstract,—the few teachers who have here followed nature's course, and allowed the young learner to commence an easy elementary and practical study of geometry in its relation to *solid* objects, have found no difficulty arising from permitting children to commence their attention to this branch of knowledge at a very early age, and to unspeakable advantage, as regards the exactness of mental habit which this mode of discipline so peculiarly tends to form.

From the observation and study of the *solid*, the transition is rational, natural and easy to the consideration and examination of its *surface;* and here another wide field of thought is opened to the mind of the juvenile learner,—yet one which is perfectly practicable to his faculties, and which he can always submit to actual survey and ocular measurement. With the solid body in his hand, the little student finds it an easy and a pleasing step to proceed from the contemplation of the *surface*, to that of its "*edges*," as he calls the boundary *lines* of the surface; and here still another delightful scope of observation opens to his mind, as he proceeds to compare line with line, and, applying the definite and exact relations of number, learns to *measure*, and thus to give certainty and precision to his observations, and accuracy to his conceptions.

*General Effects of Mathematical Discipline.*—In the more advanced stages of education, the modes of instruction in the department of mathematics, are, from the nature of the subject, of a character so definite and comparatively immutable as to suggest methods and forms of exercise uniform and sure. Hence, the admirable results secured by the discipline to which the reasoning powers are subjected in the prosecution of these studies. The value of mathematical training consists, chiefly, in the exactness of attention and discrimination, and in the orderly procedure of thought required in the processes which it prescribes, and, consequently, in the correctness of conception and accuracy of judgment thus attained in the habits of the mind. Another invaluable advantage of mathematical studies, connected more immediately, however, with their advanced stages of mental application, consists in the extent and scope of their operations, combined with the perfect sequence of every step in their procedure, and the confidence which they serve to create in the mind's own action, by the certainty of its conclusions.

The main duty of the teacher, in this department of education, lies, from the very character of the subject, in watching carefully the mind's first steps in the earliest stages of exercise; so as to see to it that the perfect rigor of intellectual discipline is attained, which mathematical science is designed to produce, that there be no yielding to juvenile impatience, tending to laxity of attention, careless assumption, heedless oversight, and unconscious inaccuracy of mental habit. In more advanced stages of progress, the successive branches of the subject afford, by their own intrinsic character, a comparative security for correctness in the processes of evolution, and especially in the case of all students whose first steps have been carefully watched.

*Common Mistake.*—There is an opinion somewhat prevalent, even among those who have the control of education, that the certainty of mathematical reasoning, depending on the peculiar character of the grounds on which it rests, has but little effect on the formation of accurate habits of judgment in relations which have no firmer foundation than matters of opinion, or of taste, or of metaphysical inquiry. But, in this view of the question, the inevitable influence of the law of *analogy* on the constitution and habits of the mind is overlooked. The educational effect of any study lies not so much in the specific character of the subject, or the particular exercises of intellect which any one of its processes requires, as in the analogous tendencies and habits which the given exercise contributes to form. The perfect precision of observation, the scrupulous correctness of judgment, and the strict sequence of thought, which mathematical operations demand, are invaluable aids to every process of mind in which the reasoning faculties are employed. A disproportioned excess of attention to mathematics in the assignments of education, may, certainly, be chargeable on the plan of intellectual culture adopted in many seminaries of learning, and, particularly, of such as are devoted to the mental training of the female sex. But this mistake, like that of attempting the exposition of moral truth by mathematical forms of reasoning, does not prove any want of adaptation in mathematics to the design and purpose of intellectual discipline on kindred subjects, or in the results of such discipline in the formation of mental habits and character.

*Logical and Critical Discipline.*—Of the great importance of a thorough practical logic, for the discipline of the reasoning faculties,—a course comprising processes of strict personal training in the art of thinking,—we have had occasion to speak, under other heads of our present investigation, and on this topic we need not now enlarge.

Another department of higher mental culture, the art of *criticism*, was briefly adverted to, on a former occasion. As one of the highest forms in which reason can be applied, and as the ground-work of all true discipline of imagination and taste, it claims a large share of attention in educational training. But, to render this department of study truly beneficial, it needs a thorough revision and enlargement of its plan. As generally adopted in our seminaries of learning, it is made to consist too much of processes of training by which the mental eye is sharpened for the perception of *error* and the detection of *defect*. This is but the negative part of critical discipline, and is chiefly directed to the faults of others, rather than those of the observer himself; while, as a forming and moulding process, its chief benefit would lie in its efficacy in training the mind to the perception and recognition of *positive beauty* and *perfection*, and in forming the tastes and habits of the individual by a strict but genial *preventive* discipline, which should preclude the tendency to deviation from the principles of beauty and truth. To secure the results of such discipline, a liberal course of early training, directed to the intelligent recognition of beauty in nature and in art,—as was suggested in a former lecture,—becomes an indispensable foundation. The reasoning, on the data thus furnished, would necessarily become positive and practical. The mind would proceed under the sure guidance of ascertained principle; and the canons, so called, of criticism, would have an authority more sure than merely the speculative opinions of an individual, or of a class of theorizers. But, so far are we, as yet, from a truly liberal standard of education, that in all our higher seminaries, scarcely can we find a place assigned to any course of *æsthetic* study or training. Yet no species of discipline could be prescribed so admirably adapted to the generous development of the powers of judgment and reason, as that critical exercise by which the mind, in the analysis and combination of the elements of beauty, learns to interpret to its own consciousness the laws of grace and of harmony.

*Philosophical Training.*—The principles of *intellectual* and *moral philosophy*, we have already adverted to, as peculiarly adapted to the discipline of the *reflective* faculties. The great facts which the mind recognizes in contemplating the principles of the former of these branches of science, and the vital truths which it evolves in tracing the relations of the latter to the former, call for the exercise of reason and judgment on materials purely mental, and, by their very nature, fitted to train the mind to habits of close investigation and nice discrimination. On these habits is the mind's whole reliance to be placed in tracing the subtle distinctions on which the eviction of the profoundest truths not unfrequently depends.

On such subjects, as also in relation to logic and criticism, it was suggested, in a former connection of our subject, that education should be rendered more personal and practical in its methods; that it should comprise, in its measures for discipline, the mental efforts of the student himself in thought, conversation and discussion, rather than the mere endeavor to retain in memory the definitions and statements of a text-book.

*Civic Training.*—The study of civil polity, as it comprehends subjects collateral to history and to ethics, forms a theme well-suited to the exercise of the mind's reflective powers, by the trains of thought to which it naturally leads. As a branch of education, it should be extended to an attentive survey of all the political relations of human society, as embodied in forms of government, in national constitutions, in international law, in civil institutions. Independently of the value of such investigations to the intelligent discharge of the duties of life, in all countries favored with constitutional immunities, the class of subjects now mentioned is of the utmost moment in the higher relations of education, as affording large scope and full exercise for the reasoning powers, in the investigations and discussions to which such subjects naturally invite the mind of the student. The discipline, however, resulting from this branch of studies, depends, obviously, on the extent to which it is made a matter of personal thought, of written dissertations, and of oral discussion, on the part of the student. In this, as in other departments of ethical science, our colleges would do well to arrange their exercises on the model of the debating society, or of the moot-courts of professional schools; so as to elicit voluntary mental action and effective coöperation on the part of students in their own education. The random exercises of debating clubs, as they are commonly conducted, in which little or no systematic preparation is made for discussion, do not serve such a purpose. For educational influences, careful premeditation and critical supervision are equally necessary to render discussion an appropriate discipline.

*Natural Theology* forms another branch of study peculiarly fitted to call forth and improve the reflective and reasoning powers of the mind. Every new advance of science gives additional attractions to this ennobling theme of contemplation. The profound thought to which it leads, the large analogies which it reveals, the great truths which it urges home to the mind, the sublime heights to which it conducts aspiring reason,—all indicate the high value of this branch of philosophic investigation, as an effective means of enlarging and invigorating the noblest faculties with which man is invested.

The subject of natural theology is, by no means, neglected in our customary routine of studies, either in schools or colleges. It is carefully designated on the programme of instruction, and regularly assigned to a definite term of the course. But restricted, as the attention given to these subjects generally is, to recitation from a formal text-book, little of the peculiar effect of personal investigation into them is felt on the mind at the time, or marked on the subsequent mental character of the student. Personal examination, and actual analysis and manipulation, are as much needed in the illustrations which serve to throw light on the subject of natural theology as they are in the study of any other branch of science. The actual, ocular inspection of objects, is felt to be the only means of effective instruction in all other subjects which require the verification of principle by reference to fact. Without the aid of such practical measures, the best of text-books becomes dry or tedious, and, at all events, fails of exciting the earnest attention and personal interest which secure the energetic action of the whole mind, give life and vigor to its habits of action, and insure the further prosecution of inquiry in after stages of life.

To secure an earnest voluntary application to this noble study is not difficult, if the instructor take pains to invite his students to personal investigation of the numberless evidences of Divine power, wisdom, and goodness, which are furnished in every department of nature. The pleasure of observing, recording, and reporting these, is one to which the teacher who will faithfully make the experiment will find few minds so torpid as to be insensible.

*Evidences of Christianity.*—This subject, too, has its appointed place in our seminaries of learning; and that it is a study required in our higher schools for the female sex, as well as in our colleges, is a happy indication. But, the unintellectual, unmeaning process of reciting merely the paragraphs of a text-book, has the same injurious effect in this as in other departments of education. No subject can be presented to the mind on which the importance of clear and distinct views, or deep impressions and personal convictions of truth, are so important to the student, as on this;—none on which the utmost rigor of deduction, the closest investigation, the most cautious induction, are so imperatively demanded. The mere verbatim committing to memory, or even the careful recapitulation, of the arguments presented in the best of manuals, is a process too passive for any valuable purpose of educational influence on the individual. The second hand knowledge thus acquired, makes too slight an impression to become a permanent personal possession; as the experienced teacher has sometimes cause to feel most deeply, when he sees a promising youth, who has recited his way successfully through a whole manual of "evidences," so easily caught and entangled in the slight web of superficial and sophistical arguments offered by a fluent fellow-student, inclined to skeptical habits of thought.

The result is quite different when the instructor prescribes, not the mere language or reasoning of a single author, but a careful comparison of several, and a *resumé* prepared by the student himself, together with a full statement of objections, and the arguments by which these are rebutted. A still deeper impression is made on the mind of the individual, when such recapitulations are made, not only in the regular form of writing, but in that also of deliberate, correct, and, if possible, earnest oral expression. It is thus only that great and vital truths can be woven into the texture of his own mind, and become, as it were, inseparable parts of itself.

*Practical Exercises.*—In conclusion of these suggestions regarding the development and discipline of the reflective faculties, a few other forms of practical exercise may deserve attention, as matters which devolve on the personal action and diligence of the teacher,—in regard to the aid which his living instructions and intelligent supervision ought to furnish, in addition to the customary course prescribed in manuals or text-books; and here we may advert to the great value of

(1.) *Systematic Reading*, as a means of cultivating reflective and thoughtful habits of mind,—reading, I mean, which is *study*, and not mere *perusal;* reading which is attentively done, carefully reviewed, exactly recorded, and, if practicable, orally recounted. Memory, under such discipline, becomes thoroughly retentive, information exact, judgment correct, conception clear, thought copious, and expression ready and appropriate.

(2.) An important aid to systematic reading may be found in the exercise of writing a careful, marginal *synopsis* of valuable works, comprising all their principal *topics*, distinctly presented, and, in addition to this, a penciled *analysis* of every prominent head or paragraph into its constituent subordinate *details*. In the case of standard works of great value and permanent authority, it may be worth while to draught a separate *plan* of the entire *work* under study, in which the synopsis and the analysis are so arranged to the eye, that the advantage of a mental map of the whole subject is secured for distinct and easy recollection, by the union of logical and ocular method.

(3.) As a means of training the faculty of *judgment* to correctness in its decisions, and exactness in discrimination, exercises in *analysis*, on every description of material, are of the greatest value. In the earliest stages of education, these may be performed, to great advantage, on objects in *nature*, particularly on the structure and organization of plants, with the aid, too, of the microscope. At a more advanced stage, the analysis of *language*, successively extending to sentences, clauses, phrases, words, and syllables, in written as well as oral forms, is another exercise of great value for sharpening the power of discrimination and forming habits of correct judgment. Still greater benefit attends the oral analysis of *discourses*, essays, and other didactic compositions, for the purpose of tracing their authors' trains of thought, following these in detail, and afterward recording the analysis, as has been already suggested.

(4.) To cultivate successfully the reasoning faculty, no method more effectual can be adopted than that of training the mind to a perfect observance of the prime law of *Order*. This great principle comes to the aid of the young mind, as creative ordination applied to chaos. The countless multitude and variety of objects soliciting observation, in the early years of childhood, and even at much later stages, often throw the mind into confusion and perplexity, till *order* comes to its aid, and, like the benevolent fairy in the fable, *arranges* the complicated masses and irregular accumulations, and lets in the light of *system* and *method* upon the elements of the mental world. Conflicting objects and relations are thus parted by due *distinction ;* accordant elements and phenomena are grouped together, by their *analogies* and *affinities*, their *connections* and *dependencies*, the *predominance* of some and the *subordination* of others ; till, at length, the authority of *Law* is recognized, and harmony established.

To attain this result, *Reason*, the supreme ordaining faculty, has to exert its power in various modes of operation. *Judgment*, as reason's executive, has to *collate*, *examine*, *compare*, *associate*, *combine* and *classify* the objects of observation and the subjects of consciousness. For such purposes no exercises can be better adapted than those which commence with the action of the *perceptive* faculties, and yet involve the use of the *reflective*, to a certain extent. Nature's great systems, in her three vast kingdoms, furnish, of course, the best material for such exercise and discipline of the mind, by combining with its perceptive action the aid of reflecting reason, in the contemplation and study of the vast domain of creation. As a noble discipline for the rational faculties, in their ascendancy over those of outward observation, and yet in perfect harmony and coöperation with them, no exercise can be more beneficial than that of surveying, in the light of *science*, the elements and forms of external nature. An illustration in point may be found in the science of *botany*, which is now rendered so generally accessible and so highly attractive, by recent manuals presenting this subject on the "natural" system, as an instructive and interesting branch of knowledge for all minds. Another example occurs in the arrangement of the *animal* kingdom presented by Cuvier, and modified by our great contemporary naturalist, Agassiz. The generous labors of this distinguished instructor, in his endeavors to bring his favorite subject before the minds of teachers, in forms happily adapted to the condition of their schools, have afforded the best suggestions for conducting appropriate exercises in this department of education. And it is to be hoped that many of our seminaries will henceforward enjoy the benefits of the admirable mental discipline resulting from those habits of attentive observation, careful examination, and close analysis, as well as those of orderly arrangement, enlarged contemplation, and systematic classification, which the thorough study of nature is so happily adapted to insure.

But it should never be forgotten by the teacher that it is the extent to which the student is induced to carry the *personal observation* and *actual collection* of natural objects, and the care and fidelity with which he arranges his specimens according to the requirements of scientific classification, which determine how far the higher powers of his mind will be benefited by the study. There are too many seminaries, even now, in which the teacher, far from following the instructive personal example of the eminent authority to whom we have just referred, and joining their students in the actual exploration of nature, in the field exercises of observing and collecting, permit them to stay within doors, and "study" the whole subject by book.

The value of personal observation and actual investigation, as the only sure means of rendering the educational materials furnished in external nature, and in the action of the percipient intellect on these, conducive to the development and discipline of the mind's reflective power, is evinced in all the other relations and departments of physical science. The study of *astronomy*, as commonly conducted in our seminaries of all grades, has been, till recently, a process of mere book-work, of committing to memory the successive sentences of a manual, and repeating them by word of mouth. The actual observation of the heavens was a thing not thought of but as a matter of occasional gratification to curiosity; while, to render astronomy an effective instrument of mental culture, capable of awakening attention and eliciting reflection, the nightly survey of the varying aspects of the firmament, in conjunction with the passing hours, and the actual positions, or apparent shifting of the planetary bodies, should be continued till the eye finds itself, so to speak, at home in that upper world of wondrous facts, and the observer can literally "call the stars by name."

Many teachers have it easily in their power to render the young mind this noble service, which may stamp a thoughtful character on its habits of action for a whole life-time. Happily, many of our colleges are now enabled to offer to those who enjoy the superior opportunities of study afforded by such seminaries, the facilities for actual observation, which modern science and art so amply provide, in this department of education. But, in most of our higher schools and academies,—even in some which are favored with the possession and occasional use of a telescope,—the actual study of the heavens, even with the naked eye, or the humblest endeavor to note the position and movements of the heavenly bodies, so as to enable the learner intelli gently to read the sky, remains, as yet, a thing seldom attempted.

Were early education in this department rightly conducted, the young student would be prepared to receive with delight those sublime revelations of astronomical science which exhibit the laws of order and subordination,—of mutual influence and adjustment,—ruling in the apparent "wilderness of worlds," and indicating the controlling power of that Reason which presides in eternal supremacy over the universe.

## Concluding Explanations.

The brief and imperfect survey of the ground and principles of intellectual culture, which is here concluded, was, as has been intimated, originally presented in the form of conversational oral lectures to successive classes of young teachers and of persons intending to enter on the occupation of teaching. The views presented in these lectures were adapted, therefore, to the mental circumstances of students to some of whom any form of systematic investigation on the subject of intellectual discipline was wholly new, and to many of whom the philosophy of education was, as yet, a field unexplored. This fact will serve to explain the strictly elementary character of the preceding discussion, and the familiar style of its illustrations, as well as the frequent iteration of special topics; while the vast importance of the subject itself, in relation to the anticipated office and duties of the teacher, as the educator and guardian of the young mind, together with the acknowledged too general neglect of such considerations, rendered it necessary that the lecturer should endeavor to present the whole work of education in the impressive light of the highest relations and principles of human action.

To some of the readers of this journal, therefore, the whole series of these lectures may have seemed common-place and uninteresting; and to others the course of analysis may have seemed too abstract and philosophical for the ordinary purposes and business of education. The contributor of this and the preceding communications of the series to the pages of this journal can only plead, in answer to both classes of objections, that, for many years, his personal field of observation and of action has made it necessary for him to endeavor to meet the wants of ingenuous minds, conscious of deficiencies in their own course of early training, and earnestly desirous of the guiding light of the simplest, yet the highest, educational principles, to direct their own efforts for the advancement of others. Successive years, occupied in three of our New England States, in endeavoring to aid the noble aspirations of those whose daily labors form the ground of the intellectual and moral hope of the community, have convinced the writer that the teacher's professional wants are most satisfactorily met when elementary principles of education are simply stated and practically illustrated, and the highest relations of human duty are presented as the motives to personal and professional action.—Long may the "plain living and high thinking" of their ancestry continue to characterize the teachers of New England!

The allusions made, in the course of the preceding discussion, to existing defects in "higher" seminaries, might seem uncalled for in a course of remarks addressed to young teachers. To explain this apparent intrusion, it may be sufficient to say, that some of the classes to which these lectures were originally addressed included among their members individuals who, though young both in years and experience, were graduates of the highest class of literary institutions, were anticipating professional employment in such establishments, and were attending the course of lectures with reference to the application, in their personal instructions, of the principles under discussion.

Apart, however, from this relation of circumstances, the consideration of principles of education, and methods of instruction, necessarily extends through the whole educational course of training; and defective methods of teaching are but little less injurious in the higher than in the lower forms of culture. The fact, moreover, is undeniable, that the renovation of the character of instruction, whether at home or abroad, has uniformly commenced in the primary stages of education, and won its way gradually upward;—a circumstance easily accounted for, when we recollect that, in the reformation, now so generally effected in elementary teaching, more regard has been paid to the wants of the *mind*, and less to the demands of *subjects*, than formerly was the case in the management of primary schools, or than is now, in the customary regulation of institutions of the highest nominal order, in most of which the *subject* of study is still too uniformly regarded in preference to the *instrument* of study.

To some readers of the journal, the intellectual philosophy, involved in the principles adopted in the preceding analysis of mental action and development, may not seem satisfactory,—as not according, in express terms, with established authorities on such topics. To objections of this character the author can only suggest that, in the circumstances of many of those to whom his lectures were addressed, it was not practicable to assume the data of a previous course of study in intellectual philosophy; and all that could properly be done, on his part, was to interweave, with his suggestions for the guidance of instructors in their professional endeavors, such elementary views of mental action and tendency as might afford intelligible ground for these suggestions.

At the same time, the writer feels free to say that, following the counsels of his own instructor, the venerable Jardine, (a student and successor of Dr. Reid,) he could not adopt any "system" of intellectual philosophy as such. All systems hitherto offered have contributed useful suggestions for the guidance of inquiry. But none, as yet, can be regarded as exhaustive or complete. The *mind*, as a subject of study, has not yet received the humble measure of justice which we yield to a plant or a mineral,—a careful observation and close examination of its own character, apart from the obscuring influence of the conflicting views and metaphysical speculations of great writers and eminent authorities. But, to the teacher, philosophical theory is a doubtful aid, compared to his own daily inspection of the mind itself, in its actual working and obvious tendencies. He is, if he understands his position, himself a primary observer, authority and reporter, in the science of mind, as developed in the processes of education. His work is that of a living philosopher, in act. To his young disciples, he is Plato, and Socrates, and Aristotle, embodied in one person;—opening to their expanding minds the highest spiritual, moral, and intellectual relations of truth.

The ground thus assigned as the field of the teacher's labor, is not too high to be assumed by any instructor, whatever be the nominal rank of the seminary in which he teaches. A mind accustomed to large views, and working on broad principles, will, unconsciously and necessarily, adopt methods correspondent, and will radiate, from its own action, light and truth throughout the sphere of its influence. Nowhere is this statement more strikingly verified than in the case of an intelligent teacher, in the direction and instruction of an elementary school. It is in this sphere that ingenuity, and tact, and originality, and skill are most needed, in endeavors to develop intellectual capabilities, and build up the great fabric of mental power. Nowhere else, in the whole field of education, is the demand so urgent for a thorough insight into the nature and working of the mind, for the light to guide its advances, or the power to mold its expanding character.

# INDEX.

# II. MORAL EDUCATION.*

LECTURES ADDRESSED TO YOUNG TEACHERS.

BY WILLIAM RUSSELL,

Editor of the American Journal of Education (Boston,) 1826–29.

---

## Introductory Observations.

*Importance of the Study of Man's Moral Constitution.*—The vital part of human culture is not that which makes man what he is intellectually, but that which makes him what he is in heart, life, and character. Intellectual cultivation, however, is a source of moral power to the individual, not merely in the mental aid which it enables him to render to others, but in that which it gives him for the understanding and government of himself. All intellectual training, therefore, is necessarily moral in its influence, so far as regards enlarged opportunity and power of intelligent, voluntary, and efficient action. It is only misguided ignorance, blinding prejudice, or perverted ingenuity, that would ignore or undo, in educational administration, the natural union of morality with intelligence.

A culture exclusively intellectual serves but to exhibit the skeleton of the mental frame, which moral influence is to furnish with the means and the power of action, and into which religious principle is to breathe the breath of life. But when moral culture assumes a separate and formal character, it ceases to be a living spiritual reality, and becomes but a mechanical routine of "the letter" which, we are told, "killeth." No reliance for effective moral influence on disposition or character, can be safely placed on mere didactic inculcation or catechetical instruction. The oracles of Divine truth tell us, that the highest moral training—the spiritual—does not separate "admonition" from "*nurture*"—the life-giving influence—but combines the two in the educational process of "bringing up." The true study of the human being, as a subject of meliorating culture, contemplates the child in the living unity of his whole nature. It regards him as an intelligent self-conscious, self-impelling, self-guiding, self-responsible agent, yet dependent on, and responsible to, the law of a higher power

---

* At the suggestion of Hon. Henry Barnard, the following series of lectures has been transcribed from the author's general course on Human Culture, originally addressed to the students of the Merrimack, (N. H.,) and New England, (Lancaster, Mass.,) Normal Institutes. A previous series on Intellectual Education, may be found by referring to Vols. II., III., and IV., of this Journal.

than his own, which has summed up and defined his individuality in a conscious will.

All careful investigation, however, in the mental, not less than in the physical world, implies an examination so close as to constitute a thorough analysis—not, in this instance, for the sake of a mere philosophic solution, but for the purpose of securing a true synthetic construction of life and character, by the better understanding, so obtained, of constituent elements and the influences which may best secure their living union and power. In every process of "instruction," (*inward building*,) the educator, whether parent or teacher, if he would work thoughtfully and successfully—if he would avoid laying upon the mental foundation of created capability a superstructure of "wood, hay, stubble," instead of the "gold, silver, and precious stones" of true worth and value—is in duty bound to see to it that he attentively observe, and carefully study, the nature and constitution of the being, whose fabric of character it is his office to aid in building up. The educator must, in a word, thoroughly understand and appreciate the elements of human character. These must be familiar to him in all their relations, and in all their varied workings, that he may understand more fully the means and sources of healthy action and healthful regimen, which it is his duty to prescribe.

*True position of the Teacher as a Moral Educator.*—Even to the youngest and least experienced of teachers, who wishes to acquit himself to the moral obligations under which he is professionally laid, equally to his pupils and himself, we would earnestly recommend not the practice of looking into some text-book of moral philosophy, for his own guidance, or for the instruction of his pupils, but—in the true spirit of an earnest, faithful, and intelligent instructor, who is aware that all he daily does or omits is a part of the effectual, living education of the subjects of his influence—the careful study and watchful observation of the moral indications and tendencies of his pupils, as intimating their capabilities and suggesting his measures and resources. It is his part to carry on, in successive stages, the sacred offices of parental love and wisdom, daily transferred to his charge, to be fulfilled in the sphere of the schoolroom, according to the measure of his judgment, his skill, and his benignity. But the proper home influence, though so often missing, is the true ideal of purpose, plan, and work, for the teacher; and, so far as regards moral results, in the schoolroom as at home, the appropriate influence must ever be that of an authoritative, affectionate, living, presence—not that of an inanimate book or a deadening routine.

No one doubts that, to become a skillful cultivator of the intel lectual capabilities of his pupils, the instructor must understand the character and action of the intellectual faculties—not merely as these exist in the enumeration of particulars in a text-book of mental philosophy, but as they actually reveal themselves in the personal action and relations of the living pupil, in whatever concerns the use and exercise of his mind. The teacher must take the position not of a student of intellectual philosophy, ruminating in his study, but of a wakeful observer and inquirer into the phenomena of an actual, living specimen of the human mind, whose course is to be, in part, dependent on the fidelity of his observation, and the genial character of his influence. Our previous course of suggestions on the cultivation of the intellectual faculties, it will be recollected, assumed this ground as the appropriate and peculiar one of the teacher, and the only one on which he could justly be regarded as doing aright his professional work. The same ground we would claim for the teacher, when surveying the field of moral culture.

### Arrangement of Topics.

*Recapitulation of Method.*—The plan which we propose to adopt in the following series of lectures, will still be, as in the former series, that which places the teacher as a responsible personal observer and reporter on phenomena and facts; watching and aiding the progress of human development. Our survey of the field of intellectual cultivation, as founded on the nature and constitution of the human being, presented, (1.) it will be recollected, *a given class of the mental powers and faculties*, themselves, as subjects of examination; (2.) *the actuating principle*, or moving spring, *of these powers;* (3.) *their* perceptible *natural tendency*, or course of action; (4.) *the results* of their action; and, (5.) *the educational processes* designed for their appropriate development.

Following this plan, we avoid all mere theoretic speculation, and stand on the sure ground of observed fact—the only point of view for the discovery and recognition of truth, or the direction and guidance of the teacher. We thus, moreover, place the work of education in the teacher's own hands, as a charge devolving on him, not merely professionally, but personally, and laying him under his just responsibility, as an agent for others, and as one intrusted, in the capacity of temporary guardian, with the dearest of all human interests, and the best of all hopes—hopes extending even to a never-dying life.

### I. Classification of the Moral Capabilities.

*Unity of Man's Moral Constitution.*—Adopting the above method for our course of suggestions on moral education, we should proceed to enumerate, as a class, the most prominent of the peculiar powers and faculties which constitute man a moral being, capable of moral influence, instruction, and development. But as every moral act involves the whole man—not merely the executive organ of muscle or nerve, intellect, heart or will, but all, in their living unity and active coöperation, we can not, as when examining the intellectual faculties, select any class or group of powers as exclusively constituting the moral capabilities of the human being. We must take into view his whole nature, comprehending, as it does, the vast range of his physical, intellectual, emotional, and voluntary attributes, in the personal constitution and organization of the individual.

1. HEALTH *as an element of Moral Life.*—Man's moral condition, and his capability of moral development, depend, in no slight degree, on that intimate connection which the Creator has ordained between soul and body. As a necessary condition of the unity of man's complex nature, wholeness of being is essential to whole and true, that is, normal action, whether of body, or of mind, or of both. Physical disorder, by its reäctionary character, disintegrates its subject as a moral agent, by withdrawing the executive organism from coöperation and consentaneous action, in subordination whether to the dictates of reason and conscience, the solicitations of feeling, or the normal activity of the will. Physical suffering, and its attendant involuntary irritation, are sufficient to overcast the clear healthy action of the judgment, to stifle the monitions of conscience, to change the natural current of affection, to generate angry passion, and propagate moral evil, to any extent—from the petty ebullitions of peevish temper, to the outbreaks of the fiercest anger, or of raving and furious insanity. Health, then, the educator must ever be careful to enumerate among the conditions of morality, whether the healthy state of the agent be owing to the normal sanity of mere bodily condition, or to that health of the higher nature, conscience, which, in man's fallen state, must so often be invoked, to rule the turbulent and rebellious tendencies of a morbid physical organization, and which, when enlightened, and strengthened, and purified, by supernal aid, is a surer reliance than the happiest condition of the best normal animal life.—To this branch of our subject we shall have occasion to refer more distinctly, under other heads, in the discussion of parental and educational influences.

2. INTELLECT, *and its culture, important elements of Moral Life.*—The vital fact of man's moral unity of constitution, involves the condition of his intellectual nature, as sound and true, or otherwise. The unhealthy condition of the bodily organism, is sufficient to subvert, as we have seen, the whole moral character of the human being,

in seasons of excessive morbid reäction. *Sanity and vigor of mind*, not less than health of body, and conditions of moral life and action; as is sadly manifest when we advert to those unhappy cases in which there has been an overthrow or obscuration of the god-like power of reason itself. Insanity, whether in the form of mental aberration or delusion, is competent not only to impair, but to obliterate, the distinctive mental and moral attributes of man.

The enlightened humanity of our day mitigates by genial, and sometimes, successful treatment, the sufferings of our nature, when reduced to such deplorable conditions; and its kind offices are crowned with yet more marked success, in its endeavors to raise the idiotic and the feeble minded to a comparatively healthy intellectual and moral level. It is one of the highest tributes paid to moral culture—we may observe in passing—that such replacements of depressed human nature are generally recognized as owing their success to the purely moral measures adopted in effecting them, whether in cases of insanity or of idiocy.

*Culture essential to Intelligence, and therefore, to Moral Elevation.*—Gross ignorance, and utter absence of mental culture, are proved to be, in general, fruitful sources of crime, and of moral evil in every shape. It is not enough that a sane mind and sound judgment be taken into the account, as, indispensable elements in the production of legitimate moral results in action and character. The intellect beclouded and darkened by ignorance and its attendant hosts of error and prejudice, or benumbed by neglect and disuse, is incapable of the clearness and activity which belong to the normal states and conditions of the human mind. A pure, intelligent, and loyal adherence to principle and to conscience, can not, in such circumstances, be expected to exist. The character indicated in sacred scripture, "a brutish man" who "doth not know," may not have chosen his condition; but, while in it, he is disqualified for every proper exercise of man's reflective and moral nature. The density of ignorance to which some classes of the population of European cities, and the majority of the slave population of our own country, are sunk, shows, in its deplorable depression, and its nearly hopeless extinction or absence of conscience, how important the daylight of knowledge is to a pure atmosphere in the human soul.

*Evils of excessive Cultivation.*—Morality necessarily implies a certain degree of intelligence and of culture. But, unhappily, there is, as is too plainly apparent in the forms of civilized and city life, a condition in which a moral inefficiency of mind is attributable not to the absence, but to the injudicious excess of cultivation; and the pale and emaciated features of school children and students, too generally indicate the incompatibility of sedentary life and close, studious application, daily sustained, with a natural, healthy condition of body. The parental complaints against schools, as undermining the temper and vivacity of childhood, confirm the truth that the "much study" which "is a weariness of the flesh," impairs, also, the healthy vigor and freshness of the spirit.

*Genial influence of appropriate early Culture.*—Were early education what it should be, a course of invigorating, life-giving observation of nature and its products, and a succession of healthful, inspiring exercises, alternating with soothing relaxation and cheering recreation, and a strictly limited and very moderate exercise of pure intellection; culture and intelligence would cease to be, as now, too often purchased at the expense of a healthy tone of mind and habit. But, as we must recur to this branch of our subject when we come to the discussion of educational methods, we must leave it, for the present, with this postulate, that a sound, clear, vigorous, and well trained *understanding*, capable of correct and decisive *judgments*, is as important as the possession of *reason* itself, to constitute man a responsible, moral agent. In other words, that his *rational faculty* is a *moral power*.

3. ÆSTHETIC CULTURE: *its Moral Influence on Imagination and Taste.*—Among the intellectual sources of moral life and power, a prominent place must ever be assigned by the judicious educator to the moulding and directing efficacy of imagination and taste. If these influential faculties are untrue or impure in their action and character, the tendency of the whole moral being is "only evil, and that continually." If they are sound, healthy, pure, and vigorous, they become sure safeguards, faithful guides, and genial companions of the youthful spirit. They, also, rise to the rank of powers in the moral domain of humanity.

*Moral influence of the impressions of Sublimity and Beauty.*—In that commingling of intuition, feeling, and imagination, and, sometimes, even of reflective judgment, by which the soul is at once overawed, and delighted, and exalted, in the contemplation of the vast, the sublime, the majestic in nature or in thought, or in that only less elevating influence which is inspired by the blending effects of greatness and grace in the grandeur of nature or of noble art, or even in that delighted and admiring love which is elicited by the presence of beauty in the myriad forms and hues with which the Creator has invested the living and ever-varying aspects of nature, which man delights to imitate in art;—in all these relations of mind is involved a moral element of power, by which man's nature is ennobled and purified, and prepared, as in the vestibule of a sanctuary, for those yet higher and more effective influences which lift awe into adoration, and attract the soul to the beauty of holiness. Such at least, we know, is the natural tendency of unperverted mind, and the experience of every soul on which the true Light shineth.

The mind which, under the purifying influence of genial culture, enjoys the refining emotions and clear perceptions of a true "taste," (*relish*,) for those pursuits which lead to the admiring contemplation of nature, and to the practice of those arts which enable man to express his admiration of nature—possesses, in its love of the beautiful, a natural preparation for the reception of all those salutary impressions which, in a higher relation, are stamped upon the heart by the irresistible power of every trait of loveliness of disposition and character embodied in the daily beauty of a pure and amiable life.

*The Graphic Arts* which embody and repeat and perpetuate such impressions, are not to be overlooked in an enumeration of man's capabilities of refining and elevating culture, even in its strictly moral and spiritual relation. The dumb statue, by its perfect symmetry and grace, or its touching beauty, makes the heart eloquent inwardly with delight and love, with admiration, or with tenderness and sympathy. The portrait which recalls the image of the lost and lovely, the good and the true, the noble and the worthy, speaks most touchingly to us, from the spirit of the departed, in the language of the heart. The landscape which skillful art presents as a microcosm of glorious nature, conjured from dead, material means and implements, by a concentration of man's inventive genius and educated hand, deepens, at once, our love of this our earthly home of palatial grandeur and finished beauty, benignantly assigned us by the great Father, for our preparatory abode, and our admiration of the powers with which He has endowed the beings created in his image. The art which at once refines and elevates, does a noble preparatory work in rendering more vividly susceptible those faculties by which the soul, when awakened to the consciousness of its highest relations, is yet more effectually purified and ennobled.

But *Music*—that art which God has been pleased to consecrate for His own special service in the offices of human devotion, and which may be employed in the humble station of a peculiar minister to man's enjoyment, as a sentient being, capable of ever new and ever pure gratification from the concord of sweet sounds, is, in its influence on the soul, an element of singular moral efficacy, in its power to inspire with reverence, with joy, with ecstatic delight, to calm and soothe the agitated spirit, to touch the heart with sympathy for sorrow, or to mingle the humanizing emotions of brotherhood and companionship. Rightly cultivated and rightly practiced, it affects with a pure and benign influence both mind and heart; and happily, of late years, has it taken its appropriate place in schools, among the effective means of moral culture not less than æsthetic.

It is no undue enlargement in the enumeration of the moral capabilities of humanity, to include within its sphere the whole range of those arts by which man's conceptions of grandeur and beauty are rendered more definite in themselves, and more effective in their influence on his character.

4. SENSIBILITY, *as an element of Moral Life.*—In our preceding observations, we have adverted to health of body and mind, and to intellectual and æsthetic culture, as determining, in degree, man's moral capabilities; since a normal physical and intellectual state is the natural condition of normal moral action. Proceeding to the further consideration of the moral capacities and powers, the next element in our enumeration will be that *Sensibility* which, by Creative ordination, links man, by the sense of *pleasure* and *pain*, to the outward world, establishes a sentient world within himself, and gives birth to the vital elements of *love* and *aversion*, in all the varied forms of *appetite, instinct, desire, feeling, affection, passion,* and *emotion*, by which man is attracted or repelled, by which he is prompted to action and expression, and which consequently determine his *morality*, (*manner* of action.)

5. THE INSTINCTIVE TENDENCIES, *as Moral Incitements.*—(1.) *Appetite*, the natural primal craving for satisfaction, which implies a sense of want and a desire of gratification, more or less definite according to the degree of intellectual development and definite consciousness, secures, by Divine appointment, the perpetual renovation of vigor, health, and life, of comfort and complacency. In the natural sympathy of mind and body, it tends, also, to generate the genial dispositions and emotions, and to diffuse the moral element of happiness. The intelligent educator recognizes it as a moral power, in its influence on habit and character. He well knows that, in its pure and healthy conditions, it is an effective promoter of serenity and tranquillity and cheerfulness, and favors the exercise of the benevolent affections; that, when neglected, it brings on an irritative reäction, too strong, if extreme, for the control of the guardian power of conscience; and that, when glutted by excess, it imbrutes the whole being, and leads to those degrading habits by which humanity is desecrated or ruined.

(2.) *The natural Love of Activity.*—One of the earliest manifestations of instinct is the restless desire of action, which is seen even in the involuntary and spontaneous motions of the muscular frame in infancy, in the insatiable thirst for exercise in childhood, in the irrepressible tendency of boyhood and youth to active exertion, in the indefatigable industry of adult man; and not less in the instinctive craving for intellectual action, and the inextinguishable curiosity of the young mind, in the eager appetite for knowledge on all accessible subjects, and the earnest desire to investigate the problems of our being and destination, which impel the maturer mind, at every stage of life. The same desire of activity is marked in the child's natural craving for sympathy and affection, and in that desire for esteem and approbation which mark the dispositions of youth and manhood. All these impelling powers, as they tend to enlarge the sphere of life to the individual, and prompt him to fill it by corresponding exertion, become vital elements of moral life and character.

(3.) *The natural Aversion to Pain.*—This instinctive principle, which makes the sentient nature a provisional guardian of the safety and welfare of infancy, and, in degree, of humanity, throughout the course of life, operates, at first, with more obvious reference to the protection of organic life and health. But, as the mental powers progressively unfold themselves, and conscious sympathy becomes a source of pleasure or of pain, the instinct becomes a moral sentiment, and leads its subject to avoid whatever seems fitted to excite painful or disagreeable emotions in the consciousness of his fellow beings. It advances as self-consciousness becomes more fully developed, to that moral rank which places it in alliance with conscience, and warns us to shun the foreseen pain of evil doing, and the reproaches of that faithful monitor which Divine wisdom has implanted in the bosom of man to represent its own jurisdiction. It rises, at length, to that fear of God which deters from sin, under the dread of His sovereignty or the apprehension of his displeasure, and which, in its truest and most genial form of filial awe, forbids the very thought of offense. The power of this instinct is most impressively shown when, as in some deplorable instances, its first monitory warnings have been disregarded, and its terrific reäction drives reason from the throne of intellect, or haunts a death-bed with horrors.

(4.) *The desire of Enjoyment*—which, in infancy and childhood, tends to seek for gratification in the sphere of the sentient nature in its animal relations, rises to intellectual and moral action, with progressive development, in subsequent stages of life and character, till it becomes the conscious pursuit of even the highest happiness of humanity, exalts successively the aims and endeavors of man to his utmost elevation of moral action and character, and stamps itself as one of the most powerful agents in the advancement of his being.

(5.) *The desire of Power.*—No attribute of his nature more distinctly marks the character of man as a progressive being, than that love of power which actuates the very infant in his attempts to stand, to walk, to speak, to put forth efforts of muscular force. The child, the boy, and the youth, all evince the activity of this principle, in the conscious ambition for progress and advancement by which they are impelled to earnest endeavor and arduous exertion, physical, intellectual, and moral. The sense of power is, in every stage of human life, one of the strongest feelings of pleasure of which man is conscious. In the maturity of his powers, it crowns his endeavors to explore the worlds of nature and of thought, to achieve the miracles of perfect art, to attain to positions of affluence or of rank, to enjoy, in whatever form, the splendor of greatness. It prompts man, at every stage of his being, from childhood onward, to aim at the relative manifestation of power which is exhibited in superiority over others, in the ability to control, direct, and sway the minds and actions of his fellow-men. This instinct of his nature becomes an element of immense productive force for evil, when perverted; although, when prompted by benevolence, and restrained by justice and rectitude, it has occasionally made men the benefactors of their race.

(6.) *The desire of Estimation.*—This principle which, in childhood, is manifested in the desire of love and approbation, becomes, in the adult, a love of esteem and respect, and, so far, is unquestionably a worthy motive power, and one which, subordinated to conscientious integrity and honor, elevates the character and prompts to benevolent action. When it degenerates to mere love of fame and applause, or sinks to the miserable desire for distinction or mere notoriety, its effects are, of course, as degrading as in its purer forms, it is ennobling. In any form, it is an element of peculiar power in man's moral constitution.

(7.) *The desire of Society.*—This principle man partakes with the gregarious races of animal life. It manifests itself in the clinging desire for sympathy and association, characteristic alike of infancy, childhood, and youth. It becomes, in manhood, the foundation of social and civil life, widens the sphere of the individual, and amplifies his being by the sympathy, the intelligence, the material and moral aid of a whole community of his fellow men. As an element of human progress and power, it ranks among the strongest and the most ample of man's moral resources.

(8.) *The desire of Freedom.*—In the stages of infancy and childhood, and of immature life generally, the instinctive desire to throw off restraint, and to enjoy liberty of action, is the natural expression of that native desire of development which impels the progressive human being in every direction that promises the pleasure of conscious effort and power. Partaking, however, of the partial blindness attributable to all forms of mere instinct, it needs the direction and guidance of faculties higher than itself, to constitute it a uniformly safe element in activity. But as it is capable of employment in the service of man's best rights and interests, and, in that capacity, has achieved some of his noblest triumphs for intelligence, virtue, and happiness, it takes justly a high rank among his moral capabilities, as an indispensable condition of development and progress.

6. THE PRIMARY EMOTIONS, *as Moral Powers.*—Sensibility, the susceptibility of feeling, the great source of moral life, presents its numerous family of emotions as constituent members of the group of moral powers and faculties by which man is rendered capable of meliorating culture and spiritual growth. Emotion, as the manifestation or expression of feeling and affection, is not merely the natural language of the heart, rendered visible or audible, but in virtue of the law of sympathy and mutual incitement, existing in the various faculties of the soul, it is itself a vital moral element reäcting with a powerful augmenting force on the source whence it springs. As an inner movement of the soul rendered legible, it has, in many cases, become, by universal consent and usage, a synonym for the interior condition whence it originates, whether in the quiet moods of serenity or the turbulence of passion.

(1.) *Joy.*—One of the earliest feelings manifested by look and action, in the infant stage of life, is that joyous emotion which constitutes, so largely, the happiness of animal existence, in all its earlier conditions. The genial nature of this emotion is indicated in the intense gratification which it evidently yields to its immediate subject, and which, by the law of sympathy, it diffuses to all sentient natures within its sphere. From its lowest forms of serene *complacency*, to its more positively marked degrees of *animation* and *cheerfulness*, its higher expressions of *delight*, of *gladness*, and *hilarity*, or its more sedate and lasting satisfactions, in the mature sense of *happiness* which attends true enjoyment, its influence on life and health, on conscious feeling, on temper and disposition, on the whole intellectual and moral nature, is, in the highest degree, salutary; while undue devotion to its influence precludes the possibility of benefit from those deeper and more lasting pleasures which flow from serious thought and earnest purposes. Mirth, habitually indulged, leads to habitual levity and frivolity, and foregoes the distinctive dignity of man. The healthy and genial inspiration of joy, however, even intelligent educators are sometimes prone to forget, is, in all the relations of moral condition and moral cultivation, one of the strongest influences to which the young mind, by the law of its constitution, is peculiarly subjected as a vital element—the oxygen, of its spiritual atmosphere.

(2.) *Sorrow, grief, regret, repentence, remorse.*—These emotions, diametrically opposed, in all their effects, to the genial influence of the preceding, are to be eschewed as permanent educational elements in any normal plan of early training; yet they have their salutary office in abnormal instances, in softening obdurate hearts, and subduing obstinate wills, or in awakening torpid and dormant intellects. Their office, in the business of education, is that of exceptional remedies for exceptional evils: they are punitive and reformatory in their character, rather than genial and preventive. They belong not to the primary stage of nurture, but rather to the secondary one of discipline. Still they are sometimes of the greatest value, when they spring from ingenuous feelings of regret for conscious error, or self-reprehension for conscious faults. It was once most happily said, "The tear of contrition serves to wash the mote of sin out of the eye." The hour of grief is that which enhances the value of consolation. The blameless sadness of the young heart calls for the gentle soothing of the voice of affection. Sorrow for deplorable losses blesses the voice which can say, in genuine sympathy and cheering kindness, "Let not your heart be troubled!" The moment of "the heaviness of the countenance" is sometimes that in which "the heart is made better," by detaching it from the burden of conscious evil, and preparing the will for the better course of a new life. In such circumstances, the judicious aid of the attentive educator may assist in the inauguration of a new moral era in the personal history of the pupil. Even the rougher and severer discipline of repentance and remorse becomes, to the hardened adult, a minister of mercy, when it wrenches the sinner from the thraldom of evil habit, and sets him free from the "bondage of iniquity."

The moral power of this whole class of emotions—from the unaccountable cloud of depression which sometimes steals over the sunshine of the young heart, to the deepest plunge into the darkness of remorse—is peculiarly marked for its efficacy in the renovation of feeling, and even of disposition and character. In the sphere of the family and the school, it sometimes marks the record of the day's history with the beginning of a salutary reformation of temper and deportment. But, in the imperfections of human management, it sometimes is permitted to mark the commencement of a reäctive sense of wrong, when the feeling is unjustly caused by arbitrary or erring authority. It then becomes a power for lasting evil.

(3.) *Timidity, fear, terror.*—Like the natural aversion to pain, these instinctive emotions, which are so easily excited in childhood, bespeak the guardian care of the Creator, in his gracious provision against danger, and consequent destruction to the organic frame, or to the mental constitution. They are the swift preventives of evil, the safeguards of humanity in peril. But the vividness of childhood's emotions needs the aid of the guardian auspices of education to prevent a salutary instinct from degenerating into unreasoning excess, and to protect the mental and moral nature from the paralyzing effect, which, in unhappy instances, has extended to the overthrow of reason itself. The timidity of childhood may, if not watched over, become habitual self-distrust, embarrassment, confusion of thought, or even moral cowardice. Wisely guarded, it may be converted into a protection from rashness, presumption, and foolhardiness. Fear may be sometimes needed as a restraining influence on forwardness and impudence, or as a check upon daring hardihood, in resistance to authority. But its influence is unfriendly to the healthy development of disposition and character. It never rises to the dignity of an aid to the development of principle. It may aid in producing a vivid apprehension of coercive and compulsory measures, and so lead to obviate their necessity. But its low rank among instincts, its semi-brutal character, at best, place it among the motives which a generous educator would ever despise. If called in, for a moment, to quell resistance to authority, it yet can never attain to the dignity of a genuine moral influence. Expediency may sometimes sanction the appeal to its effect, as a matter of necessity. But, if admitted at all into the circle of moral relations, it can not be ranked higher than among the abnormal. As for its extreme form, terror—humanity, at the present day, forbids any resort to it, as a moral expedient. The peril of insanity lies too close at hand to permit any human being to adopt it, even as a means of deterring from evil. Its only salutary use is its instinctive office to prompt the instant flight from peril to life itself. So, and so only, does it prove a benefit.

(4.) *Indignation as a moral sentiment.*—The intelligent moral instructor will, of course, carefully guard his pupils from confounding this principle with the mere animal emotion or passion of anger. Anger is the mere personal reäction of maddened feeling and blinded reason, which man is capable of in common with the brutes, and which vents itself in violence on the agent of injury. Indignation is that impersonal sentiment which regards not the agent but the act, which makes the young heart glow at the sense of wrong, when the teacher is relating an instance of oppression or cruelty, which occurred, perhaps, ages ago, and in some distant land. This species of resentment is a purely mental thing, a salutary and ennobling emotion of reäctive sympathy, which belongs to man as a being consciously endowed with free agency, and equally abhorring a condition of unjust subjection, and the oppression which causes it—

as a being instinctively impelled to oppose and overthrow every palpable form of evil which besets the condition of humanity. Indignation has inspired many of those peaceful revolutions which have renovated the social and moral condition of communities, more frequently than it has originated those bloody revolutions which have sometimes been the birth-throes of national life and liberty.

(5.) *Wonder.*—Among the first indications of mental life, in childhood, is the emotion of wonder, which, at that stage of human progress, is so often called forth by the novelties of observation and experience. The freshness of feeling which it indicates, and the manifest delight attending it, show plainly its power as an element of mental life and moral activity. This emotion, judiciously evoked and skillfully cherished by the watchful educator, becomes not only a genial and a powerful incentive to intellectual exertion, but the tribute of the young heart on the altar of the yet "unknown God," who is waiting to be, in due season, revealed to intelligent faith. The wonder which the novelty of all created things raises in the dawning consciousness of childhood, is the preparatory stage of the intelligence and reverence which are afterward to blend in the soul, as it rises to the recognition of the Author of life and the Giver of its law of duty.

(6.) *Awe.*—This emotion transcends that of mere wonder, and thrills the soul with a profounder sense of power, whether exhibited in the tremendous forces of nature, in its astounding aspects of elemental commotion, as in the heaving fire of the volcano, the dashing billows of ocean, the rush of the cataract, the blinding flash of the lightning, the roar of the thunder, or the fury of the tornado, or in the calmer majesty of mountain forms, the overwhelming vastness of impenetrable forests, or the immeasurable depths of space. As a moral inspiration, it aids the feeble faculties of man in his attempts to dwell upon the conception of almighty power and eternal duration; and while he must ever sink consciously baffled in all his attempts to comprehend Him "whose greatness is unsearchable, and whose ways are past finding out," yet he never feels more vividly the greatness of his own nature, limited though it is, than when losing his human littleness in the contemplation of the great and marvellous works which bespeak the majesty of Him who is "the same yesterday, to-day, and forever."

This overwhelming and yet ennobling emotion, education has it for one of its special offices to deepen and expand by all the aids which nature and science furnish to the inquiring mind of man. Its influence is doubly salutary, as it prostrates the human being in conscious insignificence before his Creator, and, at the same time, exalts Him who is the "Majesty of heaven and earth."

(7.) *Hope.*—As an intelligent inspiration, of intellect, heart, and will, in activity connected with the sense of duty, hope, the expectation of success, becomes an element of high moral value and power.

It is congenial with the conscious happiness of being which naturally belongs to the joyous associations of early childhood, and, indeed, of young life in all its various stages. It inspires and sustains the aspirations of boyhood and youth, and invigorates the exertions of manhood. It is a silent tribute from the heart of man to Divine benignity; and when elevated and hallowed by faith, it rejoices in the anticipation of a future life of perfect felicity. Its rank, and its efficacy as a moral influence, constitute it one of the highest powers by which man's moral nature is actuated.

7. THE BENIGNANT AFFECTIONS, *as elements of moral life and power.*—(1.) *Love.*—By the great pervading attribute of sensibility, inherent in his constitution, man learns to feel his condition before he knows it, and to sympathize with his fellow-beings before he is capable of understanding them. The law of *Sympathy*, written on his whole nature, as a primary element of his being, which ultimately developed into every form of social and benevolent feeling, brings him, unconsciously, at first, under the dominion of the paramount law of *Love*, which attracts him toward his fellow-beings by a genial and kindly influence which he delights to feel, and which, as his conscious intelligence gradually unfolds itself, he learns to understand as mutual and reciprocal. This mysterious power ties the heart of the infant to that of the mother, and that of the mother to the infant with an affection stronger than life. In the little community of home, it links the souls of brothers and sisters in fraternal union of affection. It is the sacred law of parental and filial duty, and moves the whole moral machinery of human life in its hallowed and blessed sphere of privacy.

There virtue has its purest forms and dearest aspects, its genuine, spontaneous amenities; and though unknown beyond its own quiet sphere, has its own unseen record of generous self-sacrifice, and of fortitude more than heroic. Among the noblest motive powers of moral action, the affections of home are those to which the enlightened educator will ever assign the highest place, as regards the capabilities of the human heart for living development.

(2.) *Gratitude.*—This peculiar benignant reäction of love, in view of favor or kindness experienced, mingles largely with the exercise of filial and fraternal affection, and enters into every emotion called forth by the consciousness of benefit conferred, in whatever degree—from the ordinary acts of human kindness and courtesy, to those greater expressions of benevolence, which bestow safety or comfort and happiness, in valuable and lasting forms of beneficent action. This generous emotion is not always accompanied with the satisfaction of being able to remunerate a benefactor by any adequate return. The service or the favor which calls it forth, is sometimes greater than language or action, or any form of external expression, can equal. It may be sometimes so great as to prompt the devotion of a whole life to the friend or benefactor toward whom it is directed. Such is true filial attachment. Such is man's position toward his Creator.

The promptings of this generous emotion lead, sometimes, to the noblest manifestations of true sensibility and self-renouncing devotion. Some of the brightest passages on the page of history are those which record the heroic actions to which this feeling has given birth.

In the relations of education, its influence on the ingenuous mind and heart of youth, forms one of the most sacred attachments of human life. A grateful feeling of returning love for the guardian mental care which, in our early years, watched over, and served to form and mould within us, the ideal image of excellence at which we were taught to aspire, the filial reverence which the heart, in such circumstances, so gladly pays as a tribute to wisdom and worth, insure the inspiration of the noblest aims in all subsequent life, to the heart which is conscious of them.

8. THE GENEROUS AFFECTIONS, *as Moral Powers*.—(1.) *Friendship.*—The cordialities of disinterested friendship, and the mutual good offices of human kindness and reciprocal obligation are but expansions of fraternal feeling from the primary sphere of home; and their efficacy in promoting human well-being, on a broad scale, render them powerful instruments of good, as well as rich elements of moral life in the heart.

(2.) *Patriotism.*—On a yet wider field, patriotic attachment and principle, as they cherish the generous spirit of self-devotion, give ample scope for the cultivation of the virtues which adorn and dignify human life. The noblest pages of history are those which exhibit the magnanimity of genuine patriotism. As a feeling of the heart, or a principle of duty, this sentiment possesses peculiar power in inspiring man to noble deeds; and as a spring of development to personal character, it must ever rank high among the moral capabilities of man.

(3.) *Philanthropy.*—The expansive feeling which embraces the whole human family in the wide open arms of brotherhood, is a virtue yet more disinterested, and more true to God and man, than even the truest and the warmest patriotism. It is eminently the Christian's virtue, so far as he is true to the teachings and example of Him who came to proclaim "good will to men," and charged his followers with a message of love to "the whole world." The history of genuine Christianity is chiefly the record of those who went forth on this errand, "with their life in their hand," and who were ever cheerfully ready to deposit it in pledge of their devotion to the well-being of "Barbarian, Scythian, bond, or free."

Among the powers which characterize man as a moral being capable of culture, and of advancement in the scale of excellence, no trait of disposition gives larger promise than this; and on none does humanizing culture produce larger effects.

(4.) *Humanity toward Animal Nature.*—As the offspring of Divine love, the human spirit, though its lustre has been dimmed by the breath of sin, yet retains something of the characteristic benignity of its Source; and the range of its benevolent sympathy is not limited to the circle of its fellow beings, but flows forth, if not unnaturally diverted from its channel, to the wider sphere of universal being. In its relation even to the humbler races of the creation, which have been subjected to its dominion, by the appointed gradations in the scale of life, it manifests itself capable of a beneficence for which the designation of "*humanity*" has been suggestively chosen.

The universal law of Love, if obeyed, expands and elevates the soul of man to that moral comprehensiveness of being which ranks him "but little lower than the angels;" and while he is thus permitted to see "all earthly things put under his feet," his crown of royalty is indeed one of "glory and honor," because it invests him with the conscious responsibility of an intelligent and moral sovereign. This true majesty of man is the source at once of his just self-respect, and of some of his noblest regal attributes and virtues, to cherish and confirm which is among the special offices of appropriate human culture.

9. Religious Principle, *as a Moral Power.*—(1.) *Reverence.*—The feeling of which the young mind is conscious, as one of the dawning intimations of the development of its own reflective powers, when contemplating the dignity, the authority, the wisdom, and the benignity of the parental character on which it consciously depends for being and happiness—is although not yet fully or distinctly developed to its own consciousness, one of the profoundest emotions of which it is susceptible; and to the unperverted heart it is one of the strongest cords of sacred obligation by which it is bound to all filial duty.

The emotion thus experienced is naturally transferred, by the mind's law of association to all forms of venerable human worth and dignity. It is called forth by the wisdom of age, by nobility of character in exalted station, and, in degree, by all authority justly exercised. It marks alike, in such circumstances, the deportment of ingenuous youth and of true manliness. Its indications in the intercourse of life are the assurance of that susceptibility by which judicious cultivation, and the inspiration of a genuine faith, are enabled to lift the human soul in reverence to the Father of spirits, and to create a sacred regard for all that Divine truth reveals as duty. Its value as an element in moral cultivation, is beyond expression, great, as regards its influence, whether in securing the respect and obedience due to parents and teachers, to seniority in years, and to eminence in attainments, or in conferring on education itself, its true character as a sacred relation in the business and duties of life, and as a connecting link in the chain which gives unity to man's being in its extension to a higher sphere of mental and spiritual existence.

(2.) *Faith.*—Another element of the highest power in moral relations is the Faith which believes and trusts, and thus unites man to his fellow man, and man to the Author of his being. A great writer has denominated this principle as that "which holds the moral elements of the world together." Without it, man is an isolated, helpless, hopeless outcast, wandering on the shores of being without aim and without direction, ready to be "swallowed up and lost," at the end of his brief career of earthly life.

Faith is the source and spring of all moral life, and, as a capability in the relations of culture, its productive power is comparatively inexhaustible, or limited only by the measure of endeavor. It lifts man above himself, and supplies him with a power beyond his own. It gives the parent and the teacher an influence nearly unbounded. In its highest form, it solves, with light from above, the great Christian paradox, "When I am weak, then am I strong."

(3.) *Conscience.*—The primordial moral element which holds sway over all man's powers and faculties, is Conscience. This great regulator of the springs of action no competent educator can ever permit himself to regard in the merely popular light of a reporter and penal officer, following the acts of which it takes cognizance only after they have been committed, or irretrievably determined. As the sense of duty, it presides over the whole mental being. As an intelligent agent, it partakes in the work of consciousness and reason. It knows and judges. It remembers, indeed, with fearful exactness, the deeds of the past. But it has also the eyes of intuition and of inference for the present, and the power of prospection, prediction, and suggestion for the future. In feeling—unless blunted or extinguished—it is sensitive, to the utmost degree of acuteness; and it pierces to the very "joints and marrow" of the moral organism. Its cautery is terrible in its unsparing intensity. By Creative ordination it is paramount to the will. It prompts, and threatens, and remonstrates, and commands, and forbids, and impels or deters, with absolute authority;—irresponsible to any higher power within the whole domain of humanity, and acknowledging none without, but the one supreme authority of God and duty.

As an intelligent sentiment, and determining principle, it sums up man's moral capacities and powers in their whole extent of life and action. It constitutes him what he is in the sight of God, and in his own consciousness—a responsible moral agent, whose motto, written on his inmost being, is "*Be perfect.*"

Under the prompting influence of conscience, as the law of duty, appointed by the supreme lawgiver, a devout regard to His authority, and a grateful sense of His benignant care, the young mind, enlightened by the teachings of "the wisdom which cometh from above," is betimes elevated to that *piety* toward the Father of all, which raises the personal worth and virtues of the human being, in his aspirations, to the height of sanctity, carries up all questions of moral action to the highest of all tribunals, and breathes into all his endeavors of duty the inspiring breath of a spiritual life and a divine power. Most justly did the fathers of New England require of the teacher of youth that he should regard himself as specially set apart for the "nurturing" of childhood in "piety," as the security for all those virtues which insure the safety of a community and are the adornment of humanity.

10. THE WILL, *as a Moral Power.*—Man's ability to determine the moral course of his actions, to choose the right and avoid the wrong, can never be made clearer to himself by the light of "science falsely so called," than it is in his own inmost convictions. It never is obscured to his consciousness till, wandering from his limited sphere of possible conception, he bedims it by some cloud of metaphysical speculation, and perplexing casuistry—"darkening counsel" by "skeptical doubts" and "words without knowledge." Conscience, the only competent court, adjudges him free, innocent or guilty, commendable or culpable, in every act within the limits of his power, yet—for that very reason, not independent of the authority which pronounces sentence on his actions, and which involves the existence of an authority higher than itself, to which he is strictly responsible, here and hereafter, though at liberty now to follow the bent of his individual will. To the doings of this determining and executive power, which directs and moves the arm, whether it is stretched forth to succor or to kill, attaches, then, a moral character of fearful power; and to influence it for good, and not for evil, to guide it in the path

of rectitude and benevolence, is the appropriate work of education, as the guardian of human welfare.

11. THE PRACTICAL VIRTUES, *as Moral Powers.*—High among these attributes stands *Rectitude*—that power of self-adjustment by which man corresponds to the dictates of conscience, as the sense of right, which keeps him true to his position in the moral universe—true in thought, word, and deed, to the posture in which his Creator placed him when He "made man upright." This principle confers on the human being that noble power of self-poise, which bespeaks his dignity, as a free agent, endowed with the ability, to maintain his moral identity and stability, amid all the fluctuations of circumstance, or the plausible solicitations of evil. It tends to render him sacredly regardful of *truth* in all his communications with his fellow-beings, and of *equity* and *justice* in all his transactions. It stamps his character with *integrity* and *honor*, in every station of power—with *fidelity*, *honesty*, and *punctuality* in the discharge of every obligation of duty. Truthfulness, is, in a word, the one sure and firm foundation of every personal virtue, and the only ground of reliance between man and man. Without the security which it affords, the whole fabric of human society would be but a hollow structure of falsehood and hypocrisy, and life but a degrading scene of deceit, imposition, and intrigue, issuing in universal corruption and misery.

A sacred regard to truth, in all its relations of communication, whether in expression or action, while it is an element so indispensable to the existence of human virtue, in any form, is one which more than most others, is a growth of culture in the soul, and peculiarly needs the genial guardianship of watchful care, mature wisdom, and consummate skill, on the part of the cultivator. The fertile imagination and artistic fancy of childhood, are prone to create a world of unreality around the unconscious spirit, in its immaturity of knowledge and experience; and a guiding mind is ever needed to lead it onward to a distinct perception of the sacred beauty which invests the simplicity and severity of truth, and which renders any conscious violation of it a desecration. The force of truthfulness, as a moral principle, when so directed and matured, is seen in that loyal and devoted adherence to its dictates, which is exhibited in the constancy and genuine heroism of the martyr. In his estimation, it is held dearer than life, no intensity of pain or suffering has the power to wrest it from him.

12. THE HUMANE AND GENTLE VIRTUES, *as Moral Powers.*—Under this designation may be properly included those traits of disposition and character which soften the heart of man to his fellow man—

the *sympathy* which is not a mere passive condition of feeling or organic susceptibility, but a living, active participation in the emotions evinced by our fellow creatures; leading us to *rejoice* in the happiness of others, to *compassionate* them in conditions of want and distress, to *commiserate* sorrow and suffering, in every form—ignorance, error, degradation, vice, and every pressure of evil which afflicts or depresses humanity;—to cherish the catholic spirit of universal *charity*, *tolerance* for the sentiments which differ from our own, uniform *tenderness* toward woman and childhood, *calmness* under irritating treatment, *meekness* under a sense of wrong, *quietness* and *mildness* with the violent, *patience* and *forbearance* with waywardness and opposition and injury, *pity* for the erring, *mercy* for the evil-doer. All these godlike traits of disposition are the features which characterize the peculiar spirit of true Christian culture; none of them the mere fortuitous products of a happy constitution of body or of mind, but all earned by ceaseless watchfulness, and diligent endeavor, and, sometimes, by arduous struggles, and none of them perfected without aid from on high.

13. PERSONAL QUALITIES, *in their Moral Influence: The Self-asserting and Self-sustaining Virtues of the Individual Man.*—(1.) *Self-respect.*—As a being created in the high sphere of intelligent and moral existence, and possessed of an immortal nature, man enjoys, in a just self-respect, a security against degradation by any influence which he feels to be unworthy of the rank assigned him in the universe. Consciously noble in origin and destination, he tends, if not perverted or degraded by habit, to noble action; and if, in the plenitude of Divine favor, he is consciously recovered from a fallen condition, he feels it his immunity, as "a new creature," to have been liberated from a state of bondage—set free for the enjoyment of a "glorious liberty," and impelled to run a new and noble career. Respect for his own nature and personal condition—when kept pure from the senseless interminglings of pride, or haughtiness, or arrogance, of overweening self-esteem, or exclusive self-regard—insures to man the proper dignity of his being, and tends to elevate all his aims and actions. It is an element of high moral power; and the judicious cultivation of its influence is a prominent duty of all whose office, as educators, constitutes them the guardians of humanity.

(2.) *Ambition.*—Feeling the nobility of his nature, man, when not hopelessly degraded, instinctively seeks to act in harmony with his conscious position, and, under the influence of ambition, to aspire after advancement, in every stage and relation of his life. This desire may, it is true, be suffered to center on merely selfish purposes—on the personal aggrandizement of an individual, to the exclusion or depression of others, and to the violation of their rights. In such cases, it sinks to the level of that brutal greed which prompts one of the inferior animals to usurp the better place at the trough, and monopolize its advantages, to the exclusion of the weaker members of the herd.

But the desire of advancement, as that of progress and attainment, is utterly free from all considerations of relative superiority or advantage. It is obedience to an ennobling instinct, pure in its character, and beneficial in its results, not merely to the individual whom it elevates, but to all whom it enables him to aid from the higher sphere of ability to which he has been raised. To the student it is a most powerful incitement to application and exertion; and in the relations of moral attainment, its influence is a salutary inspiration of the highest order. It is not incompatible with the purest spirit of benevolence, in the largeness of the plans on which it delights to work, and the inestimable value of the benefits which it delights to bestow. It urges the Christian aspirant to "press toward the mark," "for the prize of his high calling," and incites him by the promise of a "crown of life."

(3.) *Magnanimity.*—Ambition naturally tends to generate another personal quality of noble character and influence—that magnanimity which lifts man above the littleness that would limit the scope of life, and fritter away its purposes in paltry pursuits, in trivial employments, or low gratifications, in snatching at mean advantages, or mingling in petty strifes. This ennobling virtue incites its possessor to high aims in all his plans and purposes, and to an utter disregard of meanness in motive or action, as manifested by others toward himself. It overlooks malice and injury, or forgives their results. It disdains revenge. It is a sure preventive of that sordid narrowness of soul which induces man to drudge, throughout life, for the mere purpose of accumulating wealth, or to practice the degrading shifts of a niggardly parsimony in expenditure, through fear of diminishing his hoards. A magnanimous spirit scorns the selfish littleness which thus wraps the individual in himself, and shuts the door of his heart against the natural claims of human brotherhood. It gives a generous breadth to measures of usefulness and benevolence, and raises human activity to a higher sphere and ampler scope in all directions.

(4.) *Resolution.*—This attribute, so important in all the practical relations of life, implies the clearness of perception and readiness of judgment in consequence of which the will is empowered instantaneously to decide the course of action. Hence the certainty and the swiftness with which execution follows purpose, the invaluable habit of promptness and dispatch in business, and of punctuality and efficiency in performance, as contrasted with the lagging irresolution, and halting, unavailing endeavor, which invariably issue in failure and disappointment.

The power of energetic and decisive resolve determines, at once, the practical value of an individual, and the reliance which may be placed on him by others. It determines, in fact, the mental health and moral life of the man, the efficacy of his action, and the estimation of his character.

Many constitutions are so formed that even this trait of mental freshness and vigor, so natural to early life, in general, needs diligent cultivation to secure its due development in particular cases. The dreamy indolence, the languid inactivity, the tendency to aimless reverie and absence of mind, which proceed from organic feebleness, wear the same aspect with the profound abstraction of deep and earnest thought, and thus excite, perhaps, in the mind of the parent or the teacher, the expectation of the fruits of close thinking and severe application—an expectation sure to be disappointed. The irresolute youth is prone to sink into habitual vacancy of mind, indecision of purpose, vacillation and feebleness of judgment, sluggishness and utter inefficiency of will.

(5.) *Courage.*—A kindred quality of soul to power and promptness of resolution, is that genuine courage which man, as a self-reliant and independent agent, is naturally called to exert; and which, as a being of conscious energy and power, by his very constitution, is one of the primary instincts of his nature. It enables him to assert his place in the creation, as an agent intrusted with dominion, to a vast extent, over nature and circumstance, and destined to a high position by the exercise of his peculiar endowments. It protects him, at the same time, from any undue ascendency usurped over him by a fellow-man. It prompts him to oppose and resist every encroachment on his rights, and to imperil life itself in defense of his natural liberty of action. It nerves him to encounter danger, to triumph over obstacles, and to master difficulties. It lightens toil, and facilitates attainment.—It gives to the energies of individual mind and will the comparative force of numbers. It enables man to achieve miracles of physical strength and moral power, not merely on the field of conflict, or under the gaze of admiration, but in the solitary grapple with physical obstacles, and the daring, unassisted encounter with the fury of the elements, when the lone adventurer hazards life on some far errand of scientific or humane exploration. In its higher relations, as a moral attribute, it inspires the individual to attack usurping or even approaching evil, in its most formidable shapes, and to encounter fearlessly opposition and opprobrium, and death itself, in the cause of truth and duty.

Courage may, it is true, degenerate into inconsiderate rashness or fool-hardy temerity, and prove itself but a blind animal impulse. It is the office of education to enlighten and elevate it, and render it a ministering spirit of good to humanity, inspiring it with intelligence, and hallowing it with the sanctity of benevolence; so that it may become worthy to fulfill its highest offices, and lead the van in noble endeavor for the advancement of human well being. Its moral power and value then become incalculable; and to cherish it is a peculiar duty of the educator.

(6.) *Fortitude.*—A virtue yet higher than even the noblest form of courage, is that *Firmness* to sustain, to bear, to withstand, to endure, or to resist every pressure of pain and of suffering which inevitable evil may call him to meet and to undergo. Along with this upholding power usually comes the *equanimity* which preserves from extremes of elation or depression, and maintains the moral identity of the individual, the *patience* which soothes and tranquilizes, and coöperating with the enduring firmness of its kindred virtue, contributes to that calm *self-possession* which leaves man master of himself, and equal, in his native greatness and acquired abilities, to resist the assaults of evil, and bear the double pressure of toil and pain with unshaken firmness.

These arduous virtues are, in no sense, innate, or constitutional merely: they are the fruits of diligent and persevering culture—the attainments of the trained and practiced spirit. They owe their power to that self-education which, although it may be wisely anticipated, must ever, in substance, be purchased at the peculiar price of personal experience and strenuous endeavor.

(7.) *Perseverance.*—Another quality of high rank as a moral power, and closely allied to the preceding group, is the persistent firmness of purpose which follows so worthily in the track of dauntless courage, and enables man, with the aid of time, to accomplish, in life-long battles with external nature, those wonders of triumphant human energy which inspire successive generations of the human race with mingled admiration and awe. It is the same trait of persistent resolution that has enabled communities to struggle, for successive years, for a foothold among the family of nations, and to endure, to the verge of extinction, for independence. The same element sustains the explorer of nature, in his years of solitary exposure and unmitigated hardship, through toil, and sickness, and peril. The same sustaining power cheers the secluded student onward through his labyrinths of exhausting investigation, pursued year after year, without aid or sympathy, yet never abandoned till some glorious discovery, duly verified, crowns his devoted loyalty to science. Indefatigable perseverance, in the face of opposition and accumulated difficulty, has been the condition of success in many a noble effort of philanthropy, in its devoted endeavors to alleviate the miseries of suffering humanity, by meliorating its outward conditions, enlightening its mental darkness, or inspiring it with the elements of a new moral and spiritual life.

Without the sustaining power of this attribute, no undertaking of moment has ever succeeded, in the experience of individuals or of communities. Yet it is a quality in which the young mind, in its eager desire of novelty, and its need of alternations of activity, is more deficient than it is in that which prompts to the most arduous attempts or heroic efforts. The vigor which manifests itself in firm adherence to plan or purpose, is usually acquired by degrees, under skillful training. But, when attained, it stamps the seal of certainty on whatever human endeavor is competent to effect.

(8.) *Self-government.*—This invaluable trait of cultivated character implies, in the individual who possesses it, the skill and the mastery acquired in the training schools of conscience, magnanimity, resolution, courage, patience, fortitude, and perseverance. It implies all these qualities turned inward for the control of self. Destitute of self-command, man, when brought to the test, is but as the infant, or the lower animal—the mere victim of passion and impulse. The main moral element of character, is, in such cases, wanting; and the individual sinks in the scale of being, not only in its moral, but its mental relations. The exigencies of life which try men's souls, and demand the perfect action of all their faculties, exhibit the inexpressible value of this trait of mental and moral power, by which man is enabled to call into activity the nobler elements of his being, and, by their authoritative mandate, control and restrain every lower tendency of his nature. He thus reigns in moral sovereignty over himself, and reveals the true majesty of manhood; while, in loyal subordination to Divine law, he manifests, not less impressively, the moral beauty of the spirit of filial obedience.

The power of *self-direction* and *self-guidance*, which that of self-government implies, enables man, as an intellectual agent, to concentrate the activity of his whole mental being, on whatever solicits his thoughtful attention, or tends to promote or enlarge his intelligence. In the moral relations of his being, it secures him against the allurements of evil, the eruptions of passion, the wreck of his peace of mind, or the moral ruin of degrading habits.

Education, in its common forms, it is true, can do little by mere external precautions, admonitions, or promptings, to confer the personal happiness which it is the peculiar office of self-government to bestow. Self-intelligence, self-experience, and self-culture, and the sanctity of religious principle, are, in this relation, the only sure reliance for human virtue. But when thus grounded and rooted, it becomes the firmest security for every trait of excellence.

(9.) *Self-reliance* is the moral reward which man becomes entitled to reap from the conscious power of self-government; and, within such limitation, it is the pledge of many of the distinguishing traits of manly virtue. It may, without the genial guidance of education, become over-weening confidence and presumption. But rightly developed, it is the proper result of faith in the attributes conferred on man's nature by the Source of his being, in virtue of which he is rendered competent for the station and the duties assigned him, as an intelligent, but responsible moral agent. The conscious feebleness which induces infancy and childhood to rely on the power on which they feel they are dependent, is a natural and appropriate influence. But in the history of the moral progress of the human being, there soon succeeds a stage, in which for the highest purposes of life and character, he is weaned from the helpless condition of dependence on others; and self-intelligence and self-respect consciously demand the independence of self-exertion and self-reliance. A manly spirit of just confidence in conscious ability, never inconsistent with the crowning grace of modesty, secures the sincere respect of all who themselves feel the dignity of manhood, whether in its dawn or its maturity. It is an indispensable element in personal character, as the pledge of courageous enterprise, and persevering application, of firmness of purpose, efficient exertion, and final success, in whatever the sense of duty, or a just ambition, prompts the aspirant to attempt.

14. The Self-renouncing Virtues.—The dependent condition of childhood suggests the indispensable relation of habitual *obedience* to parental and guardian authority, and unquestioning *submission* to requirements which the young mind may not always be able to comprehend. The unity of plan and administration, and the perfect *subordination*, which even the imperfect vision of the human eye can distinctly trace in the arrangement of the visible creation, suggest to the reflective mind the universal prevalence of Law, as the prominent feature of Divine government. Order, and system, and gradation, which man sees inscribed on all things around him, and to which he is conscious that his own mind is an analogous agent, he feels to be indispensable in his own sphere of action. He recognizes them as prompters endued with a wisdom and anthority above his own, and as the legitimate directors of his whole course of action. From the habit of early subordination, acquired under the guardian care of education, when rightly conducted in the sphere of home and school life, the self-intelligent mind, in its maturity of Christian growth

learns to recognize the paramount claims of Divine authority to unhesitating obedience and cheerful submission, in the spirit of filial confidence and love, even when patient *resignation* to ordination not understood is the duty of the moment, and the utterance of the trusting spirit to its Author can only be, "not as I will, but as Thou wilt."

In the relations of human intercourse, the *Modesty* which feels what is due to others as exceeding the measure of merit in self, is no less surely an attribute of true nobility in man, than the self-reliance which forbids a feeble dependence on others, or a weak, subservient compliance with their arbitrary wishes. A sincere *respect* for just superiority, indicates the open eye for excellence, as manifested in the attainments and actions of others, and a full recognition of the true worth and genuine merit embodied in their character or conduct. It is the rightful homage of the heart, which ennobles, and never degrades. It restrains presumptuous self-confidence and arrogant assumption, and accepts, in true nobleness of spirit, that lower relative position which conscious immaturity, or inexperience, or limited attainments justly assign. It constitutes the docility of childhood and youth, and not less that of the mature student of science, who loves to sit at the feet of a competent instructor, and treasure up his words of wisdom.

The true dignity of man, as an intelligent and moral being, while it secures his personal independence, and his equality, in the sight of God, with every individual of the race, is by no means inconsistent with that profound respect for man, as the offspring of the Father of spirits, which generates *humility* of spirit and deportment, between man and man, forbids all assumption as usurpation, arrogance as injury, and haughtiness as insult, and yet knows how to meet them with the gentle spirit of Christian meekness. True humility deems no office of kindness too low which can minister to the welfare of a fellow being, whether the beneficent act be gratefully or thoughtlessly received. The perfect model of this virtue exhibited by Him whose spirit was so lowly that he condescended to wash the feet of his followers, was nobly copied in the heroic explorer* who did not disdain to perform the lowest of menial offices for his suffering crew.

The spirit of *condescension* which shuns all parade and formality in intercourse with the young and the dependent, and easily and gently glides into sympathy and due familiarity with all worthy fellow beings—which skillfully breaks down every "middle wall of partition" between man and man, and knows how to "condescend to men of low

* Dr. Kane, in the scenes of his Arctic expedition.

estate," without the display of condescension—does homage to the Maker, in honoring the man, and recognizes the individual's own position as on the common level of membership in the great family which has but one Head and one Master.

In the management of the family and the school, the whole class of virtues on which we are now dwelling, requires particular attention in all communities in which there is a peculiar tendency, owing to the free spirit of their institutions, to place a high nominal value on those traits of character which indicate independence and self-reliance. The unreflective, unreasoning nature of childhood, early catches the spirit of the moral and social atmosphere in which it breathes, and in its natural tendency to exaggeration and excess, carries what might have been a positive excellence to a noxious vice. The absurd and culpable neglect of parental control, so prevalent in our day, often exhibits a spectacle of apparent insanity, in the boys and girls of our families and our schools abandoning the natural and beautiful character of their years, and ridiculously trying to play the part of self-responsible men and women.

15. EXAMPLE, *as a Moral Influence.*—Imitation—the power by which man is enabled to maintain his personal analogy to surrounding conditions of nature, life, and character, and thus to conform to the laws of being, in their requirements—lays him open, in the early stages of life, more particularly, to the influence of example in the actions of his fellow beings. The character of parents, teachers, companions, is, in this way, unconsciously transcribed in the daily life of childhood and youth, and, to a great extent, even in the habitual actions and expressions of maturer years. The law of sympathy, written on the human constitution, in its effects on the imitative tendency natural to man, is a most fruitful source of good or evil in every moral relation and, emphatically calls for the watchful care of the faithful educator.

16. PRUDENCE, *as a Moral Monitor.*—This virtue—if, in obedience to ancient classification, it may be so called—when it springs from just and honorable motives, is a negative but preventive wisdom, somewhat analogous in its conservative effects, to the modesty which reserves itself in communication with others. It is, indeed, but a preventive virtue, yet one which education properly inculcates as a protection against manifold evil to the individual himself as well as to others. It forbids hasty conclusions, rash resolves, injudicious communication, inconsiderate conduct, hazardous undertakings, foolish expenditures of time, strength, health, or other means of useful or beneficent action. It resembles thus the self-control which keeps man in possession of his powers, and enables him to use them at will. Its

moral value, therefore, though negative, is great, and great, obviously, in proportion to the inexperience and unconsciousness of the mind in its earlier stages of progress.

17. PERSONAL HABITS: *their Moral Value.*—(1.) *The observance of Order and Method* in the distribution of time and the succession of occupations, seems to be, in the sphere of daily life, what the regularity of alternation in day and night and the return of the seasons, is to the year. They form a security against a thoughless, random mode of life, destitute of steady aim and purpose, made up of loose scraps of time, unconsciously or idly passed in effecting nothing. Man's dignity and destination imperatively forbid such a life. Morality and religion equally condemn it. But from the multitude and variety of objects soliciting its attention, and of desires craving gratification, the young mind, unaided by education, is prone to lose itself in vague and abortive endeavor at the passing moment, instead of relying on that continuous and systematic industry to which nothing practicable is denied. As the bark of life floats down the ceaseless stream of time, the hand of diligence gathers into it, hour by hour, the rich and ever increasing freight of varied acquisition, in anticipation of another and yet happier voyage, in the great Hereafter.

Activity and energy, in any pursuit, are valuable or successful only as far as they have the continuity and sequence of *system.* It is this logical principle which gives unity and invaluable results to studies pursued under even the most limited opportunities of time, and which enables the student to weave the life of a day or of an hour into the continuous web of the week, the month, and the year.

(2.) *Industry.*—The love of work, and the habit of working—the steady pursuit of a practical purpose in practical forms, is man's first step in the efficiency which elevates him above the lower tribes of animal life, as a being endowed not with the mere sagacity—if it may be so called—of instinct, but with the intelligent forecast which foresees, and fore-ordains, and prepares; and which consciously shapes and sustains a definite purpose, and willingly and skillfully toils for its accomplishment. For the attainment of such results he is qualified by his original, native love of activity; and when this primary impelling power is directed by intelligence and benevolence, it gives efficiency and success to all his endeavors, whether in the toil which wins the treasures of knowledge and learning, in that which accumulates those of wealth, or in that which indefatigably works for human good, in the labors of beneficent philanthropy.

A judicious *apportionment of time and occupation*, however is indispensable to successful and continuous industry. By such a method only can the fatal evils of excessive close application be avoided, and the due alternation of intervals of entire rest and of renovating recreation afford opportunity of restoring and maintaining the energies of life and mind. He who does not bring to his work the powers of a whole man, is incompetent even to the task of the moment, and, in the long run, his exertions prove but a succession of failures. The jaded student or teacher, and the harassed man of business, are alike unfitted for the nobler moral purposes of their being. Habits of early-formed obedience to the Creator's laws which regulate the whole nature of man, are the only sure reliance for the possession of permanent vigor of body and mind, or the soundness of moral health in the dispositions and affections of the heart. Nothing short of this personal morality in planning and conducting the business of life, can secure the unity of life in the whole man, as an intelligent, efficient, responsible moral agent.

The hygiene of man's moral being demands the most faithful attention even to the minor details of corporal well-being; and in no respect can education more effectually subserve man's best interests, than by an enlightened and constant attention to these requisites of mental health, through the whole decisive period of childhood and youth, which so effectually determines the character of subsequent life.

The lengthened catalogue of virtues and of duties, which a distinct enumeration of the moral capabilities, of human nature, as the subject of educational culture, required, will not discourage the faithful teacher, in view of the manifold duties devolving on him as the guardian of the young mind; if, as we hope he does, he regards moral culture as the chief part of his work, and values intellectual attainment in his pupils only as it conduces to the higher ends of being and of character. Nor will the extent of detail in our suggestions be objected to by those who feel, from the daily experience of the teacher's life, how close must be the watchful observation of disposition and habit, and how thoroughly practical must be the meliorating methods of influence, in the management of the school-room as a scene of moral development.

If the preceding outline of classification serve no higher purpose than that of a convenient list for reference to prompt the memory of the teacher, in his endeavors to do some measure of justice to the numerous sources of moral influence on life and character, the purpose of the writer will have been effectually accomplished.

# THOUGHTS ON RELIGION AND PUBLIC SCHOOLS.

BY RT. REV. GEORGE BURGESS, D. D.

---

If the Christian religion be from God, it ought to influence every thought and act of man, and to control every department of human life. If education be the school of character, it is least of all to be excepted from the sovereignty of that religion.

That Christian men, therefore, should view with indifference any attempt to establish an absolute separation between education and religion, is not to be expected from them till they renounce their faith. They can have no more idea that a child can be rightly educated without instruction in the laws of God and in the Gospel, than that a man can live without the same knowledge, and yet duly serve his Maker, and be prepared for the life to come.

Education, therefore, must be religious, and must include instruction in all necessary knowledge of the truths of divine revelation. In proportion as the dignity, the importance, and the efficacy of education are magnified, this necessity becomes but the more impressive and undeniable. If the educator could be content with defining his task as that of teaching to read and to write, or even to measure the earth and to number the stars, it might be allowed that this, like any other specific skill, could be imparted without saying a word concerning duty, or sin, or salvation. But we are accustomed to hear far higher praises of the work and of the men that are to form the youthful mind, and so to shape the character and the destinies of a people. Either undue and exaggerating honor is paid to the office of the teacher, or he must teach the most sacred truths, as well as those of inferior majesty and of only earthly interest.

The honest Christian must bid him take his choice. Be the teacher, he will say, of an art or any number of arts, if you will, and touch not moral things; or be a teacher of all which makes the man, and then you must teach the knowledge of God.

The honest teacher will answer, either that he is a Christian, and is ready, according to his ability, to teach religiously and to teach religion; or that he is content to leave to others the higher task.

and to teach only the elements of secular science and art. In either event, there is no longer any confusion; and the question, whether there shall be a course of secular instruction, and a separate course of religious instruction, or whether one course shall mingle both, becomes a question of possibility or of expediency, and is transferred from the sphere of abstract principle and imperative conscience.

The clergy of most countries have adhered to the wider view of education in schools, and have insisted, as long as they could, that it should be distinctly Christian, and should even form a part of the ecclesiastical system. They are not to be blamed; and had union in religious belief been preserved, it is hard to prove that their plan would not have been altogether the best. But for this it is now too late. In all free nations the freedom of discussion, doubt, and denial has been practically asserted; and, for all purposes of religious education, the body of Christians is *one* no longer.

In education, viewed as a whole, the place to be occupied by religious truth has not lost, for this cause the smallest measure of its importance. Religion is still as sovereign there as ever. Somewhere in all true and sufficient education it must have its throne; and from that throne it must sway all the rest.

But the State can support no such throne; because the State is composed of an immense mass of men whose religion is not the same. When education becomes a matter of public provision, the very highest part of education is excepted. The public school, even if under that name we should embrace any more elevated institutions which the public funds might sustain, is not the seat of that portion of this moral work which has to do, most directly and most mightily, with the heart. That, however, it must forego, and be content with its own appropriate task and praise.

The higher task must be performed elsewhere; and the consecrated precincts of the church, and the equally hallowed walls of home, must be the scene of religious instruction. It has there, too, a fitter and a happier sphere than the State, with all its wealth or its universal care, can attempt to furnish.

All this is perfectly consistent with the undoubted fact that religion is the prompting motive from which public education has had its origin, and must have its best support. It sustains that education as it sustains every good design. It desires that all men should be trained in useful knowledge of every kind, because it desires their improvement and happiness. Ignorance, in its view, is weakness, is poverty, is exposure to moral disease, is the absence of many of the highest enjoyments, is the obstruction of the purposes for which the beneficent Creator made man in His own image. Therefore, ignorance is an enemy to godliness, and a hinderance of salvation, as well as, in itself, a positive and mighty evil; and religion must long and labor to remove it from the path of society. To suppose that a Christian can be indifferent to the intellectual cultivation of his fellow-men would simply imply that he had no appreciation of its value for himself; for he must wish to communicate all which he prizes.

It is perfectly true, also, that even in the teachers of all secular knowledge, religious men will desire and prefer a spirit and principles like their own. A father who merely commits his son to the instructions of a writing-master, would rejoice to find in him a man of Christian worth, and would feel that the boy was somewhat safer. It is not possible, in any department of life, to exclude or neutralize the beneficial influence of the steadfast fear of God and the sincere love of mankind. The religious man or woman will always be, all other things being equal, unspeakably the better teacher, even of arithmetic or of needlework. Under any system of public education, however remote from a sectarian or exclusive character, this preference will be felt, and cannot be changed into indifference.

Under these systems the introduction of religious instruction, in combination with secular instruction, is relinquished, not upon grounds of abstract excellence, but upon those of convenience or necessity. Accordingly, either the system is not extended over the youngest or the oldest of those who are to be educated; or if it be, it does not command a general acceptance. The public school offers no urgent invitation to the child just rising from infancy; it leaves him, not unwillingly, to the gentle hands of his mother or of some maternal preceptress. At the other end of the course, colleges and universities are commonly allied to the Church rather than to the State. From the latter they accept aid; to the former they accord welcome intervention and an active control. Not merely financial or political considerations fix the limits of public education on this side of the highest institutions of learning. For it is felt that all education must begin and end in religion; that the infant must learn the names of God and of the crucified Redeemer with his first accents; and that the young man should not go forth into the world of professional study, action, and influence, without a settled faith. But between these two periods lies the time which public education appropriates; appropriates, simply because the interests of the commonwealth require the instruction of all in useful knowledge, and because no other power can furnish the means of such instruction for all alike.

If the task of religious education be then declined by the public teacher, it is left in hands which certainly are better fitted to execute it with dignity, with diligence, with fidelity, and with tenderness. It is in the hands of special teachers, whose labors are voluntary; of pastors; and of parents.

The Sunday School has become one of the institutions of society, wherever the English tongue is spoken. It enlists a body of teachers whose intelligence is animated by no other impulse than that of Christian love. They receive no hire, and they wield no instruments of discipline. They come to their pupils on they day which is consecrated to all holy works of piety and charity. There is nothing to disturb the pure influence of their instruction; no other studies crowding in; no intermixture of heathen mythology or abstract science; no hurry to the playground; no dread of the rod or superadded task; and none of those hereditary associations, which, absurd, unjust, and pernicious as they are, yet do still, more or less, connect themselves with the relation between the boy and the professional teacher. Love is the bond between those who teach and those who learn on the Sabbath.

When the pastor is the teacher, love is united with reverence. His office inspires that reverence, and his intelligence in sacred things merits a confidence which might elsewhere be less readily bestowed. The duties of pastors to the young may be but imperfectly undertaken, especially where the ancient and most useful custom of catechising has fallen into neglect. But it would still be great injustice to compare their influence with that of teachers who sustain no sanctity of office, have devoted no special study to sacred letters, and are not, in virtue of their office, supposed to be persons of piety.

But no teachers have an appointment more holy or divine than fathers and mothers. The cannot but educate their children religiously or irreligiously. No separation can take place in the training of home; for that is purely for the heart and soul; and its first and supreme end is the goodness of the child. He learns his prayers on the knees of his mother; he is taught to examine himself at the close of each day; his conduct is, without ceasing, subjected to a watchful scrutiny; there is no vacation, no recess, no occasion when he is released from this supervision. These teachers have an authority, too, which, for him, is the direct interpretation of the will of his Maker. To the child, the voice of the parent is the voice of God; for so has God commanded. And all which he hears and learns from these sources comes to him as nourishment from the bosom of an exhaustless love, to which his childhood must cling as if it were to him the whole wide universe.

This is the provision which the Church and the family, with many collateral aids, assign for religious education. Piety in the public teachers, and religious truth in the common school, would be additional aids; but are they indispensable, or could their influence be weighed in the balance against all this? Whatever may be the excellence of many professional instructors, whatever their noble enthusiasm in their calling, it is not to be disputed, that, as a body, the teachers of public schools are governed, in the choice and pursuit of their occupation, by the same motives which incite persons of respectable and worthy characters in all departments of business. They engage in it for a remuneration; they abandon it when it becomes unprofitable; or they exchange it for positions which are more lucrative or more to their taste. They are not appointed, and cannot well be, for their personal devoutness. If they should teach religion, it would be as they teach grammar, not because the task is known to be enthroned in their affections, but because it is made a part of their business. We do not disparage the transcendent beneficence and exalted piety of many teachers; but it is an accident, so to speak, whether these mark the character of an individual teacher; they are not and cannot be the distinguishing properties of a class selected as teachers must always be under any public arrangements. Little will it avail, that a cold, dry, unfeeling, and perhaps unbelieving teacher, consent to teach catechism, or to open his school with prayers. A truly religious teacher, even without those exercises, will leave some impress of his own spirit on the minds which he has assisted in forming and replenishing. This can be attained even now; and if any would avoid this, they must make piety a ground of exclusion from the office. The most determined unbeliever would hardly desire such an issue; but neither can piety be made a condition of admission, if it were even in our power to enforce the rules, since the talents and acquisitions which make the successful teacher are dissociated from it; and since, precious as it is, it cannot, in this position, be deemed one of the chief instruments on which the cause of religion must rely.

What, then, is the power which Christianity *cannot*, and what is that which it *can*, exercise in the system of public schools of a land like our own?

It *cannot* teach all its doctrines and laws, as they are held by any body of Christian believers.

It *cannot* blend religious truth with secular instruction, to any degree which implies the attempt to communicate systematic religious knowledge.

It *cannot* attempt to inculcate a religious character, or, in other words, faith in the Lord Jesus Christ, by precept and exhortation.

It *can* take for granted a general acquaintance, in the pupils, with the facts of Christianity, united with reverence for it as a Divine revelation.

It *can* infuse into the teacher, so far as he obeys it, a spirit which attracts to his religion, and inspires the desire to resemble its faithful followers.

It *can* afford a Christian view of every science and every department of knowledge, and show their connection with revealed truth in its great outlines.

It *can* inculcate the whole moral code of the Gospel, by rule and example.

It *can* exclude and counteract every influence of infidelity.

It *can*, in many instances, with the universal consent of the community, affix a more decidedly religious character to the school duties of each day, by the observance of daily prayers.

It *can*, with the same consent, introduce the Bible, and promote, by daily reading, the familiar knowledge of its contents; not as if it were a mere reading-book, though the best, but as the generally acknowledged word of God.

It *can*, with the same consent, which may generally be assumed, impress, as occasion is offered, all that great and priceless mass of truth in which all Christians are substantially united.

# THE TRUE ORDER OF STUDIES.

BY REV. THOMAS HILL, D.D.,

PRESIDENT OF ANTIOCH COLLEGE, YELLOW SPRINGS, OHIO.

[Reprinted from Barnard's American Journal of Education.]

## CONTENTS.

# THE TRUE ORDER OF STUDIES.

(FIRST ARTICLE.)

BY REV. THOMAS HILL,

Waltham, Mass.

---

We take it for granted that there is a rational order of development in the course of the sciences, and that it ought to be followed in the course of common education. Starting from these assumptions, we seek to find what that order is, and arrive at the conclusion that there are five great studies for the human spirit, — Mathesis, Physics, History, Psychology, and Theology, — which must be pursued in the order in which we have here named them. This circle of five points must be embraced in every scheme of education, whether for the nursery, the subprimary school, the primary school, the grammar school, the high school, or the college. No one of them is to be omitted, in any school, until the student enters the professional school in which he is to prepare directly for the exercise of his profession or calling in life.

We also take it for granted that there is a natural order of development in the human powers, and that studies should be so arranged as to develop the powers in this order. Starting from this assumption, we arrive at the conclusion that the ability to receive impressions, that is, the perceptive power, first shows itself; next, a power to conceive or imagine; thirdly, the power of reasoning; fourthly, the power to decide and act upon the decisions of reason. Moreover, these faculties are called out in their proper order of development by taking the five branches of study in their proper order, — and this harmony of the results of our two lines of inquiry is a presumptive proof of their correctness.

These are the conclusions at which we have arrived, and which we propose to illustrate somewhat at length in the present paper. Their great breadth and generality, and the demand which they make, upon those who accept them, to change the whole character of our education from the hour of the child's birth to the day of his graduation from college, must be our apology for the length of our remarks, and for our request that the reader should not dismiss them from his mind without a candid consideration of their value.

It is manifest that the faculties which are first developed should be first exercised by a judicious training. It is true that, in one sense, all the faculties are developed together, — that glimmerings of reason, and faint indications of a will, are perceived in the youngest infant. Thus, also, in education, the child is to be treated from the beginning as a reasonable and free agent. But the perceptive powers become perfected in their action long before the reason is matured, or the will strongly developed. For the first few years of a child's life its principal occupation is that of learning to recognize material things by their forms. This natural education in geometry begins through the eye at the age of a few days; and, during the whole of childhood, the attention is strongly directed to those characteristics of bodies which appeal to the senses. By the age of fifteen the perceptive powers are frequently in their highest state of development. The powers of imagination are not usually manifested at all until the age of two or three years; never in a distinct form before the age of seven or eight months, and seldom if ever attain their fullest vigor before the age of twenty. The reasoning powers cannot usually be shown to exist entirely distinct from the other faculties until the age of ten or twelve years, and seldom reach their perfection before the age of thirty. The will manifests itself, and comes to maturity no earlier than the power of reasoning.

Hence nature herself indicates that the studies of the child should follow in such succession that his perceptive powers should first be exercised more than any other; that his imaginative powers should next be called into play; and that those studies which require reasoning, and those which treat of his responsibilities, should not be given him at too early an age. A man must first learn facts, then conceive hypotheses, before he can reason of abstract truths, and deduce laws of duty.

It is also self-evident that there must be a natural sequence or order of truths, or, as it has been called, a hierarchy of sciences. In our view of the whole field of knowledge, we see it divided into five great branches; Mathesis, Physics, History, Psychology, and Theology. Theology treats of the uncreated Creator, and of our special relations to Him. Psychology treats of man, who may be called the created creator. History deals with the thoughts and deeds of men; that is with the creations of the created. Physics treat of the material world, that is, of the creations of the uncreated, with the creation in the usual sense of that word. Physics thus bear the same relation to Theology that History does to Psychology, and may hence be called Natural History. Mathesis treats of that field of space and time in which the deeds of History and of Natural History are wrought; that is, if we consider time and space as having objective reality, Mathesis deals with the uncreating uncreated.

Now, all possible objects of human thought are comprised under one or another of these five heads, and these five studies logically precede each other in the order we have here indicated. Mathematics must precede Physics, because conceptions of form, time, and number, necessarily precede any conceptions of material phenomena, which are subject to the laws of form, time, and number. In other words, Mechanics treats of motion in straight lines or in curved orbits, of the transfer of force in various directions subject to the conditions of geometry, of the strength of materials in various forms, and of the adaptation of those forms to the purposes of art; all of which implies geometrical knowledge. Chemistry deals with definite proportions, with the laws of multiples, and of combinations, so that it necessarily requires a knowledge of arithmetic. Botany and zoölogy in their morphology require both geometry and arithmetic; in their physiology, chemistry, and in both departments, mechanics.

As Mathematics thus necessarily precede Physics, so Physics must precede History. All that men do must be done in this world of ours, upon these materials set before us, while subject to the conditions of our material frame. All the thoughts of men must be expressed either by word, by symbol, or by a work of art; — and, of these, even words imply a knowledge of the outward world, for all words were originally figurative. Hence, every historical study must be preceded by the knowledge of a certain amount of physical truth, that is, of Natural History. We might add that while the deeds of men are wrought by physical agents, a great deal of the thought of man has been expended upon physical theories; so that a just appreciation of human thought and action requires a knowledge of that material world which has been the theatre of men's actions, and the object of so many of their thoughts.

Again, Psychology requires a knowledge of Physiology and of History. We know nothing of the human soul save through its actions, interpreted by our own consciousness; — including in its actions its thoughts as uttered in words. Lastly, Theology requires a knowledge of Psychology and of Natural History. For we can know nothing, by nature, concerning the Creator, in whose image we are made, except by first studying his works, and especially that image of Himself which He has placed within us. We may have religion with but little theology, but we cannot have any theology, at all, without some previous knowledge of ourselves, and of the other works of God.

It must be evident, therefore, that the Mathematics logically take the lead as the great and indispensable foundation of all learning. It is not only impossible to dispense with them, but impossible to place them anywhere else than at the beginning of all intellectual education. No man can possibly attain to the knowledge of anything in the world without first attaining some mathematical knowledge or power. That mathematical knowledge may have been gained unconsciously, and may not have arranged itself in a distinct scientific form in his mind; but it must be there, for there cannot possibly be any intellectual life whatever upon our planet which does not begin with a perception of mathematical truth. A natural method of education requires us therefore, to pay our earliest attention to the development of the child's power to grasp the truths of space and time.

Mathesis would naturally divide itself into three great branches, treating of space, of time, and of number. Geometry unfolds the laws of space; algebra those of time; and arithmetic those of number. Other branches of Mathematics are generated by the combination of these three fundamental branches. Now, geometry, arithmetic, and algebra, should be taught in a natural order. There is a difficulty in deciding, simply from the logical sequence, what that order is, because the fundamental ideas of the three studies are so nearly independent of each other. Pure algebra, as the science of time, cannot, however, be evolved without reference to number and space; it will, to say the least, in the very process of its evolution, generate arithmetic. But geometry can be evolved without the slightest reference to time, although not, to any extent, without reference to number. The idea of number is one of the earliest abstractions from our contemplation of the material world.

The relative order in which these studies should be pursued will, however, be made more manifest on reference to the order of development of the child's powers. Number, though an early abstraction from phenomena in space, is a much higher and more difficult conception than conceptions of form. The child recognizes the shape of individual things long before he can count them, and geometry should therefore precede arithmetic in his education. But time is much more difficult of comprehension than space, — it requires a riper effort of the mind to conceive of pure time without events, than of pure space without bodies. The latter remains, so to speak, visible to the mental eye; the former does not even in imagination address any of the senses. Geometry is, therefore, the first study in an intellectual course of education; generating and leading to arithmetic, and through that to algebra; preparing the way also for Physics, and thus for History, Metaphysics, and Theology. We must begin intellectual education with geometry, leading the child through other studies as rapidly and in such order as the amount of his geometrical knowledge justifies and demands. Some knowledge of geometry is gained by an infant within a week of its birth; and when it first comes to school it has usually gained at first hand from nature a sufficient knowledge of the laws of space to serve as a basis for a good deal of other information picked up here and there.

If, now, we consider the order of subdivision in physical study, we shall find here, also, three principal departments of science; mechanical, chemical, and vital. The laws of color, sound, odor, and flavor, may appear at first sight irreducible to either of these three divisions; but a closer examination of the question will show us that this arises simply from an intermingling of psychological relations with the physical phenomena. The three divisions of Physics naturally follow each other as we have named them. Some knowledge of mechanics, that is, of the laws of force and motion, is necessary to any knowledge of chemistry, and some knowledge of chemistry and of mechanics is necessary for any thorough understanding of plants and animals. But it is evident that all knowledge of Natural History must begin with observation; and that one of the uses of the previous knowledge of Mathematics is to teach the child to observe with accuracy. The senses through which we observe material phenomena are, of all the human powers, the earliest to be developed, and should, therefore, be the first to receive a deliberate cultivation. Now, the mechanical relations of bodies, including color and sound, are those most obvious to sense; the chemical are more difficult of discovery, and the effect of vital powers can scarce be perceived without an interpretation from our own consciousness. Thus it is manifest that the order of arrangement in these three departments of Physics is conformed to the order of development of the human powers; and we may add that, in every subdivision of these smaller departments of science, the same principles of classification will give us both a theoretical and practical guide to the natural and most effective mode of teaching them; — we must give first that which is most dependent upon direct perception, and, afterward, that which is more dependent upon an analysis of consciousness; — give first that which is most nearly a simple function of space, and, afterward, that which demands the conception of time or of force.

In attempting to subdivide the great department of History, we shall find difficulties arising from the complexity of the objects of human thought and action, and from the multiplicity of modes in which men have expressed their thoughts and emotions. But we are inclined to make our primary division fourfold. In the first division we should place Agriculture, Trade, and Manufactures; in the second the Fine Arts; in the third Language and the history of thought; in the fourth Education, Politics, and Political Economy. That is, the first division should embrace the history of men's operations on material things to produce a tangible product; the second should treat of men's use of forms, colors, and tones, in the expression of thought; the third, of the expression of thought through words; the fourth, of men's action on each other.

In Psychology we might, perhaps, divide man into intellect, heart, and will, giving rise to intellectual, æsthetic, or moral and religious philosophy.

In Theology we should be obliged to feel cautiously our way by the light of Scripture. A natural division might be to consider the Divine Being as being first the Creator of the world, secondly the Father of all spiritual beings. The first would lead us to what is called, generally, Natural Religion, the second to themes more peculiar to Revealed Religion; the first would treat of the relation of the physical world to its Maker; the second of our own relation to Him.

Thus, out of the five great branches of learning, Mathesis, Physics, History, Metaphysics, and Theology, we have made, as a first essay toward a subdivision, fifteen classes, to wit: Geometry, Arithmetic, Algebra; Mechanics, Chemistry, Biology; Trade, Art, Language, Law; Intellectual Philosophy, Æsthetics, Ethics; Natural Theology, Religion. We believe that all sound education gives, with or without the consciousness of the pupil and the teacher, instruction in all of these fifteen studies; and that there is no period of a child's life in which he ought not to be receiving direct instruction in at least some of the classes of study belonging to each of the five great branches. This instruction should be adapted to the child's age, consisting, at first, principally of those studies which come first upon our list, and of those which are named first under each branch; and giving only prophetic hints and foretastes of the higher parts of the course.

A true system of intellectual education would take the child at the age of five years and give it daily instruction in the simplest facts of geometry and arithmetic. Geometry should be taught at first without reasoning, simply as a matter of perception, either by diagrams, or, still better, by tangrams, bricks, geometrical solids, and simple models for generating curves and curved surfaces. The latter would belong to a period five or seven years later in the child's life, when the imagination is to be exercised as well as perception. Arithmetic should also be first taught by actual concrete numbers; nothing being better than a handful of beans. With these the properties of prime and composite numbers, the commutative principle of the factors in multiplication, and similar arithmetical truths, may be *shown* to very young scholars; and the laws of derivation or differentiation illustrated to older pupils. If there is any soundness in the views which we have given of the hierarchy of science, and of the development of the human powers, such works as Warren Colburn's inimitable First Lessons must not be the first lessons, but must be reserved to the age of twelve or thirteen years.

In the department of Physics, the child of five years should be trained in habits of observation. Every school for young children should have a cabinet of all the minerals common to the neighborhood of the school-house, and of all the most common plants, insects, and other animals, — or, at least, good, well-colored drawings of them, — and the teacher should take frequent walks with the children, requiring them to look for natural objects, and name them according to the lists accompanying the cabinet, until the child can name, at sight, several hundred of the plants and insects of his native town. The attention of the pupil should be directed not only to the form, but to the color, odor, sounds, tastes, roughness, or smoothness, of the various objects. The simple mechanical powers should be illustrated by simple apparatus. Attention should also be directed to the most obvious chemical phenomena, such as the oxidation of metals, the burning of coal, &c. By the age of seven or eight years, geography must be taught; at first wholly from the globe, afterwards from maps and books. It is also important to give the child early ideas of the true nature of the sun, moon, planets, and stars; their size, motions, and relative distances. These Natural Sciences, which are usually reserved for the high school, are, in fact, especially adapted, in their rudiments, for the primary school; and if the main facts were set clearly before the child's mind, at the age of from eight to twelve years, they would enlarge and develop his powers, both of observation and of conception or imagination, and he would be much better fitted to study them logically at the age of sixteen or eighteen.

In the department of History there will be no call for special instruction until the age of seven or eight years. The scholar may then be taught to observe, in the fields and shops of the neighborhood, the modes of cultivation, the machinery and manufactures, the articles of commerce, and the modes of packing and transporting them. He must be encouraged also to draw, and to sing; the drawing being at first the simplest copying of the outlines of leaves, flowers, &c., and the singing being at first simply by rote. Language he will have learned orally from his earliest years, — but at the age of five or six he must be taught to analyze words into their phonetic elements, and a few weeks or months afterward be taught letters as the representatives of these phonetic elements. Spelling, in the ordinary sense, must be strictly avoided for some years, as it has a mischievous effect on the child's whole nature, slight and usually unnoticed, but real and mischievous, as far as it goes. In order to insure good habits of reading let a phonetic alphabet (books in the Cincinnati alphabet are most accessible) be used for at least two years, and let there be a daily drill in phonetic analysis and synthesis of words for four or five years. As for Law, its rudiments will be incidentally taught, sufficiently for so early an age, by the discipline of the school-house, by accidental references to political questions, and by the rules of honor in the games and sports of the playground.

In the fourth great branch of study, the teaching will, at this early age, be also incidental. The child will learn something of its intellectual powers, its tastes, and its obligations, from its attempts at study, at drawing and singing, and at keeping the rules of school. And in the fifth great branch of Theology the child of tender age must have his reverence for the Divine Being deepened, and his conceptions of His attributes enlightened, by being taught to look upon crystals, plants, and animals, as the workmanship of His Wisdom, — the pleasures of home and of the school-room as the gifts of His love, — the actions of even children as pleasing or displeasing to Him in His holy oversight of men.

It would be tedious if we went on to greater length in defining the studies for each succeeding age, as we have defined them for pupils from five to seven years of age. We will, therefore, endeavor to show, in a tabular form, the order of study in each of the particular subdivisions of our five great branches. The left-hand column contains the age of the pupil, beginning with his entrance into the primary school at five, and ending with his graduation from college at twenty-two; the succeeding columns contain the studies. By the term incidental instruction, we signify that oral instruction which circumstances from time to time furnish the teacher an opportunity of giving, or that written teaching which the child will find in all the well chosen books that it reads at home or at school. This tabular view is not proposed as a Procrustean bed, but as a typical plan of studies, which should be somewhat modified by the circumstances and abilities of each student.

## TABULAR VIEW OF THE STUDIES IN LIBERAL EDUCATION FROM ENTERING SCHOOL TO LEAVING COLLEGE.

| | MATHESIS. | | | NATURAL HISTORY. | | | HISTORY. | | | | PSYCHOLOGY. | | | THEOLOGY. | | |
|---|---|---|---|---|---|---|---|---|---|---|---|---|---|---|---|---|
| Age of Pupil. | Geometry. | Arithmetic. | Algebra. | Mechanics. | Chemistry. | Biology. | Trade. | Art. | Language. | Law. | Thought. | Emotion. | Will. | Nature. | Man. | |
| 5—6<br>6—7<br>7—8 | Little bricks, blocks, and geometrical puzzles. | Counting, &c., with beans. | Rhythm | Incidental instruction | Notice | Notice flowers, insects, | Names and uses of tools, furniture, &c. | Sing, Draw on black-board. | Phonetic analysis, Phonetic print. Common print, Spelling. | School, and family rules. | Incidental | Incident- | Incidental | Incidental instruction, | Incidental instruction, | Sub-Primary School. |
| 8—9<br>9—10<br>10—11 | Geometrical Theorems as | Simple rules, i. e. $+-\times\div$ on the slate. | in verse and music. | on the sensible qualities of bodies, and Geog. by the globe alone. | combustion, rust, fermentation, decay, &c. | &c. Name flowers, &c.; also parts of the human body. | Visit farms, shops, factories, &c. | Sing, draw, and perhaps play. | Phonetic short-hand and common long-hand. Keep a short-hand diary. Write simple letters to children. Read and spell. | History of United | instruction. | al instruction. | instruction on the moral laws. | directed to cultivation of reverent views of Creation and Provi- | directed to the cultivation of a conscientious spirit, | Primary School. |
| 11—12<br>12—13<br>13—14 | facts. Theorems demonstrated in | Ciphering. Mental arithmetic. Prove rules of ciphering. | | Elements of Astronomy and Nat. Phil. Geog. by maps. Elements | Begin to call the attention more frequently to chemical changes. | Elements of Botany, Zoölogy, Anatomy, and Physiology. | History of inventions, discoveries, | The drawing begins to embrace landscape, the singing, harmony. | Commit extracts to memory. Begin to read French. Elements of English Grammar. | States. Histories of England and of the Jews. | Incidental instruction. | Cultivation of a good taste. | The same as above. | dence, drawn from Scripture reading and | and drawn from Scriptural readings, and | Grammar School. |

| | | | | | | | | | | | | | | | | |
|---|---|---|---|---|---|---|---|---|---|---|---|---|---|---|---|---|
| 14—15<br>15—16<br>16—17<br>17—18 | Geometry solid, and spherical Trigonometry.<br>Descriptive Geometry. | Use of logarithms.<br>Evolution and Involution. | Simple Algebra. The language of Trigonometry.<br>Higher Algebra. | of Optics, Acoustics, and Thermotics.<br>Physical Geography and Geology.<br>Higher Mechanics, Op- | Elements of Chemistry, Electricity, and Magnetism.<br>Higher | Botany, Physi- | Elements of Agriculture, Commerce, Manu- | Music, including thorough bass, or counter point. | English Grammar.<br>Begin Latin.<br>English Composition and Declamation.<br>Begin Greek.<br>English Versification.<br>Elements of Logic. Continue French and begin German. | History of Greece and Rome.<br>General History.<br>Story on the Constitution. | Elements of Intellectual Philosophy. | Elements of criticism of art, poetry, and eloquence. | Elements of Moral Philosophy. | instances of divine wisdom and power in Nature.<br>Natural Theology and | instances of moral government, &c., in History and daily life.<br>Natural Theology and | High School. |
| 18—19<br>19—20<br>20—21<br>21—22 | Conceptions of higher Curves. | Finite differences and theory of numbers. | Analytic Geometry.<br>Differential Calculus and Integral.<br>Hints on Higher Calculus. | tics, Acoustics, and Astronomy. | course of the same. | ology, Zoölogy, and Anatomy. | factures, as related to Political Economy.<br>Political Economy. | | Continue a more thorough study of the five languages above, especially Greek.<br>Take up Logic, Rhetoric, Writing, Speaking, &c. | Fuller course on Constitutional Law and on History, especially of the nations mentioned above, and on the laws of nations. | Complete and thorough course, including a review of the history of Speculation. | Highest criticism of art, poetry, and eloquence. | Moral Philosophy and religious discipline. | Scriptural views of the Divine Attributes, and Dogmatic Theology. | Scriptural views of the Divine Government, and Dogmatic Theology. | College. |

We of course would attempt, by this table, merely a first sketch of a plan of general study, in which there is no room for detail, and on which a great deal of careful thought must be bestowed before the proportion and arrangement of parts would be practically applicable to actual use. We have introduced it, not for the sake of giving details, but to illustrate more clearly the general principles of that plan of education, which we think is in use in Nature, and is thus given to us to learn, to understand, and to adopt. It will be observed that in each column severe study begins later than in the preceding column, and that the same is true when we take the wider columns, which are separated by double rules. The table also shows how varied and extensive are the studies which we consider necessary for a pupil at every stage of his education. From ten to fifteen different objects are always claiming his attention and taxing his powers. We have willingly brought this point forward prominently, because upon it is founded the only strong objection which we have heard advanced against our views of education, during the ten or twelve years since we first began publicly to present them.

It is said that our course of study is so extended that we should be able to give the pupil only a smattering of each; that the powers of the child would be very imperfectly developed in any one direction; and that we should end in making him a superficial "jack at all trades, master at none." In reply to the proverb, we would retort with the saying of the Stoics, "The wise man is a king and a cobbler." In reply to the charge of encouraging superficiality, we shall be obliged to explain somewhat more at length.

According to the scheme which we have given, it will be seen that, by the age of sixteen, when children usually leave the common school, we propose to give them not only the usual proficiency in Reading and Spelling, Arithmetic, Geography, and Grammar, but also to give them a knowledge of geometry, of the use of logarithms, of the elements of algebra, of the elements of mechanics, optics, &c., of the elements of chemistry, of the plants and animals of their native town, of drawing and singing, of history and of languages. Now, we confess that the attempt to introduce these studies, or half of them, as usually taught, into the common schools, in which the other studies are taught in the usual way, would only result in giving the children a confused and useless smattering of everything, a correct training in nothing. In order to make any valuable improvement in common school education, we must begin at the beginning, and lead the scholars upward by the path of nature. The labor of learning to read must be dispensed with, and by means of phonotype the task of learning to read be reduced to the pleasant sport of a few months. The stultifying process of learning to spell must, if retained at all, be made a diversion by rendering phonetic print so familiar that the ordinary spelling will be remembered for its comicality. The intense labor of arithmetic must be postponed until the child has learned all the principal facts of number, from playing with beans, and the labor will no longer be intense. Geometry must be introduced by blocks and tangrams, and addressed to the imagination before it appeals to the reason. Botany and zoölogy must be begun in the earliest years by pointing out the weeds and insects, and showing the interesting points in each creature. By thus beginning aright the child will find the subsequent path easy. But the child who has already attained the age of fourteen without any knowledge of nature, or geometry, without any training of the senses to exact observation or of the imagination to precise conception, must not expect to find his path easy.

The mode of teaching each study must also be adapted to the design of the whole course. Each study must be begun by presenting its facts to the senses or the imagination, and the order of presentation be determined by the importance and obviousness of the facts. Then the principles of the science must be presented. But the distinguishing mark of teaching on this mode must be its thoroughness and exactness. Let the fact be apprehended with precision. This is the most important aim, lying at the foundation of all education; — teach to *observe accurately*, and to repeat the observation until the precise fact is fixed in the memory. The observation should, if possible, include all the sensible qualities. The second great aim is to produce, in imagination, vivid and definite images of things defined or described in words. The third great aim is to unfold principles in such way as to make them facts to the pupil. When a child observes accurately the principal facts of a science, and remembers them; conceives clearly its hypotheses; and understands thoroughly its leading or fundamental principles; that child has not learned that science superficially. It has taken him but a few months to gain this knowledge, — and the amount of it is small; but the question of superficiality or thoroughness is not a question of quantity, but of quality. Inaccurate observation, imperfect conception, erroneous view of principles, these are the proofs of a superficial knowledge. But the accurate observer, clearly apprehending and understanding what he sees, is thorough as far as he has gone, even from the beginning. And if a proper selection of facts, hypotheses, and principles, be made when beginning a course of instruction, in any study, it requires but a moderate time to impart a valuable general acquaintance with any science;

not a vague recollection of a multitudinous array of particular facts, but a definite conception of the scope and spirit of the science. Ordinary text-books cannot, in general, be depended upon to give such views. They are not prepared with reference to a broad scheme of education, and they comprise in themselves material for the instruction of older as well as younger scholars. Even those text-books which are arranged in series err by making the whole series too diffuse, and lacking in clearness. Of all the multitudinous text-books which, in a long service on a school-committee, we have examined, we have only seen four or five that were of the highest order of excellence; and even of those some of the best are misused, — put in a high school when they belong in a primary, or in a primary when they belong in a high school. The book for the primary school should present facts and rules judiciously selected and carefully expressed, — the book for the high school should present principles; selecting the broadest, most comprehensive principles, and putting them if possible into a form in which they will be directly applicable to use. The highest use, however, of all learning is to fill the pupil with a deeper sense of the power, wisdom, and love of God, to lead him to a more perfect consecration to the service of God; — and what is commonly called practical is only valuable when used in that service. The five great branches of the hierarchy lead to theology, and theology to religion. The will is the highest faculty, and its highest function is to control the spirit to the service of the Highest, to the pursuit of the beautiful, the good, and the true; finding the highest beauty in virtue, the highest goodness in consecration to the service of God's creatures, the highest truth in the knowledge of Him and of our relations to Him.

But to return to superficiality, to which our scheme of education may lead those who but partially adopt it, we say that accuracy in laying the foundations, accuracy in apprehending the principal facts, accuracy in comprehending fundamental principles, is the true measure of thoroughness, and the true preparation for forming an extensive acquaintance with special facts and subordinate principles. Without this thoroughness of foundation the so-called thorough acquaintance of the specialist is of very little value; it amounts only to intellectual lumber. The child's powers are to be developed in due proportion, and he is to be furnished with the most useful knowledge that he can obtain at his age. Neither of these ends is obtained in our ordinary schooling, in which Spelling and Arithmetic, and Statistical Geography occupy the child for four or five years, and he nevertheless leaves school without ever having been led to observe the relation between *p*, *b*, *f*, *v*, *w*, or to note whether *wh* or *hw* comes nearer to the initial sound of such a word as *when;* he leaves school without knowing that every number is either prime or the product of certain primes; without knowing how many great coast lines are arcs of great circles tangent to the polar circles, or having a clear idea what physical fact in nature is represented by those polar circles.

Our remarks have thus far had almost exclusive reference to simply intellectual education. Let it not be supposed that we ignore other branches of instruction. A child is a spirit, whose will manifests itself through a body under the guidance of reason, and at the impulse of passion. Here are, then, four kinds of education which he needs, — an education of the body, an education of the heart, an education of the intellect, and an education of the will. These four departments of culture must proceed together harmoniously, and will do so easily according to our scheme of intellectual education. The body must be cared for, by giving the child abundance of out-door cheerful exercise. At home the parents must also provide suitable food and clothing. The special organs subservient to the mind should receive also the teacher's care. The susceptibility of the senses to external impressions differs by nature, but the differences of this susceptibility are usually marked by the still greater differences produced by culture, in the ability to interpret those impressions. Careless observers of the blind have reported them as having marvellous sensitiveness in the organs of touch and of hearing; but the marvellousness is not in their sensitiveness, but in the accuracy of judgment, acquired by habit, concerning the bearing of faint impression through those senses. The accuracy of our judgment upon sensations may always be improved by a culture similar to that imposed by nature upon those deprived of part of their organs of sensation.

The present paper has been chiefly occupied with a sketch of the true order of studies in intellectual education. The three other parts of a child's training are equally important, and each opens a wide field of investigation and discussion.

Physical education must give the child, as far as hereditary weakness of constitution, or unavoidable accidents of position, allow, a healthy, vigorous, strong body, with quick and accurate senses.

Intellectual education must develop the child's power of thought and give him a clear understanding (as far as it is permitted to our capacity), of his relation to the world, and to his Maker. This education is to be conducted with reference to the order of succession in the great hierarchy of Science, as we have explained at length in the present article.

Moral culture must develop in the child, as far as native gifts will allow, pure tastes, a cheerful and affectionate temper, a loving, confiding heart, a tender conscience. This culture is, in general, to be effected not only by precept but by example, and by treatment; — showing to the child the temper you expect from it in return, and leading it at least to do those things which a good heart would prompt a wise and good man to do.

Religious culture is the development of the will. It begins, therefore, so soon as the child is taught to apply itself either to study or to work. The necessity for labor is the first serious demand upon the will, and develops that power which most nobly manifests itself when the young man, on arriving at mature life, devotes himself with unwavering earnestness to serving God and God's children in that mode in which he judges he can serve them most effectually; forgetting all purely selfish aims, and counting not even his life dear to him if he can finish the work which has been given him to do.

We propose to continue, in future numbers of this Journal, the discussion of these views of education, taking up the five branches of the hierarchy in succession, and showing in what manner the general principles which we have now announced should influence the practical work of the teacher and of the parent, especially in the earlier years of the child's life. We are fully aware that in so large an undertaking there is room for error of opinion; but of the correctness of the first division of the hierarchy into five branches we have no doubt; nor of the propriety of cultivating observation before imagination, and imagination before reasoning. Still less can we doubt that the primary need among educators is the need of firmly-established and wide-reaching principles, such as those which we have here attempted to attain. If any man thinks that we have failed, let him join with us in hoping that we may, at least, stimulate some reader to more successful efforts.

# THE TRUE ORDER OF STUDIES.

(SECOND ARTICLE.)

BY REV. THOMAS HILL,

Waltham, Mass.

---

In our former article we gave a general view of the whole field of education as it presents itself to us. We propose, now, to take it up more in detail, and, in the present article, to treat particularly of early instruction in mathematical studies. But, before we begin the discussion of the special subject, let us briefly recapitulate the general views, which lead us to assign this special study a primary place in education.

A child's will, under the guidance of reason, and at the impulse of passion or feeling, manifests itself through a physical organization. A fourfold education is therefore needed. It is essential that the body should be in good health, and that its powers, both of perception and of action, should be trained to promptness, accuracy, and efficiency. It is necessary that just sentiments and pure emotions should be fostered, evil passions and wrong desires repressed. Nor can we neglect the enlightenment of the reason and the training of the logical powers. Least of all will a true education fail to give energy and purity of purpose to the will.

Now, these four modes of education, — the religious, which directs and strengthens the will, the intellectual, which informs and develops the reason, the moral, which cultivates the taste and restrains the passions, and the physical, which exercises the senses and develops the muscles, — must be carried on together, and not one of them can be neglected with impunity by those intrusted with the education of youth, whether in the nursery, the school, or the college.

Again, there are three sets of intellectual powers, — the perceptive, the conceptive, and the logical. All knowledge rests on a double basis of perception and conception; but perception logically precedes conception. The powers of imagination and reasoning are developed through the exercise given by observation; hence the natural order of education would be, to teach first those sciences most dependent on observation, and lastly those most dependent on consciousness. Now, this order will lead us first to mathematics, the science in which consciousness plays the least important part; for, although our ideas of time come from inward observation, and are thus partly derived from consciousness, the idea of space, which is the more important element in mathematics, is wholly from without. But in no other science is there any idea which is wholly free from dependence upon our own consciousness of power. Geometry is thus shown to be naturally the first study for a child; it is of all studies least dependent on intuitions, and therefore is best adapted for the undeveloped mind. But geometry and the mathematics in general have a higher claim to be the first study of a scholar than their mere adaptation to the weakness of the inexperienced student. They are the necessary prelude to the understanding of other sciences. It must at all events be conceded that a minute and thorough acquaintance with mathematical principles is a necessary part of any successful preparation for the study of physics. Geometry or the calculus is the Ithuriel's spear which is able to make a plausible physical theory assume its true appearance of falsehood and deformity.

But, among the various branches of mathematics, which takes precedence in time? Which comes first in the order of study, — geometry, algebra or arithmetic? Beyond all controversy, we must say geometry. The idea of form is the first of all the ideas, on which any science has been founded, to enter the child's mind. The child learns to recognize innumerable objects by their shapes, many months and usually even several years before it is able to count. What stronger testimony could Nature bear to the propriety of teaching geometry before arithmetic? We may also remark that the history of the race confirms this view of the proper succession of mathematical studies. Geometry had made great advances while yet arithmetic was but partially developed, and algebra had not yet been invented.

A young child, whose attention is easily arrested by mere differences of figure, will usually prove an apter scholar, in geometry, than an older child, whose mind has become partially accustomed to abstract thought, and whose attention is not so readily fixed on differences of simple outline. We have, for the sake of testing this view, given isolated experimental lessons to children of various ages, and to the same child at various periods of his life; and, although we have not kept any such precise record of these experiments as their importance deserved, we have been convinced that they sustained our theory. A boy of fifteen, who has never studied geometry, is not so well prepared to study it as he was at the age of eight or ten. Of course we do not mean that a child under ten years of age is capable of following geometrical demonstrations; — this would be contrary to all our philosophy of the subject. The powers of reasoning required in geometrical demonstration are not developed until four or five years later.

One great cause of the neglect of geometry, in our primary school education, is doubtless to be found in this false view of the study; — that it is simply a logical drill. Even many of the admirers of mathematics, pleading for the use of geometry in education, take this view of the study, that it is a means of developing the power of continuous thought and consecutive reasoning. Thus, also, in Sir William Hamilton's argument against the study, he contents himself with showing that other sciences afford better training for the powers of logical thought.

But the powers of observation and the powers of imagination or conception are as important as those of reasoning; and the great value of geometry for the young child is the stimulus which it gives to the habit of exact observation, and to the power of clear, definite conception. In order to produce this beneficial effect upon a child's mind, it must however be presented in a form adapted to his powers, and to his natural modes of thought. We have found, in our own experience, nothing better, for the first lessons, than the little bricks described by Miss Edgeworth. We do not refer to the blocks of various shapes which may be ordinarily found in the toy-shops. Those described in "Frank" are much better, — rectangular parallelopipeds, whose dimensions are in the ratio 1 : 2 : 4. Those which we have had manufactured and placed for sale with Messrs. Holden & Cutter, Boston, are of birch or maple, two inches long, one inch wide, and half an inch thick. When made with care, exactly in these proportions, and provided with a small percentage of blocks having the same width and depth, but of the length of one inch and of four inches, they furnish the means not only of inexhaustible amusement, but of valuable intellectual development. They should be in the hands of a child from the time he is eighteen months old to the age of ten years. The child must be taught to lay these bricks exactly, breaking joints, binding courses together, and so on, as in real brickwork. The variety of structures, all beautiful and symmetrical, which an ingenious boy of ten years old will make with a hundred of these assorted blocks, would astonish the uninitiated. Square and circular buildings, pyramids, crosses, gateways, columns surmounted by crosses, and natural arches of various forms, may be combined in a variety of modes. For the building of real arches, centerings must be provided, and also a substitute for mortar in the shape of numerous little keystones or wooden wedges, one of which is to be inserted in each joint of the arch before the centering is removed.

It will be apparent that this play cultivates the imagination, as well as the observing powers, and leads, under the guidance of a teacher, to habits of precision in observing and in acting.

The second means of geometrical education is to be found in the Chinese tangram or geometrical puzzle. This consists in giving a child the outlines of a figure, and requiring him to form the figure by placing together a given number of pasteboard triangles. Outlines should at first be given, which may be formed by placing together two or three triangles, and the complexity of the outline may afterwards be increased so as to require as many as seven pieces of pasteboard. These puzzles are adapted for children of the age of from four to twelve years. They cultivate the power of exact observation, and of the rapid analysis or dissection of forms.

When the child is able to analyze figures composed of three or four triangles, which may be at the age of from six to eight years, he will be ready for geometrical truth in an abstract form of words; but great care must be taken that he do not learn to say the words by rote. The great value of geometry, to a child of that age, lies in the power, which it may give him, of building a clear and precise image in his mind of that which he has not actually seen. Care must also be taken not to attempt to make him understand the proof of the proposition which you announce to him; — let him receive it on trust, as food for his imagination, and not attempt to establish it as a datum for reasoning. If the child asks for proof, and the demonstration is fully within the grasp of his mind, it may be well to give it to him; but there are few children under ten years who are capable of understanding the simplest geometrical demonstration. On the other hand, there are primary schools in Waltham in which scores of children, under ten years of age, have been made thoroughly acquainted with the leading truths of the geometry of the triangle and the circle; many also, under the age of twelve, who have obtained a clear knowledge of the relations of the cycloidal curves to their evolutes, and of some of the principal theorems concerning conic sections and the catenary curve. The value of this knowledge to these children will be manifold. It has already afforded to each of them an excellent culture of the power of clear and definite conception; it has enlarged their sphere of thought, and linked the highest mathematical truth with their playthings, — the hoop, the swing, the jumping-rope, and the ball; it has made them partakers in the fruit gathered by the highest spirits of our race. This clearness and precision of observation and of conception will be of use in every occupation of life, and render their testimony and their judgment of more value to themselves and to other men; even the powers of the eye and of the hand will be more likely to receive an accurate self-culture, for use in the mechanic arts, from this imposed culture of the geometrical imagination. And if there be, among the children thus early furnished with the germs of this science, any scholar whose natural gifts peculiarly fit him to advance its progress, or to use to advantage the higher mathematics, there is nothing which could more surely lead him to application than to give him the curious and interesting results which have been attained by the application of others. As the imagination is stimulated to action by the visible forms of nature, so is the reason stimulated to action by the creations of the imagination. The sight of a hanging chain, for example, stimulates the imagination to conceive of the curve line formed by a chain of infinitely small links. This conception arouses the logical powers to inquire into the relations of the parts of such a curve to each other. A boy of ten years old, playing with a chain fence, may be taught, and may, by his muscular power, roughly test the truth of the assertion, that the horizontal tension of a chain is equal to the weight of a piece of chain equal in length to the radius of curvature of the lowest point of the curve; and may easily draw the corollary that no amount of power can draw a flexible thread horizontally, *perfectly*, straight. The marvellousness of this corollary will fix the theorem ineradicably in his remembrance; and, if he be a boy of mathematical power, he will, years afterwards, when he takes up the demonstrations of geometry, wish to know the proof of the proposition. But he will find that simple geometry is not enough. He takes up algebra, and applies it to geometry, but the theorem is still too difficult; he adds the resources of trigonometry, but is no nearer the proof that he desires. He enters college, and learns the marvellous uses of Descartes' coördinates, but this simple problem is beyond the reach of their magic. Finally, his curiosity, aroused so many years before, is gratified when in his senior year he has learned something of Leibnitz and Newton's Calculus, and something of the Analytical Mechanics of Lagrange, and takes up the discussion of the catenary curve. Nor does the student who has early learned such truths come to these studies under the same disadvantages as ordinary scholars. The young men of our colleges, when entering on the study of the higher curves, have a twofold difficulty, that of mastering the conception of the curves, and that of mastering the use of the analytical instrument by which they are investigated. But when the student has already a knowledge of the curve, and an ease in producing geometrical pictures before his fancy, he can bend his whole force upon the mastery of the analytical instrument.

At the same time that the child is expanding his powers of geometrical conception, — that is, from the age of six or eight to that of eleven or twelve, according to his ability, — he should also be gaining simple ideas of numbers. And, in doing this, he should follow the order of nature, and begin with concrete numbers, such as beans, corn, balls, or counters. Beans are, on the whole, the cheapest and cleanest. They should not be employed in a niggardly way. Let the child see heaps of ten, heaps of a hundred, and heaps of a thousand. He should not be accustomed to use the names of numbers in counting, without gaining by sight a just conception of their meaning, which he cannot do from the petty number of balls upon an ordinary abacus. Not that the pupil is to be principally occupied with large numbers. On the contrary, he will find in numbers under thirty occupation for many a series of most interesting and instructive experiments with beans. Give him, for instance, 29 beans, and bid him divide them into any number of equal heaps that he can. When he has found that his task is impossible, take away one bean, and let him find that 28 may be divided either in four sevens or seven fours. Then add two, and let him discover that 30 may be divided into six fives or five sixes; two fifteens or fifteen twos; two groups of three fives, or two groups of five threes; three groups of five twos, or three groups of two fives, and so on. Thus alone can a clear knowledge be given of the actual difference between a prime and a composite number. Nor is this the simplest example. Begin with two beans, — teach the child to recognize it as a couple, as two, in whatever position. Add one, — teach him to recognize it as a triplet, as three, in whatever position. Show him that $2 + 1 = 3$, and $3 - 1 = 2$, $3 - 2 = 1$. Add another bean. Show him it can be divided into two couples. Show him that $3 + 1 = 4$, $2 + 2 = 4$, $4 - 1 = 3$, $4 - 2 = 2$, $2 \times 2 = 4$. Add another bean; it is no longer divisible into equal parts; drill him on recognizing five as a quintette, — as five, in whatever position they are placed, and on the addition and subtraction of its parts. Take up six, — lead him to divide it into three couples, or into two triplets. Explain by the beans the two meanings of dividing six by three, — that is, of either separating it into three equal parts, or of separating it into equal parts each of which consists of three. Show the identity of $3 \times 2$ and $2 \times 3$, each equalling 6. Proceed in this way with all the numbers, and you will find many months pass before the pupil will recognize a dozen as a dozen, at a glance, and before he will unravel the various combinations of groups, similarly constituted, into which 24 beans may be arranged, such, for instance, as two groups, each of three couples of twos.

The teacher of the common school may object that he has no time for such an exercise. He should then make it, by omitting the more difficult and abstract studies to which a pupil of this age is sometimes condemned. The quickness of perception given by the exercise of counting small parcels of beans, under twenty, at a glance, is more valuable to a child of that age than the intellectual discipline of mental arithmetic. In nearly every school of New England a disproportionate amount of time is given to arithmetic. The science is taught backward, beginning with reasoning instead of with observation, and is hampered also with factitious difficulties produced by a variety of unessential names and processes.

When, by means of the beans, the idea of numbers has been made familiar as well as their names, the pupil should take up written arithmetic; this may, perhaps, be at the age of eight or ten. The decimal notation is to be taught, and by means of a thousand or so of beans rendered intelligible and impressive. For decimal fractions, which should be taught (as in Pliny E. Chase's treatise) at the commencement of exercises on the slate, break up two or three dry beans into small pieces, from which select ten that are nearly one tenth each, and also some of the finer powder, which may represent hundredths. When the pupil thus perceives that the decimal scale is capable of representing the infinitesimal as well as the infinite, let him also be made familiar with the fact that the unit is in general an arbitrary standard, and that the same quantity of beans may, by removing the decimal point, be represented as so many tens, or hundreds, tenths, or hundredths.

After the pupil has made himself complete master of the four fundamental rules (including long division, in decimals), and of the principal characteristics of prime and composite numbers, let him take up mental arithmetic, and be kept at it until he is complete master of Warren Colburn's first lessons. This may not, however, be accomplished before he has, at the same time, made himself a proficient in all the ordinary operations of arithmetic. In the choice of a treatise upon this science, we have given a decided preference to Pliny E. Chase's over all others, because of its simplicity, and because of the immense number of its examples, — which two qualities render the learner expert in figures in a much shorter time than is usually given to this study. The whole subject is usually introduced to the child's mind too early, and he is kept at it to too late a period in his education.

By the time that the pupil has mastered his ordinary arithmetic he will be ready to return to geometry, and take a simple course of instruction in geometrical demonstrations, and in the application of geometry to practical use. The great master of antiquity has left in his "Elements" a model of the reasoning art, but it is not in a form best calculated for young minds. The process of analysis naturally precedes synthesis, and must necessarily precede it in the mind of one who would demonstrate a new proposition; hence, a text-book ought to give more examples of analysis than of synthesis. Moreover, the object of a geometrical demonstration is not simply to prove the theorem demonstrated, but also to impart to the pupil the power of demonstration; for which reason a text-book ought to be interspersed abundantly with undemonstrated propositions and unsolved problems, as is the case in works on arithmetic and algebra. If no such text-book is readily accessible, the teacher should select, from books not in the scholar's hands, theorems allied to those which the scholar is studying, and propose their solution as an exercise for the class.

When the pupil has made some progress in geometrical demonstrations, say at the age of thirteen to fifteen, he should be taught the use of logarithms. Only a few weeks' practice will be required to give him ease and rapidity in the use of this "wonderful rule," this marvellous "new instrument" of the seventeenth century. Logarithmic tables, while in all the more difficult calculations of astronomy, geology, and civil engineering, they are an indispensable aid, are very seldom resorted to in other cases where arithmetical results are required. Yet, as there is nothing whatever difficult in their practical application, and a facility in using them once acquired is not easily lost, there seems no reason why they should not be found in every counting-room, and used as occasion requires.

The scholar should also at this age begin to acquaint himself with algebra. With the mathematical preparation which we have now recommended, the ordinary processes of algebra will present few difficulties; and in one or two years the scholar will find the solution of equations of the first and second degree, and approximation to higher roots, by means of derivatives, a familiar and easy task.

A short and simple course of trigonometry, and a very elementary course of perspective, and of descriptive geometry in general, will finish a high-school course of mathematics.

The college course will vary according as the system of instruction embraces or omits voluntary studies. Our whole scheme of instruction, as exhibited in the tabular view (pp. 188–9 of this Journal), is based upon the idea that every human being needs education in the five branches of the hierarchy, and in each of the great divisions of that branch. The amount of study in each branch will depend in part upon the capacity of the scholar. We have endeavored to lay down a scheme extended enough to satisfy all except rare instances of extraordinary talent, and yet simple enough to be within reach of a fair proportion of our children. From our observation of the public schools of our own town, we should say that twelve or fifteen per cent. of the children in New England can, without any over-exertion, go through all that we have here laid down.

In the tabular view given in our former article, we have placed the rhythm of verse and music among the early incidental studies of algebra. The connection between algebra and the science of time is not so obvious as that between geometry and the science of space, and this is not the place to introduce any discussion of the reality of the connection. But it is the opinion of some of the highest mathematical authorities of our day, that even the idea of number involves obscurely the idea of time as well as of space; and that the laws of algebra are primarily the laws of progression in time, — that they are rather illustrated than fulfilled by geometrical forms. If this be so, the cultivation of an ear for rhythm, the custom of beating time to music, and of attending to the balancing of musical phrases, will facilitate the subsequent conception of equations and of their transformations, as surely as the attention to forms, and the attempt to draw outlines, will facilitate the subsequent study of geometry. It may be objected to this statement, that the best draughtsmen are sometimes notoriously deficient in mathematical power — the best musicians notoriously ignorant of algebra. It must be conceded that space and time seem capable of being approached and handled from entirely opposite points of view, and that art and science flow, as it were, from opposite poles of the mental battery. But we are persuaded that there is not a real antagonism between them, and that the apparent conflict comes merely from the limited capacity of the human mind, in which close attention to one mode of viewing an object usually excludes all other modes. In souls of a larger growth there is found to be no incompatibility, and Art and Science are helpers of each other; Geometry and Optics justifying and sustaining Sculpture and Painting, and they in turn giving new interest and delight to those sciences; while Music and Poetry hold a similar, although more obscure, relation to Algebra.

We have treated of the mathematics, in the present article, as though they were isolated subjects; but the remarks which we have made concerning their relation to art warn us that we must never forget the intimate blending of all themes of thought into one great universe of truth. The five branches of the hierarchy are all indispensable, and are all so interwoven that one is well taught only as it is perceived to lie in harmonious connection with the others. For this reason the teacher of mathematics should be prepared, during the whole of the course of instruction, to point out to the pupil the bonds that link his subject with the physical world, with the laws of astronomy, chemistry, botany, and zoölogy; with the history of man, of his speculation, and of his action, with mechanical inventions, with art and with commerce; with the nature of man, capable of apprehending the mathematical thoughts that have guided the Creator of the world in the formation of all things; with the nature of that Being who has made all contained in space, or evolved in time, and subjected them to laws which are a source of such instructive and delightful investigation for his children to pursue, and which, in the forms and appearances they produce, awaken also such manifold sources of pleasure in the beauty and harmony of His works.

The principal views which we have endeavored to present in this article may be summed up in three sentences: that geometry should precede arithmetic in the training of a child's mathematical powers,—that in each of these two studies concrete forms should precede abstract language, observation and conception precede reasoning,—and that the cultivation of the power of definite conception by geometry is as truly valuable as the cultivation of the logical power. We cannot agree with the opinion that arithmetic is of more practical utility than geometry; yet, if we were of that opinion, we should still teach our children geometry first, arithmetic afterwards. For a change of occupation is a rest, and the boy, who begins with geometry and reserves arithmetic to a later period, develops his powers in a more natural order, achieves his task with less fatigue, and, at the age of fifteen, not only knows more of other things, but more of arithmetic also, than he could have known, had his taste for numerical computations been destroyed by a premature, and too continuous application to that science.

In our next article we propose to consider the proper mode of introducing the young to Natural History.

# THE TRUE ORDER OF STUDIES.

(THIRD ARTICLE.)

BY REV. THOMAS HILL,

Waltham, Mass.

---

To the second great division in the hierarchy of science we have given the name of Natural History. The word Physics might also have been used, but, in either case, the meaning of the term is to be so far extended as to include all the studies of the material world in its natural state. Inasmuch as matter is formed and governed in subjection to the laws of space and time, this study of the material world logically demands a previous knowledge of mathematics; and no natural phenomenon is understood until the geometrical or algebraical law, suggested and exemplified by it, has been, at least partially, comprehended. In proportion as the scholar's knowledge of mathematics is enlarged, his power of comprehending the physical universe is increased. And, inasmuch as a knowledge of geometry is the earliest mathematical acquirement, those parts of natural history which depend upon the perception of forms may be earlier acquired than those which depend on mechanical, chemical, or physiological considerations.

Thus, although the fundamental principle of our classification places mechanics before chemistry, and chemistry before biology, our fundamental principles of education allow, and require, some instruction in botany and zoology before any is given in chemistry or mechanics.

A perfect knowledge of animals requires a knowledge of the vegetable world, which is their food; a perfect knowledge of plants requires a knowledge of their chemical constituents, and of their chemical relation to the soil and to the air; a perfect knowledge of chemistry requires a knowledge of mechanical forces. Thus, in the hierarchy, mechanics is the first department of Natural History. But we must, of course, be understood as now giving to the word mechanics a much wider signification than usual. We are including the consideration of all those phenomena of nature that arise from mechanical laws, that is, from forces whose prime effects have been shown to depend on motion. A discussion of the boundary between mechanics and chemistry, showing, for example, why we place color under mechanics, and taste under chemistry, although interesting in a metaphysical view, and necessary for a clear understanding of the philosophy of our subject, will not be required in a purely practical consideration of the course of studies, such as we are now engaged upon.

There have lately been published several treatises on the philosophy of common things, some of which, although crowded with errors and puerilities, have a very extensive circulation. Others, free from these faults, are defective from their not containing the most fruitful facts and principles of mechanics. It is not surprising that text-books on these subjects should be grossly deficient, when we recollect that in geometry and arithmetic, the oldest and simplest sciences, it has been very difficult to find perfectly unexceptionable treatises, and still more difficult to find teachers who will use the best books in the best manner. We trust that, through the increasing attention now given to education, and especially through the influence of normal schools, recognizing teaching as a distinct and high profession, we may hereafter have better text-books upon all subjects, and also teachers capable of teaching in the best way, even if the manuals for instruction should be imperfect. In all departments of Natural History the best text-books are the objects themselves of which you would teach.

The earliest instruction of a child in the direct principles of mechanics should begin, we think, at the age of seven or eight years, and at first be incidental, that is, founded on the occurrences of the moment. In his use of little bricks for building, for example, he will have practical lessons, from which the teacher may deduce and render clear to the pupil some of the principal properties of the centre of gravity, and of the states of stable and unstable equilibrium. In playing with marbles and balls, opportunities occur for showing distinctly to a child the law of the composition of forces, the accelerating effect of a constantly acting force, the increase of momentum by the increase of velocity, and the like. The laws of elasticity also, and of the reflection of motion, may be exemplified in the rebounding of balls, the return of echoes, and the use of mirrors. Of course, it will be worse than useless to give to the child simply stereotyped phrases, or vague and indistinct ideas, such as are too often found in popular text-books; but, if the teacher has himself clear ideas on these subjects, he will find the child eight or ten years old ready to receive them. Even the principal laws of optics, of acoustics and thermotics, may be thus incidentally taught. The optical toys, which are in almost every household, musical instruments, burning-glasses, and the phenomena of dew, rain, frost, and snow, will give the needed opportunities. Only let the caution be continually borne in mind that it is much better to confess to a child your own ignorance of a subject, than to attempt to give an answer to his questions while your own views are ill-defined and unsatisfactory.

One of the earliest studies, commencing, perhaps, at the age of seven years, should be geography. Let it be taught, at first, by the aid of a globe, without reference to maps. The immense magnitude of the earth will be apprehended by the child only when, in later years, he has travelled distances that have an appreciable ratio to the earth's circumference. At first he must be content with understanding accurately its form and motions. In describing these, the teacher should be careful to use the globe only as an illustration, not as though it were the thing of which he is speaking, else the child will never transfer his conceptions from the globe to the earth. In the course of thirteen years' service upon a school committee we have never found a teacher who gave to the scholars a clear conception of the physical boundaries between the five zones, and but few who even attempted it. The differences of climate and the number of degrees of extent are taught, but the child does not know what appearances of the heavenly bodies decide the position of the tropics and polar circles. Nor do we find that scholars in general gain any clear conception of the actual direction of places. Their views, being derived from maps, are necessarily erroneous. From one of the Holbrook Co.'s globes a child can readily be made to see that a straight line from one point on the globe to another, would always go through a portion of the earth, so that to point directly towards any distant place he must always point more or less downward.

The following extract from the instructions of the school committee in Waltham to the teachers of the sub-primary schools will serve as an example of the mode of teaching geography: "Begin with the globe; set it where the sun may shine upon it; bring Waltham to the top, and make the north pole point to the north. Lay a marble on the top of the globe, and show them that the light and shadow on the marble and on the globe are similarly situated. Explain the roundness of the earth; that it is only a bigger globe, under the little globe, as that is under the marble; and that the light and shade fall on it as they do on the globe and marble, making night in the shadow, day in the sunshine. Give them vivid conceptions of the size of the earth, by showing them how small upon the globe would be the landscape visible from Prospect Hill; how near to the point which represents Waltham would be the point representing the distant Monadnoc. Show them in what countries the sun is then rising, and in what setting, and where it is vertical, by simple reference to the light and shadow on the globe; and, after an hour's attention to other studies or amusements, return to the globe, and show them how the light has travelled round. Show them, according to the season of the year, whether the north or south pole remains in light or shadow all the day. Repeat this lesson at all seasons of the year, but especially do not forget it at the equinoxes and solstices. Explain how reflection from the globe diminishes the intensity of the shadow on the marble, and the reflection from the window-seat partially enlightens the under side of the globe, while there is no window-seat under the earth to reflect light upon China and New Holland. Make the amount of reflection from the window-seat more apparent to them by covering it alternately with a black veil and a white handkerchief. In like manner, although the globe will, after sunset, be in the shadow of the earth, there is no larger body below the earth to cast a shadow on our antipodes.

"Take your children occasionally to walk; go on the hills; show them how the presence of a brook or river can be foretold from the extent of the valley, the nature of the soil, and the kind of vegetations, whether forests or grass; show them the roundness of the earth from the increasing dip of the horizon, as you ascend; make them perceive how beautiful the illusion by which we always exaggerate vertical heights and under-estimate horizontal distances; call their attention to the differences in soils, and in the rocks, and point out the effects of soil and of location upon vegetation."

The earliest lessons in astronomy may be given at a very tender age. As by the globe in the sunshine the best illustration of day and night can be given, so the idea of the moon and her motions is best communicated by procuring a ball a little over one quarter the diameter of the globe, and holding it about one hundred and ten times its own diameter from the globe. If now the moon is visible when the sun is shining, let the pupil lay the side of his head upon the globe, while the teacher holds the ball at the proper distance, in such a position that, to the child, it shall appear to be just over the moon. The sunshine upon the ball will appear to him to be of the same size and shape as the visible part of the moon. The endeavor in astronomy, as in geography, should be to lead the child's mind away from the illustration to the thing illustrated. For this reason it will be with difficulty that the school-teacher can go in astronomy to any advantage beyond the relations of the sun, earth, and moon. In order to give clear conceptions concerning the planets, stars, and nebulæ, the teacher must meet the pupils in the evening, when those bodies are visible. But it is of so much importance that the child should have early a distinct conception of the relations of the solar system that few teachers would be unwilling to perform this extra labor. Astronomy and geography are to be used as the most powerful of all studies to develop the imagination; that is, the ability to conceive clearly and distinctly unseen phenomena.

Chemical relations are more abstruse than mechanical. It requires some maturity of mind in order to distinguish chemical compounds from mechanical mixtures; and yet, at the age of nine or ten years, the simplest phenomena of chemical change begin to excite the child's curiosity; and it will be greatly to his advantage if that curiosity is gratified with correct explanations and sound principles, instead of being lulled by a plausible pretence of explanation. Oxidation, especially in the forms of combustion and rust, is the most prominent instance of chemical metamorphosis, and will afford to the skilful teacher the opportunity of giving, in what we have called an incidental way, many of the fundamental principles of chemical affinity, atomic proportion, atomic combinations, the stability or instability of chemical equilibrium, and so on. We acknowledge that this implies a large amount of intellectual life in the teacher; but one who is intrusted with the direction of these earliest movements of the expanding mind should be a person not only of some acquirements, but of some intellectual vivacity. Nothing more surely characterizes a skilful teacher than the ability to seize upon the right moment and the right occasion for illustrating the principles which he wishes to impart. One perpetual danger, it must not be forgotten, attends these essays to give the first instruction to a child — the danger of extinguishing its natural thirst for knowledge. This may be done by diverting the attention to other themes, by discouraging or disgusting the mind with difficulties, or by communicating knowledge in such a way as to puff up the child with the conceit that he now understands the whole science of which you have given him some of the simplest rudiments. The art of giving instruction may be compared to that of letter-writing, of which it is humorously said that the great secret is to make the recipient "wish there was more of it."

Inasmuch as botany, while it depends in its physiology upon chemistry, classifies plants solely by texture and form, a knowledge of the common weeds and flowers, trees, mosses and lichens, of the neighborhood, may be given to a child as soon as it is old enough to distinguish them. In the tabular view there is an accidental error, making the incidental instruction in biology commence at a later period than we should advise. From the day that the child enters the sub-primary

15

school we would have it receive oral instruction, illustrated by living plants, if possible, or by dried specimens, or even by drawings, in systematic botany. At first the child may simply be taught to recognize the plants as individuals; so that he may be able to say, "This is a twig of sugar-maple, and this a sprig of white-birch; here is a bird-foot violet, and there a dandelion." But the plants must be recognized out of doors, as well as in the house, that the child may early learn to notice and enjoy the differences of form and color in the general appearance of the growing tree or plant.

In the first volume of Agassiz' Contributions to the Natural History of the United States, he shows that of the six divisions of animals (branches, classes, orders, families, genera, and species), the family is characterized by a resemblance of general form. There is, doubtless, a close analogy in the principles of classification that must be adopted in botany, to those which Agassiz develops for zoölogy. As a general rule, the plants which belong to one family are recognized by a general resemblance of form in the flower, fruit, and seed; while, to distinguish a genus, attention must be paid to detail; and, in the formation of a class, attention must be paid to organization. Hence the family, both in botany and zoölogy, is the most apparent of the higher groups in classification, and the best adapted, by its obvious dependence upon form, to be the starting-point for a child's comparisons. It is not to be brought, as an exception to this remark, that some of the great families contain tribes bearing no obvious resemblance to each other, but rather should this analogy to zoölogy be taken as an evidence of the necessity for elevating some of the sub-families in botany to the rank of families.

The second step, therefore, in botanical instruction should be to add to the name of the plant the name of its family, and a perception of the family likeness; so that the child can say, "This is a hazel; it belongs to the oak family, and shows its likeness to the oak in its catkins of staminate flowers, and in the involucre surrounding the nut; this is an alder, which belongs to the birch family, and shows its relation by having both its pistillate and staminate flowers in scaly catkins, having two or three blossoms under each scale." Of course, the teacher must remember the caution which we uttered, in speaking of chemistry, and not allow the child to think that a few words, such as those here given, can embody all the points of resemblance which characterize a family. Much less should the child be permitted to learn any truth of this kind by rote. Verbal memory has an important place in a true scheme of education, as we shall endeavor to show in our next article. But the very object of introducing geometry, botany, and zoölogy, into our course of studies is defeated, when the pupil is required to commit the words of the text-book, or formulas given by the teacher, to memory. Yet, so accustomed are some teachers to this mode of instruction, so incapable, apparently, of conceiving of any better plan, that we have known a teacher require her pupils to repeat the words of Dr. Gray's "How Plants Grow;" evidently thinking that she was thus using, while she was abusing, that excellent little book.

The book just named may be taken up, as the third step in botanical study, at the age of ten or twelve years. If deferred to a later period the study becomes distasteful, as the habit of observation becomes weaker from the distraction of the mind by other cares. It is easy to give to the child, during the ten years between five and fifteen, a perfect familiarity with three or four hundred species of common plants, such as he meets in every walk. This labor spread over so long a series of years would be by no means onerous; and the names and facts impressed upon the mind in that tender period will never be forgotten. If it be objected that there is no text-book prepared for the use of children too young to use "How Plants Grow," we reply that the plants themselves should be the text-book. The only artificial help in teaching botany to children in the sub-primary school, which, we think, would prove really valuable, would be a series of thirty or forty charts, each containing the illustrations of some one important family, — magnified drawings of the peculiarities in the organs of fructification characterizing each family, — with, perhaps, a drawing of a few of the common species.

Zoölogy is not forced upon the child's attention so frequently as botany in the natural world. Yet, from the motion, and still more from the intelligence, of animals, they are even more interesting to the child than plants. Moreover, although physiology demands a knowledge of chemistry, yet the classification of animals, like that of plants, depends principally upon organic structure, and upon the relation of the creatures to the outward world. The child of five years old is, therefore, interested to notice the difference between animals, and to learn their names. In a country school-house, in the month of May or June, it may be that the songs of thirty or forty different species of birds are heard in the course of a single day. It would be no waste of time, but, on the contrary, a thing of inestimable value, should the teacher enable his pupils to distinguish these birds by their song, learn their appearance and habits, and the families into which they are grouped. The fear is sometimes expressed, by our poets, lest a scientific acquaintance with flowers should destroy their beauty; and lest the song of the bird might have less melody when the songster had been burdened with a barbarous Latin name; but among our acquaintance we have not found these fears realized. On the contrary, a thorough scientific acquaintance with the beautiful objects of nature only increases the pleasure which we take in beholding them. The syntactical parsing and metrical analysis of an ode will not injure our appreciation of its melody and its sentiment, provided the composition has true lyric merit. The beautiful in nature will bear the closest criticism, and the longest investigation, without ever "palling upon the sense." "Nature," says the Concord seer, "never became a toy to a wise spirit." The wisdom and beauty, embodied in each organic work of nature, is "not only vast, but infinite," so that there is no possibility of exhausting it.

The insects in any given country are, at least, as numerous as its plants. The mysteries of insect transformation, the wonderful mechanical instincts that many of them display, the brilliancy of the colors of some, and the pertinacity with which others thrust themselves upon our notice, render insects peculiarly fitted to engage the child's attention, and to serve as a basis for incidental instruction in zoölogy. In this class of animals the orders are more conspicuously distinguished than the families; and it will, perhaps, be best to content one's self, at first, with teaching the child to refer insects to their orders. Insects are so easily preserved in their natural appearance, that we should suppose each school might have a small collection of the most common species to be seen in the neighborhood, grouped in their orders and families, to serve as a reference for any insects which the child might catch and bring in. We are aware of the vastness of the field of zoölogy, and of the impossibility of a child learning to recognize more than a very small proportion of the insects of his neighborhood. Yet, on account of this very magnitude, we would say, let his attention be early directed to this field; so that, if it should prove to be one in which he is peculiarly fitted to labor, he may have the advantage of an early beginning. We would also repeat the caution to be exact in the ideas which are given to the pupil. The main object in these first scientific lessons must be to induce the spirit of exact, patient observation; calling the child's attention to differences as carefully as to likenesses, and to the fact that the likeness in one part does not necessarily imply a likeness in other parts. The foliage of two trees may be almost identical, while the flowers and fruit are exceedingly diverse. While this spirit of patient and exact observation is cultivated, general principles, already discovered by the inductive philosophy, and firmly established, may incidentally be placed before the mind of the pupil, a clear guide to his sense and reason.

Comparative anatomy will thus be naturally begun at an early period. The homology of the parts in vertebrate animals with those of the child's own body will naturally be the subject of continual lessons, and the difference between these or the organs of insects and crustaceans must also be pointed out. Human anatomy and physiology have been introduced into many of the schools of New England during the last fifteen years with very great zeal; they would be much more effective, more interesting, and more valuable, if they were preceded by the lessons concerning which we have now given these brief hints. It is against the course of nature to call the child's attention too early to the functions of its own body. A better result, intellectually and morally, might be attained if the teachers and parents took care of the diet and exercise of the child, his clothing, and the temperature and ventilation of the rooms in which he sleeps and studies, until at least the age of thirteen to fifteen years. The mind would then have been prepared by previous studies for understanding the subject intellectually, while the greater development of the observing powers would prevent the danger of premature and excessive habits of mental introversion. The study of our own bodies approaches nearer to psychology, forming a natural introduction to it, and should, therefore, come last in the studies of Natural History. The study of anatomy and physiology naturally and inevitably leads the child to a psychological investigation into the facts of consciousness involved in the exercise of many of the functions of his own frame. In the tabular view (vol. VI. p. 188) the words Anatomy and Physiology ought to extend into the first years of the high school.

The importance of beginning botany and zoölogy in the very earliest years of school life, as we intended to have placed them in our tabular view, cannot be fully estimated without taking into consideration also their connection with the other branches of education. The habit of constant, attentive observation, surely learned in no other way than through early practice in these sciences, is of immense value in every walk of practical or speculative life. The habits of animals, and the manifestation of their various gifts of instinct and intelligence, are the best stimulants and aids to psychological research, as we intend hereafter to show. So, also, in theology, there is nothing more certainly adapted, in a scheme of intellectual education, to foster reverential views of the being and providence of God, than to observe the lilies of the field how they grow, and to consider how He openeth his hand and satisfieth the desire of every living thing. But this consideration will be brought again into notice when we approach the fifth division of our hierarchy.

In their relation to the mathematical and to the artistic culture of the child botany and zoölogy have also a peculiar value. Leaves and flowers, and insects, are admirable objects, from which the child may make his first attempt at drawing, — and the forms of organic life constitute the most beautiful of the unsolved problems which are now presented to the geometers of our race. The pressed leaves and mounted insects, kept in the school-room as types and standards for botanical and zoölogical reference, may also be used as drawing-patterns of the highest excellence. The insects could not be safely removed from the glass case in which they should be kept; but the pressed leaves, as being more easily replaced, if injured, might be taken to the child's desk, or to the blackboard. Nor is it unworthy of notice that the exercise of recognizing birds by their notes is of great value in the cultivation of a quick and exact musical ear.

Finally, among the prominent advantages of this early introduction of the studies of Natural History, must be placed the fact that it accords with the child's tastes, as well as with the natural order of intellectual development. All children are pleased with crystals, plants, flowers, insects, birds, and beasts, and are interested in intellectual and spiritual truths only when dressed in living figures. By following, therefore, the example of Nature, and speaking in parables to those who cannot understand the truth in other forms, we not only adopt the most successful mode of conveying the truth, but one of the most efficacious of all modes to afford the child the means of present and future happiness.

Of the course of instruction above the primary schools we need not particularly speak, since the general principles are easily applied to the whole course. We should simply say, that, in proportion as the pupil's mind enlarges, the course of physics should deal more with general laws, and less with the details by which those laws are established. This is, of course, on the supposition that the education is designed for the general purposes of liberal culture. Physics and Natural History have been unjustly neglected in many plans of education; but it would, by no means, restore the course of study to a right balance, if, after introducing these sciences in their proper place in the earlier years of school life, we should afterwards allow them to expand and fill the years of the collegiate term, when the student ought to be more fully employed in political, psychological, and theological inquiries. In the grammar and high school, after a proper preparation in the younger grades, we can readily give as much of the mechanical sciences as it is profitable to teach to those who have no special aptitude for the studies. With the preparation now given in the primary and sub-primary schools, this is impossible; and a part of the collegiate course is of necessity occupied in giving instruction in the physical sciences better adapted to children than to youth. The preparation of such excellent text-books as Guyot's Earth and Man, and of Agassiz' and Gould's Zoölogy, is thus rendered a thankless work; these books which are adapted for the widest usefulness, are, by the insufficient preparation of the younger scholars, confined to a few of the more advanced high schools and academies. Changes in the system of public education are usually made with difficulty, and it is, doubtless, well that it is so; since otherwise our schools would suffer, even more than at present, from the eccentricities and errors of those who have control over them. At present the legal guardians of the school, the teachers, the scholars, and the parents, constitute four classes, who resist any change whether for better or for worse. In the changes which we are, in these papers, advocating, the difficulty will be still greater, from the fact that the proposed alterations imply an alteration from the very beginning of the educational course; and our views concerning the high school are perfectly impracticable, unless the children in the high school have been from infancy accustomed to exact observation, rapid and accurate conception, and familiarity with the results of cautious and sound inductive reasoning. So far from this being the case in the ordinary schools, that we may more truly say the child is taught to neglect observation, to abstract his mind from things to books, to repeat words without clear conceptions, to adopt the results of hasty and unsound speculations. If the reader think this language too strong, let him reflect that into not one school in a thousand are crystals, minerals, plants, insects, &c., brought for examination; — let him remember that among the teachers not one in twenty even knows the difference between a moss and a lichen, a bug and a beetle, a moth and a butterfly, and not one in fifty but would reprove a child for bringing such things into the school-room; — let him recall the fact that, in spelling, the child is systematically taught to deny the truth of his own sense of hearing; so that, by the age of fifteen, nine-tenths of our children have begun to hear, in the spelling and in the pronunciation of words, sounds that do not exist, and not to hear sounds that are distinct; — let him remember that in the majority of schools drawing is not taught, and, when taught, it is usually drawing from a copy, so that it feebly exercises the observing powers, or it is inventive drawing, which does not develop the observing powers at all; — let him remember how much time is given to arithmetic, not to counting beans, arranging them in groups, &c.; but to abstract arithmetic, which, even in its so-called practical examples, usually excites the conception only of the names of number, or of the appearance of the Arabic notation; to arithmetic, which was introduced into primary schools only after a long struggle against the tyranny of grammar, and has now become a King Stork more intolerable than the King Log; — let him remember that geography is the only science of observation in our schools, and that geography is often a mere getting of words by rote, and even at best, in the primary schools, only occupied with the observation of maps, instead of the observation of things; — let him remember all this, and he will, at least, see how poorly the primary and sub-primary schools prepare the child for any scientific studies in the grammar and high school.

For this reason, in all these papers, we occupy ourselves more especially in indicating what we conceive to be the true mode and time of beginning each study, and pass by the studies of the high school and college; not that we take less interest in the studies of the more advanced student, but because we are convinced of the absolute necessity of beginning well, if we would produce the highest educational effect. Each day's mental state depends, in part, upon the previous education; and we cannot say how early this process of education begins to influence the mental development. For our part, however, we have long held, what we find to have been the opinion of Comenius (Amer. Journ. of Ed., vol. v., p. 281), that education begins before birth, and is received through the mental and physical condition of the mother.

# THE TRUE ORDER OF STUDIES.

(FOURTH ARTICLE.)

BY REV. THOMAS HILL,

Waltham, Mass.

Our third great division of human science includes all that is historical, the record of man's doings and sayings; and we have indicated, in our tabular view, a rough subdivision of this group of sciences into four smaller groups. The first of these smaller groups treats of man's use of nature as commodity; that is, for purposes of agriculture, manufacture, or commerce. The second embraces the fine arts; the third, language,—the use of speech or writing to express thought. The fourth treats of social life, custom, and law. The reasons for this subdivision, and for the order in which the groups are arranged, will be evident on a moment's thought. The use of the world for our bodily needs is first in the order of time and of simplicity; and the earliest knowledge that a child has of the works of man, as distinguished from the works of nature, consists in knowing that man puts nature to use. It is true, however, that this precedence in knowledge is more logical than chronological, since only a few months pass over a child's head before it uses dolls and pictures as naturally as food and clothing; showing how early the artistic use of nature is begun.

The invention and use of language must certainly be subsequent to the use of material things; and the ability to communicate ideas by language must precede any attempt at social law or order.

Without historical knowledge, a child would grow up a barbarian. The chief distinction of an educated man, or of a civilized nation, consists in a knowledge of the wisdom gained through the experience of previous generations. A child is, however, usually suffered to learn the history of manufactures, commerce, and agriculture, without distinct instruction. Books of trade and books of commerce for children's use have never enjoyed a wide popularity, although recommended by many of the best writers on education. The great obstacle to the teaching of any historical branch consists in the multiplicity of details which it involves. General principles are with difficulty applied to bring the numerous facts connected with agriculture, manufactures, and commerce, into a form adapted for the instruction of children. Much must be done incidentally, and education in this respect will therefore depend upon the family as much as upon the school. A very young child will be interested and benefited by being taught the simplest processes of planting and sowing, and of tending the growing plants. If in the city, it may be necessary to do this by description; if in the country, it should of course be done experimentally. Every one of the articles in household use should furnish lessons concerning the mode in which the raw material is rendered subservient to man's needs. The whole processes of grinding and bolting wheat; of fermenting and baking bread; of planting, tending, gathering, cleaning, carding, spinning, weaving, bleaching, dyeing or printing cotton; of tending sheep; of shearing and cleansing wool; of spinning, dyeing, and weaving yarn into the various kinds of carpeting; of tanning leather, and making boots and shoes; of the manufacture of glass; of digging and smelting ores, and working metals, — in short, of producing from the raw materials any of those articles of manufacture which the child daily sees and handles,— will furnish subjects for valuable and interesting lessons. If the parent or the school-teacher is ignorant concerning them, the requisite information may readily be obtained from books like the Penny Encyclopedia, or smaller volumes prepared expressly for the young. Undoubtedly the best mode of instructing a child, concerning any of the operations in the useful arts, is to allow him to see the process going on; and, whenever it is practicable, this course should be adopted. It is not, however, always agreeable to a manufacturer to be interrupted by visitors, and in some places it would be dangerous to allow children to pass among machinery arranged with a view to work, and not to show. But advantage should be taken of those places where work can be seen without interruption to the workmen, and especially of industrial exhibitions and mechanics' fairs.

Beside the enlargement of mind, the extension of the circle of ideas, the increase of his power of conception, which a child may gain from the examination of agricultural tools and labor-saving machinery, he will be likely to choose his occupation in life more intelligently, and with a more just reference to his own powers. The attraction which plays so large a part in the theory of the socialists cannot have fair play, and bring a child into his appropriate sphere of labor, if this opportunity is not furnished of determining towards what sphere he is most strongly drawn. A history of inventions, books containing the first rudiments of agriculture, books somewhat like Babbage's Economy of Manufactures, but treating also of carpentry and ship-building, and one on commerce, ought to make part of the child's reading. No reading-books with which we are acquainted give a complete view of these subjects, in a form adapted for school use; but we have found Miss Edgeworth's "Harry and Lucy" answer tolerably well.

The moment that man's bodily needs are satisfied he expresses his feelings in art. Music and dancing, sculpture and painting, are as natural as eating and drinking. The child of a year old makes anything into a doll, and recognizes in the rudest picture the designed resemblance. At three years old it is frequently able to sing; occasionally much earlier than that. Nature thus bids us begin early the instruction of the child in these departments. A slate and pencil should be among the first playthings put into the child's hands. Holbrook's Outlines, or similar simple copies for imitation, may be among the earliest lessons; but it is of the greatest importance that the child should at once begin also to draw from natural objects. A fresh green leaf, or a simple flower, may be drawn by a very young child, as easily from the living specimen as from a printed wood-cut, and will stimulate his powers of observation and conception to vastly higher activity; giving him thereby not only more pleasure, but a much greater increase of power. The inventive drawing taught by Professor Whittaker will be of much greater advantage to the pupil if it be preceded by an accurate copying from nature. Drawing from nature leads to accuracy and closeness of observation, and to correctness of conception, which are of the greatest use in drawing from imagination. But inventive drawing, when not preceded by the practice of copying natural objects, would conduce very feebly towards the attaining of either the habit of accurate observation, or of graceful and beautiful creations. The two modes of drawing are complementary to each other; and the inventive drawing, or creation of ideal forms, is certainly the highest. But, on that very account, because it is the highest, it should come latest; and the practice of many school-teachers of introducing it first is subversive of natural order.

The real order of procedure in art is more universally observed in music, in which airs are learned by imitation, and the child is never required to extemporize melodies. Singing has been introduced very extensively into public schools, and the instruction almost invariably is begun by simply teaching the children to sing melodies by ear. In schools of a higher grade they are taught to read the ordinary musical notation, and are initiated into the mysteries of transposition, which involves a slight knowledge of thorough bass. We think that in high schools and colleges the knowledge of music might be extended further into the rules of composition, both as regards harmony and musical form, and that the pupil should be required to compose melodies, and harmonize them. They would be worthless to others· but the attempt to write them would greatly increase the scholar's enjoyment of music.

The most extensive and important group of the historical sciences is included under the name of languages. Logically this follows the study of labor and of art; we must know things before we can talk about them; and, logically, language precedes law; we must communicate our ideas before we can enforce them. But, practically, the study of language begins at the hour of birth; and when the child enters school he already talks fluently. The first point of instruction in school will naturally be to teach him to read and write the language which he has learned to speak. And, since we are talking of those who use alphabetic writing, the first step in this process naturally should be to teach the child to analyze his spoken words into their phonetic elements. This ought indeed to have been done at home; nothing will so surely and so rapidly teach a child the correct enunciation of words, as teaching it, in its earliest efforts at speech, to enunciate, as an infantile amusement, the separate elements of spoken language. But, as this is not usually done at home, it devolves upon the teacher, as the first labor when the child enters school. As the pupil learns to distinguish the elements of speech, and to form them distinctly, separate from words, he should be taught the alphabetic signs which represent them; not giving them the names by which they are commonly designated, but, at first, teaching them as the symbols of the sounds. For instance, the word *aitch* should not be taught to the child until he is perfectly familiar with the fact that the character *h* signifies a roughness of breathing, while the mouth is in the position for sounding any vowel. Unfortunately, our English alphabet contains but twenty-six letters, three of which, *c*, *q*, and *x*, are superfluous; leaving only twenty-three symbols by which to represent forty or more sounds. Moreover, in our ordinary spelling, we are not content with being thus obliged to represent at least seventeen sounds by symbols already appropriated to some other sound; we also represent a single sound by many different symbols, and our language, instead of being alphabetic, is, in the ordinary orthography, logographic. A child cannot, therefore, be taught to read ordinary English printing in any natural and easy way. A tough constitution resists a great deal of hardship and abuse; and a vigorous intellect frequently survives the labor of learning to spell in the ordinary mode. A man who has lived through a course of bad diet, and inattention to the laws of health, is apt to regard attention to such matters as a mark of effeminacy; and, in like manner, those whose love of literature has not been absolutely quenched, and whose power to see truth has not been wholly blinded, by the ordinary mode of learning to read, suppose that there is no urgent need for improvements; but whoever will reflect upon the absurdities of English orthography, and upon the gravity with which those absurdities are usually introduced to the child as reasonable things, must perceive that such instruction has an injurious effect upon the child's mental powers, and upon his love of truth. The child may survive it, as he survived the compression of swathing-bands, drenching with herb teas, and drugging with cordials; nay, the injurious effect may, in the case of a very vigorous mind, be infinitesimal; but it is always pernicious, and, in the case of persons of small intellectual ability, disastrous.

The attempt to change the printed forms of the English language, for the ordinary purposes of books and newspapers, may be impracticable; and it may not even be desirable that such attempts should succeed; but the use of phonetic books for the purpose of teaching children to read, is both practicable and in the highest degree useful. So soon as the child has learned to read fluently in phonotype, it may take up common print, and read it easily from the general resemblance of the words on one page to those on the other; as has been proved experimentally in thousands of cases. The child thus taught to read common print, has its orthography more firmly fixed in his memory, because he perceives more clearly its oddities and anomalies. Bad spelling usually arises from an attempt to spell phonetically with the common alphabet; but this would be less likely to be done by one who had been accustomed to associate the idea of phonetic value only with a different alphabet. The use of a phonotype, for teaching a child to read, has also the advantage of giving unceasing instruction in accuracy of enunciation, and no other method has been so successful in removing from a school provincialisms and vulgarities of pronunciation. For fixing the orthography of words in the memory, no practice is more useful than that of writing from dictation; but this means, of course, cannot be applied at a very early age. If we had phonotype in common use, it would be well to have the child taught to write at the same time that he is taught to read; but, with our present "heterotypy" (as it has been facetiously called), we must be content to begin writing at the time of transition from phonotypy, when the progress in reading will of course be much more rapid than in writing.

The approach to ordinary orthography, through phonetic type, leads very naturally to etymological considerations, which will be of interest and value to a child several years before he is ready for questions of syntax. Words themselves must be understood before they can be intelligently classified. When a word is introduced to the child, in its orthographic dress, and he laughs, as well he may, at the oddity of its costume, we may tell him of its gradual growth into its present form, and show him how the silent, or the mispronounced, letters in it are the record of its ancient pronunciation, or of its derivation, or of an early error in its supposed derivation. This will lead us to explain to the pupil the conventional element in language; that usage is the right and rule of speaking; and then we may go further back, and show how much is really natural in the origin of language, and how the meaning of words sometimes sprang from an imitation of sounds, from the musical expression of speech, and from instinctive attempts at expression through the position of the organs of speech. A child of six years old will recognize the nasal element in the *meaning* of such words as snail, snake, snap, snare, snarl, sneak, sneer, sneeze, snicker, sniff, snipe, snivel, snooze, snore, snort, snout, snub, snuff, snuffle, and see how easily the word nose can be introduced into the definition of each. Then it will be interested to know that the Latins also called the nose *nasus*.

The forms, even, of the individual letters may be made the occasion of pleasant lessons in the origin of written language,— the probable development of Shemitic alphabets from phonetic hieroglyphics, and of the European alphabets from those of Phœnicia. If such instructions do not awaken a scholarly turn of mind, and lead to literary taste, they will at least relieve the dryness of the spelling-book, and give the child some glimpse of the numerous and subtle ties which bind us with all the generations which have preceded us.

The use of language is to be acquired at first by imitation. The study of books on grammar and composition does not belong to the early years of life, and it is a complete inversion of the natural method to give a child abstract themes for composition before he is old enough to think on such themes of his own accord. In the like manner, it is not in the true course of nature to teach a child to declaim before he can comprehend the pieces selected for declamation. The most instructive reading for a person of any age is that whose tone of thought is above his average thought, and yet not beyond his grasp; and the best exercise for a child, in learning to think and to express his thought, is to commit to memory such poetry or prose as is worth being treasured up forever in remembrance, but which is not entirely above his comprehension. Let him also, with the book before him, extemporaneously, turn good verse into good prose, and repeat the process so frequently as to be able to do it without hesitation. Before the child can write well he can dictate a narrative of some real event in his own experience; and, as soon as he can write, he should be accustomed to writing, at first narrative, afterward gradually coming to more abstract forms of composition, but always upon subjects with which he is familiar.

When foreign tongues are taught,—and every liberally educated person should at least have a sufficient acquaintance with them to develop his philological tastes, if he have any,—the method of nature, it seems to us, requires a blending of several modes of study. The pronunciation should be a matter of first importance; the student deciding, in the case of a dead language, on some fixed principles, and, in the case of a living language, getting as nearly as possible to actual present usage of the best speakers. Next comes the translating, and finally the grammar. The interval of time between these is not of importance; but it is of importance, in the study of any language, to read more than the small portion which you may daily analyze critically with grammar and dictionary. Let neither mode of study be neglected; a portion in one book being thoroughly studied each day; while, in some other book, several pages are rapidly and imperfectly read. The words and constructions of most frequent occurrence will thus become familiar by repetition, and to the discipline of the exact critical study of sentences will be added that appreciation of the general spirit of a language which can be attained only from a more rapid and extensive reading of its best writers. Thus, in music, also, the best culture is gained when the pupil is daily drilled to extreme accuracy in the practice of select pieces, and also daily exercised in reading at sight several pages of new music In the order of nature the child hears language and music long before it has the power to analyze and study them; and, in the order of study, it is better to have reading precede, in some degree at least, a critical and thorough study.

When translating from a foreign tongue into our own, there are two extremes in method, both of which are admirable, while the mean between them is worthless. In the study of a language you have two objects in view,—one to learn that language, and the other to gain from the study a strength and facility in the use of your own. Now, in learning the foreign tongue, one cannot translate too literally, keeping to the order and construction of the original; while, for the purpose of culture in the use of the vernacular, and indeed for understanding, in the earlier stages of study, the real thoughts of the author, one cannot be too careful to translate into the most appropriate and idiomatic English. We would, therefore, habitually accustom the student to a double rendering, first literally, then idiomatically; and in the literal rendering allow even etymological fidelity to the prefixes and parts of a compound word. Thus the proverb, *Unkraut vergeht nicht*, may have the double rendering, *An un-plant thoroughly-goes not;* that is, Weeds never die out. The habit of literal rendering may be dropped as soon as the student has acquired the power of reading and understanding the foreign language without a mental transposition into the vernacular idiom; but the habit of correct rendering into easy and idiomatic English must be cultivated carefully as long as the study of the language is pursued; — the first is for a temporary use; the second for a permanent possession. Next to the ability to act well must be placed the ability to speak well,— and indeed, so interwoven are the functions of the human being, that the ability to express thought increases the ability to think, and the power to think increases the power to act. The common opinion, that the development of one power is at the expense of another, arises from the fact that the developed power is usually one that was by natural gift predominant; and the power that has dwindled, at first naturally feeble, has not had sufficient exercise to keep it of its original strength.

The brief limits to which we are compelled to compress these papers force us to give them a fragmentary character, and to leave each branch of the subject but partially developed; hoping that the connection and unity of the parts will be apparent to the reader who carries in his mind the general principles announced in our first article; and that such readers may find here hints that shall lead them, in the course of their own thoughts, to new confirmations of the general truth and utility of these views, and to new applications of them to special points in education.

The fourth general group of studies, included in our great division of history, we have designated in our tabular view by the word law. Man is not content with thinking and expressing his thoughts, with subduing outward nature to his needs, and making it subservient to his purposes; he also seeks to govern his fellow-men. The child is born subject to his parents, and the family government has always been a type, perhaps suggesting and leading to the government of tribes and nations. At all events, there are no men to be found without some traces of government, and, in all civilized countries, there has been developed the idea of impersonal law, in the organization of a community whose associated wisdom shall decide upon what is right, and what is for the best interests of the whole; whose associated power shall enforce the right and develop the good, as far as the limits of its ability extend. The historical study of these relations of men to each other is necessary, not only to a full development of the student's mental powers, but as a preparation by which he is fitted for an intelligent participation in the rights and duties of those relations.

The method of nature is here evident, that the child is born into the family, and learns, by subjection to his parents, the duty of subjection to all just authority, before he can understand the ground on which the authority rests. He is brought under the order and discipline of the family, before he can rise to the comprehension of that vast scheme of universal order, planned by Infinite Wisdom, in obedience to the impulses of Unfathomable Love, and carried into execution by Almighty Power,—that Universal Order after which all wise legislation strives, according to which all just judicial decisions are framed, and which all righteous executive power seeks to embody.

So, in the school, the first and most important ideas of law come not from histories and constitutions, nor from political orations, read or studied by the child, but from the wise and just discipline of the school-room, from the rules of play observed in the games among his school-fellows, and from the perception that the parents and the teachers are also subject, even in school matters, to the laws of the commonwealth and to the votes of the town. The judicious teacher, by occasional words, rightly directing the child's attention for a moment to such themes, gives what we have called incidental instruction in politics and law. The next step, in this branch of study, is history in the ordinary sense of the word. Afterwards, in the higher school or college, the pupil should take a brief course of study in constitutional law, commentaries on the constitution of his own state, of the United States, and of Great Britain, comparing them with those of Greece and Rome, and of the Hebrew Commonwealth.

It was our original purpose, in commencing these papers, to have continued them so as to embrace remarks on psychological and theological studies; but, as circumstances have compelled us to defer the remaining papers to an indefinite period, we will append here some general cautions to the reader, which we had proposed to leave to the end. A recent very friendly criticism on our views shows a misapprehension of them, by saying that we have placed the studies of the encyclopedia in a right line, instead of in a circle, and that we have provided only for the education of the knowing faculties, without providing for the education of the powers of expression and action, and of the feelings and sentiments.

Let the teacher, who is really desirous of knowing the true plan of education, remember that the body and its organs need training and care for their preservation and full development; that the sentiments and passions need to be judiciously called into play, and guided in their direction; that, above all, promptness and efficiency of action, and perseverance of purpose, are to be cultivated with great care, under a consecration to the love of God, and charity to men. In our scheme of studies we are showing what we consider the natural order of intellectual growth, and the following of this order will simply give the best opportunities for the other kinds of education. Thus intellectually we place the cultivation of the powers of observation first in the scale, preceding that of the inventive and of the reasoning powers. This intellectual order of nature gives the opportunity, in physical education, of keeping the young child out of doors, rambling, under the guidance of its teacher, by the roadside, or over the pastures, to the benefit of its body as much as of its mind. The same intellectual order gives, in moral education, the opportunity for developing pure tastes, the love of natural beauty, and affording social pleasures of a higher character than in the ordinary plays of the school-yard. It gives also the best opportunity for impressing the young heart with the infinite wisdom and love manifested in the creation; and the freedom of the walk allows the opportunity for the child to manifest its own choice and will in showing kindness to its playmates according to the command of the Heavenly Father. In like manner, the whole arrangement of the intellectual problems placed before the human spirit would be found, if we understood it in its natural order, to be adapted for the appropriate furtherance, at the proper age, of each part of physical, moral, and religious education.

The complaint which has been made, that an intellectual education is of no moral benefit, but rather a moral injury, so far as it is well grounded, is grounded as much upon the fact that our intellectual drilling has been inverted in its order, crippling rather than cultivating the powers of observation, as upon the fact that the attention given to intellectual education has withdrawn the attention from moral training. This idea appears to have been one of the moving springs in the heart of the late lamented Josiah Holbrook. In like manner, the injury done to the bodily health of children, by overstudy, comes as much from the unnatural inversion of studies, the giving of that which is abstract before that which is concrete, as from the absolute amount of time spent by the children in close attention to the subjects set before them. Whatever be the amount of knowledge acquired in a given time, the ease of its acquisition will, evidently, be partly proportional to the lucidness and naturalness of the order in which it was acquired. The purely intellectual question of the true order of studies is, therefore, intimately connected, in more than one mode, with the question of moral and physical training, with the whole question of the highest welfare of the individual and of the family, the state, and the church.

Nor, in either physical, intellectual, moral or religious education, should we forget the artistic side; — that is to say, we must remember that skill in expression or action is as desirable as simple power. A man not only needs power, but needs it under control, else it loses its worth. Of how little avail would physical strength and health be to a man who could neither walk well nor swim well, who was at ease neither on the rower's seat nor in the saddle, who could neither drive nor skate, who could neither mow nor dig, but who, in all manly sports and in all useful labors, found himself strong indeed, but clumsy, and inefficient for lack of skill. In like manner, he would feel humbled and awkward indeed, who was conscious of great thoughts, and of deep emotions, and of a strong purpose to do right, and was nevertheless unable to express himself either by spoken or written words, by chisel or pencil, or by musical tones, or by well-planned and well-timed deeds.

While all studies must be used as means of developing and guiding some power of action and expression, as well as of understanding, it is perhaps the especial function of the historic studies, of trade, art, language and law, to cultivate the powers of expression; and the teacher must remember to apply them in such manner as to produce this end. As the bread of the mind is truth, so the bread of the moral nature is action, or expression, and the pupil must be drawn out into expression, not made the mere recipient of instruction.

To pass to the other point in which we would caution the reader against a misapprehension of our views, it does not follow, because we have arranged the five branches of the hierarchy in a certain logical order, with Mathematics at one end and Theology at the other, that this order is to be followed in arranging successive years of school life. It would better apply to the minutes. The order is that of logical development, that in which the subjects are to be successively unfolded to their fullest extent; but it would be absurd to postpone physical teaching entirely until a full knowledge of mathematics had been obtained, and so of any other branches. We may perhaps compare the course of education to the phyllotactic spiral on a two-fifths arrangement. The mathematics are the row of leaves on which the zero leaf is to be taken, and you cannot rise to a higher point in your mathematics, except by running round through the other four rows. For the full, harmonious development of the child's mind we need a perpetual recurrence to the five essential branches of inquiry suggested by every sight of nature. The youngest child in the school brings in, perhaps, a dandelion. What is its form, and the number of its rays? These questions belong to mathematics. What is its color, taste and smell, its medicinal effects, its relations to the sunflower and other composite plants?—these are questions of physics. The derivation of its name, dandelion,—dents de lion, dens leonis,—from the form of the leaf, and of the generic name, taraxacum, from its medical effect; the fact of its introduction from Europe; the quotation of the lines,—

> "Dear common flower, that grow'st beside the way,
> Fringing the dusty road with harmless gold;"—

these would be historical instructions from the same simple flower. Then ask the child to tell you why he likes this flower so much; whether it is because it is prettier than morning-glories, or because it comes so early, or because it is so common,—and you stimulate him, perhaps, to one of his earliest efforts at a psychological self-examination. Finally, speak to him, reverently and warmly, of the goodness of the Heavenly Father, who has spread beauty with so unsparing a hand before us, and tell him of the Saviour's appeal to our conscience, drawn from the beauty of the lily, using simple language that he can understand,—and you will have given him theological lessons also.

Now, every lesson in the school of life will lead, as simply as this dandelion has done, to the five great branches of intellectual studies; and no lesson has been fully taught until it has thus been linked into relation with all the main lines of dependent truth. The simplest geometry has its application to physics, its history of discovery and application, its psychological questions of the foundations of belief and the nature of proof, and its theological aspect, in such queries as whether the relations of space are or are not dependent on the constitution of our minds, and thus on the will of the Creator. The cycle of these five branches must be daily recurring, and our aim has been, in these articles, to show in what order the five branches are to be placed, which must always precede the others, which must first receive full development, and which, the crown and glory of the whole, must be always least within the reach of finite faculties.

# THE POWERS TO BE EDUCATED.

BY THOMAS HILL, D. D. LL. D., PRESIDENT OF HARVARD COLLEGE.

As I was journeying towards this city to partake in the pleasures of this gathering I saw upon an island, in the northern part of yonder brineless ocean, a little collection of five or six houses, and among them one hut that attracted the attention of all our party. It was so low, that although the door nearly reached the eaves, a tall man might be forced to stoop to enter; it was so poor that neither glass nor sash was in its casements. Yet it was a palace wherein a queen was reigning and was rearing kings. It was a school-house built through the missionary zeal of a noble girl who after procuring its erection and gathering in it all the children of the island, gave two years' service to this school of less than a score of children, gratuitously, and now two other years with a pay that is merely nominal. As I heard the story of her generous labors, undertaken with no thought that they should be known and appreciated beyond the narrow confines of that lonely island; I felt a new sense of the dignity and grandeur of our profession as teachers and in my heart, thanked God that He had called me to such a goodly fellowship, embracing thousands of these humble but glorious laborers, one in purpose and devotion, with the teacher of North Manitou Island.

For as I heard the story, I endeavored to estimate the value of the work there, and measure as I would, I found it invaluable. Measure it by the cost of re-production, and it is immeasurable. For it is impossible to give to one already adult, instruction in the tender years of his youth. Measure by its utility and it is immeasurable; since the uses, to a man and to the community in which he lives, of the knowledge he may have gained and of the culture he may have received are innumerable, inestimable, and of eternal duration. Thus I was led anew to consider the greatness of the work of educating the young; and I thought I might be pardoned if I used this little school on Manitou Island as an introduction to the thoughts which I hoped to bring forward at this meeting.

The course of instruction, the true selection and arrangement of studies in liberal education, is evidently one of the most important points in this great work, and yet a point which it seems to me is not discussed from a right point of view. In special Schools of Science and of Art the courses of instruction are frequently well considered, and both the selection and the arrangement of the topics studied are made upon definite and established principles. Not so with reference to our more fundamental schools of general liberal culture; in them, whether in the kindergarten and infant school, in the common school and academy, or in the college and university, either custom rules, or the course of study arises from a balance of powers among various teachers or members of a governing body; each zealously advocating the claims of some special branch of learning. There is no general recognition of any great principles controlling the whole matter,—no recognition of the need of having those principles reduced to a clear code for the government of educators.

In my own feeble attempts to supply this need,—which I could not, when I considered the great ability and zeal of my predecessors, and my cotemporaries, flatter myself would be much more successful than other men's failures,—I have thought that a general scheme for the guidance of liberal education might be safely built, only upon one of the three following foundations.

First, upon a thorough survey of the field of human activity; of the duties for which the pupil is to be prepared.

Secondly, upon a survey of the whole field of things which can be imparted by teaching.

Thirdly, upon a thorough survey of the powers which can be improved by training.

Either of these foundations being carefully prepared by an exhaustive survey would afford a safe basis on which wise and skillful men could build up a true scheme of education adapted to public and general needs, and adapted also, to the more special cases of brilliancy and genius, or of feeble mindedness on one or many sides. Of course, I assume that a true statement of the proper course and mode of instruction is possible, at least to thought, which shall include the education of a genius and of an idiot, as well as of the mass of men. I assume also, that a true course and mode of general liberal culture, built upon either of the three foundations above mentioned, would coincide with the true course and mode built upon either of the others. The safest mode of proceeding, therefore, will be for our best thinkers and writers to survey finally all three of these bases, to build upon them schemes of instruction, and by a comparison of these schemes to elicit at length, the correct mode. It may be the work of centuries to accomplish this,—but when we look around us and behold what a populous wealthy and ancient city has been built about the fork of this little river within the lifetime of most of us present, we are emboldened to hope that great achievements in intellectual and social life will not henceforth require such wearisome years to finish.

But when we attempt a thorough survey of the field of human activity and duty, we find that field so rapidly enlarging and altering in its perspective that it is difficult to avoid omissions of parts which to day may seem of little worth, and to-morrow may prove all-important. At the time when the question was asked, what should boys be taught, and it was answered, that which they can use as men, it was supposed that Conic Sections were altogether idle and useless speculations. For two hundred years the school of Plato had studied the properties of those curves, and Apollonius had summed up the results in eight books filled with truths of marvelous beauty,—but of no known utility. Perchance it might have been then thought that the Conic Sections were unfit to be the study of a youth, because he could not put them to any use as a man. But after ten times two hundred years had passed, these very Conic Sections became the most practically useful of all objects of study, and every shipyard, and every ship's dock, every machine-shop, and every railroad track affords the amplest opportunities for applying them to practice.

From the errors into which we might fall by thus contracting our ideas of utility, we could be saved only by expanding them to that degree that the useful could no longer be distinguished from the visionary. Thus our first foundation for a scheme of liberal instruction, although theoretically sound, is practically difficult, and will be useful chiefly in confirming or correcting and modifying conclusions reached through an investigation of the other two.

The second foundation is a thorough survey of the whole field of things capable of being imparted by instruction. Upon this survey I have at sundry times made preliminary sketches and published the results.* Among those results is a rough map of the field of knowledge. I divide all human science into five grand divisions according to its subject matter. The first embraces Space and Time affording us the sciences of Geometry, Algebra, and Arithmetic. The second takes in the physical world, giving us the sciences of Mechanics, Chemistry, and Physiology. The third embraces the actions of men giving us the Arts and Fine Art, Language, and Law. The fourth takes in the spirit of man, giving us the sciences of Me-

* "*American Journal of Education*," Vol. v., for Map, see page 14, 45

taphysics, Æsthetics, and Ethics. The fifth contemplates the Divine Being and gives us the sciences of Natural and Revealed Religion. I have on sundry public occasions endeavored to show that this rough sketch of the field of knowledge affords the best guide to education; that these sciences naturally follow each other in the order here given; and are to be learned only in that order, consciously or unconsciously followed; and that any attempt to invert the order leads only to a necessity of teaching the lower truth covertly and awkwardly, instead of openly and naturally.

But I propose to-day to bestow some thought upon a preliminary sketch of the third foundation of a true scheme of general liberal culture, that is, the survey of the powers which can be improved by training.

A child is a will governing a body, at the impulse of passion, and under the guidance of reason. The body, the mind, the feelings, and the will,—these constitute the four great divisions of our subject, man. The body is of course incapable of education, except when living, that is, in connection with the mind and feelings and will. The first function of the body is, then, to receive impressions from the outward world, communicating sensation to the mind, awaking thought, arousing feeling; their combination exciting desire, desire ripening into purpose, purpose culminating in volition, and volition manifesting itself in muscular movement, a movement of the body. This is an epitome of human history, and an inventory, in brief, of human powers,—capable, therefore, of serving as a basis of a true scheme of education.

The first intellectual or spiritual use of the body is, I say, to receive impressions from the outward world, and communicate sensations to the mind. In order to do this well, it must be in a healthy condition, and to this end, the teacher is to guard sedulously his pupils against all hindrances to healthy growth. Actual growth comes only through divine action and divine law,—disease and deformity through hindrances and perversions introduced by error and sin. The requisites to healthy growth are, first, healthful food, fresh air and sunlight and freedom of motion; secondly, proper alternations of rest, such as fasting and sleep and darkness; thirdly, absence of poisons and of unnatural excitements of any kind, such as pampering of the appetites and passions.

This matter of physical training and of the care of the health, I pass by for the present, only beseeching my fellow-teachers not to pass it by in the detail of their school labors. I will only allude to a single point of detail, because I conceive it to be of such overwhelming importance, so little understood by the majority of teachers, and neglected by them to the terrible injury of their pupils. You who have the care of young children, I beseech you watch over their purity. No more fearful loss can befall a child than to lose its purity of heart. I beseech you, therefore, to impress upon your children with all the eloquence of your affection, this sacred rule. Never to do or say any thing which they would be unwilling to have you see and hear. Remind them that God always sees them, and plead with them frequently and with earnestness, even to tears, not to do or say in His sight any thing which they would be unwilling to do or say in yours. There are sins which you would not warn them against for fear of soiling their minds by the suggestion,—but press upon them this rule with sincere and affectionate earnestness, and they will seldom need any plainer speech.

The first intellectual use of the body is to communicate sensations to the mind. Whether the power of sense can be increased by education is a doubtful and debated point. My own opinion, founded upon careful experiments which I have not now time to relate, is that direct delicacy of sense is an original gift, not capable of direct increase by training. Physical causes may increase or diminish it, as taking cold, for example, may blunt hearing and taste and smell, but render the eye sensitive to light,—but by no process of education can any such effect be produced.

A great deal, however, can be done in educating the ability of judging on sensations;—increase of skill can be produced by training;—and increase of skill is equivalent to increase of power. The powers of sense, coming logically first in the sketch of human nature which I have made, and being first of all, powers in the order of development in the child's growth, should be first educated. This is done first of all by objects,—and thus the object teaching of the modern schools and kindergartens is rightly given to young children. But let me warn young teachers that as there is no royal road to geometry, so neither is there any mode of teaching which can render an inefficient and indifferent teacher successful. Lessons from objects as well as lessons from text-books can be learned by rote, and object teaching like recitation easily degenerate into routine. No matter what the system is, it may in the hands of sleepy and thoughtless teachers, degrade all our schools, like the one visited by Dr. Brown, into "aixlent cemeteries of aidication,"—or it may, in the hands of earnest, enthusiastic and sensible teachers, arouse the pupils to new life and lead them to knowledge and to virtue. The object of object teaching is to lead children to observe, but a set of stereotyped questions upon a few dozen specimens in a museum box in the school-room will no more teach children to observe what is under their feet and around them on their way through life, than the setting of tasks in a book for memoriter recitation.

Simultaneous with the development of the powers of sensation, is the awakening of a power of perceiving truths independent of sense. There can be no direct sensation without indirect consciousness of your sensation, consciousness of your own existence and generally of your possession of a bodily organ through which the sensation comes, perhaps of the free movement of the organ to bring it into a position to receive the impression from a something, which is neither your mind, nor its organ of sensation. The fundamental antithesis of philosophy is, that brought to knowledge, and at the same moment, it is perceived that these bodily organs and this visible and tangible world, lie in space and time. The soul sees by direct inspection the existence and properties of space and time, not inferring them logically from the properties of extension, nor being forced by a law of mind to a fiction of their existence,—any more than it is forced to a fiction of its own existence,—but seeing then by a direct inward vision ; having its attention called to them, however, by the phenomena of nature manifested in them,—just as its attention is directed to its own existence, only at the instant of its perception of phenomena not itself. These powers of direct perception external and internal, are as I have said, to be cultivated earliest, not with the hope of increasing the actual capacity of the soul,—for that seems to vary only by original gift or by physical condition,—but with the well-grounded hope of increasing the skill of using these powers to an almost indefinite degree. These fundamental powers of direct vision of truth are divine and inexplicable even in their native state, and in their cultivated condition afford us the highest objects of adoration and wonder as tokens of the kindred of man to the Infinite Deity. By education any one sense may be made to serve the purposes of all the senses, and even to supply the place of the higher powers. Thus with those blind from birth, hearing although no more acute than in other men, serves to give a thousand kinds of information which we can not conceive of as coming through the air. What sort of house is this that we are passing? I asked a blind friend, and he replied without a moment's hesitation guided only by the echo of his footsteps, "A little two-story brick house with a low wooden paling fence about three feet in front of it."

Next in order, after the powers of direct perception, external and internal, comes the powers of memory and mental reproduction. That such a power is absolutely essential to the exercise of any of the higher functions of the soul will be manifest, when we remember that the present is an absolute zero point, and that continuity of thought is possible, therefore, only through memory and anticipation. All our life is future or past, the present gives only the opportunities of guiding the transmutation of future into past.

Memory is in its simplest form only the permanence of the perception,—more or less vivid. When in the form of recollection it becomes the revivification of past perceptions. Finally, in its higher forms of fancy and imagination, it remodels and recombines the perceptions of the past and projects them into the future,—or separates them from actual time and space and throws them into an ideal world.

These powers of memory and imagination, have, in our ordinary school studies been greatly neglected, and cultivated only in their lowest form of memory. Some teachers, it is true, perceiving the poverty of an education which strengthens the memory only, have altogether despised the cultivation of that faculty and endeavored to appeal to the reason alone. But this course is also against nature, it can not be fully carried into effect, because it is an impossibility for the reason to act, except upon transcripts furnished by the imagination from perception. And therefore imagination must be cultivated before reason. Why will we not gracefully bow to the decrees of nature and follow her plans!

In the cultivation of the imagination, it will of course be remembered, that this culture should also in its subdivisions follow a natural order. At first, memory alone, and memory of the actual outward fact,—a description of a thing not now present, but seen and handled and smelled and listened to on a previous day; then memory of words and formula by rote,—then the imagination and description and perhaps drawing of something never seen, but defined and suggested by the teacher. In this play of the imagination all sensible properties must be reproduced; but the chief care should be taken with regard to form, or geometrical figure; by far the most important intellectual element in the material world, simply because the fundamental element. What is matter but that which occupies space;—and what a material object but matter in a definite part of space, therefore having in some sense a form, as its first most essential requisite of existence. Geometry is the foundation of learning and no other learning is possible except as upheld by that foundation.

Geography is the only one of our ordinary school studies which tends directly to the increase of the powers of the imagination. Properly taught it is almost exclusively a work of that faculty. It may degenerate into a mere remembrance of names and figures,—Chicago, 150,000 souls, forty years, Lake Michigan 280 miles by 70. But with a teacher alive to her work, the 150,000 souls, and forty years, will stimulate the pupil to conceive of a city, twice as large, or half as large, as the one with which alone he is familiar, having grown up in his father's lifetime, and the 280 miles by 70, combined with the known figure of the earth, will lead him to imagine the possibility of a steamer running at a good speed, in a straight line, twenty-four hours without seeing land.

The imagination acting freely, and pursuing only its own ends, produces works of fine art, statue, picture, music, poem and tale; and these also in their time and place, are valuable for the education of the power which created them.

Then, in the order of that use, comes the reasoning power, which by a comparison of the truths gained through perception, deduces new truths for the internal vision to seize upon. For the exercise and development of this power of reasoning, we depend at present chiefly upon leading the pupil to study specimens of reasoning in the pure mathematics,—or at a more advanced stage, upon giving him treatises upon logic itself.

It has appeared to me that this method could be greatly improved by giving the pupils at the age of fifteen or sixteen years, when the logical power begins to be developed, some simple explanation of the nature of reasoning, and of the mode of revising proofs, and then giving him unsolved problems for the exercise of his own power in revising original demonstrations. It is manifest that this process need not be confined to mathematics, but can be extended into other branches of natural and metaphysical sciences.

We must not forget that while the intellectual powers guide, the passions alone impel to action. Simultaneous with perception in sensation is feeling. The sensation not only tells you that some external things acts upon your bodily organ, but gives you a feeling of pleasure or of pain. This feeling is something as indefinable, mysterious and ultimate as thought itself,—heat and cold, hunger and thirst, sweetness, sourness, fear, hope, hatred, love, aversion, longing; these words recall to your remembrance past states of your consciousness in which you knew not only the existence of yourself and of some object to which you were in relation, but also of some quality in the object which excited in you a peculiar and indefinable state of feeling.

Feeling accompanies every act of perception, from the simplest sense-perception,—as when I touch this paper and recognize its temperature, texture and surface,—up to the most complex emotions accompanying the perception of the grandest truths of politics, or of theology, the emotions of patriotism and piety.

When these feelings directly arouse strong desire they are called passions. All feeling excites a certain amount of desire or aversion, but some feelings much more than others. Desire and aversion bear to feeling somewhat the same relation that memory and foresight bear to perception. Desire and aversion arise from the recollection of past and the imagination of future feeling. When desire or aversion has a certain relative strength it leads to purpose, which is the first dawning of that greatest spiritual phenomenon, a volition. Desire and purpose are each indefinable and fundamental states; the former being the culmination of feeling, the second the dawning of will. Finally comes volition, the fulfillment of the purpose, the voluntary action.

Inasmuch as these powers are all of them higher, *per see*, than the intellectual powers, it is fitting, if they are capable of education, that their education should be most carefully watched and guarded. To preserve the freshness and tenderness of youth, to keep the heart open for simple and refining pleasures, to guard against the false excitements which exhaust the soul, to foster the pure and holy emotions of filial piety, and draw the heart toward communion with a Heavenly Father, these are grander ends in education than any training of the intellectual powers can be ;—and intellectual training is worse than wasted if it be gained at the expense of tenderness of heart and freshness of feeling.

And what else can we say of the importance of training a child in such manner that it may not allow its feelings to be cherished into evil desires, or fail to have its pure feelings awake right desires? What less can we say of the importance of so training the future man that his purposes may all be just and right. And above all, how can we say too much of the need of an education, if such an education be possible, which shall insure the man perfect command over himself, that he may not be infirm of purpose and a tool of others more wicked than himself, but setting himself steadfastly, to do that which is according to God's will, may be an accepted and successful co-worker with the Infinite Power, that ever out of evil is educing good in infinite progression.

What do our schools and academies and colleges effect toward attaining these highest ends of education, this æsthetic development of tastes, this moral control of the desires and purposes, this religious sanctification? Much, I grant; and yet nothing in comparison with what shall be done when the highest christian philosophy and culture shall have triumphed in the discovery, and embodiment in practice, of the true system of public education. Much, I grant; and yet very little with a distinct, carefully considered plan of action in reference to these points, very little with the acknowledged end of making these points of more importance than the intellectual development.

I know the practical difficulties which surround the subject. I know the danger lest in attempting to cherish virtue you cherish hypocrisy, in attempting to cultivate morality you produce formality, and in seeking to refine the taste you produce sentimentality. I know the practical difficulties, and have seen the evil results of attempts to render education more moral and more religious.

But I know that similar difficulties have beset also every attempt to improve the intellectual education of the schools. I have seen every improved method of teaching the ordinary branches, so abused by enthusiastic and partially enlightened teachers as to make the improvement worse than the old method. I have seen classes in school, committing to memory and repeating by rote, textbooks which were written for the express purpose of forcing the teacher to leave the text-book and take to the subject. And I can not forget that a hundred thousand copies of Peterson's Familiar Science, the most inaccurate school-book I ever saw, have been used in the schools of this country, while Chase's Common School Arithmetic, the best text-book on Arithmetic I ever saw, has nearly gone out of print. Seeing such errors and difficulties in the way of improving modes of intellectual training, and yet seeing that, on the whole, the mode of teaching is improved, I can not be wholly discouraged with regard to æsthetic and moral and religious education.

And now having given a rough sketch of the powers of the human soul;—the power of perceiving truth through outward sense and inward intuition; the power reproducing those perceptions in memory, and combining and modifying them in new creations of the imagination; the power of comparing them with each other, and eliciting new truths through the reason; the power of feeling the impression which these perceptions make upon the soul; the power of allowing those impressions and feelings to awaken desire or disgust, by holding them under attention, or turning the attention from them; the power of cherishing those desires until they ripen into purposes; the power of pushing the purpose into execution through volition; having given this rough sketch of human powers, I might go on to show that it would afford a correct basis for a scheme of education, and that this scheme of education, carefully developed, would not differ in its intellectual features from that toward which all the sound thinkers of the day are manifestly tending.

But some teachers may ask me, to what practical end is this discourse? and how shall we as individual teachers best fulfil our functions, while waiting for the great thinkers of the profession to perfect the future course of instruction!

I answer that the most directly practical end which I hoped to attain, was to give you a just sense of the grandeur of the work in which you are engaged; and of the importance of tasking your best powers in a calm endeavor to decide for yourselves, what better you can do than you are now doing. The field before each one of you, teachers, if it be but a little Monitou school of a dozen scholars, is worthy of the best efforts you can make. Make those efforts not with feverish anxiety lest you shall not succeed, not with a despairing sense of your inability;—much lest with a self satisfied conceit of your superiority over other teachers;—but make your best efforts to understand and to perform your duties, in the calm confidence that God, who has appointed us our tasks in life, knows best what we can do, and that he asks of us only that we should, with honest sincerity, seek to do our best.

Make your best efforts to understand your duties. The field of knowledge is open to you, as to your scholars, and you can in no way so well stimulate them to learn, and prepare yourself to teach, as by being yourself a student,—enthusiastic in your love of knowledge and your eagerness to gain more. Study what truths are to be taught, study what powers are to be developed, study what duties and opportunities in life will be likely to be opened to your pupils. Study human nature in general, and study the individual character of each pupil under your charge.

Then whatever be the system of instruction which your State Laws or your Educational Board, or your School Committee, may force you to adopt, you can make it flexible and living, and a medium of pouring the sacred life that is in you, into the hearts of your pupils.

NOTE.

The incident with which President HILL introduced his lecture, led to the following Correspondence.

CHICAGO, *August* 13, 1863

MISS ANGELICA M. BUSS,—

*Respected Lady:*—On the 3d instant a company of gentlemen and ladies, on their way to the annual meeting of the NATIONAL TEACHERS' ASSOCIATION, recently held in this city, touched at the North Manitou Island.

During the brief stay of the party, it was the pleasure of some to make your acquaintance, and learn of your work of faith and love among the children of the island.

What we saw and heard deeply impressed us with respect and love for the character of one who, under great embarrassment and self-sacrifice, has isolated herself from loved friends and associations, and devoted the best powers of her mind to the instruction, mental culture, and educational training of the young.

Prompted by a desire to honor you for your devotion to a noble work, and to show our interest in the cause of popular education, the party, with great cheerfulness and unanimity, raised a sum of money with which to purchase an American gold watch, to present to you, as a token of the high regard and respect they have for you and the cause in which you are successfully laboring

Be pleased to accept this testimonial of our esteem, with assurance of sympathy, love, and prayer, for you and your pupils.

With great respect, we are most truly yours,

J. W. BULKLEY, Chairman of the Committee.

REPLY TO THE LETTER.

NORTH MANITOU ISLAND, *August* 25, 1863.

MR. J. W. BULKLEY,—

*Kind Sir:*—I was very much surprised on the 15th instant by receiving from you a letter expressing kind feeling toward me; also a more substantial token of esteem—a gold watch—the gift of a party of gentlemen and ladies who visited my school.

The magnitude of the gift and the kind expressions contained in your communication have almost made me dumb until the present moment; but I must try and make some acknowledgment for your kindness. And first, permit me to say, you greatly over-estimate my self-sacrifice, for it is indeed a great pleasure for me to instruct the young, and see them improve, mentally, morally, and physically; and what gives me so much satisfaction can not be considered a great hardship.

However, I am greatly pleased to receive your gift, as it is an evidence of your interest in popular instruction and education, the means by which our liberties must be perpetuated. I shall ever keep it by me, and when I look at it shall think of the donors, the occasion of the gift, and the sympathy and generous feelings which prompted you and your associates to such liberality.

I shall be most grateful if I can still have your sympathy and advice; and very glad to hear from you, from time to time, in relation to the cause of popular education, a subject in which we all feel so deep an interest.

Very respectfully yours,

ANGELICA M. BUSS.

# INTELLECTUAL EDUCATION—ITS OBJECTS AND METHODS.

INTRODUCTORY DISCOURSE BEFORE THE AMERICAN INSTITUTE OF INSTRUCTION AT BOSTON, MASS, IN AUGUST, 1830.

BY FRANCIS WAYLAND, PRESIDENT OF BROWN UNIVERSITY.

---

In the long train of her joyous anniversaries, New England has yet beheld no one more illustrious than this. We have assembled to-day, not to proclaim how well our fathers have done, but to inquire how we may enable their sons to do better. We meet, not for the purposes of empty pageant, nor yet of national rejoicing; but to deliberate upon the most successful means for cultivating, to its highest perfection, that invaluable amount of intellect, which Divine Providence has committed to our hands. We have come up here to the city of the Pilgrims, to ask how we may render their children most worthy of their ancestors and most pleasing to their God. We meet to give to each other the right hand of fellowship in carrying forward this all-important work, and here to leave our professional pledge, that, if the succeeding generation do not act worthily, the guilt shall not rest upon those who are now the Instructors of New England.

Well am I aware that the occasion is worthy of the choicest effort of the highest talent in the land. Sincerely do I wish, that upon such talent the duty of addressing you this day had devolved. Much do I regret that sudden indisposition has deprived me of the time which had been set apart to meet the demands of the present occasion, and that I am only able to offer for your consideration such reflections as have been snatched from the most contracted leisure, and gleaned amid the hurried hours of languid convalescence. But I bring, as an offering to the cause of Education, a mind deeply penetrated with a conviction of its surpassing importance, and enthusiastically ardent in anticipating the glory of its ultimate results. I know, then, that I may liberally presume upon your candor, while I rise to address those, to very many of whom it were far more beseeming that I quietly and humbly listened.

The subject which I have chosen for our mutual improvement, is, *The object of intellectual education; and the manner in which that object is to be attained.*

I. It hath pleased Almighty God to place us under a constitution of universal law. By this we mean, that nothing, either in the physical, intellectual, or moral world, is in any proper sense contingent. Every event is preceded by its regular antecedents, and followed by its regular consequents; and hence is formed that endless chain of cause and effect which binds together the innumerable changes which are taking place everywhere around us.

When we speak of this system as subjected to universal law, we mean all this; but this is not all that we mean. The term law, in a higher sense, is applied to beings endowed with conscience and will, and then there is attached to it the idea of rewards and punishments. It is then used to signify a constitution so arranged, that one course of action shall be inevitably productive of happiness, and another course shall be as inevitably productive of misery. Now, in this higher sense is it strictly and universally true, that we are placed under a constitution of law. Every action which we perform, is as truly amenable as inert matter, to the great principles of the government of the universe, and every action is chained to the consequences which the Creator has affixed to it, as unalterably as any sequence of cause and effect in physics. And thus, with equal eloquence and truth, the venerable Hooker has said, "Of Law, there can be no less acknowledged, than that her seat is the bosom of God, her voice the harmony of the world; all things in heaven and earth do her homage, the very least as feeling her care, and the very greatest as not exempted from her power; both angels and men and creatures of what condition soever, though each in different sort and manner, yet all with uniform consent, admiring her as the mother of their peace and joy."

Such a constitution having been established by a perfectly wise Creator, it may be easily supposed that it will remain unchangeable. His laws will not be altered for our convenience. We may obey them or disobey them, we may see them or not see them, we may be wise or unwise, but they will be rigidly and unalterably enforced. Thus must it ever be, until we have the power to resist the strength of omnipotence.

Again; it is sufficiently evident that the very constitution which God has established, is, with infinite wisdom and benevolence, devised for just such a being, physical, intellectual, and moral, as man. By obedience to the laws of God, man may be as happy as his present state will allow. Misery is always the result of a violation of some of the laws which the Creator has established. Hence, our great business here, is, *to know and obey the laws of our Creator.*

That part of man by which we know, and, in the most important sense, obey the laws of the Creator, is called MIND. I use the word in its general sense, to signify, not merely a substance, not matter, capable of intellection, but one also capable of willing, and to which is attached the responsibility of right and wrong in human action. And, still further, it is one of the laws of mind, that increased power for the acquisition of knowledge, and a more universal disposition to obedience, may be the result of the action of one mind upon another, or, of the well-directed efforts of the individual mind itself.

Without some knowledge of the laws of nature, it is evident that man would immediately perish. But it is possible for him to have only so much knowledge of them as will barely keep generation after generation in existence, without either adding anything to the stock of intellectual acquisition, or subjecting to his use any of the various agents which a bountiful Providence has everywhere scattered around, for the supply of his wants and the relief of his necessities. Such was the case with the Aborigines of our country, and such had it been for centuries. Such, also, with but very few and insignificant exceptions, is the case in Mohammedan and Pagan countries. The sources of their happiness are few and intermitting—those of their misery multiplied and perpetual.

Looking upon such nations as these, we should involuntarily exclaim, What a waste of being, what a loss of happiness, do we behold! Here are intelligent creatures, placed under a constitution devised by Infinite Wisdom to promote their happiness. The very penalties which they suffer, are so many proofs of the divine goodness—mere monitions to direct them in the paths of obedience. And besides this, they are endowed with a mind perfectly formed to investigate and discover these laws, and to derive its highest pleasure from obeying them. Yet that mind, from want of culture, has become useless. It achieves no conquests. It removes no infelicities. Here, then, must the remedy be applied. This immaterial part must be excited to exertion, and must be trained to obedience. Just so soon as this process is commenced, a nation begins to emerge from the savage, and enter upon the civilized state. Just in proportion to the freedom and the energy with which the powers of the mind are developed, and the philosophical humility with which they are exercised, does a people advance in civilization. Just in proportion as a people is placed under contrary influences, is its movement retrograde.

The science which teaches us how to foster these energies of mind is the science of Education. In few words, I would say, *the object of the science of Education, is, to render mind the fittest possible instrument for* DISCOVERING, APPLYING, *or* OBEYING, *the laws under which God has placed the universe.*

That all this is necessary, in order to carry forward the human species to the degree of happiness which it is destined, at some time or other, to attain, may be easily shown.

The laws of the universe must be *discovered*. Until they are discovered, we shall be continually violating them and suffering the penalty, without either possibility of rescue or hope of alleviation. Hence the multitude of bitter woes which ignorance inflicts upon a people. Hence the interest which every man should take in the progress of knowledge. Who can tell how countless are the infelicities which have been banished from the world, by the discovery of the simple law that a magnetized needle, when freely suspended, will point to the north and south!

Nor is it sufficient that a law be discovered. Its relations to other laws must be ascertained, and the means devised by which it may be made to answer the purposes of human want. This is called *application*, or *invention*. The law of the expansive power of steam was discovered by the Marquis of Worcester, in 1663. It remained, however, for the inventive power of Watt and Fulton, more than a century afterward, to render it subservient to the happiness of man. From want of skill in a single branch of this department of mental labor, the human race has frequently been kept back for ages. The ancients, for instance, came very near the invention of the printing press. Thus has it been with several other of the most important inventions. It makes a thoughtful man sad, at the present day, to observe how many of the most important agents of nature we are obliged to expose to the gaze of lecture-rooms, without being able to reveal a single practical purpose for which they were created.

But this is not all. A man may know a law of his Creator, and understand its application; but if he do not *obey* it, he will neither reap the reward nor escape the penalty which the Creator has annexed to it. Here we enter, at once, into the mysterious region of human will, of motive, and of conscience. To examine it at present is not my design. I will only remark, that some great improvement is necessary in this part of our nature, before we can ever reap the benefits of the present constitution of the universe. I do not think that any philosopher can escape the conviction, that when important truth is the subject of inquiry, we neither possess the candor of judgment, nor the humility of obedience, which befits the relations existing between a creature and his Creator. In proof of this, it is sufficient to refer to well known facts. Galileo suffered the vengeance of the Inquisition, for declaring the sun to be the centre of the planetary system! How slow were the learned in adopting the discoveries of Hervey or of Newton! Still more visible is this obstinacy, when the application of a moral law is clearly discovered. Though supported by incontrovertible argument, how slowly have the principles of religious toleration gained foothold even in the civilized world! After the slave trade had been proved contrary to every principle of reason and conscience, and at variance with every law of the Creator, for nearly twenty years did Clarkson and his associates labor, before they could obtain the act for its abolition. And to take an illustration nearer home,—how coolly do we look on and behold lands held by unquestionable charter from Almighty God, in defiance of an hundred treaties by which the faith of this country has been pledged—in violation of every acknowledged law, human and divine, wrested from a people, by whose forbearance, a century ago, our fathers were permitted to exist! I speak not the language of party. I eschew and abhor it; but "I speak with the freedom of history, and I hope without offence." These examples are at least sufficient to show us, that the mind of man is not, at present, the fittest instrument possible for obeying the laws of his Creator, and that there is need, therefore, of that science which shall teach him to become such an instrument.

The question which will next arise, is this :—Can these things be taught? Is it practicable, by any processes which man can devise, to render mind a fitter instrument for discovering, applying and obeying the laws of his Creator? We shall proceed, in the next place, to show that all this is practicable.

1. It is practicable to train the mind to greater skill in *discovery*. A few facts will render this sufficiently evident.

It will not be denied that some modes of thinking are better adapted to the discovery of truth than others. Those trains of thought which follow the order of cause and effect, premises and conclusion, or, in general, what is considered the order of the understanding, are surely more likely to result in discovery than those which follow the order of the casual relations, as of time, place, resemblance and contrast, or, as it is commonly called, the order of the imagination. Discovery is the fruit of patient thought, and not of impetuous combination. Now it must be evident that mind, directed in the train of the understanding, will be a far better instrument of discovery than if under the guidance of the imagination. And it is evident that the one mode of thinking may be as well cultivated as the other, or as any mode whatsoever. And hence has arisen the mighty effect which Bacon produced upon the world. He allured men from the weaving of day-dreams to the employment of their reason. Just in proportion as we acquire skill in the use of our reason, will be the progress of truth.

Again; there can be no doubt that, in consequence of the teaching of Bacon, or, in other words, in consequence of improvement in education, the human mind has, in fact, become a vastly more skillful instrument of discovery than ever it was before. In proof of this, I do not refer merely to the fact, that more power has been gained over the agents of nature, and that they have been made to yield a greater amount of human happiness to the human race, within the last one hundred years, than for ten times that period before. This, of itself, would be sufficient to show an abundant increase of intellectual activity. I would also refer to the fact that several of the most remarkable discoveries have been made by different men at the same time. This would seem to show, that mind in the aggregate was moving forward, and that everything with which we are now acquainted must soon have been discovered, even if it had eluded the sagacity of those who were fortunate enough to observe it. This shows that the power of discovery has already been in some degree increased by education. What has been so auspiciously begun, can surely be carried to far greater perfection.

Again; if we inquire what are those attributes of mind on which discovery mainly depends, I think we shall find them to be patient observation, acute discrimination, and cautious induction. Such were the intellectual traits of Newton, that prince of modern philosophers. Now it is evident that these attributes can be cultivated, as well as those of taste or imagination. Hence, it seems as evident that the mind may be trained to discovery, that is, that mind may be so disciplined as to be able to ascertain the particular laws of any individual substance, as that any other thing may be done.

2. By *application* or *invention*, I mean the contriving of those combinations by which the already discovered laws of the universe may be rendered available to the happiness of man. It is possible to render the mind a fitter instrument for the accomplishment of this purpose.

In proof of this remark, I may refer you to the two first considerations to which I have just adverted; namely, that some trains of thought are more productive of invention than others, and that, by following those trains, greater progress has, within a few years, been made in invention, than within ten times that period before.

It is proper, however, to remark, that the qualities of mind on which invention depends, are somewhat dissimilar from those necessary to discovery. Invention depends upon accuracy of knowledge in detail, as well as in general, and a facility for seizing upon distant, and frequently recondite relations. Discovery has more to do with the simple quality, invention with the complex connections. Discovery views truth in the abstract; invention views it either in connection with other truth, or in its relation to other beings. Hence has it so frequently taken place, that philosophers have been unable to avail themselves of their own discoveries; or, in other words, that the powers of discovery and of invention are so seldom combined in the same individual. In one thing, however, they agree. Both depend upon powers of mind capable of cultivation; and, therefore, both are susceptible of receiving benefit beyond any assignable degree, by the progress of education.

3. The mind may be rendered a fitter instrument for obeying the laws of the universe. This will be accomplished, when men, first, are better acquainted with the laws of the universe, and second, when they are better disposed to obey them. That both of these may be accomplished, scarcely needs confirmation.

For, first, I surely need not consume your time to prove, that a much greater amount of knowledge of the laws of the universe might be communicated in a specified time, than is communicated at present. Improvement in this respect depends upon two principles;—first, greater skill may be acquired in teaching; and second, the natural progress of the sciences is toward simplification. As they are improved, the more proximate relations of things are discovered, the media are rendered clearer, and the steps in the illustration of truth less numerous. As a man knows more of the laws of his Creator, he can surely obey them better.

And, secondly, those dispositions which oppose our meek and humble obedience, may be corrected. Candor may be made to take the place of prejudice, and envy may be exchanged for a generous ardor after truth. This a good teacher frequently accomplishes now. And that the Gospel of Jesus Christ does present a most surprising cure for those dispositions, which oppose the progress of truth and interfere with our obedience to the moral laws of our being, no one, who, at the present day, looks upon the human race with the eye of a philosopher, can with any semblance of candor venture to deny.

It would not be difficult, did time permit, by an examination of the various laws, physical, intellectual, and moral, under which we are placed, to show that the principles which I have been endeavoring to illustrate, are universal, and apply to every possible action of the most eventful life. It could thus be made to appear that all the happiness of man is derived from discovering, applying, or obeying the laws of his Creator, and that all his misery is the result of ignorance or disobedience; and hence, that the good of the species can be permanently promoted, and permanently promoted only by the accomplishment of that which I have stated to be the object of education.

I have thus far endeavored to show, from our situation as just such creatures, namely, under laws of which we come into the world ignorant, and laws which can only be known by a mind possessed of acquired power, that there is, in our present state, the need of such a science as that of education. I have endeavored to show what is its object, and also to show that that object may be accomplished. I will now take leave of this part of the subject, with a few remarks upon the relation which this science sustains to other sciences.

1. If the remarks already made have the least foundation in truth, we do not err in claiming for education the rank of a distinct science. It has its distinct subject, its distinct object, and is governed by its own laws. And, moreover, it has, like other sciences, its corresponding art,—the art of teaching. Now if this be so, we would ask how any man should understand this science, any more than that of mathematics or astronomy, without ever having studied it, or having even thought about it? If there be any such art as the art of teaching, we ask how it comes to pass that a man shall be considered fully qualified to exercise it, without a day's practice, when a similar attempt in any other art would expose him to ridicule? Henceforth, let the ridicule be somewhat more justly distributed.

2. The connections of this science are more extensive than those of any other. Almost any one of the other sciences may flourish independently of the rest. Rhetoric may be carried to high perfection, whilst the mathematics are in their infancy. Physical science may advance, whilst the science of interpretation is stationary. No science, however, can be independent of the science of education. By education their triumphs are made known; by education alone can they be multiplied.

Hence, thirdly, it is upon education that the progress of all other sciences depends. A science is a compilation of the laws of the universe on one particular subject. Its progress is marked by the number of these laws which it reveals, and the multiplicity of their relations which it unfolds. Now we have before shown that the number of laws which are discovered, will be in proportion to the skill of mind, the instrument which is to discover them. Hence, just in proportion to the progress of the science of education, will be the power which man obtains over nature, the extent of his knowledge of the laws of the universe, and the abundance of means of happiness which he enjoys.

If this be so, it would not seem arrogant to claim for education the rank of the most important of the sciences, excepting only the science of morals. And, hence, we infer, that it presents subjects vast enough, and interests grave enough, to task the highest effort of the most gifted intellect, in the full vigor of its powers. Is it not so? If it be so, on what principle of common sense is it, that a man is considered good enough for a teacher, because he has most satisfactorily proved himself good for no one thing else? Why is it, that the utter want of sufficient health to exercise any other profession, is frequently the only reason why a man should be thrust into this, which requires more active mental labor in the discharge of its duties, than any other profession whatsoever? Alas! it is not by teachers such as these that the intellectual power of a people is to be created. To hear a scholar say a lesson, is not to educate him. He who is not able to leave his mark upon a pupil, never ought to have one. Let it never be forgotten, that, in the thrice resplendent days of the intellectual glory of Greece, teachers were in high places. Isocrates, Plato, Zeno, and Aristotle were, without question, stars of by very far the first magnitude, in that matchless constellation, which still surrounds with undiminished effulgence the name of the city of Minerva.

And, lastly, if the science of education be thus important, is it not worthy of public patronage? Knowledge of every sort is valuable in a community, very far beyond what it costs to produce it. Hence it is for the interest of every man to furnish establishments by which knowledge can be increased. Of the manner in which this should be afforded, it belongs to political economists to treat. Let me suggest only a very few hints on the subject. Books are the repositories of the learning of past ages. Longer time than that of an individual's life, and greater wealth than falls to the lot of teachers, are required to collect them in numbers sufficient for extensive usefulness. The same may be said of instruments for philosophical research. Let these be furnished, and furnished amply. Let your instructors have the use of them, if you please, gratuitously; and if you do not please, not so, and then, on the principles which govern all other labor, let every teacher, like every other man, take care of himself. Give to every man prominent and distinct individuality. Remove all the useless barriers which shelter him from the full and direct effect of public opinion. Let it be supposed, that, by becoming a teacher, he has not lost all pretensions to common sense; and that he may possibly know as much about his own business as those, who, by confession, know nothing at all about it. In a word, make teaching the business of men, and you will have men to do the business of teaching. I know not that the cause of education, so far as teachers are concerned, requires any other patronage.

I come now to the second part of the subject, which, I am aware, it becomes me to treat with all possible brevity.

II. In what manner shall mind be thus rendered a fitter instrument to answer the purposes of its creation?

To answer this question, let us go back a little. We have shown that the present constitution of things is constructed for man, and that man is constructed for the present constitution. As mind, then, is the instrument by which he avails himself of the laws of that constitution, it may be supposed that it was endowed with all the powers necessary to render it subservient to his best interests. Were it possible, therefore, it would be useless to attempt to give it any additional faculties. All that is possible, is, to cultivate to higher perfection those faculties which exist, or to vary their relations to each other. To cultivate to the utmost the original faculties of the mind, is to render it the fittest possible instrument for disovering, applying, and obeying the laws of its creation.

This is, however, an answer to the question in the abstract, and without any regard to time. But the question to us, is not an abstract question; it has regard to time. That is to say, we do not ask simply what is the best mode of cultivating mind, but what is the best mode of doing it now, when so many ages have elapsed, and so many of the laws of the universe have been discovered. Much knowledge has already been acquired by the human race, and this knowledge is to be communicated to the pupil.

All this every one sees at first glance to be true. Nearly all the time spent in pupilage, under the most favorable circumstances, is in fact employed in the acquisition of those laws which have been already discovered. Without a knowledge of them, education would be almost useless. Without it, there could evidently be no progressive improvement of the species. Education, considered in this light alone, has very many and very important ends to accomplish. It is desirable that the pupil should be taught *thoroughly;* that is, that he should have as exact and definite a knowledge as possible of the law and of its relations. It is desirable that he be taught *permanently;* that is, that the truth communicated be so associated with his other knowledge, that the lapse of time will not easily erase it from his memory. It is important, also, that *no more time be consumed in the process than is absolutely necessary.* He who occupies two years in teaching what might as well be taught with a little more industry in one year, does his pupil a far greater injury than would be done by simply abridging his life by a year. He not only abstracts from his pupil's acquisition that year's improvement, but all the knowledge which would have been the fruit of it for the remainder of his being.

If, then, all that portion of our time which is devoted to education must be occupied in acquiring the laws of the universe, how shall opportunity be afforded for cultivating the original powers of the mind? I answer, an all-wise Creator has provided for this necessity of our intellectual nature. His laws, in this, as in every other case, are in full and perfect harmony.

For, first, the original powers of the mind are cultivated by use. This law, I believe, obtains in respect to all our powers, physical, intellectual, and moral. But it must be by the use of each several faculty. The improvement of the memory does not, of necessity, strengthen the power of discrimination; nor does the improvement of natural logical acuteness, of necessity, add sensibility to the taste. The law on this subject seems to be, that every several faculty is strengthened and rendered more perfect exactly in proportion as it is subjected to habitual and active exercise.

And, secondly, it will be found that the secret of teaching most thoroughly, permanently, and in the shortest time, that is, of giving to the pupil in a given time the greatest amount of knowledge, consists in so teaching as to give the most active exercise to the original faculties of the mind. So that it is perfectly true, that if you wished so to teach as to make the mind the fittest possible instrument for discovering, applying, and obeying the laws of the Creator, you would so teach as to give to the mind the greatest amount of knowledge; and, on the contrary, if you wished so to teach as to give to a pupil, in a given time, the greatest amount of knowledge, you would so teach as to render his mind the fittest instrument for discovering applying and obeying the laws of its Creator.

I do not forget that the discussion of the practical business of teaching is, on this occasion, committed to other hands. You will, however, I trust, allow me to suggest here, one or two principles which seem to me common to all teaching, and which are in their nature calculated to produce the results to which I have referred.

1. Let a pupil understand every thing that it is designed to teach him. If he can not understand a thing this year, it was not designed by his Creator that he should learn it this year. But let it not be forgotten, that precisely here is seen the power of a skillful teacher. It is his business to make a pupil, if possible, understand. Very few things are incapable of being understood, if they be reduced to their ultimate elements. Hence the reason why the power of accurate and natural analysis is so invaluable to a teacher. By simplification and patience, it is astonishing to observe how easily abstruse subjects may be brought within the grasp of even the faculties of children. Let a teacher, then, first understand a subject himself. Let him know that he understands it. Let him reduce it to

its natural divisions and its simplest elements. And then, let him see that his pupils understand it. This is the first step.

2. I would recommend the frequent repetition of whatever has been acquired. For want of this, an almost incalculable amount of invaluable time is annually wasted. Who of us has not forgotten far more than he at present knows? What is understood to-day, may with pleasure be reviewed to-morrow. If it be frequently reviewed, it will be associated with all our other knowledge, and be thoroughly engraven on the memory. If it be laid aside for a month or two, it will be almost as difficult to recover it as to acquire a new truth; and it is, moreover, destitute of the interest derived only from novelty. If this be the case with us generally, I need not say how peculiarly the remark applies to the young.

But lastly, and above all, let me insist upon the importance of universal practice of every thing that is learned. No matter whether it be a rule in arithmetic, or a rule in grammar, a principle in rhetoric, or a theorem in the mathematics; as soon as it is learned and understood, let it be practiced. Let exercises be so devised as to make the pupil familiar with its application. Let him construct exercises himself. Let him not leave them until he feels that he understands both the law and its application, and is able to make use of it freely and without assistance. The mind never will derive power in any other way. Nor will it, in any other way, attain to the dignity of certain, and practical, and available science.

So far as we have gone, then, we have endeavored to show that the business of a teacher is so to communicate knowledge as most constantly and vigorously to exercise the original faculties of the mind. In this manner he will both convey the greatest amount of instruction, and create the largest amount of mental power.

I intended to confirm these remarks by a reference to the modes of teaching some of the most important branches of science. But I fear that I should exhaust your patience, and also that I might anticipate what will be much better illustrated by those who will come after me. I shall, therefore, conclude by applying these considerations to the elucidation of some subjects of general importance.

1. If these remarks be true, they show us in what manner text-books ought to be constructed. They should contain a clear exhibition of the subject, its limits and relations. They should be arranged after the most perfect method, so that the pupil may easily survey the subject in all its ramifications; and should be furnished with examples and questions to illustrate every principle which they contain. It should be the design of the author to make such a book

as could neither be studied unless the pupil understood it, nor taught unless the instructor understood it. Such books, in every department, are, if I mistake not, very greatly needed.

If this be true, what are we to think of many of those school-books which are beginning to be very much in vogue amongst us? There first appears, perhaps, an abridgment of a scientific text-book. Then, lest neither instructor nor pupil should be able to understand it, without assistance, a copious analysis of each page or chapter or section, is added in a second and improved edition. Then, lest, after all, the instructor should not know what questions should be asked, a copious list of these is added to a third and still more improved edition. The design of this sort of work seems to be to reduce all mental exercise to a mere act of the memory, and then to render the necessity even for the use of this faculty as small as may be possible. Carry the principle but a little farther, and an automaton would answer every purpose exactly as well as an instructor. Let us put away all these miserable helps, as fast as possible, I pray you. Let us never forget that the business of an instructor begins where the office of a book ends. It is the action of mind upon mind, exciting, awakening, showing by example the power of reasoning and the scope of generalization, and rendering it impossible that the pupil should not think; this is the noble and the ennobling duty of an instructor.

2. These remarks will enable us to correct an error which of late has done very much evil to the science of education. Some years since, I know not when, it was supposed, or we have said it was supposed, that the whole business of education was to store the mind with facts. Dugald Stewart, I believe, somewhere remarks that the business of education, on the contrary, is to cultivate the original faculties. Hence the conclusion was drawn that it mattered not what you taught, the great business was to strengthen the faculties. Now this conclusion has afforded to the teacher a most convenient refuge against the pressure of almost every manner of attack. If you taught a boy rhetoric, and he could not write English, it was sufficient to say that the grand object was not to teach the structure of sentences, but to strengthen the faculties. If you taught him the mathematics, and he did not understand the Rule of Three, and could not tell you how to measure the height of his village steeple, it was all no matter,—the object was to strengthen his faculties. If, after six or seven years of study of the languages, he had no more taste for the classics than for Sanscrit, and sold his books to the highest bidder, resolved never again to look into them, it was all no matter,—he had been studying, to strengthen his facul-

ties, while by this very process his faculties have been enfeebled almost to annihilation.

Now, if I mistake not, all this reasoning is false, even to absurdity. Granting that the improvement of the faculties is the most important business of instruction, it does not follow that it is the only business. What! will a man tell me that it is of no consequence whether or not I know the laws of the universe under which I am constituted? Will he insult me, by pretending to teach them to me in such a manner that I shall, in the end, know nothing about them? Are such the results to which the science of education leads? Will a man pretend to illuminate me by thrusting himself, year after year, exactly in my sunshine? No; if a man profess to teach me the laws of my Creator, let him make the thing plain, let him teach me to remember it, and accustom me to apply it. Otherwise, let him stand out of the way, and allow me to do it for myself.

But this doctrine is yet more false; for even if it be true, that it matters not what is taught, it by no means follows that it is no matter how it is taught. The doctrine in question, however, supposes that the faculties are to be somehow strengthened by "going over," as it is called, a book or a science, without any regard to the manner in which it is done. The faculties are strengthened by the use of the faculties; but this doctrine has been quoted to shield a mode of teaching, in which they were not used at all; and hence has arisen a great amount of teaching, which has had very little effect, either in communicating knowledge, or giving efficiency to mind.

Let us, then, come to the truth of the question. It is important what I study; for it is important whether or not I know the laws of my being, and it is important that I so study them, that they shall be of use to me. It is also important that my intellectual faculties be improved, and therefore important that an instructor do not so employ my time as to render them less efficient.

3. Closely connected with these remarks is the question, which has of late been so much agitated, respecting the study of the ancient languages and the mathematics. On the one part, it is urged that the study of the languages is intended to cultivate the taste and imagination, and that of the mathematics to cultivate the understanding. On the other part, it is denied that these effects are produced; and it is asserted that the time spent in the study of them is wasted. Examples, as may be supposed, are adduced in abundance on both sides; but I do not know that the question is at all decided. Let us see whether any thing that we have said will throw any light upon it.

I think it can be conclusively proved, that the classics could be so taught as to give additional acuteness to the discrimination, more delicate sensibility to the taste, and more overflowing richness to the imagination. So much as this, must, we think, be admitted. If, then, it be the fact that these effects are not produced—and I think we must admit that they are not, in any such degree as might reasonably be expected—should we not conclude that the fault is not in the classics, but in our teaching? Would not teaching them better be the sure way of silencing the clamor against them?

I will frankly confess that I am sad, when I reflect upon the condition of the study of the languages among us. We spend frequently six or seven years in Latin and Greek, and yet who of us writes,—still more, who of us speaks them with facility? I am sure there must be something wrong in the mode of our teaching, or we should accomplish more. That can not be skillfully done, which, at so great an expense of time, produces so very slender a result. Milton affirms, that what in his time was acquired in six or seven years, might have been easily acquired in one. I fear that we have not greatly improved since.

Again, we very properly defend the study of the languages on the ground that they cultivate the taste, the imagination, and the judgment. But is there any magic in the name of a classic? Can this be done by merely teaching a boy to render, with all clumsiness, a sentence from another language into his own? Can the faculties of which we have spoken, be improved, when not one of them is ever called into action? No. When the classics are so taught as to cultivate the taste and give vigor to the imagination,—when all that is splendid and beautiful in the works of the ancient masters, is breathed into the conceptions of our youth,—when the delicate wit of Flaccus tinges their conversation, and the splendid oratory of Tully, or the irresistible eloquence of Demosthenes, is felt in the senate and at the bar—I do not say that even then we may not find something more worthy of being studied,—but we shall then be prepared, with a better knowledge of the facts, to decide upon the merits of the classics. The same remarks may apply, though perhaps with diminished force, to the study of the mathematics. If, on one hand, it be objected that this kind of study does not give that energy to the powers of reasoning which has frequently been expected, it may, on the other hand, be fairly questioned whether it be correctly taught. The mathematics address the understanding. But they may be so taught as mainly to exercise the memory. If they be so taught, we shall look in vain for the anticipated result. I suppose that a student, after having been taught one class of geometrical principles, should as much be required to combine them in the forms of original demonstration, as that he who has been taught a rule of arithmetic should be required to put it into various and diversified practice. It is thus alone, that we shall acquire that δυναμις αναλυτικη, the mathematical power which the Greeks considered of more value than the possession of any number of problems. When the mathematics shall be thus taught, I think there will cease to be any question, whether they add acuteness, vigor and originality to mind.

I have thus endeavored, very briefly, to exhibit the object of education, and to illustrate the nature of the means by which that object is to be accomplished. I fear that I have already exhausted your patience. I will, therefore, barely detain you with two additional remarks.

1. To the members of this Convention allow me to say, Gentlemen, you have chosen a noble profession. What though it do not confer upon us wealth?—it confers upon us a higher boon, the privilege of being useful. What though it lead not to the falsely named *heights* of political eminence?—it leads us to what is far better, the sources of real power; for it renders intellectual ability necessary to our success. I do verily believe that nothing so cultivates the powers of a man's own mind as thorough, generous, liberal, and indefatigable teaching. But our profession has rewards, rich rewards, peculiar to itself. What can be more delightful to a philanthropic mind, than to behold intellectual power increased a hundred fold by our exertions, talent developed by our assiduity, passions eradicated by our counsel, and a multitude of men pouring abroad over society the lustre of a virtuous example, and becoming meet to be inheritors with the saints in light—and all in consequence of the direction which we have given to them in youth? I ask again, what profession has any higher rewards?

Again, we at this day are in a manner the pioneers in this work in this country. Education, as a science, has scarcely yet been naturalized among us. Radical improvement in the means of education is an idea that seems but just to have entered into men's minds. It becomes us to act worthily of our station. Let us by all the means in our power second the efforts and the wishes of the public. Let us see that the first steps in this course are taken wisely. This country ought to be the best educated on the face of the earth. By the blessing of Heaven, we can do much towards the making of it so. God helping us, then, let us make our mark on the rising generation.

# REMARKS

OF

## DR. WILLIAM E. CHANNING ON EDUCATION AND TEACHERS.

---

IN 1833, Dr. Channing brought the aid of his personal influence and powerful pen, to the service of the teacher. In an article in the Christian Examiner, for November, 1833, written for the express purpose of commending the Annals of Education, and the great subject to which it was devoted, under the editorial charge of William C. Woodbridge, to the attention of the best class of minds in the community, the following views are presented as to the importance of institutions for the education of teachers, and the true nature and dignity of the office:

"We are not aware that in this country a single school for teachers is supported at the public expense. How much would be gained, if every state should send one of its most distinguished citizens to examine the modes of teaching at home and in Europe, and should then place him at the head of a seminary for the formation of teachers."

* * * * * *

"There is no office higher than that of a teacher of youth; for there is nothing on earth so precious as the mind, soul, character of the child. No office should be regarded with greater respect. The first minds in the community should be encouraged to assume it. Parents should do all but impoverish themselves, to induce such to become the guardians and guides of their children. To this good, all their show and luxury should be sacrificed. Here they should be lavish, whilst they straiten themselves in every thing else. They should wear the cheapest clothes, live on the plainest food, if they can in no other way secure to their families the best instruction. They should have no anxiety to accumulate property for their children, provided they can place them under influences which will awaken their faculties, inspire them with pure and high principles, and fit them to bear a manly, useful, and honorable part in the world. No language can express the cruelty or folly of that economy, which, to leave a fortune to a child, starves his intellect, impoverishes his heart."

* * * * * *

"We know not how society can be aided more than by the formation of a body of wise and efficient educators. We know not any class which would contribute so much to the stability of the state, and to domestic happiness. Much as we respect the ministry of the gospel, we believe that it must yield in importance to the office of training the young. In truth, the ministry now accomplishes little, for want of that early intellectual and moral discipline, by which alone a community can be prepared to distinguish truth from falsehood, to comprehend the instructions of the pulpit, to receive higher and broader views of duty, and to apply general principles to the diversified details of life. A body of cultivated men, devoted, with their whole hearts, to the improvement of education, and to the most effectual training of the young, would work a fundamental revolution in society. They would leaven the community with just principles."

* * * * * *

"We maintain that higher ability is required for the office of an educator of the young, than for that of a statesman. The highest ability is that which penetrates farthest into human nature, comprehends the mind in all its capacities, traces out the laws of thought and moral action, understands the perfection of human nature, and how it may be approached, understands the springs, motives, applications, by which the child is to be roused to the most vigorous and harmonious action of all its faculties, understands its perils, and knows how to blend and modify the influences which outward circumstances exert on the youthful mind. The speculations of statesmen are shallow, compared with these. It is the chief function of the statesman to watch over the outward interests of a people; that of the educator to quicken its soul. The statesman must study and manage the passions and prejudices of the community; the educator must study the essential, the deepest, the loftiest principles of human nature. The statesman works with coarse instruments for coarse ends; the educator is to work by the most refined influences on that delicate, ethereal essence—the immortal soul."

* * * * * *

"One great cause of the low estimation in which the teacher is now held, may be found in narrow views of education. The multitude think, that to educate a child, is to crowd into its mind a given amount of knowledge—to teach the mechanism of reading and writing—to load the memory with words—to prepare a boy for the routine of a trade. No wonder, then, that they think almost every body fit to teach. The true end of education, is to unfold and direct aright our whole nature. Its office is to call forth power of every kind—power of thought, affection, will, and outward action; power to observe, to reason, to judge, to contrive; power to adopt good ends firmly, and to pursue them efficiently; power to govern ourselves, and to influence others; power to gain and to spread happiness. Reading is but an instrument; education is to teach its best use. The intellect was created, not to receive passively a few words, dates, facts, but to be active for the acquisition of truth. Accordingly, education should labor to inspire a profound love of truth, and to teach the processes of investigation. A sound logic, by which we mean the science or art which instructs us in the laws of reasoning and evidence, in the true methods of inquiry, and in the sources of false judgments, is an essential part of a good education. And yet, how little is done to teach the right use of the intellect, in the common modes of training either rich or poor. As a general rule, the young are to be made, as far as possible, their own teachers—the discoverers of truth—the interpreters of nature—the framers of science. They are to be helped to help themselves. They should be taught to observe and study the world in which they live, to trace the connections of events, to rise from particular facts to general principles, and then to apply these in explaining new phenomena. Such is a rapid outline of the intellectual education, which, as far as possible, should be given to all human beings; and with this, moral education should go hand in hand. In proportion as the child gains knowledge, he should be taught how to use it well—how to turn it to the good of mankind. He should study the world as God's world, and as the sphere in which he is to form interesting connections with his fellow-creatures. A spirit of humanity should be breathed into him from all his studies. In teaching geography, the physical and moral condition, the wants, advantages, and striking peculiarities of different nations, and the relations of climate, seas, rivers, mountains, to their characters and pursuits, should be pointed out, so as to awaken an interest in man wherever he dwells. History should be constantly used to exercise the moral judgment of the young, to call forth sympathy with the fortunes of the human race, and to expose to indignation and abhorrence that selfish ambition, that passion for dominion, which has so long deluged the earth with blood and woe. And not only should the excitement of just moral feeling be proposed in every study. The science of morals should form an important part of every child's instruction. One branch of ethics should be particularly insisted on by the government. Every school, established by law, should be specially bound to teach the duties of the citizen to the state, to unfold the principles of free institutions, and to train the young to an enlightened patriotism. From these brief and imperfect views of the nature and ends of a wise education, we learn the dignity of the profession to which it is entrusted, and the importance of securing to it the best minds of the community."

* * * * * *

"We have said that it is the office of the teacher to call into vigorous action the mind of the child. He must do more. He must strive to create a thirst, an insatiable craving for knowledge, to give animation to study and make it a pleasure, and thus to communicate an impulse which will endure when the instructions of the

the school are closed. The mark of a good teacher is, not only that he produces great effort in his pupils, but that he dismisses them from his care, conscious of having only laid the foundation of knowledge, and anxious and resolved to improve themselves. One of the sure signs of the low state of instruction among us is, that the young, on leaving school, feel as if the work of intellectual culture were done, and give up steady, vigorous effort for higher truth and wider knowledge. Our daughters at sixteen, and our sons at eighteen or twenty, have *finished* their education. The true use of a school is, to enable and dispose the pupil to learn through life; and if so, who does not see that the office of teacher requires men of enlarged and liberal minds, and of winning manners—in other words, that it requires as cultivated men as can be found in society. If to drive and to drill were the chief duties of an instructor—if to force into the mind an amount of lifeless knowledge—to make the child a machine—to create a repugnance to books, to mental labor, to the acquisition of knowledge—were the great objects of the school-room, then the teacher might be chosen on the principles which now govern the school-committees in no small part of our country. Then the man who can read, write, cypher, and whip, and will exercise his gifts at the lowest price, deserves the precedence which he now too often enjoys. But if the human being be something more than a block or a brute—if he have powers which proclaim him a child of God, and which were given for noble action and perpetual progress, then a better order of things should begin among us, and truly enlightened men should be summoned to the work of education."

In an address delivered at the Odeon, in Boston, on the 28th of Feb., 1837, he thus advocates the establishment of an institution for the professional training of teachers:

"We need an institution for the formation of better teachers; and, until this step is taken, we can make no important progress. The most crying want in this commonwealth is the want of accomplished teachers. We boast of our schools; but our schools do comparatively little, for want of educated instructors. Without good teaching, a school is but a name. An institution for training men to train the young, would be a fountain of living waters, sending forth streams to refresh present and future ages. As yet, our legislators have denied to the poor and laboring classes this principal means of their elevation. We trust they will not always prove blind to the highest interest of the state.

We want better teachers, and more teachers, for all classes of society—for rich and poor, for children and adults. We want that the resources of the community should be directed to the procuring of better instructors, as its highest concern. One of the surest signs of the regeneration of society will be, the elevation of the art of teaching to the highest rank in the community. When a people shall learn that its greatest benefactors and most important members, are men devoted to the liberal instruction of all its classes—to the work of raising to life its buried intellect, it will have opened to itself the path of true glory. This truth is making its way. Socrates is now regarded as the greatest man in an age of great men. The name of *king* has grown dim before that of *apostle*. To teach, whether by word or action, is the highest function on earth.

Nothing is more needed, than that men of superior gifts, and of benevolent spirit, should devote themselves to the instruction of the less enlightened classes in the great end of life—in the dignity of their nature—in their rights and duties—in the history, laws, and institutions of their country—in the philosophy of their employments—in the laws, harmonies, and productions of outward nature, and, especially, in the art of bringing up children in health of body, and in vigor and purity of mind. We need a new profession or vocation, the object of which shall be to wake up the intellect in those spheres where it is now buried in habitual slumber.

We want a class of liberal-minded instructors, whose vocation it shall be, to place the views of the most enlightened minds within the reach of a more and more extensive portion of their fellow-creatures. The wealth of a community should flow out like water for the preparation and employment of such teachers—for enlisting powerful and generous minds in the work of giving impulse to their race.

Nor let it be said that men, able and disposed to carry on this work, must not be looked for in such a world as ours. Christianity, which has wrought so many miracles of beneficence—which has sent forth so many apostles and martyrs—so many Howards and Clarksons, can raise up laborers for this harvest also. Nothing is needed but a new pouring out of the spirit of Christian love—nothing but a new comprehension of the brotherhood of the human race, to call forth efforts which seem impossibilities in a self-seeking and self-indulging age."

From the outset, Dr. Channing exhibited great interest in the establishment of the Board of Education, and the permanent organization of the Normal Schools. In a letter addressed to Mr. Mann, in August, 1837, congratulating him and the commonwealth on his acceptance of the office of Secretary of the Board, he says:

"You could not find a nobler station. Government has no nobler one to give. You must allow me to labor under you according to my opportunities. If at any time I can aid you, you must let me know, and I shall be glad to converse with you always about your operations. When will the low, degrading party quarrels of the country cease, and the better minds come to think what can be done toward a substantial, generous improvement of the community? 'My ear is pained, my very soul is sick,' with the monotonous, yet furious clamors about currency, banks, &c., when the spiritual interests of the community seem hardly to be recognized as having any reality.

If we can but turn the wonderful energy of this people into a right channel, what a new heaven and earth must be realized among us! And I do not despair. Your willingness to consecrate yourself to this work, is a happy omen. You do not stand alone, or form a rare exception to the times. There must be many to be touched by the same truths which are stirring you."

A few months afterward, he attended, at Taunton, one of the series of county conventions, which Mr. Mann held, in pursuance of the plan of the Board, to attract attention to the improvement of common schools, and took part in the proceedings by submitting and advocating a resolution affirming the immediate and pressing necessity of public and legislative action in behalf of common education. We make a few extracts from a newspaper report:

"We are told that this or that man should have an extensive education; but, that another, who occupies a lower place in society, needs only a narrow one: that the governor of a state requires a thorough education, while the humble mechanic has need only to study his last and his leather. But why should not the latter, though pursuing an humble occupation, be permitted to open his eyes on the lights of knowledge? Has he not a soul of as great capacity as the former? Is he not sustaining the same relations as a parent, a citizen, a neighbor, and as a subject of God's moral government? To educate a child is, in fact, a greater work than to perform the duties of a governor. What is it? It is to take the direction of mind, to cultivate the powers of thought, and to teach the duties which we owe to God and to our neighbor. Can a parent teach his child these duties, unless he has learned them himself? Every one, no matter what is his occupation or place, needs an education, in order that he may have the proper use of his powers, and be enabled to improve them through life.

Some say, were these views of education to prevail, there would be little or no work done—manual labor would fail. But for the purpose of working effectually, one should be intelligent; he will bring the more to pass, because he labors for some known object, and is stimulated by motives which he understands and feels.

We want worthy laborers, who exalt themselves while they benefit others. The circumstances in which they are placed, are fitted to call forth their mental powers, to awaken thought, and to impress them with their responsibilities. They are

# THE TEACHER'S MOTIVES.

BY HORACE MANN, LL.D.,

Late Secretary of the Mass. Board of Education, and President of Antioch College, Ohio.

---

ALL labor is delightful or irksome; noble or ignoble; and right or wrong in the sight of God, according to the quality of the motive that prompts its performance. That the moral quality of an action is always determined by the nature of the motive that begets it is a truism. But this is not the whole of the truth which is contained in that truism; the perseverance, the sustaining and uplifting energy with which we prosecute a purpose: the joy or loathing that wings or bemires our steps, in whatever we undertake, depend upon the motive that inspires us. Motive may hallow the most servile or desecrate the most sacred employment; may elevate into piety the menial office of washing a Savior's feet, or profane into perfidy and murder the privilege of saluting the Savior with a kiss.

Every body knows that the scale of motive is infinite in extent. It reaches upward to God, who is at the moral zenith; and it sinks to the moral nadir of all that is anti-god-like. Some motives are born of nature, and are what are called spontaneous. Some are the offspring of a cultivated intellect, and others of a moral and religious education. In cases of high necessity, nature prepares special motives to meet special exigencies. In the brute creation, the love of the young lies dormant, until awakened by the birth of their own offspring, but as soon as that event occurs, there is sure to flame up the blind, resistless orgasm of maternal love. I have seen a barn-yard fowl fly defiantly at a railroad locomotive with its attendant train, for daring to invade her walks when she clucked forth her chickens. I have had the most timid and wild of all our wild-fowl,—the partridge, fly in my face when accidentally obtruding upon her brood, in a woodland ramble. There is something which seems far more heroic and poetic, in the scream and swoop of the eagle, when her nest is invaded, than in her loftiest sunward flights; and the lioness bears about in her breast a latent magazine of rage, which nature stored there for the protection of her whelps. A mother is transfigured, when her babe is in peril. Fearlessly she climbs mountain heights, or plunges into ocean depths. During a child's sickness, her spirit seems to perform the miracle of abrogating or suspending the laws of the body. She can labor without rest, watch without sleep, subsist without food. An exaltation of motive works the seeming miracles.

There are other motives which exist to some extent in all men, at all times; but they are variously combined, and they operate with various degrees of intensity. According to their several natures, they form the character and determine the destiny of their possessor. What made Columbus hold on in his course, while all his crew mutinied, and while nature herself, acting through the magnet which she had lent him as a guide, seemed to remonstrate against his audacity? What upheld those self-exiles, the Pilgrim Fathers of New England, as they went from England to Leyden, and from Leyden to Plymouth Rock, but a motive that was founded upon the Rock of Ages? In fine, motive determines every thing. It makes the same external act or course of conduct, high or low, joyous or painful, sacred or profane. It gives fertility to our life, or smites it with barrenness. It makes a king on his throne tremble, or a martyr on his scaffold triumph.

Before considering the motives by which you as teachers should be animated, I deem it proper to lay open for your inspection, my own motives for addressing you on this subject.

I come before you, my friends, feeling an unspeakable interest in your personal advancement and professional success. If there be any class of persons toward whom my heart yearns with a tender, gushing, and deathless affection, it is the teachers of our youth. My nerves are intertwined with their nerves; my heart thrills or throbs with theirs; and so close is the affinity I feel for them, that their good or ill fortune is matter of *personality* to me. If I have any earthly ambition, it is that which can be gratified only by their success; and all the high hopes which I do avowedly entertain of a more glorious future for the human race, are built upon the elevation of the teacher's profession and the enlargement of the teacher's usefulness. Whatever ground of confidence there may be for the perpetuation of our civil and religious liberties; whatever prospect of the elevation of our posterity; whatever faith in the general Christianization of the world;—these aspirations and this faith depend upon teachers, more than upon any, more than upon all other human instrumentalities united. And if in the councils of God, there be a gracious purpose of restoring his lost image to the human race, I believe that he will choose and anoint the teachers of youth among the choicest of His ministers for the holy work. In addressing teachers, therefore, I feel that I stand upon holy ground; for I am in the august presence of the highest interests, mortal and immortal;—I am in the midst of the eternal principles of moral life and moral death. God's law, human accountability, the unending consequences of our conduct, encompass me about. Amid these awful concernments, the most splendid of earth's objects fade into dimness; the most magnificent of earthly ambitions wane and recede, and I am admonished, as with no mortal voice, to speak alike in the love and in the fear of truth.

This, therefore, my friends, is no occasion for flattery. I come not here to feast praise-loving hearts with honeyed words, or to sing lullabies over disquieted consciences. If the worm gnaws in any breast, let it gnaw, until it shall eat out the very pith and core of vanity and egotism. If the fire burns, let it not be quenched, until the dross shall be purged from the gold. If there be a noble-hearted teacher here present, I know that he or she would rebuke me if I should spend the passing hour in magnifying his rights, forgetful of his duties; if I should extol the dignity of his profession, as though he had created it, instead of being obligated by it; or in telling him that because he grasped the implement of Solomon in his hand, he, therefore, must have the wisdom of Solomon in his head. As it is the duty of the faithful physician to probe a wound to the bottom, though the patient does flinch; so it is the office of the faithful friend to unmask any low or unworthy motive which may lurk in the heart of his friend. Would that I could so unfold our responsibilities to the rising generation, and our duties to heaven, that each one of us should clothe himself in the sackcloth of humility, and cry out from the bottom of his heart, "Woe is me, that in performing the great work which the Lord has committed to my hands, I have been so unprofitable a servant."

In considering the motives by which teachers should be governed, I shall begin with the lowest.

I maintain that it is not only right and proper for a teacher, but that it is his duty also, to have reference to the recompense of reward; I mean pecuniary reward, or in the vernacular, *dollars and cents.* In this, as in every other vocation, the workman is worthy of his hire. To say that in proportion as a work is invested with high and sacred attributes, it is therefore to go unpaid for, transcends transcendentalism. When it shall be found that a man's natural appetites for food and beverage shall die out, one after another, as he enlists in more sacred callings, it will be good evidence that a life devoted to holy labor should forego those natural supplies which it no longer needs. When a minister of the gospel, with a family to be educated, can subsist, as the chameleon was once said to do, on the air; when a missionary to the Arctic regions can keep his blood at the temperature of 98°, without clothing or shelter; or when an apostle, or one greater than an apostle, can sequester himself from all worldly cares and pursuits, and devote his life to training up children in the way they should go, and the ravens shall bring him his food and raiment; then I shall believe that all our teachers ought to do, as some of them are now almost compelled to do—work for nothing and find themselves. But so far as I can learn, the experience is universal in our times, that a healthy stomach, after a strict abstinence of twelve or fifteen hours, will crave food, however pure the conscience may be; or in other words, a conscience void of offence will not replenish a stomach void of nourishment. So a missionary, sent naked to Iceland or Spitzbergen, will freeze, however ardent his benevolence; and the most exalted piety will not be a sufficiently tenacious cement to hold body and soul together, without a little alloy of animal food; or at least, without some chemical amalgam whose principal ingredients are bread and butter.

But while I maintain that it is right for a teacher to make sure of an honorable and equitable salary;—nay, that it would be inexcusable in him to make no provision for his own household—whether that household be in the plural or have just passed into the dual, or still remain in the singular number,—still, when he has deliberately agreed upon a price for his services, all pecuniary considerations should forthwith be dismissed from his thoughts. He has then come under the most solemn obligations to perform a certain amount of duties, and no inadequacy in his compensation, however great, can excuse any neglect in his duties, however small. The pilot must not sleep and suffer the vessel to be wrecked, on the plea of short pay.

What then shall we think of a teacher, who having secured the most liberal salary, seeks to contract his duties within a narrower and narrower limit, and grudgingly performs even those which are embraced within the contracted circle; who spends his purloined leisure in pleasure-seeking, in pecuniary speculations, or without the most cogent reasons in the lottery of school-book making? What of him who clips a half hour from the morning or afternoon session,—which however it may stand in the civil code, is a greater offence in the moral one than clipping the king's coin? What of him who carries his body only to the school-room, while his soul plays truant; and who, when his classes are hungering and thirsting for spiritual food, gives them for bread, a stone; for a fish, a serpent; and for an egg, a scorpion? There is no neglect on earth so criminal as the neglect of a teacher to do his duties to his scholars; and the darkest dungeon in the realms of "outer darkness" will be reserved for those teachers who through sloth or worldliness suffer these little ones to perish.

There is another class of motives, not indeed of a very high or meritorious character, but which incur no censure, unless indulged in to excess. I refer to the teacher's desire of general approval, and especially to the mature and time-satisfied opinions of those who have been his pupils. The common credit or discredit, which inures to a workman, for doing his work well or ill, is an allowable incentive to fidelity. The reports which will go abroad respecting the literary proficiencies and moral condition of a school, at the end of a term or a year, must be an auxiliary stimulus to exertion, in every mind that is not either too high or too low to be classed among the human. There is not an artisan or an artist, from a cobbler to a sculptor, who is not elated or depressed by the prevalent opinions of the public respecting the quality of his work. "An advancing school," "a stationary school," "a retrograding school," become expressions of weighty import, when they are uttered by every mouth in the district; when recorded in the school committee's report, to be read in open town-meeting or printed for general perusal, and at last, perhaps, published in the annual Abstract of School Returns. Now, though the condition of a school is modified by many things, yet more than any other thing, it is modified by the character of the teacher. And hence, whatever other impress is stamped upon it, the teacher's image is most conspicuous. In all schools kept by the same teacher for any considerable length of time, he determines the number of the dunces, as well as the number of the scholars and the gentlemen. A teacher who is a dolt himself, makes scholars who are dolts, in the same way that a poor farmer impoverishes a fertile farm. A teacher, therefore, who decries the general capacity of his scholars, disparages himself; and all intelligent people who hear his detractions, say, "No wonder; does not like beget like?" On the other hand, we know that an accomplished teacher will take the roughest boor, and by skillful and constant manipulations will smooth and polish him into a gentleman; he will take the most metallic and hard-hearted wretch, and by placing him in such positions that his own electric currents may flow through him, he will at last endue him with a celestial polarity.

But the future and abiding opinion, formed of a teacher by his pupils, is a far weightier consideration. Such an opinion will be formed and will be expressed. Every person remembers his school teachers. Almost every one is so situated in adult life, that he can express his opinion of his former teachers without fear or favor. If a teacher has had large numbers under his care, for a series of years, he has sent out a sufficient company to make, by themselves, a very formidable public opinion. In the pleasures or business of life, these former pupils will meet. In recurring to bygone days, the school and the teacher will rise to vivid recollection. Merits and demerits will be remembered, and an honorable or a condemnatory judgment be awarded. When a teacher has kept large schools, and sent out company after company for successive years, there is probably not a day in the year, and perhaps not an hour in the day, when his excellencies or his faults are not rehearsed; and if there were any truth in that old-fashioned superstition, that the right or the left ear burns, as people are speaking well or ill of us, all old teachers must always have, at least one, if not two, very hot and flame-colored ears.

Reflect on this a little, my friends, for it is really worthy of your attention. All handicraftsmen, all cultivators of the soil, who have any regard for their reputation, exercise some care and caution, in regard to the fabrics or the products, which they exhibit at home, or send abroad for sale. The perishable materials of the loom, which hardly survive their manufacture for a year, the consumable products of the earth, the most enduring of which are expected to last only till another harvest, are all so many witnesses, for the time being, of the skill and fidelity of their producers. But these workmen send forth dumb commodities,—things speechless from their birth, that have no memory for past evil or good, that can break forth at the mention of their producer's name, into no ejaculation of heart-felt gratitude, nor utter curses for remembered injuries. But what sort of plants are they which go forth from the teacher's nursery? Are they animals? Will you hear no more from them after a twelvemonth? Or in the common course of nature, will they not last for your honor or shame, as much longer than you last, as their years are now exceeded by yours?

And again, are the products, which go forth from your hands, voiceless? Do they wait for some bystander to discover their origin and to make proclamation of it? Or do they, each in his own sphere, make this proclamation themselves? If a man sends a shabby boot or shoe into the market; if he sends a yoke of badly trained cattle, or a vicious colt, to be sold at the Fair, he puts no earmark on the work of his hands. He gladly compounds for secresy. He feels like a rogue who has counterfeited the current coin,—who desires to pass off his base money and abscond. But the miserable teacher can not deny or conceal his productions. If he does not proclaim them, they proclaim him. They bear his earmark on their bodies and on their souls as plainly as though they came bleeding from the pillory. The records kept by a teacher who had been in the same school for eleven consecutive years, in Massachusetts, showed that one in every nine of his boys had been sent to the State's prison, the jail, or house of correction. When the question arises, who presided at the formation of a character, the teacher can not prove an alibi. There goes a man whom everybody calls a vile, calumnious bigot; and you, Mr. Arch-bigot, so culled and collated the divine texts as to make him so. You taught the bad Levite to hate the good Samaritan. Indeed the whole subsequent life of a pupil may be considered as a sort of practical commentary, of which the teacher is the text. A pupil may be, not a standing but a walking advertisement of a teacher's incompetency; and by the necessity of the case, the teacher can not help himself. No court of Chancery can grant an injunction to stay his proceedings; the nuisance shouts its origin, and, what is worse, the teacher can not abate it. His only hope and chance are to wait until death shall remove this spiritual offspring from his sight; but death will probably take the parent before the child. I do not say this is true in regard to all scholars and under all circumstances, but it has been and still is true, to such an extent as to justify caution and excite alarm amongst all teachers, at least all permanent ones. And such results are becoming more and more extensively true, every day we live. Just in proportion as the art and science of education advance, just so far will the character of individuals be more and more referred to the specific influences of the teacher under whom they were trained. Early training and adult character will be more and more recognized as cause and effect. The union between teacher and scholar will become closer and closer, and the character of the former will be reflected from the conduct of the latter, in more legible inscriptions of honor or shame.

I have said that pupils will go forth into life, pronouncing praises, or, perhaps, maledictions, upon their teachers, wherever they go. In one respect, this reputation falls short of the truth. A pupil may bestow the highest verbal commendations on a teacher, and express ardent gratitude toward him, but yet with such accompaniments of speech and of manner, as to betray both the teacher's folly and his own. I recollect having once heard a man, who had long passed middle life, when addressing an intelligent audience of at least a thousand people, advocate emulation among scholars, and the bestowment of medals, in schools. To make his argument more effective, he gave us a chapter from his own school history. He described the competition between his classmates and himself for the medal which had been offered;—how they strove but he won; how swiftly they ran to reach the goal, but how he outran them all; how worthy the honor his rivals were, but how he excelled them and triumphed. In order to prolong and magnify this self-laudation, he introduced the teacher, and bespangled him with garish compliments; because the teacher had had the sagacity to see that the boaster was entitled to the prize. When the egotist had done,—in all that audience of a thousand persons, I do not think there was an intelligent man or woman, who did not say, "Poor Pupil! Poor Teacher! What precious fools you have both made of yourselves!" So, on the other hand, a man may upbraid and vilify a teacher, on account of the treatment received from him,—in such a way, however, that every sagacious hearer shall say, at once, that the teacher must have had the most ample justification for doing all he is blamed for. And this is as true in matters of intellectual instruction as in moral guidance. Suppose a man tell you, how perfect a reader his teacher was, and how careful he was to train him, according to the most perfect models of the art, and then gives you a disgusting specimen of ultra theatrical heroics, in proof of his assertion. As the public become more discerning on this subject, there will be a closer and closer approximation to justice, in the praise or the blame awarded to teachers, on an inspection of their work. In short, every word of a teacher, whether shouted or whispered, awaken an echo which will live forever. Year after year, while he survives, and years after he shall be dead, the reverberations will come back to salute his own ears and the ears of his friends who outlive him, in tones of approval or condemnation.

Thongh an inadequate expression of the truth, yet for want of a better illustration, I would compare each *professional* teacher to a great organ-builder,—each child whom he educates being one of the pipes wrought by his hand into the living instrument. These pipes are all instinct with sound, for such is their nature. Tones of some sort, they will emit, and nothing but death,—nay, not death itself can silence them. The teacher, by his dexterity or his clumsiness, moulds and shapes, opens or contracts these pipes, in accordance with, or in opposition to the laws of his heavenly art. According to the benevolent or the tyrannical spirit of his prelusions, he gives them the form, and breathes into them the soul, which will afterwards go forth, uttering divine or savage sounds. Day by day, and year by year, under his ever-repeated touch, the pliant fibres of their vocal apparatus harden and consolidate into those enduring forms, which shall determine the quality of the articulate music they will afterwards discourse. I pretend to no special quickness of ear, either for poetry or music, but on entering a school which has been taught for a long time by the same person, it seems to me that I need no imagination, but only the common faculty of hearing, to catch the air or strain with which these organ pipes are spontaneously vocal. You will no sooner set foot in a school-room which has suffered under a long reign of violence and severity and terror, than you will hear this teacher-built organ growl out its angry dissonance.

In another school, a lovely female teacher is tuning her living instrument to sing such strains as this:

As zephyrs to the Æolian chords,
As dew and sun to flowers;
So sweetly fall her heavenly words
On these glad hearts of ours.

Lit by her smile, the murkiest sky
With Orient splendor glows;
Rain-drops are pearls, and 'neath her eye,
Each snow-flake falls a rose.

Oh grant, Dear God, that we may live,
And win her angel powers;
In turn to childhood's heart we'll give
The heaven she gave to ours.

Or in the case of some noble old teacher, who has spent his life in preparing a soil rich as Eden, and in sowing it with the seeds of high thoughts and pure sentiments, a strain bursts forth loftier and diviner than ever came forth from cathedral organ, or from strong-voiced orchestra with its thousand exulting instruments. His pupils pour out their lyric strains in this wise:

Hail to the Framer of our mortal frames!
Feeble and frail were we,
An insect progeny,
Scorched by the summer, and by winter froze;
Pain choked our first drawn breath,
Disease preluded Death,
And Nature's kindliest elements were foes,
For bodies prone that crawled like worms,
He reared these heaven aspiring forms,
And in each arm and foot and hand,
Put steel-spring fibres for old threads of sand;
Till now in Health's invulnerable mail,
All toils, all perils, fearless we assail;—
Knowing that whatsoe'er in earth is stored
Of giant might, still mightier is its Lord:
In sun or rain
On mount or main,

Torrid or Arctic,—wheresoe'er we dwell,
Nature's fierce powers are liege men of our will;
Hail to the Framer of our mortal frames!
Hail to the builder of our god-like minds!
Through space and time he sought,
Wherever God had wrought;
Saw where the deep foundations of the world were laid,
And measured up the starry dome that arches overhead;
And said, upon this depth and breadth and height of plan,
I'll build the structure of my pupil—Man,
Arts, knowledge, sciences, he took,
With all the tongues wise men have spoke,
And gathered in the Dome of Thought,
The truths wherewith God's realms are fraught,
Till, in the mystic chambers of each brain,
Creation was created o'er again!
Hail to the builder of our god-like minds!
Hail to the Former of our deathless souls!
Tutor, Securer.* Blessed be his name!
Meek follower was he of Him who came
To save the lost. He saved us from the shame
Of Earth's ambitions, vanities, and lies,
And our young hearts baptized with flame,
Whose fount is in the skies.
Copious his lessons overran
With love to God and love to man,
And lest his *Words* we might forget,
His *Life* the holy signet set.
While others proudly sought to show
The vision of a heaven above,
By truth and peace, by joy and love,
He imaged heaven below.
Oh, haste the eternal day,
When like bright stars around
We each shall gem
The diadem
With which his brow is crowned,
Hail to the Former of our deathless souls!

And thus is every professional teacher, through every day of his life constantly preparing,—or rather composing,—some lofty anthem, or some low doggerel, which shall be pealed to his honor or shame, as long as his memory lasts.

How careful would every mechanician be, if each well or ill-made wheel, in all his machines, instead of an industrious and business like humming, or a distressful creaking, should boldly articulate the name of its maker, at every revolution. Who then shall set bounds,

* It is a beautiful fact that the etymon of the word Tutor means to protect, defend, or secure.

even to the rational solicitude which every teacher should feel in regard to those living and speaking products that pass from under his hand?

Another motive which should powerfully urge on a teacher to the full performance of his duty, is the desire to elevate the profession to which he belongs. "Every man," says Lord Bacon, "is a debtor to his profession;"—which means, as I suppose, that every man, by the mere fact of membership, comes under an implied obligation to render that profession some valuable service. Surely it would be held dishonorable, not to say a dishonest act, if a man should join any partnership, corporation, or guild, appropriate to his own personal advantage, some portion of its general funds,—whether those funds might consist of money or of respectability,—and should then, without requital, desert the company he has defrauded. Still worse would it be, if the interloper should bring general discredit upon his fellow-members, or degrade the character of their employment. Each of these offences the incompetent teacher commits. In the first place, does he not pocket more than his equitable share of the public money given for the support of schools; or if I may use a technical phrase, current among rogues, because it so well describes the quality of his conduct, does he not *crib?* In the second place, he degrades the standard of good school-keeping, and covers all his brethren with some degree of odium.

On the other hand, the accomplished teacher not only performs an invaluable service to all his pupils, but he sheds lustre upon all his fellow-laborers, and he elevates the common sentiments of mankind, in regard to the dignity of the employment. By making the profession honorable, he increases its attractive power, as a profession, and thus draws minds of a higher order to engage in it and adorn it. This aggrandizes it and irradiates it still more, and action and reaction hasten the grandest results. The employment itself is thus lifted more and more out of the sphere and reach of ignorance and incompetency. Nor is this all the good service which the accomplished teacher renders. He is perpetually improving old methods, and inventing new ones, for the instruction and government of children. These improvements enable all teachers to do their work better and easier, as well as to do more in the same time. It is the opinion of the best teachers that the art of teaching is yet in an exceedingly rude state, and that its instruments and appliances are yet to be as much improved, as navigation has been improved by steamboats, or land travel by railroads. It is only the incompetent teacher who mistakes the circumference of his nutshell for the outside of the universe. Some great improvements have already been made, and doubtless, in this, as in all the mechanic arts and in all the sciences, still greater ones are to follow. The black-board is to vivid and exact instruction, what the art of painting was to civilization; and yet the black-board does not perform one-fourth of the service which it will do, when the art of drawing becomes a common attainment. A black-board, to a teacher who can not draw, is, with the exception of arithmetic, very much like a library to a man who can not read. Now, all the losses incurred through deficiency, as well as all the advantages gained by skill, are daily illustrated in the practice of the accomplished teacher. His life is a lesson on the *exhibitory* plan. What Watt and Fulton were to the steam-engine; what Franklin was to electricity, Newton to astronomy, Bacon to philosophy, Columbus and Vasco de Gama to a true knowledge of the earth—all this are accomplished teachers,—the Pestalozzis, the Wilderspins, and the Colburns, to their profession, and its professors. Thousands and tens of thousands,—a profession reaching to the end of time—will do homage to their memories.

Another motive which should operate strongly upon the mind of a teacher, is the desire to be master of his business. Here all selfish and all benevolent promptings coincide, and impel with united force in the same direction. Just so far as any one improves himself as a teacher, he improves himself as a man, and elevates his standing as a citizen. Consider, for a moment, upon what vantage ground a finished teacher stands, and the attainments which are indispensable in his daily business—if he has the good sense to cast away all pedantry—are available in his daily intercourse with men. Let us look at this point a little in detail, for I think many teachers do not fully appreciate, in this particular, the advantages of their position. Even in the lowest and most mechanical departments of a teacher's duty, his attainments are hardly less serviceable, in his daily intercourse with the world, than they are in the school-room. Every teacher of respectable qualifications for the humblest class of our district schools, is a perfect speller of all the common words in our language, he is also a good penman and a good reader. As a grammarian, he can both speak and write the English language with propriety. As a geographer, he is acquainted with every city, mountain, river, and island of any note in the world, knows all the political divisions of the earth; and has the principal statistics of population, commerce, religion, education, and so forth, at the end of his tongue. And as an arithmetician, he can solve, with facility and correctness, at least all the questions that ever arise in the ordinary business transactions of life.

Now into whatever circle or association such a teacher may be thrown, his information will come into frequent demand, and he will be always able to take a respectable, and often a conspicuous part in conversation. He will be better prepared than any others, excepting perhaps a few professional men, to write a letter, draft a circular, or make a report, which, in its orthography, grammar, style and arrangement, shall be substantially faultless. If the news of the day, whether from armies, or from missionaries, suggest any geographical inquiry, he is ready to answer it. Being familiar with arithmetic, he will declare the answer to any question that may arise in this branch, while others are puzzling over the preliminaries; and he will be able to detect, at a glance, the thousand mistakes into which the half educated are constantly falling. I say then, that a competent teacher for a common district school enters any ordinary circle of men and women, or takes part in the business of any organized body,—whether it be a temperance meeting or a town meeting, under very considerable and very desirable advantages. He possesses all these important advantages, too, the first year he begins to teach, and however ordinary the school over which he presides. But suppose him to continue in the business of teaching for twenty or thirty years, what abundant and enviable opportunities does he possess for becoming a real master of his profession, as well as for obtaining great prominence and consideration in society. The permanent teacher will enlarge his knowledge in all directions. He will expand his grammar into philology, rhetoric, and logic. He will turn modern geography backward into ancient. He will make geography, biography, and history mutually illustrate, diversify, and enrich each other. In connection with book-keeping, he will not only learn the common forms of business, but many of the leading points of the Law-merchant. Through mechanical and natural philosophy, especially if to these he adds chemistry, he will become acquainted with that extensive and beautiful field of inquiry,—the application of science to the arts of life. Through political and moral science, he will examine, as it were by a celestial light, the condition of individuals and nations and learn what conduct, what institutions, what form of government leads to their exaltation or abasement. Through astronomy, he will look outward into infinite space, and through geology backward into infinite time; and he will never enter his school-room, or thoughtfully survey the children before him, without thinking of heaven and an hereafter. Besides being a careful reader of every leading work and periodical pertaining to his profession, he will, through newspapers and reviews at least, keep up with the times, as we familiarly express it, and learn the progress which great principles and great causes are making throughout the world. Now it will not be questioned that a well-bred person of spotless character, and possessing this variety and amplitude of infomration, will be a welcome inmate in any society or family, and will adorn whatever circle he may enter. His manners will please, his kindness will endear, his good humor, nurtured by his intercourse with children, will enliven, his knowledge will instruct, his dignity and worth will win spontaneous deference and respect,—sometimes rising to reverence.

It has been remarked a thousand times, that the profession of the law prepares a man for becoming a politician,—(I use this word here in a good sense,)—because a lawyer, by his daily studies, is becoming familiar with most of the great principles on which the statesman proceeds. So the teacher, if he be true to himself, is daily making acquisitions which assimilate him more and more to all the leading minds, in all the leading departments of life. He becomes a literary and classical critic, and he is consulted by scientific men. On the side of political economy, he approaches the statesman, and on the side of ethics he equals the moralist. As a physiologist, he is better than a physician, and as a trainer of children in the way they should go, he will advance the cause of virtue and humanity, more than as many polemics as could stand within the orbit of Saturn. In himself alone, he is a temperance society and a peace society; he goes for the abolition, not of one evil only, but of all evils, and he is the most effective of Home Missions.

But suppose a teacher, on being asked to compute the value of a cord of wood, at five shillings and sixpence a foot, makes it come to between three and four hundred dollars; or finds, by slate and pencil, that the legal interest, on a note of hand for one year, is just six times as much as the principal; or when inquired of, who wrote the Acts of the Apostles, says it was the apostle Acts; or, when questioned as to what were once considered the four elements,—says, earth, air, fire, and brimstone; or, to take example of men who have been through college, declares that he does not mean to read Gibbon's Decline and Fall of the Roman Empire, till he can read it in the original Latin; or does not know what constitutes hearing evidence in law; nor the logical difference between *a priori* and *a posteriroi* reasoning in logic: or what is worse than any ignorance, however thick or black it may be, carries the manners of a haughty pedagogue into society, and demands that men shall say his creed after him, word for word, just as he demands of a child four years old, that he shall repeat his *a*, *b*, *c*, or of a boy in the Latin grammar, that he shall say hic, hæc, hoc; or decides all the momentous questions connected with Prison Discipline, by the rule of his own school-room;—that in all cases of transgression, corporal punishment is the first resort;—suppose these things, I say, and such as these, to be true, and what man of intelligence and moral culture will desire the company of such a teacher at his table or his fire-side. And yet these are not imagined cases; they are not borrowed from Irving or Dickens, but are veritable facts, and, I blush to say it, of Massachusetts origin.

It should also be a leading motive with every teacher, to avoid the dangers peculiar to his calling. Incident to every occupation and profession among men, there are peculiar dangers. Painters are afflicted with the "Painter's colic." The burnishers of steel die of consumption. Tailors and shoe-makers are in danger of being hump-backed and round-shouldered; and if put to the work very young, they have bandy-legs to match. Watch repairers become squint-eyed, and mere technical lawyers become squint-minded. Rich men are prone to be too conservative, and mere politicians too radical. Surgeons treat human nerves, as though they were pack-thread, and clergymen often lose all relish for innocent enjoyments, become austere and sanctimonious, and are in danger of skipping the duties of this life, in the intentness with which they look after another. Now the teacher's vocation is by no means exempt from this common lot. It has its peculiar exposures, and against them, therefore, the teacher should exercise constant vigilance. In the school-room, the teacher is, and must be, the ultimate court of appeal. All questionable points, whether in lessons or in conduct, come before him for adjudication. He holds accounts both of civil and criminal jurisdiction. He determines all questions of law, as well as all matters of fact. His "terms" last through the year, and probably he decides as many questions each day, as the highest court, in any state or nation in Christendom, does in a twelvemonth. Now all this tends to make him dogmatical and opinionated. I do not say, it necessarily produces dogmatism, or stubbornness in the defense of opinions; but I do say that it tends to these odious qualities, and unless this tendency be counteracted, it will produce them. His decisions, too, he makes extemporaneously. He can not, like a court of Chancery, keep a case before him, until the original parties are dead, and their executors or administrators come in to pray for judgment. This state of things necessitates promptness, if not precipitancy, in the formation of opinions; and hence an incautious teacher, in his intercourse with men, is prone to decide all social, national, or international questions,—questions involving commerce, diplomacy, or war,—in as summary a manner, as when he presided in the school-house forum, and decided contested points about accent or number, apples or nuts. Now against all circumscription and narrowness in the range of thought and speculation, teachers should stand guard continually. They should practice counteracting mental exercises to prevent their minds from becoming microscopic and pedantically nice; in the same way that a sensible tailor or shoemaker practices counteracting physical exercises against being bow-backed. The teacher should constantly aim at that enlargement of mind, that amplitude of view, which will assimilate the operations of the school-room to the grandest affairs of life, instead of contracting the grand affairs of life to the narrow dimensions of the school-room. By intercourse with business men, he should rectifiy his generalizations, and by conversation with the progress of the great and busy world, he should give his mind a centrifugal impetus, which will enlarge the diameter, without increasing the eccentricity of its orbit. There is still another point which I hope no one will deem too trivial to be noticed in this connection. Some teachers suffer under those nervous phenomena, commonly called *Fidgets.* Twirling a pencil-case or a watch-key; stroking down a watch-guard; fumbling with a button; making the fingers ride pick-a-pack; rocking the foot; swinging the arms; shrugging the shoulders; see-sawing the body; drumming with the fingers; snapping or cracking the joints; soloing on a whistle or a key; thrusting the hands into the pockets, or—contemptible sight—hanging up the arms, like herrings to be dried, at the armholes of the vest;—in fine, all sorts of ungainly movements, fibrous twitchings and small spasms generally, constitute the odious tricks I refer to. Whether these unseemly exhibitions are electric in their nature; whether they operate as an escapement to carry off superabundant nervous fluid, I pretend not to decide; but I would respectfully suggest to all school-examiners, whether such manners do not disqualify for teaching. For their own sakes, and especially for the sakes of the children, let all teachers call in the surgeon, if necessary, to eradicate these nictitating membranes, or to cut off the nerves that lead to them.

The motives which have thus far been specially enjoined, though in a degree personal to the teacher, are in no respect discreditable to him. I am happy however to rise out of this region into one of purer ether,—to motives untainted by any personal considerations whatever.

I address myself then to those high and enduring motives that grow out of the very nature of the teacher's calling. And here it is obvious, on the threshold, that the teacher presides, not over insentient and inanimate things, but over sentient and animated creatures; not over the stationary and impenetrable, but over the progressive, and over the most impressible of all the works of the Creator; in fine, he presides, not over the ephemeral or temporal, but over the immortal. No other workman works on such materials. The natures on which he operates shall expand without bound or limit; for, when once created, they are coeternal with their Creator. Hence the smallest influence of a teacher, upon the receptive mind of a pupil, must eventuate in great results. There are no such things, in education, as trifles or insignificances. The subject fails of being appreciated merely because it is so vast; as the earth can not be clasped, like an orange, because of its size. To make it understood, it must be analyzed, and presented in fragments and by piece-meal. And I think it can be easily proved to any teacher, that each day's labor, well or ill-done, will have an important, it may be a decisive effect upon the fortunes of his pupils. And what may perhaps surprise some who have never pondered on the subject, this remark holds true, even in regard to the commonest studies.

Here is a boy learning to write. As he opens his manuscript-book, writes during his hour, and then lays it aside, the progress which he has made or failed to make, in regard to the cut or smoothness of a few letters or lines, seems of little consequence; and yet who that is acquainted in our cities, does not know of many instances, where a man has obtained or lost a clerkship,—and thus secured or missed a competency for life,—by his skill and dispatch, or his want of them, in the single matter of chirography?

A child is learning to spell, but no special pains are taken to make him respell, and respell, until spelled aright, every misspelled word. Hence his danger of error increases with the number of words he begins to use. The best age for mastering the orthography of our language passes by, and the pupil goes out into the world, exposed to the odium of illiteracy, and perhaps incurring still graver consequences. I knew a late case, where a young gentleman of sterling talents, and of great promise, lost the appointment of teacher, in one of our Public Schools, where the salary was fifteen hundred dollars a year because in the written application which he made for the place, the word gramm*ar* was spelled gramm*er*. He had been taught, too, in the schools of a city, whose masters received $1500 a year. Now if orthography had been taught to that young man, in a proper manner; if he had ever written exercises in orthography; or had ever seen the misspelled word, *grammer*, gibbeted on the black-board, he would have saved two important things,—his mortification, and fifteen hundred dollars a year. What sort of a song will such a man sing about his old teacher?

A school-boy is untaught or mistaught in reading. He makes ridiculous mistakes in the pronunciation of common words, gives such intonation and inflections as pervert an author's meaning; or worst of all, he is trained to a theatrical and overwrought style of elocution. He leaves school. By and by, in the presence of a smaller or a larger company, he chances to be called upon to read. He exposes his ignorance or his affectation, gets laughed at, and is never put forward more. Clergymen have lost settlements; or what is quite as humiliating, have preached to empty seats, because of their miserable reading; and in long and complicated trials at law, where most of the evidence has been documentary, lawyers have been supposed to win verdicts from a jury, because of the clear enunciation, the intelligibility, and the impressiveness, with which they have read the testimony.

Another pupil has never been indoctrinated into arithmetical principles; his whole instruction, in this branch, having been by arbitrary rule and formula. A place is bought for him in a city counting-room, but, owing to his frequent mistakes, he is dismissed; or in the country, he is appointed to audit the accounts of town or parish officers, makes blunders, is exposed, forfeits his reputation, and so loses all chance of promotion or advancement among his fellow-citizens.

Who, too, does not know that men fail in business, losing not only property, but perhaps character and integrity also, because they did not know how to keep accounts, and hence were ignorant of their real pecuniary condition?

Ask any lawyer, any man of business, or politician, what is the class of remarks usually made, when a man's fitness for any particular service or office becomes a subject of discussion. If three men are to be selected as arbitrators, perhaps a dozen will be named before a complement is agreed on. One man is acknowledged to be conscientious, but he knows nothing beyond the Multiplication Table. Another is well skilled in business, but a suspicion hangs on his integrity. A third, for want of proper guidance, has spent all his school-going days, and all the leisure of his subsequent life, in the abstractions of Mathematics; he knows all the puzzling sums on record:

"Can tell how far a careless fly
Would chance to turn the globe awry,
If flitting round in giddy circuit,
With leg or wing he kick or jerk it;"

while in all matters pertaining to practical life, he is a ninny and is not competent to superintend the affairs of an ant-heap;—I do not mean one of those imperial ant-heaps, reared by the termites of Africa, but one of those Lilliputian mounds we see in a garden after a shower. Another is allowed to possess talent and attainment; but he has been educated to believe that every one who does not attend the church he attends, and employ the physician he employs, must be a wicked man, while anybody who does so must be a good one. And thus, through some defect in disposition, in attainments, or in character, which education might and should have remedied, they are set aside.

So in those anti-preliminary meetings, as we may call them,—those private interviews or conversations which iniate initiation,—what are the points which indicate this or that individual as an eligible candidate for office? In four cases out of five,—in nine cases out of ten,—are they not some attributes that have been developed or made prominent in school,—or in college, which is only a higher school? And the case is the same, when the question first arises, whether a man is qualified to be an accountant in a trading house or bank; an overseer in a factory; a superintendent in a mechanic's shop, or an engineer on a railroad. In regard to these first chances, which a man has to show what he is, and to better his condition, education has far more influence than talent. After one has secured his opportunity; after he has reached a position where his capacities can speak for themselves; then I acknowledge that less will depend upon his previous training and more upon his native endowments. But the greatest want of a mass of men is an opportunity to exhibit what is in them. Give them this opportunity, and if they have any vigor, they will display it and insure their fortune. Take this away and their talent rusts in a napkin. The most perfect seed in the world can never evolve its powers, until it finds a soil in which to germinate.

Now all these, and ten thousand more facts like unto them, will never be denied or gainsaid by any person acquainted with the evolution of effects from causes. And what is the motive which the teacher should derive from them? Surely no less than this. His every day's teaching and government will elevate or depress the condition, in all after life, of every pupil in his school. There is not one of all the children around him, on whom his daily instruction and treatment will produce *no* effect. The physical, intellectual, and moral condition of each is to be, at least partially, what he foredooms.

A child has a feeble constitution, or his native stamina have been broken down or enfeebled, in early life, by injudicious exposure or foolish parental indulgence. Perhaps it is now too late ever to make a healthy, athletic man of him. That once attainable blessing may have been forfeited beyond redeeming. What then? Is he not still in a condition to be made either better or worse? By a knowledge and application of the laws of Physiology, may you not so far restore him, as to save him from two or three fits of sickness, or from a painful, costly period of chronic ailment and debility? If you can not prolong his years to seventy, you may to sixty, or at least to fifty, instead of his dying at thirty-five. If you can not prevent his liability to colds and weak lungs, you may at least save him from consumption and premature death. You may so increase his health that he will be able to fill positions and perform duties of which he would otherwise be incapable. Perhaps you may give him just that additional degree of strength, by which, when encompassed by the perils of the flood, he can put forth the one stroke more which will save him from drowning. Extensively true as this is in regard to boys, how much more so is it of girls. It is no imagination or extravagance to say, that your judicious or injudicious treatment of a delicate girl, during a single winter's school term, may save or lose the mother of a young family. Here you have a whole class of boys, not one of whom gives token of that talent or address which will secure him a seat in the Congress of the United States. What then? Can not you make some of them fit to be senators or representatives in the State Legislature? Or if this, on second thought, looks a little presumptuous, can you not qualify more or less of them for some respectable city or town office?

But perhaps some of you will here remind me of the smith, who had a piece of iron of which he said he would make an axe. But on heating and hardening and hammering it, it proved wholly insufficient for an axe. "Well," said he, "I can heat it again and make a hatchet." But by heating and tempering it the second time, so much of the substance was lost in cinders and scoriæ, that it now proved as insufficient for a hatchet, as it was before for an axe. "Well," said he, "I will at least make a knife of it." So he heated, and tried to temper it the third time; but its texture had been destroyed, and there was only a residuum of dross left. "Ay," cried he, in a pet, "I'll heat you seven times hotter than before, and douse you into the water, and make a mighty great hiss!!"

Now do you say you will have scholars from whom you can make nothing but a mighty great hiss; or perchance, a mighty little hiss,—two or three bubbles only? I reply by asking, whether you may not fall into the same error as did the hero of my story. Doubtless, his piece of iron, in the beginning, would have made a very respectable hatchet; but it was by a series of over-estimates that its owner reduced it, at last, to the smallest kind of "sizzle." Do not teachers and school-officers, too, make the same sort of mistake, when they inflate the ambition of all the boys in the school, by talking to them about being governors and presidents, and thus disgusting them with the sober pursuits of life? Probably not more than one in a hundred thousand, even in Massachusetts, will ever be governors; and even if it were probable that she could ever have another president, her turn would not come once in fifty years. But all children may be that "noblest work of God, an honest man," which is far better than any chief magistracy of state or nation.

But perhaps you will here retort upon me, that you can not make all children honest. Here, for instance, say you, is a boy whose natural organization is frightfully bad. His head is shaped like the segment of a sphere; his eyes are close together, and his ears close behind his eyes; so that almost the entire mass of his brain lies at the base and in the rear. His cranium resembles that of a tiger or a serpent, rather than that of a man. His father was a devil and his mother no better. He was not only conceived in sin and brought forth in iniquity, but he was nursed at the paps of intemperance and lewdness, from his birth drank milk which was nothing but rum leached through human lacteals, and this too, adulterated by the basest impurities of heart and brain; was trained to steal from the day he could walk, to swear from the day he could talk, and long before talking, could lie in pantomime. If other children are quantities, more or less, dipped out of the infernal cauldron of total depravity, he is its essential oil, its rectified, thrice distilled spirit,—the Prussic acid of it, and the sulphureted hydrogen of it! What can be done, I hear some of you defiantly ask, with a case like this? I acknowledge this to be a tough problem. I admit that there is no extraction of roots so difficult as the extirpation of vice from a heart, which is prone to evil as the sparks to fly upwards. Grant then, that you can not, from such a quasi-monster as has been supposed, make an intelligent, honest, exemplary, high-souled man. But can you, by no possibility, save him from the house of correction or the county jail? Or if this would be hope run mad, can you not save him from the state-prison; or at least reduce his sentence to one of ten years, instead of imprisonment for life? Yes, my friends, the vilest and most intractable of them all, can you not save him from being a thief; or if not from theft, then from highway robbery; or, if not from highway robbery, then from incendiarism and murder; or, if not from these, then from piracy on the high-seas, scuttling ships, and murdering crews; or, once more and finally, from the commission of all these atrocities, together? Can you not reduce him to a single devil, instead of his being a legion? If, animated by a sublime hope, and filled with the wonder-working spirit of love, you can do all or any of these things, we have reason to believe that you will cause a thrill of joy among the angels of heaven.

Not long since, I visited a prison in a neighboring state, and spent the greater part of the day in private conversations with different prisoners, in order to learn the histories of their temptation and fall, and the spirit in which they received their punishment. While I was there, two new convicts arrived. I went to the receiving lodge, where they were delivered. There was the Prison-book, in which was recorded the names, ages, occupation, offence, term of sentence, and so forth, of all who came to dwell in those gloomy abodes. The book, in which these entries were made, was a great folio, probably of not less than five thousand pages. It had been recently procured, and only a small part of it was filled. How can I express the mournful interest with which I looked along the pages of recorded crime and allotted penalty. What a sententious column was that, in which was written "For two years;" "For five years;" "For ten years;" "For life;"—and that other column containing the words, "Theft;" "Robbery;" "Burglary;" "Attempt to kill," and so forth. Oh, if to these culprits, in their early days, God had sent an angel, in the form of a wise and faithful teacher, would those terrible words ever have been written against their names?—would their names ever have been found in that book?

I have said that I looked with an inexpressibly mournful interest upon the sad pages of that book which had been already filled. But with a sadness far more profound and solemn, did I look upon the pages which had not been filled,—whose clear white sheets had not yet been blackened by the records of guilt and condemnation. We have no adequate ground for hope, that those yet undefiled pages will never be filled; and who are they whose names are to be written therein? The young man, bold, fiery, and reckless, whose veins are fermenting with the new wine of life; but into whose heart no moral alchymist has ever infused a principle which will transmute his tendencies for evil into desires for good;—his name must be there. The rash, brave boy of the school-room;—the ringleader in sport and in mischief; who bears the severest punishments as stoically as an Indian bears fire; whose fatal misfortune is to have parents or teachers insane enough to believe that they can extinguish the fervid spirit within him, which God only meant they should direct;—his name, too, must be there. Ay, and who shall say that the name of the sweet babe in its mother's arms,—whether now gently closing its eyes to sleep, as the tender flower folds its petals at the approach of eve, or whether waking to new-born life and joy after reanimating slumbers;—

Yes, or the same infant coming perfumed with baptismal water from the holy font;—who shall say that his name, too, in consequence of over-indulgence and under restraint, shall not lengthen out that black catalogue of guilt? Teacher, you can forefend the awful hand-writing, in books like these, by a sacred hand-writing upon the soul. Not by charms and talismans, not by phylacteries upon the garments, or frontlets upon the brow, or amulets suspended from the neck; but by a cultivation of the conscience, by the living and sovereign efficacy of the law of God written upon the heart, you may do this holy work.

But we have been looking only at the darkest points in the picture,—at its doleful shadows, and not at its celestial lights. In our schools are to be found the greatest elements of hope for our country and for the world. Bright talents are there, which shall find and follow the foot-prints of the Deity, and reveal to us more of his attributes, by revealing to us more of His marvelous works. The vivid genius is there, which will find new chords in the human soul, to be thrilled with joy. The capacities of benevolence and duty are there, which shall add hosts to the now feeble bands of philanthropists, who shall go forth to do battle with the giant iniquities of the world,—with the Titanian sins of intemperance, of oppression in all its forms, with the spirit of war and with bigotry. The executive and administrative talent is there, which for good or for evil, shall ere long find its way into the counsels and guide the energies of the State, or the vaster energies of the nation. These powers and possibilities are all there, and it is hardly a license of speech to say that you hold them as in the hollow of the hand. Go to your work then, as if worthy the custody and stewardship of these mighty interests. Replenish your energies by the hopes which such resources legitimately supply. Look forward to the glorious results which fidelity on your part must assuredly produce. Stand among your pupils like prophets and seers, and labor to bring nearer the vision which your prescience reveals. Consider yourselves, as you truly are,—vicegerents of God, placed in authority over the richest of all his provinces, and responsible to a great extent, for their beauty and grandeur and moral well-being.

Here is a boy who seems head-strong and obstinate,—stubborn almost to sullenness;—analyze the case; it may be, that this exhibition of character is founded upon the noble, though untrained principles of conscience and firmness; and if it so be, you have only to manage the case wisely, to make another Martin Luther of him;—a man who will defy the Papal anathemas of his day, as did the old hero of Wittenburg, in the fifteenth century. Here are two playmates, bound together as it were by some congenial affinity, diligent in study, conspicuous in recitation; but vehement and vociferous, almost beyond endurance. Do not alienate these youthful Boanerges, by the base motive of rivalry and emulation; but rather strengthen their attachment and guide them aright, and by and by, perhaps from different parts of the union, they may meet on the floor of Congress, not to contend with each other, at the head of hostile factions, but to lift their voices together, like true sons of thunder, against corruption in high places. Here is an unsophisticated child, whose voice falters and his eye moistens, as he reads the story of some wounded or imprisoned bird, or of a hare pursued to its death by hounds, quadruped and biped. It was a beaming seraph from the throne of God, then nestling in his heart, which choked that voice and bedewed that eye. Save him from the profanation of ridicule and levity. In the fullness of time, he will go forth to give sight to the blind, to loose the tongue of the dumb, to gather the insane from their living tombs and heal demoniacs in the spirit and with the power of Christ. There sits a little girl, distinguished from all the rest by the simplicity of her dress, and by the tenderness with which she watches the little ones of the school however ill-clad or ill-mannered they may be. No gaudy ribbons delight her eye; no gleeful games can make her forgetful of the safety or the comfort of others. Rescue her from the pride of wealth, from the frivolity and emptiness of fashionable life; and when others shall be wasting their time at theatres and assemblies, she will be a ministering angel to the poor, in their crowded hovels and cellars, and sweetening the earth with her footsteps, as she goes on her errand of mercy and love. Another, as quiet of mien, but of bolder resolve, like Mrs. Fry or Miss Dix, will stand before Governors and Legislatures, hushing the storm of partizan warfare by her rebukes, and making them, for very shame, if for no better reason, provide for the woes of humanity.

These, my friends, and such as these, are the lofty motives, with which every teacher should go to his school, in the morning; with which he should live among his pupils during the day; and in the sustaining consciousness of which, he should seek, at night, the rest which will prepare him for the renewal of his labors. With the faithful and fruitful teacher, not a day will pass, in which he will not so modify and ennoble the character of his pupils, that they will choose a wiser and more exalted course of conduct in the eventful crises of life. He will be making better husbands and wives, better fathers and mothers, and scattering from afar, blessed eras of goodness and joy all along the future course of his pupils' lives.

Surrounded by these motives, and summoned onward by these hopes, if there be any one who can ever talk of the irksome task of instructing the young, or advocate blows as the chief moral instrumentality,—the first resort in cases of difficulty;—let him throw aside his books and seize the ox-goad; let his talk no longer be of children but of bullocks;—or rather, let him betake himself to stone-hammering, and by cheating his imagination with the grateful delusion that granite blocks are boys' backs, get greater day's work out of his hard bones and harder heart.

What special need is there to exhort teachers to possess their souls in patience? A teacher has no more excuse for passion, because of the thousand oversights and cases of forgetfulness, and carelessness, and waywardness in a group of young children, than an orchardist has for indulging in fits of anger, because his fruits are acrid while they are yet immature, or untouched by the hues of the rainbow while they are yet unripe. Waywardness and what Carlyle calls "un-wisdom," are in the nature of childhood, as much as sourness is in the nature of an apple or a berry, before it has had time to be ripened; or, if any one objects to this expression as too condemnatory of the nature of childhood; still it can not be denied that such have been the transgressions of parents that children do inherit painful susceptibilities of evil. Yet infinitely more blameworthy are the fathers who ate the grapes, than the children whose teeth have been set on edge by their sourness. While human nature remains as it now is, we must expect much of inconsiderateness and aberration in the young. It is the special function and office of a teacher to supply the necessary ameliorating influences. But this transforming work can not be done by one day's labor, any more than harvests can be ripened by one day's sunshine. The sun and clouds might as well refuse to shine and shower, because the various growths of the summer are not perfected in a day. Yet with what calm constancy they pursue their work; and not the waste and loss of the wide wilderness restricts their bounty. Under the slanting beams of the vernal sun, the corn germinates, the fruit trees bud and blossom and the vine shoots up its branches. As yet, however, for all purposes of human utility, they are worthless. But is the sun wearied or discouraged? Does he not ascend the heavens; does he not lengthen his day, and pour down upon them his solstitial fervor? Still, neither in the corn, nor in the fruit is there any sustenance for man, and the young grape is more bitter than wormwood to the taste. For weeks and months that sun labors on, increasing the ardor of his beams; till, at length, the rich fields wave a welcome to the harvester; the orchards glow with orient-colored fruitage; and in the fullness of gratitude, the grape bursts with its nectarious juices. It is the euthanasia of the year. It is like the dying psalm of a righteous man. Look at that miracle of beauty, the century plant. For lustrums and decades, the seasons and the elements labor on to bring it to perfection, but seem to labor in vain. It absorbs the nurture of generations of cultivators, yet appears to make no requital for their care. But at length its slow maturing powers approach their crisis. The day of its efflorescence comes. The gorgeous flower bursts forth, queenly, beautiful as Aphrodite from the waves, and loading the air with the gathered perfumes of a hundred years. And to you, my friends, this is the moral:—Not a ray of sunshine ever fell upon that plant; not a rain-drop nor a dew-drop ever fertilized or refreshed it; not a kind office of its guardian was ever expended upon it, which is not now remembered and proclaimed in the grandeur of its bloom and the richness of its fragrance. Learn a lesson from the ancient oaks, which you pass daily in your walk to the school-room. In rearing them to their loftiness and majestic proportions, has nature ever grown weary or impatient, since the day when these tiny germs cleft the shell? Of all the occupations among men, the teacher, who knows the nobility of his work, and feels its divine impulses, has the least need of patience. The delver among insensate clods; the hewer of wood; the operative who spins the lifeless thread or casts the monotonous shuttle; the statesman who declares himself constrained to warp the eternal principles of rectitude to accommodate his policy to the ignorance and selfishness of men; the minister who strives to soften hearts, which inveterate sins have ossified; the judge who sends human beings to the state's prison or the gallows, one day's work of whom is enough to crush the life out of a man's heart;—the soldier who slays his fellow-man in battle, or is himself slain;—these have need of *patience*,—or something else I know not what;—but to enjoin patience upon those whose very office and mission it is to prepare children for all the happiness of this world, and to bring the kingdom of heaven round about them, is an intolerable indignity and grievance.

What I long, above all other things upon earth, to see,—what prophets and kings might well desire to see, but as yet have never seen,—is a glorious brotherhood of teachers, whose accomplished minds and great hearts are bound together by their devotion to one object,—and that object a desire to reform the world,—to re-impress upon the heart of man the almost obliterated image of his Maker.

Were teachers animated by the spirit which inspires the martial hero, such a union and for such an object would not be postponed to be seen by happier men in some happier age, but we ourselves should behold it. And can not the sublimer motive give birth to the sublimer effort? Can not those whose office it is to reform their fellow-men, be as devoted and as valiant as those whose office it is to destroy their fellow-men? Is not theirs as good a fight? Will their songs of triumph be less exultant? Will not palms as fadeless crown their victories? If we marvel greatly at the bravery of men engaged in war, have we not far greater reason to marvel at the lukewarmness and unconcern of those who are engaged in the holy cause of enlightening and redeeming the race? Look at the pages of history for thousands of years, and see what those who have sought for military glory,—such lurid glory as it is,—have borne and done. Not commanders only, but subalterns and common soldiers perform feats of valor that seem incredible; and their bodies might be blown to pieces a thousand times, before the bravery of their hearts could be subdued. They scale mountain-lifted forts, whose sides are precipices, while rocks like hail-stones are falling around them. The blazing hill of the terraced battery. they charge to the topmost tier. They rush to the field where the grape is showered whose vintage is blood. As siegers and besieged, they fight by day and sleep by night, within range of that newly-invented and terrific engine of destruction, which can be compared to nothing earthly but a volcano upon wheels. At the battle of Waterloo, Marshal Ney had five horses shot under him, and he dismounted from the sixth and charged the British infantry sword in hand In naval engagements, how often do officers and men ply their guns, till the very ship,—which to them is the earth, and their only earth,—is swallowed in the waves. When Paul Jones engaged the Serapis, he lashed his ship to the foe in the embrace of death. He received the enemy's broadsides, until his own vessel was almost reduced to a heap of floating splinters. Apparently sinking, he was summoned to surrender. "Surrender," said Jones, "I hav'n't yet begun to fight." Where in our ranks are the Neys and Joneses and a thousand others of the mighty men of valor? Where, amongst us, are the men who will forfeit all prospects of worldly distinction, surrender their ease, pledge their fortunes, sacrifice health, and life too, if need be, to uphold and carry forward the cause of education, which, more than any other, is the cause of God and humanity? If our motives are stronger than those of the shedders of human blood, why should not our arms and hearts be stronger than theirs also? And what do we know under the heavens, or,—I speak it with reverence,—what do we know above the heavens, which can excel the high emprise in which we are embarked? The world is to be redeemed. For six thousand years, with exceptions "few and far between," the earth has been a dwelling-place of woe. There has not been an hour since it was peopled, when war has not raged, like a conflagration, on some part of the surface. In the haughtiness of despotism, on the one hand, and the debasement of vassalage, on the other, the idea of human brotherhood has been lost. The policy of the wisest nations has been no higher than to punish the crimes they had permitted, instead of rewarding the virtues they had cherished. Throughout the earth, until lately, and now, in more than three of its five grand divisions, the soldier and the priest have divided and devoured it. The mass of the human race has sojourned with animals,—that is, in the region of the animal appetites; and though the moral realms have been discovered, yet how feebly have they been colonized. But it is impiety to suppose that this night of darkness and blood will always envelope the earth. A brighter day is dawning, and education is its day-star. The honor of ushering in this day, is reserved for those who train up children in the way they should go. Through this divinely appointed instrumentality, more than by all other agencies, the night of ignorance and superstition is to be dispelled, swords beat into ploughshares, captives ransomed and rivers of Plenty made to run, where the rivers of Intemperance now flow. At this sight "Angels look on and hold their breath, burning to mingle in the conflict."

But the joys and triumphs of this conflict are not for angels; they are held in trust for those teachers, who, in the language of Scripture, will take them by violence,—that is, by such a holy ardor and invincible determination as will conquer time and fate, and fulfill the conditions, on which, alone, such honors can be won. And if the strong-voiced angel, who flies through heaven crying, "Woe, woe, woe," to the inhabiters of the earth, is ever to be silenced, he will be silenced by the stronger acclamations of those whom teachers have been among the blessed and honored instruments of preparing for the ransom of the world.

NOTE.—This Lecture was delivered at over thirty Conventions or Associations of Teachers in seven different States.

# I. EDUCATION:—A NATIONAL INTEREST.

### HISTORICAL DEVELOPMENT.

In the ordinance of the Congress of the Confederation in 1785, respecting "the disposing of lands in the Western territory," "section sixteen of every township" was reserved for the maintenance of public schools.

The ordinance of 1787, "for the government of the Territory northwest of the river Ohio," confirmed the ordinance of 1785, and declared "that religion, morality and knowledge being necessary to good government and the happiness of mankind, schools and the means of education shall be forever encouraged."

The Constitution of the United States, after setting forth in the Preamble in words of sublime import the national objects for which the people of the United States had ordained this fundamental law, expressly grants to Congress the power "to dispose" of the public lands and other property—"to exercise exclusive jurisdiction" over the district to be ceded as the seat of government—and "to lay and collect taxes, &c., to provide for the common defense and general welfare."

In the Convention of 1787, which framed the Constitution, Mr. Charles Pinckney, of South Carolina, on the 29th of May and the 18th of August, and subsequently Mr. Madison, of Virginia, submitted propositions "to provide for the establishment of a National University at the seat of government," "for the advancement of useful knowledge," "and the promotion of agriculture, commerce, trades and manufactures." On the 14th of September, both of these delegates moved to insert in the list of powers vested in Congress, "to establish a university in which no preference or distinction should be allowed on account of religion." This motion was opposed by Gouverneur Morris, of New York, and was lost, as reported by Mr. Madison, expressly on the ground that the power to establish such a university was included in the grant of exclusive legislation over the district in which the government should be located. And as we learn from other sources, and from the subsequent recommendations by President Washington, the power to encourage agriculture, trade, manufactures, and education, was understood by him, and other statesmen, to be included in the first clause of the enumerated powers of Congress "to lay taxes and to provide for the common defense and general welfare of the United States."

GEORGE WASHINGTON.

Fresh from the discussions of the Convention which framed the Constitution, of which he was the presiding officer, and called by the unanimous voice of his countrymen to inaugurate, as its chief executive, the national government, George Washington, in his first formal recommendation of special measures to both Houses of Congress, on the 8th of January, 1790, after commending further legislation for an efficient and uniform plan of military organization, as well as of a national judiciary, calls attention to the necessity of "uniformity in the currency, weights and measures;" "the advancement of agriculture, commerce, and manufactures," "the effectual encouragement, as well as to the introduction of new and useful inventions from abroad, as to the exertions of skill and genius in producing them at home;" "facilitating the intercourse between the distant parts of our country by a due attention to the post-office, and post-roads"—did not hesitate to add:—

> Nor am I less persuaded, that you will agree with me in opinion, that there is nothing which can better deserve your patronage than the promotion of science and literature. Knowledge is in every country the surest basis of public happiness. In one, in which the measures of government receive their impression so immediately from the sense of the community, as in ours, it is proportionably essential. To the security of a free constitution it contributes in various ways: by convincing those who are intrusted with the public administration, that every valuable end of government is best answered by the enlightened confidence of the people; and by teaching the people themselves to know and to value their own rights; to discern and provide against invasions of them; to distinguish between oppression and the necessary exercise of lawful authority, between burdens proceeding from a disregard to their convenience and those resulting from the inevitable exigencies of society; to discriminate the spirit of liberty from that of licentiousness, cherishing the first, avoiding the last, and uniting a speedy but temperate vigilance against encroachments, with an inviolable respect for the laws.
>
> Whether this desirable object will be the best promoted by affording aid to seminaries of learning already established, by the institution of a national university, or by any other expedients, will be well worthy of a place in the deliberations of the legislature.

In his speech to both Houses of Congress, December 7th, 1796, after referring to the measures adopted for the encouragement of manufactures, and urging immediate attention to agriculture as a matter of individual and national welfare—and especially of constituting a board (or as has since been done, by a National Department) "charged with collecting and diffusing information, and enabled by premiums and small pecuniary aids to encourage, and assist a spirit of discovery and improvement. This species of establishment contributes doubly to the increase of improvement, by stimulating to enterprise and experiment, and by drawing to a common center the results everywhere of individual skill and observation, and spreading them thence over the whole nation"—he again returns to the expediency of establishing a national university, and also a military academy; and proceeds:—

The assembly to which I address myself, is too enlightened not to be fully sensible how much a flourishing state of the arts and sciences contributes to national prosperity and reputation. True it is, that our country contains many seminaries of learning highly respectable and useful; but the funds upon which they rest are too narrow to command the ablest professors, in the different departments of liberal knowledge for the institution contemplated, though they would be excellent auxiliaries.

Amongst the motives to such an institution, the assimilation of the principles, opinions and manners of our countrymen, by the common education of a portion of our youth from every quarter, well deserves attention. The more homogeneous our citizens can be made in these particulars, the greater will be our prospect of permanent union; and a primary object of such a national institution should be, the education of our youth in the science of government. In a republic, what species of knowledge can be equally important, and what duty more pressing in its legislation, than to patronize a plan of communicating it to those who are to be the future guardians of the liberties of the country.

In a letter addressed to Alexander Hamilton, from Philadelphia, September 1st, 1796, referring to the topics which he wished to introduce in his Farewell Address, a draft of which he had enclosed in a former letter, Washington regrets "that another subject (which in my estimation is of interesting concern to the well-being of this country) was not touched upon also;"—

I mean education generally, as one of the surest means of enlightening and giving just ways of thinking to our citizens, but particularly the establishment of a university; where the youth from all parts of the United States might receive the polish of erudition in the arts, sciences, and belles-lettres; and where those who were disposed to run a political course might not only be instructed in the theory and principles, but (this seminary being at the seat of the general government, where the legislature would be in session half the year, and the interests and politics of the nation of course would be discussed,) they would lay the surest foundation for the practical part also.

But that which would render it of the highest importance, in my opinion, is, that at the juvenile period of life, when friendships are formed, and habits established, that will stick by one, the youth, or young men from different parts of the United States would be assembled together, and would by degrees discover that there was not that cause for those jealousies and prejudices which one part of the Union had imbibed against another part:—of course sentiments of more liberality in the general policy of the country would result from it. What but mixing of people from different parts of the United States during the war rubbed off those impressions? A century, in the ordinary intercourse, would not have accomplished what the seven years' association in arms did; but that ceasing, prejudices are beginning to revive again, and never will be eradicated so effectually by any other means as the intimate intercourse of characters in early life,—who in all probability will be at the head of the counsels of this country in a more advanced stage of it.

To show that this is no new idea of mine, I may appeal to my early communications to Congress; and to prove how seriously I have reflected on it since, and how well disposed I have been, and still am, to contribute my aid toward carrying the measure into effect, I enclose you the extract of a letter from me to the Governor of Virginia, and a copy of the resolves of the legislature of that State in consequence thereof.

I have not the smallest doubt that this donation (when the navigation is in complete operation, which it certainly will be in less than two years,) will amount to £1200 or £1500 sterling a year, and become a rapidly increasing fund. The proprietors of the Federal City have talked of doing something handsome towards it likewise; and if Congress would appropriate some of the western lands to the same uses, funds sufficient, and of the most permanent and increasing sort, might be so established as to invite the ablest professors in Europe to conduct it.

In a letter to Hamilton, dated Sept. 6, 1796, Washington adds:

If you think the idea of a university had better be reserved for the speech at the opening of the session, I am content to defer the communication of it until that period: but even in that case, I would pray you, as soon as convenient, to make a draft for the occasion, predicated on the ideas with which you have been furnished: looking at the same time at what was said on this head in my *second* speech to the *first* Congress, merely with a view to see what was said on the subject at that time; and this, you will perceive, was not so much to the point as I want to express now, though it may, if proper, be glanced at, to show that the subject had caught my attention early.

I much question whether a recommendation of this measure to the legislature will have a better effect *now* than *formerly*. It may show, indeed, my sense of its importance, and that is a sufficient inducement with *me* to bring the matter before the public in some shape or another at the close of my political life. My object in proposing to insert it when I did. was to set the *people* ruminating on the importance of the measure, as the most likely means of bringing it to pass.

In his Farewell Address to the people of the United States, dated September 17, 1796, Washington gave utterance to that noble sentiment which has passed into an axiom of political philosophy:—

Promote, as an object of primary importance, institutions for the general diffusion of knowledge. In proportion as the structure of a government gives force to public opinion, it is essential that public opinion should be enlightened.

Washington did not confine the expressions of his interest in education, and especially the establishment of a national university, to his official communications to Congress and to the people of the United States. In a letter addressed to Mr. Adams, the Vice President, dated Nov. 27, 1794, on a proposition communicated by Mr. Jefferson, for "transplanting the members entire of the University of Geneva to America," there is the following passage:—

That a national university in this country is a thing to be desired, has always been my decided opinion; and the appropriation of ground and funds for it in the Federal City has long been contemplated and talked of; but how far matured, or how far the transporting of an entire seminary of foreigners, who may not understand our language, can be assimilated therein, is more than I am prepared to give an opinion upon; or, indeed, how far funds in either case are attainable.

On 28th of January, 1795, Washington addressed from Philadelphia, the following letter to the Commissioners of the Federal District:—

GENTLEMEN—A plan for the establishment of a university in the Federal City has frequently been the subject of conversation; but, in what manner it is proposed to commence this important institution, on how extensive a scale, the means by which it is to be effected, how it is to be supported, or what progress is made in it, are matters altogether unknown to me.

It has always been a source of serious reflection and sincere regret with me, that the youth of the United States should be sent to foreign countries for the purpose of education. Although there are doubtless many, under these circumstances, who escape the danger of contracting principles unfavorable to republican government, yet we ought to deprecate the hazard attending ardent and susceptible minds, from being too strongly and too early prepossessed in favor of other political systems, before they are capable of appreciating their own.

For this reason I have greatly wished to see a plan adopted, by which the arts, sciences, and belles-lettres could be taught in their fullest extent, thereby embracing all the advantages of European tuition, with the means of acquiring the liberal knowledge, which is necessary to qualify our citizens for the exigencies of public as well as private life; and (which with me is a consideration of great magnitude) by assembling the youth from the different parts of this rising republic, contributing from their intercourse and interchange of information to the removal of prejudices, which might perhaps sometimes arise from local circumstances.

The Federal City, from its centrality and the advantages which in other respects it must have over any other place in the United States, ought to be preferred, as a proper site for such a university. And if a plan can be adopted upon a scale as extensive as I have described, and the execution of it should commence under favorable auspices in a reasonable time, with a fair prospect of success, I will grant in perpetuity fifty shares in the navigation of the Potomac River towards the endowment of it.

What annuity will arise from these fifty shares, when the navigation is in full operation, can at this time be only conjectured; and those, who are acquainted with it, can form as good a judgment as myself.

As the design of this university has assumed no form with which I am acquainted, and as I am equally ignorant who the persons are, who have taken or are disposed to take the maturing of the plan upon themselves, I have been at a loss to whom I should make this communication of my intentions. If the Commissioners of the Federal City have any particular agency in bringing the matter forward, then the information, which I now give to them, is in its proper course. If, on the other hand, they have no more to do in it than others, who may be desirous of seeing so important a measure carried into effect, they will be so good as to excuse my using them as the medium for disclosing these my intentions; because it appears necessary, that the funds for the establishment and support of the institution should be known to the promoters of it; and I see no mode more eligible for announcing my purpose.

In February, 1795, Mr. Jefferson addressed from Monticello a letter to President Washington, in reference to a proposition of M. D'Ivernois, and the Professors of the University of Geneva, Switzerland, to remove in a body to the United States, and establish here a University, "comprehending a College of Languages, preparatory to the principal one of Sciences, and also a third one for the gratuitous teaching of reading and writing to the poor." Mr. Jefferson, in view of a previous communication from Washington, as to his intention to aid by testamentary devise, the establishment of a National University, thinks the acceptance of this proposition, with modifications, will give "the institution at the outset such *éclat*, and such solid advantages, as would insure a very general concourse to it of the youths from all our States, and probably from other parts of America."

The composition of the academy can not be settled there. It must be adapted to our circumstances, and can therefore only be fixed between them and persons here acquainted with those circumstances, and conferring for the purpose after their arrival here. For a country so marked for agriculture as ours, I should think no professorship so important as one not mentioned by them, a professor of agriculture, who, before the students should leave college, should carry them through a course of lectures on the principles and practice of agriculture; and that this professor should come from no country but England. Indeed I should mark Young as the man to be obtained. These, however, are modifications to be left till their arrival here.

To this letter, Washington replied on the 15th of March, 1795:—

I had little hesitation in giving the Federal City a preference over all other places for the institution, for the following reasons. First, on account of its being the permanent seat of the government of this Union, and where the laws and policy of it must be better understood than in any local part thereof. Secondly, because of its centrality. Thirdly, because one half (or near it) of the District of Columbia is within the Commonwealth of Virginia, and the whole of the State not inconvenient thereto. Fourthly, because, as a part of the endowment, it would be useful, but alone would be inadequate to the end. Fifthly, because many advantages, I conceive, would result from the jurisdiction which the general government will have over it, which no other spot would possess. And, lastly, as this seminary is contemplated for the completion of education and study of the sciences, not for boys in their rudiments, it will afford the students an opportunity of attending the debates in Congress, and thereby becoming more liberally and better acquainted with the principles of law and government.

My judgment and my wishes point equally strong to the application of the James River shares to the same subject at the same place; but, considering the source from whence they were derived, I have, in a letter I am writing to the executive of Virginia on this subject, left the application of them to a seminary within the State, to be located by the legislature.

Hence you will perceive, that I have in a degree anticipated your proposition. I was restrained from going the whole length of the suggestion by the following considerations. First, I did not know to what extent or when any plan would be so matured for the establishment of a university, as would enable any assurances to be given to the application of M. D'Ivernois. Secondly, the propriety of transplanting the professors in a body might be questioned for several reasons; among others, because they might not be all good characters, nor all sufficiently acquainted with our language. And again, having been at variance with the leveling party of their own country, the measure might be considered as an aristocratical movement by more than those, who, without any just cause that I can discover, are continually sounding the bell of aristocracy. And, thirdly, because it might preclude some of the first professors in other countries from a participation, among whom some of the most celebrated characters in Scotland, in this line, might be obtained.

My letter to the commissioners has bound me to the fulfillment of what is therein engaged; and if the Legislature of Virginia, on considering the subject, should view it in the same light as I do, the James River shares will be added thereto; for I think one good institution of this sort is to be preferred to two imperfect ones, which, without other aid than the shares in both navigations, is more likely to fall through, than to succeed upon the plan I contemplate; which is, in a few words, to supersede the necessity of sending the youth of this country abroad for the purpose of education, where too often principles and habits unfriendly to republican government are imbibed, and not easily discarded. Instituting such a one of our own, as will answer the end, and associating them in the same seminary, will contribute to wear off those prejudices and unreasonable jealousies, which prevent or weaken friendships and impair the harmony of the Union.

On the 16th of March, 1795, Washington addressed the following letter to Gov. Brooke of Virginia:—

SIR:—Ever since the General Assembly of Virginia were pleased to submit to my disposal fifty shares in the Potomac, and one hundred in the James River Company, it has been my anxious desire to appropriate them to an object most worthy of public regard.

It is with indescribable regret, that I have seen the youth of the United States migrating to foreign countries, in order to acquire the higher branches of erudition, and to obtain a knowledge of the sciences. Although it would be injustice to many to pronounce the certainty of their imbibing maxims not congenial with republicanism, it must nevertheless be admitted, that a serious danger is encountered by sending abroad among other political systems those who have not well learned the value of their own.

The time is therefore come, when a plan of universal education ought to be adopted in the United States. Not only do the exigencies of public and private life demand it, but, if it should ever be apprehended, that prejudice would be entertained in one part of the Union against another, an efficacious remedy will be, to assemble the youth of every part under such circumstances as will, by the freedom of intercourse and collision of sentiment, give to their minds the direction of truth, philanthropy, and mutual conciliation.

It has been represented, that a university corresponding with these ideas is contemplated to be built in the Federal City, and that it will receive considerable endowments. This position is so eligible from its centrality, so convenient to Virginia, by whose legislature the shares were granted and in which part of the Federal District stands, and combines so many other conveniences, that I have determined to vest the Potomac shares in that university.

Presuming it to be more agreeable to the General Assembly of Virginia, that the shares in the James River Company should be reserved for a similar object in some part of that State, I intend to allot them for a seminary to be erected at such place as they shall deem most proper. I am disposed to believe, that a seminary of learning upon an enlarged plan, but yet not coming up to the full idea of a university, is an institution to be preferred for the position which is to be chosen. The students, who wish to pursue the whole range of science, may pass with advantage from the seminary to the university, and the former by a due relation may be rendered coöperative with the latter.

I can not however dissemble my opinion, that if all the shares were conferred on a university, it would become far more important, than when they are divided; and I have been constrained from concentering them in the same place, merely by my anxiety to reconcile a particular attention to Virginia with a great good, in which she will abundantly share in common with the rest of the United States.

I must beg the favor of your Excellency to lay this letter before that honorable body, at their next session, in order that I may appropriate the James River shares to the place which they may prefer. They will at the same time again accept my acknowledgments for the opportunity, with which they have favored me, of attempting to supply so important a desideratum in the United States as a university adequate to our necessity, and a preparatory seminary.

This letter was accordingly communicated to the Assembly at their next session, when the following resolves were passed:—

IN THE HOUSE OF DELEGATES, *December 1st*, 1795.

Whereas the migration of American youth to foreign countries, for the completion of their education, exposes them to the danger of imbibing political prejudices disadvantageous to their own republican forms of government, and ought therefore to be rendered unnecessary and avoided;

*Resolved*, that the plan contemplated of erecting a university in the Federal City, where the youth of the several States may be assembled, and their course of education finished, deserves the countenance and support of each State.

And whereas, when the General Assembly presented sundry shares in the James River and Potomac Companies to George Washington, as a small token of their gratitude for the great, eminent, and unrivaled services he had rendered to this Commonwealth, to the United States, and the world at large, in support of the principles of liberty and equal government, it was their wish and desire that he should appropriate them as he might think best; and whereas, the present General Assembly retain the same high sense of his virtues, wisdom, and patriotism;

*Resolved*, therefore, that the appropriation by the said George Washington of the aforesaid shares in the Potomac Company to the university, intended to be erected in the Federal City, is made in a manner most worthy of public regard, and of the approbation of this Commonwealth.

*Resolved*, also, that he be requested to appropriate the aforesaid shares in the James River Company to a seminary at such place in the upper country, as he may deem most convenient to a majority of the inhabitants thereof.

The following are provisions of Washington's last Will:—

—As it has always been a source of serious regret with me to see the youth of these United States sent to foreign countries for the purposes of education, often before their minds were formed, or they had imbibed any adequate ideas of the happiness of their own; contracting, too frequently, not only habits of dissipation and extravagance, but *principles unfriendly to republican government, and to the true and genuine liberties of mankind*, which thereafter are rarely overcome; for these reasons it has been my ardent wish to see a plan devised on a liberal scale, which would have a tendency to spread systematic ideas through all parts of this rising empire, thereby to do away local attachments and State prejudices, as far as the nature of things would, or indeed ought to admit, from our national councils. Looking anxiously forward to the accomplishment of so desirable an object as this is (in my estimation), my mind has not been able to contemplate any plan more likely to affect the measure, than the establishment of a University in a central part of the United States, to which youths of fortune and talents from all parts thereof may be sent for the completion of their education in all branches of polite literature, in arts and sciences, in acquiring knowledge in the principles of politics and good government; and, as a matter of infinite importance in my judgment, by associating with each other, and forming friendships in juvenile years, be enabled to free themselves in a proper degree from those local prejudices and habitual jealousies, which have just been mentioned, and which, when carried to excess, are never-failing sources of disquietude to the public mind, and pregnant with mischievous consequences to the country. Under these impressions,

I give and bequeath in perpetuity the fifty shares which I hold in the Potomac Company (under the aforesaid acts of the Legislature of Virginia,) towards the endowment of a university to be established within the limits of the District of Columbia, under the auspices of the general government, if that government should incline to extend a fostering hand towards it; and until such seminary is established, and the funds arising on these shares be required for its support, my further will and desire is, that the profit accruing therefrom shall, whenever the dividends are made, be laid out in purchasing stock in the bank of Columbia, or some other bank, at the discretion of my executors, or by the treasurer of the United States for the time being, under the direction of Congress, provided that honorable body should patronize the measure; and the dividends proceeding therefrom are to be vested in more stock, and so on until a sum adequate to the accomplishment of the object is obtained, of which I have not the smallest doubt before many years pass away, even if no aid or encouragement is given by legislative authority, or from any other source.

The hundred shares, which I hold in the James River Company, I have given, and now confirm, in perpetuity, to and for the use and benefit of Liberty Hall Academy, in the county of Rockbridge, in the commonwealth of Virginia.

We shall continue this Historical Development of the National Aspects of Education through successive administrations, down to the action of Congress at its last session.

# I. THE STATE AND EDUCATION.

AN ADDRESS TO THE PEOPLE OF NEW JERSEY IN 1838.*

---

Fellow Citizens:—We were appointed by the Convention of your own delegates to address you on the subject of Common Schools. We approach you with solicitude, as deeply sensible of the great importance of the interest intrusted to us; yet, as freemen speaking to freemen, with prevailing confidence.

The points which we propose for your attention, and, if we might, would press into every heart, are few, simple and practical; the necessary consequences, it seems to us, from principles which all admit. We say that *knowledge is the universal right of man:* and we need bring no clearer demonstration than that intellectual nature, capable of it, thirsting for it, expanding and aspiring with it, which is God's own argument in every living soul. We say that the assertion for himself of this inherent right, to the full measure of his abilities and opportunities, is *the universal duty of man:* and that whoever fails of it, thwarts the design of his Creator; and, in proportion as he neglects the gift of God, dwarfs and enslaves and brutifies the high capacity for truth and liberty which he inherits. And all experience, and every page of history confirm the assertion, in the close kindred, which has everywhere been proved, of ignorance and vice with wretchedness and slavery. And we say farther, that the security of this inherent right to every individual, and its extension, in the fullest measure, to the greatest number, is *the universal interest of man;* so that they who deny or abridge it to their fellows, or who encourage, or, from want of proper influence, permit them to neglect it, are undermining the foundations of government, weakening the hold of society, and preparing the way for that unsettling and dissolving of all human institutions, which must result in anarchy and ruin, and in which they who have the greatest stake must be the greatest sufferers. A lesson, clearly taught by

* The Convention assembled in Trenton on the 27th and 28th of January, 1838, Chief Justice Hornblower presiding. The address was prepared by the Rt. Rev. George W. Doane, in behalf of a Committee consisting of Bishop Doane, *Chairman*, L. Q. C. Elmer, M. J. Rhees, T. Frelinghuysen, J. S. Green, D. B. Ryall, A. B. Dod, A. Atwood, and S. R. Gummere.

that divine philosophy, in which the Maker of mankind becomes their Teacher; reveals the world as but one neighborhood, and men as brethren of one family; and writes upon all social institutions these golden truths, the fundamentals and essentials of the true political economy, which neither individuals nor nations have ever disregarded with impunity,—"all things whatsoever ye would that men should do to you, do ye even so to them"—"none of us liveth to himself"—"whether one member suffer, all the members suffer with it; or one member be honored, all the members rejoice with it"—"bear ye one another's burdens, and so fulfill the law of Christ."

If the truth of these positions be established, their application is self-evident. And there never was a nation, since the world was made, in which their obligation was so clear, or its application so important. In the theory of our constitution, the people are the governors. In practice, they ought to be. And is ignorance the qualification for good government? Would you select a man to make your laws who can not read? Or one who can not write to execute them? Yet the authority which they exercise, and the abuses of which they are capable, are nothing, in comparison with theirs, from whom all power proceeds, and without whose permission no wrong can be done. Fellow citizens, we are republicans. Our country is our *common wealth.* We have all an equal share in her. Her laws are alike for the protection of all. Her institutions are alike for the advantage of all. Her blessings are our common privilege. Her glory is our common pride. But common privileges impose a common responsibility. And equal rights can never be disjoined from equal duties. The constitution which, under God, secures our liberties, is in the keeping of us all. It is a sacred trust which no man can delegate. He holds it for himself, not only, but for his children, for posterity, and for the world. And he who can not read it, who does not understand its provisions, who could not on a just occasion, assert its principles, no more sustains the character of an American citizen, than the man who would not seal it with his blood.

It is in vain to say that education is a private matter, and that it is the duty of every parent to provide for the instruction of his own children. In theory, it is so. But there are some who can not, and there are more who will not, make provision. And the question then is, shall the State suffer from individual inability, or from individual neglect? When the child who has not been trained up in the way in which he ought to go, commits a crime against the State, the law, with iron hand, comes in between the parent and his offspring, and takes charge of the offender. And shall there be provision to punish only, and none to prevent? Shall the only offices in which the State is known be those of jailor and of executioner? Shall she content herself with the stern attribute of justice, and discard the gentler ministries of mercy? It was said of Draco's laws that they were writ with blood. Is it less true of any State which makes provision for the whipping-post, the penitentiary, the scaffold, and leaves the education of her children to individual effort or precarious charity? It was well said by the distinguished head of our Judiciary,* even more distinguished as the President of the late convention for Common Schools, "the State has an interest in every child within her limits." May not still more than this with equal truth be said,—the welfare, nay, the being of the State is bound up in the character of every child? Think of the blessings which Washington, and Franklin, and Fulton, and Marshall, have brought down upon our land! Think of the scorn and execration which the name of Arnold brings with it, the single name in our whole history at which the nation needs to blush!

If the positions be maintained, that *the education of the people is indispensable to the preservation of free institutions*, and that *it is therefore the duty of every free State to provide for the education of her children*, we are prepared, fellow citizens, for the inquiry, *how far has provision been made for the discharge of this duty in the State with which we are most intimately connected, the State of New Jersey?* That the duty of making some provision for this end has long been recognized, the twenty-one years which have elapsed since the passage of the first act "to create a fund for the support of free schools" sufficiently attest. That what has been done is insufficient you have yourselves borne witness in the general impulse which, in December and January last, originated so many of those primary assemblies—in our republic the true sources of power and influence—for the consideration of this subject; and in that large, intelligent, and most respectable convention, composed of delegates, chosen by yourselves, to express your own views on the provisions for the public instruction, by which it was resolved with singular unanimity, that "the general laws of this State on the subject of Common Schools are essentially defective and ought to be repealed." Into the question, "What shall be substituted for the present law?" the convention did not enter. It was for them to de-

* Chief Justice Hornblower, by his deportment as the presiding officer of the Convention, addea new dignity to his office, and to himself.

clare the wishes of the people for a more effective system of instruction. The plan and its provisions they left with perfect confidence to the wisdom of the Legislature. The course which the convention pursued is even more becoming for us. The rather, as the matter is at this very moment in the course of legislative action. And after all, fellow citizens, the question, "What the law is?" is by no means so important as the question, "What is public sentiment?" If the people are but right the Legislature never will be greatly wrong. Or if they should, the remedy is easy, and the cure infallible.

Omitting all considerations, then, of what has been or of what may be legislative enactments on the subject, we address you as the Sovereign People, and we say that "*it is your duty and your highest interest to provide and to maintain, within the reach of every child, the means of such an education as will qualify him to discharge the duties of a citizen of the Republic;* and will enable him, by subsequent exertion, in the free exercise of the unconquerable will, to attain the highest eminence in knowledge and in power which God may place within his reach. We utterly repudiate as unworthy, not of freemen only, but of men, the narrow notion that there is to be an education for the poor, as such. Has God provided for the poor a coarser earth, a thinner air, a paler sky? Does not the glorious sun pour down his golden flood as cheerily upon the poor man's hovel as upon the rich man's palace? Have not the cotter's children as keen a sense of all the freshness, verdure, fragrance, melody, and beauty of luxuriant nature as the pale sons of kings? Or is it on the mind that God has stamped the imprint of a baser birth so that the poor man's child knows with an inborn certainty that his lot is to crawl, not climb? It is not so. God has not done it. Man can not do it. Mind is immortal. Mind is imperial. It bears no mark of high or low, of rich or poor. It heeds no bound of time or place, of rank or circumstance. It asks but freedom. It requires but light. It is heaven-born, and it aspires to heaven. Weakness does not enfeeble it. Poverty can not repress it. Difficulties do but stimulate its vigor. And the poor tallow chandler's son that sits up all the night to read the book which an apprentice lends him lest the master's eye should miss it in the morning, shall stand and treat with kings, shall add new provinces to the domain of science, shall bind the lightning with a hempen cord and bring it harmless from the skies.* The Common School is *common*, not as inferior, not as the school for poor men's children, but as the

* See Franklin's Life.

light and air are common. It ought to be the best school because it is the first school; and in all good works the beginning is one-half. Who does not know the value to a community of a plentiful supply of the pure element of water? And infinitely more than this is the instruction of the common School; for it is the fountain at which the mind drinks, and is refreshed and strengthened for its career of usefulness and glory.

Fellow citizens, it is the wise ordinance of God that man shall work for what he values. In all the dealings of your ordinary life, you act upon the principle. You plow your fields. You urge your spindles. You ply your fisheries. You tend your shops. With sweat of brow, or sweat of brain, each precious thing that man possesses must be gained and kept. At no less price can liberty and its attendant blessings be enjoyed. "That which makes a good constitution," said wise and prudent William Penn,* "must also keep it, men of wisdom and virtue: qualities which, because they descend not with inheritance, must be carefully propagated by a virtuous education of youth." Ask not, then, when we enjoin on you the duty of providing for the public instruction, where the cost shall come from? Were your house beset with robbers would you stop to ask the cost of its defense? If an invading army were to land to-morrow on our shores must we stop to count the cost before we march to meet and to repel them? The Common Schools are in the place to us of arms, and troops, and fleets. They are our nurseries of men. They are indeed "the cheap defense of nations."

What constitutes a State?
Not high-raised battlements or labored mound,
Thick wall, or moated gate;
Not cities proud, with spires and turrets crowned,
Not bays and broad-armed ports,
Where, laughing at the storm, rich navies ride;
Not starred and spangled courts,
Where low-browed baseness wafts perfume to pride,
No—MEN, high-minded MEN.
* * * * *
Men who their duties know,
But know their rights, and knowing, dare maintain;
Prevent the long-aimed blow,
And crush the tyrant, while they rend the chain:
These constitute a State.†

Fellow citizens, it is for you to say what shall be the present character, what shall be the future destiny of New Jersey. We

* Preface to the Frame of Government, 1682. † Sir William Jones, in imitation of Alcæus

have indeed a goodly heritage. But it has been long and shamefully neglected. We have undervalued our privileges. We have overlooked our duties. We have been content to be a pendent merely, when we ought to be an independent State. There is now, thank God, the sound as of a trumpet in the land that stirs the old heroic blood. We feel the remnant sparks of the forgotten fire which warmed our fathers' hearts. The spirit of the elder day is breathing on us with its quickening and invigorating power. Let us accept the omen. Let us obey the noble impulse. Let us arise to duty and to glory. Men of New Jersey, it is you that are to rise. You are the State. You create and you control the Legislature. You enact and you sustain the laws. Yours are the means. Yours is the influence. Yours is the work. You make, *you are the State.* Go on as you have now begun. The system of Common Schools which shall be adopted by the present legislature, take into your own hands. If it is not what it should be, see that the next legislature make it such. Act together. Act with system. Act like men. The organization for the purpose is complete. The General Committee, the Committees of correspondence for the counties, the Committees of the townships—there is not an inch of ground that is not reached, there is not a citizen of New Jersey whose heart may not be roused by this electric chain. Lay to your hands, then, and employ it well. The work is great, and great must be the effort, and great the confidence. You must trust yourselves. You must trust your fellow citizens. You must trust the legislature. A system of public instruction is a great and arduous enterprise. You must repose such confidence in those who are to frame it as shall enable them to do it well. When it is framed you will do wisely to commit its oversight, subject to legislative supervision, to a judicious Board,* selected carefully from your most tried and faithful men, with wisdom to direct and with devotion to exert its powers. Above all, give the direction of the engine, with a large and liberal discretion, to a skillful engineer. And when it is made, and manned, and set in operation, you must still support it, you must watch over it, you must be yourselves a part of it. The School Fund is not equal to the work. And if it were, it would not be so well for you. Tax yourselves for the support of

* It is said that there are prejudices against a Board of Education, and a Superintendent. We can hardly think that they are general. If so, our appeal is to the good, sterling, common sense of the people of New Jersey. Is there a turnpike road, or a steamboat, or a bank, or a cotton factory, whose affairs are not intrusted to a Board of Managers? Is there a mill in all the State without a miller, or a locomotive in the land without an engineer? Is the education of the people less important than all these? Or is the system of public education to be the only case of a machine that goes alone?

Common Schools and you will never be in danger of taxation from a foreign power—you will need less taxation for the support of pauperism, and the punishment of crime. Look to your school-houses. See that they are convenient of access, that they are comfortable, that they are neat and tasteful. Look to the teachers. See that they are taught themselves, and apt to teach; men that fear God, and love their country. See that they are well accommodated, well treated, well remunerated. Respect them and they will respect themselves, and your children will respect them. Look to the scholars. Have them much in your eye, and always in your heart. Remember you are to grow old among them. Remember you are to die, and leave your country in their hands.

"Good Common Schools," says Governor Everett, of Massachusetts, "are the basis of every wise system of popular education." This is precisely what they are, the basis of a system; but the basis only. Let us now lay their broad foundations deep and strong—foundations that will stand themselves and bear the noble structure which our children and our children's children, as we trust, will rear upon them. We are the citizens of a small State. We can not, by our votes, control the electoral college. We can not, by our political influence, aspire to be the empire State of the confederacy. But there is a nobler empire, whose dominion does not come by numbers or by physical power. We may aspire, if we are just to ourselves and to our opportunities, to wield the suffrages of mind. The men of Athens were but few, their territory small, their soil indifferent. Yet did Athenian arms prevail against the myriads of the East; and to Athenian letters and Athenian arts admiring nations still award the palm. In the same noble lists let us engage; and make the mastery of intellect the prize of our ambition. Let us devote ourselves and consecrate the State to the great work of education. Let us lay hold in earnest of the remarkable advantages which we possess in this respect, in our accessible position, our temperate climate, our freedom from absorbing interests, the moderate habits, and the simple manners of our people. Let us sustain our present seats of learning; and let kindred institutions in every varied form be multiplied about us. Let us collect the children of the land: and on their minds make the mark which shall go down to latest generations. Let other States excel in commerce, or in agriculture, or in manufacturies. But let the staple of our State be mind; the products of our soil, with God to bless the culture, knowledge, and patriotism, and virtue; our highest object and our noblest aim to be the State of Common Schools, Academies, and Colleges, the educating State, the nursery of freemen.

That which makes a good Constitution must keep it, viz: men of wisdom and virtue: qualities that, because they descend not with worldly inheritance, must be carefully propagated by a virtuous education of youth, for which spare no cost, for by such parsimony, all that is saved is lost. WILLIAM PENN. *Instructions to Council.*

Promote, as an object of primary importance, institutions for the general diffusion of knowledge. In proportion as the structure of a government gives force to public opinion, it is essential that public opinion should be enlightened.

GEORGE WASHINGTON. *Farewell Address.*

The wisdom and generosity of the Legislature in making liberal appropriations in money for the benefit of schools, academies and colleges, is an equal honor to them and their constituents, a proof of their veneration for letters and science, and a portent of great and lasting good to North and South America, and to the world. Great is truth—great is liberty—great is humanity—and they must and will prevail.

JOHN ADAMS. *Inaugural.*

I look to the diffusion of light and education as the resources most to be relied on for ameliorating the condition, promoting the virtue, and advancing the happiness of man. And I do hope, in the present spirit of extending to the great mass of mankind the blessings of instruction, I see a prospect of great advancement in the happiness of the human race, and this may proceed to an indefinite, although not an infinite degree. A system of general instruction, which shall reach every description of our citizens, from the richest to the poorest, as it was the earliest, so it shall be the latest of all the public concerns in which I shall permit myself to take an interest. Give it to us, in any shape, and receive for the inestimable boon the thanks of the young, and the blessings of the old, who are past all other services but prayers for the prosperity of their country, and blessings to those who promote it. THOMAS JEFFERSON.

Learned institutions ought to be the favorite objects with every free people; they throw that light over the public mind which is the best security against crafty and dangerous encroachments on the public liberty. They multiply the educated individuals, from among whom the people may elect a due portion of their public agents of every description, more especially of those who are to frame the laws: by the perspicuity, the consistency, and the stability, as well as by the justice and equal spirit of which, the great social purposes are to be answered.

JAMES MADISON.

Moral, political, and intellectual improvement, are duties assigned by the author of our existence to social, no less than to individual man. For the fulfillment of these duties, governments are invested with power, and to the attainment of these ends, the exercise of this power is a duty sacred and indispensable. JOHN QUINCY ADAMS.

For the purpose of promoting the happiness of the State, it is absolutely necessary that our Government, which unites into one all the minds of the State, should possess in an eminent degree not only the understanding, the passions, and the will, but above all, the moral faculty and the conscience of an individual. Nothing can be politically right that is morally wrong; and no necessity can ever sanctify a law that is contrary to equity. Virtue is the soul of a Republic. To promote this, laws for the suppression of vice and immorality will be as ineffectual as the increase and enlargement of goals. There is but one method of preventing crime and of rendering a republican form of government durable; and that is, by disseminating the seeds of virtue and knowledge through every part of the State, by means of proper modes and places of education; and this can be done effectually only by the interference and aid of the legislature. I am so deeply impressed with this opinion, that were this the last evening of my life, I would not only say to the asylum of my ancestors and my beloved native country, with the patriot of Venice, "*Esto perpetua*," but I would add, as the best proof of my affection for her, my parting advice to the guardians of her liberties, establish and support PUBLIC SCHOOLS in every part of the State. BENJAMIN RUSH.

There is one object which I earnestly recommend to your notice and patronage; I mean our institutions for the education of youth. The importance of common schools is best estimated by the good effects of them where they most abound, and are best regulated. Our ancestors have transmitted to us many excellent institutions, matured by the wisdom and experience of ages. Let them descend to posterity, accompanied with others, which by promoting useful knowledge, and multiplying the blessings of social order, diffusing the influence of moral obligations, may be reputable to us, and beneficial to them. JOHN JAY.

The first duty of government, and the surest evidence of good government, is the encouragement of education. A general diffusion of knowledge is the precursor and protector of republican institutions, and in it we must confide as the conservative power that will watch over our liberties and guard them against fraud, intrigue, corruption and violence. I consider the system of our Common Schools as the palladium of our freedom, for no reasonable apprehension can be entertained of its subversion, as long as the great body of the people are enlightened by education. To increase the funds, to extend the benefits, and to remedy the defects of this excellent system, is worthy of your most deliberate attention. I can not recommend, in terms too strong and impressive, as munificent appropriations as the faculties of the State will authorize for all establishments connected with the interests of education, the exaltation of literature and science, and the improvement of the human mind.

DE WITT CLINTON. *Message as Governor.*

The parent who sends his son into the world uneducated, defrauds the community of a lawful citizen, and bequeathes to it a nuisance.

CHANCELLOR KENT.

For augmenting the aggregate amount of intelligence and mental power, in any community, the grandest instrumentality ever yet devised is the institution of Common Schools. The Common School realizes all the facts, or fables, whichever they may be, of the Divining Rod. It tries its experiments over the whole surface of society, and wherever a buried fountain of genius is flowing in the darkness below, it brings it above, and pours out its waters to fertilize the earth. Among mankind, hitherto, hardly one person in a million has had any chance for the development of his higher faculties. Hence, whatever poets, orators, philosophers, divines, inventors or philanthropists, may have risen up to bless the world, they have all risen from not more than one millionth part of the race. The minds of the rest, though equally endowed with talent, genius and benevolence, have lain outside the scope of availibility for good. These millions, with the exception of the units, have been drudges, slaves, cattle; their bodies used, their souls unrecognized. Ah, nowhere else have there been such waste and loss of treasure, as in the waste and loss of the Human Faculties. All spendthrift profusions, all royal prodigalities, are parsimony and niggardliness, compared with the ungathered, abandoned treasures of the human soul. As civilization has advanced, perhaps one child in a hundred thousand, and, in more favored nations, one child in ten thousand, has been admitted to the opportunities of knowledge. Forthwith, the men capable of constructing the institutions or the engines of human improvement and adornment appeared; and in numbers, too, far beyond the proportionate share of the constituencies from which they sprang. But if, instead of striking the fetters of prohibition from one in a hundred thousand, or from one in ten thousand, those fetters are stricken from all, and incitements to exertion and aids to self-development are supplied to all; then, immediately, quick as water gushes from unsealed fountains, Shermans rise up from the shoemaker's bench, Beechers come from the blacksmith's anvil, and Bowditches and Franklins from the ship-chandler's and the tallow-chandler's shop, and a new galaxy shines forth over all the firmament of genius. These are truths which the uneducated nations do not understand;—truths too, which the caste-men, whether of birth or of wealth, do not wish to understand. HORACE MANN. *Inaugural at Antioch College.*

The theory of our government is,—not that all men, however unfit, shall be voters,—but that every man, by the power of reason and the sense of duty, shall become fit to be a voter. Education must bring the practice as near as possible to the theory. As the children now are, so will the sovereigns soon be. How can we expect the fabric of the government to stand, if vicious materials are daily wrought into its framework? Education must prepare our citizens to become municipal officers, intelligent jurors, honest witnesses, legislators, or competent judges of legislation,—in fine, to fill all the manifold relations of life. For this end, it must be universal. The whole land must be watered with the streams of knowledge. HORACE MANN.

# THE STATE AND EDUCATION.

WHAT constitutional right has the government to impose the burthen of taxation on individual property, or to employ the public funds, however obtained, for the furtherance of any such object as that of popular instruction? Is not education a personal advantage, accruing to the individual instructed, as much as the possession of property, or any other good—and by what right does the government undertake to bestow personal benefits at all, much more to compel one class of men, because they are men of substance, to bear the expense of benefits gratuitously bestowed on another class?

In the first place, the power over education is one of the powers of *public police*, belonging essentially to government. It is one of those powers, the exercise of which, is indispensable to the preservation of society—to its integrity, and its healthy action. It rests on the same foundation as that which is employed in defining and taking cognizance of crime, in erecting courts, both of civil and of criminal jurisdiction, in establishing jails and penitentiaries, and in compelling the performance of contracts, and the reparation of injuries. In this point of view, it is one among a number of means to the same end, either of which, or all of which, may be freely used, according to the wisdom and discretion of the public authorities. All are lawful, and equally lawful and constitutional modes of action. In the present case, however, the choice is not a question of expediency or economy only—though certainly important in the latter point of view; but it becomes a question of humanity also. For while it will always be necessary to provide for the punishment of offences against society, when committed, and for the compulsory observance of personal obligations, and redress of personal grievances, yet it is vastly preferable, undoubtedly, that, if such a thing were possible, there should be no grievances to be redressed, no broken promises, and no committed crimes. It is the aim, and the undoubted tendency of education, properly understood and conducted, to accomplish this object—an object of incalulable benefit to human society. As a measure, designed to operate only as a law of police, the public support of education goes behind all crime, and all injurious and disturbing action in society, and seeks to occupy the intellect and the affections of men, and simply by informing the mind and molding the temper, by demonstrating that it is the interest and the happiness of each to be just and generous towards all, by letting a little light in on the understanding, and touching the heart, either to take from them the disposition to offend one another, or to injure society, or to arm them with strength of purpose to resist every temptation to do so.

But there is another and broader ground, still, on which to rest the power and duty of the state, in regard to education. That which we have already noticed, is enough for the authority, if the state choose to exercise it, and in the opinion of your committee, enough for the duty also. But the consideration which we now approach, is not only sufficient for the abundant justification of authoritative action—it demands action, and the state could not justify itself to the people without it.

The people of this state, having united themselves together in a civil society, have agreed to secure to themselves, or to attempt to secure to themselves, the highest advantages of the social compact, through the agency of certain forms of government and administration. We have adopted the representative system; and we start from the position, that the whole political power of the country, much of it for immediate exercise, and all of it by ultimate reference, is in the hands of the people. And, on this grand position, as a basis, do all our constitutional forms absolutely rest. But just as children are unfit to govern themselves, so are uneducated men, being still children, though of huge growth, unfit to govern themselves. In one mode or another, associations of such men always have had, and always will have, protectors and masters; and we hardly need add, that a people with masters of any sort, as the basis of a free representative system, is a contradiction in terms. It is evident, therefore, that popular cultivation, as diffusive and general as the numbers composing the republic, is indispensable to the preservation of our republican forms—and hence arises the great constitutional duty of the government. *It is the duty of self-preservation, according to its actual mode of existence, for the sake of the common good.* The highest good of the whole, as a body, is the object in view; that good is to be attained only, according to the very terms of the original compact, through our adopted forms; and the duty of preserving and maintaining those forms, in their vigor and purity, becomes, at once, the very highest duty and obligation of those who are intrusted with the administration. It is a duty, every instant, and perpetually, in force. No change of administration can affect it; and the moment it is denied or neglected, that moment is the cause of the republic repudiated and betrayed.

It is easy, we think, to know when this duty of maintaining our constitutional forms, by the care which is taken of the structure on which they rest, is in the way of being faithfully performed. The duty is *not* well provided for, unless some rational plan of public instruction shall have been devised and adopted, the object and the probable effect of which shall be, to lead to the cultivation of every child in the community, at least so far as to fit them all, without exception to the extent of their capabilities, for an intelligent discharge of the common and ordinary duties and responsibilities of social and political life, to which all, or nearly all, are called by the very conditions of our social and political forms. The future mother must be educated in every female child—a matter not to be neglected if we would have men in the republic; and in every male child, must be educated the future elector, juror, and local administrator.

The duty of being educated is, undoubtedly, one of positive obligation, resting on every citizen, as part of the original compact between every citizen and the whole body of citizens; and as far as instruction is attainable in youth, the obligation rests on parents and guardians. It is a duty which by no means concerns the individual only; it is one in which every other individual, and the whole community have a deep interest. The verdict of jurors, and the decision of a contested election, perhaps by the casting vote of a single person, are matters of vast concernment to others, besides those who render the verdict, or turn the election.

But while there can be no doubt about this personal duty, and the claims which the community has on every member in regard to it, it is clearly one which could not, especially with us, be enforced by any direct and arbitrary exercise of power. Happily, we think, nothing of this sort is necessary, any more than it would be desirable.

There are evidently two difficulties in the case to contend with. One of them is, that so long as men differ in endowment and in the allotments of Providence, and so long as the rights of property shall be respected, there will always be a considerable portion of the community unable, for want of the necessary means, to sustain the expenses of education. Whenever this is the case, we hold it to be the duty of the state to supply the necessary means; and on this principle the state has long acted.

The other difficulty in the case is the more serious one of the two. It is, that perhaps a large majority of those who have the means of meeting the necessary outlays for the proper education of their children, are not disposed to use them for any such purpose. The burthen in many cases is undoubtedly a heavy one, and it is difficult to convince parents of the unquestionable truth, that they can make no provision for their offspring by pecuniary aids, which can in any degree compensate for the want of adequate mental and moral cultivation.

This is a difficulty to be met by the state, with measures of a delicate character -measures calculated to induce and to persuade—measures aiming to bring in public opinion to its aid, and appealing at once to the good sense, the pride, and the interest of the parties concerned. Whatever compulsory action is resorted to, must be of a gentle and paternal character, and be surrounded and accompanied with every circumstance of kindness, and with whatever is best adapted to move and to interest. Such, in a great measure, has been and is the nature of the system of public instruction long in operation in this state, so far as designed to meet the difficulty here suggested; and your committee propose some important measures, regarded by them as worthy of great consideration, not certainly to change materially the features of the system in this respect, but to modify them, and if possible to give them efficiency.

There is one other test to which your committee would refer, as one by which we may know whether the state has performed, or is performing, its great constitutional duty of self-preservation for the common good, by taking due care of the subject of popular instruction. That test is, whether or not the system be such as makes education a thing of practicable and probable attainment by the class of the comparatively indigent. For if it be otherwise, there can be no security for the continuance of our constitutional forms. In this age of the world, the rich in any civilized community will be educated; and if the poor can not be, and are not, the necessary consequence is, that a separation takes place. Knowledge is power, and it will be exercised; and a selfish aristocracy, formed of those who are at the same time rich and educated, will bear the class of the indigent and ignorant to the wall. The community being once divided into these two great classes, it matters little, to the present argument at least, whether the powerful bear sway wisely and well, or oppressively: in either case the balance is destroyed which makes our government what it is; our constitutional forms are not preserved; and so much of common good as depended upon them, much or little, is sacrificed.

Nor is it enough, in our judgment, to satisfy the demands of the test now referred to, that our common schools are made accessible to all classes, the poorest as well as the better conditioned. If the system stopped here, it would aid in creating the very distinction and separation which ought to be avoided. In the first place the condition of the common schools themselves must be elevated; and if it is not, the consequence will soon be, that they will come to be regarded as the seminaries of the poor, when the rich will desert them; yielding them neither countenance nor support any further than forced to do so, or contributing to sustain them, like other institutions for the poor, as public charities. The condition of these schools then must be elevated. They must be common places of resort for all classes as far as possible, where the youth of the same neighborhood, however otherwise separated, may meet, as youth now meet in our academies and colleges, to sacrifice all distinctions except such as grow out of various success in the prosecution of the same studies.

But this is not all; the way to the higher schools—to the academies and colleges—must be open, at least to the young man of genius and enterprise among the classes of the indigent, as well as to his more wealthy rival.

There is one way, and only one in which this can be done; and that is, by such liberal endowment of the better schools, by private munificence and state patronage, as will bring down the wages of instruction to the person taught, to a moderate sum. When this is accomplished, the balance between the wealthy and poorer classes will be easily struck; for though their relative numbers will still be unequal in these schools, the sum of knowledge and intellectual power among the sturdy and ambitious sons of poverty, will be, out and out, equal to that acquired and displayed by the more numerous class of those among whom must always be many whom indulgence and luxury have enervated.

D. D. Barnard. *Report as Chairman of Leg. Committee*, 1838.

In this particular, New England may be allowed to claim, I think, a merit of a peculiar character. She early adopted and has constantly maintained the principle, that it is the undoubted right, and the bounden duty of government, to provide for the instruction of all youth. That which is elsewhere left to chance, or to charity, we secure by law. For the purpose of public instruction, we hold every man subject to taxation in proportion to his property, and we look not to the question, whether he himself have, or have not, children to be benefited by the education for which he pays. We regard it as a wise and liberal system of police, by which property, and life, and the peace of society are secured. We seek to prevent, in some measure, the extension of the penal code, by inspiring a salutary and conservative principle of virtue and of knowledge in an early age. We hope to excite a feeling of respectability, and a sense of character, by enlarging the capacity, and increasing the sphere of intellectual enjoyment. By general instruction, we seek, as far as possible, to purify the whole moral atmosphere; to keep good sentiments uppermost, and to turn the strong current of feeling and opinion, as well as the censures of the law, and the denunciations of religion, against immorality and crime. We hope for a security, beyond the law, and above the law, in the prevalence of enlightened and well-principled moral sentiment. We hope to continue and prolong the time, when, in the villages and farm-houses of New England, there may be undisturbed sleep within unbarred doors. And knowing that our government rests directly on the public will, that we may preserve it, we endeavor to give a safe and proper direction to that public will. We do not, indeed, expect all men to be philosophers or statesmen; but we confidently trust, and our expectation of the duration of our system of government rests on that trust, that by the diffusion of general knowledge and good and virtuous sentiments, the political fabric may be secure, as well against open violence and overthrow, as against the slow but sure undermining of licentiousness. Daniel Webster. *Discourse at Plymouth*, 1822.

COLONY OF MASSACHUSETTS.

It being one chief project of the old deluder, Satan, to keep men from the knowledge of the Scriptures, as in former times by keeping them in an unknown tongue, so in these latter times by persuading from the use of tongues, that so at least the true sense and meaning of the original might be clouded by false glosses of saint-seeming deceivers; that learning may not be buried in the grave of our fathers in the church and commonwealth, the Lord assisting our endeavors—

It is therefore *ordered*, that every township in this jurisdiction, after the Lord hath increased them to the number of fifty householders, shall then forthwith appoint one within their town to teach all such children as shall resort to him, to write and read; whose wages shall be paid, either by the parents or masters of such children, or by the inhabitants in general, by way of supply, as the major part of those that order the prudentials of the town shall appoint; provided, those that send their children be not oppressed by paying much more than they can have them taught for in other towns; and it is further *ordered*, that when any town shall increase to the number of one hundred families or householders, they shall set up a Grammar School, the master thereof being able to instruct youth so far as they may be fitted for the University; provided, that if any town neglect the performance hereof above one year, that every such town shall pay £5 to the next school till they shall perform this order.

*Order of General Court*, 1647.

In 1647, when a few scattered and feeble settlements, almost buried in the depths of the forest, were all that constituted the Colony of Massachusetts; when the entire population consisted of twenty-one thousand souls; when the external means of the people were small, their dwellings humble, and their raiment and subsistence scanty and homely; when the whole valuation of all the colonial estates, both public and private, would hardly equal the inventory of many a private individual at the present day; when the fierce eye of the savage was nightly seen glaring from the edge of the surrounding wilderness, and no defense or succor was at hand; it was then, amid all these privations and dangers, that the Pilgrim Fathers conceived the magnificent idea of a Free* and Universal Education for the People; and, amid all their poverty, they stinted themselves to a still scantier pittance; amid all their toils they imposed upon themselves still more burdensome labors; amid all their perils they braved still greater dangers, that they might find the time and the means to reduce their grand conception to practice. Two divine ideas filled their great hearts—their duty to God and to posterity. For the one they built the church; for the other they opened the school. Religion and Knowledge!—two attributes of the same glorious and eternal truth—and that truth the only one on which immortal or mortal happiness can be securely founded.

As an innovation upon all preëxisting policy and usages, the establishment of Free Schools was the boldest ever promulgated since the commencement of the Christian era. As a theory, it could have been refuted and silenced by a more formidable array of argument and experience than was ever marshaled against any other opinion of human origin. But time has ratified its soundness. Two centuries now proclaim it to be as wise as it was courageous, as beneficent as it was disinterested. It was one of those grand mental and moral experiments whose effects can not be determined in a single generation. But now, according to the manner in which human life is computed, we are the sixth generation from its founders, and have we not reason to be grateful both to God and man for its unnumbered blessings? The sincerity of our gratitude must be tested by our efforts to perpetuate and improve what they established. The gratitude of the lips only is an unholy offering.

HORACE MANN. *Tenth Report of the Secretary of the Massachusetts Board of Education.*

---

* Was the Public School of Massachusetts at first *free?* Was Massachusetts the first to establish such a system as is ordained in the law of 1647?—*Ed. of Amer. Jour. of Education.*

The three following propositions describe the broad and ever-during foundation on which the Common School system of Massachusetts reposes:

The successive generations of men, taken collectively, constitute one great Commonwealth.

The property of this Commonwealth is pledged for the education of all its youth up to such a point as will save them from poverty and vice, and prepare them for the adequate performance of their social and civil duties.

The successive holders of this property are trustees, bound to the faithful execution of their trust by the most sacred obligations; because embezzlement and pillage from children and descendants are as criminal as the same offenses when perpetrated against contemporaries.

Recognizing these eternal principles of natural ethics, the Constitution of Massachusetts—the fundamental law of the State—after declaring, (among other things,) in the preamble to the first section of the fifth chapter, that "the encouragement of arts and sciences and all good literature tends to the honor of God, the advantage of the Christian religion, and the great benefit of this and the other United States of America," proceeds, in the second section of the same chapter, to set forth the duties of all future Legislators and Magistrates, in the following noble and impressive language:—

"Wisdom and knowledge, as well as virtue, diffused generally among the body of the people, being necessary for the preservation of their rights and liberties; and as these depend on spreading the opportunities and advantages of education in the various parts of the country, and among the different orders of the people, it shall be the duty of legislators and magistrates, in all future periods of this Commonwealth, to cherish the interests of literature and the sciences, and all seminaries of them; especially the University of Cambridge, public schools, and grammar schools in the towns; to encourage private societies and public institutions, rewards and immunities, for the promotion of agriculture, arts, sciences, commerce, trades, manufactures, and a natural history of the country; to countenance and inculcate the principles of humanity and general benevolence, public and private charity, industry and frugality, honesty and punctuality in their dealings; sincerity, good humor, and all social affections and generous sentiments among the people."

Horace Mann. *Tenth Report of the Secretary of the Massachusetts Board of Education.*

The outline and most of the essential features of the present system of common, or public schools in Connecticut, will be found in the practice of the first settlers of the several towns which composed the two original colonies of Connecticut and New Haven, before any express provision was made by general law for the regulation and support of schools or the bringing up of children. The first law on the subject did but little more than declare the motive, and make obligatory the practice which had grown up out of the character of the founders of these colonies, and the circumstances in which they were placed. They did not come here as isolated individuals, drawn together from widely separated homes, entertaining broad differences of opinion on all matters of civil and religious concernment, and kept together by the necessity of self-defense in the eager prosecution of some temporary but profitable adventure. They came after God had set them in families, and they brought with them the best pledges of good behavior, in the relations which father and mother, husband and wife, parents and children, neighbors and friends, establish. They came, with a foregone conclusion of permanence, and with all the elements of the social state combined in vigorous activity—every man, expecting to find or make occupation in the way in which he had been trained. They came with earnest religious convictions, made more earnest by the trials of persecution ; and the enjoyment of these convictions was a leading motive in their emigration hither. The fundamental articles of their religious creed, that the Bible was the only authoritative expression of the divine will, and that every man was able to judge for himself in its interpretation, made schools necessary to bring all persons 'to a knowledge of the Scriptures,' and an understanding 'of the main grounds and principles of the Christian religion necessary to salvation.' The constitution of civil government, which they adopted from the outset, which declared all civil officers elective, and gave to every inhabitant who would take the oath of allegiance the right to vote and to be voted for, and which practically converted political society into a partnership, in which each member had the right to bind the whole firm, made universal education identical with self-preservation. But aside from these considerations, the natural and acknowledged leaders in this enterprise—the men who, by their religious character, wealth, social position, and previous experience in conducting large business operations, commanded public confidence in church and commonwealth, were educated men—as highly and thoroughly educated as the best endowed grammar schools in England could educate them at that period, and not a few of them had enjoyed the advantages of her great universities. These men would naturally seek for their own children the best opportunities of education which could be provided; and it is the crowning glory of these men, that, instead of sending their own children back to England to be educated in grammar schools and universities, they labored to establish free grammar schools and a college, here amid the stumps of the primeval forests; that, instead of setting up 'family schools' and 'select schools' for the ministers' sons and the magistrates' sons, the ministers and magistrates were found,—not only in town meeting, pleading for an allowance out of the common treasury for the support of a public or common school, and in some instances for a 'free (endowed grammar) school,'—but among the families, entreating parents of all classes to send their children to the same school with their own. All this was done in advance of any colonial legislation, and was begun in anticipation of any formal town action.

The first permanent settlement of Hartford was made by the religious friends and congregation of Rev. Thomas Hooker, in 1636, and in 1637 John Higginson, before he became chaplain of the fort at Saybrook, was a resident and 'schoolmaster' at Hartford; and Winthrop mentions 'one Mr. Collins, a young scholar who came from Barbadoes, and had been a preacher, who was established at Hartford to teach a school in 1640.' These masters taught before the first formal vote of the town, so far as the records now show, in April, 1643—and the engagement with Mr. Andrews was not to set up a school, but 'to teach the children in the school,' as an institution already in existence. This first public school was maintained, as all the early common schools of Connecticut were, by the joint contributions of parents and the town—which secured parental and public interest in the management, and did accomplish, what no other mode of supporting public schools has yet effected elsewhere, the universal elementary instruction of the people.

The first settlement in the colony of New Haven was made at Quinnipiac (New Haven) in 1638; and within a year 'Thomas Fugill is required by the court to keep Charles Higinson, an indented apprentice, at school one year, or else advantage him as much in his education as a year's learning comes to.' This transaction proclaims at once the existence of a school in the first year of this infant commonwealth, and the protection which the first settlers extended to those who could not help themselves, and their desire to make elementary education universal. In 1641 it is ordered by the General Court 'that a free school be set up in this town, and our pastor, Mr. Davenport, together with the magistrates shall consider what yearly allowance is meet to be given to it out of the common stock of the town, and also what rules and orders are meet to be observed in and about the same.' Over this school presided master Ezekiel Cheever, one of the principal men of the colony, and who subsequently taught the 'Free School at Ipswich,' and still later the Town Free School at Charlestown, closing his career at Boston, as 'sole master' of the still-famous Latin school. To this school, or its successor, was assigned in 1667, a portion of the legacy left by Edward Hopkins, that excellent magistrate and beneficent citizen, 'to give some encouragement for the breeding up of hopeful youth for the public service of the country in future times.'

The strength of the school system of Connecticut lies in the habits of her people of always looking after the education of their children.

HENRY BARNARD, *History of Common Schools in Connecticut.*

### COLONY OF CONNECTICUT.

Forasmuch as the good education of children is of singular behoof and benefit to any commonwealth; and whereas many parents and masters are too indulgent and negligent of their duty in that kind—

*It is therefore ordered by this court and the authority thereof*, That the selectmen of every town in the several precincts and quarters where they dwell, shall have a vigilant eye over their brethren and neighbors, to see, first, that none of them shall suffer so much barbarism in any of their families, as not to endeavor to teach by themselves or others, their children and apprentices so much learning, as may enable them perfectly to read the English tongue, and knowledge of the capital laws, upon penalty of twenty shillings for each neglect therein; also, that all masters of families, do, once a week at least, catechise their children and servants, in the grounds and principles of religion, and if any be unable to do so much, that then, at the least, they procure such children or apprentices to learn some short orthodox catechism, without book, that they may be able to answer to the questions that shall be propounded to them out of such catechisms by their parents or masters, or any of the selectmen, when they shall call them to a trial of what they have learned in this kind; and further, that all parents and masters do breed and bring up their children and apprentices in some honest lawful calling, labor or employment, either in husbandry or some other trade profitable for themselves and the commonwealth, if they will not nor can not train them up in learning, to fit them for higher employments; and if any of the selectmen, after admonition by them given to such masters of families, shall find them still negligent of their duty, in the particulars aforementioned, whereby children and servants become rude, stubborn and unruly, the said selectmen, with the help of two magistrates, shall take such children or apprentices from them, and place them with some masters—boys till they come to twenty-one, and girls to eighteen years of age complete—which will more strictly look unto and force them to submit unto government, according to the rules of this order, if by fair means and former instructions they will not be drawn unto it. *Code of* 1650.

### COLONY OF NEW HAVEN.

Whereas, too many parents and masters, either through an over tender respect to their own occasions and business, or not duly considering the good of their children and apprentices, have too much neglected duty in their education while they are young and capable of learning—It is ordered that the deputies for the particular court in each plantation within this jurisdiction for the time being; or where there are no such deputies, the constable, or other officer or officers in public trust, shall from time to time, have a vigilant eye over their brethren and neighbors within the limits of the said plantation, that all parents and masters, do duly endeavor, either by their own ability and labor, or by improving such schoolmaster, or other helps and means as the plantation doth afford, or the family may conveniently provide, that all their children and apprentices, as they grow capable, may through God's blessing attain at least so much as to be able duly to read the Scriptures and other good and profitable printed books in the English tongue, being their native language, and in some competent measure to understand the main grounds and principles of Christian religion necessary to salvation. And to give a due answer to such plain and ordinary questions as may by the said deputies, officer or officers be propounded concerning the same. And when such deputies, or officers, whether by information or examination shall find any parent or master one or more negligent, he or they shall first give warning, and if thereupon due reformation follow, if the said parents or masters shall thenceforth seriously and constantly apply themselves to their duty in manner before expressed, the former neglect may be passed by; but if not, then the said deputies and other officer or officers, shall three months after such warning, present each such negligent person or persons to the next plantation court, where every such delinquent, upon proof, shall be fined ten shillings to the plantation, to be levied as other fines. And if in any plantation there be no such court kept for the present, in such case the constable, or other officer or officers warning such person or persons, before the freemen or so many of them as upon notice shall meet together and proving the neglect after warning, shall have power to levy the fine as aforesaid. But if in three months after that, there be no due care taken and continued for the education of such children or apprentices as aforesaid, the delinquent (without any further private warning,) shall be proceeded against as before, but the fine doubled. And lastly, if after the said warning and fines paid or levied, the said deputies, officer or officers, shall still find a continuance of the former negligence, if it be not obstinacy, so that such children or servants may be in danger to grow barbarous, rude, and stubborn, through ignorance, they shall give due and seasonable notice that every such parent and master be summoned to the next court of magistrates, who are to proceed as they find cause, either to a greater fine, taking security for due conformity to the scope and intent of this law, or may take such children or apprentices from such parents or masters, and place them for years, boys till they come to the age of one and twenty, and girls till they come to the age of eighteen years, with such others who shall better educate and govern them, both for the public conveniency and for the particular good of the said children or apprentices.

*Colony Law.* 1655.

COLONY OF PLYMOUTH.

Forasmuch as the maintenance of good literature doth much tend to the advancement of the weal and flourishing state of societies and republics, this court doth therefore order, that in whatever township in this government, consisting of fifty families or upwards, any meet man shall be obtained to teach a grammar school, such township shall allow at least twelve pounds, to be raised by rate on all the inhabitants. *Order of Legislature.* 1669.

In the early history of almost every town in every state of New England, a portion of the public land was reserved, or special grants were made by individuals for "gospel" and school purposes.

On the 17th of May, 1784, Mr. Jefferson, as chairman of a committee for that purpose, introduced into the old Congress an ordinance respecting the disposition of the public lands, but this contained no reference to schools or education. On the 4th of March, 1785, another ordinance was introduced—by whom does not appear on the Journal, and on the 16th of the same month was recommitted to a committee consisting of Pierce Long, of New Hampshire, Rufus King, of Massachusetts, David Howell, of Rhode Island, Wm. S. Johnson, of Connecticut, R. R. Livingston, of New York, Charles Stewart, of New Jersey, Joseph Gardner, of Pennsylvania, John Henry, of Maryland, William Grayson, of Virginia, Hugh Williamson, of North Carolina, John Bull, of South Carolina, and William Houston, of Georgia. On the 14th of April following, this committee reported the ordinance—by whom reported, no clue is given; which after being perfected, was passed the 20th of May following, and became the foundation of the existing land system of the United States.

By one of its provisions, the 16th section of every township was reserved "*for the maintenance of public schools;*" or, in other words, one section out of every thirty-six composing each township. This same provision was incorporated in the large land sale, in 1786, to the Ohio Company; and, the following year, in Judge Symmes' purchase. The celebrated ordinance of 1787, for the government of the Territory Northwest of the river Ohio, and which confirmed the provisions of the land ordinance of 1785, further declared, that, "RELIGION, MORALITY and KNOWLEDGE, being necessary to good government, and the happiness of mankind, SCHOOLS, AND THE MEANS OF EDUCATION, SHALL BE FOREVER ENCOURAGED." From that day to the present, this noble policy has been confirmed and extended, till its blessings now reach even the distant shores of the Pacific, and FIFTY MILLIONS OF ACRES of the public domain have been set apart and consecrated to the high and ennobling purposes of education; together with five per cent. of the net proceeds of the sales of all public lands in each of the States and Territories in which they are situated.

LYMAN DRAPER. *Report of Supt. of Public Instruction*, 1858.

When the rich man is called from the possession of his treasures, he divides them, as he will, among his children and heirs. But an equal Providence deals not so with the living treasures of the mind. There are children just growing up in the bosom of obscurity, in town and in country, who have inherited nothing but poverty and health, who will, in a few years, be striving in generous contention with the great intellects of the land. Our system of free schools has opened a straight way from the threshold of every abode, however humble, in the village or in the city, to the high places of usefulness, influence and honor. And it is left for each, by the cultivation of every talent; by watching with an eagle's eye, for every chance of improvement; by bounding forward, like a greyhound, at the most distant glimpse of honorable opportunity; by redeeming time, defying temptation, and scorning pleasure to make himself useful, honored, and happy. EDWARD EVERETT.

It is a noble and beautiful idea of providing wise institutions for the unborn millions of the West; of anticipating their good by a sort of parental providence; and of associating together the social and the territorial development of the people, by incorporating these provisions with the land titles derived from the public domain, and making school reservations and road reservations essential parts of that policy.

CALEB CUSHING.

Doubtless it will be urged that a general tax on property, for this object, (Public Schools,) would fall on many who have no children, and is therefore unjust. Carry out the principle of this objection, and it would overthrow the whole system of taxation. One would say that he never uses the public roads, and therefore he must not be taxed for them. Another never goes out in the evening, and therefore must not be taxed for lighting the streets. Another denies the right of all government and prefers to be without any protection but that of virtue, he must not be taxed for courts and legislatures. But taxation, we apprehend, is never based on the principle that the individual wants it for his direct benefit, but that the public wants it; for the public has a right in all property as truly as the individual, and may draw upon it for its own uses. And one of these uses is the education of the youth; for there is a very important sense in which children belong to the State, as they do to the family organization. Indeed, if we revert to the Jewish, Persian, Lacedemonian, and Roman States—all those ancient fabrics that rose in the youth time of nature—we see the State to be naturally endowed with a real instinct of civil maternity, making it the first care of her founders and constitutions, to direct the education of the youth. And why should she not? These are her heroes of the future day, her pillars of state and justice, her voters on whose shoulders she rests her constitution, her productive hands, her sentinels of order, her reliance for the security of life, liberty, and property.

DR. H. BUSHNELL.

## THE STATE AND EDUCATION.

I know not to what else we can better liken the strong appetence of the mind for improvement, than to a hunger and thirst after knowledge and truth; nor how we can better describe the province of education, than to say, it does that for the intellect, which is done for the body, when it receives the care and nourishment which are necessary for its growth, health and strength. From this comparison, I think I derive new views of the importance of education. It is now a solemn duty, a tender, sacred trust. What! sir, feed a child's body, and let his soul hunger! pamper his limbs, and starve his faculties! Plant the earth, cover a thousand hills with your droves of cattle, pursue the fish to their hiding places in the sea, and spread out your wheat fields across the plain, in order to supply the wants of that body, which will soon be as cold and as senseless as their poorest clod, and let the pure spiritual essence within you, with all its glorious capacities for improvement, languish and pine! What! build factories, turn in rivers upon the water-wheels, unchain the imprisoned spirits of steam, to weave a garment for the body, and let the soul remain unadorned and naked! What! send out your vessels to the farthest ocean, and make battle with the monsters of the deep, in order to obtain the means of lighting up your dwellings and workshops, and prolonging the hours of labor for the meat that perisheth, and permit that vital spark, which God has kindled, which He has intrusted to our care, to be fanned into a bright and heavenly flame; permit it, I say, to languish and go out!

EDWARD EVERETT.

If I were asked by an intelligent stranger to point out to him our most valued possessions, I would show to him—not our railroads, our warehouses filled with the wealth of all the earth, our ships, our busy wharves and marts, where the car of commerce is ever "thundering loud with her ten thousand wheels;" but I would carry him to one of our public schools, would show him its happy and intelligent children, hushed into reverent silence at their teacher's word, or humming over their tasks with a sound like that of bees in June. I would tell him that here was the foundation on which our material prosperity was reared, that here were the elements from which we constructed the State. Here are the fountains from which flow those streams which make glad our land. The schools of Boston are dear to my heart. Though I can have no personal and immediate interest in them; though no child on earth calls me father; yet most gladly do I contribute to their support, according to my substance; and when I see a father's eye filled with pleasant tears as he hears the music of his child's voice linked to some strain of poetry or burst of eloquence, I can sympathize in the feeling in which I can not share. May the blessing of Heaven rest upon our schools. They are an object worthy of all efforts and sacrifices. We should leave nothing undone which may tend to make them more excellent and more useful. For this we should gather into our own stores all the harvests of experience which have been reaped from other soils.

GEORGE S. HILLARD.

TABLE II.—*Showing the area of the several States and Territories containing public lands, and the quantity devoted for educational purposes by Congress up to June* 30, 1867.

[Compiled from Report of the Commissioner of the Land Office for 1867.]

| States and Territories containing public land. | Areas of States and Territories containing public land. | | Donations and grants for schools and universities. | | Granted for agricultural colleges, act of July 2, 1862.* | | Granted for deaf and dumb asylums. | Remaining unsold and unappropriated June 30, 1867. |
|---|---|---|---|---|---|---|---|---|
| | | | Schools. | Universities. | Selected in place. | Located with scrip. | | |
| | *Sq. miles.* | *Acres.* | *Acres.* | *Acres.* | *Acres.* | *Acres.* | *Acres.* | *Acres.* |
| Ohio | 39, 964 | 25, 576, 960 | 704, 488 | 69, 120 | ........ | ........ | ........ | 500. 00 |
| Indiana | 33, 809 | 21, 637, 760 | 650, 317 | 46, 080 | ........ | ........ | ........ | 2, 000. 00 |
| Illinois | 55, 410 | 35, 462, 400 | 985, 066 | 46, 080 | ........ | ........ | ........ | 2, 000. 00 |
| Missouri | 65, 350 | 41, 824, 000 | 1, 199, 139 | 46, 080 | 244, 384. 51 | 147, 797. 25 | ........ | 1, 835, 892. 71 |
| Alabama | 50, 722 | 32, 462, 080 | 902, 774 | 46, 080 | ........ | ........ | 21, 949. 46 | 6, 915, 081. 32 |
| Mississippi | 47, 156 | 30, 179, 840 | 837, 584 | 46, 080 | ........ | ........ | ........ | 4, 930, 893. 56 |
| Louisiana | 41, 346 | 26, 461, 440 | 786, 044 | 46, 080 | ........ | ........ | ........ | 6, 582, 841. 54 |
| Michigan | 56, 451 | 36, 128, 640 | 1, 067, 397 | 46, 080 | 225, 253. 88 | 960, 807. 59 | ........ | 5, 180, 640. 63 |
| Arkansas | 52, 198 | 33, 406, 720 | 886, 460 | 46, 080 | ........ | ........ | 2, 097. 43 | 11, 757, 662. 54 |
| Florida | 59, 268 | 37, 931, 520 | 908, 503 | 92, 160 | ........ | ........ | 20, 924. 22 | 17, 540, 374. 00 |
| Iowa | 55, 045 | 35, 228, 800 | 905, 144 | 46, 080 | 240, 000. 96 | 1, 760. 00 | ........ | 3, 113, 464. 18 |
| Wisconsin | 53, 924 | 34, 511, 360 | 958, 649 | 92, 160 | 240, 007. 73 | 702, 425. 07 | ........ | 10, 016, 700. 87 |
| California | 188, 981 | 120, 947, 840 | 6, 719, 324 | 46, 080 | ........ | ........ | ........ | 106, 062, 392. 13 |
| Minnesota | 83, 531 | 53, 459, 840 | 2, 969, 990 | 46, 080 | 119, 852. 17 | 488, 803. 03 | ........ | 36, 776, 170. 89 |
| Oregon | 95, 274 | 60, 975, 360 | 3, 329, 706 | 46, 080 | ........ | 1, 920. 00 | ........ | 52, 742, 078. 96 |
| Kansas | 81, 318 | 52, 043, 520 | 2, 891, 306 | 46, 080 | 90, 000. 40 | 411, 959. 70 | ........ | 43, 148, 876. 44 |
| Nevada | 112, 090 | 71, 737, 741 | 3, 985, 430 | 46, 080 | ........ | ........ | ........ | 67, 090, 382. 62 |
| Nebraska | 75, 995 | 48, 636, 800 | 2, 702, 044 | 46, 080 | ........ | 475, 989. 58 | ........ | 42, 523, 627. 38 |
| Washington Territory | 69, 994 | 44, 796, 160 | 2, 488, 675 | 46, 080 | ........ | 1, 120. 00 | ........ | 41, 627, 464. 39 |
| New Mexico | 121, 201 | 77, 568, 649 | 4, 309, 368 | 46, 080 | ........ | ........ | ........ | 73, 005, 192. 00 |
| Utah | 88, 056 | 56, 355, 635 | 3, 130, 869 | 46, 080 | ........ | ........ | ........ | 51, 139, 646. 00 |
| Dakota | 240, 597 | 153, 982, 080 | 8, 554, 560 | ........ | ........ | ........ | ........ | 145, 295, 284. 97 |
| Colorado | 104, 500 | 66, 880, 000 | 3, 715, 555 | ........ | ........ | ........ | ........ | 62, 870, 665. 83 |
| Montana | 143, 776 | 92, 016, 640 | 5, 112, 035 | ........ | ........ | ........ | ........ | 86, 904, 605. 00 |
| Arizona | 113, 916 | 72, 906, 304 | 4, 050, 350 | ........ | ........ | ........ | ........ | 68, 855, 954. 00 |
| Idaho | 90, 932 | 58, 196, 480 | 3, 233, 137 | ........ | ........ | ........ | ........ | 54, 963, 343. 00 |
| Indian | 68, 991 | 44, 154, 240 | ........ | ........ | ........ | ........ | ........ | 44, 154, 240. 00 |
| American purchase from Russia | 577, 390 | 369, 529, 600 | ........ | ........ | ........ | ........ | ........ | 369, 529, 600. 00 |
| Total | 2, 867, 185 | 1, 834, 998, 400 | 67, 983, 914 | 1, 082, 880 | 1, 159, 499. 65 | 3, 192, 582. 22 | 44, 971. 11 | 1, 414, 567, 574. 96 |

* The whole quantity liable to be issued under the act of July 2, 1862, is 9,600,000 acres.

## CONSOLIDATION AND OTHER MODIFICATIONS OF AMERICAN COLLEGES.

BY RT. REV. ALONZO POTTER.*

---

This occasion seems to me to furnish an omen of national interest; may I not add, of world-wide interest. As connected with higher education—with the administration of Colleges and Universities—it appears to furnish, at least, some hope that several movements, which I believe are imperiously needed, may, at no distant day, be secured.

In the first place, this is a consolidation of two independent collegiate institutions, and as such, I hail it as an event which might be repeated in our own State, and throughout the land, with the utmost advantage. Hitherto the tendency has been to multiply colleges, and to isolate them. There are now some hundred and fifty colleges in the United States. They all claim to stand on the same level, to teach the same branches, and to have the same right to public confidence and support. Resources which, if concentrated, would have been ample for the thorough endowment of a few institutions, have been so scattered, and so large a part of them have been so improvidently expended, that nearly all our colleges are crippled for want of libraries, apparatus, and a competent staff of accomplished teachers. In their relations to each other, there is neither affiliation, subordination, nor—except casually—even co-operation. With a population greater than that of Britain, we are without one University proper. Our college system is now, in respect to organization, where our common or public school system was before the establishment of High Schools. The citizens of Lancaster know how that one measure infused new life and vigor into the whole school system of this town—how, by a proper distribution and gradation of work, the teaching has been improved in every department; and a portion of the pupils carried forward much further than formerly. What has thus been done for common schools needs to be done for colleges. If they would not be distanced in the work of progress and improvement, they must no longer remain in a state of estrangement from each other. They must contemplate the necessity of hearty co-operation, if not of combi-

---

* Remarks at the formal opening of Franklin and Marshall College—formed by the consolidation of two chartered institutions—Franklin College located at Lancaster, and Marshall College, located at Mercersberg.

nation and consolidation. They *must prepare the way for the open University* which, like the Universities of London and France, may be merely an organic center for purposes of supervision; or it might be constituted by a Board of Professors delegated from different colleges, and giving, personally, higher courses of instruction at some convenient point. I hail the union of Franklin and Marshall College, in the hope that we are on the eve of a general movement among similar institutions towards more of centralization.

II. In another respect, this event seems to me to be auspicious. I observe among your Professors, one gentleman, at least, who was reared in a Foreign University, and who has held an honorable post as teacher in a College in Southern Europe.* I hear too, that a distinguished German Professor, who, several years since, was invited to leave his fatherland for a chair in the Theological Faculty of Marshall College, has been invited to become your President.† Though I have not the honor of his acquaintance, and can presume to have no opinion of his qualifications for such a post, yet there is one reason why I earnestly hope he may accept this place. I desire to see the example followed which Marshall College has given. In almost every country of Europe, there are men of high endowments, of admirable erudition, capable of giving instruction to the most advanced students, who are yet languishing in obscurity and poverty. Such talent exists in Germany to so great an extent, that the intellectual and scholastic market is actually glutted. Here it is far otherwise. Pursuits of a more exciting and engrossing nature absorb, with us, the energy and enthusiasm which are given among the laborious earnest-minded Germans to literary toil. We import their laboring population by thousands—we import their accomplished artisans and agriculturists—we import from all the countries of continental Europe, teachers in the rudiments of their respective languages. Why should we not have a portion of their illustrious scholars and *savans* also. Where can they find a larger field, or the promise of better pecuniary remuneration?

This policy is recommended by various considerations—and there are special reasons why it should originate in Pennsylvania. This State has one characteristic, till recently, almost peculiar to it, but which is fast growing to be the characteristic of our nation. It is the somewhat heterogeneous nationalities that are represented in its population. Not only Old and New England, but Germany, Scotland, Wales and Sweden, have long had within this Commonwealth colonies of their people. This will soon be the case with every part of the United States. Ingredients, which have hitherto been regarded

* Professor Kœppen. † Professor Schaff.

as incongruous and discordant, are seething in our great national cauldron, and we confidently expect to see them fused and blended into one harmonious whole—penetrated by the one American spirit. This result will be sure and speedy, in proportion as the culture which we apply to the rising generation is large-minded and liberal—having respect to national peculiarities and combining, in a wise eclectic spirit, the methods of different fatherlands. Where can such a policy originate so properly or so readily as in Pennsylvania?

There is another reason why it appears to me desirable that our higher instruction in this country should have an infusion from Germany. That country has given to the world an open Bible, the common school and the printing press. Wherever these its gifts are fully enjoyed—there a reading and thinking people must be formed. Combined, as they are in this country, with a free political system and with prodigious industrial activity, they make a nation of readers, a nation of workers and to some extent a nation of thinkers. Our intellectual activity is widespread and intense, and it associates itself intimately with active practical life. But the predominance of that life with us is not friendly at present to deep erudition or to profound and comprehensive thinking. We have literature, but we want ripe thorough scholarship. We have philosophies, but they are crude, presumptuous, and narrow. Errors and extravagancies—whether pertaining to speculation or to practical questions—swarm over the land, and in the absence of vigorous habits of investigation and of a copious learning, they perpetuate themselves to the equal injury and disgrace of our national character. To her other gifts, then, let Germany add one more. Let her scholars teach us the patience, the thoroughness, the unquenchable zeal and lofty enthusiasm with which subjects should be considered; and the manly frankness and boldness with which results should be announced. Let her assist in putting into our hands the true Ithuriel spear, one touch of which will suffice to unmask pretentious sophisms, and one-sided schemes, and ambitious, unscrupulous sciolism.

Would the German scholastic mind be injured by such an association with ours? No wise German will think so. I am not prepared to adopt the saying of a distinguished scholar (I think) of the fatherland, that while the English ruled over the sea, the French over the land, the sway of Germany was over the air. I honor the passion for the ideal, and the stern enthusiasm with which the most abstruse philosophical questions are discussed among that noble people. But no candid observer will deny, that while the Anglo-American is too much given to empiricism, the German is rather too much addicted to speculative dogmatism—too impatient of qualifying theories by practice—too disdainful of the wisdom which comes only from a combination of high thought with active efficiency. Could the speculative tastes and liberal enthusiasm of the one be combined with the robust sagacity and indomitable enterprise of the other, we might inaugurate a form of culture, nobler and more beneficent than the world has yet seen. May we not hope that to promote such a blending and interpenetration of these national characteristics will be one of the cherished objects of Franklin and Marshall College?

III. I cannot but anticipate another benefit from this movement. The teaching in this college, I trust, will always be the result of earnest thinking, of profound research. It is time we had done with the notion that superficial men make the best teachers. It is a notion which has been quite too prevalent in this country; the effect of it has been not only to emasculate our teaching, but to paralyze the studies of our professors and instructors. It has taken from them that stimulus to daily effort, to continued freshness of thought and ardor of inquiry, which ought to have been supplied by their profession. The universities of Germany contain a great practical refutation of this pestilent heresy. The most popular teachers have been their ablest thinkers and profoundest scholars. They—and the remark applies in some measure to the professors of Scottish universities—have shown that a talent for elementary exposition is perfectly compatible with habits of the most devoted and intricate research—that, in truth, each promotes and is promoted by the other.

And the same lesson has been taught in the public schools of this city. There are those present who remember well a modest, unobtrusive teacher, in one of those schools, who was always assiduous and successful, especially in the department of mathematics. He left here a few years since to become a teacher of the same branch in the Academy at Pottsville; and scarcely had he departed, before the scientific men of both hemispheres were startled by the tidings that from that remote and obscure institution had emanated a discovery which was to rank forever by the side of those which have made the names of Kepler and Newton so illustrious. While a resident of Lancaster, Mr. KIRKWOOD was slowly but surely elaborating that law or principle which bears his name. Let his example teach us then, that clear and interesting teaching in the class-room, is not inconsistent with profound thinking in the closet. Let it imprint upon the soul of every professor a sense of the debt which he owes, as an original inquirer, to the department of science or letters which he has in charge. Let it inspire all—teachers and pupils—with the generous ambition to make colleges, here and now, what they were in the days of Abelard in Europe—places all alive with mental activity, places consecrated to the most earnest and independent inquiry.

IV. there is one more feature which will, I trust, always characterize the influence sent forth from Franklin and Marshall College. An institution bearing such a name would be recreant to all the promises its name implies, if it did not encourage public spirit and a large-hearted sympathy with humanity in all its forms and interests. Franklin began every day by asking himself, "What good can I do to my fellow men to-day?" he closed it by asking, "What good that I might have done to my fellow men to-day, have I left undone?" He who lived by such a rule could not be less than the benefactor of all men. He came to Philadelphia a poor apprentice boy. He lived to found its great Library, its Philosophical Society, its University, with many provisions for its material prosperity. He lived to be the almost idolized citizen of his adopted town and State, and the profoundly honored and trusted sage of the whole land. Yet never, when wearing his highest honors, did he forget the humble origin from which he sprang; never did his heart fail to beat with kindness and consideration towards all who needed his succor or his counsel. And John Marshall, too, how kindly and genial was his spirit? How free from arrogance! Be this the spirit that shall ever reign here. Not our Pennsylvania Germans alone, many others have dreaded colleges as nurseries of a silly aristocratic pride—as places where young men, coming from plain but respectable and worthy homes, would learn to despise them; as schools where they would be taught to put scorn upon the institutions of their country or the demands of their age. The gentleman who preceded me has adverted to these impressions. Erroneous as they are, they have continued to live because the follies of young men, and the mistakes of their teachers, have sometimes given countenance to them. Colleges in our land, like Universities in England, have sometimes been slow to feel the progress of society. They have fallen back upon their privileges; they have cultivated too little sympathy with the public mind which it is their office to guide and instruct. They have asked the people to sustain and cherish them; but they have sometimes forgotten that "love is the loan for love." They would have the masses feel great interest in the colleges, but they do not always think it necessary that the colleges should care much for the masses.

Here, we trust, is an institution where such a spirit will be unknown. If there are men who, more than all others, should have pulses throbbing with a large humanity, with a generous patriotism; it is they who are in contact with the fountains of thought, and whose business it is to trace the history of our race in its literature, and in all its struggles for a fairer and happier lot. Let teachers and pupils emulate each other in love for their kind, and in quick sympathy for every effort which would promote the greatest happiness of the greatest number. Let them honor that which is most worthy of honor; and when they go out to mingle with the sons of toil, let them put no slights upon it. Let them own its intrinsic dignity; let them strive that it may be associated with a higher culture; let them so bear themselves that it shall be seen that a college is the true home for large minds and large hearts—for spirits that are enlightened and refined enough for the highest, and kindly and courteous enough for the lowliest in the land.

V. I cannot conclude without expressing my devout hope that this college may be administered in the spirit of *faith*. "If thou canst believe, all things are possible to him that believeth." Aim, friends, at *great things*. Doubt not, that if true to yourselves, God will empower you to do great things for yourselves and for mankind. Lancaster has her model farms and her model mills: why should she not have her model college? not one where there shall be many students badly taught and badly governed; but where there shall be at least a few so taught and so guided that they shall be *model students here* and *model men abroad*. Young men, who form the first classes in Franklin and Marshall College, be models of diligence—be models of self-respect—be models of scholar-like enthusiasm. You shall thus kindle a spirit here which will burn on steadily from class to class, and which will make you benefactors to this college, and to your successors, beyond the bounds of your utmost ambition. Gentlemen of the Faculty! let *nil desperandum* be your motto. Never despair of your pupils, of your Trustees, of yourselves. Let no obstacles dishearten, no failures weary. Be enthusiastic students, that you may be attractive and powerful teachers. Be vigilant, but loving and long-suffering disciplinarians, that you may knit these young hearts to you as with hooks of steel. And, gentlemen of the Board of Trustees, doubt not that, with a liberal steady policy, with unyielding enthusiasm, you shall find your fondest hopes and wishes realized. Cherish this seat of letters, this home of liberal arts; endow it largely with all means of instruction. Let its libraries, its museum, its halls of apparatus, teem with appliances for the best teaching and the best illustrations. As individuals, imitate the noble benefactions which men of successful enterprise in New England think it a privilege to bestow upon their seminaries of learning; and do not permit yourselves to close you eyes on life, without having left behind you here some honorable memorial of your zeal in behalf of Religion and of Learning.

## ALONZO POTTER, D. D., LL. D.

RT. REV. ALONZO POTTER, D. D., the first President of the American Association for the Advancement of Education, was born of parents who were of Rhode Island, in Beekman, (now La Grange,) in Duchess County, New York, July 10th 1800, and died in San Francisco, California, July 4th, 1865. After attending the common school of his town till he was fourteen years old, he enjoyed the advantages of a classical and mathematical training for college, in the academy at Poughkeepsie, then under the charge of Daniel S. Barnes, who was afterward associated with Dr. Griscom in the Public High School of the City of New York. He graduated in 1818, at Union College, the first scholar in a class which included many men who afterward became eminent.

He commenced teaching immediately after graduating, in Philadelphia, and in the following year was called to Union College as tutor, where he became, in 1821, Professor of Mathematics and Natural Philosophy, which Chair he filled till 1826, when he became Rector of St. Paul's Church, in Boston, but returned to Schenectady in 1831, on the urgent solicitation of his father-in-law, Dr. Nott, to become Vice President and Professor of Moral Philosophy in Union College, which positions he filled till 1845, when he was elected Bishop of the Diocese of Pennsylvania. As a college officer and teacher, he has had no superior for thorough instruction, and the power of cultivating lofty aspirations and a manly character in his pupils; and while doing his whole duty as a college officer and teacher, and as Rector and Bishop, no man in his day and place did more to promote the cause of popular education and religious philanthropy. He was the adviser of James Wadsworth of Geneva, in his voluntary labors, and pecuniary contributions, and of the School Department at Albany in its official action, and of the friends of popular education, in all efforts to establish School Libraries, Educational Periodicals, County Supervision, State Normal Schools, and to elevate and inform public sentiment on the whole subject of Educational Improvement. His wise counsel and earnest appeals were sure to be heard in all County, State, and National School Conventions, up to the day that his own nervous system broke down beneath his manifold labors. The Hospital, the Divinity School, the Literary and Lecture Associations of Philadelphia, and every department of education in Pennsylvania felt the impulse of his earnest spirit. The School for Imbeciles at Media was a charity of his suggestion and efforts.

On the outbreak of the rebellion, Bishop Potter took a decided stand on the side of the National Government, was an active member of the Sanitary and Christian Commissions, and an earnest friend of Emancipation—devoting much time to the hospitals of invalid and wounded soldiers, until his vital powers were exhausted, when he took a voyage to the Pacific, but died before he could be taken to the land.

Bishop Potter was the author of "The Principles of Science applied to the Domestic and Mechanic Arts," "Political Economy, its Objects, Uses and Principles," and a "Hand Book for Readers and Students"—all published in Harpers' District School Library, which was got up under his supervision. "The School," the first part of the "School and Schoolmaster," was prepared by him at the request of Mr. Wadsworth, and had a circulation of over 60,000 copies. He received the degree of D. D. from Harvard College, and of LL. D. from Union College.

## PUBLIC SCHOOLS FIFTY YEARS AGO.

It was, as I have said, sir, fifty-two years last April since I began, at the age of nine years, to attend the reading and writing schools in North Bennett street. The reading school was under *Master* Little (for "Young America" had not yet repudiated that title), and the writing school was kept by Master Tileston. Master Little, in spite of his name, was a giant in stature, — six feet four, at least, — and somewhat wedded to the past. He struggled earnestly against the change then taking place in the pronunciation of *u*, and insisted on our saying *monooment* and *natur*. But I acquired, under his tuition, what was thought in those days a very tolerable knowledge of Lindley Murray's abridgment of English Grammar, and at the end of the year could parse almost any sentence in the American Preceptor. Master Tileston was a writing-master of the old school. He set the copies himself, and taught that beautiful old Boston handwriting, which, if I do not mistake, has in the march of innovation (which is not always the same thing as improvement) been changed very little for the better. Master Tileston was advanced in years, and had found a qualification for his calling as a writing-master, in what might have seemed at first to threaten to be an obstruction. The fingers of his right hand had been contracted and stiffened in early life by a burn, but were fixed in just the position to hold a pen, a penknife, and a rattan! As they were also considerably indurated, they served as a convenient instrument of discipline. A copy badly written or a blotted page was sometimes visited with an infliction which would have done no discredit to the beak of a bald eagle. I speak, sir, from observation not from experience. His long, deep desk was a perfect curiosity-shop of confiscated balls, tops, penknives, marbles, and jewsharps; the accumulation of forty years. I desire, however, to speak of him with gratitude, for he put me on the track of an acquisition which has been extremely useful to me in after life, — that of a plain, legible hand. I remained at these schools about sixteen months, and, on leaving them, had the good fortune in 1804 to receive the Franklin medal in the English department.

After an interval of about a year (during which I attended a private school taught by Mr. Ezekiel Webster, a distinguished gentleman of New Hampshire, and, on occasion of his absence, by his much more distinguished and ever memorable brother, Daniel Webster, at that time a student of law in Boston), I went to the Latin School, then slowly emerging from a state of extreme depression. It was kept in School-street, where the Horticultural Hall now stands. Those who judge of what the Boston Latin School ought to be from the spacious and commodious building in Bedford-street, can form but little idea of the old school-house. It contained but one room, heated in the winter by an iron stove, which sent up a funnel into a curious brick chimney, built down from the roof, in the middle of the room, to within seven or eight feet from the floor, being, like Mahomet's coffin, held in the air to the roof I hardly know how, perhaps by bars of iron. The boys had to take their turns in winter in coming early to the school-house, to open it; to make a fire sometimes of wet logs and a very inadequate supply of other combustibles, if such they might be called; to sweep out the room, and, if need be, to shovel a path through the snow to the street. These were not very fascinating duties for an urchin of ten or eleven; but we lived through it, and were perhaps not the worse for having to turn our hand to these little offices.

The standard of scholastic attainment was certainly not higher than that of material comfort in those days. We read pretty much the same books, or books of the same class, in Latin and Greek, as are read now, with the exception of the Greek Testament; but we read them in a very cursory and superficial manner. There was no attention paid to the philosophy of the languages, to the deduction of words from their radical elements, to the niceties of construction, still less to prosody. I never made an hexameter or pentameter verse, till years afterwards, when I had a son at school in London, who occasionally required a little aid in that way. The subsidiary and illustrative branches were wholly unknown in the Latin School in 1805. Such a thing as a school library, a book of reference, a critical edition of a classic, a map, a blackboard, an engraving of an ancient building, or a copy of a work of ancient art, such as now adorn the walls of our schools, was as little known as the electric telegraph. If our children, who possess all these appliances and aids to learning, do not greatly excel their parents, they will be much to blame.

### COLLEGE LIFE FIFTY YEARS AGO.

But, short as the time is since I entered college (only half as long as that which has elapsed since the close of the seven years' war), it has made me the witness of wonderful changes, both materially and intellectually, in all that concerns our *Alma Mater*. Let me sketch you the outlines of the picture, fresh to my mind's eye as the image in the *camera*, which the precincts of the college exhibited in 1807. The Common was then uninclosed. It was not so much traversed by roads in all directions ; it was at once all road and no road at all, — a waste of mud and of dust, according to the season, without grass, trees, or fences. As to the streets in those days, the "Appian Way" existed then as now ; and I must allow that it bore the same resemblance then as now to the *Regina Viarum*, by which the consuls and proconsuls of Rome went forth to the conquest of Epirus, Macedonia, and the East.

As to public buildings in the neighborhood of the University, with the exception of the Episcopal Church, no one of the churches now standing was then in existence. The old parish church has disappeared, with its square pews, and galleries from which you might almost jump into the pulpit. It occupied a portion of the space between Dane Hall and the old Presidential House. I planted a row of elm and oak trees a few years ago on the spot where it stood, for which, if for nothing else, I hope to be kindly remembered by posterity. The wooden building now used as a gymnasium, and, I believe, for some other purposes, then stood where Lyceum Hall now stands. It was the county court-house ; and there I often heard the voice of the venerable Chief Justice Parsons. Graduates' Hall did not exist ; but on a part of the site, and behind the beautiful linden trees still flourishing, was an old black wooden house, the residence of the professors of mathematics. A little further to the north, and just at the corner of Church-street, which was not then opened, stood what was dignified in the annual college catalogue (which was printed on one side of a sheet of paper, and was a novelty) as "The College House." The cellar is still visible. By the students this edifice was disrespectfully called "Wiswall's Den," or, for brevity, "the Den." I lived in it in my freshman year. Whence the name of "Wiswall's Den" was derived, I hardly dare say : there was something worse than "old fogy" about it. There was a dismal tradition that, at some former period, it had been the scene of a murder. A brutal husband had dragged his wife by the hair up and down the stairs, and then killed her. On the anniversary of the murder — and what day that was no one knew — there were sights and sounds — flitting garments draggled in blood, plaintive screams, *stridor ferri tractæque catenæ* — enough to appall the stoutest sophomore. But, for myself, I can truly say, that I got through my freshman year without having seen the ghost of Mr. Wiswall or his lamented lady. I was not, however, sorry when the twelvemonth was up, and I was transferred to that light, airy, well-ventilated room, No. 20 Hollis ; being the inner room, ground-floor, north entry of that ancient and respectable edifice.

### COMMON SCHOOLS AND COLLEGES.

The worthy chairman of the committee alluded to the University in this place ; and, as he made the allusion, the thought crossed my mind to institute a comparison of the expense with which the University and the public schools of Cambridge are supported. It may enable us to realize how great an effort is made by the citizens of Cambridge to support their public schools. The annual expenditure for the support of our schools exceeds twenty thousand dollars, without including the building and repair of school-houses. Last year it was twenty-one thousand dollars. Now the University, as we all know, is by far the oldest and best endowed in the country ; but the whole annual income of its funds applicable to the business of instruction (I speak of Harvard College proper, and not of the professional and scientific schools connected with the University), is less than that sum. All that the liberality of the State and the bounty of individuals for two centuries have accumulated on this favored seat of learning, in the shape of funds for carrying on the work of instruction (and I do not include the cost of buildings, cabinets, and libraries in reference to the University, as I have not included the cost of school-houses, apparatus, and libraries in reference to the schools), does not yield so large a sum annually, as the city of Cambridge appropriates to support this system of common school education.

### WHAT COMMON-SCHOOL EDUCATION DOES.

I certainly cannot on this occasion, and in the few minutes' time still left me, undertake to treat this mighty theme in all its bearings; but I do not despair, even in a few sentences, of suggesting to you the great points of the argument. I will take school education in its common simple acceptation, as confined to reading and writing (in which I include speaking and composition), arithmetic, and the elements of natural philosophy; and I believe the extension to a whole community of the means of obtaining such an education without cost, is sufficient to effect all I ascribe to it. It is scarcely necessary to say that I do not, in these statements, hold up education as a *creative* cause. I take into the account the spontaneous coöperation of the mysterious principle of intelligence, with all its perceptive faculties, bestowed and quickened by the Author of our being; just as the farmer, when he describes the effect of the various processes of husbandry, includes the coöperation of those inscrutable principles of vegetable growth, which philosophy strives in vain to analyze, but without which not an ear of corn is ripened.

With this explanation I say, sir, that common reading and writing, that is, in a word, the use of language as a system of visible and audible signs of thought, is the great prerogative of our nature as rational beings. I say that when we have acquired the mastery of this system of audible and visible signs, we have done the greatest thing, as it seems to me, as far as intellect is concerned, which can be done by a rational man. It is so common that we do not much reflect upon it; but, like other common things, it hides a great mystery of our nature. When we have learned how, by giving an impulse with our vocal organs to the air, by making a few black marks on a piece of paper, to establish a direct sympathy between our invisible and spiritual essence and that of other men, so that they can see and hear what is passing in our minds, just as if thought and feeling themselves were visible and audible, — not only so, when in the same way we establish a communication between mind and mind in ages and countries the most remote, we have wrought a miracle of human power and skill, which I never reflect upon without awe. Can we realize, sir, that in this way we have, through the medium of the declamation of these children, been addressed this morning by Demosthenes and Cicero, by Burke and Fox? Well, sir, all this is done by writing, reading and speaking. It is a result of these simple operations. When you tell me a boy has learned to read, you tell me that he has entered into an intellectual partnership not only with every living contemporary, but with every mind ever created that has left a record of itself on the pages of science and literature; and when he has learned to write, he has acquired the means of speaking to generations and ages that will exist a thousand years hence. It all comes back to the use of language. The press, the electric telegraph, are only improvements in the mode of communication. The wonderful thing is that the mysterious significance of thought, the invisible action of spirit, can be embodied in sounds and signs addressed to the eye and ear. Instead of wondering that among speaking, writing, and reading men you have occasionally a Shakspeare, a Bacon, or a Franklin, my wonder is to see these boys and girls, after a few years' training, able to express, in written marks and spoken sounds, the subtlest shades of thought, and that in two or three languages.

The next branch of common-school education is arithmetic, the science of numbers, the elements of mathematics. This is in reality a branch of the great department of language, a species of composition; but of so peculiar a nature as to constitute a separate science. This is another of the great master-keys of life. With it the astronomer opens the depths of the heavens; the engineer, the gates of the mountains; the navigator, the pathways of the deep. The skilful arrangement, the rapid handling of figures, is a perfect magician's wand. The mighty commerce of the United States, foreign and domestic, passes through the books kept by some thousands of diligent and faithful clerks. Eight hundred bookkeepers, in the Bank of England, strike the monetary balances of half the civilized world. Their skill and accuracy in applying the common rules of arithmetic are as important as the enterprise and capital of the merchant, or the industry and courage of the navigator. I look upon a well-kept ledger with something of the pleasure with which I gaze on a picture or a statue. It is a beautiful work of art. It is by arithmetical rules, and geometrical diagrams, and algebraical formulæ, that the engineer digs an underground river-channel for an inland lake, and carries a stream of fresh water into every house in a crowded capital. Many a slate-full of vulgar fractions has been figured out, to enable our neighbors in Boston to sip a glass of Cochituate ; and I suppose, sir, a good many of the citizens of Cambridge think it is pretty nearly time that we should go to work on the same sum.

Then come the elements of natural philosophy and natural science, the laws of organic and inorganic nature, of which something is taught in our common schools. Is it wonderful that a community, in which this knowledge is diffused, should multiply itself a hundred-fold? I mean is it wonderful that one well-taught man should do the work of uninstructed thousands? Mythology tells us of Briareus with his hundred hands, and Argus with his hundred eyes ; but these are only faint images of the increased strength and sharpened vision which knowledge imparts to the well educated. Mr. Agassiz sees a great deal more with his two eyes than Argus did with his hundred. Mr. Bond beholds a satellite of Neptune in the depths of the heavens, three thousand millions of miles from the sun, a body perhaps not five hundred miles in diameter, as easily as the diver beholds a pearl oyster in seven fathoms of water. No Titan that fought with Jupiter, and piled Ossa upon Pelion, had as much strength in his arm, as the engineer has in his thumb and finger, when he turns the screw that lets the steam into the cylinder of his engine. What is there in the Arabian Nights like the skill of the Metallurgist, who converts a shapeless piece of iron ore into the mainspring of a watch? What was there in Michael Scott's book to compare with the practical necromancy of the chemist?

Now these are branches of knowledge of which the elements are taught at our schools ; and need I urge that such a control of the signs of thought, such a possession of the keys of knowledge, such a consciousness of power over nature as results from this acquaintance with her mysteries, is quite sufficient in the aggregate to give a character to a community ; not certainly to produce wonderful effects in each individual, but in their united and continuous operation to promote the prosperity of a State.

## CONDITIONS OF A GOOD SCHOOL.

These liberal pecuniary appropriations, however, are but the first step ; they give you school-houses, school-libraries, apparatus, and fuel, and the salaries of teachers ; but the teachers themselves are not to be had merely by paying for them. A class of skilful, accomplished, and conscientious teachers can only be gradually formed. They must be men and women, a considerable part of them, who have chosen the work of education as the business of their lives ; who give to it their time, their abilities, and their hearts. Such a class of teachers is not to be had by asking for it. It must form itself in the bosom of an intelligent and virtuous community, that knows how to prize them, that holds them in high esteem, as some of its most honored public servants. There are portions of our country, in which, if you were to stud them thick with our beautiful school-houses, with all their appliances, apparatus, and libraries, you could not work the system for want of teachers, nor get the teachers merely by advertising for them. Sir, I say it for no purpose of compliment in this place ; the school-teachers in this community constitute a class inferior in respectability to no other, rendering the most important services, by no means over-compensated, rather the reverse. I consider their character and reputation as a part of the moral treasure of the public, which we cannot prize too highly.

Closely connected with the teacher, and of the utmost importance in a good school system, is the school committee, a most efficient part of the educational machinery. Much of the prosperity of our schools depends upon these committees. They stand between all the interests, parents, pupils, and the public; connect them all, mediate between them all. An intelligent committee is the teacher's great ally. They witness his labors, and mark the proficiency of the pupils. They counsel him in cases of doubt; share or assume the responsibility in cases of difficulty. A community may think itself highly favored when gentlemen of respectability in the several professions, and in the active callings of life, can be found, as in the city of Cambridge at the present time, to undertake this laborious and responsible office. Nor will an efficient school system readily be sustained where this cannot be done. I own, sir, I witness with admiration the spectacle of gentlemen, whom I know to be burdened with heavy and incessant duties of their own, and are yet willing, day after day, and week after week, in summer and in winter, to devote themselves to a laborious, thorough, and conscientious examination of the schools; besides looking in upon them frequently, and being always accessible for counsel and direction, in the intervals of the periodical visitations.

But, sir, all this is not enough. In order that the school should prosper, no small part of the work must be done at home. Let the father and the mother, who think that their child has made but little progress at school, bear this in mind. I am almost tempted to say, without intending a paradox, that half of the government, if not of the instruction of the school, must be done at home. This I will say, that if nothing is done at home to support the teacher, his labor is doubled. The parent must take an interest in his boy's or his girl's pursuits, and let that interest be seen. It is shocking to reflect how often the child is sent to school "to get him out of the way." There will be no good schools in the community where that is the prevalent motive. No, he must be sent there for his good and yours. Your heart must go with him. He is not an alien and a plague, to be got rid of for so many hours. He is a part of yourself; what he learns, you learn; it is your own continued existence, in which you love yourself with a heavenly disinterestedness. And yet you are not to let your parental fondness blind you. Do not listen to every tale of childish grievance against the master. The presumption is, that nine times out of ten the grievance is imaginary; in truth, the presumption is always so, generally the fact is so. Then, too, the parent's coöperation is of the utmost importance in other ways. For many of the short-comings of scholars, the parents are the party to blame. It is their fault, if he stays at home for a breath of cold air or a drop of rain. It is the fault of a father or mother, if the poor child cannot get his breakfast in season, or if his clothes are not in wearing condition. Let the child see betimes that, in the opinion of his parents, going to school is one of the most important things to be attended to in the course of the day, and he will so regard it himself.

## HALF A CENTURY AGO.

In fact, Mr. Chairman, there are few things in which the rapid progress of the country is so apparent as in its institutions for education. The learned Secretary of the Board of Education (Rev. Dr. Sears) has just alluded to the defects of the schools in some remote parts of the Commonwealth, unfavorably situated in this respect. I dare say his representations are correct; but the younger part of this audience would not believe me, no one scarcely whose own recollection did not confirm it would believe me, if I were to describe the state of what were called good schools when I was myself a school-boy, more years ago, Mr. Chairman, than I believe I shall tell you. I allude to the condition of the best public schools of that day. The instruction in what are commonly called the English branches was confined to reading, writing, arithmetic, grammar, and geography, all taught according to very defective methods, and with the help of poor manuals. The books for reading and speaking were either foreign, some of them consisting of matter selected without judgment and taste, and ill-adapted to this country, or, if of domestic manufacture, not much better adapted, on that account, to form the taste of the young American speaker or reader. In fact, our native literature, at that time, afforded but scanty materials for a useful and interesting selection. In grammar, we had a very imperfect abridgment of a work of but moderate merit in its original form. For arithmetic we depended on the work of Pike. I desire to speak respectfully of it, as I learned from it what little I learned at all of the noble science of numbers; and, in fact, in the elementary rules, there cannot be room for much diversity of method. But good or bad, there were few schools that carried the pupil far beyond the *Rule of Three*. Single and double fellowship was rather a rare attainment, and alligation, medial and alternate, a thing to talk of. As for logarithms, geometry and its various applications, and algebra, they belonged to a *terra incognita*, of which no school-boy ever heard, who had not an older brother at college. As to the blackboard, I never heard of such a thing at school. Geography was taught, at that day, from very imperfect compends; it was confined to a rehearsal of a few meagre facts in physical geography, and a few barren statistical details, which ceased to be true while you were repeating them. The attention of the learner was never called to the philosophy of this beautiful branch of knowledge; he was taught nothing of the relations in which man stands to the wonderful globe on which he is placed. No glimpse was given him of the action and reäction upon each other, in this department of knowledge, of nature and man. A globe, I believe, I never saw at a public school near enough to touch it. I am not sure that I was ever in the same room with one, at that period of my life, though I will not speak with entire confidence on that point. A large and accurate map was never exhibited in school fifty years ago. I do not speak of such beautiful maps as those now constructing under the superintendence of Professor Guyot, with their admirable ethnographical indications, isothermal lines, vegetable boundaries, oceanic currents, and careful delineations of those breaks in the mountain chains, which have determined the paths of civilization. I do not speak of these refinements with which the eyes of the young student of geography are daily feasted at the present day, but of large, distinct, well-executed maps of any kind; I never saw one at school. The name of natural or moral philosophy was never heard in our English schools at that day; it was much if some small smattering of those branches was taught in the upper classes at our best academies. The same may be said of all the branches of natural science, such as chemistry, zoölogy, and botany, which have been so well unfolded to you at the High School during the last two years, partly in the stated routine of instruction, and partly in the admirable lectures kindly given to you by Professor Agassiz. There was no philosophical or scientific apparatus furnished at the schools in my day, with the exception, as I remember, in a single instance, of a rickety gimcrack that was called a *planetarium*, and showed how the heavenly bodies do *not* move. As for a school library, with which, my young friends, you are so well provided, there was not in any school I ever attended so much as half a dozen books bearing that name. There was indeed at the academy at Exeter, which it was my good fortune to attend for a few months before I entered college, a library, containing, I believe, some valuable, though probably rather antiquated volumes. It was my privilege, while I was a pupil, never to see the inside of that apartment; privilege, I say, sir, for it was the place where the severer discipline of the institution, in rare cases of need, was administered.

> Hinc exaudiri gemitus, et sæva sonare
> Verbera.

We, little fellows, sir, got to have the most disagreeable associations with the very name of library. I ought to add, in justice to our honored preceptor, good Dr. Abbott, that the use of the library for any such purpose was a very rare occurrence. He possessed the happy skill, Mr. Smith, which I am gratified to say has not died with him, of governing a school by persuasion and influence, and not by force and terror.

As to the learned languages and classical literature generally, they were very poorly taught in those days. I do not like to speak disparagingly of men and things gone by. The defects were at least *vitia ævi non hominum*, but defects they were of the grossest kind. The study of the Latin and Greek was confined to cursory reading of the easier authors; a little construing and parsing, as we called it. The idiom and genius of the languages were not unfolded to us; nor the manner of the different writers; nor the various illustrative learning necessary to render the text which was read, intelligible. We got the lesson to recite, and that was all. Of Prosody, we were taught little; of versification nothing. I was never set to make an hexameter or a pentameter verse at any school, or, I may add, college, in my life; nor did I ever do it, till I was old enough to have children at school, who asked my assistance.

As for text-books and editions, they were all foreign, and, I may add, compared with those of the present day, both native and foreign, all poor. Master Cheever's Accidence, Corderius, and Eutropius, with an English translation in parallel columns, were the books with which the study of Latin was commenced half a century ago.

Such were the schools; and the school-houses were in keeping with them; for the most part cheerless and uninviting in the extreme; cold in winter, hot in summer, without ventilation, destitute of everything required for accommodation, comfort, or health.

### VACATION.

But it is fully time to close these remarks; let me do it with a single word of counsel to our young friends, who are still to enjoy the advantages of this institution, — a bit of advice suggested by one of the laws of our nature. The force of habit is very great. I remember hearing an anecdote of one of the members of the Massachusetts Convention of 1820, who was so regular in his daily attendance, that he went up to the State-house the day after the convention was dissolved, and wondered his colleagues did not appear. Now, I hardly suppose any of you will actually go down to the school-house in vacation, but if you should be tempted to continue in the holidays your habit of studying six, eight, or ten hours a day, as you do in term-time, let me caution you against it. Such uninterrupted exertion all the year round will not be good for your health. Give yourselves a little repose as a matter of duty. If your parents propose to you some little excursion, do not churlishly refuse. Take the times and seasons as they come along, enjoy term-time as much as you please, but do not murmur at vacation. Make it a season of relaxation, and, if possible, of pleasure, in order that, when it is over, you may rush back to your duties with a keener zest. With this parting counsel, I bid you, my young friends, an affectionate farewell, and tender to you, Mr. Smith, and you, gentlemen of the committee, my best wishes for the continued prosperity of the Cambridge High School.

[These historical reminiscences are selected from different addresses made by Mr. Everett when President of the University at Cambridge, at the annual exhibition of the High School in that town, and from other addresses made at the Boston School Festival, and at one of the meetings of the alumni of Harvard College. The passages on the "Conditions of a Good School," and on "Vacation," are also taken from the addresses at the Cambridge High School.]

### POPULAR EDUCATION AND SOUND SCIENCE.*

But it is more than time to proceed to the second point, which I proposed briefly to illustrate, — the favorable influence of the extension of the means of education, and the diffusion of knowledge, on the progress of sound science. It is a pretty common suggestion, that while the more abundant means of popular education, existing at the present day, may have occasioned the diffusion of a considerable amount of superficial knowledge, the effect has been unfavorable to the growth of profound science. I am inclined to think this view of the subject entirely erroneous, — an inference by no means warranted by the premises from which it is drawn. It is no doubt true, that, in consequence of the increased facilities for education, the number of students of all descriptions, both readers and writers, is almost indefinitely multiplied, and with this in-

* From an address delivered before the literary societies of Amherst College, Aug. 25, 1835.

crease in the entire number of persons who have enjoyed, in a greater or less degree, advantages for improving their minds, the number of half-taught and superficial pretenders has become proportionably greater. Education, which, at some periods of the world, has been a very rare accomplishment of a highly gifted and fortunate few, — at other times, an attainment attended with considerable difficulty, and almost confined to professed scholars, — has become, in this country at least, one of the public birthrights of freemen, and, like every other birthright, is subject to be abused. In this state of things, those who habitually look at the dark side of affairs, — often witnessing the arrogant displays of superficial learning, books of great pretension and little value, multiplied and circulated, by all the arts and machinery of an enterprising and prosperous age, and in all things much forwardness and show, often unaccompanied by worth and substance,— are apt to infer a decline of sound learning, and look back, with a sigh, to what they imagine to have been the more solid erudition of former days. But I deem this opinion without real foundation in truth.

It is an age, I grant, of cheap fame. A sort of literary machinery exists, of which the patent paper-mill, the power-press, the newspapers, magazines and reviews, the reading clubs and circulating libraries, are some of the principal springs and levers, by means of which almost anything, in the shape of a book, is thrown into a sort of notoriety, miscalled reputation. The weakest distillation of soft sentiment from the poet's corner flows round a larger circle of admirers than Paradise Lost, when first ushered to the world; and the most narcotic infliction of the quarterly critical press (*absit invidia verbo*) no doubt far excels the *Novum Organum* in the number of its contemporary readers. But nothing is to be inferred, from this state of things, in disparagement of the learning and scholarship of the age. All that it proves is, that with a vast diffusion of useful knowledge, — with an astonishing multiplication of the means of education, and, as I firmly believe, with a prodigious growth of true science, there has sprung up, by natural association, a host of triflers and pretenders, like a growth of rank weeds, with a rich crop, on a fertile soil.

But there were surely always pretenders in science and literature, in every age of the world; nor must we suppose, because their works and their names have perished, that they existed in a smaller proportion formerly than now. Solomon intimates a complaint of the number of books in his day, which he probably would not have done, if they had been all good books. The sophists in Greece were sworn pretenders and dealers in words, — the most completely organized body of learned quacks that ever existed. Bavius and Mævius were certainly not the only worthless poets in Rome; and from the age of the grammarians and critics of the Alexandrian school, through that of the monkish chroniclers and the schoolmen of the middle ages, and the mystics of the sixteenth and seventeenth centuries, the kingdom of learned dulness and empty profession has been kept up, under an unbroken succession of leaden or brazen potentates. If the subjects at the present day seem more numerous than formerly, it is only in proportion to the increase in the entire numbers of the reading and writing world; and because the sagacious hand of time brushes away the false pretensions of former days, leaving real talent and sound learning the more conspicuous for standing alone.

But, as in elder days, notwithstanding this unbroken sway of false lore and vain philosophy, the line of the truly wise and soundly learned was also preserved entire; as the lights of the world have in all former ages successively risen, illuminating the deep darkness, and outshining the delusive meteors; so, at the present day, I am firmly convinced that there is more patient learning, true philosophy, fruitful science, and various knowledge, than at any former time. By the side of the hosts of superficial, arrogant, and often unprincipled pretenders, in every department, there is a multitude innumerable of the devoted lovers of truth, whom no labor can exhaust, no obstacles can discourage, no height of attainment dazzle; and who, in every branch of knowledge, sacred and profane, moral, physical, exact, and critical, have carried and are carrying the glorious banner of true science into regions of investigation wholly unexplored in elder times. Let me not be mistaken. I mean not arrogantly to detract from the fame of the few great masters of the mind, — the gifted few, who, from age to age, after long centuries have intervened, have appeared; and have risen, as all are ready to allow, above all rivalry. After-time alone can pronounce whether this age has produced minds worthy to be classed in their select circle. But this aside, — I cannot comprehend the philosophy by which we assume as probable, nor do I see the state of facts by which we must admit as actually existing, an intellectual degeneracy at the present day, either in Europe or in this country. I see not why the multiplication of popular guides to partial attainments, — why the facilities, that abound for the acquisition of superficial scholarship, should, in the natural operation of things, either diminish the number of powerful and original minds, or satisfy their ardent thirst for acquisition, by a limited progress. There is no doubt that many of these improvements in the methods of learning, — many of the aids to the acquisition of knowledge, which are the product of the present time, are, in their very nature, calculated to help the early studies even of minds of the highest order. It is a familiar anecdote of James Otis, that, when he first obtained a copy of Blackstone's Commentaries, he observed with emphasis, that if he had possessed that book when commencing his studies of the law, it would have saved him seven years' labor. Would those seven years have borne no fruit to a mind like that of James Otis? Though the use of elementary treatises of this kind may have the effect to make many superficial jurists, who would otherwise have been no jurists at all, I deem it mere popular prejudice to suppose that the march of original genius to the heights of learning has been impeded by the possession of these modern facilities to aid its progress. To maintain this seems to be little else than to condemn as worthless the wisdom of the ages which have gone before us. It is surely absurd to suppose that we can do no more with the assistance of our predecessors, than without it; that the teachings of one generation, instead of enlightening, confound and stupefy that which succeeds; and that "when we stand on the shoulders of our ancestors, we cannot see so far as from the ground." On the contrary, it is unquestionably one of the happiest laws of intellectual progress, that the judicious labors, the profound reasonings, the sublime discoveries, the generous sentiments of great intellects, rapidly work their way into the common channel of public opinion, find access to the general mind, raise the universal standard of attainment, correct popular errors, promote arts of daily application, and come home at last to the fireside, in the shape of increased intelligence, skill, comfort and virtue; which, in their turn, by an instantaneous reäction, multiply the numbers and facilitate the efforts of those who engage in the further investigation and discovery of truth. In this way, a constant circulation, like that of the life-blood, takes place in the intellectual world. Truth travels down from the heights of philosophy to the humblest walks of life, and up from the simplest perceptions of an awakened intellect to the discoveries which almost change the face of the world. At every stage of its progress it is genial, luminous, creative. When first struck out by some distinguished and fortunate genius, it may address itself only to a few minds of kindred power. It exists then only in the highest forms of science; it corrects former systems, and authorizes new generalizations. Discussion, controversy begins; more truth is elicited, more errors exploded, more doubts cleared up, more phenomena drawn into the circle, unexpected connections of kindred sciences are traced, and in each step of the progress, the number rapidly grows of those who are prepared to comprehend and carry on some branches of the investigation, — till, in the lapse of time, every order of intellect has been kindled, from that of the sublime discoverer to the practical machinist; and every department of knowledge been enlarged, from the most abstruse and transcendental theory to the daily arts of life.

## THE DISCIPLINE OF A COLLEGE.*

It is earnestly desired by the Government and Faculty of the University, that the students may be influenced to good conduct and diligence in study by higher motives than the fear of punishment; and they mainly rely, for the success of the institution as a place of liberal education, on moral and religious principle, a sense of duty, and the generous feelings which belong to young men engaged in honorable pursuits.

* This passage introduces the chapter on "Discipline" in "The Statutes and Laws of the University at Cambridge." 1848.

## MORAL EDUCATION AND INTELLECTUAL.*

But moral education is much too important an object to be left to follow as an incidental effect from mere literary culture. It should be deemed the distinct duty of a place of education to form the young to those habits and qualities which win regard and command respect, — gentleness of deportment, — propriety of conduct, — the moral courage "that will make them hate the cowardice of doing wrong," — willing obedience to the laws of virtue, — and a profound reverence for sacred things; and of these traits of character, I know of no reliable foundation but sincere and fervent religious faith, founded on conviction, enlightened by reason, and nourished by the devout observance of those means of spiritual improvement which Christianity provides. In the faithful performance of this duty, I believe that a place of education, whether in Europe or America, renders at the present day a higher and more seasonable service to society, than by anything that ends in mere scientific or literary culture. The understanding in every department of speculative or practical knowledge has advanced of late years with a vigor and success beyond what the world has witnessed at any other period; but I cannot suppress a painful impression that this intellectual improvement has not exerted, and is not exerting, its natural influence in purifying the moral character of the age. I cannot subdue the feeling that our modern Christendom, with all its professions and in all its communions, is sinking into a practical heathenism, which needs a great work — I had almost said a new dispensation — of reform, scarcely less than the decrepit paganisms of Greece and Rome. Christians as we are, we worship, in America and in Europe, in the city and the field, on the exchange and in the senate, and must I not add in the academy and the church, some gods as bad as those of the Pantheon. In individual and national earnestness, in true moral heroism, and in enlightened spirituality unalloyed by mysticism, the age in which we live is making, I fear, little progress; but rather, perhaps, with all its splendid attainments in science and art, is plunging deeper into the sordid worship of

> "the least erected spirit that fell
> From heaven, for even in heaven his looks and thoughts
> Were always downward bent, admiring more
> The riches of heaven's pavement, — trodden gold, —
> Than aught divine or holy else enjoyed
> In vision beatific."

It may be feared that a defect of this kind, if truly stated and sufficiently general to mark the character of an age, will prove too strong for any corrective influences but those of public calamity, and what are called, in our expressive national phrase, "the times that try men's souls." But I have long thought, that if, in a period of prosperity and by gentle influences, anything can be effected toward the same end, the work must be begun in our seminaries of liberal education, and that they have a duty to perform, in this respect, which cannot be too strongly urged nor too deeply felt.

How it should be discharged, it would be at once unseasonable and arrogant to endeavor on this occasion minutely to set forth. All, however, who hear me will agree, — every parent, every good citizen, will agree, — that the object itself, the formation of character on Christian principles, is that last great object of a place of education, to which all else is subordinate and auxiliary. For this reason, it is the duty of all intrusted with the control of such an institution to conduct it conscientiously, as an instrument of mighty efficiency for good or for evil. The branches of study, the influences under which they are pursued, and the whole discipline of the place, should be, as far as human wisdom can make them so, such as are most friendly to sound moral principles, and they should be conducted by men whose heart is in the work, and whose example teaches more and better than their precept.

To all that can be thus effected by indirect association and influence should be added that kind and degree of direct religious instruction which circum-

* From the address delivered by Mr. Everett at his inauguration as president of the University at Cambridge, Thursday, April 30, 1846.

The "*Letter*" which President Barnard addressed to the board of trustees of the University of Mississippi, in 1858, is so full of suggestions of the highest practical importance to the efficiency and fuller development of our American collegiate and university system, that we must enrich our pages with a few extracts.

In this, as in his former publications on the subject, the writer claims that the expansion of the range of studies, without extending the time in which these studies are to be pursued, has impaired the efficiency of the system, in its original and legitimate aim—the discipline and training of the intellectual powers—without giving to the students a thorough mastery of any one of the many new subjects introduced. This evil he attributes, not to the inefficiency of the professors, or to their defective methods of instruction, but to the system itself.

The evil has been the growth of years. It has accumulated by degrees almost imperceptible. Each successive addition has probably seemed inconsiderable to those who made it, but the united sum has become intolerable. Could it, in the nature of things, have been possible that a proposition should at any one time have been made for a sudden change from the system, as it existed a century ago, to the system of to-day, it is inconceivable that it should have been entertained by enlightened educators for a moment.

To relieve the course of under-graduate study in our colleges of some part of its excessive burthen, and at the same time to meet the demands of the age for instruction in the studies which have been introduced, President Barnard proposes to divide the studies into distinct and separate courses—a sub-graduate and a post-graduate department.

The sub-graduate course may be defined by the very simple process of excluding from the curriculum of study, as it stands at present, all those branches of science which are confessedly modern additions, and, along with these, the modern languages. This course will, therefore, as reconstructed, embrace the English, Latin, and Greek languages, all the elementary branches of the pure mathematics, the mechanical branches of natural philosophy, logic, rhetoric, the principles of criticism, moral and mental philosophy, composition, and elocution. These several branches of study are to be pursued to something like the extent, and with something like the thoroughness, contemplated in the earlier period of the history of our collegiate instruction. To these it may not be thought improper to add, during the concluding year, succinct expository courses in chemistry and the subjects of natural philosophy, not strictly mechanical; these topics being taught avowedly in outline only, and not as matters to be embraced in the examination for the Bachelor's degree.

To the post-graduate department, may be turned over those branches of science and letters which are excluded from the former, and which are confessedly, at present, but imperfectly taught; and the number of these may, from time to time, be increased, by adding new ones, as the wants of the public and the growing resources of the university may demand or justify. Thus it *may* immediately include astronomy, geology, mineralogy, chemistry, natural philosophy, meteorology, civil engineering, the higher branches of the pure mathematics, Greek and Roman letters, the modern languages and their literature, political economy, international law, constitutional law, and the history of philosophy; but it probably *will* include, at first, only such of this list as are most practical in their nature. As, in creating this department, the design should be, from the beginning, to build up here ultimately a university in the largest acceptation of that term, it is to be expected that, in the progress of years, schools of agriculture, of natural history, of medical science, of civil and political history, &c., &c.

The post-graduate department is to be open to all who may wish to go thoroughly to the bottom of any subject which the university proposes to teach, and for which he has prepared himself in school, or by private study; but the master's degree is not to be conferred upon any one who has not graduated as Bachelor of Arts, in this or some other college. When students of mature minds resort, of their own option, to a school of higher learning, like that contemplated, it is presumed they will be in earnest in the pursuit of knowledge.

The above assumption can not safely be made of the body of the under-graduates of our colleges. Nor is it difficult to find reasons for a fact of so general observation. One of these is, doubtless, the immaturity of the youthful student himself; in consequence of which, he is yet to learn both the importance of mental culture, and the value of positive knowledge. Another is presented in the circumstance that the under-graduate student is not always, perhaps not usually, a member of an institution of learning, entirely of his own voluntary choice; but that he has become such, in compliance with the wishes of his parents and friends; often with no other feeling on his own part than a desire to make his college life pass away as agreeably as circumstances will allow; a desire which does not always prompt him to seek for enjoyment by the most rational means.

In the higher department, or post-graduate course, of the university, President Barnard proposes to employ the plan of daily recitation only to a limited extent, and to resort mainly to oral exposition on the part of the teacher.

According to Sir William Hamilton, all instruction was originally given, in the universities of England, as it continues to be in the continental universities, by lecture. The colleges and halls, which now monopolize the principal work of teaching in those venerable institutions, were erected to provide for the physical wants of the students, and to secure a vigilant supervision over their morals. The officers, called tutors, employed by the colleges for the latter purpose, gradually took upon themselves the character of instructors, by exacting from the youth under their charge, a repetition of what they had learned in the public lecture-halls. To this kind of recitation, they subsequently added recitation from books. The evident design of the exercise, in its origin, was that in which we find its chief utility at present—to insure the attention of the pupil to the subject which he is required to know. The distinctive name given by the French, to the officer whose duty it is merely to hear recitations, makes it sufficiently evident what idea is associated with the exercise by them. This name—*répétiteur*—suggests to the mind the bare repetition of a task, as that which it is the business of the officer to secure. * * *

All that Melancthon has said, all that Hamilton has said, all that any panegyrist of the system of daily examination, as a means of instruction, has said, in regard to the incidental advantages growing out of the method, is admitted without any hesitation. It stimulates emulation, it cultivates self-possession, it encourages or enforces precision of speech, it abates conceit, it convinces of deficiency. But all these resultant benefits presume the immaturity of the learner; and most of them presume, furthermore, that an unceasing constraint is necessary to compel him to profit by the instructions he receives. * * *

It will be conceded that, considered as an instructive, and not as a coercive method, the system of daily examination is attended with some incidental advantages, besides those which have just been enumerated. It is a possibility that a student, who has failed to comprehend some point embraced in the text of his lesson, may be enlightened, by listening to the performance of a fellow-student. It is also a possibility, or rather a fact of frequent occurrence, that the imperfect performance of an individual scholar, may indicate to the instructor the deficiencies of that individual, and so elicit explanatory comments or illustrations. It is further true, that the instructor may volunteer explanations and elucidations of points of difficulty, even though occasion may not arise to force their introduction.

An acute instructor, moreover, by the ingenious selection of interrogatories, will bring out the weak points of a pupil, as a lawyer does those of a witness; or will bring into prominent relief the points of the subjects under consideration, which are of highest importance. But, beyond this, it is certainly true, that it is only in so far as, for whatever reason, the instructor does actually superadd his own teachings to the text of the lesson, that any talents or attainments, which may belong to him personally, can be of any sort of use to his pupils. For all the purposes of *mere* recitation, any man, who is capable of understanding what the pupil says, and of reading the book or books from which he has learned it, so as to compare the performance with the text, is as good and as capable a presiding officer and examiner in a class-room, as any other. The teacher, therefore, who meets his classes for no purpose at any time but to "hear their recitations," is not really a teacher, except in so far as he ingrafts upon this exercise the expository feature which is the distinguishing characteristic of the plan of instruction by lecture. To do this, however, to any extent, in the recitation-room, without seriously interfering with the specific design for which the exercise of recitation was primarily instituted, is proved by experience to be impracticable. Class recitations have, at best, the great disadvantage, that either but few out of a large number can perform at all, or that each one who performs shall be under examination for so brief a space of time as nearly to defeat every useful object, and to render the exercise little better than an idle form.

Another serious vice of the system, is its pernicious influence on the teacher. To whatever degree it may be coercive to the student, it is not in the least so to him. It stimulates him to no self-improvement, and awakens in him no ambition for higher attainments, on the one hand; and it affords him no adequate field for the display of genius, or for the turning of accumulated knowledge to use, on the other. Instead of this, the opportunity which it offers him of sinking, without observation, into a mere cipher, is a real, a perpetual, and a most insidious temptation to sloth. The difficulty of employing, in the recitation room, the expository mode of instruction, without overreaching too far upon the exercise proper to the hour, is enough, in itself, to repress in the teacher the teaching spirit, and to cause him constantly to tend to the level of the mere *répétiteur*. How dangerously is this tendency increased, by the fact that its downward direction coincides precisely with that in which the native love of ease is perpetually dragging all mankind! For this great evil, there is but one antagonistic influence, which can be of any avail: it is that of a living, fervent, zeal in his work, existing in the instructor himself; a zeal, not in the work of conducting recitations, as the remark might seem to imply, but which would be ridiculous—a zeal, rather, in the higher and nobler work of training immortal minds to vigor, and capacitating them for usefulness. The college officer, therefore, of the present day, whose interest in his profession is bounded by the fact, certainly uninspiring, however important to himself, that it secures to him the means of living, is in imminent danger of lapsing into a mere automaton.

The advantages of oral teaching are thus set forth:—

According to the plan, if the teacher possesses any knowledge on the subject of study, which is not contained in the books of the course, or not easily accessible to the student, or if the sources from which such knowledge may be obtained are above the present level of the student's capacity, this knowledge will be brought out and made available. And if he possesses any power of clear analysis, or of luminous illustration; if he possesses, as he ought, in order to occupy fitly a position of this high responsibility, that mastery over his theme which belongs to the man who has ceased to think of the truth which he teaches as of a something found in books, and of which all that he knows is knowledge gathered at second-hand; but who has independently interrogated the sources of information himself, and stands in immediate contact with nature and with thought, feeling no need of an interpreter—if this is his own intellectual character, this the degree of his intellectual cultivation, and this the comprehensive scope of his acquired resources—then his teachings will carry with them, to the minds of his hearers, a fullness of satisfaction, and fasten themselves there with a permanency of impression, such as no amount of perusal of mere lifeless text-books, written down to the level of their immediate attainments, no matter how earnestly attentive, or how conscientiously faithful the perusal may be, can ever produce.

Not that from such a system of instruction books are to be discarded. By no means. Not only will the necessity of books continue to be as absolutely imperative, as under any system whatever of recitation from a text; but the multiplication of books will be an inevitable consequence. For, while the instructor will aim to expound all that relates to theory or doctrine, he will not embarrass his class-room with the lumber of innumerable applications, which, however useful they may be, are the proper labor of the student himself, in his solitary study; neither, in regard to simple matters of plain fact, of which a multitude are strewn along the path of every walk in science, will he consider it expedient to occupy time in stating, in minute detail, what can be found in every book, and what needs but to be read once to be understood. For their necessary enlightenment in matters such as these, he will refer his pupils to certain selected authors, of which he will designate the portions which require their attention, with as much regularity as if they were to be subjected to examination upon the same passages. But he will not always confine himself to one author, nor always give the same author preference; for his business is to teach a subject, and not a book; and books, therefore, are not his guides, but his helps. Nor will the student find it quite a practicable thing to disregard the recommendations thus made, or to neglect the perusal, or rather severe study, of the books designated; for he will shortly discover that this study is indispensable to his understanding and properly profiting by the instructions of his own immediate teacher.

The two salient merits of the method of instruction here proposed, then, for the class of learners contemplated, are, first, that it both permits and compels the teacher to *be* a teacher, and neither constrains nor allows him to sink into inactivity, nor to content himself with presiding in empty state over an exercise to which he is conscious of contributing nothing valuable; and, secondly, that it makes *knowledge itself*, and not the substance of any *treatise* upon knowledge, not any *artificial form* into which knowledge has been thrown, the immediate subject of teaching.

To make the plan of oral teaching more effective, President Barnard proposes to introduce another feature, somewhat peculiar:—

This is to afford to the members of the class, pursuing their studies in any school, the opportunity, after the instructor shall have completed the exposition of the topic of the day, to bring up for re-examination points which still remain to them obscure, or to ask further information in regard to matters which may not have been fully explained. This is, in fact, to inaugurate a species of recitation in which the student and teacher reverse the positions usual in this exercise. The student questions; the teacher replies. The student should even be permitted, if he pleases, in cases which admit of argument, to take issue with his instructor, and to present his reasons for his opinions. Discussion will be advantageous to both parties, and will keep more actively alive the interest felt by the class in the subject of study.

But the larger portion of the "*Letter*" is devoted to an elaborate effort to induce the trustees, by inaugurating the project of a post-graduate department, to take a first decided step in the direction of a higher development of the educational system of the state.

The character of every school, from the highest to the lowest, within our borders, is to be determined ultimately by the respectability or the inferiority of this. Though it is true that but a fraction of the people will receive their personal instruction within the university halls, yet all, without exception, will be partakers of the benefits of which the university is to be the fountain-head and the central source. If the institution does not immediately teach the entire people, it will teach their teachers; or, what is equivalent to this, it will force every instructor, whom it does not itself instruct, to come up to the standard it prescribes, on penalty of being else driven from the educational field. * * *

But what *is* the university of to-day? What, but a training school for immature minds—impaired, indeed, in its usefulness for this purpose, by the very attempt to accomplish, along with it, other and entirely incompatible objects? If the people suppose that this is a place to make practical men, or learned men, or profoundly scientific men—if they suppose that it is within the reach of possibility for the university, under the existing system, to turn out accomplished engineers, or expert chemists, or proficient astronomers, or profound philosophers, or even finished scholars—we know very well that they are deceived. Not that this institution falls any further short of accomplishing these ends, or fails any more signally to meet this popular impression, than other American colleges; but that the power to do these things seems, by force of a general hallucination, to be attributed to colleges as a class, while, in point of fact, it does not actually exist in any one of the whole number. * * *

The existence of the want of institutions of a higher than merely collegiate grade, as a reality, is made evident by the earnest and urgent demand, spoken of earlier in this communication, which has been, for the last thirty or forty years, so extensively heard, for something or other which the existing educational system does not supply. This demand, so far as it has proceeded from scholars and men of science, has taken the specific form of a demand for universities called by that name; because scholars and men of science have been able to perceive distinctly, that the university was the precise thing needed to satisfy the want. But when it has come from the people—and from the people it has come very steadily, for at least a quarter of a century—it has been, not for the university by name, but for new schools of some vaguely-conceived description; for colleges to be broken up and destroyed in all that regards the province of their past usefulness, and built up anew upon some visionary plan, and according to some impracticable theory; for schools of science, as applied to the arts of construction, of agriculture, of manufactures, and every thing useful to mankind, but chiefly things useful according to that literal sense which confounds utility with increase of wealth; for schools, in short, which should do what the collegiate schools do not do, and what we know that it is not necessary or even proper that they should do—prepare men, so far as schools can prepare them, to take directly hold of the real business of life. No one is ignorant that this demand has existed for a period at least as long as asserted; that, at times, it has been vociferous and violent; or that, not content with insisting on the creation of new schools, to accomplish the ends desired, it has turned, occasionally, almost in a spirit of vindictive destructiveness, upon the old, because they did not accomplish those same ends.

These demands, the undersigned ventures to assert, are evidence of the want of higher universities. Not because they ask for the university; not because their authors, if the university were proposed to them as a remedy, would be likely to accept it; but because the present inconvenience, which is so sensibly felt, is one which the university would remove, though those who feel it do not perceive how. And why not? Because first, looking at universities, as they have been in past centuries, as the repositories of literary lore, as the resorts of scholars dealing with abstractions, as the burrowing-places of book-worms, eating out the hearts of the black-letter volumes of the sixteenth century, or of the manuscripts of the sixth, as the unchallenged domain of grammarians and lexicographers, of commentators upon Aristotle and Longinus, ingenious speculators upon the mysteries of the digamma, and indefatigable elaborators of ethical and logical niceties, they picture them, in their imaginations, even to this hour, as solemn and shadowy retreats, still smelling of the dust and mold of antiquity, where philology, linguistic philosophy, and the sublimer metaphysics brood, like the pensive owl in Gray's churchyard turret, with none to

"Molest their ancient solitary reign."

But this conception is entirely erroneous. The university, in the sense in which the name is now generally received, no matter what may have been its original acceptation, is *Universitas Scientiarum;* it is, in other words, an institution in which the highest learning of its day is taught in every walk of human knowledge.

When classic learning, philosophy, and logic, were subjects of the highest interest in human estimation, it is not surprising that the character of university teaching should have been principally determined by them. But, inasmuch as, at the present day, physical science has attained a position of actual dignity, immeasurably higher than it then enjoyed, and as its useful applications have become almost endlessly more numerous and varied, the university of to-day would fail to be what its name imports, if it did not assign a corresponding prominence to these subjects—subjects, be it observed, which happen to be the same for which the agitators we have been speaking of demand that a special provision of special schools shall be made. * * *

There is, however, a second class of agitators, who, while admitting the justice of the foregoing representation, are not disposed to accept the university as a remedy for the inconvenience they suffer, because, while it gives them all that they demand, it gives them at the same time much more—much for which they do not ask, and for which they do not care. They fear so great a project, as the creation of an institution, professing, and really preparing itself, to teach every thing embraced in the entire circle of human knowledge. They fear that, in attempting this, they shall attempt what is beyond their means; and that, by grasping too much, they shall loose every thing. It is believed that all this class of persons, if they rightfully interpret our views, will find that we are entirely in accordance with them, and they with us. For no such visionary scheme is entertained by any one connected with this institution, as that of creating here, in a day, a university, complete in all the many-faced aspects of a repository of universal truth, and a dispenser of universal knowledge. What is aimed at, what is recommended, is only, as already stated, to take a first step in the right direction—a step which shall, indeed, ultimately conduct to the fulfillment of the great idea, but which shall not be itself the fulfillment—a step which will mark only the beginning of a progress, in which, advancing only as the growing intelligence and increasing wants of the people of the state shall urge it, the University of Mississippi may, to the eyes of a future generation, at length present the lustrous spectacle which the comprehensive idea of a true university implies.

There is still another class, whose views on the subject under consideration can not be overlooked—a class possibly the most numerous of all those who concern themselves about it; or, if not the most numerous, at any rate, by far the most impracticable. Those are here indicated who deny the utility of high learning altogether. They are, of course, utilitarians in the technical sense of that word. Let any thing tend to promote the bodily comfort of the race—let it furnish man with food, or keep him warm, or put a barrier between him and the weather—and that is a useful thing. By consequence, therefore, science does, occasionally, in some of its practical results, command their partial consideration; but, for science or learning as a whole, a matter between which and the increase of wealth no connection in the relation of cause and effect is to their minds obvious, they have no respect whatever. To elevate the intellectual man in the scale of being, to enable him to form larger and juster views than his unaided senses or his individual, casual, and unsystematic observation has qualified him to conceive, of the power and wisdom and goodness of the great Architect of the universe, to introduce him to a world of enjoyments growing out of the exercise of the godlike intellect upon subjects of beauty, and sublimity, and deep-seated and with delightfully difficult effort laboriously unraveled truth—enjoyments such as doubtless occupy cherubic intelligences, in their rapt contemplation of the wonderful works of God—all this the mere utilitarian philosopher, ever like the man with the muck-rake in Bunyan, looking downward, fails to comprehend and to appreciate; and all arguments addressed to him, founded upon the consideration, to which he is insensible, that knowledge is valuable for its own sake, are wholly thrown away.

* * * * * * * * * *

Is, then, scientific knowledge useful? Few objectors will take the broad ground of denying all utility to science; or of denying utility to all sciences. Few will hesitate to admit that every science furnishes some facts that are useful. Even the patient and diligent collector of bugs, and butterflies, and caterpillars, though looked down upon in a general way by the utilitarian with an amusingly sublime loftiness of contemptuous regard, if he but intimate a belief that he is upon the sure trace of a method of exterminating the insect scourges of the cotton-field, is listened to with respectful, nay, with greedy ears, and is elevated at once to position of comparative dignity. No scoffer at science, therefore, ever scoffs at the science, or at the facts of science, which he understands; understands, that is to say, not as simple, isolated facts, a thing which is generally easy—but understands in all their bearings, and relations, and far-reaching affiliations with other facts with which they have no obvious or visible connection—a thing which is often not easy at all. * * *

When Priestly, in 1774, turning the focus of his burning lens upon the substance known in the shops of the apothecaries under the name of red precipitate, detached bubbles of a gas identical with that which, in the atmosphere, supports life, who could presume that, in thus freeing one of the metals from its companion element, he had detected the composition of many of the most useful ores, and furnished a hint which was yet to reduce all metallurgic art, from the smelting of iron to the reduction of aluminium, under the dominion of chemical science, and to the severe rule of an intelligent and a productive economy? When, in the same year, Scheele, by operating on the acid of sea-salt, made first visible to human eyes that colored gas whose suffocating odor is now so well known to all the world, who could foresee the astonishing revolution which a discovery, then interesting only for its curious beauty, was destined to introduce into the manufacture of paper, of linen textures, and of a vast multitude of other objects, of daily and hourly use? Or what imagination could have been extravagant enough, or fantastic enough, in the exercise of its inventive power, to anticipate that a substance, for the moment not merely useless but seemingly noxious, would, in the nineteenth century, accomplish what, without it, no instrumentality known to science or art could have accomplished—find aliment for the rapacious maw of a letter-press, whose insatiable demands, already grown vast beyond all conception, grow yet with each succeeding year? When the chemists of the last century observed the discoloration and degradation which certain metallic salts undergo in the sunlight, who could possibly read, in a circumstance so apparently trivial, though occasionally troublesome, the intimation that the sun himself was about to place in the hands of Niepce, and Daguerre, and Talbot, a pencil, whose magical powers of delineation should cause the highest achievements of human pictorial art to seem poor and rude in the comparison? When Malus, in 1810, watching the glare of the sun's rays, reflected from the windows of the Luxembourg to his own, noticed for the first time the curious phenomena attendant on that peculiar condition of light which has since been known by the name of polarization, what prescience could have connected a fact so totally without any perceptible utility, with the manufacture of sugar in France; or have anticipated that an instrument, founded in principle on this very property, would, forty years later, effect an annual saving to the French people to the extent of hundreds of thousands of francs? When Œrsted, in 1819, observed the disturbance of the magnetic needle by the influence of a neighboring galvanic current, how wild and visionary would not that man have been pronounced to be, who should have professed to read, in an indication so slight, the grand truth that science had, that day, stretched out the scepter of her authority over a winged messenger, whose fleetness should make a laggard even of Oberon's familiar sprite, and render the velocity which could "put a girdle round the earth in forty minutes" tardy and unsatisfying?

Questions of this kind, suggested by the history of scientific progress, might be multiplied to fill a volume. Indeed, it has almost come to be a dogma in science, that there is no new truth whatever, no matter how wide a space may seem, in the hour of its discovery, to divide it from any connection with the material interests of man, which carries not within it the latent seeds of a utility, which further discovery, in the same field, will reveal and cause to germinate.

We would gladly follow President Barnard through his glowing argument, in behalf of higher learning but we must refer our readers to the "*Letter*" itself.

### ELECTIVE STUDIES.

In the last annual communication of the president to the trustees, evidence was presented, derived from a pretty extensive examination of the statistics of collegiate education in the United States, showing that the colleges, in insisting upon the pursuance of an invariable curriculum of study by all their students, are not satisfying the demands of the age as it respects the higher education. The question was then discussed as a question of pure statistics; with a view to ascertain, if possible, what is the estimation in which the education furnished by the colleges is held by the people at the present time, compared with what it was earlier in the century. The result of the inquiry, however it might turn out, did not necessarily involve any thing beyond. Should it appear that the colleges at present attract a smaller number of students in proportion to the population than formerly, and even that this proportion is sensibly diminishing as years go by, it is still free to those who believe that the system can not be materially improved, to ascribe this to popular error; and to hope, and to profess to anticipate that this error, like many caprices of which precedents may be found perhaps in history, will presently pass away. To such the results actually reached in the inquiry will probably be unwelcome, but will fail to suggest the propriety of any modification of the system itself.

There are those who hold with some reason that the popular judgment of systems of education is not to be trusted; but none can wisely claim that it ought not to be regarded. No scheme however judicious can be successful, in a country where choice is free, unless the people can be made to see that it is judicious. To a community without education, or but imperfectly educated, the value of education of any kind is not very obvious. And hence it is that this is one of the subjects of great public interest, of which it is unsafe to trust the regulation to the ordinary law of supply and demand. Limitation of knowledge is not, like deficiency of food, attended with a craving for a larger supply. It is characteristic of ignorance, on the other hand, to be content not to know; and of partial information, to be puffed up with the conceit that there is little more to be known. The relations of men to each other in civilized society render certain descriptions of elementary knowledge necessary to all; or at least cause the absence of such humble knowledge to be felt as a positive inconvenience; and so far as this may extend, but only so far, we may presume that education will be provided in obedience to a spontaneous popular demand. But a high order of education is not the necessity of the many, and the want of it can never be felt by them as a personal want. Still less are the multitude likely to feel the importance to the commonwealth that there should be an order of educated men superior to themselves. On the other hand, the popular feeling is instinctively opposed to the growth of such an order, or to any order which breaks the dead level of uniform mediocrity. This is well illustrated in the history of educational institutions in a number of the more recently formed states of our Union, in which provision for the higher education has been made by means of endowments granted by the general government, but intrusted for their administration to the legislatures of the States themselves. In cases which have fallen under the personal observation of the president, the colleges, though costing the people nothing, have been subjects of constant denunciation by demagogues as nurseries of aristocrats, their halls have been but meagrely attended in spite of attractions which ought to have filled them with throngs, and their endeavors to fulfill their mission have been rather tolerated than sustained by the people.

The fact then regarding the higher education is, not that the demand creates the supply, but that the supply determines the demand. Superior educational institutions are provided either by governments or by the thinking few; and these, by the offers which they hold out, and by the visible results which they produce as illustrated in the subsequent history of those who avail themselves of their advantages, slowly educate the people to an understanding of the value of education—of the value of education in general, and of the value of the form of education furnished, in particular. So long as this form of education seems to fit men best to meet with and master the practical problems presented by the age in which they live, whether these be political or social, industrial, moral or purely intellectual, so long will it be preferred, and so long will the public preference for it be manifested in the increasing numbers of those who seek its benefits. If, in the changing conditions of society, systems of education remain wholly unchanged, there is reason to doubt whether the training which was once perfectly adapted to the circumstances can continue to remain so. And its want of adaptedness to the new exigencies of life, or its positive defects, can not fail to be detected by the people, through the application of the same criteria by means of which they learned to value the higher education at all. As therefore the practical success of educational systems and of educational institutions, in a country where as before remarked, the choice is free—where government, that is to say, does not step in to control the will of the individual—must depend upon the favor voluntarily extended to them by the people, the evidence of a great and decided change in the popular estimation of a system long established and long undeniably favorite, compels the inevitable conclusion that this system requires modification. No theory can stand against a fact like this. It is idle to prove to a people that they ought to prefer a species of culture which, upon evidence satisfactory to them, they have deliberately made up their minds not to prefer.

The change in respect to the popular appreciation of the system of collegiate education, in form as hitherto conducted in our country, indicated by the diminished attendance upon the colleges, is too great to be treated as an accidental irregularity; and it has been steadily progressive for so long a time, that it can be attributed to no passing caprice. Taking the whole country through, the number of undergraduate students in all the colleges is less at the present time in proportion to the entire population, than it was thirty years ago, nearly in the ratio of two to one. From New England, where collegiate education has always been more highly in favor than any where else, the number of undergraduate students sent to the colleges within and without New England, is not greater by one hundred in all at this time, than it was in 1838. It is even considerable less, if, at both dates, we leave out Harvard University; an institution which has received, within the last few years, a rapid and surprising increase of numbers, as an apparent consequence of having abandoned the distinctive feature of the collegiate system of instruction, *i. e.* the invariable curriculum of study. In all New England there is not a single considerable college in which the attendance from its own state has not fallen off in recent years, except Amherst, where it has not increased, though the population has increased largely, and Harvard, in regard to the exceptional prosperity of which, the probable reason has just been suggested.

In regard to our own State of New York, we have not the means of ascertaining, for former years, how many young men have been sent to colleges beyond the State limits, or how many from other States have attended our own; but the comparison of the *total* attendance upon the colleges of New York at different periods exhibits results entirely in harmony with those derived from New England. Taking up, for instance, entirely at random, the American Almanac for 1848, we find that the colleges of the State of

New York, then six in number, viz. Columbia, Union, Hamilton, Madison, Geneva (now Hobart) and the N. Y. City University, embraced for the year preceding, nine hundred and forty undergraduate students; while in 1869-70, the total attendance of students in Arts in all the colleges, now increased to *twelve* in number, viz., besides the above-named, Genesee, Rochester, St. Stephens, Cornell, Alfred, and the college of the City of New York, was only one thousand and thirty-four; an absolute increase of ninety-four, or ten per cent. only, while the population of the State during the same time increased not less than fifty per cent.

If, in connection with facts like these, which illustrate the declining favor with which that system of collegiate education is regarded, which makes adherence to an invariable curriculum of study its distinctive characteristic, we consider the success of those institutions which offer to their students a considerable latitude of choice in the selection of their studies, we shall see that it is not an inferior grade of education which the popular voice demands, nor a diminished amount of exaction. It is rather that education shall be varied to suit the varying capacities of individuals; and further, that, in place of limited and necessarily superficial attainment in many things, there shall be thoroughness, or at least the opportunity for thoroughness, in a smaller number. The throng which has filled the halls of Cornell University from the first day of their opening has been gathered mainly by the opportunity thus offered. And though the education furnished by some of the schools of that institution is not what can be properly called liberal, yet setting these schools aside, the truth still remains that Cornell University, in the third year of its existence, outnumbers any three of those of the colleges of the State which have been in existence half a century. The University of Michigan furnishes an example almost equally striking which has been in evidence for a much longer period. This institution numbers at present nearly five hundred students in its undergraduate department. But the most remarkable illustration of the same truth is probably that which is to be found in the case of Harvard University already mentioned; especially when considered in comparison with the sister institution next in age (in New England) and her most prominent competitor, Yale College. These two institutions have, for many years, appeared to divide pretty equally the popular favor. But while the first is exhibiting at the present time a growth more vigorous than has marked any former period of her history, the second is nearly stationary. The average undergraduate attendance of Yale

College for the last five years (including the present) has been five hundred and thirteen. Her catalogue for 1870-71, gives the present attendance at five hundred and twenty-two; but the total for 1860-61—ten years ago—was almost exactly the same, viz. five hundred and twenty-one. The increase at Harvard in the meantime has been nearly two hundred.

The reasons which were once thought conclusive in favor of an invariable curriculum of study extending through the collegiate course, have many of them at present lost their principal force. The first and chief of these was that the object of collegiate training is so almost exclusively mental discipline, and so little the imparting of useful knowledge, as to make a uniform system of instruction a logical necessity. It is not what a young man *likes* to study—that is the argument—but what he *needs* to study, to which his attention should be directed. Very probably what he likes least he will need most, and to give to him freedom of choice will be to defeat the ends of his education.

The force of this argument depends upon the assumption, which is always made, and which thus far has never been in terms distinctly contradicted, that the entire college course is or ought to be a course of mental discipline strictly, and nothing else. However justifiable this assumption may have been fifty years ago, it can by no means be admitted at the present time, without at least important qualification. The mental powers can not, it is true, be exercised without improvement upon any subject, or at any period of life before the commencement of natural decline; and in this sense we may say that we are always under mental discipline. But the discipline which we properly distinguish as educational is something different from this. It may be defined or explained somewhat as follows:—

There is a period of early life during which, without any artificial and intentional culture at all, the powers of the body and those of the mind simultaneously unfold themselves. During this period if certain muscles of the body or certain of its limbs be kept in incessant activity, and certain others in continual repose, the result will be an abnormal and possibly a monstrous growth. But if the child be allowed to grow up under ordinary conditions so as to reach adult years with tolerably symmetrical proportions, the subsequent effect of unequal activity of the different members of the body will no longer be an unnatural development, or a marked disturbance of the balance of the physical powers; but rather a greater skill or aptness in the use of those which are most employed. Nor even in regard to this, is use or practice or exercise, after a very early period of life, sufficient to produce results which, while the system is still plastic, are accomplished almost imperceptibly and with infinitely less effort. There are arts, such for instance as glass blowing, which can never be mastered except by persons who have grown up to them from early childhood. And no fact is more familiar than the facility with which the pronunciation of foreign languages is acquired by infantile lips; while it is a hopeless undertaking for an adult, no matter what amount of practice and perseverance he may expend upon the effort, perfectly to master the same accomplishment.

Now precisely the same law holds true in regard to mental development. As there is a period of infancy during which the child is incapable of supporting his own weight; so there is one in which he is hardly conscious of his own existence. And as, with the physical growth, the organs of the body acquire strength and come by degrees under the control of the will, so correspondingly, in the natural and quite spontaneous growth of the mind, the faculties unfold themselves and expand into vigor, in simple obedience to the principle of development divinely implanted in the soul in the moment of its birth. With the progress of years this growth goes on; and the mind, like the body, attains an adult stage, whether it be subjected to external influences controlling its habits—that is, to educational influences—or not. There comes a time at last beyond which educational influences are proverbially vain. There is another period, the earliest of all, in which they are almost omnipotent. This is the period during which, in obedience to nature's law, the faculties are growing; and when the educator may force them to grow into any mould which he may choose to throw around them. But when expansion has ceased, moulds will be placed in vain: the mind will retain the contour which nature and circumstances have given it; and from this point onward the business of education is no longer to form it, but to make the most of what it is. There is here doubtless room for the educator to do much; but his business is to give fair play to the faculties such as they are, and such as they must continue to be; rather than to repress the salient characteristics, and waste both precious time and weary labor in the endeavor to bring out others which have lost the power to respond to the solicitations of the cultivator.

Now it can hardly be doubted that the average age of undergraduates in our American colleges is more advanced at present by several years, than it was a century ago. At the admission of students into Columbia College, record is made of the age of each candidate at his last preceding birthday. Of the students of all the classes at present in college, the average of the ages thus recorded is sixteen years and nine months; and as this is the average at the birthday preceding admission, it may fairly be concluded that, at the time of admission, the average age exceeded seventeen years. The average age at graduation is therefore twenty-one years, or the age of manhood complete. Until within the last six or seven years, the matriculation books of the college have contained no record of the ages of the students. It is impossible, therefore, from this source, to obtain any information as to the average age of admission into this college during the last century. Quite a number of instances have, however, come to our knowledge in which individuals entered the college as early as twelve or thirteen, and graduated at sixteen or seventeen. Possibly these were extreme cases; but no such case could be possible at all at present, since the statutes prohibit the admission of any student below fifteen years of age. Suppose then the average age at that early period to have been thirteen or fourteen years. That is already three or four years below the present average; and three or four years taken at the very time of life when the mental as well as the physical organization is loosing its plasticity and attaining its ultimate form as well as stature. It is a question well worth considering, whether a plan of education which might be admirably adapted to the circumstances of boys between twelve and sixteen, could possibly be equally suitable for young men between seventeen and twenty-one. For the first class named, there might be reason in demanding that the entire course should be shaped with a view to mental discipline only. As it respects the second, there is no less reason for requiring that a principal object should be, to impart knowledge for the sake of knowledge itself. And though this should not be the governing object throughout the whole course, it ought at least to give character to the later years.

A second reason why it is no longer expedient to treat collegiate instruction as being designed exclusively for mental discipline, in contradistinction to the acquisition of knowledge, is found in the fact that it is no longer practicable to do so. While the subjects taught in college were few, and with the exception of the pure mathematics, were purely literary, it was not difficult to prosecute them so steadily and so far as to make them instruments of a real mental discipline. This is no longer the case, especially after the first two years. The curriculum has been so overloaded by gradual additions, that if now an equal distribution of the available time were made to the several subjects of study, each one could command but two or three weeks. This surely is not sufficient to make of any study an efficient instrument of mental discipline. Nor is the expedient by which the several subjects, instead of being successfully disposed of, are spread out over the surface of a whole session or a whole year, being alternated in such a manner as to separate the hours devoted to each by considerable intervals, sometimes by several days, one which is likely to increase its efficiency. It has been claimed for our American college system that, in departing from the type on which it was originally constructed, as it has done by the large extension of its curriculum, it has been materially improved; and this is true, if we regard its principal aim to be to impart knowledge; but it is by no means so if we consider it as designed mainly for the discipline of immature minds. Under the arrangements actually existing and in present circumstances unavoidable, it is impossible to confine the attention of the student with steadiness to any particular subject; and without some such steadiness of effort the benefit of study can not be subjectively great. It is true that diversity of labor, under proper limitations is beneficial; and is in fact indispensable to the attainment of the important educational end of a well balanced mental development; but it is evident that such a diversification may be carried so far as to result rather in a dissipation than a healthful exercise of the mental powers. Our college system may not have reached this extreme; but it is not necessary that it should reach it in order that its usefulness for its original object may be seriously impaired.

A third reason why it is desirable that our colleges should cease to insist upon an invariable curriculum of study throughout the whole extent of the educational course is to be found in the fact that we have no other institutions but these to supply to American youth that advanced training which in Europe is furnished so abundantly by the universities. We profess to comprehend in our teaching nearly every subject of human knowledge; but we are scarcely able to pursue a single one beyond its elements. The majority of our students do not become so proficient, even in the classical tongues, as to be able to read with facility the works of classic authors which they have not read before; and yet these are subjects in which they are required to be tolerably well versed before they enter the college. The only expedient by which it can be made possible for an individual to pursue any given subject to a greater extent, and to attain to greater thoroughness in it than at present, is to permit him, at some period of the course, to devote himself more uninterruptedly to this, and to relinquish other subjects in its favor. Supposing such a freedom to be generally allowed, the tone of the teaching in all the departments of the college will be necessarily raised, and will be, to some extent assimilated to the teaching of the European universities. Those colleges which peculiar circumstances, such as the possession of large resources, or of a wide and well established reputation, conspire to favor, may be able at length to place themselves entirely upon the level of those celebrated foreign institutions. It is probably only by some such gradual transformation of existing institutions, that we shall in this country ever be able to realize the ideal of a continental university. Projects innumerable have been set on foot looking to the independent erection among us of such grand and costly educational establishments; but so long as the highest institutions of this description which we have already, in spite of all the influences, political, denominational, sectional and personal, which can be combined in their favor, continue to be struggling against the difficulties which limited means entail upon them, it is idle to expect that such schemes can succeed, and it would be a manifest wrong if they could. What the country now needs most is that the colleges should be supported and strengthened; what the colleges need is, such improvements in their plan of operations, as shall regain for them the confidence and favor of the people of the country, and shall enable them, or some of them at least, to supply that deficiency in the system of our superior education, which, if not supplied by them, can hardly be supplied at all.

There can be no doubt that a considerable reason why the average age of students in American colleges has become so materially advanced within the last half century, is to be found in the great improvement within that time, of the Secondary Schools. Fifty years ago, almost the only superior schools below the colleges to be found in the country, were those which were devoted to the preparation of boys for entering college; and in these very little was taught beyond the ancient languages. Now, the academies of the State of New York, and the schools of corresponding grade in most of the northern, middle, and western states, give instruction in as large a range of subjects as the colleges themselves. They differ from the colleges in permitting to their pupils the largest freedom of choice in the selection of their studies, and in limiting attendance to no determined period of years. Some of them, perhaps most of them, have established what they call, "a graduating course of study," corresponding to the college curriculum; at the close of which they grant certificates of proficiency, or diplomas, to those who have completed the course; but these certificates confer no rights or privileges, and though often representing an amount of attainment equal to that of many college graduates, do not carry with them a prestige like that which accompanies a degree in Arts. Academies conducted on this plan have all the characteristics of the ordinary college, with the elective system added. Except as to this additional feature, and in being open to both sexes, they do not differ in any material respect from the average college of the country. There are unquestionably academies in the State of New York which, considered as educational instrumentalities, are immensely superior to many institutions elsewhere, which in virtue of a name and a charter are entitled by law to take rank above them. In the list of the subjects taught in these academies there is not one wanting which is to be found in the curriculum of the average college of the United States. This will be apparent from the following enumeration derived from the last annual report of the regents of the university. Omitting the elementary branches, as being of course taught, we find in this enumeration the following, viz., under *mathematics*, alphabetically arranged; algebra, astronomy, calculus, conic sections, engineering, geometry, analytical geometry, descriptive geometry, natural philosophy, (*i. e.* physics in all its branches), leveling, navigation, perspective, surveying, and trigonometry: under *ancient languages;* Greek, Latin, Grecian antiquities, Roman antiquities and mythology: under *modern languages;* French, German, Italian and Spanish: under *natural sciences;* anatomy, physiology, hygiene, botany, chemistry, geology, meteorology, mineralogy, natural history, technology, and zoölogy: and finally, under *moral, intellectual* and *political science;* criticism, christianity (evidences,) general history, history of the United States, history of literature, natural theology, intellectual philosophy, moral philosophy, constitutional law, logic, rhetoric, political economy and the principles of teaching.

Of this system and this programme, the regents of the university, in their eighty-first annual report, remark as follows: "Though these subjects are voluntary with the scholar, and he is permitted to exercise an almost unrestrained freedom of choice, many pursue them all, while others select those to which their peculiar taste prompts them, or which the expected employments of life seem to demand. Young men have often thus been brought from the humblest position in life to commence their studies without any design or expectation of making them exclusive; but as their intellects have been developed, and their desire for knowledge strengthened, they have successfully grappled with difficulties, every new struggle giving them additional power, until the highest means of education have been reached, and they have gone forth into the world to grace the most honorable and responsible positions in society."

The academies of the State of New York fulfill a double function. They are at once schools of elementary training, and schools of superior culture. In the advantages of elementary instruction which they offer, all their pupils more or less participate; the higher instruction benefits a more limited number. Were they restricte dsolely to this superior function, they would occupy the grade and perform substantially the work of the German gymnasia. And that portion of their pupils who pursue the higher course of study correspond approximately in respect to age with the student body of the college as we may presume it to have been from fifty to one hundred years ago. We find, in fact, that of the total number of pupils who were, at one time or another, in attendance upon all the academies of the state, in 1869, (the year embraced in the last published report of the regents)—a total exceeding thirty thousand—about one-third part, or over nine thousand, were engaged in pursuing classical or higher English studies; and the average age of this portion is given at sixteen years and four-tenths. This is the average age of students in a college in which the course of study covers four years, and the students enter as freshmen between fourteen and fifteen.

The total number of the academies in the State, according to the report just cited, is two hundred and twenty-four; but of these there were only one hundred and ninety-eight from which returns had been received. The numbers given above ought perhaps, therefore, to be increased about one-eighth. But these numbers, being the aggregates for the year, should be checked by the reports of average daily attendance. The average daily attendance in one hundred and ninety-eight academies was thirteen thousand three hundred and eighty-two; and the average daily attendance of the higher class of pupils would accordingly be reduced to four thousand and fifty-seven; so that if allowance be made for academies not reporting, it may be stated, in round numbers at forty-five hundred.

The existence of a class of schools of this high character, in which perfect freedom is allowed in the choice of studies, can not but have something to do in turning away students from the colleges which (in their programmes) profess to teach nothing more, but in which the choice is completely fettered. It is in this manner only that a satisfactory explanation can be found of the fact that the State of New York furnishes to the regular colleges of the country a very exceptionally small number of undergraduate students in proportion to the aggregate population. From the returns of the ninth census of the United States it appears that the population of the State of New York amounts at present to 4,374,499. From the collected catalogues of the principle colleges of the Union, amounting to more than one hundred and fifty in all, it appears that the total number of undergraduate students in the department of Arts in these, from the same State, is thirteen hundred and seventy. The State furnishes, therefore, only one undergraduate student to the colleges for every three thousand one hundred and ninety-three inhabitants; while New England furnishes at the same time, one to every one thousand nine hundred and fifty-seven. Now of the forty-five hundred students of the higher class in daily attendance in the academies, at least a fifth part may be assumed to be pursuing the advanced studies of the programme, such as correspond to the later years in college. And if we increase the actual number of undergraduates found as above for New York by nine hundred, the fifth part of forty-five hundred, the result will be to give a proportion of students to population of one to one thousand nine hundred and twenty-seven, very nearly the same as in New England.

There is, moreover, additional evidence that the attractions of the academies sensibly affect the attendance on the colleges, to be found in a more particular examination of the returns of the several academies taken separately, in regard to the ages of their advanced pupils. The average age of all these pupils, in all the academies, is as above stated, sixteen years and four-tenths. But the average age of this class is very different in the different academies; and it is by no means to be presumed that all these institutions, any more than all the colleges, are of one uniform grade of excellence. Accordingly it appears that, whereas in a large number, the average age of the pupils reported as belonging to the advanced class is as low as fifteen or lower, yet in many it is above eighteen, in some above nineteen, and in several even above twenty. Thirty-nine of the academies, in fact, have an aggregate attendance of pupils pursuing advanced studies amounting to two thousand two hundred and eighty-seven, return the average age of these students as above eighteen years. Of this aggregate, two thousand and sixty-nine are between eighteen and nineteen; one hundred and twenty-six between nineteen and twenty; and ninety-two above the age of twenty. The ages of these students correspond to those of college students, and the studies they are pursuing are similar in character to those which are pursued in college. It can not be doubted that some of this large number have chosen the academy rather than the college, on account of the greater freedom which they find there in the selection of their studies.

It is not to be presumed that the teaching of the academies in the higher branches of study can in general compare favorably with that of the colleges, as it respects either method or thoroughness; but it would be unjust to apply this remark universally. That there is great inequality among them, both as it respects efficiency and as it respects the instrumentalities of instruction, is distinctly stated by the regents in their report, in which they say, "if with our present experience, we were to commence our academical system anew, there is little doubt that seventy-five or one hundred academies properly distributed through the state, would, by their strong staff of teachers, their considerable libraries and well selected apparatus, do more effectual service in the cause of education than the present large number of institutions; as many of these, from their want of sufficient endowments and adequate support, are compelled to do much of their work imperfectly." But many of them are schools of very superior merit and efficiency, and these are doing, at the present time, a great part of that work of disciplinary education which has been so much insisted on as being the proper work of the colleges. It is by these schools that the colleges are principally fed, as in Germany the universities are fed by the gymnasia; and it is to be presumed that, in progress of time, by the strengthening and elevation of both, these two classes of institutions, thus independent of each other but still intimately related, may create upon this continent a system of superior education practically parallel with that of continental Europe. All our colleges, it is true, can not become universities. If the change here anticipated should go on, some will continue to maintain but a secondary rank, some will probably be absorbed by others, and some will perhaps at length become extinct. It is true already of these institutions, as the regents have found it to be of the academies, that their number is greatly in excess of the wants of the country, and that the efficiency of the system would be materially promoted, if it could be reduced.

The principle objection to the elective system of study has always been that which is derived, as above stated, from the theory of a liberal education considered as demanding a well-rounded development of the faculties. We have seen that the force of this objection rests upon an assumption which can no longer be admitted—the assumption, namely, that the college student is throughout the course of that tender age in which educational influences may do a great deal more than merely to brighten and invigorate such faculties as he has; in which such influences may in fact actually give them shape and form, and evolve or repress them at pleasure. Other objections have been suggested of less apparent weight, which still should not be permitted to pass without examination, nor without an attempt to provide securities against the dangers which they indicate. If the choice of studies is free, young men, it is said, will exercise it capriciously, and will possibly pass from subject to subject without continuing long enough at any one to derive from it substantial advantage. By granting freedom of choice, however, it is not to be presumed that such a freedom is intended as would permit a student to change from day to day, or from week to week. The study which is chosen must be chosen as a whole, and must be pursued to the end, or to the end, at least, of some branch of it which is complete in itself. This rule will prevent capricious changes, and will secure at least as much continuity of attention to particular subjects as the ordinary curriculum allows; for the very fault of the ordinary curriculum is that, during the later years at least, it presents so large a number of subjects that long continued study of any one of them is impossible.

But it is further objected that the free exercise of choice permits a selection of such studies as present the fewest difficulties; and thus plays directly into the hand of the careless and inefficient student. To this it may be replied, as the result of a pretty long observation, that the incorrigibly idle are not perceptibly improved in diligence by being compelled to pursue difficult studies. In every considerable body of students there will always be some such. And it is truly marvelous to remark how very closely such individuals manage to run to the very minimum of attainment required to save them from being dropped from the rolls as hopelessly deficient. Now the benefit which such individuals can derive from being compelled to pursue what they call "hard studies," are insignificant in comparison with the harm they do to others, who, being yoked with them in the same classes, are hampered in their progress by their dullness or their willful neglect of study. It is one of the great advantages of the principle of election, that these drags upon progress are effectually eliminated by it; so that the strong men and the willing men can go along together and turn their strength and their zeal to substantial account. The man who, at the age of nineteen, which in Columbia College is the age of entering upon the junior year, can be so indifferent to his own improvement, and so averse to mental effort, as to choose his studies deliberately with a view of getting rid of work, can hardly be constrained to work upon studies chosen for him. And the experience of our own college, which, though brief, is still worth something, indicates that facts are not likely to justify the apprehension on which this objection is founded.

It may be regarded as nearly certain that, in the case of every student as to whom it is of the slightest consequence one way or the other what he chooses, the choice will be determined not by caprice nor a pitiful desire to shirk labor; but by a natural taste or liking for one subject rather than another, or by an honest desire to know. The preliminary and more elementary part of the course furnishes the opportunity to compare different subjects, so far as to enable the student to judge what he is likely to pursue in its larger development with the greatest satisfaction and therefore with the largest substantial results; and upon the basis of this knowledge his choice will be made. That this is true is made almost demonstrably evident in the selections of elective studies made at the beginning of the last academic year by the members of our senior class; when the study commonly reputed to be the most difficult (metaphysics) was chosen by two-thirds of the class; while that which passes for the easiest, and to many is the most fascinating, (chemistry) was chosen by fewer than one-fourth.

That the elective system is not at present more largely adopted in American colleges is owing, in good degree, to the fact that it increases considerably the number of exercises which the officers are required to conduct; and imposes very soon the necessity of enlarging the academic staff. The question is not therefore purely an educational one; but it is complicated by economical considerations. It is not possible that the system should be introduced into all the colleges; and out of this circumstance is likely to grow, sooner or later, a classification into grades. Out of the higher grade, embracing the smaller number, will probably be developed the universities, if we are to have such, which are to rival those of continental Europe. The lower will remain what they are or will disappear.

It is now about eighteen months since the elective system was introduced into Columbia College to a limited extent and applied to a portion of the studies of the senior year. The results of the first experiment, as stated in the brief notice given of it in the last annual report of the president, were so satisfactory, as to induce the committee on the statutes to authorize its further extension. After the lapse of another year, the president is prepared to speak with greater confidence than before, and in terms of more decided satisfaction. As it was last year stated that the senior class had never before been so steadily attentive to study up to the close of the year, so it may be said at the present time that the diligence of the class throughout the whole year has been to a very marked degree satisfactory. The officers have noticed a greater manifestation of interest in the subjects studied than has been observed in former years; and they agree, it is believed, in ascribing this result to the fact that the studies are voluntarily chosen.

It is not perhaps practicable for us for the present to give to the elective system a larger extension than it has already received. In order that, among the studies submitted to the choice of the student, it may be practicable to select any desired combination at will, it is necessary that the scheme of attendance shall be so arranged that the hours allotted to all these studies may be different. In Columbia College at present, the exercises occupy only three consecutive hours in the morning of each day, giving to each class fifteen hours per week. Of these fifteen hours, about half must be devoted to the required studies of the course; so that only seven or eight at furthest remain available for the optional studies. In consequence of this, it has been found thus far impracticable to construct the scheme so as to prevent different optional studies from falling upon the same hour; but the studies coinciding have been generally those between which the election would naturally fall; and thus the latitude of choice maintained has been greater than would at first appear. The plan is one, however, which can be carried no further; and it would be better if it were not carried so far.

No remedy presents itself for this difficulty, but to extend the exercises over a larger number of the hours of the day; and this is what, ultimately, if the system is maintained, will have to be done. But in making such an extension, it will inevitably happen that there will occur occasionally hours in which a class or portion of a class will have no exercise; and for the profitable employment of these at such intervals, it is impossible at present to make provision. This would be no embarrassment but rather an advantage, if accommodations could be found in the college building for the unoccupied classes, so as to enable them, with the aid of their textbooks and other authorities, to read up the subject of the ensuing lecture. In fact, after considerable observation of the varying practices of colleges in the distribution of their time, we are clearly of opinion that it is much more profitable to the student to alternate study with his lectures or recitations, than to prepare all his exercises for an entire day at once, and afterward give his attendance in the class-rooms for three consecutive hours. As the long-continued strain upon the mental faculties in continuous study is wearying in one way, so the long-continued bodily confinement in successive classes is wearying in another. By breaking up these protracted periods, and alternating briefer seasons of active effort with intervals of comparative repose, it seems reasonable to believe that more beneficial results may be secured, as it respects both the culture of the mind and the health of the body. It is an advantage enjoyed by colleges in which students and instructors reside together and form a compact community, that any division of the day which seems best, may be adopted with equal convenience. This advantage may also be enjoyed by colleges in country villages, whether they provide lodgings for their students or not; for neither students nor instructors, can, in such places, be remote from the academic centre. But the same is not true in large cities, though to a certain extent it may be made so, by providing, as just suggested, convenient apartments in which students may study in common during the intervals between the academic exercises.

In the numerous occasional discourses which he has been called on to prepare and publish, Dr. Hopkins has expressed his views on a great variety of educational topics, specimen of which we give below.

### EDUCATION.

*Inaugural Discourse*, 1836.

By education, I mean, not merely formal instruction, but any system of excitement or restraint the object of which is to effect some definite change in the physical, intellectual, or moral character of man. The term, I know, is often used, in a broader sense, to include every thing in external nature, and in the circumstances of the individual, which can exert an influence upon him, whether intended to exert such influence or not. That there are circumstances in local situation, and in the structure of society, the influence of which can not be avoided, and which yet often control the character and destiny of the young, there can be no doubt. Climate, the form of government, childhood spent in the city or in the country, in luxury or in poverty, and perhaps more than all, early and casual impressions caught from first associates, operate imperceptibly, but irresistibly, in modifying and giving variety to character. But though the influence upon the mind of causes beyond our countrol, may be an interesting subject of speculation, just as is the influence of gravity on matter, and though these causes may form a part of that tutelage under which in the providence of God his creatures are put, and we may, if we please, call it the education of circumstances, yet if we regard the common use of language, or if we would define a practical science, we must include in the term Education, only those circumstances over which we have a control, and which we can and do bring to bear upon man with the intention of effecting a particular end.

But whether we consider education as comprising more or less, or whatever division we may make of it, the general principle which we are to regard, especially in its second part, which is positive instruction, is now settled among all thinking men. It is, that we are to regard the mind, not as a piece of iron to be laid upon the anvil and hammered into any shape, nor as a block of marble in which we are to find the statue by removing the rubbish, nor as a receptacle into which knowledge may be poured; but as a flame that is to be fed, as an active being that must be strengthened to think and to feel—to dare, to do, and to suffer. It is as a germ, expanding, under the influence certainly of air and sunlight and moisture, but yet only through the agency of an internal force; and external agency is of no value except as it elicits, and controls, and perfects the action of that force. He only who can rightly appreciate the force of this principle, and carry it out into all its consequences, in the spirit of the maxim, that nature is to be conquered only by obeying her laws, will do all that belongs to the office of a teacher.

### SELF-EDUCATION.

*Inaugural Discourse*, 1836.

We hear much said about self-educated men, and a broad distinction is made between them and others; but the truth is, that every man who is educated at all, is, and must be, self-educated. There are no more two methods in which the mind can make progress, than there are two methods in which plants can grow. One seed may be blown by the winds, and cast upon the southern, or perchance on the northern side of some distant hill, and may there germinate, and take root, and do battle alone with the elements, and it may be so favored by the soil and climate that it shall lift itself in surpassing strength and beauty; another may be planted carefully in a good soil, and the hand of tillage may be applied to it, yet must this also draw for itself nutriment from the soil, and for itself withstand the rush of the tempest, and lift its head on high only as it strikes its roots deep in the earth. It is for the want of understanding this properly, that extravagant expectations are entertained of instructors, and of institutions; and that those who go to college sometimes expect, and the community expect, that they will be learned of course—as if they could be inoculated with knowledge, or obtain it by absorption. This broad distinction between self-educated men and others has done harm; for young men will not set themselves efficiently at work until they feel that there is an all important part which they must perfect for themselves, and which no one can do for them.

### CHIEF EXCELLENCIES OF A TEACHER.

*Inaugural Discourse*, 1836.

And I here mention, that from this view of the subject, it is easy to see what it is that constitutes the first excellence of an instructor. It is not his amount of knowledge, nor yet his facility of communication, important as these may be; but it is his power to give an impulse to the minds of his pupils, and to induce them to labor. For this purpose, nothing is so necessary as a disinterested devotion to the work, and a certain enthusiasm which may act by sympathy on the minds of the young. It is from the decay of this that courses of lectures and of instruction, once attractive, often cease to interest. When a teacher has advanced so far beyond his class, or has become so familiar with his subject, as to feel no interest in its truths, then, however well he may understand them, and however clearly he may state them, he is not all that a teacher ought to be. He who carries the torchlight into the recesses of science, and shows the gems that are sparkling there, must not be a mere hired conductor, who is to bow in one company, and bow out another, and show what is to be seen with a heartless indifference; but must have an ever living fountain of emotion, that will flow afresh as he contemplates anew the works of God and the great principles of truth and duty. This is no more impossible in regard to the beauties and wonders which science discloses, than it is in regard to the more obvious appearances of nature, and the instructor may adopt in spirit the words of the poet—

"My heart leaps up when I behold
A Rainbow in the sky;
So was it when my life began;
So is it now I am a Man;
So be it when I shall grow old,
Or let me die!
The Child is Father of the Man;
And I could wish my days to be
Bound each to each by natural piety."

It is such an one alone who can know the pleasure of carrying forward a class of ingenuous youth, and watching them as they gain new positions, and take in wider views till the whole prospect is at their command. And when, as sometimes happens, he has a class of an opposite character, and his instructions fall dead, and no interest is excited, it is he alone who can know the anxiety, I had almost said agony, with which, as the prophet of old upon the dead body of the child, he once and again as it were puts his mouth to its mouth, and his eyes to its eyes, and stretches himself upon the class, and finds no life come. And he alone knows how cheerless and hopeless and slavish is the dull routine of his labors after that. There are, it seems to me, few modes of gaining a living short of actual villainy, which a man of sensibility would not prefer to it.

### FEMALE EDUCATION.

*Address at Anniversary of Mount Holyoke Seminary.*

Important as female education is now admitted to be, it is not perhaps surprising that it did not receive early attention. Men attack evils as they find them, without first investigating secret influences and remote causes. It was natural, for instance, that intemperance should first be attacked as it existed in the intemperate, before it was traced back to its source in temperate drinking. And so it was natural that mankind should first attempt to control the waters of society as they found them flowing on, impetuous and turbid, before tracing them up to their source and purifying the springs from which they flowed.

This attempt has been made from the beginning and is still made. It is not even yet understood how true it is, in the body politic as well as in the natural body, that "if one member suffer, all the members suffer with it," that if one portion of the community be enslaved, or oppressed, or degraded, there will be sown indirectly the seeds of vice, of debility, and of ultimate dissolution; and especially, that if those who hold to us the relations of wives, and mothers, and daughters, and sisters, are restricted, or cramped, or in any way prevented from receiving that expansion of the intellect and of the affections which will enable them to exert an elevating and a purifying influence upon man, society can not reach its full stature and perfection. It is not understood how high those qualities of the intellect and of the heart are, which are needed for the right management of the young, how much light and how much love must shine around the opening bud of early childhood that it may expand in fair proportions; it is not understood how early the ductile material of character begins to grow rigid, so that before the age of eight, or even of six, it generally assumes lineaments to which subsequent life only serves to give greater prominence. In forming that material, *man* can not do what ought to be done, he can not undo what *will be* done by a mother who is ignorant or weak, or selfish or unprincipled; and whatever influence he may wish to exert, will be far more efficient if he has the coöperation of one who can enter fully into all his views—just as the oak will cast a shade that is deeper and more refreshing if the vine that adorns it mingles its leaves with those of every branch, and entwines itself to the topmost bough.

But these truths are beginning to be understood and felt, and there are probably more persons now than ever before, who feel that if we are ever to do any thing effectual for the improvement of society, the proper place to begin at is the beginning—that the influence that presides over the cradle, and the nursery, and the fireside, must be a right influence.

### EDUCATION IN CONNECTION WITH NATURE AND RELIGION.

*Address at Missionary Jubilee*, 1856.

No service can be rendered to education so great as to bring it into a closer and more vital connection with religion, and through that, with some form of great and heroic action. But the educating power of an institution is not solely from what that institution is at any given moment—from its buildings, its apparatus, its libraries, its teachers; it also lies much in the influences of nature and of society around it; in the memories of the past, and in its connection with great interests and events. No man worth educating, ever passed through this College without being in part educated by these great mountains. Greylock is an educator. They are of a style and an order of architecture that is very ancient, and, though they cost nothing, are worth more than any ever devised by man. We do not wish to educate merely the intellect, but also the moral nature; to control the associations and to reach the springs of action. Surely there must be a legitimate use of association in education, not superstitious or idolatrous; and we wish to associate literature and science with all that is beautiful and grand in nature, and all that is pure and elevating in religion. We wish to link in minds of the highest culture, sentiments of veneration and honor with humble prayer, and with devotion to the cause of Christ. Oh, sir, if this could but be, if indolence and vice could but be banished from this College, if there could be here two hundred and twenty young men, fully receiving the influences of nature which God has spread around them, and fully yielding themselves to the power of that religion which he has revealed, I would not exchange my position for any one upon earth.

### ACADEMIES.

*Dedication of Williston Seminary*, 1841.

If this institution prepares better teachers for the common schools, they will send back to it scholars better prepared, and it may be able, after a time, to relinquish to the common school some of its branches, and to elevate its own course. If, again, it sends scholars to college better fitted, college, to say nothing of other and indirect benefits, will send back to it better instructors, and may, in its turn, be able to relinquish to it some part of its course. This process has, indeed, gone on to some extent within my remembrance, but it needs to go much farther. I see no other way in which our general system of education can be elevated. We need, and must have, institutions like this, which shall give a thorough preparat.on for college in the English as well as classical department, and which shall not only be thorough as far as they go, but shall carry the student much farther than he now goes in them. I see no difficulty in it, and I hope to see the day when almost all that is now studied in the freshman class in college, especially in languages, shall be required for admission, and shall be thoroughly taught in schools like this. This would relieve the colleges from the heavy load they are obliged to drag when the classes are poorly prepared, and would give them time, not only to be more full and thorough in their present branches of science, but to introduce new ones as the wants of the age may require.

### MEDICAL SCIENCE.

*Address to Medical Class at Pittsfield*, 1840.

The principal of life then, lies at the foundation of the science of medicine; but it is to be studied as manifested in this wonderful range of productions only by the physician? Certainly not. We might as well say that no one should study the science of music except those whose business it is to repair musical instruments. In its regular manifestations the principle of life presents itself as one of the great principles of nature, inviting equally with gravitation, or light, or magnetism, or electricity, the study of every liberal and inquiring mind. This I know has not been so regarded, but it is coming to be so more and more. It ought, at least, to enter somewhat largely into every course of liberal education, and I trust that in one college at least, more will be done with reference to it than has been done.

On this point physicians themselves have perhaps been in fault, or at least have misjudged. They have been inclined to regard the whole domain as their own, and to publish books, especially on human physiology, solely for the use of the profession. This, however, has been much less the case within the last few years, and the change can not fail to be advantageous both to the public and to the profession. It will be advantageous to the public, because, by giving them a knowledge of the laws of health, which are nothing more than the conditions on which the principle of life will act with regularity, much disease will be prevented; and it will be of advantage to the profession, because it will furnish the only possible guard against the prevalence of quackery, which is found to deposit its eggs and mature its growth upon ignorance alone. Nor would it encroach upon the proper province or science of the physician, if the whole of physiology were well understood by the community; for though the principle of life lies at the foundation of the science of the physician, yet if it were like gravitation, and never irregular in its action, there would be no physicians or science of medicine. The laws of life manifested in regular action ought to be understood by every body, so far at least as is necessary to preserve health. It is only as it manifests itself in diseased action, that the principle of life lies at the foundation of medical science. Diseased action, and the means of controlling it—diseases and remedies—these are the appropriate subjects of the study of the physician.

As a prerequisite to the knowledge of diseases, anatomy and physiology are necessary; to the knowledge of remedies, chemistry and botany. No physician can be fully qualified to practice his profession unless he is acquainted with these sciences; and the field of observation and of general cultivation to the mind which they open is so wide, that from its connection with them, if from nothing else, the profession of medicine would be entitled to the rank of a liberal profession.

### THEOLOGICAL EDUCATION.

*Address before Porter Rhetorical Society, Andover*, 1837.

In its literal signification, and in its highest character, the Gospel is good tidings; and it is the grand business of those who preach it, to commend it as worthy of all acceptation to them that are lost. Nothing can compensate in a preacher for the want of a heartfelt conviction of the ruin of man, and that the Gospel is the all-sufficient and the only remedy; and nothing can excuse him if he do not urge the acceptance of this remedy upon his fellow-men with his utmost force of intellect and energy of feeling. His appropriate office is to preach the Gospel of peace, to bring glad tidings of good things, to stand as an ambassador for Christ, and to beseech men in his stead to be reconciled to God.

But though this is the chief, it is not the only relation which the preacher holds to society, for, as the light of the sun not only reveals to us the azure depths from which it comes, but also quickens vegetation into life and spreads a mantle of beauty over the earth, so does the Gospel of Christ not only reveal our relations to God and the heaven which is to be our home, but it is spread over all the social relations, and is an essential element in the production of that moral verdure without which society would be a waste. Where the Sun of Righteousness shines, the whole soil is meliorated. The hemlock and the night-shade grow less rankly, the natural affections expand more fully and shed a sweeter fragrance, and the seed sown bears fruit for *this* life as well as for that which is to come. The system which the preacher advocates is therefore not isolated and arbitrary; it is not a foreign and discordant mass, thrown into society and fitted only to be a source of terror to some, of ridicule to others, and a curse to all; but it has relations to the works of God, to the social and political well-being of man, to the secret thoughts and hidden structure as well as to the future destiny of the soul. It is only in the atmosphere of a pure Christianity that social man can attain his true stature. In this he moves and respires freely; while every other system is like an atmosphere more or less deprived of its vital principle, and lies like an atmosphere more or less deprived of its vital principle, and lies like an oppressive and suffocating weight upon him. As well then may the natural philosopher rest satisfied with his knowledge of the literal atmosphere as the breath of life, and disregard its connection with vegetation, and its use in evaporating water and reflecting light and conveying sound and facilitating commerce, as may the student of Christianity consider it simply in its relation to another world, without regarding its connection with the works of God, and its present influence on the well-being of society.

### OBJECTIONS TO COLLEGES.

*Inaugural Discourse*, 1836.

And first, it is objected that colleges destroy physical vigor. There has, no doubt, been ground for this objection. From its local situation, this college has probably suffered less in this way than some others, and there has been here, especially of late, comparatively little failure of the health. Something has been done, but there is still room for improvement. It ought, however, no more to be expected that the student should have the same robustness of frame and muscular vigor as the laboring man, than that the laboring man should have the same intellectual cultivation as the student. But the truth is that students, in common with other classes of the community, not only do not exercise enough, but they live in the constant violation of all the rules of dietetics. Some have used, and still use, intoxicating drinks; a much larger number use tobacco; some are constantly eating dried fruits and various kinds of confectionery; many eat too much; many sit up late under the excitement of novel reading, and perhaps for study. Let their food be of proper quantity and quality, let them avoid poisonous and narcotic substances, let them keep regular hours, and shun the predominence of an excited or polluted imagination; and they will find that there is an elasticity in the human frame that requires exercise. Nor need it be aimless exercise. Let them saw their own wood, let botany and mineralogy lead them over the hills, let them cherish a love of fine prospects, let them cultivate the taste and manly spirit that have originated and carried forward so happily in this college, the horticultural and landscape gardening association; and there will be cheeks as fresh, and limbs as agile, and animal spirits as buoyant, as if they spent three hours a day in a workshop, and, (which would be necessary in some of our institutions,) as if a thousand dollars a year were expended to enable them to do something useful. It has been a fault, which I trust will be avoided here, that this subject has not been sufficiently urged upon students in the early part of their course.

Again; it is objected that colleges are not practical. There are some who seem to be slow in understanding what is meant by the discipline of the mind, or mental training, as if it were different in its principle from a military drill, in which a series of actions is performed, not so much for its own sake as a preparation for the future battle. It is true the discipline must be such as will fit them for the combat. We must not put bows and arrows into their hands when they will have to use the cartridge-box and the musket—but discipline there must be. We are indeed to consult utility, but it must be in its highest and broadest sense —not that eager utility which would cut down the tree for the sake of sooner getting its fruit, its unripe fruit; but that far-sighted utility, which would plough a crop under for the sake of benefiting the soil, and which would look forward to the coincidence of its plans with the high purposes of God in the creation of man. But if there are any who never make a distinction between general and professional education, who look upon man solely as a being who is to be fitted to make money in some particular sphere, and not as one who has faculties to be perfected, to them I have nothing to say.

Again; it is objected that colleges do not keep up with the spirit of the age. This objection probably does not always assume a definite form in the minds of those who make it. But if it be intended that improvements in the sciences are not ingrafted, as they are made, upon the scientific courses, or that new sciences are not introduced as the wants of the public demand; if it be intended that there is an adherence to things that are old because they are old—then, however much ground there may have been for the charge formerly, and especially in England, from which this complaint is mostly imported, I do not think there is any ground for it now. It is within the memory of our older graduates that chemistry, and geology, and mineralogy, and botany, and political economy, were either not taught at all, or scarcely at all, in the college course. These have been introduced as fast as the sciences have become so mature as to furnish good text-books; and now if the public will furnish us the means, we shall be glad to introduce more of modern languages, and something on constitutional law, which we intend to introduce, and perspective, and civil engineering.

Again; it is objected to colleges that they are aristocratic. Besides those who form no theory of society, there are two classes who would be thought to aim at the perfection and perpetuity of republican institutions, but their methods are directly opposite. The one can conceive of no improvement except by leveling every thing down—and probably there always will exist in every community a sediment of such people, whose uneasy malignity, manifesting itself in a pretended zeal for republicanism, nothing but a return of society to a savage state could satisfy. The other class do what they can to level up. And if there be one of these who imagines that colleges are not coöperating with him, it is because he is entirely ignorant of the facts. Must men be told at this day that the diffusion of knowledge is the only safety of republican institutions? Or are they ignorant that without higher seminaries the lower can never be sustained in any efficiency? Or that if there were not some institutions like colleges, to make education cheap, we should soon have an aristocracy of knowledge and refinement as well as of wealth? On this subject there is a mistake in regard to two points. One respects the class of persons who go to college. While a portion of these are sons of wealthy men, the great mass are the sons of clergymen, and farmers, and tradesmen, who feel that an education is the best patrimony they can bestow upon their children, and who are unable to give them even that, unless they assist themselves in part by teaching. The most of those therefore who graduate at our colleges spend no inconsiderable portion of time, either before or after graduating, in teaching, and thus diffusing the blessings of general education. The other point on which there is a mistake, respects the real extent to which the cost of education is diminished. At this college a young man receives instruction, and has the use of the buildings, and library, and apparatus, and cabinet, and pays the college but about thirty-three dollars a year. The whole necessary expense per annum is less than one hundred dollars; a sum quite insufficient to maintain a boy in a common family school. In addition to this, we have funds bestowed by benevolent individuals, which enable us to appropriate something to meet the bills of those who promise to be useful but are not able to pay so much. Still the whole expense is greater than is desirable, and if our funds would permit it we would gladly make it less. It thus that the poor man who has no farm to give his son, can give him an education, which, if he is a suitable person to be educated, is better. He is thus enabled to start fairly in the race of competition with the sons of the wealthy. In a class in college, each is on a perfect equality with the rest, and must stand on his own merits; and if the son of the rich should happen to have the advantage in previous training, he may yet find that he will have as much as he will care to do to maintain it in the field of open competition; and often when he does his best, much more if he become vain or frivolous or self-indulgent, will he find himself left behind by the stern efforts of those who feel that they must depend on themselves alone. Surely he who would tax and cripple colleges, would tax and depress general education, and keep down the people.

The last objection against colleges which I shall notice, comes from another quarter, and is, that they do not teach manners. And it must be confessed that this is not one of those things for which we give a diploma. Good manners certainly ought to exist and to be acquired in colleges, and more ought to be done on this point than is done. Still there are difficulties in the way which will be appreciated by every sensible man. In the first place, manners can not be taught by direct inculcation; they must mainly depend on parents and on associates during the earlier years of life. Again, many of those who come to college are of such an age that it would be impossible to remodel their manners entirely under the most favorable circumstances. They seem to have lost the power, which indeed some never had, of perceiving the difference between the easy intercourse of good fellowship which is consistent with self-respect and respect toward others, and a coarse familiarity which is consistent with neither. There is further a sentiment often prevalent among young men, than which no mistake could be greater, that manners are of little importance, and that to be slovenly and slouching, and perhaps well nigh disrespectful, is a mark of independence. But after all, college is not, in some respects, a bad place to wear off rusticity and break down timidity. And if those who make the complaint could see the transformation and improvement which really take place in many, I may say in most instances, in a college course, they would perhaps wonder that so much is accomplished, rather than complain that there is so little.' Still, when a young man comes with a frame of granite rough from the mountains, or as rough as if he came from them, and has seen perhaps nothing of polite society, and knows nothing of polite literature, it can not be expected that he should learn during his college course the manners of the drawing-room, or the arbitrary forms of fashionable etiquette. If he shall possess, as perhaps such men oftenest do, that higher form of politeness which consists in respecting the feelings of others and consulting their happiness, and we can send him into the world with a sound head and a warm heart to labor for the good of the world, we shall be satisfied, and the world ought to be thankful. Such men often become the pillars of society.

### EMOTIONS OF TASTE MODIFIED BY OUR VIEWS OF GOD.

*Lecture—Connection between Taste and Morals.*

And if the emotions of taste are thus modified by our views of man, how much more must they be by those respecting God! How must a blank atheism hang the heavens in sackcloth, and cover the earth with a pall, and turn the mute promisings of nature into a mockery, and make of her mighty fabric one great charnel-house of death without the hope of a resurrection! On the other hand, how must the beauty and sublimity of nature and of the universe be hightened, the moment we perceive them in their connection with God! Nothing is more common than to hear those, who emerge from that practical atheism in which most men live, speak of the new perceptions of beauty and sublimity with which they look upon the works of nature.

All our investigations into nature show that man has no faculties to which there are not corresponding and adequate objects. As infinite as he is in reason, yet the works of God are not exhausted by the operations of that reason: no intellectual Alexander ever sat down and wept for the want of more worlds to conquer. As vast as is his imagination, the revelations of astronomy, as sober facts, go beyond any thing that the imagination had conceived. And is it so, that, in the region of taste alone, the faculties of man have no adequate object? But it is only when nature, like the Bible, is seen to be full of God, that she is clothed with her true sublimity. It is only when "the heavens declare the glory of God, and the firmament showeth his handy work," that they correspond to the highest conceptions either of the taste or of the intellect. Man rests in the Infinite alone, and the universe without a God is not in harmony with his constitution, even when he is considered as endowed with taste only. But if our views on moral subjects thus modify the emotions of taste, it can not be doubted that those emotions react upon our moral views, tending to elevate and purify them.

# COEDUCATION OF THE SEXES.

AN ADDRESS BEFORE A MEETING OF COLLEGE PRESIDENTS AT SPRINGFIELD, ILL.

BY REV. JAMES H. FAIRCHILD, D. D., OF OBERLIN COLLEGE, JULY 10TH, 1867.

---

MR. PRESIDENT, AND GENTLEMEN OF THE ASSOCIATION:

THE invitation extended to me by your Executive Committee, to share in your deliberations upon this question, was based upon the fact of my connection with a school in which the system of education under discussion has been in operation for many years; and it was intended that I should present the subject in the light of that experience. It seems more fitting to confine myself to arrangements and results at Oberlin, stated descriptively and historically, than to attempt any general discussion of the subject—a work more appropriate to the members of the Association.

That I may speak without restraint upon these matters, it is proper for me to say that I entered the College as a boy at its opening, and served seven years as a pupil before entering upon the responsibilities of a member of its board of instruction. Thus I appear before you as one of the children of the school, and not one of the fathers, and shall not seem to speak of the work of my own hands, as I claim no personal responsibility for the wisdom or folly of the arrangement.

Oberlin College is now in the thirty-fourth year of its life, and from the beginning has embraced among its pupils both young men and young women. The first year it was a high school, with something over a hundred pupils, more than one-third of whom were ladies: not a local school, for the enterprise started in the woods, and one-half of the students at least were from New England and New York. The second year the numbers increased to nearly 300, with theological and college classes in full operation, the ladies being about one-fourth of the whole. In two or three years the numbers reached 500, and maintained that annual average until 1852, when the number was suddenly doubled, and has averaged more than a thousand yearly for the last fifteen years. The proportion of young ladies has not for many years fallen below one-third, nor risen above one-half, except during the war, when the ladies predominated in the ratio of five to four. The last Annual Catalogue gives 655 gentlemen and 490 ladies, and this is about the normal proportion. These are young men and women of such ages as the advanced schools of the land generally present.

The *town* began with the school and has kept pace with it, containing at present from 3,000 to 4,000 inhabitants. At first, almost all the accommodations for the students in room and board were furnished by the College. The dormitory system was adopted for both young men and young women, separate halls or buildings being assigned to each—the ladies' hall being also a boarding-hall, in which seats at table were provided for young men. As the numbers increased and the dwellings in the village were improved and multiplied, the students were to a greater extent provided for among the families, until at present far the greater number are thus furnished with homes. Our present ladies' hall affords rooms for about 100 young ladies, and sittings at table for about 220 boarders. Large boarding-houses are not found; but a majority of families that have room receive a few students. The young ladies find their homes under this arrangement as well as the young men. Some families receive young ladies only; but families are permitted, with suitable arrangements, to receive both classes. The entire female department is under the immediate charge of a lady Principal, and her assistant; and these are occupied, not with teaching, to any considerable extent, but with the care and supervision of the young ladies, their classification and general culture. These principals communicate, as occasion may require, with the matrons of the families where the young ladies board. The special discipline of the young ladies is committed to the lady Principal, assisted by a 'Ladies' Board of Managers,' composed in general of wives of professors in the college. The advice of the College Faculty is sometimes taken, but the young ladies do not come before them for special discipline. The regulations of the school, for both ladies and gentlemen, are intended to be addressed to the good sense and personal responsibility of the pupil. We have no monitors, but each one makes a weekly report of success or failure in the performance of prescribed duties: young ladies boarding in families have their report countersigned by the matron of the house, who is in a degree responsible for the conduct of her charge. The ladies' hall is the headquarters of the female department, where the Principal receives all the ladies for general instruction and for personal advice.

Throughout the literary departments the classes consist of young men and young women, taken indiscriminately, as their studies correspond. The larger numbers of both sexes are found in our Preparatory Department—a department which embraces, besides those preparing for the regular courses, a large number that study for a more limited time. This department is under the charge of a gentleman Principal, whose strength is expended chiefly upon oversight, classification, and discipline, and an associate Professor of Languages, who gives himself to the teaching of the advanced classes in Latin and Greek. The other classes in this department are taught by successful pupils (gentlemen and ladies) from the higher departments. After the Preparatory Department, we have two courses open to young ladies—the 'Ladies' Course,' and the regular 'College Course.' The Ladies' Course is a course of four years, requiring, as conditions of entering, a good elementary English education, and a year's study of Latin. It embraces all the studies of the regular College course, omitting all the Greek and most of the Latin, omitting also the Differential and Integral Calculus, and adding lessons in French and Drawing, and some branches of natural science. Those pursuing this course recite with the college classes in the same studies. Separate classes are organized for the ladies in essay-writing until the commencement of the third year, when they are added to the Junior College class in this exercise. Their training in this department is limited to reading and writing, none of the ladies having any exercise in speaking. The great majority of our young ladies pursue this course, and it was supposed at the organization of the school that nothing farther would be required for them; but in 1837 four young ladies prepared themselves for the Freshman class, and were received upon their own petition. Since that time it has been understood that the College Course is open to young ladies, and we have always had more or less in the classes: sometimes the proportion of ladies to gentlemen in the course has been as high as one to four; at present it is one to ten. We have observed no special tendency to an increase in this proportion; for the last three years there has been a diminution. The ladies in this course are under the same general regulations and discipline as in the other course, and are responsible to the lady Principal. At the termination of their course they receive the regular degree in the Arts. Eighty-four ladies have received this degree, and three hundred and ninety-five have received the diploma of the Ladies' Course.

The Theological Department has never been opened to ladies, as regular members. Two young ladies attended upon all the exercises of the department through a three-years course, and were entered upon the Annual Catalogue as 'resident graduates pursuing the Theological course.' This was nearly twenty years ago, and we have had no applications since. Doubtless the same privileges would be afforded as formerly.

The association of gentlemen and ladies out of the class-room is regulated as experience seems to require. They sit at the same table in families and in the Ladies' Hall. Young gentlemen call on ladies in a social way at the parlors of the Ladies' Hall and of private families, between the hour for tea and half-past seven in the winter, and eight o'clock in the summer. They walk in groups from one class-room to another, as convenience and their sense of propriety may dictate, with the help of a suggestion, if needed, from thoughtful and observing friends. Now and then the young ladies have permission to attend an evening lecture given under the auspices of the College, and in such case to accept the attendance of young men. No such association is permitted in the case of religious meetings. They do not ride or walk together beyond the limits of the village, except on a holyday, under special arrangements. There is no association of the sexes in literary societies, or other voluntary and independent organizations.

It seemed necessary to give this detail of arrangements, that the conditions upon which the solution of the problem has been conducted with us may be fully understood. In speaking of results, I wish to be understood as giving not merely my own individual judgment, but the unanimous opinion, so far as I understand it, of all who have had responsibility in connection with the school. If there has been any diversity of sentiment on the subject, it has been unknown to me. Others might choose different terms in which to express their opinions, but I shall endeavor to make no statement from which I suppose that any one of those that are or have been associated in this work would dissent.

Among the advantages which seem to be involved in the system, as we have observed its operation, are the following:

1. Economy of means and forces. The teaching force and other apparatus required in all the higher departments of study is made available to a larger number. In most Western Colleges the higher classes might be doubled without any detriment, and often with great advantage. Scarce any one of these schools has had larger classes than our own, and yet only once or twice have we had occasion to make two divisions in any college class, including the ladies pursuing the same study. In the preparatory department, classes must be multiplied on account of numbers; but in the higher departments of instruction, where the chief expense is involved, the expense is no greater on account of the presence of

ladies. If a separate establishment were attempted for ladies, affording the same advantages, the outlay in men and means would have to be duplicated; or, as would often happen, the force would have to be divided, and the advantages as well. Of course, if there were obvious disadvantages in the arrangement, the argument from economy would have essentially no weight. We must have the best system of higher education at any necessary cost.

2. Convenience to the patrons of the school. It has been a matter of interest with us to note the number of cases in which a brother is accompanied or followed by a sister, or a sister by a brother. I can not give exact statements upon this point; but it is an interesting and prominent feature in our operations. This is most convenient and wholesome; each is safer from the presence of the other; and the inducements to attend school, to the one or the other, are increased by the possibility of having each other's company. The want and tendency in this direction are shown in the fact that in the vicinity of every flourishing college, opened for young men only, a ladies' school, equally flourishing, is almost sure to be established, requiring afterward a good degree of vigilance to keep apart those who have thus naturally come together.

3. Another advantage we find in the wholesome incitements to study which the system affords. This is a want in all schools, provided for often by a marking and grading system involving a distribution of honors and prizes. An acknowledged defect in this plan, not to speak of any thing unwholesome in the spirit of rivalry which it induces, is in the fact that it appeals to comparatively few in a class. The honors are few, and the majority soon cease to strive for them. The social influence arising from the constitution of our classes operates continuously and almost equally upon all. Each desires for himself the best standing that he is capable of, and there is never a lack of motive to exertion.

It will be observed, too, that the stimulus is the same in kind as will operate in after life. The young man, going out into the world, does not leave behind him the forces that have helped him on. They are the ordinary forces of society, and require no new habits of thought or action in order to their effective operation. We have introduced a marking system into the recitation-room, pertaining solely to the performance there, and used for the information of teachers and guardians, and the pupil himself: not for the assignment of grade or distribution of honors, or for any publication whatsoever. We rely upon the natural love of a fair standing with teachers and associates as the supplement to the higher motives for exertion, and have not found it a vain reliance.

4. Again, the social culture which is incidental to the system is a matter of no small importance. To secure this the student does not need to make any expenditure of time, going out of his way, or leaving his proper work for the pleasure or improvement resulting from society. He finds himself naturally in the midst of it, and he adjusts himself to it instinctively. It influences his manners, his feeling, and his thought. He may be as little conscious of the sources of the influence as of the sunlight or the atmosphere; it will envelope him all the same, saving him from the excessive introversion, the morbid fancies, the moroseness, which sometimes arise in secluded study, giving him elasticity of spirits, and ease of movement, and refinement of character, not readily attained out of society. It seems desirable that our young men especially should enjoy these advantages during the period of their course of study, while the forces that form character work most efficiently.

5. Closely connected with this influence is the tendency to good order which we find in the system. The ease with which the discipline of so large a school is conducted has not ceased to be a matter of wonder to ourselves. One thousand students are gathered from every state in the Union, from every class in society, of every grade of culture—the great mass of them, indeed, bent on improvement, but numbers sent by anxious friends with the hope that they may be saved or recovered from wayward tendencies. Yet the disorders incident to such gatherings are essentially unknown among us. Our streets are as quiet by day and by night as in any other country town. There are individual cases of misdemeanor, especially among the new comers, and now and then one is informed that his probation has been unsatisfactory; but in the regularly organized classes of the College and Ladies' Departments, numbering from two to four hundred in constant attendance, the exclusions have not on the average exceeded one in five years, and in one instance a period of more than ten years elapsed without a single exclusion from these classes. This result we attribute greatly to the wholesome influence of the system of joint education. The student feels that his standing and character are of grave consequence to him, and he is predisposed to take a manly attitude in reference to the government and regulations of the school. An admonition in the presence of the students assembled in the chapel has always been more dreaded by an offender than a private dismission. Offenses against propriety, that in a body of young men forming a separate community would seem to be trivial, change their aspect when the female element is added to the community; and

that better view adds greatly to the force of wholesome regulations. From the beginning, the use of tobacco has been prohibited to our students. In the presence of ladies the regulation has a force and significance that could not be otherwise secured, and has been maintained with a good degree of success. College tricks lose their wit and attractiveness in a community thus constituted. They are essentially unknown among us. There are no secret societies, and, so far as I know, there has been no tendency toward them. The relations of the classes to each other are comfortable and desirable. With a sufficient degree of class feeling to give unity and collective force, there is an entire absence of the antagonisms which sometimes appear in college life. It may be a mistake to attribute this fact in any degree to the social constitution of the school, but it seems to me to be a natural result. The general force of the society controls and limits the clannish tendency. We have had no difficulty in reference to conduct and manners in the college dining-hall. There has been an entire absence of the irregularities and roughnesses so often complained of in college commons.

6. Nor can it be reasonably doubted that the arrangement tends to good order and morality in the town outside of the school. Evils that might be tolerated, in the shape of drinking-saloons and other places of dissipation, if young men only were present, seem intolerable where ladies are gathered with them. The public sentiment requires their suppression. Of course, this influence alone would not be sufficient; but it increases and intensifies the moral forces of the place which withstand their introduction.

7. Another manifest advantage is in the relations of the school to the community—a cordial feeling of good will, and the absence of that antagonism between town and college which in general belongs to the history of universities and colleges. The absence of disorder in the school is the prime condition of this good feeling; but beyond this, the constitution of the school is so similar to that of the community that any conflict is unnatural: the usual occasion seems to be wanting.

8. It can hardly be doubted that young people educated under such conditions are kept in harmony with society at large, and are prepared to appreciate the responsibilities of life, and to enter upon its work. They will not lack sympathy with the popular feeling, or an apprehension of the common interests. They are naturally educated in relation with the work of life, and will not require a reädjustment. This seems a matter of grave importance, and we can scarcely be mistaken as to the happy results attained. If we are

not utterly deceived by our position, our students naturally and readily find their work in the world, because they have been trained in sympathy with the world.

These are among the advantages of the system which have forced themselves upon our attention. The list might be extended and expanded; but you will wish especially to know whether we have not encountered disadvantages and difficulties which more than counterbalance these advantages, and you will properly require me to speak with all frankness upon those difficulties which are commonly apprehended.

1. Have young ladies the ability in mental vigor and bodily health to maintain a fair standing in a class with young men? Do they not operate as a check upon the progress of the class, and degrade the standard of scholarship? and do they not break down in health under a pressure which young men can sustain?

To this inquiry I answer, where there has been the same preparatory training, we find no difference in ability to maintain themselves in the recitation room. Under the circumstances, I shall be excused for referring to my own individual experience, which has been somewhat varied. The first eight years of my work as a teacher was in the department of the Ancient Languages—Latin, Greek, and Hebrew; the next eleven, in Mathematics, abstract and applied; the last eight, in Philosophical and Ethical studies. In all these studies my classes have included young women as well as young men, and I have never observed any difference between them in performance in the recitation. The strong and the weak scholars are equally distributed between the sexes.

In this statement I do not imply that I see no difference between the normal male and female mind as to taste for particular studies. I have no doubt of the existence of such differences; but they do not appear in the ability as pupils to comprehend and express the truth. A few days since, on a visit to the University of Michigan, I attended a recitation in Thucydides. So far as could be judged from a single exercise, in which there were many excellent performances, the daughter of the Professor of Greek, the only young lady under the wing of the University, led the class. But it did not strike me as an anomaly; I had often seen such things.

Nor is there any manifest inability on the part of young women to endure the required labor. A breaking down in health does not appear to be more frequent than with young men. We have not observed a more frequent interruption of study on this account; nor do our statistics show a greater draft upon the vital forces in the case of those who have completed the full college course. Out of eighty-four young ladies who have graduated since 1841, seven have died—a proportion of one in twelve. Of three hundred and sixty-eight young men who have graduated since that date, thirty-four are dead, or a little more than one in eleven. Of these thirty-four young men, six fell in the war; and leaving those out, the proportion of deaths still remains one to thirteen. Taking the whole number of gentlemen graduates, omitting the Theological Department, we find the proportion of deaths one to nine and a-half; of ladies, one to twelve: and this in spite of the lower average expectation of life for women, as indicated in life insurance tables. The field is, of course, too narrow for perfectly conclusive results; but there is no occasion for special apprehension of failure of health to ladies from study.

2. But it is held by many that ladies need a course of study adapted to their nature and their prospective work, and that it must be undesirable to bring them under the same training with young men. The theory of our school has never been that men and women are alike in mental constitution, or that they naturally and properly occupy the same position in the work of life. The education furnished is general, not professional, designed to fit men and women for any position or work to which they may properly be called. Even in the full college curriculum it does not appear that there is any study that would not be helpful in the discipline and furniture of an educated lady. But only a small proportion of young ladies seeking an education will naturally require the full college course. It is not difficult to frame a suitable course parallel with the college course, made up substantially of studies selected from it, and diversified by the addition of the accomplishments supposed to be peculiarly adapted to female culture. Almost every Western college has a scientific course, involving these substantial elements. The best schools in the land for the education of ladies alone have the same course. We do not find that any peculiar style of teaching is required to adapt these studies to female culture. The womanly nature will appropriate the material to its own necessities under its own laws. Young men and women sit at the same table and partake of the same food, and we have no apprehension that the vital forces will fail to elaborate from the common material the osseous and fibrous and nervous tissues adapted to each frame and constitution. Except under pressure of great external violence, the female nature asserts itself by virtue of its own inherent laws. No education can make alike those whom God has made as unlike as men and women.

3. Yet apprehension is felt and expressed that character will deteriorate on one side or on the other; that young men will become frivolous or effeminate, and young women coarse and masculine. The more prevalent opinion seems to be that, while the arrangement may be desirable in its effect on young men, it will be damaging to young women. That young men should become trifling or effeminate, lose their manly attributes and character, from proper association with cultivated young women, is antecedently improbable, and false in fact. It is the natural atmosphere for the development of the higher qualities of manhood—magnanimity, generosity, true chivalry, earnestness. The animal man is kept subordinate, in the prevalence of these higher qualities. We have found it the surest way to make men of boys, and gentlemen of rowdies. It must be a very poor specimen of masculine human nature that is not helped by the association, and a very poor specimen of a woman that does not prove a helper. In my judgment, as the result of experience, the chances are better even for the poor specimen.

But, on the other hand, are not womanly delicacy and refinement of character endangered? Will not the young woman, pursuing her studies with young men, take on their manners and aspirations and aims, and be turned aside from the true ideal of womanly life and character? The thing is scarcely conceivable. The natural response of woman to the exhibition of manly traits is in the correlative qualities of gentleness, delicacy, and grace. It might better be questioned whether the finer shadings of female character can be developed without this natural stimulus. If you would transform a woman into an Amazon or virago, take her apart from well-constituted society, and train her in isolation to a disgust for men, and a rough self-reliance. You will probably fail even thus in your endeavor; but it is the only chance of success.

But it is my duty not to reason, but to speak from the limited historical view assigned me. You would know whether the result with us has been a large accession to the numbers of coarse, 'strong-minded' women, in the offensive sense of the word; and I say, without hesitation, that I do not know of a single instance of such a product as the result of our system of education. It is true that in our 'Triennial' are found the names of three somewhat distinguished lady lecturers, who are some times referred to as belonging to this class. They pursued their studies at Oberlin from four to five years in each case. But, whatever their present position and character may be, I have personal knowledge of the fact that they came to us very mature in thought, with their views of life settled and their own plans and purposes determined and announced. Whatever help in their chosen life they derived from the advantages afforded them, they have never given us any credit for their more advanced views of woman's rights and duties. While avowing a radical dissent from those views, I can not forbear to say that I am happy to number these ladies among my friends, and to express my admiration of much that is noble and womanly in their character, and of their earnest but mistaken philanthropy.

To show that our system of education does not bewilder woman with a vain ambition, or tend to turn her aside from the work which God has impressed upon her entire constitution, I may state that of the eighty-four ladies that have taken the college course, twenty-seven only are unmarried. Of these twenty-seven, *four* died early, and of the remaining twenty-three, twenty are graduates of less than six years' standing. The statistics of the graduates of the Ladies' Course would give essentially the same result. There may be an apparent indelicacy, perhaps, in parading such private, domestic facts; but the importance of the question upon which they bear will vindicate the propriety.

4. But this view does not touch the exact point of the difficulty. It is in general admitted that the association of young men and women, under proper conditions, is elevating instead of degrading, but there is doubt whether bringing them together in a school provides for these proper associations. The wholesome association of the young requires the presence and influence of those who are mature and have experience and a sense of responsibility,—more of the family influence than can be secured in a large school. Is there not danger that young men and young women thus brought together in the critical period of life, when the distinctive social tendencies which draw the sexes toward each other seem to act with greatest intensity, will fail of that necessary regulative force and fall into undesirable and unprofitable relations? Will not such associations result in weak and foolish love affairs, and in such habits of communication and social life as lead to these and grow out of them.

It is not strange that such apprehensions are felt, nor would it be easy to give an *à priori* answer to such difficulties; but, if we may judge from our experience, the difficulties are without foundation. I have no hesitation in expressing the conviction that in the associations of our young people there is as little of this undesirable element as is found in any general society. The danger in this direction results from excited imagination,—from the glowing exaggerations of youthful fancy; and the best remedy is to displace these fancies by every-day facts and realities. The young man shut out from the society of ladies, with the help of the high-wrought representations of life which poets and novelists afford, with only a distant vision of the reality, is the one who is in danger. The women whom he sees are glorified by his fancy, and are wrought into his day-dreams and night-dreams as beings of supernatural loveliness. It would be different if he met them day by day in the recitation-room, in a common encounter with an algebraic problem, or at the table sharing in the common want of bread and butter. There is still room for the fancy to work, but the materials for the picture are more reliable and enduring. Such association does not take all the romance out of life, but it gives as favorable conditions for sensible views and actions upon these delicate questions as can be afforded to human nature.

There is another danger to which the young man is exposed greater even than this of a too high-colored ideal of female character. It is too low an estimate, springing from his own sensual tendencies, and darkened by a dash of misanthropy which is one of the most common experiences of the young. Such an ideal degrades the one who indulges it, and mars his whole conception of life. No greater misfortune can befall a young man than to admit to his heart such a misconception. It can spring up only in an isolated life, apart from the society of the pure and the good. It is good for a young man to face the facts, and let his dreams go, whether bright or dark. In the presence of these facts, he will conceive and maintain a genuine respect for women as worthy of his confidence and regard, which will save him from amorous follies on the one side, and from a degrading misanthropy on the other. There may be, here and there, displays of these weaknesses of youth; and where are there not? Among hundreds of the young, such weak ones must be found; but if there is any more potent corrective than the public sentiment of such a company of young people of ordinary good sense, I have not been able to find it.

Of course there is room for the wisdom which comes from experience in regulating the associations of such a school. The danger seems to be in both extremes, of too great strictness and restraint and too great laxity, as in all forms of school discipline. Those who have observed the pressure against restrictions, where there is an attempt to prohibit intercourse, sometimes imagine that any letting-up would prove fatal to all order and propriety. They would probably be surprised to find that the sense of propriety and self-respect of their pupils would prove a surer reliance than any artificial barriers imposed from without. On the other hand, it is important that the intercourse of the young people be regulated by such restrictions as the good sense of the community will justify—not minute and arbitrary, in an attempt to meet all deficiencies of taste and judgment, and forestall every conceivable impropriety, but comprehensive and suggestive, expanded as occasion may require in familiar and practical suggestions from principal or teacher. It is desirable that the intercourse of the school be easy and natural, not fettered at every step by some restriction. The government of our school would be impossible, except as approved and sustained by the great body of the pupils. It would be easy, but extremely unwise, to surrender this stronghold in the endeavor to fortify ourselves by artificial barriers.

The experience of the Friends in this country in the management of their schools is instructive. For many years they have had boarding-schools at the East and the West, to which they sent both their sons and their daughters, but intended to allow no association between them in the schools. They found the undertaking too great. Walls could not be built that would entirely separate them. Within two or three years the policy has been changed and the walls removed, and, as I am informed, with the happiest results. A regulated association becomes easy now which was impossible before.

5. But will not the young people form such acquaintances as will result, during their course of study or after they leave school, in matrimonial engagements? Undoubtedly they will; and if this is a fatal objection, the system must be pronounced a failure. The majority of young people form such acquaintances between the ages of sixteen and twenty-four, and these are the years devoted to a course of study. It would be a most unnatural state of things if such acquaintances should not be made in a school where young men and young women are gathered in large numbers; nor is it to be expected that marriage engagements even will not be formed more or less frequently. Now and then it may occur that parties will seem to have left school for the purpose of consummating such an engagement. The reasonable inquiry in the case is, whether such acquaintances and engagements can be made under circumstances more favorable to a wise and considerate adjustment, or more promising of a happy result. Are the circumstances such as naturally to promote hasty and ill-assorted marriages? If the sys-

tem were to stand or fall by this one test, its friends would have no occasion to apprehend the result.

6. But what security is there that positive immoralities may not at times occur, and startling scandals even, that shall shock the community and produce distrust of the system? Of course, such a thing might be; but it would scarce be logical to condemn the system on the ground of such possibilities or even actualities. The only pertinent inquiry is whether such immoralities are the more natural and frequent product of this than of other systems. Is the moral atmosphere of the best and most approved Eastern colleges perfectly free from every taint of impurity? Is the propriety of the best-ordered and most carefully-guarded female seminary not liable to be broken in upon by a sporadic offense of this character? Such liabilities go everywhere with fallen human nature; and it has not been shown that the monastic institutions of either ancient or modern times have afforded perfect security upon this point. There may have been a time when one such scandal in a school for joint education would have brought reproach upon the system and overwhelmed it with popular disgust. A generation of successful trial, under a sheltering Providence, should have won for it the impartial judgment which is the right of every system.

7. But is this method adapted to schools in general, or is the success attained at Oberlin due to peculiar features of the school and of the place, which can rarely be found or reproduced elsewhere? This idea is not an unnatural one, and is somewhat prevalent. It is true, we have been favored with some special advantages. The place and the school were founded together—a Christian enterprise, with a common aim. From the beginning, the great interest of the place has been the school. The religious earnestness, in which the enterprise had its birth, has been in some good degree maintained, securing a unity of interest and of action very rare in the history of schools and of communities. The habits of the community have in a good degree taken their shape from the necessities of the school, and there is a very general and hearty interest in all that pertains to its welfare. On the other hand, the village has increased until its population numbers nearly 4000—a population gathered from all parts of the country, with a colored element amounting perhaps to one-fifth of the whole, of every grade of culture and of want of culture, not in any proper sense a disturbing element, but precluding that perfect homogeneity of thought and life embraced in the popular idea of Oberlin society. Our students, too, have been so numerous as to preclude the possibility of the

close personal supervision attainable in a smaller school; and while we have had occasion to congratulate ourselves on their general character, their earnest endeavors after improvement and usefulness, still they are essentially like the pupils in other schools at the West between the parallels which embrace the New-England emigration, with the addition of the colored element, varying from five to seven per cent. of the whole.

The experiment was commenced, too, by those who had had no experience in such a school, who had to feel their way through the various questions involved in its organization and arrangement. Thus, with the special advantages of our position, there have been some special difficulties.

But the experiment at Oberlin, if the earliest, is by no means the only one. At least a score of schools have sprung up that have adopted essentially the same plan, and I have yet to learn that there has been any other than a uniform result in the convictions of those who have best understood these movements. There are doubtless advantages in entering upon the plan at the organization of a school instead of introducing it into a college already in existence. The usual style of college life, the traditional customs and habits of action and of thought, are not suited to a school where ladies are gathered as well, and the changes required might occasion difficulty at the outset, and peril the experiment. On this point I have no experience; but I have such confidence in the inherent vitality and adaptability of the system, that I should be entirely willing to see it subjected to this test.

In concluding this statement, permit me to say that I have no special call as an apostle or propagandist of this system of education. The opinions set forth are such as, with my limited experience, I am compelled to cherish, and when called upon, as now, I cheerfully express them.

## NOTE.

Oberlin College, and Oberlin as a settlement or town, originated in the deep religious convictions of the founders of both, which had been awakened and confirmed in the "revivals" of 1830, and the few years following. The author of the plan of the "Collegiate Institute," on the manual labor system, and the "Covenant," under which a tract of land three miles square, and comprising about eight thousand acres, was purchased in Lorain County, at the low rate of one dollar and fifty cents per acre, was Rev. John J Shipherd, while he was pastor of the Presbyterian church in Elyria in 1832. Associated with him, in public and private prayer and effort, was Mr. P. P. Stewart, a retired missionary among the Cherokees in Mississippi, then residing in Mr. Shipherd's family. The early colonists and students, deeply imbued with the religious spirit which the preachings of Rev. Charles Finney had awakened, entered on the enterprise with missionary zeal, "lamenting the degeneracy of the Church, and the deplorable condition of the perishing world, and ardently desirous of bringing both under the influence of the blessed gospel of peace" and "of glorifying God in doing good to men to the extent of their ability." Assuming the name of the French pastor and educator of the retired parish of Walbach, in the Ban de la Roche, they have achieved, within the period measured by that pastor's labors, an educational success, and made their principles and practices felt in the political and ethical, as well as the educational questions of the day, to an extent which Oberlin never aspired to.

The land was bought in 1832—the first log cabin on the tract, by no means inviting for settlement, was built in April, 1833, and the first college building was extemporized, out of trees felled from the till then untouched forest; in the following summer, a church on the Congregational basis, but in temporary connection with a Presbytery, was gathered in September, and in December a school was opened in "Oberlin Hall," with thirty pupils, which number before the close of May, 1834, was increased to one hundred. And thus was launched an enterprise which, in little more than thirty years, has grown into a village and township of 3000 inhabitants, and according to the annual catalogue of 1867–68, (of fifty-six closely-printed pages,) and an institution (no longer the "Oberlin Collegiate Institute" on the manual labor system, with one undergraduate student of Western Reserve College as teacher,) known throughout the land as Oberlin College, with an endowment of $160,000, seven buildings, and twenty professors and instructors laboring in a *Theological Department* with 11 students; a *College Department* with 119 students, 9 of whom are ladies in a four years' course; a *Scientific Course* of three years, with 34 students; a *Preparatory Department* with 484 "gentlemen" students; a *Young Ladies' Course* of four years, with 190 students; and a *Ladies' Preparatory Course* with 294 pupils—a grand total of 1134 pupils. Besides these regular courses, there is a "Teachers' Institute" every Fall term, continuing about six weeks, in which special instruction is given to those who propose to teach; a "Winter Vacation School," under the superintendence of the Faculty, in optional studies, commencing at the close of the Autumn term; and a "Conservatory of Music," under a Professor fresh from the Conservatory of Music at Leipzig in Saxony. And in these thirty years, over 15,000 pupils have been instructed to some extent in its various courses. [We shall return to Oberlin.—*Ed.*]

# IX. SCHOOLS FOR PROFESSIONAL EDUCATION OF TEACHERS.

BY JOHN S. HART, LL. D.,

PRINCIPAL OF THE STATE NORMAL SCHOOL AT TRENTON, NEW JERSEY.

---

### NORMAL SCHOOL.

The term Normal School is an unfortunate misnomer, and its general adoption has led to much confusion of ideas. The word "Normal," from the Latin *norma*, a rule or pattern to work by, does not differ essentially from "Model." A Normal School, according to the meaning of the word, would be a pattern school, an institution which could be held up for imitation, to be copied by other schools of the same grade. But this meaning of the word is not what we mean by the thing. When we mean a school to be copied or imitated, we call it a Model School. Here the name and the thing agree. The name explains the thing. It is very different when we speak of a Normal School. To the uninitiated, the term either conveys no meaning at all; or, if your hearer is a man of letters, it conveys to him an idea which you have at once to explain away. You have to tell him, in effect, that a Normal School is not a Normal School, and then that it is something else, which the word does not in the least describe.

What then do we mean by a Normal School? What is the thing which we have called by this unfortunate name?

A Normal School is a seminary for the professional education of teachers. It is an institution in which those who wish to become teachers learn how to do their work; in which they learn, not reading, but how to teach reading; not penmanship, but how to teach penmanship; not grammar, but how to teach grammar; not geography, but how to teach geography; not arithmetic, but how to teach arithmetic. The idea which lies at the basis of such an institute, is that knowing a thing, and knowing how to teach that thing to others, are distinguishable and very different facts. The knowledge of the subjects to be taught, may be gained at any school. In order to give to the Teachers' Seminary its full power, and efficiency, it were greatly to be desired that the subjects themselves, as mere matters of knowledge, should be first learned elsewhere, before entering the Teachers' School. This latter would then have to do only with its own special function, that of showing its matriculants how to use these materials in the process of teaching. Unfortunately, we have not made such progress in popular education as to be able to separate these two functions to the extent that is desirable. Many of those who attend a Teachers' Seminary, come to it lamentably ignorant of the common branches of knowledge. They have consequently first to study these branches in the Normal School, as they would study them in any other school. That is, they have first to learn the facts as matters of knowledge, and then to study the art and science of teaching these facts to others. Instead of coming with their brick and mortar ready prepared, that they may be instructed in the use of the trowel and the plumb-line, they have to make their brick and mix their mortar after they enter the institution. This is undoubtedly a drawback and a misfortune. But it cannot be helped at present. All we can do is to define clearly the true idea of the Teacher's School, and then to work towards it as fast and as far as we can.

A Normal School is essentially unlike any other school. It has been compared indeed to those professional schools which are for the study of law, divinity, medicine, mining, engineering, and so forth. The Normal School, it is true, is like these schools in one respect. It is established with reference to the wants of a particular profession. It is a professional school. But those schools have for their main object the communication of some particular branch of science. They teach law, divinity, medicine, mining, or engineering. They aim to make lawyers, divines, physicians, miners, engineers, not teachers of these branches. The Professor in the Law School aims, not to make Professors of law, but lawyers. The medical Professor aims, not to make medical lecturers, but practitioners. To render these institutions analogous to the Teachers' Seminary, their pupils should first study law, medicine, engineering, and so forth, and then sit at the feet of their Gamaliels to be initiated into the secrets of the Professorial chair, that they may in turn become Professors of those branches to classes of their own. Nor would such a plan, if it were possible, be altogether without its value. It surely needs no demonstration to prove, that in the highest departments, no less than in the lowest, something more than knowledge is needed in order to teach. An understanding of how to communicate one's knowledge, and practical skill in doing it, are as necessary in teaching theology, metaphysics, languages, infinitesimal analysis, or chemistry, as they are in teaching the alphabet. If there are bunglers, who know not how to go to work to teach a child its letters, or to open its young mind and heart to the reception of truth, whose school-rooms are places where the young mind and heart are in a state, either of perpetual torpor, or of perpetual nightmare, have these bunglers no analogues in the men of ponderous erudition that sometimes fill the Professor's chair? Have we no examples, in our highest seminaries of learning, of men very eminent in scientific attainments, who have not in themselves the first elements of a teacher? who impart to their students no quickening impulse? whose vast and towering knowledge may make them perhaps a grand feature in their College, attracting to it all eyes, but whose intellectual treasures, for all the practical wants of the students, are of no more use, than are the swathed and buried mummies in the pyramid of Cheops!

A Teacher's Seminary, if it were complete, would include in its curriculum of study the entire cycle of human knowledge, so far as it is taught by schools. Our teachers of mathematics and of logic, of law and of medicine, need indeed a knowledge of the branches which they are to teach, and for this knowledge they do not need a Teachers' Seminary. But they need something more than this knowledge. Besides being men of erudition, they need to be teachers, no less than the humble members of the profession, who have only to teach the alphabet and the multiplication table; and there is in all teaching, high or low something that is common to them all—an art and a skill that is different from the mere knowledge of the subjects; which is not necessarily learned in learning the subjects; which requires special, superadded gifts, and distinct study and training. There is, according to my observation, as great a lack of this special skill in the higher seminaries of learning, as in the lower seminaries. Were it possible to have a Normal School, not which should undertake to teach the entire encyclopædia of the sciences, but which, limiting itself to its one main function of developing the art and mystery of communicating knowledge, should turn out College Professors, and even Divinity, Law, and Medical Professors,—men who are really skillful teachers,—it would work a change in those venerable institutions as marked and decisive as that which it is now effecting in the common schools. Of course, no such scheme is possible; certainly, none such is contemplated. But I am very sure I shall not be considered calumnious, when I express the conviction, that there are learned and eminent occupants of Professors' chairs, who might find great benefit in an occasional visit to a good Normal School, or even to the class-room of a teacher trained in a Normal School. I certainly have seen, in the very lowest department of the common school, a style of teaching, which, for a wise and intelligent comprehension of its object, and for its quickening power upon the intellect and conscience, would compare favorably with the very best teaching I have ever seen in a College or University.

I come back, then, to the point from which I set out, namely, that a Normal School, or Teachers' Seminary, differs essentially from every other kind of school. It aims to give the knowledge and skill that are needed alike in all schools. To make the point a little plainer, let me re-state, with what clearness I can, some of the elementary truths and facts which lie at the foundation of the whole subject. Though to many of my readers it may be going over a beaten track, it may not be so to all; and we all do well, even in regard to known and admitted truths, to bring them occasionally afresh to the mind.

As it has been already said, a man may know a thing perfectly, and yet not be able to teach it. Of course, a man cannot teach what he does not know. He must first have the knowledge. But the mere possession of knowledge does not make one a teacher, any more than the possession of powder and shot makes him a marksman, or the possession of a rod and line makes him an angler. The most learned men are often unfortunately the very men who have the least capacity for communicating what they know. Nor is this incapacity confined to those versed in book knowledge. It is common to every class of men, and to every kind of knowledge. Let me give an example. The fact about to be stated, was communicated to me by a gentleman of eminent commercial standing in Philadelphia, now the President of one of its leading banks. The fact occurred in his own personal experience. He was, at the time of its occurrence, largely engaged in the cloth trade. His faculties of mind and body, and particularly his sense of touch, had been so trained in this business, that in going rapidly over an invoice of cloth, as his eye and hand passed in quick succession from piece to piece, in the most miscellaneous assortment, he could tell instantly the value of each, with a degree of precision, and a certainty of knowledge, hardly credible. A single glance of the eye, a single touch, transient as thought, gave the result. His own knowledge of the subject, in short, was perfect, and it was rapidly winning him a fortune. Yet when undertaking to explain to a younger and less experienced member of the craft whom he wished to befriend, by what process he arrived at his judgment, in other words, to teach what he knew, he found himself utterly at a loss. His thoughts had never run in that direction. "Oh!" said he, "you have only——to look at the cloth, and—and—to run your fingers over it,—thus. You will perceive at once the difference between one piece and another." It seems never to have occurred to him that another man's sensations and perceptions might in the same circumstances be quite different from his, and in order to communicate his knowledge to one uninitiated, he must pause to analyse it; he must separate, classify, and name those several qualities of the cloth of which his senses took cognizance; he must then ascertain how far his interrogator perceived by his senses the same qualities which he himself did, and thus gradually get on common ground with him.

Let the receiving-teller of a bank be called upon to explain how it is that he knows at a glance a counterfeit bill from a genuine one, and in nine cases out of ten he will succeed no better than the cloth merchant did. Knowing and communicating what we know, doing and explaining what we do, are distinct, separable, and usually very different processes.

Similar illustrations might be drawn from artists, and from men of original genius in almost every profession, who can seldom give any intelligible account of how they achieve their results. The mental habits best suited for achievement are rarely those best suited for teaching. Marlborough, so celebrated for his military combinations, could never give any intelligible account of his plans. He had arrived at his conclusions with unerring certainty, but he was so little accustomed to observing his own mental processes, that he utterly failed in attempting to make them plain to others. He saw the points himself with perfect clearness, but he had no power to make others see them. To all objections to his plans, he could only say, "Silly, silly, that's silly." It was much the same with Oliver Cromwell. It is so with most men who are distinguished for action and achievement. Patrick Henry would doubtless have made but a third-rate teacher of elocution, and old Homer but an indifferent lecturer on the art of poetry.

To acquire knowledge ourselves, then, and to put others in possession of what we have acquired, are not only distinct intellectual processes, but they are quite unlike. In the former case, the faculties merely go out towards the objects to be known, as in the case of the cloth merchant passing his eye and finger over the bales of cloth. But in the case of one attempting to teach, several additional processes are needed, besides that of collecting knowledge. He must turn his thoughts inward, so as to arrange and classify properly the contents of his intellectual storehouse. He must then examine his own mind, his intellectual machinery, so as to understand precisely how the knowledge came in upon himself. He must lastly study the minds of his pupils, so as to know through what channels the knowledge will best reach them. The teacher may not always be aware that he does all these things, that is, he may not always have a theory of his own art. But the art itself he must have. He must first get the knowledge of the things to be taught; he must secondly study his knowledge; he must thirdly study himself; he must lastly study his pupil. He is a teacher at all only so far as he does at least these four things.

In a Normal School, as before said, the knowledge of the subject is presupposed. The object of the Normal School is, not so much to make arithmeticians and grammarians, for instance, as to make teachers of arithmetic and grammar. This teaching faculty is a thing by itself; and quite apart from the subject matter to be taught. It underlies every branch of knowledge, and every trade and profession. The theologian, the mathematician, the linguist, the learned professor, no less than the teacher of the primary school, or of the Sabbath-school, all need this supplementary knowledge and skill, in which consists the very essence of teaching. This knowledge of how to teach is not acquired by merely studying the subject to be taught. It is a study by itself. A man may read familiarly the *Mechanique Celeste*, and yet not know how to teach the multiplication table. He may read Arabic or Sanskrit, and not know how to teach a child the alphabet of his mother tongue. The Sabbath-school teacher may dip deep into biblical lore, he may ransack the commentaries, and may become, as many Sabbath-school teachers are, truly learned in Bible knowledge, and yet be utterly incompetent to teach a class of children. He can no more hit the wandering attention, or make a lodgment in the minds of his youthful auditory, than the mere unskilled possessor of a fowling-piece can hit a bird upon the wing.

## THE ART OF TEACHING.

The art of teaching is the one indispenable qualification of the teacher.

Without this, whatever else he may be, he is no teacher. How may this art be acquired? In the first place, many persons pick it up, just as they pick up many other arts and trades,—in a hap-hazard sort of way. They have some natural aptitude for it, and they grope their way along, by guess and by instinct, and through many failures, until they become good teachers, they hardly know how. To rescue the art from this uncertainty and chance, is the object of the Normal School. In such a school, the main object of the pupil is to learn how to make others know what he himself knows. The whole current of his thoughts and studies is turned into this channel. Studying how to teach, with an experimental class to practice on, forms the constant topic of his meditations. It is surprising how rapidly, under such conditions, the faculty of teaching is developed; how fertile the mind becomes in devising practical expedients, when once the attention is roused and fixed upon the precise object to be attained, and the idea of what teaching really is, fairly has possession of the mind. In furtherance of this end, every well-ordered Normal School has, in connection with it, and as part of its organization, a Model School, to serve the double purpose of a school of observation, and a school of practice. Thus, after these pupil-teachers are once thoroughly familiar with the branches to be taught, and after they have become acquainted with the theory of teaching, as a science, it is surprising how soon, with even a little of this practice-teaching, they acquire the art. If the faculty of teaching is in them at all, a few experimental lessons, under the eye of an experienced teacher, will develope it. The fact of possessing within one's self the teaching gift, sometimes breaks upon the possessor himself with all the force of a surprising and most delightful discovery. The good teacher does not indeed stop here. He goes on to improve in his art as long as he lives. But his greatest single achievement is when he takes the first step,—when he first learns to teach at all. The pupil of a Normal School gains there a start, an impulse, which carries him forward the rest of his life. Thus a very little judicious experimental training redeems hundreds of candidates from utter and pitiful incompetency, and converts for them an awkward and painful drudgery into keen, hopeful, and productive labor.

### TEACHING.

But what is teaching? Unless our ideas on this point are clear and well defined, it is in vain to look for any satisfactory results. Teaching, then, in the first place, is not simply telling. A class may be told a thing twenty times over, and yet not know it. Talking to a class is not necessarily teaching. We have known many teachers, who were brimful of information, and were good talkers, and who discoursed to their classes with ready utterance a large part of the time allotted to instruction, yet an examination of their classes showed little advancement in knowledge.

There are several time-honored metaphors on this subject, which need to be received with some grains of allowance, if we would get an exact idea of what teaching is. Chiselling the rude marble into the finished statue, giving the impression of the seal upon the soft wax, pouring water into an empty vessel,—all these comparisons lack one essential element of likeness. The mind is indeed, in one sense, empty, and needs to be filled. It is yielding, and needs to be impressed. It is rude, and needs polishing. But it is not, like the marble, the wax, or the vessel, a passive recipient of external influences. It is itself a living power. It is acted upon only by stirring up its own activities. The operative upon mind, unlike the operative upon matter, must have the active, voluntary coöperation of that upon which he works. The teacher is doing his work, only so far as he gets work from the scholar. The very essence and root of the work are in the scholar, not in the teacher. No one, in fact, in an important sense, is taught at all, except so far as he is self-taught. The teacher may be useful, as an auxiliary, in causing this action on the part of the scholar. But the one, indisputable, vital thing, in all learning, is in the scholar himself. The old Romans, in their word education, (*educere*, to draw out) seem to have come nearer to the true idea than any other people have done. The teacher is to draw out the resources of the pupil. Yet even this word comes short of the exact truth. The teacher must put in, as well as draw out. No process of mere pumping will draw out of a child's mind knowledge which is not there. All the power of the Socratic method, could it be applied by Socrates himself, would be unavailing to draw from a child's mind, by mere questioning, a knowledge, for instance, of chemical affinity, of the solar system, of the temperature of the Gulf Stream, of the doctrine of the resurrection.

What then is teaching? Teaching is causing any one to know. Now no one can be made to know a thing, but by the act of his own powers. His own senses, his own memory, his own powers of reason, perception, and judgment must be exercised. The function of the teacher is to bring about this exercise of the pupil's faculties. The means to do this are infinite in variety. They should be varied according to the wants and the character of the individual to be taught. One needs to be told a thing; he learns most readily by the ear. Another needs to use his eyes; he must see a thing, either in the book, or in nature. But neither eye nor ear, nor any other sense or faculty will avail to the acquisition of knowledge, unless the power of attention is cultivated. Attention, then, is the first act or power of the mind that must be roused. It is the very foundation of all progress in knowledge, and the means of awakening it constitute the first step in the educational art.

When by any means, facts, positive knowledge, are once in possession of the mind, something must next be done to prevent their slipping away. You may tell a class the history of a certain event, or you may give them a description of a certain place, or person, or you may let them read it, and you may secure such a degree of attention, that at the time of the reading or the description, they shall have a fair, intelligible comprehension of what has been described or read. The facts are for the time actually in the possession of the mind. Now, if the mind was, according to the old notion, merely a vessel to be filled, the process would be complete. But mind is not an empty vessel. It is a living essence, with powers and processes of its own. And experience shows us, that in the case of a class of undisciplined pupils, facts, even when fairly placed in the possession of the mind, often remain there about as long as the shadow of a passing cloud remains upon the landscape, and make about as much impression.

The teacher must seek not only to get knowledge into the mind, but to fix it there. In other words, the power of the memory must be strengthened. Teaching, then, most truly, and in every stage of it, is a strictly coöperative process. You cannot cause any one to know, by merely pouring out stores of knowledge in his hearing, any more than you can make his body grow by spreading the contents of your market-basket at his feet. You must rouse his power of attention, that he may lay hold of, and receive, and make his own, the knowledge you offer him. You must awaken and strengthen the power of memory within him, that he may retain what he receives, and thus grow in knowledge, as the body by a like process grows in strength and muscle. In other words, learning, so far as the mind of the learner is concerned, is a growth; and teaching, so far as the teacher is concerned, is doing whatever is necessary to cause that growth.

Let us proceed a step farther in this matter. One of the ancients observes that a lamp loses none of its own light by allowing another lamp to be lit from it. He uses the illustration to enforce the duty of liberality in imparting our knowledge to others. Knowledge he says, unlike other treasures, is not diminished by giving.

The illustration fails to express the whole truth. This imparting of knowledge to others, not only does not impoverish the donor, but it actually increases his riches. *Docendo discimus.* By teaching we learn. A man grows in knowledge by the very act of communicating it. The reason for this is obvious. In order to communicate to the mind of another a thought which is in our own mind, we must give to the thought definite shape and form. We must handle it and pack it up for safe conveyance. Thus the mere act of giving a thought expression in words, fixes it more deeply in our own minds. Not only so, we can, in fact, very rarely be said to be in full possession of a thought ourselves, until by the tongue or the pen we have communicated it to somebody else. The expression of it, in some form, seems necessary to give it, even in our own minds, a definite shape and a lasting impression. A man who devotes himself to solitary reading and study, but never tries in any way to communicate his acquisitions to the world, or enforce his opinions upon others, rarely becomes a learned man. A great many confused, dreamy ideas, no doubt, float through the brain of such a man. But he has little exact and reliable knowledge. The truth is, there is a sort of indolent, listless absorption of intellectual food, that tends to idiocy. I knew a person once, a gentleman of wealth and leisure, who having no taste for social intercourse, and no material wants to be supplied, which might have required the active exercise of his powers, gave himself up entirely to solitary reading, as a sort of luxurious self-indulgence. He shut himself up in his room, all day long, day after day, devouring one book after another, until he became almost idiotic by the process, and he finally died of softening of the brain. Had he been compelled to use his mental acquisitions in earning his bread, or had the love of Christ constrained him to use them in the instructien of the poor and the ignorant, he might have become not only a useful, but a learned man.

We see a beautiful illustration of this doctrine in the case of Sabbath-school teachers, and one reason why persons so engaged usually love their work, is the benefit which they find in it for themselves. I speak here, not of the spiritual, but of the intellectual benefit. By the process of teaching others, they are all the while learning. This advantage in their case is all the greater, because it advances them in a kind of knowledge in which, more than in any other kind of knowledge, men are wont to become passive and stationary. In ordinary worldly knowledge, our necessities make us active. The intercourse of business and of pleasure even, makes men keen. On these subjects we are all the while bandying thoughts to and fro, we are accustomed to give as well as take, and so we keep our intellectual armor bright, and our thoughts well defined. But in regard to growth in scriptural knowledge, we have a tendency to be mere passive recipients, like the young man just referred to. Sabbath after Sabbath we hear good, instructive, orthodox discourses, but there is no active putting forth of our own powers in giving out what we thus take in, and so we never make it effectually our own. The absorbing process goes on, and yet we make no growth. The quiescent audience is a sort of exhausted receiver, into which the stream from the pulpit is perennially playing, but never making it full. Let a man go back and ask himself, what actual scriptural knowledge have I gained by the sermons of the last six months? What in fact do I retain in my mind, at this moment, of the sermons I heard only last Sabbath? So far as the hearing of sermons is concerned, the Sabbath-school teacher may perhaps be no better off than other hearers. But in regard to general growth in Biblical knowledge, he advances more rapidly than his fellow worshippers, because the exigencies of his class compel him to a state of mind the very opposite of this passive recipiency. He is obliged to be all the while, not only learning, but putting his acquisitions into definite shape for use, and the very act of using these acquisitions in teaching a class, fixes them in his own mind, and makes them more surely his own.

I have used this instance of the Sabbath-school teacher because it enforces an important hint already given, as to the mode of teaching. Some teachers, especially in Sabbath-schools, seem to be ambitious to do a great deal of talking. The measure of their success, in their own eyes, is their ability to keep up a continued stream of talk for the greater part of the hour. This is of course better than the embarrassing silence sometimes seen, where neither teacher nor scholar has anything to say. But at the best, it is only pouring into the exhausted receiver enacted over again. We can never be reminded too often, that there is no teaching except so far as there is active coöperation on the part of the learner. The mind receiving must reproduce and give back what it gets. This is the indispensable condition of making any knowledge really our own. The very best teaching I have ever seen, has been where the teacher said comparatively little. The teacher was of course brimfull of the subject. He could give the needed information at exactly the right point, and in the right quantity. But for every word given by the teacher, there were many words of answering reproduction on the part of the scholars. Youthful minds under such tutelage grow apace.

It is indeed a high and difficult achievement in the educational art, to get young persons thus to bring forth their thoughts freely for examination and correction. A pleasant countenance and a gentle manner, inviting and inspiring confidence, have something to do with the matter. But, whatever the means for accomplishing this end, the end itself is indispensable. The scholar's tongue must be unloosed, as well as the teacher's. The scholar's thoughts must be broached as well as the teacher's. Indeed, the statement needs very little qualification or abatement, that a scholar has learned nothing from us except what he has expressed to us again in words. The teacher who is accustomed to harangue his scholars with a continuous stream of words, no matter how full of weighty meaning his words may be, is yet deceiving himself, if he thinks that his scholars are materially benefited by his intellectual activity, unless it is so guided as to awaken and exercise theirs. If, after a suitable period, he will honestly examine his scholars on the subjects, on which he has himself been so productive, he will find that he has been only pouring water into a seive. Teaching can never be this one-sided process. Of all the things we attempt, it is the one most essentially and necessarily a coöperative process. There must be the joint action of the teacher's mind and the scholar's mind. A teacher teaches at all, only so far as he causes this co-active energy of the pupil's mind.

### THE ART OF QUESTIONING.

It cannot be too often repeated, the measure of a teacher's success, is not what he himself does, but what he gets his scholars to do. In nothing is this more noticeable, than in the different modes of putting a question to a scholar. One teacher will put a question in such a manner as to find out exactly how much or how little of the subject the child knows, and thereby encourage careful preparation; to give the pupil an open door, if he really knows the subject, to express his knowledge in a way that will be a satisfaction and a pleasure to him; to improve his power of expression, to cultivate his memory, to increase his knowledge, and to make it more thorough and definite. Another teacher will put his questions so as to secure none of these ends, but on the contrary so as to induce a most lamentable degree of carelessness and inaccuracy. Let me illustrate this point, taking an example for greater convenience from a scriptural subject. Suppose it be a lesson upon Christ's temptation, as recorded in the 4th chapter of Matthew. The dialogue between teacher and scholar may be supposed to proceed somewhat in this wise:

*Teacher.* Who was led up of the Spirit into the wilderness to be tempted of the devil?

*Pupil.* Jesus.

*T.* Yes. Now when Jesus had fasted forty days and forty nights, he was afterward a—— what? How did he feel after that?

*P.* Hungry.

*T.* Yes, that is right. He was afterward "ahungered." Now then?—the next scholar. Who then came to Jesus and said, if thou be the Son of God, command that these stones be made bread?

(Scholar hesitates.)

*T.* The t——?

*P.* The tempter.

*T.* Yes, you are right. It was the tempter. Who do you think was meant by the tempter?—the devil?

*P.* Yes.

*T.* When a man has fasted, that is, has eaten nothing, for forty days and forty nights, and feels very hungry, would the suggestion of an easy mode of getting food be likely to be a strong temptation to him, or would it not?

*P.* It would.

*T.* Yes, you are right again. It would be a strong temptation to him.

I need not pursue this dialogue further. The reader will see at once how there may thus be the appearance of quite a brisk and fluent recitation, to which however the pupil contributes absolutely nothing. It requires nothing of him in the way of preparation, and only the most indolent and profitless use of his faculties while reciting. He could hardly answer amiss, unless he were an idiot, and yet he has the appearance, and he is often flattered into the belief, of having given some evidence of knowledge and proficiency.

The opposite extreme from the method just exhibited, is that known as the topical method. It is the method pursued in the higher classes of schools, and among more advanced students. In the topical method, the teacher propounds a topic or subject, sometimes in the form of a question, but more commonly only by a title, a mere word or two, and then calls upon the pupil to give, in his own words, a full and connected narration or explanation of the subject, such as the teacher himself would give, if called upon to narrate or explain it. The subject already suggested, if propounded topically, would be somewhat in this wise:

The first temptation of Jesus.

Or, more fully: Narrate the circumstances of the first temptation of Jesus, and show wherein his virtue was particularly tried in that transaction.

The teacher, having propounded the subject clearly to the class, then waits patiently, maintaining silence himself, and requiring the members of the class to be silent and attentive, until the pupil interrogated is quite through, not hurrying him, not interrupting him, even with miscalled helps and hints, but leaving him to the free and independent action of his own faculties, in giving as full, connected, and complete an account of the matter as he can. When the pupil is quite through, the teacher then, but not before, makes any corrections or additional statements that may seem to be needed. In such an exercise as this, the pupil finds the absolute necessity of full and ample preparation; he has a powerful and healthy stimulus thus to prepare, in the intellectual satisfaction which one always feels in the successful discharge of any difficult task; and he acquires a habit of giving complete and accurate expression to his knowledge, by means of entire sentences, and without the help of "catch words," or leading-strings of any kind.

Some classes, of course, are not sufficiently advanced to carry out fully the method here explained. But there are many intermediate methods, founded on the same principle, and suited to children in every stage of advancement. Only let it be understood, whatever the stage, that the object of the recitation is, not to show what the teacher can say or do, but to secure the right thing being said and done by the pupil.

To recur once more to the same subject, the temptation of Christ. For a very juvenile class, the questioning might proceed on this wise:

*T.* Where was Jesus led after his baptism?
*P.* He was led into the wilderness.
*T.* By whom was he led there?
*P.* He was led by the Spirit.
*T.* For what purpose was he led into the wilderness?
*P.* He was led into the wilderness to be tempted.
*T.* By whom was he to be tempted?
*P.* He was to be tempted by the devil.
*T.* What bodily want was made the means of his first temptation?

If the class is quite young, and this question seems too difficult, the teacher, instead of asking it, or after asking it and not getting a satisfactory answer, might say to his class, that Jesus was first tempted through the sense of hunger. He was very hungry, and the devil suggested to him an improper means of relieving himself from the inconvenience. He might then go on with some such questions as these:

*T.* What circumstance is mentioned as showing how very hungry he must have been?

*P.* He had fasted forty days and forty nights.

*T.* Mention any way in which *you* might be tempted to sin, if you were suffering from hunger?

The foregoing questions, it will be perceived, are very simple, being suited to scholars just advanced beyond the infant class. Yet no one of the questions, in its form or terms, necessarily suggests the answer. No one of them can be answered by a mere "yes" or "no." No scholar, unacquainted with the subject, and with his book closed, can guess at the answer from the way in which the question is put. Not a question has been given, simple as they all are, which does not require at least some preparation, and which does not, to some extent, give exercise to the pupil's memory, his judgment, and his capacity for expression.

If the class is more advanced, the questions may be varied, so as to task and exercise these faculties more seriously. For instance, the teacher of a class somewhat older might be imagined to begin the exercise thus:

*T.* After the baptism of Jesus, which closes the 3d chapter of Matthew, we have an account of several temptations to which he was exposed. Now, open your books at the 4th chapter and see if you can find out how many verses are occupied with the narrative of these temptations, and at what verse each temptation begins.

The teacher then requires all the class to search in silence, and each one to get ready to answer, but lets no answer be given until all are prepared. When all have signified their readiness, some one is designated to give the answer.

The books being closed, the questioning begins:

*T.* Name the different places into which Jesus was taken to be tempted, and the verse in which each place is named.

*P.* It is said in the 1st verse that Jesus was led up into the wilderness; in the 5th verse that he was taken up into the holy city, and set on a pinnacle of the temple; and in the 8th verse, that he was taken up into an exceedingly high mountain.

*T.* What was the condition of Jesus, when the devil proposed his first temptation?

*P.* He had been fasting forty days and forty nights, and he was very hungry.

I need not multiply these illustrations. I have not made the mentirely in vain, if I have succeeded in producing in the mind of the reader the conviction of these two things; first, that it is a most important and difficult part of the teacher's art, to know how to ask a question; and, secondly, that the true measure of the teacher's ability is, not so much what he himself is able to say to the scholars, as the fulness, the accuracy and the completeness of the answers which he gets from them.

### TEACHING AND TRAINING.

Before leaving this part of the subject, and that there may be no possible misunderstanding on these elementary points, it seems proper that I should here explain briefly the difference between teaching and training, two processes which practically run into each other a good deal, but which nevertheless ought not to be confounded. Training implies more or less of practical application of what one has been taught. One may be taught, for instance, the exact forms of the letters used in writing, so as to know at once by the eye whether the letters are formed correctly or not. But only training and practice will make him a penman. Training refers more to the formation of habits. A child may be taught by reasoning the importance of punctuality in coming to school. But he is trained to the habit of punctuality only by actually coming to school in good time, day after day.

The human machine on which the teacher acts, is in its essential nature different from the material agencies operated on by other engineers. It is, as I have once and again said, a living power, with laws and processes of its own. Constant care, therefore, must be exercised, in the business of education, not to be misled by analogies drawn from the material world. The steam engine may go over its appointed task, day after day, the whole year round, and yet, at the end of the year, it will have no more tendency to go than before its first trip. Not so the boy. Going begets going. By doing a thing often, he acquires a facility, an inclination, a tendency, a habit of doing it. If a teacher or a parent succeeds in getting a child to do a thing once, it will be easier to get him to do it a second time, and still easier, a third time.

A teacher who is wise, when he seeks to bring about any given change in a child, whether it be intellectual or moral, will not ordinarily attempt to produce the change all at once, and by main force. He will not rely upon extravagant promises on the one side, nor upon scolding, threats, and violence on the other. Solomon hits the idea exactly, when he speaks of "leading in the way of righteousness." We must take the young by the hand and lead them. When we have led them over the ground once, let us do it a second time, and then a third time, and so keep on, until we shall have established with them a routine, which they will continue to follow of their own accord, when the guiding hand which first led them is withdrawn. *This is training.*

The theory of it is true, not only in regard to things to be done, which is generally admitted, but also in regard to things to be known, which is often ignored if not denied. A boy, we will say, has a repugnance to the study of arithmetic. Perhaps he is particularly dull of comprehension on that subject. We shall not remove that repugnance by railing at him. We shall never make him admire it by expatiating on its beauties. It will not become clear to his comprehension by our pouring upon it all at once a sudden and overpowering blaze of light in the way of explanation. Such a process rather confounds him. Here again let us fall back upon the method of the great Teacher, "Line upon line, precept upon precept." We will first patiently conduct our boy through one of the simplest operations of arithmetic, say, a sum in addition. The next day we will conduct him again through the same process, or through another of the same sort. The steps will gradually become familiar to his mind, then easy, then clear. He learns first the practice of arithmetic, then the rules, then the relations of numbers, then the theory on which the rules and the practice are based, and finally, he hardly knows how, he becomes an arithmetician. He has been trained into a knowledge of the subject.

You wish to teach a young child how to find a word in a dictionary. You give at first, perhaps, a verbal description of the mystery of a dictionary. You tell him that, in such a book, all the words are arranged according to the letters with which they begin; that all the words beginning with the letter A are in the first part of the book. Then those beginning with the letter B, then those beginning with C, and so on; you tell him that all the words beginning with one letter, covering some one or two hundred pages, are again re-arranged among themselves according to the second letter of each word, and then again still further re-arranged according to the third letter in each, and so on to the end. Arouse his utmost attention, and explain the process with the greatest clearness that words can give, and then set him to find a word. See how awkward will be his first attempt, how confused his ideas, how little he has really understood what you have told him. You must repeat your directions patiently, over and over, "line upon line"; you must take him by the hand, day after day, and train him into a knowledge of even so apparently simple a thing as finding a word in a dictionary.

While teaching and training are thus distinguishable in theory, in practice they are well nigh inseparable. At least, they never should be separated. Teaching has never done its perfect work, until, by training, the mind has learned to run in accustomed channels, until it sees what is true, and feels what is right, with a clearness, force, and promptitude, which come only from long continued habit.

Supposing a man to know clearly what teaching is, and to have himself the gift, how endless are the modes by which it is to be exercised! How numerous are the methods of doing even that one function of the teacher's office, the hearing of recitations! It may be well to occupy a little space in considering two or three of these modes, by way of still farther illustraing the subject, and before drawing the general conclusion to which all these illustrations point.

### METHODS OF HEARING RECITATIONS.

The first that I shall name is called the concert method. This is practiced chiefly in schools for very young children, especially for those who cannot read. There are many advantages in this method, some of which are not confined to infant classes. The timid, who are frightened by the sound of their own voices when attempting to recite alone, are thereby encourged to speak out, and those who have had any experience with such children, know that this is no small, or easy, or unimportant achievement. Another benefit of the method is the pleasure it gives the children. The measured noise and motion connected with such concert exercises, are particularly attractive to young children. Moreover, one good teacher, by the use of this method, may greatly multiply his efficiency. He may teach simultaneously fifty or sixty, instead of teaching only five or six. But in estimating this advantage, one error is to be guarded against. Visitors often hear a large class of fifty or more go through an exercise of this kind, in which the scholars have been drilled to recite in concert, and if such persons have never been accustomed to investigate the fact, they often suppose that the answers given are the intelligent responses of all the members of the class. The truth is, however, in very many such cases, that only some half-dozen or so really recite the answers from their own independent knowledge. These serve as leaders; the others, sheep-like, follow. Still, by frequent repetition, even in this blind way, something gradually sticks to the memory, although the impression is always apt to be vague and undefined.

The method of reciting in concert is, in my opinion, chiefly useful in reciting rules and definitions, or other matters, where the very words are to be committed to memory. The impression of so large a body of sound upon the ear is very strong, and is a great help in the matter of mere verbal recollection. Children too are very sympathetic, and a really skillful teacher, by the concert method, can do a great deal in cultivating the emotional nature of a large class.

Young children, too, it should be remembered, like all other young animals, are by nature restless and fidgety, and like to make a noise. It is possible, indeed, by a system of rigorous and harsh repression, to restrain this restlessness, and to keep these little ones for hours in such a state of decorous primness as not to molest weak nerves. But such a system of forced constraint is not natural to children, and is not a wise method of teaching. Let the youngsters make a noise; I had almost said, the more noise the better, so it be duly regulated. Let them exercise, not only their lungs, but their limbs, moving in concert, rising up, sitting down, turning round, marching, raising their hands, pointing to objects to which their attention is called, looking at objects which are shown to them. Movement and noise are the life of a child. They should be regulated, indeed, but not repressed. To make a young child sit still and keep silence for any great length of time, is next door to murder. I verily believe it sometimes is murder. The health, and even the lives of these little ones, are sacrificed to a false theory of teac ing. There is no occasion for torturing a child in order to teach him. God did not so mean it. Only let your teaching be in accordance with the wants of his young nature, and the school-room will be to him the most attractive spot of all the earth. Time and again have I seen the teacher of a primary school obliged at recess to compel her children to go out of doors, so much more pleasant did they find the school-room than the play-ground.

Quite the opposite extreme from the concert method, is that which, for convenience, may be called the individual method. In this method, the teacher examines one scholar alone upon the whole lesson, and then another, and so on, until the class is completed.

The only advantage claimed for this method is that the individual laggard cannot screen his deficiencies, as he can when reciting in concert. He cannot make believe to know the lesson by lazily joining in with the general current of voice when the answers are given. His own individual knowledge, or ignorance, stands out. This is clear, and so far it is an advantage. But ascertaining what a pupil knows of a lesson, is only one end, and that by no means the most important end of a recitation. This interview between the pupil and teacher, called a recitation, has many ends besides that of merely detecting how much of a subject the pupil knows. A far higher end is to make him know more,— to make perfect that knowledge which the most faithful preparation on the part of the pupil always leaves incomplete.

The disadvantages of the individual method are obvious. It is a great waste of time. If a teacher has a class of twenty, and an hour to hear them in, it gives him but three minutes for each pupil, supposing there are no interruptions. But we know there always are interruptions. In public schools the class oftener numbers forty than twenty, and the time for recitation is oftener half an hour than an hour. The teacher who pursues the individual method to its extreme, will rarely find himself in possession of more than one minute to each scholar. In so brief a time, very little can be ascertained as to what the scholar knows of the lesson, and still less can anything be done to increase that knowledge. Moreover, while the teacher is bestowing his small modicum of time upon one scholar, all the other members of the class are idle, or worse.

Teaching, of all kinds of labor, is that in which labor-saving and time-saving methods are of the greatest moment. The teacher who is wise, will aim so to conduct a recitation that, first, his whole time shall be given to every scholar; and secondly, the scholar's mind shall be exercised with every part of the lesson, and just as much when others are reciting, as when it is his own time to recite. A teacher who can do this is teaching every scholar, all the time, just as much as if he had no scholar but that one.

Even this does not state the whole case. A scholar in such a class learns more in a given time, than he would if he were alone, and the teacher's entire time were given exclusively to him. The human mind is wonderfully quickened by sympathy. In a crowd each catches, in some mysterious manner, an impulse from his fellows. The influence of associated numbers, all engaged upon the same thought, is universally to rouse the mind to a higher exercise of its powers. A mind that is dull, lethargic, and heavy in its movements, when moving solitarily, often effects, when under a social and sympathetic impulse, achievements that are a wonder to itself.

The teacher, then, who knows how thus to make a unit of twenty or thirty pupils, really multiplies himself twenty or thirty-fold, besides giving to the whole class an increased momentum such as always belongs to an aggregated mass. I have seen a teacher instruct a class of forty in such a way, as, in the first place, to secure the subordinate end of ascertaining and registering with a sufficient degree of exactness how much each scholar knows of the lesson by his own preparation, and secondly, to secure, during the whole hour, the active exercise and coöperation of each individual mind, under the powerful stimulus of the social instinct, and of a keenly awakened attention. Such a teacher accomplishes more in one hour than the slave of the individual method can accomplish in forty hours. A scholar in such a class learns more in one hour than he would learn in forty hours, in a class of equal numbers taught on the other plan. Such teaching is labor-saving and time-saving, in their highest perfection, employed upon the noblest of ends.

### OBSERVING A PROPER ORDER IN THE DEVELOPMENT OF THE FACULTIES.

But besides these questions of methods, there are other and higher questions, growing out of what may be called the philosophy of education. One of these relates to the observance of a proper order in the development of the mental faculties, and a mistake on this point leads often to a sad waste of time, even where it does not cause a mischievous perversion of ideas. Education may be defined to be the process of developing in due order and proportion all the good and desirable parts of human nature. On this point all educators are substantially agreed.

Another truth, to which there is a general theoretical assent, is that, in the order in which we develope the faculties, we should follow the leadings of nature, cultivating in childhood those faculties which seem most naturally to flourish in childish years, and reserving for maturer years the cultivation of those faculties which in the order of nature do not show much vigor until near the age of manhood, and which require for their full development a general ripening of all the other powers. The development of a human being is in some respects like that of a plant. There is one stage of growth suitable for the appearance and maturity of the leaf, another for the flower, a third for the fruit, and still a fourth for the perfected and ripened seed.

The analogy has of course many limitations. In the human plant, for instance, one class of faculties, after maturing, does not disappear in order to make place for another class, as the flower disappears before there can be fruit. Nor, again, is any class of faculties wanting altogether until the season for their development and maturity. The faculties all exist together, leaf, flower, fruit, and seed, at the same time, but each has its own best time for ripening.

While these principles have received the general assent of educators, there has been a wide divergence among them as to some of the practical applications. Which faculties do most naturally ripen early in life, and which late in life?

According to my own observation, the latest of the human powers in maturing, as it is the most consummate, is the Judgment. Next in the order of maturity, and next also in majesty and excellence, is the Reasoning power. Reason is minister to the judgment, furnishing to the latter materials for its action, as all the other powers, memory, fancy, imagination, and so forth, are ministers to reason, and supply it with its materials. The reasoning power lacks true vigor and muscle, the judgment is little to be relied on, until we approach manhood. Nature withholds from these faculties an earlier development, for the very reason, apparently, that they can ordinarily have but scanty materials for action until after the efflorescence of the other faculties. The mind must first be well filled with knowledge, which the other faculties have gathered and stored, before reason and judgment can have full scope for action.

Going to the other end of the scale, I have as little doubt that the earliest of all the faculties to bud and blossom, is the Memory. Children not only commit to memory with ease, but they take actual pleasure in it. Tasks, under which the grown up man recoils and reels, the child will assume with light heart, and execute without fatigue. Committing to memory, which is repulsive drudgery to the man, is the easiest of all tasks to the child. More than this. The things fixed in the memory of childhood are seldom forgotten. Things learned later in life, not only are learned with greater difficulty, but more rapidly disappear. I recall instantly and without effort, texts of Scripture, hymns, catechisms, rules of grammar and arithmetic, and scraps of poetry and of classic authors, with which I became familiar when a boy. But it is a labor of Hercules for me to repeat by memory anything acquired since attaining the age of manhood. The Creator seems to have arranged an order in the natural development of the faculties for this very purpose, that in childhood and youth we may be chiefly occupied with the accumulation of materials in our intellectual storehouse. Now to reverse this process, to occupy the immature mind of childhood chiefly with the cultivation of faculties which are of later growth, and actually to put shackles and restraints upon the memory, nicknaming and ridiculing all memoriter exercises as parrot performances, is to ignore one of the primary facts of human nature. It is to be wiser than God.

Another faculty that shoots up into full growth in the very morning and spring-time of life, is Faith. I speak here, of course, not of religious faith, but of the faculty of the human mind which leads a child to believe instinctively whatever is told him. That we all do thus believe, until by slow and painful experience we learn to do otherwise, needs no demonstration. Everybody's experience attests the fact. It is equally plain that the existence and maturity of this faculty in early childhood is a most wise and beneficent provision of nature. How slow and tedious would be the first steps in knowledge, were the child born, as some teachers seem trying to make him, a sceptic, that is, with a mind which refuses to receive anything as true, except what it has first proved by experience and reason! On the contrary, how much is the acquisition of knowledge expedited, during these years of helplessness and dependency, by this spontaneous, instinctive faith of childhood. The same infinite wisdom and love, which in the order of nature provide for the helpless infant a father and mother to care for it, provide also in the constitution of the infant's mind that instinctive principle or power of faith, which alone makes the father's and mother's love efficacious towards its intellectual growth and development. Of what use were parents or teachers, in instructing a child which required proof for every statement that father, mother, or teacher gives? How cruel to force the confiding, young heart into premature scepticism, by compelling him to hunt up reasons for everything, when he has reasons, to him all-sufficient, in the fact that father, mother or teacher, told him so?

It may seem trifling to dwell so long upon these elementary points. Yet there are wide-spread plans of education which violate every principle here laid down. Educators and systems of education, enjoying the highest popularity, seem to have adopted the theory, at least they tacitly act upon the theory, that the first faculty of the mind to be developed is the reasoning power. Indeed, they are not far from asserting that the whole business of education consists in the cultivation of this power, and they bend accordingly their main energies upon training young children to go through certain processes of reasoning, so called. They require a child to prove everything before receiving it as true, to reason out a rule for himself for every process in arithmetic or grammar, to demonstrate the multiplication table before daring to use it, or to commit it to memory if indeed they do not forbid entirely its being committed to memory as too parrot-like and mechanical. To commit blindly to memory precious forms of truth, which the wise and good have hived for the use of the race, is poohed at as old fogyish. To receive as true anything which the child cannot fathom, and which he has not discovered or demonstrated for himself, is denounced as slavish. All authority in teaching, growing out of the age and the reputed wisdom of the teacher, all faith and reverence in the learner, growing out of a sense of his ignorance and dependence, are discarded, and the frightened stripling is continually rapped on the knuckles, if he does not at every step show the truth of his allegations by what is called a course of reasoning. Children reason, of course. They should be encouraged and taught to reason. No teacher, who is wise, will neglect this part of a child's intellectual powers. But he will not consider this the season for its main, normal development. He will hold this subject for the present subordinate to many others. Moreover, the methods of reasoning, which he does adopt, will be of a peculiar kind, suited to the nature of childhood, the results being mainly intuitional, rather than the fruits of formal logic. To oblige a young child to go through a formal syllogystic statement in every step in elementary arithmetic, for instance, is simply absurd. It makes nothing plain to a child's mind which was not plain before. On the contrary, it often makes a muddle of what had been perfectly clear. What was in the clear sunlight of intuition, is now in a haze, through the intervening medium of logical terms and forms, through which he is obliged to look at it.

A primary teacher asks her class this question: "If I can buy 6 marbles with one penny, how many marbles can I buy with 5 pennies?" A bright boy who should promptly answer "30" would be sharply rebuked. Little eight-year old Solon on the next bench, has been better trained than that. With stately and solemn enunciation he delivers himself of a performance somewhat of this sort. "If I can buy 6 marbles with 1 penny, how many marbles can I buy with 5 pennies? Answer—I can buy 5 times as many marbles with 5 pennies as I can buy with 1 penny. If, therefore, I can buy 6 marbles with 1 penny, I can buy 5 times as many marbles with 5 pennies; and 5 times 6 marbles are 30 marbles. Therefore, if I can buy 6 marbles with one penny, I can buy 30 marbles with 5 pennies."

And this is termed reasoning! And to train children, by forced and artificial processes, to go through such a rigmarole of words, is recommended as a means of cultivating their reasoning power and of improving their power of expression! It is not pretended that children by such a process become more expert in reckoning. On the contrary, their movements as ready reckoners are retarded by it. Instead of learning to jump at once to the conclusion, lightning-like, by a sort of intuitional process, which is the very essence of an expert accountant, they learn laboriously to stay their march by a cumbersome and confusing circumlocution of words. And the expenditure of time and toil needed to acquire these formulas of expression, which nine times out of ten are to those young minds the mere *dicta magistri*, is justified on the ground that the children, if not learning arithmetic, are learning to reason.

Let me not be misunderstood. I do not advocate the disuse of explanations. Let teachers explain, let children give explanations. Let the rationale of the various processes through which the child goes, receive a certain amount of attention. But the extreme into which some are now going, in primary education, is that of giving too much time to explanation and to theory, and too little to practice. We reverse, too, the order of nature in this matter. What it now takes weeks and months to make clear to the immature understanding, is apprehended at a later day with ease and delight at the very first statement. There is a clear and consistent philosophy underlying this whole matter. It is simply this. In the healthy and natural order of development in educating a young mind, theory should follow practice, not precede it. Children learn the practice of arithmetic very young. They take to it naturally, and learn it easily, and become very rapidly expert practical accountants. But the science of arithmetic is quite another matter, and should not be forced upon them until a much later stage in their advancement.

To have a really correct apprehension of the principle of decimal notation, for instance, to understand that it is purely arbitrary, and that we might in the same way take any other number than ten as the base of a numerical scale,—that we might increase for instance by fives, or eights, or nines, or twelves, just as well as by tens,—all this requires considerable maturity of intellect, and some subtlety of reasoning. Indeed I doubt whether many of the pretentious sciolists, who insist so much on young children giving the rationale of everything, have themselves ever yet made an ultimate analysis of the first step in arithmetical notation. Many of them would open their eyes were you to tell them, for instance, that the number of fingers on your two hands may be just as correctly expressed by the figures 11, 12, 13, 14, or 15, as by the figures ten,—a truism perfectly familiar to every one acquainted with the generalizations of higher arithmetic. Yet it is up-hill work to make the matter quite clear to a beginner. We may wisely therefore give our children at first an arbitrary rule for notation. We give them an equally arbitrary rule for addition. They accept these rules and work upon them, and learn thereby the practical operations of arithmetic. The theory will follow in due time. When perfectly familiar with the practice and the forms of arithmetic, and sufficiently mature in intellect, they awaken gradually and surely, and almost without an effort, to the beautiful logic which underlies the science.

How do we learn language in childhood? Is it not solely on authority and by example? A child who lives in a family where no language is used but that which is logically and grammatically correct, will learn to speak with logical and grammatical correctness long before it is able to give any account of the processes of its own mind in the matter, or indeed to understand those processes when explained by others. In other words, practice in language precedes theory. It should do so in other things. The parent who should take measures to prevent a child from speaking its mother tongue, except just so far and so fast as it could understand and explain the subtle logic which underlies all language, would be quite as wise as the teacher who refuses to let a child become expert in practical reckoning, until it can understand and explain at every step the rationale of the process,—who will not suffer a child to learn the multiplication table until it has mastered the metaphysics of the science of numbers, and can explain with the formalities of syllogism exactly how and why seven times nine make sixty-three.

These illustrations have carried me a little, perhaps, from my subject. But it seemed necessary to show that I am not beating the air. I have feared lest. in our very best schools, in the rebound from the exploded errors of the old system, we have unconsciously run into an error in the opposite extreme.

My position on the particular point now under consideration, may be summed up briefly, as follows: 1. In developing the faculties, we should follow the order of nature. 2. The faculties of memory and faith should be largely exercised and cultivated in childhood. 3. While the judgment and the reasoning faculty should be exercised during every stage of the intellectual development, the appropriate season for their main development and culture is near the close, rather than near the beginning, of an educational course. 4. The methods of reasoning used with children should be of a simple kind, dealing largely in direct intuitions, rather than formal and syllogistic. 5. It is a mistake to spend a large amount of time and effort in requiring young children formally to explain the rationale of their intellectual processes, and especially in requiring them to give such explanations before they have become by practice thoroughly familiar with the processes themselves.

I have thus endeavored to set forth, in the first place, what a Normal School is, namely, a seminary for professional training in the art and science of teaching; and, secondly, to show, with some particularity and variety of illustration, what teaching is, in its very root and essence; and to make the matter plainer, I have attempted to show the difference between teaching and training, and to explain some two or three out of very many different modes of teaching, and to discuss briefly one of the many points that are involved in the philosophy of education. Some distinct consideration of these subjects, which come up continually for discussion in a Normal School, seemed to be the very best line of argument for showing the necessity of such an institution. To appreciate the full force of this argument, it would be necessary, indeed, to consider the vast array of similar and connected subjects which beset the teacher's path, and which there is not time now even to enumerate. Let me merely name some few of these subjects.

The Monitorial method of teaching.

The Catechetical method.

The Explanatory method.

The Synthetical method.

The Analytical method.

Modes of securing in a large school all the while something for all the children to do.

Modes of teaching particular branches: as Spelling, Reading, Mental Arithmetic, Written Arithmetic, Grammar, Geography, Composition, Drawing, Penmanship, Vocal Music, &c.

School apparatus and means for visible illustration.

The development and cultivation of the faculties of observation, attention, memory, association, conception, imagination, &c.

Modes of inspiring scholars with enthusiasm in study, and of cultivating habits of self-reliance.

Topics and times for introducing oral instruction.

Teaching with and without books.

Object teaching.

The formation of museums, and collections of plants, minerals, &c.

Exchange of specimens of penmanship, maps, drawings, minerals, &c., with other schools.

School examinations. Their object, and the different modes of conducting them.

School celebrations, festivals, and excursions.

The daily preparation which a teacher should make for school.

Circumstances which make a teacher happy in his work.

Requisites for success in teaching.

Causes of failure in teaching.

Course to be pursued in organizing a new school.

Course to be pursued in admitting new scholars.

Making an order of exercises.

Making a code of rules.

Keeping registers of attendance and progress.

Duties of the teacher to the parents and to school directors.

Opening and closing exercises of a school.

Moral and religious instruction and influences.

Modes of cultivating among children a love of truth, honesty, benevolence, and other virtues.

Modes of preventing lying, swearing, stealing, and other vices.

Modes of securing cleanliness of person, neatness of dress, courtesy of language, and gentleness of manners.

Modes of preserving the school-house and appurtenances from defacement.

Keeping the school-room in proper condition as to temperature and ventilation.

Length of school day.

Length and frequency of recess.

Games to be encouraged or discouraged at recess.

Modes of preventing tardiness.

Causes by which the health of children at school is promoted or injured.

Modes of establishing the teacher's authority.

Modes of securing the scholar's affections.

Mode of treating refractory children.

Modes of bringing forward dull, backward children.

Modes of preventing whispering.

The use of emulation.

Prizes and rewards.

But I pause. The very enumeration of such a list, it seems to me, shows of itself, with overwhelming force, how urgent is the necessity that the teacher should have a time and an institution for considering them, and for obtaining in regard to them definite, well settled views. Some of these questions come up for practical decision every day of a teacher's life, and they are of too serious import to be left to the unpre meditated exigencies of the moment of execution. In a Normal School the novice hears these subjects discussed by teachers and professors of learning and experience, and he is made acquainted with the general usage of the most successful members of the profession. He enters upon his important and responsible work, not only fortified with safeguards against mistake, but furnished with a kind of knowledge which reduces to a minimum his chances of failure, and increases to almost a certainty his chances of success.

# NORMAL METHODS OF TEACHING.

We shall bring together in this article examples of methods of teaching and training—of study and recitation, adopted and illustrated in our schools for the professional training of teachers, and inculcated or followed by prominent educators.

### FATHER PIERCE AT LEXINGTON, MASS.

The following letter, addressed in 1851, by Mr. Peirce, to Hon. Henry Barnard, then Superintendent of Common Schools in Connecticut, embodies his own views as to the aims of his labors as Principal of the Normal School at Lexington, and West Newton.

"Dear Sir:—You ask me 'what I aimed to accomplish, and would aim to accomplish now, with my past experience before me, in a Normal School.'

I answer briefly, that it was my aim, and it would be my aim again, to make better teachers, and especially, better teachers for our common schools; so that those primary seminaries, on which so many depend for their education, might answer, in a higher degree, the end of their institution. Yes, to make better teachers; teachers who would understand, and do their business better; teachers, who should know more of the nature of children, of youthful developments, more of the subjects to be taught, and more of the true methods of teaching; who would teach more philosophically, more in harmony with the natural development of the young mind, with a truer regard to the order and connection in which the different branches of knowledge should be presented to it, and, of course, more successfully. Again, I felt that there was a call for a truer government, a higher training and discipline, in our schools; that the appeal to the rod, to a sense of shame and fear of bodily pain, so prevalent in them, had a tendency to make children mean, secretive, and vengeful, instead of high-minded, truthful, and generous; and I wished to see them in the hands of teachers, who could understand the higher and purer motives of action, as gratitude, generous affection, sense of duty, by which children should be influenced, and under which their whole character should be formed. In short, I was desirous of putting our schools into the hands of those who would make them places in which children could learn, not only to read, and write, and spell, and cipher, but gain information on various other topics, (as accounts, civil institutions, natural history, physiology, political economy, &c.) which would be useful to them in after life, and have all their faculties, (physical, intellectual and moral,) trained in such harmony and proportion, as would result in the highest formation of character. This is what I supposed the object of Normal Schools to be. Such was my object.

But in accepting the charge of the first American Institution of this kind, I did not act in the belief that there were no good teachers, or good schools among us; or that I was more wise, more fit to teach, than all my fellows. On the contrary, I knew that there were, both within and without Massachusetts, excellent schools, and not a few of them, and teachers wiser than myself; yet my conviction was strong, that the ratio of such schools to the whole number of schools were small; and that the teachers in them, for the most part, had grown up to be what they were, from long observation, and through the discipline of an experience painful to themselves, and more painful to their pupils.

It was my impression also, that a majority of those engaged in school-keeping, taught few branches, and those imperfectly, that they possessed little fitness for their business, did not understand well, either the nature of children or the subjects they professed to teach, and had little skill in the art of teaching or governing schools. I could not think it possible for them, therefore, to make their instructions very intelligible, interesting, or profitable to their pupils, or present to them the motives best adapted to secure good lessons and good conduct, or, in a word, adopt such a course of training as would result in a sound development of the faculties, and the sure formation of a good character. I admitted that a skill and power to do all this might be acquired by trial, if teachers continued in their business long enough; but while teachers were thus learning, I was sure that pupils must be suffering. In the process of time, a man may find out by experiment, (trial,) how to tan hides and convert them into leather. But most likely the time would be long, and he would spoil many before he got through. It would be far better for him, we know, to get some knowledge of Chemistry, and spend a little time in his neighbor's tannery, before he sets up for himself. In the same way, the farmer may learn what trees, and fruits, and seeds, are best suited to particular soils, and climates, and modes of culture, but it must be by a needless outlay of time and labor, and the incurring of much loss. If wise, he would first learn the principles and facts which agricultural experiments have already established, and then commence operations. So the more I considered the subject, the more the conviction grew upon my mind, that by a judicious course of study, and of discipline, teachers may be prepared to enter on their work, not only with the hope, but almost with the assurance of success. I did not then, I do not now, (at least in the fullest extent of it,) assent to the doctrine so often expressed in one form or another, that there are no general principles to be recognized in education; no general methods to be followed in the art of teaching; that all depends upon the individual teacher; that every principle, motive and method, must owe its power to the skill with which it is applied; that what is true, and good, and useful in the hands of one, may be quite the reverse in the hands of another; and of course, that every man must invent his own methods of teaching and governing, it being impossible successfully to adopt those of another. To me it seemed that education had claims to be regarded as a science, being based on immutable principles, of which the practical teacher, though he may modify them to meet the change of ever-varying circumstances, can never lose sight.

That the educator should watch the operations of nature, the development of the mind, discipline those faculties whose activities first appear, and teach that knowledge first, which the child can most easily comprehend, viz., that which comes in through the senses, rather than through reason and the imagination; that true education demands, or rather implies the training, strengthening, and perfecting of all the faculties by means of the especial exercise of each; that in teaching, we must begin with what is simple and known, and go on by easy steps to what is complex and unknown; that for true progress and lasting results, it were better for the attention to be concentrated on a few studies, and for a considerable time, than to be divided among many, changing from one to another at short intervals; that in training children we must concede a special recognition to the principle of curiosity, a love of knowledge, and so present truth as to keep this principle in proper action; that the pleasure of acquiring, and the advantage of possessing knowledge, may be made, and should be made, a sufficient stimulus to sustain wholesome exertion without resorting to emulation, or medals, or any rewards other than those which are the natural fruits of industry and attainment; that for securing order and obedience, there are better ways than to depend solely or chiefly upon the rod, or appeals to fear; that much may be done by way of prevention of evil; that gentle means should always first be tried; that undue attention is given to intellectual training in our schools, to the neglect of physical and moral; that the training of the faculties is more important than the communication of knowledge; that the discipline, the instruction of the school-room, should better subserve the interests of real life, than it now does;—these are some of the principles, truths, facts, in education, susceptible, I think, of the clearest demonstration, and pretty generally admitted now, by all enlightened educators.

The old method of teaching Arithmetic, for instance, by taking up some printed treatise and solving abstract questions consisting of large numbers, working blindly by what must appear to the pupil arbitrary rules, would now be regarded as less philosophical, less in conformity to mental development, than the more modern way of beginning with mental Arithmetic, using practical questions, which involve small numbers, and explaining the reason of every step as you go along.

So in the study of Grammar, no Normal teacher, whether a graduate or not, of a Normal School, would require his pupils to commit the whole text-book to memory, before looking at the nature of words, and their application in the structure of sentences. Almost all have found out that memorizing the Grammar-book, and the exercise of parsing, do very little toward giving one a knowledge of the English language.

Neither is it learning Geography, to read over and commit to memory, statistics of the length and breadth of countries, their boundaries, latitude and longitude, &c., &c., without map or globe, or any visible illustration, as was once the practice. Nor does the somewhat modern addition of maps and globes much help the process, unless the scholar, by a previous acquaintance with objects in the outer world, has been prepared to use them. The shading for mountains, and black lines for rivers on maps, will be of little use to a child who has not already some idea of a mountain and a river.

And the teacher who should attempt to teach reading by requiring a child to repeat from day to day, and from month to month, the whole alphabet, until he is familiar with all the letters, as was the fashion in former days, would deserve to lose his place and be sent himself to school. Could any thing be more injudicious? Is it not more in harmony with Nature's work, to begin with simple, significant words, or rather sentences, taking care always to select such as are easy and intelligible, as well as short? Or, if letters be taken first, should they not be formed into small groups, on some principle of association, and be combined with some visible object?

Surely, the different methods of teaching the branches above-mentioned, are not all equally good. Teaching is based on immutable principles, and may be regarded as an art.

Nearly thirty years' experience in the business of teaching, I thought, had given me some acquaintance with its true principles and processes, and I deemed it no presumption to believe that I could teach them to others. This I attempted to do in the Normal School at Lexington; 1st. didactically, *i. e.* by precept, in the form of familiar conversations and lectures; 2d. by giving every day, and continually, in my own manner of teaching, an exemplification of my theory; 3d. by requiring my pupils to teach each other, in my presence, the things which I had taught them; and 4th. by means of the Model School, where, under my general supervision, the Normal pupils had an opportunity, both to prove and to improve their skill in teaching and managing schools. At all our recitations, (the modes of which were very various,) and in other connections, there was allowed the greatest freedom of inquiry and remark, and principles, modes, processes, every thing indeed relating to school-keeping, was discussed. The thoughts and opinions of each one were thus made the property of the whole, and there was infused into all hearts a deeper and deeper interest in the teachers' calling. In this way the Normal School became a kind of standing Teachers' Institute.

But for a particular account of my manner and processes at the Normal School, allow me to refer you to a letter which I had the honor, at your request, to address to you from Lexington, Jan. 1, 1841, and which was published in the Common School Journal, both of Connecticut and Massachusetts, (vol. 3.)

What success attended my labors, I must leave to others to say. I acknowledge, it was far from being satisfactory to myself. Still the experiment convinced me that Normal Schools may be made a powerful auxiliary to the cause of education. A thorough training in them, I am persuaded, will do much toward supplying the want of experience. It will make the teachers' work easier, surer, better. I have reason to believe that Normal pupils are much indebted for whatever of fitness they possess for teaching, to the Normal School. They uniformly profess so to feel. I have, moreover, made diligent inquiry in regard to their success, and it is no exaggeration to say, that it has been manifestly great. Strong testimonials to the success of many of the early graduates of the Lexington (now W. Newton) Normal School, were published with the 8th Report of the late Secretary of the Board of Education, and may be found in the 7th vol. of the Massachusetts Common School Journal.

But it is sometimes asked, (and the inquiry deserves an answer,) Allowing that teaching is an art, and that teachers may be trained for their business, have we not High Schools and Academies, in which the various school branches are well taught? May not teachers in them be prepared for their work?

Where is the need then of a distinct order of Seminaries for training teachers? I admit we have Academies, High Schools, and other schools, furnished with competent teachers, in which is excellent teaching; but at the time of the establishment of the Normal Schools in Massachusetts, there was not, to my knowledge, any first-rate institution exclusively devoted to training teachers for our common schools; neither do I think there is now any, except the Normal Schools. And teachers can not be prepared for their work anywhere else, so well as in seminaries exclusively devoted to this object. The art of teaching must be made the great, the paramount, the only concern. It must not come in as subservient to, or merely collateral with any thing else whatever. And again, a Teachers' Seminary should have annexed to it, or rather as an integral part of it, a model, or experimental school for practice.

Were I to be placed in a Normal School again, the only difference in my aim would be to give more attention to the development of the faculties, to the spirit and motives by which a teacher should be moved, to physical and moral education, to the inculcation of good principles and good manners.

In conclusion, allow me to recapitulate. It was my aim, and it would be my aim again, in a Normal School, to raise up for our common schools especially, a better class of teachers,—teachers who would not only teach more and better than those already in the field, but who would govern better; teachers, who would teach in harmony with the laws of juvenile development, who would secure diligent study and good lessons and sure progress, without a resort to emulation and premiums, and good order from higher motives than the fear of the rod or bodily pain; teachers, who could not only instruct well in the common branches, as reading, writing, arithmetic, &c., but give valuable information on a variety of topics, such as accounts, history, civil institutions, political economy, and physiology; bring into action the various powers of children, and prepare them for the duties of practical life; teachers, whose whole influence on their pupils, direct and indirect, should be good, tending to make them, not only good readers, geographers, grammarians, arithmeticians, &c., but good scholars, good children, obedient, kind, respectful, mannerly, truthful; and in due time, virtuous, useful citizens, kind neighbors, high-minded, noble, pious men and women. And this I attempted to do by inculcating the truth in the art of teaching and governing,—the truth in all things; and by giving them a living example of it in my own practice."

The following extracts are taken from the letter of Mr. Pierce, addressed to Mr. Barnard, Jan. 1, 1841, and published in the Conn. Common School Journal.

You ask for a full account of my manner of instruction in the *art of Teaching.* This, it is not easy to give. From what I say, you may get some idea of what I *attempt;* and of the *manner* of it. Two things I have aimed at, especially in this school. I. To teach *thoroughly* the principles of the several branches studied, so that the pupils may have a *clear* and *full understanding* of them. 2nd, to teach the pupils by my own *example*, as well as by *precepts*, the *best way of teaching the same things* effectually to others. I have four different methods of recitation. 1st, by question and answer; 2nd, by conversation; 3d, by calling on one, two, three, more or less, to give an analysis of the whole subject contained in the lesson, and 4th, by requiring written analyses in which the *ideas* of the author are stated in the *language* of the pupil. I do not mean that these are all practiced at the same exercise. The students understand that, at all the recitations, they are at perfect liberty to suggest queries, doubts, opinions. At all the recitations we have more or less of discussion. Much attention is paid to the *manner* in which the pupils *set forth, or state* their positions. I am ever mingling, or attempting to mingle, at these exercises, theory and example; frequently putting the inquiry to them, not only; 'how do you understand such and such a statement;' but, 'how would you express such and such a sentiment, or explain such a principle, or illustrate such a position to a class, which you may be teaching?' 'Let me,' I say to them, 'hear your statements, or witness your modes of illustrating and explaining.' In this connection I frequently call them to the blackboard for visible representation. They make the attempt: I remark upon their manner of doing it, and endeavor to show them in what respect it may be improved.

Sometimes, instead of reciting the lesson directly to me, I ask them to imagine themselves for the time, acting in the *capacity* of *teachers*, to a class of young pupils, and to adopt a style suitable for such a purpose. At many of our recitations, more than half the time is spent with reference to teaching '*the art of teaching.*' Besides delivering to the school a written *Formal Lecture* once a week, in which I speak of the qualifications, motives, and duties of teachers, the discipline, management, and instruction of schools, and the *manner* in which the various branches should be taught, I am every day, in conversations or a familiar sort of lectures, taking up and discussing more *particularly* and *minutely* some point or points suggested by the exercises or occurrences, it may be of the day, relating to the *internal operations* of the school-room, or to physical, moral or intellectual education:—I say much about the views and motives of teachers, and the motives by which they should attempt to stimulate their pupils. And here I would state that my theory goes to the entire exclusion of the *premium and emulation system*, and of corporal punishment. My confidence in it is sustained and strengthened by a full and fair experiment for more than one year in a public school composed of seventy scholars of both sexes. I am constantly calling up real or supposed cases, and either asking the pupils what they would do in such case, or stating to them what I would do myself, or both. As a specimen of such questions, take the following, viz.: on going into a school as teacher, what is the first thing you would do? How will you proceed to bring to order, and arrange your school? Will you have many rules or few? Will you announce beforehand a code of laws, or make special rules as they may be needed? What *motives* do you purpose to appeal to, and what *means* will you adopt to make your pupils interested in their studies? What method will you adopt to teach spelling, reading, arithmetic? What will you do with the perseveringly idle and troublesome? What will you do if your scholars quarrel? lie? swear? What will you do if a scholar tells you he *wont* do as he is directed? If a question in any ordinary lesson, say arithmetic, comes up, which you can not solve readily, what will be your resort? Should you be chiefly ambitious to teach *much*, or to teach thoroughly? How would you satisfy yourself that your teaching is thorough, effectual? To what branches shall you attach most importance, and why? Will you aim chiefly to exercise the *faculties*, or communicate instruction? Besides these daily discussions or conversations, we have a *regular debate* every Saturday, in which the principles involved in these and similar questions are discussed.

Reading, I teach by oral inculcation of the principles as contained in Porter's Rhetorical Reader (which strike me as in the main correct), and by example; reading myself before the whole class; hearing the pupils read, and then reading the same piece myself; pointing out their faults, and calling upon them to read again and again, and even the third and fourth time. They also read to each other in my presence. This is a most difficult art to teach. Very few good readers are to be found either in our schools or elsewhere. Spelling I teach both orally and by *writing* from the reading lesson, for I think each method has its advantages. Orthography has not yet received quite its merited attention in our schools. *Most* persons in business life have to *write;* few comparatively are called upon to read publicly, for this reason it is more important to be a correct speller than a fine reader.

I have adopted no text-book in teaching Geography. Worcester's is *chiefly* used. My method has been to give out a subject (a particular country, e. g.) for examination. The class make search, using what maps and books they have at command, and get all the information of every kind they can, statistical, historical, geographical, of the people, manners, religion, government, business, &c., and at the recitation we have the *results* of their researches. Giving to each a separate subject, I sometimes require the pupils to make an imaginary voyage or journey to one, two, three, or more countries, and give an account of every thing on their return. If I were to teach Geography to a class of *young beginners*, I should commence with the town in which they live.

In Grammar, I have adopted no particular text-book. I am teaching a class of beginners in the model school without a book.

In Moral Instruction we use both Wayland and Combe; and our recitations are conducted as above described. There are no subjects in which scholars manifest more interest than in questions of morals. This I have noticed in all schools. It shows how easy it would be to do what is so much needed, if the teachers are disposed; viz., to cultivate the *moral faculties.* In connection with reading the Scriptures at the opening of the school, it is my practice to remark on points of practical duty as far as I can go on common ground.

Allow me to express my high gratification in your late visit to the Normal School. You have had much opportunity to see and compare many schools. For any suggestions in regard to what you saw at Lexington for the *improvement* of the school, I would be very thankful. I have undiminished confidence in the feasibility of the plan of Normal Schools, if sustained by the sentiment of the community, it could be allowed to continue in operation long enough to make a fair experiment. But on *this point* I have increasing fears.

That there could ever have been any serious doubt of the permanence of an institution for the professional training of teachers in the State of Massachusetts, as is expressed in the closing paragraph of Mr. Pierce's letter, can with difficulty be credited in 1872, when Normal Schools, Teachers' Institutes, and City Training Schools, are liberally provided in every State, and nearly every large city—as essential features in any efficient system of public instruction. And yet such was the anxiety felt by Mr. Mann, Mr. Everett (at that time Governor of Massachusetts), and Mr. Dwight, whose benefaction of $10,000 (or so much as remained unexpended), it was then under consideration in the House of Representatives to return, that the writer of this note, in March, 1841, at the urgent request of Mr. Mann, spent two weeks in Boston, to manifest to members of the Legislature the interest felt by educators out of the State in a fair trial of the first experiment of a State Normal School.

**Mr. Pierce died at West Newton, on the 6th of April, 1860, aged seventy.**

## NICHOLAS TILLINGHAST AT BRIDGEWATER.

PROFESSOR TILLINGHAST was educated at the United States Military Academy at West Point, and brought to the instruction of pupil teachers of common schools, an accurate mathematical training, and the "before the blackboard method of illustration and recitation," which characterized that institution. Before entering on his duties as principal, he spent six months at the Barre State Normal School, as an assistant and pupil of Prof. Newman, who had filled the chair of rhetoric and literature at Bowdoin College. Prof. T. left his mark not only on the blackboard, but on the mental character and methods of his pupils. The following passages are from a letter addressed by him to Mr. Barnard, printed in Barnard's Normal Schools of the United States.

There are, it seems to me, grave defects in the constitution of my school. Four years would, in my judgment, be profitably given to the subjects which we touch on in one. If pupils must be *taught* subjects in these schools, as I think they must for a time under the best organization, the course ought to extend over three years at least. I think it would be a better plan than the present, to receive pupils for, say twenty-one weeks, and to give that time to reading, spelling, arithmetic, and geography; and in another twenty-one weeks, to take up reading, spelling, physiology, grammar; so that only a few studies should be in the school at a time, and teachers might go for a term without interfering with their teaching school. The great evil now, in my school, is the attempt to take up so many studies, most persons inverting the truth, and supposing the amount acquired the important thing, and the *study* unimportant. But I should be content if I could bring pupils into such a state of knowledge that they could recognize her when overtaken. A very few studies, and long dwelling on them—this is my theory. I have no especial belief in teaching others *methods* of teaching: I do not mean, that the subject should be entirely passed by; but that pupils should not be *trained* into, or directed into particular processes; it seems to me that each well-instructed mind will arrive at a method of imparting, better for *it* than any other method. I therefore have tried to bring my pupils to get at results for themselves, and to show them how they may feel confident of the truth of their results. I have *sought* criticism from my scholars on all my methods, processes, and results; aimed to have them, kindly, of course, but freely, criticise each other; and they are encouraged to ask questions, and propose doubts. I call on members of the classes to hear recitations, and on the others to make remarks, thus approving and disproving one another; they are called upon to make up general exercises, and to deliver them to their classes, sometimes on subjects and in styles fitted to those whom they address; sometimes they are bid to imagine themselves speaking to children. I find I am getting more into details than I intend, or you wish. My idea of a Normal School is, that it should have a term of four years; that those studies should be pursued that will lay a *foundation* on which to build an education. I mean, for example, that algebra should be *thoroughly* studied as the foundation for arithmetic; that geometry and trigonometry should be studied, by which, with algebra, to study natural philosophy, &c.; the number of studies should be comparatively small, but much time given to them. I, of course, do not intend to write a list of studies, and what I have said above is only for illustration: the teacher should be so trained as to be *above* his text-books. Whatever has been done in teaching in all countries, different methods, the thoughts of the best minds on the *science* and *art* of instruction, should be laid before the neophyte teachers. In a proper Normal School there should be departments, and the ablest men put over them, each in his own department. Who knows more than one branch *well?*

I send herewith a catalogue of my school, which will give you some idea of its osteology; what of life these bones have, others must judge. But when shall the whole vision of the Prophet be fulfilled in regard to the teachers of the land,—"And the breath came into them, and they *lived* and stood upon their feet (not on those of any author), an exceeding great army."

God prosper the work, and may your exertions in the cause be gratefully re-

## DR. WAYLAND.—METHOD OF RECITATION.

Dr. WAYLAND, in the preface to his text-book on Moral Science, suggests a few hints as to the manner in which it may be most successfully used in the class-room.

1. In the recitation-room, let neither instructor nor pupil ever make use of the book.

2. Let the portion previously assigned for the exercise be so mastered by the pupil, both in plan and illustration, that he will be able to recite it in order, and explain the connection of the different parts with each other, without the necessity of assistance from his instructor. To give the language of the author is not, of course, desirable. It is sufficient if the idea be given. The questions of the instructor should have respect to principles that may be deduced from the text, practical application of the doctrines, objections which may be raised, &c.

3. Let the lesson which was recited on one day, be invariably reviewed on the day succeeding.

4. As soon as any considerable progress has been made in the work, let a review from the beginning be commenced. This should comprehend, for one exercise, as much as had been previously recited in two or three days; and should be confined to a brief analysis of the argument, with a mere mention of the illustrations.

5. As soon as the whole portion thus far recited has been reviewed, let a new review be commenced, and continued in the same manner; and thus on successively, until the work is completed. By pursuing this method, a class will, at any period of the course of study, be enabled, with the slightest effort, to recall whatever they have already acquired; and when the work is completed, they will be able to pursue the whole thread of the argument, from the beginning to the end; and thus to retain a knowledge, not only of the individual principles, but also of their relations to each other.

But the advantage of this mode of study is not confined to that of a more perfect knowledge of this or of any other book. By presenting the whole field of thought at one view before the mind, it will cultivate the power of pursuing an extended range of argument; of examining and deciding upon a connected chain of reasoning; and will, in no small degree, accustom the student to carry forward in his own mind a train of original investigation.

I have been emboldened to make these suggestions, not in the least because I suppose the present work worthy of any peculiar attention from an instructor, but simply because, having been long in the habit of pursuing this method, and having witnessed its results in my own classes, I have thought it my duty to suggest it to those who are engaged in the same profession with myself. Other instructors may have succeeded better with other methods. I have succeeded best with this.

The method thus indicated he caused to be introduced into all the recitations of the college to which it is applicable. In the use of this method, the classes generally passed over less ground than is common in other colleges, but could not fail to understand the relations of each discussion. Especially this method cultivates in the student the power of analysis. If he is required to state the substance of each paragraph in its proper relation to that which precedes and to that which follows, he must fully understand its meaning and its bearing upon the rest. He learns to perceive the exact significance of each section and sentence, to discriminate between thoughts which resemble each other, and to analyze trains of thought. His own conceptions become well defined.

The following suggestions by that eminent lawyer and scholar, the late Thomas S. Grimke of Charleston, S. C., are of the highest practical value; they apply the method of Dr. Wayland to a still closer analysis, and more frequent review of every paragraph and chapter.

# THE PHILOSOPHY AND METHOD OF TEACHING

## PURSUED AT THE WESTFIELD STATE NORMAL SCHOOL.

BY J. W. DICKINSON, A. M., PRINCIPAL.

### 1. THE PHILOSOPHY OF TEACHING.

If the mind is led to act in accordance with the laws of its nature, it will acquire the inclination and the ability to obey these laws. That state of the mind in which it has the inclination and the ability to obey the laws of its nature, is called Education; and the mind possessing this state, is said to be educated.

This definition of Education makes it a state of the mind and not a process. There is but one process by which the mind can be changed from one state to another, and that process is found in the mind's own activity.

By mental activity, knowledge is acquired, and the knowledge in turn excites activity, but it is activity only that produces a change in the powers that act.

As knowledge is both the product and the occasion of mental activity, knowledge seems to combine with mental activity in producing the state called Education.

That which produces a thing is the cause of that thing; then the cause of education is knowledge and mental activity. The cause of education is also called Instruction.

The term Instruction is sometimes used to signify knowledge, and sometimes to signify the process by which the teacher leads his pupils to acquire knowledge.

The word Instruction means to build within, and may well be limited in its application to mental activity and knowledge, which we have shown build up to perfection the mind itself.

It is the duty of the teacher to present in a right manner to the mind, objects and subjects which he desires to be the occasion of mental activity and knowledge.

The process of presenting occasions is Teaching.

The relations that Education, Instruction, and Teaching, hold to one another, are these: Instruction is the cause of Education, and Teaching is the occasion of Instruction.

Teaching must have for its object one of two ends, Knowledge or Education.

Knowledge as an end is valueless; then, the end towards which all intelligent teaching directs its attention, is Education.

If Education is the end the teacher should lead his pupil to attain, and if mental activity is the primary cause of Education, the teacher must provide right occasions for a complete and perfect mental activity. The ability to do this implies a knowledge of the ways in which the mind acts.

The modes, or ways of mental action, are three; thinking, feeling and choosing.

The mind thinking is called the Intellect: the mind feeling is called the Sensibilities; the mind choosing is called the Will.

The activity of the sensibilities is the result of thinking; the activity of the will is the result of feeling,—therefore, the teacher turns his attention primarily to the activity of the Intellect.

Every Intellectual act is an act of comparison.

The Intellect compares for perceptions, for general notions, for judgments, and for reasoning.

The teacher must present to the minds of the pupils, as occasions for these different acts of comparison, subjects and objects, named in proper order, for a *course* of *study*.

The course of study is divided into two courses: the one being an Elementary, the other a Scientific course.

In the Elementary course, the mind is excited to activity in acquiring a knowledge of facts.

This knowledge of facts is to be used as the occasion of Scientific knowledge.

A complete and perfect course of study, will name objects and subjects sufficient in number, and of the right kind, to guide the teacher in presenting occasions to the minds of his pupils, for making all kinds of comparisons; for comparing all kinds of objects; for comparing all kinds of relations, and for making the comparisons in the order, and in the manner required by the mind, as its powers are developed.

These are the principles which constitute the philosophy of teaching.

## 2. MODE OF TEACHING.

There are two ways of teaching. One way consists in presenting objects and subjects first as wholes, for general knowledge, then the parts and their relations for particular knowledge. The other way consists in first presenting parts of things, and the relations of the parts, for particular knowledge, then the whole made up of these parts and of their relations, for general knowledge.

These two ways of teaching are called Modes, or Methods. The first method is called the Analytic, the second the Synthetic method.

A synthetic method of study is impossible; as a method of teaching it is faulty for two reasons:

1st. The application of the method requires the teacher to present as occasions for mental activity and knowledge, parts of wholes, not as parts, but as independent individual things, that are not seen to hold any relation to the wholes of which they are parts, until the relation has been established by the teacher.

2d. The method requires the teacher to do the work that belongs to the student.

The application of the Analytic method requires the teacher to assign lessons for study, by the use of topics made out according to the following rules:

1st. The objects and subjects to be presented for study, should be of such a kind as are adapted to call into exercise the powers of the mind in accordance with the time and order of the development of these powers.

2d. The first topics assigned should be those that lead the pupil to study for Elementary knowledge.

3d. The first topic in any study should require the pupil to search for a general knowledge of the object or subject of study.

4th. The minor topics should present the parts of objects in a natural order, and of subjects in a logical order, and require the pupil to study for particular knowledge.

5th. The topics should lead the pupil to exhaust the subject.

Language is not to be considered the primary source of knowledge, but the mind is to be made conscious of having the ideas and thoughts to be expressed by the language used, before the language is employed.

This is done by actually bringing into the presence of the mind the object of study.

It is the duty of the teacher to excite the minds of his pupils to such mental activity as will lead to the state called Education, by bringing into their presence, in a right manner, the thing to be studied, and by guiding them to a knowledge of the facts and truths he would have them know.

All lessons are to be taught orally by the teacher, in such a manner that he will do nothing except furnish an occasion for knowledge.

The pupil should acquire the knowledge by his own mental activity.

The lesson thus taught will furnish for the pupil topics properly arranged for study, and a knowledge of the topics sufficient to enable him to continue to study them intelligently and profitably.

Text-books may be put into the hands of the pupils to be used as reference books. As text-books are sometimes used, they take away the possibility of independent mental activity on the part of both teacher and pupil.

The pupil having prepared his lesson, is to recite before the class upon the topic or topics, assigned at the time by the teacher.

He is to develop, without questions by the teacher, the topics assigned him, illustrating carefully the ideas and thoughts he expresses in words, before the expressions are made, observing to follow the same Analytic method in recitation that was observed by the teacher in assigning the topics, and by himself in studying them.

Both the teacher and the class are to observe carefully the pupil reciting, with reference to his knowledge, and his mode of teaching or reciting.

After the pupil has completed his recitation, the teacher and pupils may make criticisms, for the purpose of correcting mistakes, and for calling attention to new truth.

The pupil should be permitted, and even required, to use his active powers in obtaining knowledge, as well as his passive powers in receiving it.

The teacher should be constantly aware of the nature of his work, and of the end to be secured, and of the relation the means he employs holds to that end.

Successful teaching implies the existence of a course of study that is adapted to the wants of the mind as its powers are developed. It requires the employment of the right method in applying this course, and the presence of a teacher who understands the philosophy of his work.

The teacher must be supplied with all external means necessary for his teaching, and with the cordial sympathy of all in authority over him, and then he can so apply his philosophical method as to obtain a better and higher result than the schools have yet known.

We introduce the following as specimens of Mr. Page's method of illustrating different processes of teaching.

### POURING-IN PROCESS.

This consists in *lecturing* to a class of children upon every subject which occurs to the teacher, it being his chief aim to bring before them as many facts in a limited time as possible. It is as if he should provide himself with a basket of sweetmeats, and every time he should come within reach of a child, should seize him, and compel him to swallow—regardless of the condition of his stomach—whatever trash he should happen first to force into his mouth. Children are indeed fond of sweetmeats, but they do not like to have them *administered*—and every physiologist knows there is such a thing as eating enough, even of an agreeable thing, to make one sick, and thus produce loathing forever after. Now many teachers are just such misguided caterers for the mind. They are ready to seize upon the *victims* of their kindness, force open their mental gullets, and pour in, without mercy and without discretion, whatever sweet thing they may have at hand, even though they surfeit and nauseate the poor sufferer. The mind, by this process, becomes a mere *passive recipient*, taking in without much resistance whatever is presented, till it is full.

"A passive recipient!" said one to his friend, "what is a *passive recipient?*" "A passive recipient," replied his friend, "is a *two-gallon jug*. It holds just two gallons, and, as it is made of potters' ware, it can never hold but just two gallons." This is not an unfit illustration of what I mean by making the mind a passive recipient. Whenever the teacher does not first excite inquiry, first prepare the mind by *waking it up* to a desire to know, and, if possible, to find out by itself, but proceeds to think *for* the child, and to give him the results, before they are desired, or before they have been sought for—he makes the mind of the child a *two-gallon jug*, into which he may pour just *two gallons*, but no more. And if, day after day, he should continue to pour in, day after day he may expect that what he pours in will *all run over*. The mind, so far as retention is concerned, will act like the jug; that is, a part of what is poured in to-day will be diluted by a part of that which is forced in to-morrow, and that again will be partially displaced and partially mingled with the next day's pouring, till, at length, there will be nothing characteristic left. But, aside from retention, there is a great difference between the jug and the mind. The former is inert material, and may be as good a jug, after such use, as before. But the mind suffers by every unsuccessful effort to retain.

This process of lecturing children into imbecility is altogether too frequently practiced; and it is to be hoped that intelligent teachers will pause and inquire, before they pursue it further.

The other process to which I wish to call attention, is that which, for the sake of distinguishing it from the first, I shall denominate the

### DRAWING-OUT PROCESS.

This consists in asking what the lawyers call *leading questions*. It is practiced, usually, whenever the teacher desires to help along the pupil. "John," says the teacher, when conducting a recitation in Long Division, "John, what is the number to be divided called?" John hesitates. "Is it the dividend?" says the teacher. "Yes, sir; the dividend." "Well, John, what is that which is left, after dividing, called?—the remainder—is it?" "Yes, sir." A visitor now enters the room, and the teacher desires to show off John's talents. "Well, John, of what denomination is the remainder?"

John looks upon the floor.

"Is n't it always the same as the dividend, John?"

"Yes, sir."

"Very well, John," says the teacher, soothingly, "what denomination is this dividend?" pointing to the work on the board. "Dollars, is it not?"

"Yes, sir; dollars."

"Very well; now what is this remainder?"

John hesitates.

"Why, *dollars* too, is n't it?" says the teacher.

"Oh yes, sir, *dollars!*" says John, energetically, while the teacher complacently looks at the visitor, to see if he has noticed how *correctly* John has answered!

A class is called, to be examined in history. They have committed the text-book to memory; that is, they have learned the *words*. They go on finely for a time. At length one hesitates. The teacher adroitly asks a question in the language of the text. Thus: "*Early in the morning, on the* 11*th of September*, what did *the whole British army* do?" The pupil, thus timely reassured, proceeds: "*Early in the morning, on the* 11*th of September, the whole British army*, drawn up in two divisions, commenced the expected assault." Here again she pauses. The teacher proceeds to inquire: "Well—'Agreeably to the plan of Howe, the right wing' did what?"

*Pupil.* "*Agreeably to the plan of Howe, the right wing*"—

*Teacher.* "*The right wing, commanded by* whom?"

*Pupil.* "Oh! '*Agreeably to the plan of Howe, the right wing, commanded by* Knyphausen, made a feint of crossing the Brandywine, at Chad's Ford,'" &c.

This is a very common way of helping a dull pupil out of a difficulty; and I have seen it done so adroitly, that a company of visitors would agree that it was wonderful to see how thoroughly the children had been instructed!

I may further illustrate this *drawing-out* process, by describing an occurrence, which, in company with a friend and fellow-laborer, I once witnessed. A teacher, whose school we visited, called upon the class in Colburn's First Lessons. They rose, and in single file marched to the usual place, with their books in hand, and stood erect. It was a very good-looking class.

"Where do you begin?" said the teacher, taking the book.

*Pupils.* On the 80th page, third question.

*Teacher.* Read it, Charles.

*Charles.* (*Reads.*) "A man, being asked how many sheep he had, said that he had them in two pastures; in one pasture he had eight; that three-fourths of these were just one-third of what he had in the other. How many were there in the other?"

*Teacher.* Well, Charles, you must first get one-fourth of eight, must you not?

*Charles.* Yes, sir.

*Teacher.* Well, one-fourth of eight is two, is n't it?

*Charles.* Yes, sir; one-fourth of eight is two.

*Teacher.* Well, then, three-fourths will be three times two, won't it?

*Charles.* Yes, sir.

*Teacher.* Well, three times two are six, eh?

*Charles.* Yes, sir.

*Teacher.* Very well. (A pause.) Now the book says that this six is just one-third of what he had in the other pasture, do n't it?

*Charles.* Yes, sir.

*Teacher.* Then, if six is one-third, three-thirds will be—three times six, won't it?

*Charles.* Yes, sir.

*Teacher.* And three times six are—eighteen, ain't it?

*Charles.* Yes, sir.

*Teacher.* Then he had eighteen sheep in the other pasture, had he?

*Charles.* Yes, sir.

*Teacher.* Next; take the next one.

At this point I interposed, and asked the teacher if he would request Charles to go through it alone. "Oh, yes," said the teacher, "Charles, you may do it again." Charles again read the question, and—looked up. "Well," said the teacher, "You must first get one-fourth of eight, must n't you?" "Yes, sir." "And one-fourth of eight is two, is n't it?" "Yes, sir." And so the process went on as before, till the final eighteen sheep were *drawn out* as before. The teacher now looked round, with an air which seemed to say, "Now, I suppose you are satisfied."

"Shall *I* ask Charles to do it again?" said I. The teacher assented. Charles again read the question, and again—looked up. I waited, and he waited;—but the teacher could *not* wait. "Why, Charles," said he, impatiently; "you want one-fourth of eight, do n't you?" "Yes, sir," said Charles, promptly; and I thought best not to insist further at this time upon a repetition of "*yes, sir*," and the class were allowed to proceed in their own way.

This is, indeed, an extreme case; and yet it is but a fair sample of that teacher's method of stupefying mind. This habit of assisting the pupil, to some extent, is, however, a very common one, and as deleterious to mind as it is common. The teacher should at once abandon this practice, and require the scholar *to do the talking* at recitation. I need hardly suggest that such a course of *extraction* at recitation, aside from the waste of time by both parties, and the waste of strength by the teacher, has a direct tendency to make the scholar miserably superficial. For why should he study, if he knows from constant experience that the teacher, by a leading question, will relieve him from all embarrassment? It has often been remarked, that "the teacher makes the school." Perhaps in no way can he more effectually make an inefficient school, than by this *drawing-out process.*

I look upon the two processes just described, as very prominent and prevalent faults in our modern teaching; and if, by describing them thus fully, I shall induce any to set a guard upon their practice in this particular, I shall feel amply rewarded.

### THE MORE EXCELLENT WAY.

It is always a very difficult question for the teacher to settle, "How far shall I help the pupil, and how far shall the pupil be required to help himself?" The teaching of nature would seem to indicate that the pupil should be taught mainly to depend on his own resources. This, too, I think is the teaching of common sense. Whatever is learned, should be so thoroughly learned, that the next and higher step may be comparatively easy. And the teacher should always inquire, when he is about to dismiss one subject, whether the class understand it so well that they can go on to the next. He may, indeed, sometimes give a word of suggestion during the preparation of a lesson, and, by a seasonable hint, save the scholar the needless loss of much time. But it is a very great evil, if the pupils acquire the habit of running to the teacher, as soon as a slight difficulty presents itself, to request him to remove it. Some teachers, when this happens, will send the scholar to his seat with a reproof perhaps; while others, with a mistaken kindness, will answer the question, or solve the problem themselves, as the shortest way to get rid of it. Both these courses are, in general, wrong. The inquirer should never be frowned upon; this may discourage him. He should not be relieved from labor, as this will diminish his self-reliance without enlightening him; for whatever is done *for* a scholar, without his having studied closely upon it himself, makes but a feeble impression upon him, and is soon forgotten. The true way is, neither to discourage inquiry nor answer the question. Converse with the scholar a little as to the principles involved in the question; refer him to principles which he has before learned, or has now lost sight of; perhaps call his attention to some rule or explanation before given to the class; go just so far as to enlighten him a little, and *put him on the scent*, then leave him to achieve the victory himself. There is a great satisfaction in discovering a difficult thing for one's self—and the teacher does the scholar a lasting injury, who takes this pleasure from him. The teacher should be simply suggestive, but should never take the glory of a victory from the scholar, by doing his work for him; at least, not until he has given it a thorough trial himself.

The skill of the teacher, then, will be best manifested, if he can contrive to awaken such a spirit in the pupil, that he shall be very unwilling to be assisted; if he can kindle up such a zeal, that the pupil will prefer to try again and again before he will consent that the teacher shall interpose. I shall never forget a class of boys, some fourteen or fifteen years of age, who, in the study of algebra, had imbibed this spirit. A difficult question had been before the class a day or two, when I suggested giving them some assistance. "*Not to-day, sir*," was the spontaneous exclamation of nearly every one. Nor shall I forget the expression that beamed from the countenance of one of them, when, elated with his success, he forgot the proprieties of the school, and audibly exclaimed, "*I've got it! I've got it?*" It was a great day for him; he felt, as he never before had felt, his own might. Nor was it less gratifying to me, to find that his fellows were still unwilling to know his method of solution. The next day a large number brought a solution of their own, each showing evidence of originality. A class that has once attained to a feeling like this, will go on to educate themselves, when they shall have left the school and the living teacher.

As to the communication of knowledge, aside from that immediately connected with school-studies, there is a more excellent way than that of *pouring it in* by the process already described. It is but just that I should give a specimen of the method of doing this. I shall now proceed to do so, under the head of

### WAKING UP MIND.

The teacher of any experience knows that, if he will excite a deep and profitable interest in his school, he must teach many things besides *book-studies*. In our common schools, there will always be a company of small children, who, not yet having learned to read understandingly, will have no means of interesting themselves, and must depend mainly upon the teacher for the interest they take in the school. This, to them, is perhaps the most critical period of their lives. Whatever impression is now made upon them will be enduring. If there they become disgusted with the dullness and confinement of school, and associate the idea of pain and repulsiveness with that of learning, who can describe the injury done to their minds? If, on the other hand, the teacher is really skillful, and excites in them a spirit of inquiry, and leads them in suitable ways to observe, to think, and to feel, that the school is a happy place even for children, it is one great point gained.

I may suggest here, then, that it would be well to set apart a few minutes once a day, for a *general exercise* in the school; when it should be required of all to lay by their studies, assume an erect attitude, and give their undivided attention to whatever the teacher may bring before them. Such a course would have its physiological advantages. It would relieve the minds of all for a few minutes. The erect attitude is a healthful one. It would also serve as a short respite from duty, and thus refresh the older scholars from study. I may further add, that, for the benefit of these small children, every general exercise should be conducted with reference to *them*, and such topics should be introduced as they can understand.

It is the purpose of the following remarks to give a *specimen* of the manner of conducting such exercises, for a few days, with reference to *waking up mind* in the school, and also in the district.

Let us suppose that the teacher has promised that, on the next day, at ten minutes past ten o'clock, he shall request the whole school to give their attention five minutes, while he shall bring something there to which he shall call the attention, especially of the little boys and girls under seven years of age. This very announcement will excite an interest both in school and at home; and when the children come in the morning, they will be more wakeful than usual till the fixed time arrives. It is very important that this time should be fixed, and that the utmost punctuality should be observed, both as to the beginning and ending of the exercise at the precise time.

The teacher, it should be supposed, has not made such an announcement without considering what he can do when the time arrives. He should have a well-digested plan of operation, and one, which he knows beforehand, that he can successfully execute.

Let us suppose that, in preparing for this exercise, he looks about him to find some object which he can make his *text;* and that he finds upon his study-table an *ear of corn*. He thinks carefully what he can do with it, and then, with a smile of satisfaction, he puts it in his pocket for the "general exercise."

In the morning he goes through the accustomed duties of the first hour, perhaps more cheerfully than usual, because he finds there is more of animation and wakefulness in the school. At the precise time, he gives the signal agreed upon, and all the pupils drop their studies and sit erect. When there is perfect silence and strict attention by all, he takes from his pocket the ear of corn, and in silence holds it up before the school. The children smile, for it is a familiar object; and they probably did not suspect they were to be *fed* with corn.

*Teacher*. "Now, children," addressing himself to the youngest, "I am going to ask you only one question to-day about this ear of corn. If you can answer it, I shall be very glad; if the little boys an girls upon the front seat can not give the answer, I will let those in the next seat try; and so on, till all have tried, unless our time should expire before the right answer is given. I shall not be surprised if none of you give the answer I am thinking of. As soon as I ask the question, those who are under seven years old, that think they can give an answer, may raise their hand. WHAT IS THIS EAR OF CORN FOR?"

Several of the children raise their hands, and the teacher points to one after another, in order, and they rise and give their answers.

*Mary.* It is to feed the geese with.

*John.* Yes, and the hens too, and the pigs.

*Sarah.* My father gives corn to the cows.

By this time the hands of the youngest scholars are all down, for, having been taken a little by surprise, their knowledge is exhausted. So the teacher says that those between seven and ten years of age may raise their hands. Several instantly appear. The teacher again indicates, by pointing, those who may give the answer.

*Charles.* My father gives corn to the horses, when the oats are all gone.

*Daniel.* *We* give it to the oxen and cows, and we fat the hogs upon corn.

*Laura.* It is good to eat. They shell it from the cobs, and send it to mill, and it is ground into meal. They make bread of the meal, and we eat it.

This last pupil has looked a little further into domestic economy than those who answered before her. But, by this time, perhaps before, the five minutes have been nearly expended, and yet several hands are up, and the faces of several are beaming with eagerness to tell their thoughts. Let the teacher then say, "We will have no more answers to-day. You may think of this matter till to-morrow, and then I will let you try again. I am sorry to tell you that none of you have mentioned the use I was thinking of, though I confess I expected it every minute. I shall not be surprised if no one of you give this answer to-morrow. I shall now put the ear of corn in my desk, and no one of you must speak to me about it till to-morrow. You may now take your studies."

The children now breathe more freely, while the older ones take their studies, and the next class is called. In order to success, it is absolutely necessary that the teacher should positively refuse to hold any conversation with the children on the subject, till the next time for "general exercise."

During the remainder of the forenoon, the teacher will very likely observe some signs of thoughtfulness on the part of those little children who have been habitually dull before. And, perhaps some child, eager to impart a new discovery, will seek an opportunity to make it known during the forenoon. "Wait till to-morrow," should be the teacher's only reply.

Now let us follow these children as they are dismissed, while they bend their steps toward home. They cluster together in groups, as they go down the hill, and they seem to be earnestly engaged in conversation.

"I do n't believe it has any other use," says John.

"Oh, yes, it has," says Susan; "our teacher would not say so, if it had not. Besides, did you not see what a knowing look he had, when he drew up his brow, and said he guessed we could n't find it out?"

"Well, I mean to ask my mother," says little Mary; "I guess she can tell."

By and by, as they pass a field of corn, Samuel sees a squirrel running across the street, with both his cheeks distended with "*plunder*."

At home, too, the ear of corn is made the subject of conversation. "What is an ear of corn for, mother?" says little Mary, as soon as they have taken a seat at the dinner table.

*Mother.* An ear of corn, child? why, do n't you know? It is to feed the fowls, and the pigs, and the cattle; and we make bread of it, too—

*Mary.* Yes, we told all that; but the teacher says that is not all.

*Mother.* The *teacher?*

*Mary.* Yes, ma'am; the teacher had an ear of corn at school, and he asked us what it was for; and, after we had told him every thing we could think of, he said there was another thing still. Now I want to find out, so that *I* can tell him.

The consequence of this would be that the family—father, mother, and older brothers and sisters—would resolve themselves into a committee of the whole on the ear of corn. The same, or something like this, would be true in other families in the district; and, by the next morning, several children would have something further to communicate on the subject. The hour would this day be awaited with great interest, and the first signal would produce perfect silence.

The teacher now takes the ear of corn from the desk, and displays it before the school; and quite a number of hands are instantly raised, as if eager to be the first to tell what other use they have discovered for it.

The teacher now says, pleasantly: "The use I am thinking of, you have all observed, I have no doubt; it is a very important use indeed; but, as it is a little out of the common course, I shall not be surprised if you can not give it. However, you may try."

"It is good to boil!"* says little Susan, almost springing from the floor as she speaks.

"And it is for squirrels to eat," says little Samuel. "I saw one carry away a whole mouthful, yesterday, from the cornfield."

Others still mention other uses, which they have observed. They mention other animals which feed upon it, or other modes of cooking it. The older pupils begin to be interested, and they add to the list of uses named. Perhaps, however, none will name the one the teacher has in his own mind; he should cordially welcome the answer, if perchance it is given; if none should give it, he may do as he thinks best about giving it himself on this occasion. Perhaps, if there is time, he may do so—after the following manner:—

"I have told you that the answer I was seeking was a very simple one; it is something you have all observed, and you may be a little disappointed when I tell you. The use I have been thinking of for the ear of corn is this:—*It is to plant. It is for seed*, to propagate that species of plant called corn." Here the children may look disappointed, as much as to say, "we knew that before."

The teacher continues: "And this is a very important use for the corn; for if for one year none should be planted, and all the ears that grew the year before should be consumed, we should have no more corn. This, then, was the great primary design of the corn; the other uses you have named were merely secondary. But I mean to make something more of my ear of corn. My next question is:—Do OTHER PLANTS HAVE SEEDS?"†

Here is a new field of inquiry. Many hands are instantly raised; but, as the five minutes by this time have passed, leave them to answer at the next time.

"*Have other plants seeds?*" the children begin to inquire in their own minds, and each begins to think over a list of such plants as he is familiar with. When they are dismissed, they look on the way home at the plants by the roadside, and when they reach home, they run to the garden. At the table, they inquire of their parents, or their brothers and sisters.

At the next exercise, they will have more than they can tell in five minutes, as the results of their own observation and research. When enough has been said by the children, as to the plants which have seeds, the next question may be:—Do ALL PLANTS HAVE SEEDS? This question will lead to much inquiry at home, wherever botany is not well understood. There are many who are not aware that all plants have seeds. Very likely the ferns (common brakes,) will be noticed by the children themselves. They may also name several other plants which do not exhibit their apparatus for seed-bearing very conspicuously. This will prepare the way for the teacher to impart a little information. Nor is there any harm in doing so, whenever he is satisfied that the mind has been suitably exercised. The mind is no longer a "passive recipient;" and he may be sure that, by inquiry, it has increased its *capacity to contain*, and any fact which now answers inquiry, will be most carefully stored up.

The next question may be:—Do TREES HAVE SEEDS? As the children next go

* The children themselves will be sure to find some new answers to such questions as the above. In giving in substance this lecture to a gathering of teachers, in the Autumn of 1845, in one of the busy villages of New York, where, also, the pupils of one of the district schools were present, by invitation, I had described a process similar to that which has been dwelt upon above. I had given the supposed answers for the first day, and had described the children as pressing the question at home. When I had proceeded as far as to take up the ear of corn, the second day, and had spoken of the possibility that the true answer to the question might not be given, I turned almost instinctively to the class of children at my right, saying, "*Now what is the ear of corn for?*" A little boy, some six years of age, who had swallowed every word, and whose face glowed as if there was not room enough for his soul within him, bounded upon his feet, and forgetting the publicity of the place, and the gravity of the chairman of the meeting, clapping his hands forcibly together, "*It's to pop!*" he exclaimed emphatically, very much to the amusement of the audience. His mind had been *waked up*.

† *Plant* is here used in the popular sense.

out, their eyes are directed to the trees above them. The fruit-trees, the walnut, the oak, and perhaps the pine, will be selected as those which have seeds. They will, however, mention quite a number which do not, or which they think do not have seeds. Among these may be the elm, the birch, and the Lombardy poplar. After hearing their opinions, and the results of their observations, take one of their exceptions, as the subject of the next question :—*Does the elm have seeds?* This will narrow their inquiries down to a specific case, and every elm in the district will be inquired of as to its testimony on this point.

If the children can any of them collect and give the truth in the matter, so much the better; but if they, after inquiring of their parents and their grandparents, as I have known a whole school to do, come back, insisting that the elm has no seeds; after hearing their reasons for their belief, and perhaps the opinions of their parents, you may promise to tell them something about it at the next exercise. This will again awaken expectation, not only among the children but among the parents. All will wish to know what you have to bring out.

Great care should be taken not to throw any disparagement upon the opinions of parents. After giving the signal for attention, you may proceed as follows:—

"*Has the elm-tree any seeds?* Perhaps, children, you may recollect, after the cold winter has passed away, that, along in the latter part of March, or the first of April, we sometimes have a warm, sunny day. The birds perhaps appear and begin to sing a little, and as you look up to the elm, you notice that its buds seem to swell, and you think it is going to put out its leaves. Every body says we are going to have an early spring. But, after this, the cold, frosty nights and windy days come on again, and then you think the leaves can not come out so early. Now, if you observe carefully, the leaves do not come out till about the 20th of May, or perhaps the 1st of June. Did you ever see any thing like what I have described?"

"Yes, sir; we remember that."

"Well, the next time you see the buds begin to open, just break off a twig of a good large tree, and you will find they are *not the leaf-buds*. But, if you will watch them carefully for two or three weeks, you will find that each bud will put out some beautiful little flowers, brightly colored, and slightly fragrant. If you will still continue to watch them, you will find, as the flowers fall off, that seed-vessels are formed, shaped very much like the parsnip seed. These will grow larger and larger every day, and by and by they will turn brown, and look as if they were ripe. Just about this time the leaves will come out; and soon after, these seeds, during some windy day or night, will all fall off. The ground will be covered with thousands of them. Perhaps you have seen this."

"Yes, sir," says John; "Grandpa calls that *elm-dust*."

"Perhaps next year you can watch this, and ask your parents to examine it with you. But the five minutes are ended."

Now, information thus communicated will never be forgotten. The mind, having been put upon the stretch, is no longer a *passive recipient*.

The next question:—How ARE SEEDS DISSEMINATED?—(of course explaining the term—"*disseminated*.")

This will bring in a fund of information from the pupils. They will mention that the thistle-seed *flies*, and so does the seed of the milkweed; that the burs of the burdock, and some other seeds, are provided with hooks, by which they attach themselves to the hair of animals or the clothing of men, and *ride* away to their resting-place, which may be a hundred miles off. Some fall into the water, and *sail* away to another shore. Some, like the seed of the touch-me-not, are thrown to a distance by the bursting of the elastic pericarp; others, as nuts and acorns, are carried by squirrels, and buried beneath the leaves. These facts would mostly be noticed by children, when once put upon observation.

Next question:—*Are plants propagated in any other way than by seeds?*

This question would call their attention to the various means of natural and artificial propagation, by layers, by offsets, by suckers, by grafting, by budding, &c.

Again:—*Have any plants more ways than one of natural propagation?* Some have one way only—by seeds, as the annual plants; some have two—by seeds, and by roots, as the potato; some have three—as the tiger-lily, by side-bulbs from the roots, by *stalk-bulbs*, and by the seeds. This can be extended indefinitely.

Let it be remembered that the above has been given *simply as a specimen* of what could easily be done by an ingenious teacher, with as common a thing as an ear of corn for the text. Any other thing would answer as well. A chip, a tooth, or a bone of an animal, a piece of iron, a feather, or any other object, could be made the text for adroitly bringing in the *uses of wood*, the *food and habits of animals*, the *use and comparative value of metals*, the *covering of birds*, their *migration*, the *covering of animals*, &c., &c. Let the teacher but think what department he will dwell upon, and then he can easily select his *text;* and, if he has any tact, he can keep the children constantly upon inquiry.

The advantages of the above course are many and great.

1. *It immediately puts the minds of the children into a state of vigorous activity.* They feel that they are no longer *passive recipients.* They are incited to discover and ascertain for themselves. They are, therefore, profitably employed, both in and out of school; and, as a consequence, are more easily governed. A habit of observation is easily cultivated in them; and what an advantage is this for a child! It is almost unnecessary to remark that many people go through the world, without seeing half the objects which are brought within their reach. It would be the same to them if their eyes were half the time closed. If they travel through a country presenting the most beautiful scenery, or the most interesting geological features, they see nothing. They grow up, among all the wonders of God's works, amid all the displays of his wisdom, of his design, to no purpose. They study none of the plans of nature; and by all the millions of arrangements which God has made, to delight the eye, to gratify the taste, to excite the emotions of pleasure instead of pain, they are neither the happier nor the wiser. What a blessing, then, it is to a child, to put his mind upon inquiry; to open his eyes to observe what his Creator intended his intelligent creatures should behold, of his goodness, his wisdom, his power. And how far superior is he, who teaches a child to see for himself, and to think for himself, to him who sees and thinks *for* the child, and thus practically invites the pupil to close his own eyes, and grope in darkness through the instructive journey of life.

2. *It is of great service to the parents in the district, to have this waking-up process in operation.* Our children are sometimes our best teachers. Parents are apt to grow rusty in their acquirements, and it is, no doubt, one of the designs of providence, that the inquisitiveness of childhood should preserve them from sinking into mental inactivity. Who can hear the inquiries of his own child after knowledge, without a desire to supply his wants? Now it is right for the teacher to use this instrumentality to *wake up mind* in his district. Parents, by the course I have recommended, very soon become interested in these daily questions of the teacher; and they are often as eager to know what is the *next question* as the children are to report it. This course, then, will supply profitable topics of conversation at the fire-side, and very likely will encourage also the pursuit of useful reading. It will moreover soon awaken a deeper interest in the school, on the part of the parents. They will begin to inquire of one another as to this new measure; and when they find by conference that the feeling in this matter is becoming general, they will desire to visit the school, to witness this as well as the other operations of the teacher. This will secure parental co-operation; and thus, in every way, the influence of the school will be hightened. It is no small thing for a teacher to enlist the interest of his patrons in the success of his school; and this is the most happily done through the pupils themselves.

3. *It wakes up the teacher's own mind.* This is by no means the least important point to be gained. The teacher, by the very nature of his employment, by daily confinement in an unhealthy atmosphere, by teaching over and over again that with which he is quite familiar, by boarding with people who are inclined to be social, and by the fatigue and languor with which he finds himself oppressed every night, is strongly tempted to neglect his own improvement. There are but few who rise above this accumulation of impediments, and go on, in spite of them, to eminence in the profession. A large proportion of all who teach, rely upon the attainments with which they commence; and, in the course of two or three years, finding themselves behind the age, they abandon the employment. This is very natural. Any man who treads in a beaten track, like a horse in a mill, must become weary, however valuable the product may be which he *grinds out.* It is essential that he should keep his own interest awake by some exercise of his ingenuity, and that he should compel himself to be industrious by undertaking that which will absolutely demand study.

### VISIT TO THE TEACHERS' SEMINARY, ANDOVER, MASS.

THE following account of a visit to the Teachers' Seminary, at Andover, Mass., appeared in the "*Annals of Education*" for August, 1832:—

The building for the Teachers' Seminary, in Andover, is pleasantly situated and handsomely constructed. It has two stories, besides the basement. I could not help contrasting this large, elegant, airy mansion, with the multitude of school-houses, which are every where to be found, whose narrow dimensions and miserable construction, better fit them for prisons than for places of instruction.

The first or lower story embraces the principal school room, a spacious entrance, and a room for a library. The entrance contains suitable places for depositing hats, clothes, &c., and a stairway. The second or upper story includes, besides the stairway and entrance, a room for the preparatory school, with a recitation room adjoining; a room for geological, mineralogical, and botanical specimens, and a room for lectures in philosophy, astronomy, &c., with the necessary apparatus.

Part of the basement story is occupied as a chemical lecture room and laboratory. The rest is designed as a workshop, and is, to some extent, already used for that purpose.

All these rooms are furnished with appropriate seats, and with desks, where these are necessary. The desks and seats of the principal school room are on an improved plan. The seats consist of a chair firmly fixed to the floor, with a very low back. The apparatus and specimens necessary in the illustration of natural science, are arranged in the several rooms appropriated to their use. The electrical apparatus, in particular, is very fine. The minerals, and geological specimens are already numerous, and are rapidly accumulating, through the exertions of the teachers and their pupils. The chemical laboratory is well supplied. The library contains 200 to 300 volumes, very judiciously selected.

Every facility might be afforded for the comfort, and convenience, and progress of a much larger number than have ever yet attended. It does not seem to be generally known that there is a school of this kind existing in New England, sustaining the high character which might justly be challenged by this institution.

The higher department is under the immediate care of Rev. S. R. Hall. He is assisted in this department by Mr. F. A. Barton, and in the preparatory department by Mr. L. Tenney, both of whom appear to be well qualified for their task.

School books of a good character are selected, and the most approved methods of instruction adopted. But, while books, and apparatus, and hard study, are deemed indispensable to thorough and efficient progress, much is accomplished by familiar, conversational lectures, giving the student ample opportunity for asking questions, suggesting doubts, &c. No attempts are made to hurry through a science, for the sake of having gone through it; but constant, and as it appears to me, *successful* efforts are made to teach every thing to which the pupil's attention is called *thoroughly*.

In both departments of the school, there is nothing of that routine of mere memory work which is so often witnessed in our schools. Those methods are pursued, generally speaking, in every exercise, which give employment to the whole intellect, and not to certain favored faculties merely, while the rest are suffered to lie neglected. If any faculty has not been properly developed, in the early years of instruction, a course is here pursued which is most happily adapted to awaken and excite its slumbering energies, and bring it into habits of cheerful, healthy, vigorous action.

The spelling lessons are usually short. Few, if any, words are studied according to the arbitrary arrangement of most dictionaries and spelling books. Sometimes the teacher dictates a series of words, which the pupils write on their slates; at others, they are requested to select all the words of a certain class which they can recollect, and write them down, thus forming their own spelling lessons. By classes of words is meant all which belong to a certain occupation, art, tribe of animals, &c. Thus, at one time, their spelling lesson will consist of the names of all the birds of prey they can think of; at another, of all the implements used in husbandry, or in some mechanical occupation. The examination of these lessons by the instructor, is often accompanied by much useful and familiar conversation on various topics, not excluding moral and religious subjects. Many other methods of teaching spelling are adopted.

I was never before so thoroughly convinced of prevailing deficiencies in teaching *reading*, as while witnessing the performances of these pupils. I was so much ashamed of my own neglect of distinctness, and propriety of enunciation, that I resolved at the moment never to read or speak before others again, till I had subjected myself to a thorough drilling on these points.

Arithmetic was also taught in a very judicious manner, in both the higher and lower departments. Great attention was paid to the difficult subject of *carrying*. Three-quarters of an hour of close attention is given to penmanship once in two days.

In both departments of the institution, every branch is pursued, as far as possible, independently of every other. By this is meant that every study has its appropriate hour and space, and when that hour arrives, it is exclusively attended to. In the higher department, the exercises for every day of the week are written down plainly and minutely, and a monitor rings a bell at the arrival of the time for every new exercise. So exact is the order, and so accustomed to it have the students become, that, so far as discipline is concerned, it matters little whether the teachers are present or absent, provided the monitor is at his post, and performs his duty.

The higher branches of the mathematics, geography, grammar, history, composition, drawing, philosophy in its various divisions, chemistry, political economy; indeed, every thing to which the attention of the pupils is called, is pursued, so far as I could ascertain, in the same rational and thorough manner, as spelling, reading, and arithmetic. Not only is every thing rendered intelligible, but *interesting;* and the thinking powers of the pupil are called into useful activity. During my visit a course of chemical lectures was commenced by an assistant, which promised to be highly practical and useful. Music is taught in the seminary, and a hymn is also sometimes sung in connection with the religious exercises.

But what rendered this seminary most deeply interesting to me, was the conviction, which I was unable to resist, that all its methods, and plans, and processes, were eminently adapted to the development and formation of character. As a place of *instruction*, it justly ranks high; and I do not believe it has been too highly appreciated. But, as a place of EDUCATION, it has still higher claims. Knowledge of the best kind is successfully inculcated by the best means; but the capacity and disposition to make a good *use* of knowledge, is regarded as of still *more* importance.

In the first place, the maxim that a sound mind requires a sound body is not forgotten. The location of the seminary is peculiarly happy. The building is kept thoroughly ventilated, and a due regard is paid to temperature. Exercise receives a measure of that attention which its superlative importance demands. The importance of early hours is inculcated. Indeed, every thing which favors the health is remembered by the teachers, and, so far as circumstances may permit, controlled and directed.

But the intellectual and moral habits of the pupils are also wisely regarded. Nothing struck me more than the cheerful love of order which seemed to prevail. It was not the order of a prisoner in the dungeon, but of the healthy, happy laborer. On the book containing the rules for each day, was written, in conspicuous characters, "ORDER IS HEAVEN'S FIRST LAW;" but it was written in characters scarcely less legible in their words and actions. In securing such order, I noticed several things which appeared to have no small influence.

*Habits of punctuality.*—When the hour arrives for opening the school, or for any exercise whatever, it is attended to. The teacher does not wait a few minutes beyond the time for tardy pupils—he is on the spot himself, and the work commences. In fact, he is often ready a few minutes before the time. The pupils know it, and they are convinced the teacher is in earnest. This makes *them* so.

*Nothing is hurried.*—This is, in part, an effect of the former habit. If "time is taken by the forelock," there is less need of hurrying. There will be time for every thing—and time to do it well.

*Every thing has its place.*—There is no time lost by looking for things which have become misplaced. This is economical and favorable to good order.

*The teacher observes order himself.*—Every *word*, every *step*, every *performance*—I had almost said every *look* of the teachers—inculcate order and system. And the powerful influence of example is too well known to need any encomiums.

I know not what other means of discipline may have been used in the seminary formerly; but am persuaded that those which have just been mentioned, have a very large share of influence, at present, in maintaining it. The *habit and love* of order and discipline *secure* order and discipline. So it is with motives to progress. The habit and love of acquiring knowledge, and of making improvement, appear to *insure* that knowledge and improvement, without the aid of emulation, which appears to be discarded. I know of no school for boys, where a better English education can be obtained.

Were it not in vain, I could wish that the fathers and mothers of New England might all spend a few days in this seminary. If a knowledge of its actual condition should lead to nothing more effective, it might induce many to send their sons there for a few years, to have the unspeakable pleasure of seeing them molded into teachers of high-minded purposes, and holy, self-denying character. May we not hope that a knowledge of what is effected at Andover will lead to the establishment of similar schools throughout New England—to be fountains of intelligence, and virtue, and piety?

LECTURES ON SCHOOL-KEEPING, by Samuel R. Hall, Boston, 1829, p. 135.

CONTENTS. *Lecture* I. Indifference to the importance, character, and usefulness of common schools; its origin and influence. II. Obstacles to the usefulness of common schools. III. Requisite qualifications of teachers. IV. Nature of the teacher's employment. Responsibility of the teacher. Importance of realizing and understanding it. V. Gaining the confidence of the school. Means of gaining it. The instructor should be willing to spend all of his time when it can be rendered beneficial to the school. VI. Government of a school. Prerequisites. Manner of treating scholars. Uniformity in government. Firmness. VII. Government, *continued.* Partiality. Regard to the future as well as the present welfare of the scholars. Mode of intercourse between teacher and scholars, and between scholars. Punishments. Rewards. VIII. General management of a school. Direction of studies. IX. Mode of teaching. Manner of illustrating subjects. Spelling. Reading. X. Arithmetic. Geography. English Grammar. Writing. History. XI. Composition. General subjects, not particularly studied. Importance of improving opportunities when deep impressions are made on the minds of the school. XII. Means of exciting the attention of scholars. Such as are to be avoided. Such as are safely used. XIII. To female instructors.

# EXTRACT FROM AN ADDRESS

BY EX-GOVERNOR GEORGE S. BOUTWELL,

AT THE DEDICATION OF THE STATE NORMAL SCHOOL AT SALEM,

*August 19th*, 1854.

---

THE house you have erected is not so much dedicated to the School as to the public; the institution here set up is not so much for the benefit of the young men and women who may become pupils, as for the benefit of the public which they represent. The appeal is, therefore, to the public to furnish such pupils, in number and character, that the institution may soon successfully enter upon the work for which it is properly designed. But the character and value of this school depend on the quality of its teachers more than on all things else. They should be thoroughly instructed, not only in the branches taught, but in the art of teaching them. The teacher ought to have attained much that the pupil is yet to learn; if he has not, he can not utter words of encouragement, nor estimate the chances of success. It is not enough to know what is contained in the text-book; the pupil should know that at least; the teacher should know a great deal more. A person is not qualified for the office of teacher when he has mastered the contents of a book; and has, in fact, no right to instruct others until he has mastered the subject." Here then seems to be the gist of the whole matter. We in Maine have at length an opportunity to do something which may be made of great benefit to the public schools of the State, and, through them, to the cause of general good learning. This is to be done through the instrumentality of an institution—the Normal School. Very largely is this trust committed to the hands of the educational men of the present day among us. Future generations will hold us responsible for a right discharge of our duties. Let us not prove recreant to our sacred trust.

When that great educator, who has left a bright and ineffaceable record upon the annals of the present age, heard of his election as master of the School at Rugby, he wrote to Dr. Hawkins, whose recommendation, in which he expressed his belief that Arnold would revolutionize the system of public instruction in Europe—had done most towards securing his appointment, in the following touching words:

"I need not tell you how unexpected this result [my election] has been to me, and I hope I need not say also what a solemn and overwhelming responsibility is imposed upon me. I would hope to have the prayers of my friends, together with my own, for a supply of that true wisdom which is required for such a business." The position of a Normal School teacher is one of "solemn and overwhelming responsibility," and the person occupying it needs a wisdom that comes through communion with the Divine One. This institution, like the noble, the lamented Arnold, is nothing less than revolutionary in its relationship to the Common Schools. It will fail to accomplish its mission, or it will regenerate. It will give life, or it itself will die.

It remains to be said—if indeed that be necessary—that I believe with De Gasparin and De Tocqueville, that in the universality of common instruction is the true superiority of Americans: that I believe, with the leading patriots of my country, that republican institutions can not exist for any length of time except they be enshrined in the hearts of an intelligent, liberty-loving people; that to retain the true superiority of which we, as a nation, are acknowledged to be possessed, we must retain and improve its cause—the public school system; that I believe, with the lamented Mann and Page, the living Barnard, the patriotic and eloquent Everett, and a host of other eminent educators, that the Normal School is a necessity—a *sine qua non*—for the perfection of a system of instruction for the people; and lastly, and consequently, that I would give to the Normal School its right to rank among the institutions which, as an harmonious whole, work for the preservation of American Freedom.

Let it not be thought, my friends, that I am an enthusiast in respect to the position which the Normal and the public school hold among the institutions of our nation, and the consequent glory of the profession of the popular educator. Here is a cause in which, surrounded by the safeguards of the Christian religion, one need not fear to be enthusiastic.

### THE OFFICE OF THE PUBLIC SCHOOL TEACHER

Before the public school teachers of this nation, there is opening a future, which, like every other prospective view in the time in which we live, is at once solemn and cheering. It is cheering to believe that we may live to see the day when education for the people shall be as much prized in the South as in the North; that from the "one true seed of freedom" which the Pilgrims of 1620 were commissioned of the Almighty to plant upon these then benighted shores, has grown the Tree of Life, whose leaves are for the healing of the nation. But it is solemn—O, is it not intensely solemn!—to reflect that upon our shoulders is to be thrown so great responsibility; that not alone upon the field of battle, but more certainly upon the field of moral thought, are to be laid the firm foundations of a regenerated republican liberty! American citizenship is, and is to be a grander, loftier thing in the future than it has been in the past. Our baptism of blood is to do its work of purification; and, thus, looking with the vision of a poet of the motherland, we discerned through the gloomy days of battle, through the fierce conflict of our nation's heroic period, the dawn-breaking of a more comprehensive, more brilliant social illumination. We said with Tennyson:

"Tho' many a light shall darken, and many shall weep
For those that are crushed in the clash of jarring claims,
Yet God's just wrath shall be wreaked on a giant liar;
And many a darkness into the light shall leap,
And shine in the sudden making of splendid names,
And noble thought be freer under the sun,
And the heart of a people beat with one desire."
* * * * * * * *
"Let it flame or fade, and the war roll down like a wind,
We have proved we have hearts in a cause; we are noble still,
And all have awaked, as it seems, to the better mind;
It is better to fight for the good than to rail at the ill."

The end of our conflict was not, when, with ringing of bells, with roar of deep-mouthed cannon, with bonfires and illuminations, with notes of praise, and with voice of silver-toned oratory, we celebrated the restoration of peace and union. For then came the necessity for the highest qualities of statesmanship, in State legislatures and a national Congress. And again, the end is not when the counsels of the statesman, under the blessings of Divine Providence, shall have settled the most complicated problems growing out of the present disjointed condition of our affairs. After all that, in the dim distant future, when you and I shall have acted well or ill our part upon the stage of life and shall sleep with the fathers of the Republic, the generations that will come will find a work high and glorious, made doubly sacred by the blood and prayers and tears of their predecessors.

The American citizen is to act a part in all this, and the American citizen is to be taught in youth in the public school. Will any one say that the position of a common school teacher is one of small account—will any gainsay his claim to a preparation for his professional duties at the expense of that people to whom his service is so important? True it is, as some one has said, "Let a people treat with scorn the defenders of its liberties, and invest them with the symbols of degradation, and it will soon have none to defend them." There is no more sure defense to republican liberty than the public school; there is no truer personal defender of American institutions than the schoolmaster. Treat him with scorn, invest him with the symbols of degradation if you dare. God may give him grace still to labor on, but it will be with a saddened heart—a life without an earthly ambition.

# THE NATIONAL TEACHERS' ASSOCIATION:

## ITS NATURE AND OBJECTS.

BY JOHN D. PHILBRICK,

Superintendent of Public Instruction in Boston, Mass.

---

LADIES AND GENTLEMEN:—The position in which I find myself placed by the choice of the association—a position unsought, undesired, and undeserved—bestowed no doubt, as a compliment to the section of the country, and particularly to the state in which I live and labor, and to be relinquished gladly at the close of this session,—imposes upon me the duty of inaugurating these proceedings by an introductory address.

And perhaps I may be expected to attempt, by an elaborate performance, either in the exhaustive treatment of some single topic, or in the presentation of a comprehensive summary of our proper aims and purpose, to strike the key-note of the occasion, and thus in a manner to give direction and tone to the discussions which may follow. But this is not what I propose. Indeed, since this meeting was determined upon, at a late day, it has not been in my power to make adequate preparation for such a task. But what, under other circumstances, and in quieter and happier times might have been expected, and might have been attempted, is scarcely required now. It is not from my lips, it could not be from any human lips, that that strain of eloquence, of learning, or of wisdom, is to flow, most competent to shape and inspire the debates and deliberations of this body of American educators, at this time and in this place.

The great and unparalleled conjuncture of our public affairs, the unprecedented perils in which our national existence has been, and is now involved, the sharp and tragic realities of our mighty struggle, demanding the work of all hands, the thoughts of all heads, and the devotion of all hearts, the sacrifice of so much of the best blood of the nation, the necessity to provide for the security of peace, whan peace shall come; these things are what must and will fire our hearts, and bias our thoughts, and direct our aims, and

---

* Introductory Address before the National Teachers' Association in Chicago, August 4th, 1863; by the President, John D. Philbrick.

influence our speech and action. Till peace and union, and the settled state of order are restored, loyal hearts can not but everywhere, and at all times, vibrate in unison with the key-note uttered by the mouths of the cannon which spoke on the memorable 12th of April, 1861, from the casemates of Sumter, in defence of free government, of christian civilization, of the rights of man. That utterance meant duty,—duty to God, duty to our country,—duty to one another. And our topics, treatment, thoughts, views, must be moulded and tinged by the circumstances and exigences of this perilous crisis, this mighty conflict, and as patriotic educators, we must necessarily keep uppermost in our minds, at such a time as this, the relations of education to the national life, to political morality, and the stability of free institutions of government.

It seems proper, however that I should present, briefly, some facts and suggestions respecting the nature and objects of our association, and the sphere of its operations and influence.

It is now six years since this association was organized. It originated in a call signed and issued by the Presidents of ten State Associations, inviting teachers throughout the United States to assemble in Philadelphia on the 26th of August, 1857, for the purpose of organizing a National Teachers' Association. It being the express design of the movement to institute a society which should be strictly professional in its character, the invitation was not extended to the friends of education generally, but was limited to persons actually engaged in the business of education. The language employed is this; "We cordially extend this invitation to all *practical teachers* in the North, the South, the East, and the West, who are willing to unite in a general effort to promote the educational welfare of our country, by concentrating the wisdom and power of numerous minds, and by distributing among all the accumulated experiences of all who are ready to devote their energies, and to contribute of their means to advance the dignity, respectability and usefulness of their calling; and who, in fine, believe that the time has come when the teachers of the nation should gather into one great educational brotherhood."

In pursuance of this call a meeting was held at the designated time and place. It was well attended, and was composed of gentlemen from the different sections of the country, many of whom had won a title to confidence by their eminent services in the cause of education. These gentlemen proceeded to organize the association by the adoption of a constitution and the election of officers. On each of the three succeeding years, a large and successful annual meeting was held—in 1858, in Cincinnati, fifteen states being represented; in 1859, in Washington, representatives from seventeen states being present; and in 1860, in Buffalo, with a representation from nineteen different states, and from the Federal District. The proceedings have been published each year in pamphlet form, including a part of the lectures and papers, which have been characterized by a good degree of ability, learning, and sound practical wisdom. Thus, in brief, stands our record up to 1860.

No annual meeting was held in 1861 or in 1862, the all absorbing exigences of the war, and the impossibility of securing a representation from the seceded states seeming to justify and render necessary a temporary suspension of our operations as a society.

But the period of inaction has passed, and we have reason to congratulate ourselves that it has not resulted in decay and dissolution. As individuals, and as an Association, we still live, and after the lapse of three years we meet again in largely increased numbers, and with renewed strength, here in this great Metropolis of the Northwest, the most marvelous creation and monument of American enterprise, as well as the most striking illustration of the rapid growth and expansion of American civilization.

And it would be an unpardonable neglect of a manifest duty, if we should not feel and acknowledge, with profound gratitude, the favor of Heaven in thus permitting us to assemble here and now, in such force, undisturbed, and in protecting to such an extent the interests of education which we represent, notwithstanding the calamities which have befallen the nation.

The distinctive peculiarity of our organizatian is found in the fact that it is both *national* and *professional*. It is the only educational body of a truly national character now existing in America. Our educational associations for the past thirty years have been for the most part limited to a state or section of the country; and though their usefulness is beyond question, their tendency is no doubt to strengthen local prejudices, and to perpetuate local ideas and systems. The American Institute of Instruction, though a highly useful and honorable society, whose influence has been, and is now widely felt, is mainly supported from the School Fund of Massachusetts, and during the thirty-three years of its existence, it has held but one meeting beyond the limits of the New England States—most of its working members having their residence in a few of the Atlantic States, and therefore it can not justly claim to be what its name implies, and what it was intended to be—truly national in its scope and operations.

But the national character of this body is evident in its design and origin, in the place of its meetings, in the generality of its representation, and indeed in its whole history. In fact the proof is before me. I see within these walls delegates from nearly every loyal state, not only in the Valley of the Mississippi, but beyond the Alleghanies, and on the Atlantic shore, gathered here at a point nearly a thousand miles from the place of the first meeting.

The constitution provides that membership shall be restricted to those who are actually engaged in education as a business, either as teacher, superintendent, or editor, thus securing to it a strictly professional character. This provision, it is believed, will tend to insure both its efficiency and its perpetuity. The American Association for the Advancement of Education, which was instituted at Philadelphia in 1849, and which flourished six or seven years, exerting an extended and beneficial influence, was indeed national in its character, but it was composed of *friends* of education as well as teachers, and not of persons wholly devoted to the business of education. And hence it lacked the essential elements of vitality, and is now known only as a thing in the past. It was destitute of that principle of life which is found in that strong cohesion, that enduring cement, that bond of union, that close affection, which holds together those of the same guild and craft and profession, with ties which, though light as air, are strong as links of steel.

Its design and scope are no less comprehensive than the plan of its organization. These as set forth in the preamble to the constitution, are "to elevate the character and to advance the interests of the profession of teaching, and to promote the cause of popular education in the United States." Thus while designed to admit to membership and participation in its proceedings, the representatives of all grades and descriptions of educational institutions, whether public or private, from the humblest infant school to the highest university, the sphere of its operations is co-extensive with our country's territory and its educational interests, aspiring to embrace the whole subject of instruction and training for the rising generation in all quarters of the Union. With a title so comprehensive, and with objects so vast and important, we have ventured to present ourselves before the community and the world. It becomes us therefore, to consider well the responsibility of the position we have assumed. We ought to endeavor to raise our minds to the height of the great argument. We ought to take large views. We ought to be catholic in spirit, knowing no sects in religion, no parties in politics. We should come to this work and to tnese deliberations, bringing with us no local prejudices, no state jealousies, no sectional bigotry. We should come with ideas and sentiments circumscribed within no geographical limits, hemmed in by no mountain ranges or river courses, by lines of latitude or longitude, but with a broad comprehension of intellect and feeling, with minds and hearts large enough to embrace all the interests we profess to serve—remembering ever that we have "one hope, one lot, one life, one glory."

The first great object to which our efforts are pledged, is to elevate the character and advance the interests of the profession of teaching.

Many fine things have been said concerning the mission of teachers, but after all that has been said, in all ages, upon the subject, more than justice has not been, and never can be done to the theme. We may say with Channing, that there is no office higher than that of a teacher of youth; for there is nothing on earth so precious as the mind, soul, character of the child; or, in the language of Everett, that the office of the teacher, in forming the minds and hearts of the young, and training up those who are to take our places in life, is all important; or in the words of President Humphrey, that the schoolmaster literally speaks, writes, teaches, paints for eternity; his pupils are immortal beings, whose minds are as clay to the seal under his hand. But such generalities, however just and true, fail to convey to our minds an adequate or vivid conception, either of the actual or possible results of the teacher's work.

Let us look at this subject a little more in detail. Let me conduct you, in imagination, to a modest edifice erected for the purpose of primary education, in a retired street in one of our Atlantic cities. Let us enter and observe the occupants and their doings. Here are fifty or sixty children, of both sexes, in the first year of their schooling, being from five to six years of age. The presiding genius who receives us so courteously, welcoming us in tones of peculiar sweetness, is a lady whose natural endowments and opportunities of education have combined to form the true teacher. The cleanly, tidy, well behaved children, seem to be under some magic influence. Some of them are from homes of poverty and ignorance, and yet they appear like a company of brothers and sisters. Their happy, cheerful faces suggest no unpleasant restraint, and yet perfect order reigns. Here you seem to see for once the solution of the eternal problem of uniting liberty with law, freedom with government. Every one is intent upon work as though it were no task, but an agreeable pastime. The lessons proceed. How the mind of the teacher seems to enter into the minds of the pupils! With what a combination of patience, gentleness, sympathy and energy every process is conducted. How the minds and hearts of these children open to receive instruction as the flower opens to light and rain! Weariness is prevented by frequent and regular alternations of work, play, and physical exercise. The air is kept pure and the temperature equable. Here we see these scores of children, without the loss of a day, are at once set forward on the true path of moral and intellectual life; conscience is awakened, and its dictates practically obeyed; manners are formed; right habits are acquired; curiosity is aroused and gratified by imparting rational instruction. They are taught what they need first to know, for comprehending more easily what is to follow. Nothing is learned which they will need to unlearn; their first operations being so guided, that without altering any of their habits, they can more easily produce what is excellent in future. They are beginning to learn to love the good, the beautiful, the true. Their teacher is to them the model and pattern of all excellence. Here we feel sure that the twig is bent in the right direction; and yet this is no fancy sketch.

Let us now imagine that the nation's whole bright tribe of childhood, were thus instructed and trained up in the way they should go—so educated not only in the first *year* of their schooling, but that in each successive grade of their course they should be carried forward with a corresponding perfection of skill, till they go out into the world, whether graduating from the district school, from the high school, or from the university,—let your imagination conceive what would be the results, what moral rectitude, what mental ability and accomplishment would be achieved, and you have some notion of the mission of teachers considered in a national point of view.

Now just in proportion as we elevate the character and promote the interests of the profession of teaching, we shall approach the realization of this ideal of the teacher's mission.

And if we look back over the educational history of America for the space of a quarter of a century, we shall find much to encourage and stimulate our efforts in this high endeavor. Within that period a great and salutary change has taken place respecting the vocation of teaching. Its advancement in respectability, influence and efficiency, has been marked and rapid. The number of able and learned persons of both sexes who are devoted to it, has been increased many fold. The rate of compensation has been increased probably fifty per cent. Its labors have been rendered more agreeable and attractive by the classification and grading of schools, and by the vast improvements which have been made in school architecture. At the dedication of one of the large grammar schools in Boston, a year or two ago, a member of the Corporation of Harvard University, a wise man who weighs his words, said in presence of the late president of that university, and an ex-president, that the head of such a school was the president of a college to all intents and purposes. The establishment of normal schools, now found in most of the educating states, may be regarded as a substantial recognition of teaching as a distinct and liberal profession. Well did Mr. Mann say at the dedication of the first normal school house ever erected in America, " I consider this event as marking an era in the progress of education on this continent and throughout the world."

Already the highest literature of the day is beginning to class teaching with the learned professions, an admission of no little significance. In consequence of the great increase of desirable situations in teaching and superintending schools, some of the best graduates of our colleges are beginning to choose this profession in preference to those of law, medicine, and divinity, as affording an inviting career for a young man of generous ambition, who wishes to make the most of himself as a man, and at the same time to employ his talents for the improvement of the lot of his fellow creatures. In view of such facts as these, we can not but feel encouraged to pursue the objects of this association with zeal and animation.

One of the principle means of elevating the character of teachers is to increase the demand for accomplished teachers. And this demand will be increased as the progress of education is advanced, and its value is appreciated. After all that can be done for the improvement of education, it is substantially what the teachers make it. The stream can not rise higher than its fountain. If asked to describe in the fewest words, the best system of public instruction, I should say it is that which secures and retains the services of the best teachers. To accomplish this, three things are requisite:

1. The situation of the teacher must be made desirable, by adequate compensation, by good treatment, by suitable accommodations, and by limiting the labors to the requirements of health and self-improvement.

2. The mode of selecting and appointing teachers should be such as to encourage the competition of the best qualified candidates, and to give merit the preference over every other consideration.

3. The proper means should be employed to secure continued

self-improvement on the part of teachers; and with this view they should, as far as practicable, be commended, promoted, and rewarded in proportion to their advancement, and degraded or removed for delinquency and neglect of duty.

As in this country the control of educational affairs rests ultimately with the people, the accomplishment of these objects requires that the popular mind should be enlightened upon the subject. Here then is the great paramount work which, as members of this association, we should keep in view—to diffuse useful information on the subject of education. The nature and objects of education, its value and importance to the individual, to the community, and the state; the kind and degree to be desired; the means and methods of securing it,—these are the great leading topics in regard to which the people need to be informed. Every teacher owes it to his profession, as well as to the cause of education, to improve every available opportunity to promote this object, by his pen and voice, and by aiding in the circulation of educational documents.

Public opinion should be especially educated to a liberal, though judicious provision, for the support of institutions of learning. It is a capital error to suppose that a high standard can be maintained at a cheap rate. I have seen, not without sentiments of disapprobation, a competition in certain cities and towns to see which can show the smallest expenditure per scholar. I should rather take pride in showing how large a sum is expended, provided that the outlay can be proved to be judiciously employed. Educational reports, both local and state, constitute the principal channel through which this information is to be diffused. Who can estimate the vast influence of the twelve Reports of Horace Mann, as Secretary of the Massachusetts Board of Education? His fifth Report has probably done more than all other publications within the last twenty-five years to convince capitalists of the value of elementary instruction as a means of increasing the value of labor.

Notwithstanding the advance which has been made in the rate of wages paid to teachers, inadequate compensation is by far too general. I measure the standard of education in any city or town by the rate of salaries paid the teachers. There may be exceptions in particular schools. Still, in my judgment, this is the best general test. As a rule, talent is sure to go where it is best appreciated and rewarded. On this point school officers and the people are not sufficiently enlightened We should endeavor to make every body understand that cheap education must generally be poor education, and that good education must cost money.

But what belongs to teachers themselves to do more than any thing else, in furtherance of the objects of our Association, is the study of the science and art of education—that department of knowledge which is strictly professional. The want of enterprise in this respect, I think, may justly be charged upon teachers as a body. Nor is this deficiency peculiar to any particular class or grade of teachers. It applies to professors in colleges as well as to teachers of common schools, to those who are engaged in the business of education as a permanent profession, and to those who make it a temporary sojourn while on the way to another profession. Of the one hundred thousand teachers in the country, how few are thoroughly versed in the educational literature of the day? But a small part of this number ever see even an educational periodical. A still smaller part have read any books on the subject of education. And how very few even of those who are receiving the higher salaries can boast of a respectable educational library. Scarcely any foreign books relating to the subject are imported, and the number of volumes annually published and sold in this country is, I had almost said, ridiculously small, considering the number of persons who ought to be readers of such works. If proof of this unwelcome truth was needed it would be sufficient to refer to a single publication—I mean *Barnard's Journal of Education*—which has now reached its thirteenth volume, a library in itself. Costing little, considering the amount of matter it contains, embracing exhaustive treatises on almost all departments of education; yet, I am told that the number of copies sold has not been sufficient to pay for the stereotype plates. This fact is not complimentary to American teachers as a body. Of the numerous teachers whom I have known, how few can I name who have made education a study, who have read to any considerable extent on its philosophy, its methods, its institutions, its biography, and its literature. Here, then, in my judgment, is found, to-day, the most practical and efficacious means of a speedy elevation of the character of our profession. Of course a broad and solid basis of general education is an indispensable requisite to form the accomplished teacher, but let every teacher, according to his ability, procure and read the best books and periodicals on education, and incalculable benefits would be the results. It would work a revolution in the profession, and at the same time, prove an efficient means of promoting education.

Professional study consists mainly in learning from the experience of others. This is the means and condition of all progress. Without it civilization itself would be impossible. I know of nothing more unwise in teachers than that disposition which too many have to rely solely on their own personal experience for information respecting their vocation. Such teachers rarely attain to even mediocrity in their profession, and never to eminent success. The most successful are those who learn from others as well as by their own experiments.

I would commend the wise words on this point taken from "The Schoolmaster," the earliest, and one of the best works in the language on education, by Roger Ascham, who was himself thoroughly imbued with the wisdom of the ancient philosophy:

"Surely long experience doth profit much, but most, and almost only to him that is diligently before instructed with precepts of well doing. For good precepts of learning be the eyes of the mind, to look wisely before a man, which way to go right, and which not. Learning (the recorded experience of others,) teacheth more in one year than experience in twenty; and learning teacheth safely, when experience maketh more miserable than wise."

I have spoken of only one of the objects of our Association,—that of elevating the character and advancing the interests of the profession of teaching. The other great object of our efforts, as set forth in the preamble to our constitution, is "to promote the cause of popular education in the United States." Time will not permit me to enlarge upon this province of our labors. But of this we may be assured; whatever tends to elevate and improve the character and qualifications of teachers, contributes also to the progress of education; and on the other hand, whatever tends to advance the cause of education, must, at the same time promote the interests, and improve the character of teachers. The two objects, therefore, for which we profess to work, are essentially one and the same.

In conclusion I present the following summary of the recent movements and improvements in education, and of what, in my judgment, ought to be done to promote the cause.

I. Recent movements and improvements.

1. Primary schools have been much improved.

2. Progress has been made in reference to truancy and compulsory education.

3. Much has been done to introduce and to perfect Object Teaching.

4. Physical education has been greatly advanced.

5. Much has been done to perfect courses of study for high, grammar, primary, and district schools.

6. A beginning has been made in establishing Technological and Industrial Institutes. The establishment of the Massachusetts Institute of Technology, in Boston, is an important movement for the application of science to the practical arts.

7. Public attention has been strongly turned to the subject of military education, and the necessity of competitive examinations for admission to the National Military and Naval Academies is beginning to be agitated.

8. The thorough grading of schools wherever it is practicable, has now become the settled policy of all enlightened educators.

9. Great progress has been made in establishing free public high schools.

10. Public libraries in cities, towns, and school districts, have been greatly multiplied.

II. Measures to be encouraged and advocated by the association for the advancement of popular education.

1. The appointment of a professor of education in every important college and university.

2. The appointment of superintendents of public instruction in all states, counties, cities, and important towns.

3. One or more normal schools should be established and maintained at public expense in each state.

4. The teachers of each state should maintain and conduct an educational periodical.

5. Teaching should be legally recognized as a profession.

6. The condition of teachers should be ameliorated by the payment of better salaries, and the requirement of less work.

7. Educational associations should be maintained in every state, county, and town.

8. Teachers should devote more attention to the study of the science and art of education.

9. A national bureau of education should be established at Washington.

10. A system of free public schools, comprising the primary, grammar, and higher grades, should be established, and supported by taxation in every state where such a system does not exist.

11. All schools should be graded where grading is practicable.

12. Educational men should be appointed to fill educational offices of every description.

13. Moral and religious training ought to be made much more prominent than it is.

14. The whole rising generation should be instructed in the principles of our republican government.

These are some of the topics which I would suggest for the future consideration of this association. And now

Fellow Teachers:—Let us rejoice that we live in a day, and at a period of unexampled opportunities for usefulness and honorable effort. Let us congratulate each other that we have the blessed privilege of assembling in this place, from regions widely remote, to take counsel for the promotion of the moral and intellectual culture of the whole people—the highest earthly interest of society. While our sons and brothers, and friends, are on the field of battle, with arms in their hands, fighting and pouring out their life-blood for the preservation of our national integrity and Union, for the defence of free institutions and christian civilization, let us strive to act well our part by endeavoring to make our country worthy of such sacrifices and such heroes. Let us remember that peace hath her victories, and that it belongs to us to act a strenuous, patriotic, and heroic part for the welfare of our country, to go forth conquering, and to conquer in the domain of ignorance, achieving those peaceful triumphs which will insure our future prosperity and success, and enable us worthily to fulfill our destiny

# BARNARD'S EDUCATIONAL PUBLICATIONS.

# BARNARD'S EDUCATIONAL PUBLICATIONS.

| | PRICE |
|---|---|
| Brooks, Edward, Memoir and Portrait | 50 |
| Cady, I. F., Method of Classical Instruction | 25 |
| Calderwood, H., Teaching, Its Ends and Means | 25 |
| Caldwell, C., Education in North Carolina | 25 |
| Cambridge University. The Undergraduate | 25 |
| Camp, D. N., Memoir and Portrait | 50 |
| Calkins, N. A., Object Teaching | 25 |
| Carlyle, Thomas, University Studies | 25 |
| Letter on Reading | 25 |
| Carter, James G., Memoir and Portrait | 50 |
| Essay on Teachers' Seminaries in 1824 | 25 |
| Catechism of Methods of Teaching | 50 |
| Catholic Church, Schools and Teaching Orders | 1.00 |
| Cecil, Sir William, Advice to his Son | 25 |
| Channing, W., Teachers & their Education (1832) | 25 |
| Hints on Self Culture | 25 |
| Chatham, Lord, Letters to his Nephew | 25 |
| Cheever, Ezekiel, & Free Schools of N. England | 50 |
| Chesterfield, Lord, Studies and Conduct | 25 |
| Choate, Rufus, Books and Reading | 25 |
| Christian Schools, Earliest Established | 25 |
| Cities, Systems of Public Schools | 2.50 |
| Clarke, H. G., Principles & Modes of Ventilation | 25 |
| Clark T. M., Education for the Times | 25 |
| Coggeshall, W. J., Ohio System of Pub. Schools | 25 |
| Colburn, Dana P., Memoir and Portrait | 50 |
| Colburn, W., Educational Work, and Portrait | 50 |
| Cole, D., Method of Classical Education | 25 |
| Colet, J., Educational Views and St. Paul School | 50 |
| Colman, Henry, Agricultural Schools in France | 25 |
| Comenius, A., Educational Labors and Principles | 50 |
| Colleges, Origin and Use in Universities | 25 |
| College Code of Honor | 25 |
| Competitive Examinations for Public Service | 25 |
| Conduct—Suggestions by Eminent Men | 3 50 |
| Connecticut, Educational Institutions | 3.50 |
| Conversation.—Suggestions by Bacon and others | 25 |
| Conversational Method | 25 |
| Corporal Punishment—Barbarism of Discipline | 25 |
| Coutts, Miss Burdett, Prize Scheme for Girls | 25 |
| Cowdery, M. F., Moral Training in Pub. Schools | 25 |
| Cowley, A., Plan of Philosophical College, 1662 | 25 |
| Cowper, Wm., The Tirocinium. Review of Schools | 25 |
| Crabbe, Geo., Schools of the Borough | 25 |
| Crime and Education | 25 |
| Currie, James, Methods of Early Education | 25 |
| Dana, J. D., Science and Scientific Schools | 25 |
| Dawson, J. W., Nat. Hist. in its Educat. Aspects | 25 |
| Day, Henry N., English Composition | 25 |
| Deaf Mute Institutions and Instruction | 25 |
| De LaSalle, A., Memoir & the Christian Brothers | 50 |
| Denmark, Public Instruction | 25 |
| DeQuincy, Studies and Conduct | 25 |
| Letters on the Art of Conversation | 25 |
| DeMetz, M., Colonies for Juvenile Offenders | 25 |
| Dickinson, J.W., Philos. & Methods of Teaching | 25 |
| Diesterweg, Memoir | 25 |
| Catechism of Methods of Teaching | 50 |
| School Discipline and Plans of Instruction | 25 |
| Intuitional and Speaking Exercises | 25 |
| Dinter, G. F., Memoir | 25 |
| Disraeli, B., Studies and Conduct | 25 |
| Dixon, W. Hepworth.—Swiss Schools in 1870 | 25 |
| Doane, George W., The State and Education | 25 |
| Döllinger, Universities, Past and Present | 25 |
| Dominic, St., and the Dominicans | 25 |
| Donaldson, James, Edu. in Prussia and England | 25 |
| Drawing, Methods of Teaching | 50 |
| Duai, A., German Schools in the United States | 25 |
| Ducpetiaux, Agricultural Reform Schools | 25 |
| Duffield, D. B., Education a State Duty | 25 |
| Dunn, H., Methods of the Borough-road Schools | 25 |
| Durfee, Job, R. I. Idea of Government | 25 |
| Duruy, Secondary Special Schools in France | 25 |
| Dupanloup, Studious Women | 25 |
| Dwight, Edmund, Memoir and Portrait | 50 |
| Dwight, Timothy, Memoir | 25 |
| Academy at Green Farms | 25 |
| Yale College in 1814 | 25 |
| Educational Biographies, with Portraits of over 100 Eminent Teachers, Educators, and Benefactors of Educators, each | 50 |
| Educational Tracts, Numbers I.–XII., each | 25 |
| Edu. Documents for Gen. Circulation, I.–IV. each | 1.00 |
| Education and the State | 25 |
| Education Defined | 25 |

| | PRICE. |
|---|---|
| Edwards, Richard, Memoir and Portrait | 50 |
| Normal Schools | 25 |
| Elyot, Sir Thomas, The Governour | 25 |
| Emerson, Geo. B., Educat. Labors, with Portrait | 50 |
| Memorial on Normal Schools, 1837 | 25 |
| Moral Education | 25 |
| England, Elementary Schools and Methods | 3.50 |
| Public or Endowed Schools | 25 |
| Navigation Schools | 25 |
| Universities of Oxford and Cambridge | 50 |
| Military Schools | 25 |
| Scientific and Technical Schools | 2.50 |
| English Estimate of Swiss Public Schools | 25 |
| Public Schools of the United States | 25 |
| English Pedagogy, First Series | 3.50 |
| Second Series | 3.50 |
| Erasmus, Memoir and Educational Works | 50 |
| Classical Studies | 25 |
| Ernest the Pious, Educational Works | 25 |
| European Estimate of American Schools | 25 |
| Everett, E., Educational Views, and Portrait | 50 |
| John Lowell and the Lowell Lectures | 25 |
| John Harvard and his Benefaction | 25 |
| Uses of Astronomy | 25 |
| Address on Normal Schools, 1839 | 25 |
| Everett, W., The Cambridge System of Study | 25 |
| Fairchild, Coeducation of the Sexes | 25 |
| Felbiger, J. J., Educational Labors in Austria | 25 |
| Fellenberg, Memoir and Principles of Education | 25 |
| Felton, C. C., Memoir and Portrait | 50 |
| Characteristics of American Colleges | 25 |
| Female Schools and Education | 5.50 |
| Fenelon, Memoir and Female Education | 25 |
| Fichte, J. H. von, Frobel's Eductional System | 50 |
| Fliedner, Ins. for Deaconesses at Kaiserswerth | 25 |
| Forbes, E., Educational Uses of Museums | 25 |
| Fowle, W. B., Memoir and Portrait | 50 |
| Fowler, W. C., The Clergy and Common Schools | 25 |
| France, System of Public Instruction | 2.50 |
| The University of Paris | 25 |
| The University of France | 25 |
| Technical and Military Schools | 3.50 |
| Special Secondary Schools | 25 |
| French Teachers and Pedagogy | 3.50 |
| Francis, St., and the Franciscans | 25 |
| Franke, A. H., Educational Views and Labors | 25 |
| Franklin, B., Maxims of Poor Richard | 25 |
| Frederic the Great, as School Reformer | 25 |
| School Codes of 1764 | 25 |
| Free Schools of New England, Historical Data | 25 |
| French Schools and Pedagogy | 5.50 |
| Froebel, The Kindergarten System | 25 |
| Froude, University Studies | 25 |
| Fuller, Thomas, The Good Schoolmaster | 25 |
| Gallaudet, Thomas H., Memoir and Portrait | 50 |
| Plan for a Teachers' Seminary in 1824 | 25 |
| Gammell, W., Memoir of Nicholas Brown | 25 |
| Garfield, James A., Education a National Duty | 25 |
| Gaston, William, Advice to College Graduates | 25 |
| Gerard-Groote, and the Hieronymians | 25 |
| Germany, National System and Pedagogy, 5v. | |
| Primary and Secondary Schools | 5 50 |
| Technical and Military Schools | 3 50 |
| Universities, Gymnasia, & Polytechnic Schools | 3.50 |
| Educational Reformers—Ratich, Comenius, etc. | 3.50 |
| Modern German Pedagogy | 3.50 |
| Gesner, J. M., Educational Views | 25 |
| Gilman, D. C., Scientific Schools | 25 |
| Gladstone, W. E., Educational Views | 25 |
| Goethe, Educational Training and Views | 25 |
| Cultivation of Reverence | 25 |
| Goldsmith, Oliver, Essay on Education | 25 |
| Goodrich, S. G., Schools as they were in 1800 | 25 |
| Goodrich, W. H., Plea for Extended Education | 25 |
| Göttingen University | 25 |
| Gould, B. A., The American University | 25 |
| Graser, System of Instruction | 25 |
| Greece, Ancient, Schools and Education | 25 |
| Greece, Modern, System of Public Instruction | 25 |
| Greek Language, Subject of School Study | 25 |
| Greene, S. S., Object Teaching | 25 |
| Educational Duties of the Hour | 25 |
| Gregory, J. M., The Problem of Education | 25 |
| Griscom, John, Memoir and Portrait | 50 |
| Guizot, Ministry of Public Instruction in France | 50 |
| Gulliver, J. P., Norwich Free Academy | 25 |

The above Treatises have all appeared as separate articles in Barnard's American Journal of Education. Any Book or Pamphlet on the List will be sent by mail, *postage paid*, on receiving the price in postage stamps or money order. On orders of $20 a discount of 20 per cent. will be made.

*Address H. B., Post Office Box U, Hartford, Conn.* *January*, 1875.

# BARNARD'S EDUCATIONAL PUBLICATIONS.

| | PRICE. |
|---|---|
| HALE, SIR MATTHEW, Studies and Conduct | 25 |
| HALL, S. R., Educational Labors and Portrait | 50 |
| HAMANN, J. G., Pedagogical Views | 25 |
| HAMIL, S. M., School Discipline | 25 |
| HAMILTON, J., and the Hamiltonian Method | 25 |
| HAMILTON, Sir W., Mathematics | |
| The College in the University | 25 |
| HAMMOND, C., New England Academies | 25 |
| Hanover, System of Public Schools | 25 |
| HART, J. M., The American Student at Göttingen | 25 |
| HART, J. S., Memoir and Portrait | 50 |
| Characteristics of a Normal School | 25 |
| Anglo-Saxon in the Study of English | 25 |
| HARTLIB, S., Plan of College of Husbandry in 1651 | 25 |
| HAÜY, V., and the Instruction of the Blind | 25 |
| HAVEN, JOSEPH, Mental Science as a Study | 25 |
| HAWES, JOEL, Female Education | 25 |
| HEDGE, N., Schools as they were | 25 |
| HEIKEL, FELIX, Public Instruction in Finland | 25 |
| HELFENSTEIN, J., Mediæval Universities | 25 |
| HENRY, J., Common Schools | 25 |
| HENRY, JOSEPH, Philosophy of Education | 25 |
| HENTSCHELL, E., Teaching Singing | 25 |
| Teaching Drawing | 25 |
| HERBERT, J. F., Pedagogical Views | 50 |
| HERDER, Life and Educational Views | 25 |
| Hesse-Cassel, System of Public Schools | 25 |
| Hesse-Darmstadt, System of Public Schools | 25 |
| HILL, M. D., Reformatory Schools | 25 |
| HILL, T., True Order of Studies | 25 |
| HILLIARD, G. S., Boston Public Library | 25 |
| HILLHOUSE, J. A., Literary Culture in Republics | 50 |
| Hints and Methods for the Use of Teaching | 25 |
| HODJINS, J. GEORGE, Education in Upper Canada | 25 |
| HOLBROOK, J., Educational Labors and Portrait | 50 |
| The American Lyceum | 25 |
| Holland, System of Public Instruction | 25 |
| HOOD, THOMAS, The Irish Schoolmasters | 25 |
| HOOLE, C., The Old Art of Teaching, 1659 | 25 |
| HOPKINS, M., Educational Labors and Views | 1.00 |
| HOWE, S. G., Memoir and Portrait | 50 |
| Laura Bridgman | 25 |
| HUMBOLT, WM. VON, Studies for Old Age | 50 |
| HUMPHREY, HEMAN, Normal Schools | 25 |
| Common Schools as they were | 25 |
| HUNTINGTON, F. D., Unconscious Tuition | 25 |
| College Prayers | 25 |
| HUXLEY, T. H., Science in Schools | 25 |
| IGNATIUS LOYOLA, and the Schools of the Jesuits | 25 |
| Illiteracy in the United States | 25 |
| Ireland, English Educational Policy | 25 |
| National Schools | 25 |
| Endowed Schools | 25 |
| Universities | 25 |
| Italy, System of Public Instruction | 25 |
| Revival of Classical Learning | 50 |
| Mediæval Universities | 25 |
| Infant School and Kindergarten | 25 |
| JACOBS, F., Method of Teaching Latin | 25 |
| JACOTOT, L., Memoir and Method of Instruction | 25 |
| JAMESON, Mrs., Social Occupations of Women | 25 |
| JARVIS, E., Misdirected Education and Insanity | 25 |
| JEROME, ST., Education of Daughters | 25 |
| Jesuits, Society and Schools of the | 25 |
| JEWELL, F. S., Teaching as a Profession | 25 |
| JOHNSON, SAMUEL, Educational Views | 2 |
| JOHNSON, W. R., Educational Labors, & portrait | 25 |
| JULIUS, DR., Normal Schools in Prussia | 50 |
| KEENAN, P. J., Organization of Irish Schools | 25 |
| KINDERMANN, School Reform in Bohemia | 25 |
| KINGSBURY, JOHN, Memoir and Portrait | 25 |
| KNIGHT, CHARLES, Economical Science | 50 |
| KIRKPATRICK, E., Education in Greece & Rome | 25 |
| KEY, JOSEPH, Prussian Schools | 50 |
| KRÜSI, Life and Educational Labors | 25 |
| LALOR, J., Nature and Objects of Education | 25 |
| LANCASTER, JOS., Memoir and Monitorial Schools | 25 |
| LAWRENCE, A., and Lawrence Scientific School | 25 |
| Latin Language, Methods of Teaching | 50 |
| LEIGH, E., Illiteracy in the United States | 25 |
| LEWIS, DIO, The New Gymnastics | 25 |
| LEWIS, SAMUEL, Memoir and Portrait | 50 |
| LEWIS, T., Methods of Teaching Greek and Latin | 25 |
| LINDSLEY, PHILIP, Memoir and Portrait | 50 |
| LOCKE, JOHN, Thoughts on Education | 1.00 |
| LONGSTREET, Schools as they were in Georgia | 25 |
| LOTHROP, S. K., W. Lawrence & N.E. Academies | 25 |
| LOWE, ROBERT, University Studies | 25 |
| LOWELL, JOHN, and the Lowell Lectures | 25 |
| LUTHER, MARTIN, Memoir and Views on Educat. | 50 |
| LYON, MARY, Principles of Mt. Holyoke Seminary | 50 |
| LYTTON, SIR E. B., Studies and Conduct | 25 |
| Money, its Acquisition and Uses | 25 |
| LYCURGUS, and Spartan Education | 25 |
| LYELL, SIR CHARLES, Physical Science in Educat. | 25 |
| MACAULAY, LORD T. B., Educational Views | 25 |
| MANSFIELD, E. D., Military Acad. at West Point | 25 |
| History of National Land Grants to Ohio | 25 |
| MARCEL, C., Conversational Method in Language | 50 |
| MARCH, F. A., Study of English Language | 25 |
| MARIA THERESA, Educational Reforms | 25 |
| MARION, GENERAL, Free Schools for Republics | 25 |
| MANN, HORACE, Memoir and Portrait | 50 |
| Lectures and Reports | 5.50 |
| Teachers' Motives | 25 |
| Professional Training of Teachers | 25 |
| College Code of Honor | 25 |
| Fourth of July Oration, 1842 | 25 |
| Manual Labor in Education | 25 |
| MASON, LOWELL, Memoir and Portrait | 50 |
| MASON, S. W., Physical Exercises in School | 25 |
| MASSON, D., College and Self-Education | 25 |
| Milton's Home, School, and College Education | 25 |
| MAY, S. J., Educational Work, with Portrait | 50 |
| MAYHEW, IRA, Educational Work with Portrait | 50 |
| McCRIE, DR., Universities of Scotland | 25 |
| McELLIGOTT, J. N., Debating in School Work | 25 |
| MEIEROTTO, Method of Teaching Latin | 35 |
| MELANCTHON, P., Memoir and Educational Work | 50 |
| Mettrey Reform School, Rise and Progress | 25 |
| MILL, J. S., University Studies | 25 |
| MILTON, JOHN, Tractate on Education | 25 |
| Home, School, and University Training | 25 |
| MOLINEUX, E. L., Military Exercises in Schools | 25 |
| Monitorial System and Method | 25 |
| MONTAIGNE, Educational Views | 25 |
| MONTESQUIEU, Educational Views | 25 |
| MORE, SIR THOMAS, Educational Views | 25 |
| MORRISON, T., School Management | 50 |
| MULCASTER, R., Positions and Elementaire | 25 |
| MURRAY, J. N., English Policy in Irish Education | 25 |
| Music, Method for Common Schools | 25 |
| NEANDER, M., Educational Views | 25 |
| NEWMAN, University Education | 25 |
| NIEBUHR, Method of Philological Study | 25 |
| NIEMEYER, Aphorisms (other German Educators) | 2.50 |
| NISSEN, H., Public Schools in Norway | 25 |
| NORTHEND, E., Memoir and Portrait | 50 |
| Normal Schools and Teach. Sem., *Ed.* of 1854 | 2.00 |
| Norwich Free Academy | 25 |
| OBERLIN, J. F., Educational Work | 25 |
| Object Teaching, and other Methods | 3.50 |
| Oral Methods | 50 |
| OLMSTEAD, D., Memoir and Portrait | 50 |
| Democratic Tendencies of Science | 25 |
| Timothy Dwight—a Model Teacher | 25 |
| OVERBERG, B., Educational Views | 25 |
| OWEN, R., Educational Views | 25 |
| Oxford University in 1873-4 | 25 |
| PAGE, D. P., Memoir and Portrait | 50 |
| Pouring In and Drawing Out Methods | 25 |
| Paris, The Old University | 25 |
| Superior Normal School | 25 |
| Polytechnic Schools | 50 |
| PARR, SAMUEL, Educational Views | 25 |
| PARTRIDGE, A., Educational Work and Portrait | 50 |
| PATTISON, Prussian Normal Schools | 25 |
| PAYNE, JOSEPH, Science and Art of Education | 25 |
| PEABODY, GEORGE, Educational Benefactions | 25 |
| PEIRCE, B. K., Reformatory for Girls | 25 |
| PEIRCE, CYRUS, Memoir and Portrait | 50 |
| PESTALOZZI, Memoir and Portrait | 1.50 |
| Leonard and Gertrude | 1.00 |
| Evening Hour of a Hermit | 25 |
| PESTALOZZI, and Pestalozzianism | 3.50 |
| PESTALOZZI, Fellenberg and Wehrli | 25 |
| PETRARCH, DANTE, and BOCCACIO | 25 |
| PETTY, SIR W., Plan of a Mechanical College, 1647 | 25 |
| PHELPS, ALMIRA L., Memoir and Portrait | 25 |
| PHELPS, W. F., Memoir and Portrait | 50 |

The above Treatises have all appeared as separate articles in Barnard's American Journal of Education. Any Book or Pamphlet on the List will be sent by mail, *postage paid*, on receiving the price in postage stamps or money order. On orders of $20 a discount of 20 per cent. will be made.

*Address H. B., Post Office Box U, Hartford, Conn.* *January*, 1875.

# BARNARD'S EDUCATIONAL PUBLICATIONS.

| | PRICE. |
|---|---|
| Payne, A., The Science and Art of Education.. | 25 |
| Philbrick, John D., Memoir and Portrait..... | 50 |
| Work for the National Teachers' Association. | 25 |
| Report on Boston Public Schools, 1874......... | 50 |
| Platter, T., School Life in the 15th Century.... | 25 |
| Plutarch, Educational Views.................. | 25 |
| Pombal, Marquis, Educa. Work in Portugal... | 25 |
| Port Royalists, Educational Views............. | 25 |
| Porter, J. A., Plan of an Agricultural College.. | 25 |
| Porter, Noah, Prize Essay on School Reform.. | 25 |
| Barnard's Educational Activity in Conn. & R. I | 50 |
| Portugal, System of Public Instruction.......... | 25 |
| Potter, Alonzo, Memoir and Portrait.......... | 50 |
| Consolidation of American Colleges.... ...... | 25 |
| Potter, E. R., Religion in Public Schools ...... | 50 |
| Pouchet, M., French View of Ger. Universities | 25 |
| Prussia, System of Public Schools.............. | 3.00 |
| 1. Primary Schools.............................. | 50 |
| 2. Secondary Schools........................ | 50 |
| 3. Universities................................ | 50 |
| 4. Technical Schools.......................... | 50 |
| 5. Military Schools.......................... | 50 |
| Public Schools, Official Exposition in 1856...... | 50 |
| Quick, Educational Reformers—Jacotot......... | 25 |
| Quintilian, Educational Views ................ | 25 |
| Rabelais, Educational Views ................ | 25 |
| Ramus, Peter, Memoir and Educational Views. | 25 |
| Randall, Henry S.. School Libraries ......... | 25 |
| Randall, S. S., Memoir and Portrait............ | 50 |
| Raphall, M. L., Education among the Hebrews | 25 |
| Ratich, Educational Views..................... | 50 |
| Raumer, Karl Von, German Universities.. .... | 2.50 |
| Early Childhood.................................. | 25 |
| Methods of Teaching Latin.................... | 25 |
| Methods of Teaching Arithmetic............... | 25 |
| Physical Education ........................... | 25 |
| Education of Girls .......................... | 50 |
| Educational Revival in Italy.................. | 25 |
| Progressives of the 17th Century............. | 25 |
| Ratich, Comenius and Basedow............... | 1.00 |
| Loyola and Schools of the Jesuits.............. | 25 |
| Raumer, Rudolf, Instruction in German....... | 25 |
| Ravaisson, F., Instruction in Drawing.......... | 25 |
| Reformatory and Preventive Schools & Agencies | 1.50 |
| Renan, E., German views of French Education.. | 25 |
| Rendu, E., Prussian & French School Expenses. | 25 |
| Reuchlin, and Education in the 16th century.... | 25 |
| Rhode Island Institute of Instruction............ | 25 |
| Richards, W. F.. Manual of Methods........... | 50 |
| Rickoff, A. J., Memoir and Portrait............ | 50 |
| Riecke, Philosophy of Early Education......... | 25 |
| Rider, Admiral, Navigation Schools for England | 25 |
| Ross, W. P., Catechetical Method.............. | 25 |
| Rousseau, Memoir and Educational Views...... | 25 |
| Rollin, Charles, Education of Youth.......... | 50 |
| Russell, Scott, Technical University for England | 25 |
| Systematic Technical Education............... | 25 |
| Russell, William, Memoir and Portrait........ | 50 |
| Normal Training............................ | 1.50 |
| Legal Recognition of Teaching as a Profession | 25 |
| Russia.—System of Public Instruction.......... | 25 |
| Military and Naval Education............... | 25 |
| Universities................................. | 25 |
| Ryerson, Edgerton, Memoir and Portrait...... | 50 |
| Savigny, Universities of the Middle Ages........ | 50 |
| Saxony, System of Public Instruction........... | 25 |
| Secondary and Superior Instruction........... | 25 |
| Technical and Special Schools................ | 25 |
| Saxon Principalities, Public Instruction......... | 25 |
| Sarmiento, Memoir and Portrait............... | 50 |
| The Schoolmaster's Work................... | 25 |
| School Architecture, Revised Edition, with 500 Ill. | 5.50 |
| School Architecture, Practical Illustrations.. ... | 1.00 |
| Do. Rural and Ungraded Schools........... | 50 |
| Do. City and Graded Schools............. | 1.00 |
| Do. Primary and Infant Schools............ | 50 |
| Do. Public High Schools .................. | 50 |
| Scotland, System of Public Instruction......... | 50 |
| Secondary Schools and Universities............ | 1.00 |
| Seeley, J., Cambridge System of Examinations | 25 |
| Seguin, Treatment and Training of Idiots. ..... | 25 |
| Seton, S. S., Schools as they were 60 Years Ago | 25 |
| Sheldon, E. A., Object Teaching............... | 25 |
| Shenstone, W., The Schoolmistress............. | 25 |
| Siljstrom, P. A., American Schools............. | 25 |
| Simonson, L., Cadet System in Switzerland...... | 25 |
| Smith, Elbridge, Norwich Free Academy ..... | 25 |
| Spencer, Herbert, Thoughts on Education.... | 50 |

| | PRICE. |
|---|---|
| Southey, Robert, Home Education............. | 25 |
| Dr. Dove, and the Schoolmaster of Ingleton... | 50 |
| Sprague, W. B., Influence of Yale College...... | 25 |
| Spain, System of Public Instruction.............. | 25 |
| Spurzheim, Educational Views................. | 25 |
| Stanley, Lord, Lyceums and Popular Education | 25 |
| State and Education—The American Doctrine... | 25 |
| Stearns, E., Early History of Normal Schools.. | 25 |
| Stow, David, Gallery Training Lesson.......... | 25 |
| Stowe, Calvin E., Memoir and Portrait......... | 50 |
| Teachers' Seminaries........................ | 25 |
| Sturm, John, Educational Views............. | 25 |
| Sullivan, O., Teaching the Alphabet......... | 25 |
| Sweden and Norway, Public Instruction......... | 25 |
| Swett, John, Educational Labors and Portrait.. | 50 |
| Swift, Jonathan, Manners and Conversation... | 25 |
| Switzerland.—Public Instruction in each Canton | 1.50 |
| Military, and Cadet System................... | 25 |
| Sybel, H. Von, The German University.......... | 25 |
| Tainsh, E. C., Prize Essay on Education & Crime | 25 |
| Tappan, H. P., Memoir and Portrait........... | 50 |
| Educational Development of Europe........... | 25 |
| Tarbox, J. N., American Education Society..... | 25 |
| Taylor, Henry, True Uses of Wealth .......... | 25 |
| Text Books, Catalogue of... ..................... | 1.00 |
| Thayer, Gideon F., Memoir and Portrait... ... | 50 |
| Letters to a Young Teacher.................... | 50 |
| Tillinghast, Nicholas, Memoir and Portrait... | 50 |
| Town, Salem, Schools as they were............ | 25 |
| Trotzendorf, Educational Views............... | 25 |
| Tubingen University........................... | 25 |
| Tucker, George, Educational Census of 1840... | 25 |
| Turkey, Schools and School Code............. | 25 |
| Tyndall, Science in Education.............. | 25 |
| Unconscious Influence—Bushnell............. | 25 |
| Unconscious Tuition—Huntington .............. | 25 |
| United States, Systems of Public Instruction.... | 5.50 |
| Common Schools as they were about 1800...... | 1.00 |
| Common Schools in 1870... .................... | 1.00 |
| Colleges and Universities........................ | 1.00 |
| Military and Naval Schools..................... | 1.00 |
| Normal Schools.................................. | 3.50 |
| Universities and Colleges........................ | 5.50 |
| University Life—Past and Present.............. | 50 |
| Deposition, Pennalism, Landmannschaften.... | 50 |
| Tripos, Prævaricator, Terræ Filius............. | 50 |
| Vail, T. H., Methods of Using Books............ | 25 |
| Vassar, M., Memoir and Portrait............... | 50 |
| Vehrli, J., Industrial Element in Schools...... | 25 |
| Ventilation and Warming of School houses..... | 25 |
| Vienna, Educational Institutions............... | 25 |
| Vives, L., Memoir and Educational Views....... | 25 |
| Wadsworth, James S., Memoir and Portrait.... | 50 |
| Washington, George, Rules of Conduct....... | 25 |
| National Education......................... | 25 |
| Wayland, Frances, Memoir and Portrait....... | 50 |
| Intellectual Education—Institute Address...... | 25 |
| Webster, Daniel, Educational Views........... | 25 |
| Webster, Noah, Educational Views........... | 25 |
| Wells, W. H., Memoir and Portrait.......... | 50 |
| Methods in English Grammar.................. | 25 |
| West Point Military Academy................... | 25 |
| Whately, A., Annotations on Bacon's Essays... | 25 |
| Whewell, W., Educational Views .............. | 25 |
| White, E. E., Normal Schools for Ohio.......... | 25 |
| National Bureau of Education................ | 25 |
| White, S. H., National Bureau of Education.... | 25 |
| Wichern, T. H., German Reformatory Schools.. | 50 |
| Wickersham, Educational Work and Portrait... | 50 |
| Education in Reconstruction .................. | 25 |
| Willard, Mrs. Emma, Memoir and Portrait..... | 50 |
| Wilson, J. M., Science in Rugby School......... | 25 |
| William of Wykeham and St. Mary's College.... | 25 |
| Willm, J., Teachers' Conferences and Libraries. | 25 |
| Wimmer, H., Special Schools in Saxony......... | 25 |
| Public Instruction in Dresden................. | 25 |
| Wines, E. C., Memoir and Portrait............. | 50 |
| Winterbotham, W., American Education in 1796 | 25 |
| Wirt, William, Professional Studies—Law.... | 26 |
| Wolf, T. A., Educational Views..... .......... | 25 |
| Wotton, Sir Henry, Educational Views......... | 25 |
| Wurtemberg, System of Public Instruction...... | 25 |
| Technical Schools.............................. | 25 |
| Woodbridge, W. C., Memoir and Portrait....... | 50 |
| Wykeham and St. Mary College................ | 25 |
| Young, Thomas, Manual for Infant Schools...... | 25 |
| Zurich, Cantonal School Code and System....... | 25 |
| Federal Polytechnic University.............. | 25 |

The above Treatises have all appeared as separate articles in Barnard's American Journal of Education. Any Book or Pamphlet on the List will be sent by mail, *postage paid*, on receiving the price in postage stamps or money order. On orders of $20 a discount of 20 per cent. will be made.

*Address H. B., Post Office Box U, Hartford, Conn.* *January*, 1875.

# OBJECT TEACHING.

BY E. A. SHELDON, OSWEGO, N. Y.

In opening the discussion on this occasion, on what is sometimes technically called "Object Teaching," I propose first very briefly to state the principles upon which the methods thus indicated are based. Secondly to consider some of the difficulties that lie in the way of the progress of these reformed methods of teaching, and the best way of removing them; and lastly consider the true aim and limit of these methods as applied to the development of the early faculties of childhood.

We assume first that education should embrace the united, harmonious development of the *whole being*, the *moral*, the *physical*, and the *intellectual;* and that no one of these should be urged forward to the neglect or at the expense of the other. We likewise assume that there is a natural order in the evolution of the human faculties, and also of appliances for their development, a knowledge of which is essential to the highest success in education; that the perceptive faculties are the first and most strongly developed and upon them are based all future acquirements; that just in proportion as they are quick and accurate in receiving impressions, will all the future processes of education and outgrowing attainments be easy and rapid, and ever prove unfailing sources of delight; and hence they should be the first to receive distinctive and special culture. To this we may add that childhood has certain marked and distinctive characteristics which should never be lost sight of in all our dealings with children. Among the more prominent of these are activity, love of sympathy, and a desire for constant variety. In the natural order of subjects we recognize as first, mathematics, including a consideration of form, size, and number; second, physics, including objects in nature, their sensible qualities and properties, and third, language, including oral and written expression, reading and spelling.

We have thus stated, as concisely as possible, the very first steps in this natural order, upon which must be based all successful educational efforts; for the limited time allotted to this paper reminds us of the necessity of confining ourselves closely to the point under discussion.

It would be not a little interesting to trace the natural relation of these two orders throughout a complete educational course, nor would it be entirely foreign to our subject; but this would lead us into too broad a field of investigation, and be liable to divert the discussion from the point particularly before us. We will not stop now to consider in detail the method best adapted to the development of the infant faculties, but will advert to them after considering briefly a few of the more prominent obstacles that lie in the way of the most successful progress of these improved methods of teaching. And in this connection we remark first, that the very title by which these methods are popularly designated is open to serious objection. It is true that the term "Object Teaching" is, to a certain extent, suggestive of the real character of these early processes, in that we are continually dealing with tangible objects and illustrations, but it is liable to be taken in a too limited sense. Instead of embracing a large number of subjects, and covering the entire field of the early culture of the faculties, many have taken it to mean nothing more than miscellaneous lessons on objects. These lessons often clumsily given by those who have no knowledge of correct principles, and who therefore continually violate them, have led many to condemn the whole system, and thus in certain quarters to bring it into disrepute.

Again, book speculators are continually making use of the term as a catch word, for the purpose of disposing of their wares; thus imposing upon the uninitiated, and bringing into discredit methods of which these books are the farthest possible from being the representatives. In this way old books have received new title pages, and new books with old methods have been christened with the catch word, "Object Lessons," or "On the Object Plan;" and what is lamentable, multitudes know not the difference between the *name* and the *thing*. In this way much mischief has already been done, and much more is yet to be experienced.

Realizing these objections, some have proposed to change the name, substituting a term more comprehensive and less liable to objection. But this change of names will only subject publishers to an additional expense of new title pages, and will not wholly obviate the evils referred to. Our plan would be to drop all specific names, and speak of all improved, natural or philosophical methods of teaching as such, and let the great effort be to infuse right principles into the minds of teachers, to lead them to study the mental moral and physical constitution of children, and the best method of bringing this treble nature out in harmonious development. In this lies our only hope of any substantial improvement in educational processes.

This leads me to consider secondly, as a serious obstacle lying in the way of the proposed reformation, the ignorance of teachers upon the points just referred to, and their disposition to study *methods* rather than *principles*. Now, any proper system of education must be based upon philosophical principles, upon a knowledge of the natural order of development of the being to be educated, in his mental, moral and physical constitution, and the corresponding appliances for promoting such growth; and no one can hope for success who does not clearly comprehend these principles. The first effort then on the part of teachers should be to study *principles*, and then the *mode* of applying them. The reverse of this is the course now being pursued in this country. Teachers are endeavoring to imitate models from books, rather than making themselves first familiar with the principles upon which these methods are based, and then using these models as aids in applying them. The only remedy for this evil, as it seems to us, is the establishment of Training Schools for the *professional* education of teachers. Not schools in which the branches are taught, but where the whole aim and effort shall be to impart a *practical* knowledge of the science of education and the art of applying it. In these schools should be exhibited the highest excellence in the art of teaching. There should also be schools of practice where the students shall have abundant opportunity for applying the instruction they receive, and the methods they observe.

Who would think of employing a man who never had any practice in carpentry to build the house he designed as a permanent home for himself and his children, although he might be perfectly familiar with all the books ever written on this subject? We require that our mechanics have not only the rules of their trades, but the practice also, before we presume to employ them, and this too even in the more unimportant arts. They must serve an apprenticeship—a term that implies years of careful observation, study and practice.

They must not only become familiar with all the tools used in their trade, and the exact use to be made of each, but they must also become skilled in using them. And not only must the apprentice know his tools, and know how to use them, before he is entrusted with any important work away from the eye of his master, but must also have a thorough and exact knowledge of the character and composition of the materials used in his art; their strength, durability, and solidity, that he may know how always to adapt them to the exact place they are to occupy. Without this knowledge the sculptor with a wrong tool, or the wrong use of the right one, a little too heavy a blow of the mallet, or the artist with a wrong pigment, or a wrong stroke of the pencil, may ruin his subject. The mechanic by the omission of a single brace, or the use of a wrong timber, or one composed of weak, perishable material, or by the putting together of materials composed of different powers of contraction and expansion, may ruin his edifice and endanger many lives, or much valuable property. In view of these facts we are all agreed as to the importance of a thorough apprenticeship in all the mechanic arts and trades. In the professions too, in law, medicine, surgery, a special professional education is deemed indispensable. What intelligent person would employ a quack to tamper with his own life or the lives and health of his family, or entrust a case involving large interests in the hands of an unread and unskilled lawyer? Who would entrust the amputation of a limb to the hands of one not conversant with the anatomy of the human frame, or unskilled in the use of the knife? If then so much importance is attached to the careful preparation of the various artizans and men of other professions, for their work, (and no one can say that its importance is over-estimated,) what shall be said of the wickedness and folly of employing both *ignorant* and *unskilled* hands to form and fashion this noblest of all God's creations—the immortal mind! Is it that the mind is less intricate, or of less importance than the body, that we have been in the habit of entrusting its cultivation to the uneducated and untrained? This certainly can not be the reason. The one is like the grass that springeth up in the morning, and in the evening is cut down, while the other is immortal and is freighted with interests of the most momentous character—interests linked with the destinies of mankind for time and for eternity. The human mind is composed of elements the most subtle and complicated, yet capable of being analyzed, and each assigned its appropriate place and function, as also the order and method of its evolution. These faculties do not, like the mineral, grow by accretion, but by their natural use; and ill-timed, or under exercise, or a neglect of the proper use at the proper time, are alike prejudicial; and no one has any right to undertake the work of developing these faculties until he knows something of their real character, their functions, the order in which they manifest themselves, and the appliances best calculated to develop them and give them strength.

No mistakes can be made here that are not serious in their character. As is a too heavy blow from the mallet, or a wrong use of the pencil, or the use of the wrong material to the statue, the painting or the edifice, so a mistake made here, an undue strain of a faculty yet weak, and but faintly developed, or the neglect of those still in full and active vigor, if not fatal in its consequences, is due only to the recuperative power of the mind to overcome injuries inflicted.

A common error committed in Object Teaching is in converting exercises that should be strictly for development, into instruction in abstract science. Now the aim of all these early lessons should be to quicken the perceptions, and give them accuracy, awaken thought and cultivate language. To this end the senses must be exercised on the sensible qualities and properties of objects; and when the consideration of these objects goes beyond the reach of the senses, then of course, the exercise ceases to be a development exercise, and becomes either an exercise of the memory or of some of the higher faculties. All these early lessons then should be confined to objects, their parts, qualities and properties that come clearly within the reach of the senses of the children, and no generalizations should include any thing more than such objects and their qualities. Definitions should in no case go beyond the mere description of the actual perceptions of the children. These points we regard of vital importance, and that we may be clearly understood, we will be a little more definite, and indicate just where we would begin, and how far we would go in carrying out the leading exercises employed. In the theory we have presented, these should consist of lessons on Form, Size and Number as belonging to mathematics; of lessons on Objects, Animals, Plants, Color, and Place or Geography, as belonging to Natural History, and lessons on language, including oral and written expression, reading and spelling.

And here I trust I shall be pardoned for presenting my views on these points in nearly the words of a report on this subject presented last week at the Annual meeting of the New York State Teachers' Association. In lessons in number the children should be held long and closely to the simple combination of objects, and hence must be confined to numbers that come fairly within the range of the perceptions.

The lessons on Form should be confined to the observation and description of some of the more simple and common forms in nature. Here we must guard against abstractions; the mere memorizing of definitions that go beyond the observations of the children. As we have already said, definitions should be nothing more than mere descriptions, a remark that applies equally to all kindred subjects of instruction. The lessons on Size consist of nothing more than the actual measurement of various objects and distances, and the simple exercise of the judgment in the application of the knowledge thus gained.

In lessons in Color, the children may be led to observe, discriminate and name the leading colors and their tints and shades, and apply them to the description of objects in nature. This will add largely to their stock of language, and greatly aid them in their future lessons. It is worthy of remark just here, that the deficiency in terms to express in our language distinctions in color is one that is deeply felt, and any effort at improvement in this direction should receive our hearty encouragement. Beyond this the children may be indulged in mixing colors, to observe how the various colors are produced from the primaries, and finally their intuitive perceptions of the harmony of colors may be called out. Not that any attempt should be made to teach the scientific law underlying the harmony of colors, but they simply observe that "certain colors look well together."

In lessons on Place or Elementary Geography, the attention of the child is confined to a consideration of that part of the earth which he sees in his daily walks, its physical and industrial features, the various grouping and relation of objects to each other and himself, as a preparation for the consideration of what lies beyond his own immediate neighborhood. In lessons on animals and plants we begin by calling attention to the parts, position, and finally, uses of parts. At the next step, in lessons on animals, the children are led to consider something of characteristics and habits, and *finally* of adaptation of parts to habits. The children are continually exercised in close and accurate observation, by means of specimens or pictures, and to a limited extent from given or tangible facts and phenomena, to draw conclusions, thus calling forth the, as yet, feeble powers of reason. In some of these later lessons some little knowledge of the natural history of the animals considered, is also imparted. All these lessons are given on the more familiar quadrupeds and birds, either those inhabiting the immediate neighborhood, or of which they have been made acquainted by information. Some attention has also been given by the teacher to the order in which these lessons have been presented, grouping together, or rather giving in succession, lessons belonging to the same class or order. Thus far, however, the children have no realizing sense of any such design. After having gone over in this way with a few of the leading types of each order of mammals, they are led to associate in natural groups or orders the animals that have constituted the subjects of these lessons, aided by the knowledge they have acquired of their characteristic parts and habits. These systematic lessons, however, are confined to mammals and birds, as being more familiar to the children. For variety an occasional lesson may be given on a fish, an insect, a reptile, or a shell, those somewhat familiar to the children, but a large proportion of the animals belonging to these and the lower subdivisions of the animal kingdom are farther removed from the child's immediate sphere of observation, and therefore the basis of the classification is less apparent.

In "Lessons on Objects" proper, as distinct from "Lessons on Animals and Plants," the first lessons should be on objects of the most familiar character, and for a long time their attention should only be called to the simple parts and their position. This involves no use of difficult terms, but at the same time cultivates observation and the power of accurate expression. At the next step some of the more simple and common qualities are added. At a further step more occult qualities, requiring more close and careful observation, and such as are brought out by experiment, may be introduced; also, to a limited extent, the adaptation of qualities, material or structure, to use, may be considered. At a still more advanced stage, some information in regard to the objects considered may be brought in, as also a *simple classification* of the objects and qualities considered. In connection with all these lessons, the cultivation of language should be made one of the leading points; commencing with the simplest oral expressions, leading on to written reproductions, and finally to consecutive narrative.

This leads us directly to a consideration of *language*, the subject next in order. It was a favorite maxim of Pestalozzi, that "The *first* object in education must be to lead a child to *observe with accuracy;* the *second*, to *express with correctness* the result of his observations." Again, "*ideas first*, and language afterward." That there is a natural connection between thought and speech, observation and expression, there can be no reasonable doubt. Who has not observed that children always seek a name for every new object of discovery, and are never satisfied until they receive it? It is, in fact, out of this necessity of our nature, that language has grown up, expanded and enlarged, to keep pace with the growth of ideas. Bacon has well said, "Men believe their reason to be lord over their words; but it often happens too, that words exercise a reciprocal and reactionary power over our intellect. Words, as a Tartar's bow, shoot back upon the understanding of the wisest, and mightily entangle and pervert the judgment."

Again, of what practical advantage would be the careful cultivation of observation, without a corresponding power of expression? Ideas unuttered are valueless to all but their possessor, but well expressed, they are a power to move the world. Like the ripple started on the surface of the placid lake, their influence is felt to the remotest shores of time. Now as observation is cultivated by careful and constant use, so is language by the frequent expression of ideas. But how is the child to acquire this power of language, or what is the process and order of this acquisition? This is an interesting question, and deserves an intelligent answer. Here, as in everything else, we must go back to nature, if we would make no mistakes. Observe then the child in his first utterances. His first efforts at speech are to articulate the names of those persons, objects and actions, bearing the most immediate relation to his desires and necessities; the names of pa and ma, the articles of food and drink, the different members of the household, and familiar objects about him. Next in order come action-words.

Neither name nor action-words are as yet qualified, but these quality words follow slowly along.

The third step is reached before the time of school life begins. However, when the transfer is made from the nursery to the school-room, this vocabulary must be enlarged to keep pace with the growth of ideas. Observing then the order already indicated, we begin with the names of objects, the wholes and their parts. Next come the names of the properties and qualities of objects, proceeding, of course, from the most simple to the more difficult. But is it asked to what extent are these terms to be given? We answer most unhesitatingly, *just so far as the child feels the necessity for their use, and has the power to apply them.* But it is objected that "The use of words can not be long kept up or remembered by the children, that are above the current language of the circle in which they move."

We can say with that assurance that springs from careful observation and experience, that they are governed quite as much in the application of these terms, and consequently in their familiarity with them, by the necessity they experience for their use in the description of objects about them, and in the expression of their perceptions, as by the language of the home circle, or immediate associates. To this may be added the fact that for five hours in the day, and five days in the week, and this for several successive years, they live in the atmosphere of the school-room, where these terms are "current language," and the children from the humblest homes readily incorporate them into their own dialect. Were not these *facts*, there would be poor encouragement for the teacher to labor to improve the diction, manners or morals of the poorer classes.

The success of every good school located in such unfortunate neighborhood, in elevating the children in all these points, is sufficient to substantiate this position. On what other principle can we account for the elevation of successive generations and races of men above their immediate ancestors? And how else can we account for the growth of language? We must depend upon the school to exert a refining, civilizing influence, and that too above and beyond the immediate "circle in which they move." Now in the language of the masses of the people there is a great dearth of terms descriptive of the properties and qualities of objects. How and where is this defect to be remedied? We answer emphatically, by the *cultivation of language in the schools.* We have already stated that language as the expression of ideas, bears an important relation to their development and growth, and therefore that the two should be carried on contemporaneously. We should, therefore, as we proceed with the exercises in developing ideas, give the terms expressive of those ideas, always using, however, those terms which are most simple, and at the same time expressive of the perceptions to be indicated. In all these exercises reference should be had to the mental status of the children; never giving any more than can be readily comprehended and appropriated. In these and all other school exercises, the answers of the children should be incorporated into full and complete expressions. As they advance they will take pleasure in reproducing their object lessons on their slates. This should always be encouraged, and should become a daily and regular exercise. Where this course is pursued the children will early acquire the power of easy and elegant diction, and readiness in composition.

The subject of reading is one surrounded with many difficulties. These, it is the business of the teacher to so divide and classify as to present but one difficulty at a time, and make the successive steps easy and pleasurable to the child. The difficulties that meet the young learner at the very threshold, are the number of different sounds represented by the same character, the number of different characters representing the same sound, the representation of the same sound sometimes by one character and sometimes by another, and sometimes by a combination of characters, and the frequent use of silent letters. To obviate these difficulties he should not for a long time be confused with more than a single form to a single sound. With twenty-three characters and the same number of sounds a large amount of reading matter, consisting of easy simple words, may be given. It is better to commence with the small forms of the letters, as they are better adapted for general use. When the children become familiar with these, the capitals may be introduced. Gradually new sounds may be brought in, and with them new words. A few words may be learned as words, to enable us to fill up the reading matter. In connection with the Object Lessons, also, new words are being continually learned. By this process, in which the children are able to help themselves at every step of their progress, they ever find fresh delight. By a simple plan of classification, in which words of like anomalies are brought together, and which the children at first dictate themselves, the work of spelling is made one of the most pleasing, and animated exercises in the schoolroom. These words are both spelled orally and written upon the slate. The plan we have suggested, of which we have been able only to give the merest outline, we have found a very rapid and thorough one in teaching children to read and spell, and in its details strictly Pestalozzian.

We have thus briefly alluded to a few of the leading exercises, and the extent to which they should be employed in the development of the early faculties of childhood, that our position may be definitely understood, and for the reason that we believe them liable to much abuse.

# OBJECT SYSTEM OF INSTRUCTION

## AS PURSUED IN THE SCHOOLS OF OSWEGO.

BY H. B. WILBUR, M. D.

Superintendent of the State Asylum for Idiots, Syracuse, N. Y

---

### INTRODUCTORY NOTE.

IN consenting to the publication of the following paper, read before the National Association of Teachers, at its last meeting, I am constrained, in justice to myself, to prefix a brief statement of the circumstances under which it was prepared.

Some two years since, I delivered an address before the New York State Teachers' Association. On that occasion I gave some account of my own peculiar work, the instruction of idiots And as it seemed to me that my experience had some practical relations to the audience before me and to the topics just then somewhat prominent in the minds of American educators, I ventured to make the proper application. The "object system of instruction," so-called, was referred to at some length, and I indulged in some passing criticisms upon the peculiar methods of instruction adopted by the Home and Colonial Society of England, which some persons were laboring to introduce into this country.

That I was not a conservative in an obnoxious sense in my educational views, an outline of what was then said upon these two points will sufficiently show.

I attempted to set forth the doctrine, by implication rather than by any very distinct enunciation, that there were two kinds of knowledge, the one which may be styled natural and the other conventional. I remarked that the education related to the former began where instinct ceases, and consisted of a judicious ministering of the proper aliment to the intuitive powers. And I endeavored to point out the true function of the teacher, in respect to this natural education.

I then added that, as in point of time, so in harmony with the natural order of development of the human faculties, was it fit and proper that the acquisition of natural should precede that of conventional knowledge, and that the former was the best foundation for the superstructure of the latter. The summary statement of my argument upon the subject was, "that we should educate the senses and through the senses, the intelligence and will, and then apply and subordinate the engendered habits of accurate observation and the cultivated intellectual activity and power to a proper method of acquiring the elementary studies and their outgrowing attainments."

It seemed to me then that, if these views were correct, they had a twofold application. In the first place, that our system of primary school instruction, confining itself, as it had hitherto done, mainly to elementary studies of a conventional character, should be modified by the introduction of a preliminary class of exercises, designed especially to cultivate the faculties of observation. That the elementary branches should be taught in such a manner as not to blunt the perceptive faculties. Of course, the natural outgrowth of these two provisions would be, that the apparent acquirements of the school-room would represent the actual mental power and knowledge of the pupils.

In the second place, sympathizing, as I have before said, fully with the aims of those seeking reform in the principles and methods of elementary instruction, I yet could not fail to see or avoid making an application of the principles I had developed, to the correction of certain grievous errors some of these well disposed friends of education had fallen into.

I know how short is the usual school-attending period of the great mass of the children for whom our school system is framed. Avoiding, therefore, all educational scheming, I would have that system so sound in its principles, and so judicious in its methods, that it may leave these children, on the threshhold of the apprentice stage of life, with all their natural endowments so brought into willing and active exercise by preliminary training, that nothing in the whole world of relation, designed for their improvement or pleasure, should be thereafter unappropriated; that by its thorough drill in the strictly elementary branches of learning, it should so furnish them with the keys to all educational knowledge, that their future attainments should be limited only by the necessities of their peculiar lot.

In noticing the English system of instruction mentioned, I dwelt mainly upon what I then regarded as its error in the introduction of science at too early a stage in the work of education, not only in the form of positive science, but in the scientific aspect in which the common matters of daily life and observation were treated, and also the abuse of language involved in their practice.

The errors into which I feared the over-zealous advocates of the "object system" might fall proved to be no chimeras. An evil, which, with the respect I felt for American teachers, I then deprecated as somewhat remote, has become more imminent. A foreign educational scheme, partial, bigoted, and unphilosophical, is now naturalized in the country, and its universal propagation demanded by zealous advocates. The "Oswego System" is the new impress that is to give it currency on this side the water.

To increase the deception, the very text-books of the English system have been brought over and (to the scandal of American publishers it must be confessed) with no alteration, save a little upsetting and a turning wrong end foremost of here and there a section, have been issued as of American authorship.

Impulsive friends of education have somewhat indiscreetly indorsed it, by speaking of Oswego as "the Mecca of American teachers;" and of the movement as "a reform which is welcomed by the best minds of the age, which has been prophesied and prayed for by the best lights of other years."

Even some persons, who should have been more discriminating, looking only at the motives of its partisans, have good naturedly given it a vague countenance, as ladies sometimes give a "character" to a stupid or shiftless domestic, who "means well."

Besides, in the State of New York, legislation has been successfully invoked to establish a school for training teachers in the methods of a foreign school society— of dubious reputation at home—outside of its Normal School, which is supposed to have been created for the very purpose of educating teachers in the most approved methods of instruction of every grade and wherever originating.

With these circumstances in view, when invited to prepare a paper for the last meeting of the National Association of Teachers, on the "Object System," a sense of duty constrained me to accept. And I ventured on a discussion of the subject which I knew must be inadequate, if for no other reasons, that I was precluded from presenting the most obvious objections to the system, inasmuch as I had done this on a previous occasion, and because also the invitation I received from the Executive Committee of the Association rather limited me to a half hour and which I endeavored not to transcend.

# THE OSWEGO SYSTEM OF OBJECT INSTRUCTION.

The topic assigned me for the present half hour is the "Object System" of instruction. To avoid all misapprehension, I may say at the outset, that I shall confine myself mainly to some thoughts in connection with what is called in this country the "Oswego System." This is substantially a system of instruction transplanted from England, and known there as the Home and Colonial Society's system of instruction. The circumstances attending the adoption of this foreign system on this side of the water need not be stated, except in the most general terms. The zealous Superintendent of the public schools of Oswego, (whom I need not name,) in common with many holding similar relations to the schools of other cities, felt the need of some change in the methods of instruction prevailing in the primary departments. The want he felt he thought well supplied by the English system alluded to. With zeal and energy he set himself to the task of introducing it in his own proper field of labor. He has accomplished this—and more. We find the same system now urged upon the friends of education everywhere for a similar adoption. And so it comes fairly before a National Association of Teachers for discussion.

It hardly need be said to those who are familiar with the history of the educational reform, inaugurated in this country nearly forty years ago, that the new want I have spoken of, as being generally felt by a certain class, was not to be satisfied by the search for, or the finding of any new principles of education.

The new problem offered to those interested was, how shall we apply, in the earlier stages of school instruction, most wisely and most fruitfully, principles of education generally recognized and acknowledged in this country?

I say generally recognized and acknowledged in this country. This is not too much to say, for here more than elsewhere—almost only here—were sound principles and methods of instruction generally prevalent. The reasons are obvious. The American mind is unusually active upon educational subjects, for theoretically our republican form of government is based upon universal education, and an education not peculiar to a caste or rank in society. Again, the great majority of our educated men have been practical teachers for longer or shorter periods of their lives. Look for a moment at the history of education during the period mentioned, a history adorned with the names of many eminent men. A history that furnishes abundant evidence of much thought in the elucidation of principles and in the devising of methods. Notice the machinery of the educational movement; the essays and discussions, the public addresses and the multiplied associations for mutual improvement; the Teachers' institutes and the Normal schools; the literature of the profession of the teacher embracing everything worthy of record, whether in the way of personal thought or individual experience, the world being tributary; not forgetting the periodical contributions from every quarter. Further, mark the resulting evidence of all this labor well performed in the general public interest, in the judicious legislation, and in the wonderful improvement in text-books. And again, notice the light incidentally furnished by special systems of education. The result of this general awakening in the public mind upon the subject of education, I hardly need to say, though reaching to the principles most fundamental, was not manifested by measures violent, hasty, or subversive. The reform kept step with the advance of an enlightened public sentiment, if at times it were one step in advance. It were well if the future waves of improvement in the same direction should roll as quietly and steadily forward on the shores of coming time.

But a graded system of school instruction brings out a new want. A large class of children are brought together, with little or no previous instruction, and almost too young for the continuous attention and thought required to master the elementary branches of the school-room, as taught in the ordinary way. They are deprived of those educational influences that so pervaded the atmosphere of the school-room of mixed grades and which insinuated themselves into every avenue to the active mind of childhood. They are now dependent for improvement upon the exercise of their own intuitive powers and upon the resources of the teacher.

We need not stop to discuss the question, whether, viewed in relation to the proper orderly and harmonious development of their faculties, these children should be in school at all, thus early, for in school they are. And so it happens, that under the new circumstances, that which should be the work of nature, is brought within the function of the teacher, and accordingly new topics and methods of instruction must be introduced. It hardly need be pointed out with what extreme diffidence we should approach any task that involves any interference with nature's methods, or how zealous should be the endeavor when such interference is necessitated to follow her analogous teachings, and how promptly we should cease our interference at the first moment practicable. The natural channels to the pupil's mind are first to be opened before they can be used for receiving or imparting instruction. Again, the natural avenues are to be used before what may be called the conventional ones are brought in requisition. And so the powers of observation and speech (or spoken language) are to be cultivated before any positive instruction in reading and writing is attempted. Cultivated it should be remembered for purposes and ends mainly practical and disciplinary. Has it occurred to those of you who have seen blind children spelling out with busy fingers and delighted faces the page of raised letters and thus receiving food for their active minds through a channel wrought out for them by the agency of a sense perverted from its legitimate function, that in teaching ordinary children to read from the printed, or written page, the same thing is substantially done; that is, the eye is made to perform the natural office of the ear—that a new gift is imparted.

One result of bringing together children of the same grade is, to bring out more distinctly the class mental peculiarities, the class educational needs, and so more obviously the proper modes of meeting those needs. I have elsewhere stated, in a summary way, my idea of the scope and aim of a proper elementary education, which I will venture to reproduce. "That we should educate the senses and through the senses, the intelligence and will, and then apply and subordinate the engendered habits of accurate observation and the cultivated intellectual activity and power, to proper methods of acquiring the elementary studies and their outgrowing attainments."

In seeking to accomplish the ends thus defined, the main reliance of the educator is upon a proper study and comprehension of the characteristics of childhood, the natural order, mode, and rate of development of the childish faculties. The proof of this is furnished by recalling any synoptical statement of the principles of education, and noticing how many of them relate to these very points. It is of importance to remember this because much time and labor have been lately wasted in devising methods of instruction based upon foundations merely speculative, and some injury done by attempting to put these methods in practice. I may illustrate this by citing two or three forms of theoretical error in this regard representing quite a diversity of opinion—all "idols of the cave."

The first of these is a method based upon a theory that every child must "rediscover for himself the truths and results to be acquired in each department of knowledge undertaken by the learner," and the corollary from this, "that no truth or knowledge which is in its nature a consequent on some other truths or knowledge can by any possibility be in reality attained by any mind, until after that mind has first secured and rightly appreciated those antecedent truths or knowings." This involves, it will be observed, a form of instruction always absolutely synthetical. This is partially true —true as far as intuitive education is concerned and true no farther.

Another error, not unheard of by this Association, is a theory that there is a rational order of development in the course of the sciences, and that it ought to be followed in common education; for the reason that it is claimed that this order of succession in the sciences corresponds precisely to the order of evolution of the faculties. Now this is an assumption based upon the most fanciful analogies, but as I find it asserted with great emphasis, in a report to which my own name is signed, I leave it for others to deal with.

One other theory deserves a passing notice. It will be found elaborated by Herbert Spencer and cropping out quite generally in the essays and discussions that have since appeared upon educational topics. After admitting the distinction between education as relates to discipline and to the value of the knowledge acquired, he at once assumes that what is best for the one end is also best for the other. He then proceeds to develop a scheme for education based upon the relative and practical uses of knowledge. If his course of reasoning proves anything it proves that physiology should be the first study of childhood, then the means of getting a livelihood, then the treatment of offspring and the government of children, and finally the study of social science.

Let me now examine briefly the mode in which the Oswego System aims to accomplish the ends I have supposed. To be sure it claims to be more than a system of Primary School instruction. It claims to be the only correct system for any stage of education. "That if adopted, it will lead to a complete revolution in our methods of teaching in this country," (where it is asserted "we have never had any system based on sound philosophical principles,) as also in the profession of teaching itself, or rather it will *make teaching a profession*—a title it has yet to earn."

In making a somewhat hurried preparation for the part assigned me on this occasion, I have spent some time in the examination of the various manuals designed for the instruction of teachers in the new system. I confess the result has been somewhat discouraging. The principles laid down are somewhat contradictory in their character. They are wanting in definiteness, and, most of all, they are so enveloped in the voluminous details of methods, that it is difficult to discover the distinctive features, and somewhat confusing to one attempting to discuss them.

Referring then to the Oswego manuals, I find first a statement of what are called Pestalozzian plans and principles. On examination, I find that some latitude has been used in applying the term Pestalozzian. Transmutation as well as translation will be seen in their treatment of the great reformer. It may be remarked of these generally, that whatever of them are sound have not the claim of novelty to American teachers, and what are new of no value, if not leading to positive error.

1. Activity is a law of childhood. Accustom the child to do—educate the hand.
2. Cultivate the faculties in their natural order—first form the mind, then furnish it.
3. Begin with the senses, and never tell a child what he can discover for himself.
4. Reduce every subject to its elements—one difficulty at a time is enough for a child.
5. Proceed step by step. Be thorough. The measure of information is not what the teacher can give, but what the child can receive.
6. Let every lesson have a point, except in junior schools, where more than one lesson is required before the point is reached, each successively tending towards it.
7. Develop the idea—then give the term—cultivate language.
8. Proceed from the known to the unknown—from the particular to the general—from the concrete to the abstract—from the simple to the more difficult.
9. First synthesis, then analysis—not the order of the subject, but the order of nature.

Let us examine these principles briefly.

"1st. Activity is a law of childhood. Accustom the child to do —educate the hand."

It will be observed, first, that there is an implied restriction of this law of childhood to his physical system. Of the second clause —should it not rather be said, let the child do. Let him use not only his hands, but his physical system generally. The distinction between letting the child do and accustoming him to do, at this early stage, is an important one, and is related (if activity is a general law of childhood) not only to physical actions, but also to the senses and the faculties which act spontaneously on the presentation of their proper objects. Should not a system of so much pretension direct us wisely here on the very threshhold?

"2d. Cultivate the faculties in their natural order—first form the mind, then furnish it."

The truth enunciated here is older than Pestalozzi; and may be found in some form or another in half the works on education published in this country during the last thirty years. As to the second clause, one might naturally ask, is it a corollary from the first? or only meant as a reiteration? or what?

"3d. Begin with the senses, and never tell a child what he can discover for himself."

What is the designed relation between the two clauses of this rule? Must we never tell a child what he can discover for himself?

"4th. Reduce every subject to its elements—one difficulty at a time is enough for a child."

This seems a harmless proposition. But the practical inferences in the way of method, that the manuals are full of, gives it another aspect.

"5th. Proceed step by step. Be thorough. The measure of information is not what the teacher can give, but what the child can receive."

Would not these directions indicate that the process of education is not always and strictly a development exercise, in which the child is the main actor?

"7th. Develop the idea—then give the term—cultivate language."

If this rule were designed only to enforce the truth that ideas should precede language, no comment would be necessary. But herewith is connected one of the most vicious methods of the Oswego System. In the light of their practical teachings it means that with the idea the term must be invariably connected; that the observation and language must be inseparably connected. And it is assumed that when the idea is mastered, there is no difficulty in retaining the appropriate term on the part of the pupil.

It is claimed that the peculiar phraseology of the summary is strictly a resultant of the workings of the class mind. And so we find in connection with each lesson, or series of observations, the W. B. (writing on the board) and the S. R (simultaneous repetition) to fix in the pupil's mind the set phrase and the stereotyped formula that the teacher furnishes as the summary of the particular class exercise.

But the partisans of the Oswego System, or their progenitors in England, were not the original sinners. It was precisely here where Pestalozzi went so grievously astray from his own early principles, as to draw from one of his cotemporaries the remark, that "he kicked over with his feet what he built up with his hands." And these very practices of his have been discarded by intelligent educators everywhere, even when professedly following the doctrines of the German school.

"Observation (said he) is the absolute basis of all knowledge.

The first object, then, in education must be, to lead a child to observe with accuracy; the second, to express with correctness the result of his observations." There is abundant evidence from his works that he did not mean by this, that observation should be the principal object of instruction at its earlier stage and language at a later period. The English and Oswego disciples have faithfully copied the defects of their master.

Now is it necessary to affirm in this presence, that language has absolutely nothing to do with observation as far as it concerns the pupil? That the observing powers are exercised for a long period in childhood before the gift of language is received, and that the child not only uses the senses, but discriminates, compares, reasons, judges, decides, and wills in connection with such use of the senses, and all this without the use of any language?

But the time comes when language is necessary for the expression of wants and ideas, and then it is given. In the roll of education the teacher avails himself of this natural gift, this child-language, to test the progress of the child, and so it is properly connected with observation and with the growth of ideas.

Again, a period comes when language which has been acquired intuitively, and without any conscious effort on the part of the child, may be properly a subject of positive instruction, by methods so wisely suggested in the opening address of the President of this Association; for when the higher and reflective powers of the mind are brought into active exercise, language precise and adequate becomes necessary as the means of thought.

Language (let me repeat again) which in the infancy of the individual, as well as that of the race, is a mere means of expressing the immediate wants of the individual or the race in its then condition; expands not only commensurately with increasing desires, but absolutely acquires another function; that is, as the instrument of higher, continuous, and abstract thought; and this fact, or the growth of language to meet social needs, suggests the principle that should guide in the introduction of language, as an exercise in the school-room. I have on another occasion referred to this topic and so I can only hint at the dangers of thus early and intimately connecting the study of language with the development of the faculties of observation. The thing signified is lost in the effort to remember the sign. Have you not all seen a bright boy in a class, who could and would answer almost intuitively a question in numbers like the following, hesitate and stammer, grow confused and fail, in attempting to cloak the fully comprehended truth in the long syllogistic formula required of him by the teacher? Thus—

If 2 bunches of matches cost 4 cents, what will 4 bunches cost? The pupil repeats the question and gives the solution.

If 2 bunches of matches cost 4 cents, what will 4 bunches cost? 1 bunch of matches will cost one-half as much as 2 bunches of matches. If 2 bunches of matches cost 4 cents, 1 bunch of matches will cost one-half of 4 cents, which are 2 cents. 4 bunches of matches will cost 4 times as much as 1 bunch of matches. If 1 bunch cost 2 cents, 4 bunches will cost 4 times 2 cents, which are 8 cents. Therefore, if 2 bunches of matches cost 4 cents, 4 bunches of matches will cost 8 cents.

The very tendency of formulated language is to routine. The foundations of the childish memory and the childish principle of association are upset, and the natural observation of childhood entirely devitalized. But an illustration, furnished by the same master-hand that gave us the Yorkshire boarding-school, will answer my purpose better.

No teacher before me, who has read Dickens' "Hard Times," will fail to recall the following scene:—

Mr. Gradgrind, the town magnate and school patron, is present in the model school of his own creation, where Mr. McChoakumchild surcharges the youthful Coke-towners with grim facts. After a preliminary address to the teachers in this vein—

"Now what I want is facts. Teach these boys and girls nothing but facts. Facts alone are wanted in life. Plant nothing else, and root out everything else. You can only form the mind of reasoning animals upon facts; nothing else will ever be of any service to them. This is the principle upon which I bring up my own children, and this is the principle on which I bring up these children. Stick to facts, Sir!"

Having thus relieved himself, that his self-love may be gratified by witnessing the triumphs of his own educational scheming, he calls out, by an appropriate management and catechising, its distinctive features.

Sissy Jupe, Girl No. 20, the daughter of a strolling circus actor, whose life, no small share of it, has been passed under the canvass; whose knowledge of horse, generic and specific, extends back as far as memory reachés; familiar with the form and food, the powers and habits and everything relating to the horse; knowing it through several senses; Sissy Jupe has been asked to define horse. Astonished at hearing her father stigmatized as a veterinary surgeon, a farrier and horse-breaker; bewildered by the striking want of resemblance between the horse of her own conceptions and the prescribed formula that represents the animal in the books of the Home and Colonial Society, she dares not trust herself with the confusing description, and shrinks from it in silence and alarm.

"Girl No. 20 unable to define a horse," said Mr. Gradgrind. Girl No. 20 is declared possessed of no facts in reference to one of the commonest of animals, and appeal is made to one red-eyed Bitzer, who knows horse practically only as he has seen a picture of a horse, or as he has, perhaps, sometimes safely weathered the perils of a crowded street crossing.

"Bitzer," (said Thomas Gradgrind,) "your definition of a horse!"

"Quadruped. Graminivorous. Forty teeth, namely: twenty-four grinders, four eye teeth, and twelve incisive. Sheds coat in the Spring; in marshy countries sheds hoofs too. Hoofs hard, but requiring to be shod with iron. Age known by marks in mouth" Thus (and much more) Bitzer.

"Now Girl No. 20," said Mr. Gradgrind, "you know what a horse is."

The features of a school system thus graphically described are the features of the Home and Colonial Society's system, and I regret to say that what is known in this country as the Oswego System is its lineal descendant.

That this is no misrepresentation (see lessons on objects, page 97.)

LESSON TWENTY-THIRD.

*A Lady Bird.*

Ideas to be developed—hemispherical, fragile, jointed.

| *Parts.* | *Qualities.* |
|---|---|
| The head.................... | It is animal. |
| " eyes.................... | Natural. |
| " feelers or palpi............ | Hemispherical. |
| " horns or antennæ......... | The wing cases are red. |
| " wings.................. | Spotted. |
| " wing cases or elytra....... | Bright. |
| " thorax.................. | Hard. |
| " legs.................... | The wing cases are brittle. |
| " body.................... | Opaque. |
| " back.................... | Stiff. |
| " spots.................... | The outside is convex. |
| " surface.................. | The inside is concave. |
| " claws.................... | One margin straight. |
| | The other curved. |
| | The wings are membranaceous, |
| | " pliable, |
| | " thin, |
| | " transparent, |
| | " fragile. |
| | The body is oval, |
| | " black. |
| | The legs are jointed, |
| | " short, |
| | " black. |

The lesson above cited is one of a large number sketched for the use of teachers; all models for still others of a similar character to be framed as they shall be needed, and designed to cover the whole period of school instruction. Is such endless repetition of obvious qualities a natural and nourishing food for the childish mind? Will it never tire of such thin gruel of utilitarianism? And looking at the real object of a public school system as our own, supported from the public treasury, designed to obviate the accidents of birth or fortune, by placing the keys of knowledge in every youthful hand, is such chaff a substitute for a thorough grounding in the elementary branches? is it a good preparation, even, for the same? But conceding that these exercises accomplish the end for which they were designed, is it not a cultivation of the perceptive faculties too exclusive, and at the expense of the other powers of the pupil?

It is claimed, however, that thus are laid the foundations for a future structure of science; that we ascend from form to geometry, from place to geography, &c., &c. Than this nothing can be more mistaken. Perceptions of form and color are quite distinct from geometry and chromatography. Language is one thing, and the science of grammar quite another.

That scientific and technical language is prematurely introduced in the methods adopted at Oswego, no one can question who visits the Oswego schools. One hears little children, not two weeks under instruction, taught that certain parts of a sheep (or the picture of a sheep) are "principal," others "secondary," and some "characteristic." One hears from infant mouths such terms as "graminiverous and chalybeate, iridescent and amorphous, serrated and foliaceous, imbricated and indigenous." Children there are taught not only to discriminate, with the eye, the various shades and hues of color, but loaded down with such terms as hyaline, watchet, lazuline, indigene, carneline, rosine, coraline, venetia, morone, salmonine, peachine, and magenta.

The 9th and last principle laid down is the following:—"First synthesis, then analysis—not the order of the subject, but the order of nature." I leave for others to discuss the first clause of the rule. I may venture this inquiry, however. If it be true "that all intelligent action whatever depends upon the discerning of distinctions among surrounding things," does not this principle require that analysis should be the first step in the work of education? And further, as one examines the specimen lessons in the Oswego textbooks, even, does it not appear that so far as the exercise of the observing faculties is properly conducted, it is pure analysis, while the mere framing of the definition or the formulated summary can only be called synthetical.

The last clause, ("not the order of the subject, but the order of nature,") whatever its supposed relation to the former, contains an important truth which I would thus interpret. All subjects should be presented to a child in view of the order in which his faculties are developed; in connection with his already existing ideas, as they may be indicated by the form in which his curiosity manifests itself, or otherwise, that they may be retained by some principle of association; and also in relation to their practical value and uses, as acquirements and discipline, for the time being. And contrariwise, they should not be presented in relation to any assumed order of knowledge or any scientific arrangement or classification. (I am speaking now especially of those subjects which, in the primary school-room and in the case of young children, should precede and furnish the foundation of what are ordinarily regarded as the elementary studies.) Scientific names, definitions and classification are designed for a special and practical purpose; and that purpose, manifestly, not related to the instruction of infants or the early history of our race. A young child (and for that matter the savage) has no practical use for science and therefore does not need its technicalities. What he does need are words, figurative expressions, or a classification connected in a living way to his senses, his observation, his experience, the range of his reasoning powers, and by the use of which he can remember, reproduce, or communicate to another his sensations and ideas.

The scientific mode should be reserved for a later period of instruction, when science, as such, has, by the development of the pupil, acquired a practical value.

For modern science, be it remembered, (and herein it differs from the older forms,) is, from its very nature, far removed from the range of a child's observation, and has no obvious relations to the little, every-day world in which he lives and moves. It is based upon structure and organs, and unobvious, and to the child, unimportant properties, and includes, what Spencer has called, "completeness of prevision." And though there are certain external features which ordinarily indicate, to the eye of the expert, the peculiarities of internal structure, yet the connection can not be appreciated at an immature age.

So true is this, that I find a modern writer of great logical acuteness thus expressing himself:—

Science, as I shall afterwards have occasion to illustrate, is painful from the necessity of dissociating appearances that go naturally and easily together, of renouncing the full and total aspect of an object by which it engages agreeably the various senses, and of settling upon some feature that has no interest to the common eye.*

I have ventured to elaborate what seemed to me to be the truth contained in the clause under discussion. But that this is not the interpretation of it adopted by the advocates of the Oswego System may be seen by referring either to a single model lesson, or to the general method of treating a particular subject. Take, by way of illustration, almost the first lesson in the manual. It is a development exercise to cultivate the powers of observation. The children are first told that paper is artificial, that it is made of linen rags, that linen is made from the stem of a plant called flax. They then observe its obvious qualities; they are next supplied with the terms pliable, translucent, inflammable, &c.

But one must not stop upon individual lessons, but take subjects.

What I am now about to say is related also to principle No. 4—"Reduce every subject to its elements."

Take the method of teaching reading. If one takes up a printed page it may be resolved into lines, these lines into words, the words

* Bain. "The Senses and Intellect."

into letters, (to say nothing of points,) the letters into combination of forms, that may be further classified as straight lines and curved, perpendicular and horizontal. As related to the printer's art, this may be called reducing the subject to its elements, or following the order of the subject.

Again, the words on the page (which is speech represented to the eye) represent a variety of combinations of sounds, which may be resolved into their elementary sounds; these into classes as atonic, sub-tonic, &c.; and still further according to the position of the vocal organs in producing these elementary sounds. This may be called reducing the subject to its elements, or following its order.

If our language were strictly phonetic, these two classes of elements could be, in some degree, approximated, and thus the art of reading, as an art, could be acquired without any great waste of effort on the part of the learner, particularly an adult learner. But this is not true. The number of elementary characters does not correspond to the number of elementary sounds. The forms of the characters have no actual or symbolic relation to the sounds.

Custom has also sanctioned a variety of form in the same letters. These have each been provided with a name conventional and arbitrary, sometimes resembling its power in composition, and sometimes not.

Furthermore, to increase the perplexities, the same sounds are represented by different letters and combinations; and these last do not uniformly represent the same sound. So that our language is irregularity run wild. The rule is the exception and the exception is the rule.

Now the method of the Home and Colonial Society (and the Oswego plan is but little better) brings the child, face to face, with this mountain of difficulties, and on the plea of reducing every subject to its elements, picks up each individual difficulty, one at a time, and throws it a stumbling-stone at the feet of the pupil. With fatiguing exercise, perhaps, the whole ground may be at last stumbled over. Listen to the role and judge.

The pupils are first taught to distinguish by the eye all the Roman capitals; next, to distinguish clumsy imitations of these, as many as can be formed by combinations of straight lines; and then similar imitations of the remainder formed by straight lines and curved. A similar plan is now adopted in teaching the forms of the smaller letters. The pupils are practiced in repeating the forty, more or less, elementary sounds of the language. They are lead to notice the position of the organs of speech in making these sounds.

At this stage (First Step—pupils between four and five years of age) they are encumbered with the application of the terms, "tonic, atonic and sub-tonic," &c., to the sounds in question.

They are taught to form uncouth imitations of the spurious capitals, before mentioned, with pieces of lath; then to print them on the slate. Then comes the learning of twenty-six arbitrary names of letters and connecting these with the same number of conventional forms. The same course is pursued with the small letters. The pupils are next exercised in the sounds of the vowels and dipthongs; not, however, their power in composition. They are taught to spell classes of words of one syllable. Only at this point do any proper exercises in reading (or in fact in learning to read) begin; and even then these are in accordance with a somewhat clumsy phonic method.

It is claimed for this plan, the stupidity of which no description can fully portray, that it "puts the child in possession of a key by which he is able to help himself—a very important principle in education." A hundred such keys will leave a child groping and knocking at the door of our written language, in which the sound *too* is spelt three different ways and *ough* stands for half its vowel sounds.

All this is done, as it is supposed, to carry out a principle ascribed to Pestalozzi; that the work of the educator should be analytical and that of the learner synthetical.

This is what they propose to do theoretically. Meanwhile, however, the pupil, in spite of this attempt to hamper his feet with the intricacies and perplexities of our language, has been covertly making his way by a more direct, natural, and easy route to the same end. In this respect the child has shown himself wiser than the master. By the aid of a memory which can only be characterized as "adhesive" in the extreme, he has been quietly learning words as words, on the blackboard, on the lesson cards, and in the text-book of the school-room. He has been classifying words in accordance with his own principle of association, to assist his memory when its mere adhesiveness has failed; and now noting their resemblances and differences, he has analyzed them for himself into their elements and thus learned the powers of letters in composition. In short, he has grasped the idea of the sole object of learning to read, and directed his steps by the shortest route to that end.

Years ago I read in Emerson's "Schoolmaster" that the best way of learning to read was to let children learn words first and afterwards the letters of which they are made; and why? because "this is nature's method." I can not stop to outline this word-method by showing how completely it follows the order of nature.

I will call your attention now, briefly, to the Oswego method of teaching drawing. It commences from combinations with two straight lines, then with three, and so on up to seven or eight. Then combinations with four right and two acute angles, then with obtuse angles. Combinations with four rectangular triangles. Combinations with the various quadrangular figures. Then combinations with the various curves. This is all elementary to geometrical drawing. This doubtless has its uses. This is better than no instruction in drawing, perhaps.

But that this is not the way to teach drawing as an art, or for the practical and pleasurable uses which render its acquisition desirable, I think that the great mass of experts will agree. Spencer speaks of an elementary drawing-book, on a similar plan, as most vicious in principle, as only "a grammar of form with exercises." Ruskin is equally emphatic in recommending an entirely different course.

The same regard to the order of the subject and disregard of the order of nature is seen in the selection and arrangement of topics for the object lessons; in the scientific tone that pervades the whole series, and in the early introduction of science (distinctly) into their educational course; as if this were unavoidable in attempting to impart any useful knowledge to the child.

The late Archbishop Whately disposed of this opinion epigrammatically by asking, "Can not a child be taught that a nettle will sting without being taught the science of botany?"

That these are not unwarranted criticisms on the Oswego methods, let me appeal to the manuals in which they are embodied. The extracts illustrative of methods may be appropriately introduced by a few sentences selected either from preface or introduction, somewhat in the form of precepts.

"The design of this work is to present a definite course of elementary instruction adapted to philosophic views of the laws of childhood."

"It would seem too obvious to require an argument that every teacher"—(and for that matter, it might have been added, every superintendent of public schools and each school-book compiler) "should clearly comprehend the character of the infant mind and its mode of operation."

That a proper lesson "should equally avoid detailed information, on the one hand, and on the other, mere general notices, such as constitute a table of contents or heading of a chapter."

"That it is important, as far as possible, to give the children a good deal of latitude; and let the discoveries be their own, except as they may be guided in part by the teacher."

"Those who fall into a mechanical way of giving such instruction and do not perceive the principle involved, completely defeat its intention and *they had far better keep to old plans and old books.*" The italics are mine.

Turn now to "Lessons on objects," (page 132 and the following.)

It is the "fourth step," or designed for children of seven or eight years old. The subject is the metals. Seven pages are devoted to the general subject. The mode of their occurrence is given; their distinguishing "characters;" their properties as reflectors of light and heat, as conductors of heat and electricity. The specific gravity of ten are given in numbers to the third decimal. The weight of a cubic foot of the common metals is also given. They are told the number of tons that rods an inch square, of the common metals, will severally sustain without breaking. Detailed information upon the other general properties are likewise furnished by the teacher, to an extent that will suggest the thought that not only is "a good deal of latitude given the children," but some degree of longitude. Then follow eight model lessons on as many metals, in which the properties, qualities, uses, geographical and geological relations are given with almost encyclopedic particularity; though not always with the accuracy desirable in a text-book.

We will now open the other manual, "Elementary Instruction." As in the former case, take the "fourth step," the children of the same age as before. Under the head of "objects," (page 134,) "Sketches on the Bible." In another place it is stated "that the general aim of the teacher in a Bible lesson is to produce a religious impression." Let us see how this is done.

### 10. SKETCHES ON THE BIBLE.

Having drawn from the class, by a few direct and simple questions, that the Bible was not always a printed book—was not first written in English—was not bestowed on mankind at once, complete from Genesis to Revelation, but in detached parts; and having told them to consider the successive portions in which it was given, the language in which it was first written, and the form in which it then appeared, the children ought to be in possession of most of the facts referred to; therefore, during the greater part of the lessons, the business of the teacher would be to lead them to collect and arrange what they already know.

I. *Scripture—in what portions given, and at what period.*

1st Possessors of Scripture—the Hebrew nation Not when we first recognize it in Egypt, but previous to the settlement in Canaan. Date of this event. At that time the Israelites had the writings of Moses, probably including one or two of the Psalms, and the book of Job. Thence to the first captivity they received successively the books of Joshua, Judges, Samuel, Kings, Chronicles, the writings of David, those of his son, a portion of the greater and most of the lesser prophets. After the return, the narratives of Ezra, Nehemiah and Esther, with the three last prophetical books. Date of the return.

2d Books of the New Testament period. Also considered with respect to writers, titles, and oracles. Date of conclusion of Scripture. Text learned: Hebrews i, 1—"God, who at sundry times and in divers manners spake in times past unto the fathers of the prophets, hath in these last days spoken unto us by His Son."

II. *Language—that in which Scripture was first written—translations.*

1st. Every revelation prior to the date of the first captivity made in Hebrew This accounted for. Books of Daniel and Ezra written partly in Hebrew and partly in Chaldee. Lead the class to infer the probable reason of this, from consideration as to the subject of the portions written in Chaldee; principally such as include original letters, decrees, &c., of the Babylonish and Persian governments. Scriptures posterior to the date of the captivity written in Chaldee, and all the earlier books translated into the same tongue. No sooner did the ancient Hebrew become a dead language, than the Scriptures were put into the vernacular tongue by men, such as Ezra, acting under the immediate inspiration of God. Conclusion drawn from this, and text learned, showing the importance of understanding the Word of God: 1 Cor. xiv, 19—"I had rather speak five words with my understanding, that by my voice I might teach others also, than ten thousand words in an unknown tongue."

2d. The coming of the time in which the Gentiles were to be led to a knowledge of the truth, marked by the dispersion of the Scriptures among them. Providence of God shown in this. Its design and effect. Give general account of various translations, and particular one on the Septuagint. Refer to, and prove the importance of, the last translation. Refer to prevalence of the Greek tongue in every part of the civilized world, as connected providentially with the publication of the Gospel in that language.

To connect this period with what follows, touch very briefly on the general professions of Christianity. Division of the Roman Empire and subsequent spread of the Greek and Roman Catholic churches. Progress of the latter. Extent of her power. Change with respect to the language of the Bible. Scripture written in Latin throughout all the countries of the Western Empire.

III. *Forms under which the Scriptures have been presented at different periods.*

1st. Derivation of the terms Bible and Scripture. Sacred words of the Jews' writings. Not books. Kind of materials chiefly used, either parchment or vellum. Scroll—when not in use, rolled up on a slender cylinder like a school map; hence, origin of the term *volume*. Refer to the Scribes. Their office. Importance and accuracy of their labors.

2d. Describe sacred records of Christians in the Middle Ages. Illuminated MSS. What they were. Why so called? Sometimes rolls, oftener books. Beauty and value of these copies. The copyists—what class of men they were. Their mode of life, position, and character, compared with that of the Jewish Scribes.

3d. Sacred records in the modern form. Class observe their own Bibles, and state how they differ externally from those before described. Why composed of many sheets bound together, not of one rolled up? Why made of paper rather than parchment? Why no longer MSS.? Give brief account of the invention of printing and its immediate consequence. The great multiplication of copies. Effect of the distribution of these all over the world. Specimens of Scriptural translations in one hundred and forty-eight languages were to be seen at the Great Exhibition. Compare God's present method of making known Himself and His will, to that He adopted in the Apostolic age. Then, supernatural gift of tongues, enabling the Apostles so to preach that all could understand. Why necessary then? Now, the same object effected without a miracle, by the translation of the Bible into different languages, so that the nations may still say, "We do hear them speak in our tongues the wonderful works of God."—Acts ii, 11.

IV. *Unchangeableness of the inspired word—its influence.*

Bible to be regarded as a perfect whole. The New Testament not an abrogation, but a development of the principles contained in the Old. Text: Matthew v, 17, 18. This might be proved by reference to the nature of God, but is evidently seen by the invariable influence of the Scriptures on the condition of man in all ages and countries. Compare the mental and moral condition of the Jews prior to their first captivity, with that of the nations surrounding them. Refer to countries in which the Bible is unknown at this day; without exception, utterly barbarous and degraded. Refer to countries in which its doctrines are rejected, and yet, because the people have learned something of the historical events recorded in it, because its precepts (though their origin is not recognized) are interwoven with social laws, they take a far higher rank. Instance, Mohammedans. Refer to countries in which the Scriptures are held to be true, and the people do not read them, because the ecclesiastical power has put a seal on the book. These are better off than those before named, for they hear of the name, and know somewhat of the character of Jesus, and through the thick mists of tradition the light of the Word will sometimes shine.

Conclusion drawn—that the Bible is a great engine of civilization, as well as the source of spiritual knowledge. Effect of its free circulation throughout the land. Refer to the renovation now commenced in heathen lands, from the spread of Scriptures and spiritual teaching. Duty incumbent on us to place the Bible in the households of our own and other countries. We may anticipate the promised blessing, that they who water others shall themselves be watered.

Now imagine, if you please, a teacher of a public school standing in the presence of a class of pupils between the ages of seven and twelve, composed of such material as will be found in our cities and large towns, "talking like this book," and tell me, will such themes, thus presented, conduce to any feelings worthy of the name of religious impressions? Is such instruction in accordance with "philosophic views of the laws of childhood?" Do you smile at the absurdity of the extracts I have given?—there is hardly a page in either of the two volumes of Oswego gospel but contains matter equally ridiculous. The fact is, this peculiar adaptation of Pestalozzianism could hardly be otherwise, for though fresh from an American press, it yet had its origin in what may be called the dark ages of educational history in England; that is, some thirty years ago.

[There is a difficulty attending the proper treatment of this subject. I mentioned at the outset the considerations which made it a suitable theme for discussion in even a national assemblage of teachers. But when one exposes the fallacy of any of the principles, the absurdity of any of the methods, up start the advocates of the system and repudiate the obnoxious features, or claim that these are but experiments, looking towards something to be perfected in the alembic of the future. And when the vicious tendencies of the system, as a whole, are pointed out, then these same parties fall back upon the quality of their motives.

But the very exclusiveness of their theory forbids any hope of improvement with the best intentions that underlie it.

They are on record at the very outset in this wise. The system as presented to the American public is claimed to embody "the light and experience of the best schools of Europe, where these methods have been longest and most thoroughly tested." That it is "a *definite course of elementary instruction* adapted to philosophic views of the laws of childhood," &c., &c.

Furthermore, a legislative grant has been obtained, as has been already mentioned, not for experimental purposes, looking towards improvement in elementary instruction, but to train teachers in this particular system.

But the time allotted will not permit me to pass in review other features of the so-called Oswego System, equally objectionable.

The task I have already performed would have been a disagreeable one, even if, with more time and preparation, I could have flattered myself that it had been well done. It is still more so, conscious as I am of its imperfectness. But it is important that the work of primary instruction should be well conducted. And it is claimed for the Oswego System, by its advocates, that in no other way can this be accomplished than by the methods prescribed in the books from which I have quoted. The State of New York has given a legislative sanction to the justness of this claim, by appropriatiug money for the support of a training school for teachers, where these principles and methods are adopted and applied. The legislatures of other States will doubtless be invited to follow this example.

I regard the whole scheme as unwise and defective. A sense of duty has therefore constrained me to call the attention of the teachers of the country to the subject, that others more nearly related to our common school system, and otherwise more competent than myself, may hereafter more thoroughly expose its vicious tendencies.]

I would not, even now, be understood as discouraging, in the slighest degree, the addition to our present modes of primary school instruction of any new or desirable features, or the adoption of any new methods to meet new educational wants, from whatever source obtained.

I will venture to illustrate my idea. It was my good fortune not many months ago to visit, under favorable circumstances, the schools of a western city.* I saw there the evidences of a most intelligent supervision, by one familiar with the whole subject of American education, and who had carefully studied the principles and methods of instruction in other lands. I saw a corps of teachers, from highest to lowest, intelligent, active, animated by a full sense of the importance of their work and imbued with the same spirit that controlled the supervision. I saw the usual elementary course in our common schools, preceded by, associated with, and supplemented by well selected oral lessons that made the whole a living form of education. Viewing the pupils as individuals, I saw that a natural and suitable aliment was so wisely spread before each mind as to insure the proper grasp and growth, and as a consequence, mental activity and strength. Looking at them as classes, I beheld each grade of pupils, in the school-rooms, responsive to every word and ook and thought of the teacher.

# PHYSICAL EXERCISE IN SCHOOL.

BY S. W. MASON, PRINCIPAL OF HANCOCK GRAMMAR SCHOOL, BOSTON, MASS.

---

So intimate and mutual is the relation of mind with matter, the mental with the physical, that the one can not be neglected without detriment not only to itself, but also dragging the other down to the same low level.

The body is constantly influencing the mind, and the mind as constantly influencing and controlling the conditions of the body; hence intellectual and physical culture and training should "go hand in hand;" if permitted, or by us forced to go apart, either will stray from its appropriate sphere, resulting in feebleness, failure, and premature decay, and the fate will be that of a "house divided against itself."

The laws of nature will not, can not be broken with impunity. Every attempt to cultivate the intellect, independently of its coördinate power, the body, must end, yea *will end*, in an ignoble failure, or a miserable defeat; but when these two powers so intimately by the Almighty connected, are made to act in unison and harmony, any thing within the limits of possibility, may be accomplished.

So apparent or demonstrable has been this mutual relation, that thoughtful men and educators, in all ages, have studiously sought to know how the one can be exercised for the greatest development and vigor of the other.

The necessity of training the powers of the mind by due bodily exercise has been acknowledged in all states of society, from the most primitive to the most enlightened.

As teachers we have committed to our care and parental keeping, beings of a material and an immaterial nature, not divorced, or by us to be divorced; but they are, and ever must be, mutually dependent on each other; and they should be so recognized by us, and properly trained and developed, in order that our pupils may grow up to the full stature of those made in the image of God.

The importance of systematic, rigid physical training, is now conceded by most educators; indeed so generally is it acknowledged, that any argument in its favor is unnecessary for the purpose of arousing teachers to a proper sense of its value as a means of culture.

It is apparent to the most casual observer, that the Anglo American race has been deteriorating for a series of years. What teacher especially, has failed to observe, how common in the school-room is the "cramped stooping posture," the crooked spine, the contracted chest, the dull languid eye, the pale, haggard cheek, with its bright hectic, marking its possessor as a sure victim of that fell destroyer of our happy homes, consumption.

Conscious as we are of the sad decay going on around us, how to remedy the evil and restore pristine vigor to the youth of our land, through the legitimate channels of instruction, is now interesting the leading educators of the age.

Within a very short time a wonderful impulse has been given to the subject of physical education, and the attention of the wisest heads and kindest hearts has been turned in this direction, till some kind of systematic physical culture is expected, yea, demanded in our public schools.

I trust the current which has so auspiciously begun to flow, may run stronger and deeper, till all teachers shall not only be convinced that they have been derelict in this matter, but shall hasten to do works meet for repentance. Physical culture should be promoted systematically and persistently till it assumes a position in our public schools commensurate with its importance.

The particular form it shall take or the methods adopted for carrying it out, will long remain a matter of abstract and experimental investigation, each person interested, (and there is no live teacher but what is or should be interested,) contributing something of his experience and thought toward the realization of the grand object—the highest efficiency and well being of mankind, morally, intellectually and physically.

The expediency or practicability of introducing direct physical culture into our schools by gymnastic or calisthenic exercises has been, and is still, doubted.

The term, Gymnastic, conveys to the minds of many, erroneous impressions. It turns our school-rooms into mere gymnasia, bringing with it all the appliances of their intricate machinery. Books, slates, pens and pencils, must be exchanged for bars, poles and heavy weights, turning the activity of the school-room, induced by an interest in mental improvement, into gladiatorial shows and feats of athletes. And it is not strange that such impressions should obtain, for gymnastics as practiced formerly in this country, have been so encumbered with the *endless* paraphernalia of the system that it has been, and is impossible, to introduce them into our schools. However beneficial they may have been, but few have been able to receive the benefits resulting from the system, and then only by resorting to some gymnasium, at a great expense of time and money.

So exclusive have been the gymnasia of this country that a great prejudice has existed against them, as the resort only of the low and vulgar, and gymnastics have been considered as tending to produce coarseness of manners and a combative disposition, and to raise up a nation of bullies and prize fighters; but this prejudice against gymnastics, as such, has been in a great measure overcome by the admirable system of New Gymnastics, which is so well adapted to interest, please and improve those who become acquainted with its beautiful and simple machinery, and practice its symmetrical movements.

The *Gymnasium*, under the new regime, is now the resort of the refined and cultivated. Much as we may admire the new system, it never can with all its apparatus be incorporated into our school system. Every practical teacher knows that there are insurmountable difficulties in introducing into our public schools apparatus of any kind, except where a room is appropriated especially to gymnastic purposes, and this we know is not practicable, and even if it were practicable, we believe that free movements without apparatus of any kind, stand preëminently as the best system for our schools, indeed, as the only system that can be introduced with any degeee of success into the school-room; hence they, and they only, can legitimately be called *school gymnastics*, and so happily are they adapted to the labors of the school-room that the question, not only of introducing, but of continuing them in our schools, is no more a matter of doubt than that Arithmetic, Geography, or any other essential branch of education should have its appropriate place in our school system. The use of apparatus of any kind is, and ever will be, a source of annoyance and torture to the teacher. We are supplied by one Creator with all the apparatus needed. "God never made his work for man to mend." Wands, bean-bags, dumb-bells, rings &c., must be bought, dropped, mislaid, lost or broken, so that when the hour of exercise comes round, numerous are the excuses why this or that one can not join the class, till the teacher becomes discouraged, and wishes he had never attempted to introduce gymnastics into his school, and in his haste condemns *all* physical exercise; while these free movements are always "on hand," and at a given signal all are ready to commence without the vexatious delay of the long preparation in distributing the apparatus, and the oft repeated "ready," and with music and song, they constitute the very poetry of motion.

A series of motions, performed in exact time, either with or without music, each pupil knowing how many movements to make with a certain limb, the precise position to take, when, where, and how to change, without dictation from the teacher, the transition from one position to another being easy and natural, will be found a most agreeable auxiliary in the school-room.

The great hindrance to the successful introduction of physical exercises into our schools has not been from a want of interest in the subject, but because we have not the inclination, hence think we have not the time to arrange a series of exercises which should be both pleasant to the spectator, and easy, agreeable, and profitable to the pupil.

The first requisite for the successful introduction of calisthenic exercises into any school is, that the teacher of the school, (not a special teacher,) should have a series of movements arranged and classified. It is folly for any teacher to attempt to have pupils perform any physical exercise with pleasure and profit, unless he has in his own mind, a well defined idea, just what movements should be made, and he himself is able to make the exact motions required.

We should have faith in the utility and practicability of any series of exercises, as fitted to answer the end desired, and then when we have become familiar with them, if we are "apt to teach" in other things, we are prepared to instruct our own pupils.

"If we want any thing done well, do it ourselves." If we don't know how, let us learn or leave. These exercises should not be taken as a mere pastime, but for the purpose of accomplishing some specific object; yet, did I know, that they had no effect upon the mental, moral, or physical well being of my pupils, I should have them practiced in my school, for the pleasure they afford, and as a relaxation from close mental application. Knowing as I do the immense good, mental and physical, to be derived from a judicious practice of free gymnastics in the school-room, I would insist that every pupil, unless disabled, should take some arranged series of exercises daily.

When these free movements are understood and comprehended by the teacher, they are ready to be practiced at any time, even in the midst of a recitation, if perchance it languishes, on account of inattention or weariness. A few moments exercise will cause the blood which has on account of close application to study, been crowding toward the brain, and causing stupor, to leap through the veins, promoting muscular development, quickening respiration and circulation, and giving the whole system life and energy. Joy reigns, the dull eye sparkles with delight, fun and frolic succeed, and the whole aspect of the room is changed, and the pupil prepared to enter upon the recitation with renewed vigor.

It needs no argument to prove that a well arranged series of free movements, persistently practiced, will not only be useful in giving proper development to the bodily powers, but they will be equally efficient in developing mental activity by inducing habits of order, and exactness in mental operations. Every position properly taken increases the influence of the will to move the muscle desired; the muscle is invigorated and the will strengthened; hence all motions should be symmetrical, uniform, precise; merely *moving* the limbs does not constitute a gymnastic exercise.

There should be a determination of the mind how a certain member of the body is to be moved to constitute a given position, and the members moving in obedience to the will, should make the predetermined position.

To raise the arm in a careless, heedless way, and let it fall as carelessly, or to thrust out the hand at random without determining beforehand, just where it should stop, and how long it should be in the transition from one point to another, can have but little effect either upon the mind or body; but when raised to a certain height, with a certain velocity and directness, as previously determined by the will, this constitutes a gymnastic position, and is beneficial; hence, precision must be exacted, and "to render any movement definite and exact, a point of departure, a point of termination, and the line through which the body or any of its parts must pass, must be clearly and precisely determined, as well as the rythm of the action itself."

Never should we leave a set of exercises till the utmost uniformity and precision is secured; so much so, that the pupils find *actual pleasure* in the perfect performance. "Whatever is worth doing at all is worth doing well." We soon become weary, *yea* disgusted with any exercise when we are conscious we do it imperfectly.

Short, active exercises, well done, will afford the greatest pleasure, and lay the foundation for successfully carrying out a well developed plan, embracing variety and system.

A proper system of school gymnastics is not confined to the mere motions of the limbs, by occasional exercise in the school-room. It is more general; it looks beyond the present out into the illimitable future; it endeavors to make man, as he is, the noblest work of God, rendering mind and body susceptible of all the power, all the perfection of which they are capable. Its great object and aim is immediate good, and prospective happiness.

Nothing is more important, or more conducive to the happiness and health of our pupils, and their progress in study, than the ordinary positions of sitting and standing which they assume in school, and certainly no habits will cling to them with greater tenacity in after life.

What volumes of wisdom in the injunction of the wise man. "Train up a child in the way he should go, and when he is old he will not depart from it."

Such being the force of habit, we ought to adopt such methods of standing and sitting as will insure for our pupils elegance of manners, and grace and dignity of carriage, combined with the best physical development.

Pupils should be required to sit in a certain position, a few minutes at a time, then change to some other, the positions being such as are adapted to their ease and comfort, and graceful and proper for them to take at all times, and in all places, instead of being permitted to loll at pleasure during school hours. Though it may seem a rigid plan thus to make pupils sit, they will not only acquiesce in the arrangement, but delight in it, on account of the uniformity and beauty; and with little effort on the part of the teacher it can be secured.

Great care should be taken with the standing and walking positions of pupils. To walk on tip-toe with hands clasped behind, though quiet may be secured, the greater good of comfort and health is sacrificed. It is impossible thus to walk erect; the head is necessarily thrown forward, the chest cramped and every motion is unnatural. The habit of having the arms folded in front either in sitting or standing is neither graceful nor healthy. Let pupils sit erect, shoulders thrown down and back, arms hanging naturally by the side or akimbo, hands resting on hips. Let them assume such attitudes as will conduce to their present comfort and future happiness. Make the child as near as possible what you would have the man or woman.

The man of erect form and commanding presence, such as a correct system of gymnastic free movements develops, is sure to make a more favorable impression in life than one of sloping form, rounded shoulders, and sunken chest. He enjoys better health, possesses increased powers for usefulness, realizes more and more that he, made in the image of God, has more for which to be grateful than he who goes with bowed head all his days.

In introducing free movements into our schools, we should guard against commencing too rapidly. Pupils are apt to begin any physical exercise too rapidly, and accelerate the movements till they become confused, and there is no definiteness in them. They should be so slow that exactness can be secured. All motions of the head should be made very slowly and with measured precision, else dizziness will be induced, rendering the movements injurious rather than beneficial.

Let the breathing be slow and deep, the lungs as fully expanded as possible, especially when any sudden outside pressure is applied to the chest. In all exercises, inhalation and exhalation should be through the nose, the proper organ of respiration. "God breathed into man's nostrils the breath of life."

Do not attempt too much at one time. Five or ten minutes is long enough ordinarily for exercise, if properly done, and if not properly done one minute is too long. If pupils have been systematically trained for any considerable time, they can and will exercise one hour with less apparent fatigue than at first, five minutes.

At first many of the lads in my school, were obliged to sit and rest after a few moments exercise; parents would call requesting me not to compel their boys to exercise, for it made them lame, and they really thought I was permanently injuring their boys; and in fact, the simple system of free movements which we had adopted was made the scape-goat upon which was laid all the aches and pains which flesh was heir to; yet with kind, judicious treatment, it has not only survived the first trial, but the very parents who at first condemned the movements are loudest now in their praise; and I know that for the past three years nothing has been more conducive to the comfort of the teacher and the benefit of the pupils, than gymnastic exercises.

I might give many examples showing the great benefit which has accrued to my pupils since the introduction of regular physical exercises into the school. One must suffice; a lad who stood at the head of his class, who had an active mental organization, but a feeble physical development, was told by his worthy mother, when he came to my room, not to join in the physical sports with the other boys. She could not, she would not, have her boy ruined to gratify any man's whims. I saw the father and mother and tried to reason with them, endeavored to show them that judicious exercise was just what their son needed. No, it was a hobby of mine, and I had better try the system with my own children. When I told them it really did other boys good, made them better and happier, they replied that their son was not like other boys. These parents are not alone in the estimate of their children. Every parent thinks his child is an exception to the general rule. These kind parents said their boy took no interest in play at home, had no desire to play with boys on the street, took no delight in the usual sports of boyhood, but was a sober, noble, manly boy, caring most for his books; he needed very tender care, our calisthenic movements were too severe. I loved that boy, as I love all my boys, and I was determined, if possible to save him from an early grave. He had, before coming to my room, been obliged to be absent much of the time on account of his health, and it seemed to me that unless he would exercise with other boys he could not complete his school course; I believed the positions as taken by others would really be a "movement cure" for him, and by much persuasion he was allowed to practice with the other members of the class. He soon showed signs of improvement, became lively and happy, and during his last school year, never neglected to exercise with his class; he was not tardy a moment nor absent a day during the entire year, increased his chest measurement more than three inches during the year, never studied so hard, never recited so well, and never was more happy, than when, with the greatest enthusiasm he joined in physical sports. And when that good mother took me by the hand as that noble, lively, manly boy of hers left my school, with the Franklin medal on his neck, an honor to any school, and a praise to any teacher, she thanked me for the interest I had taken in her boy, and especially was grateful because I had compelled him to join in our gymnastic exercises; and but a few days since the father of the lad told me that he stood at the head of his class in a well known literary institution, was a strong, healthy young man, and "I attribute his success" said he, "in a great measure to those simple physical exercises which I so unjustly condemned."

I speak of what I know, and testify of what I have seen when I say that scholars are better and teachers happier by the daily practice of free gymnastics in school.

If we as teachers take this matter of physical exercise in school into serious consideration, determined to cultivate the physical well-being of our pupils as enthusiastically and systematically as we do the intellectual, we shall see even in our day, a better and happier, because a healthier race, coming on to the stage of action, and future generations will rise up and call us blessed.

# FORMATION OF MORAL CHARACTER

## THE MAIN OBJECT OF THE PUBLIC SCHOOL.*

BY M. F. COWDERY,

Superintendent of Public Schools in Sandusky, Ohio.

THERE is a sentiment of very long standing with the great public, that book knowledge is the first object of school instruction, and the formation of character, if a legitimate object of school life at all, quite subordinate to the first. We desire to have this order inverted, changed end for end in the estimation of society, and in the labors of teachers. Practically it is so changed in some cases, and by some teachers, already. It is also changed in the minds of many of the parents who send to our schools—very possibly this may be now nearly the public sentiment of the city. But if there is now this union of hearts, it is time there was a union of hands; an open, public solemnization of the contract. If the formation of character is to stand first in the order of importance, and instruction in science *second*, and this by common consent of the people, teachers will be relieved of some embarrassment, and will know more definitely how to expend their strength with their pupils, if the sentiment is authoritatively recognized. It would be very easy to show that it is the true doctrine to adopt, but I trust that before this audience such a proposition needs no argument.

I have another sentiment to propose, which may or may not be received with the same unanimity. It is, that the right formation of character should be the chief end of school instruction for a child. It is simply carrying the former proposition to its logical conclusions, and yet, stated in this form, it may not receive the full assent of those who have not given the subject special attention. I offer it here this morning, however, not as a mere speculative belief, but as a practical question of the gravest importance to the school interests of the city, and if this is really the right position to be taken for common school instruction, I desire that the same may be distinctly avowed and our schools placed squarely upon it as early as practicable. I ask your careful consideration of the following statements and explanations regarding the proposed change:—First, it is not

* An Address to Teachers and Citizens, Sandusky, Ohio, March 3, 1866.

intended or believed that instruction from books will be any less in quantity or quality than now. It would be simply zeal without knowledge, to undertake to form a child's character without giving him something to do. It is the special province of all wise instruction to arouse the sluggish to activity, and then to keep such and all others most diligently employed. This, without reference to choice, becomes a pure necessity, if the teacher would keep temptation and wrong-doing at a safe distance from his pupils. Next, it is not contemplated that peculiarities of religious creeds shall in any manner mingle with the proposed better formation of character. While the foundation principles of integrity and purity must be drawn from the Scriptures, and can by no possibility be drawn from any other source, these may be instilled into the hearts of children without giving offense to any right-minded parent. For, surely, no father can desire to see his son grow up utterly outside of all the precepts and influences of Christianity, soon to be shipwrecked, and a nuisance to the world. And if, in the depths of his depravity and hostility to revealed truth, he *should* so wish, is there any good reason why his desire should be gratified? Our city authorities do not allow a material nuisance to be kept, even a few hours, on any man's premises. Is there any greater abridgment of civil or religious liberty in restraining a man from turning a moral nuisance loose upon community, to strew desolation and ruin in his path until an indignant public shuts him in prison, or death ends his career? It may be well further to remark, that no sudden or violent changes are contemplated in the school instruction, by the adoption of the principle proposed. While a change in the direction of the teacher's labor is expected at some time and to some extent, this change must be gradual, so that all duties and labors shall harmonize.

Next, let us thread out in practice some of the results of a general public recognition of the doctrine, that the right formation of character is the *chief* end of school instruction. In the administration of school discipline teachers meet with cases of vicious conduct, sometimes restricted to one or two pupils, and sometimes amounting to clanship and threatening to undermine the authority of the teacher, or to exert a demoralizing influence upon the school, and yet there is such a sort of *surface* civility that no investigation may be undertaken or, if undertaken, the teacher is at once reminded by the offenders, and probably by their parents, that the teacher's duty in the school-room extends simply to *giving instruction* and *keeping order*. It would be some satisfaction at least, in such cases, that the teacher should be able to point to well-settled authority to probe all disorderly conduct to the bottom, and when sullen and sympathizing witnesses are asked to give information, that they shall not evade the command by any direct or indirect appeal to want of rightful authority of the teacher to demand his testimony. Make *character* the *chief end* of school instruction, and the rights and duties of all parties become clear in such cases.

Again, let us see how our teachers and grades of schools would stand in relation to each other, under the proposed new arrangement. If the time shall ever come when there shall be any marked success in building up strength and solidity of character, that work must be commenced in the primary school, and the teacher must enter her school-room with the clear and explicit understanding that this is to be the first and chief end of all her labors, and all other things subordinate. She must clearly understand that the first great work for the child *must* be done in her school-room. That it will be a sad and sorrowful task for the teacher in the grade above, to find two years lost, *far worse than lost*, to the child in its moral training. All this must not only be distinctly understood as a matter of *theory*, but it must enter into all her plans of labor in the school-room, and into all her convictions of duty and usefulness for this world. And she must hold herself responsible, other teachers must hold her responsible, and the public must hold her responsible, that all that the circumstances will allow her to do for the right training of her pupils must be done.

But how shall such work be commenced? First, it would be necessary for the teacher, as early and as rapidly as possible, to become personally and intimately acquainted with each pupil. The family circumstances and the family discipline at home should, as far as possible, be at once understood. Then the habits of the child, its health, its peculiar disposition, its associates *in* school and *out* of school, should be inquired into, so that, besides all general methods employed to make children dutiful, the teacher can treat each individual pupil as its case may require. Using the general methods now common in our schools, for interesting all the children in right conduct, more frequently, and more faithfully and spiritedly, will be the first work to be done. Very probably, in a school of fifty scholars, there might be groups of six to ten that might need similar words of reproof or encouragement, by themselves; and again, half that number might require specific instruction of another sort.

Lastly, *each individual* pupil should be a subject of *special study* by the teacher, for each will probably need specific instruction of some sort, if not for any present wrong-doing, then to fortify against temptation in the future. But in what shall the instruction consist? First, the child should be taught unconditional submission to all proper authority; and whether there seems to be any present necessity for the lesson or not, it should be so thoroughly, so frequently, and so faithfully taught, that there never can be any *present necessity* for teaching it.

Next, teach every little child the great law of *kindness.* Do not be satisfied because you see children so naturally kind to each other in their happy hours and childish sports. This is only an indication that you, primary teachers, have an easy and delightful duty before you. But just here, my dear friends, suffer me especially to admonish you, that you can not over-estimate the importance—the solemnity rather—of your position. You must assume that this out-gushing kindness of childhood may be matured into a strong, over-ruling principle, or it may fade into uncertain impulses, just as you shall permit its direction to run. You must labor with your pupils and for them, as if deliverance from a life of savage selfishness and cruelty depended wholly upon your exertions. Do not let an unkind word be uttered in your school-room or on your play-grounds; watch, and treat appropriately, all angry looks, and while, negatively, you are suppressing every thing contrary to the law of love, do all you can positively to inculcate it; suggest to them little modes of really doing kind things to each other. And do not grow weary in doing this. Keep doing yourself, and keep your children doing. Never, for a moment, suppose that your work is an insignificant one. You are teaching a great law, the law of love, the law of Heaven; joyfully and lovingly should you do this noble work.

Still farther on, teach children kindness to the unfortunate, to the stranger, to animals, in brief on this point, get as much of *heaven upon earth* into your school-rooms as you possibly can. And there is perfect truthfulness, and perfect honesty, and heroic courage to do right, to be instilled thoroughly into these little minds. And then there are some ugly wild beasts at your door to be watched, lest they devour your tender lambs—such as profanity and vulgarity. For character is first in favor now, character is to be "king" henceforth, you remember, and nothing that would harm or mar its beauty must be allowed to enter. These miniature men and women must soon go from your instruction to the next teacher above, and, still retaining their artlessness and innocence, you must pass them up, perfect little patterns of propriety, perfect little heroes for the truth and for right.

This is a slight sketch of the change of labor and relations for a single grade. It would, of course, be understood that the successive grades above should be responsible, *first*, for securely retaining all that had been acquired through such watchfulness and faithfulness, in the school below. And here grave responsibilities open upon us. For, with each ascending grade, the advancing age of the pupil requires a new exertion of restraining and controlling power to hold him steadfastly in the paths of uprightness. And if this *is not done*, what shall be said of the teacher or grade where the failure was made? If, after the work in the lower grades had been faithfully, skillfully, nobly done, such a calamity should occur midway between the Primary and High School, what a shock would thereby be given to our system! What breaking of arteries or snapping of nerves would produce such a sensation? How could society be compensated for such losses? How could the teachers of the grades below find consolation for their lost labor and treasures? When the schools below fail to give each their proper quantity and quality of instruction in the sciences, the schools above are seriously and unjustly embarrassed by the culpable neglect. But what shall be thought of offering to the higher grades *damaged characters* and corrupting influences? And if the grand failure should occur at the High School—if, standing at the head of the system, it should have low conceptions of its position or its duties, or, still further, knowing its responsibilities, it should fail to meet them, and the good principles which had been so assiduously, so tenderly, through long years, *so faithfully* inwrought, be there dissipated, scattered to the four winds of heaven, *how* should the loss be estimated? If it were the sentiment of our people, that the crowning excellence of our free public school system was to prepare noble men and women for our country and the world, how keenly would the disappointment be felt if there should be found want of skill, want of profound sense of obligation,—want of complete and triumphant success in the particular department where all these qualities were demanded in the highest perfection!

I have hastily glanced at a few points of advantage and changes of relations among our school grades and teachers, which the proposed end of school instruction would involve. There are also some other important relations to be stated, some other advantages to be gained, and also some further objections to be met. The more full discussion of these topics may be given when it shall seem to be demanded.

It will be seen that I am now seeking *a new contract*, or rather *new conditions* to a former contract, between teachers and the public.

To be binding as an agreement they must, of course, receive the assent of both parties. I have no authority for saying that they will be entirely acceptable to either. I suspect teachers will feel a reluctance to assume such new responsibilities, not from any want of right disposition, but from the real magnitude of the undertaking, and from a painful consciousness of want of the necessary preparation and power to do such work. Truly, teachers, the right formation of character for this generation of the children of our city is an enterprise full of difficulties and discouragements, and you *must have power*, directing, controlling power, or you can do nothing of this labor. If you are to stand by the *side* of the parent, in *place of the parent*, often even *above the parent*, in the education of his children, you must have *first* the power which genuine affection gives. Children delight in an atmosphere of affection. They would instinctively exchange houses of marble for cabins of logs or clay, to dwell with hearts as gentle and loving as their own. Sparkling gems, or the richest attire, would be worthless to them as pebbles or rags, if counted against a mother's, or sister's, or brother's love. It is fixed in the deep counsels of Infinite Wisdom, that children shall be led by affection, be taught early obedience to duty, not through reasoning faculties, just feebly dawning, but through the affections now glowing in full sunlight, and there must be no thought of evasion of this divine law. Teachers, as well as parents, then, *must love children.* But surely, every body must love, or *can learn to love*, little children. And in loving them *wisely* and well, we may fashion their hearts, and habits, and tempers after any model we will. Within certain limits, and for certain ends, *knowledge* is power to the teacher in forming character, as well as developing the intellect. If you need more of such power, the world of science and the whole field of history are open to you. Take as much as you need or as you please.

Again, right is might, truth is might, and the soft-haired boy, as well as the gray-haired man, must bow to their power. Teach the child or the young man the letter and spirit of the golden rule; bury deep in his heart the great principle of love to God and love to man, and a power mightier than the silent forces of creation continually operates to ameliorate his nature and guide his wayward steps. Explain, patiently and gently, how the Eternal Father loves and approves thoughts and deeds of kindness, even in children, and teach him, by skillful modes of illustration, how He hates, with an infinite, eternal hatred, all forms of oppression, and no future arguments, however crafty or profound, can dislodge this conviction from his heart. Bring to his full comprehension, often and faithfully, the truth, that for all his wrong-doing, both open and secret, conscience will be a swift witness of his guilt, and for all this guilt there must be accountability, and you throw around him a restraining power such as no human wisdom can devise. For truth is mighty, far mightier than all other instrumentalities that mortals are permitted to wield, and in its judicious employment we may proceed with the same confidence in laying the foundations of character that we look for mental development to follow mental exertion, or the seasons to go and return, or the green herbage to spring up under the genial sunshine.

Again, purity, personal purity of heart and life, is power—power perhaps slightly understood and appreciated in this life, yet ever silently, under Providence, working out the grandest and noblest results. Faith, true Christian faith, is power, giving to the little child or the feeble invalid a might which the strongest intellect may not possess. And still further, daily communion with the Source of all Power imparts to the feeblest intellect attributes of sovereignty. How often, by this means, does the humblest mortal "move the hand that rules the world!" How seeming impossibilities become pleasant pastimes under the friendly direction of an omnipotent guide! How, by communion with the High and Holy One, have the weak surpassed the wise in wisdom, or the keenest trials ended in songs of triumph! That slave-prince, Joseph, was mightier than all the monarchs of Egypt, because he was in habitual communion with the Sovereign of all Sovereigns; because the Eternal Jehovah was his daily refuge, and underneath him were the Everlasting Arms. There was no "smell of fire" on the garments of those three Jewish captives who were thrown into the "burning fièry furnace," because the "form of the Fourth" was there, and the "*form of the Fourth*" was there because His infinite power and loving presence had been invoked for this hour of terrible ordeal.

Self-denial is power. Self-sacrificing affection is power—power in the lowliest stations of life, and power in the most exalted, power at the humblest fireside, and power among the nations of the earth. Observe how it gives the mother her irresistible influence and her imperishable memory in the family circle. How it gives the missionary respect and kind regards among brutalized and depraved tribes of men all unused to words of kindness. How it every where subdues the coarsest natures and chastens and refines the gentlest hearts. *Self-sacrificing affection!* What enmity or depravity *can it not* conquer? How surely, in God's good time, it must change the face of the world? How its brightest manifestation eighteen hundred years ago shines clearer and stronger through the lapse of centuries! How an innocent, unresisting personage, by suffering a death of terrible anguish, singly for the good of others, has awakened emotions never before excited in this world, and constrained allegiance to which earth and time can fix no bounds.

But *humility* too is power, patience is power—wonderful power to the teacher. In short, every Christian grace and virtue is power. *Be a thoroughly good man or a good woman* and your whole life shall be a *life of power*. Your words, your examples, your teachings, shall be powerful for good. And if to Christian virtues and graces you add an earnest purpose to fashion youthful character after celestial models, your efforts can *by no possibility* be in vain.

If, after proper consultation and reflection, our citizens decide to charge you with the duty of laying the foundations of integrity and uprightness more deeply and strongly with the children than heretofore, do not, my dear friends, shrink from the work on account of its difficulties or its magnitude. Modestly, hopefully, accept the trust. Take these children, *all of them*, the rich man's and the poor man's, lovingly to your hearts, and train them for God and our country. The *end* of the labor you nor I may ever live to see. The *beginning* only is for us and in prayerfully and perseveringly beginning it you shall find "strength equal to your day." With an earnest purpose to be successful, you shall find difficulties vanish before you like mists before the morning sunshine. My sister, my brother, you shall not meet these solemn responsibilities single-handed and alone. You shall not give your manly strength, nor your health and womanly grace and beauty, to this great public service, while others may revel in freedom and sunshine, without a full equivalent. Good men and women will sympathize with you and encourage you. Fathers and mothers will bless you. Children, many children, shall love and honor you. Angelic spirits shall look lovingly, joyfully, upon your labors, from the abodes above. The blessed Redeemer shall be ever at your side—nearer than all earthly friends. The Infinite Father himself shall shower his blessings upon you, and hereafter, in the presence of the countless millions who shall stand before Him, he shall say to each of you, "Well done, good and faithful servant, enter thou into the joy of the Lord."

# DR. HENRY BARNARD'S
## STANDARD EDUCATIONAL PUBLICATIONS.

---

Official Reports—as Superintendent of Common Schools in Connecticut, 1 vol.; as Commissioner of Public Schools, R. I., 1 vol.; as National Commissioner of Education, 3 vols. $4.50 per volume,

Connecticut Common School Journal, 1838–42, 4 vols. $4.00. *Second Series*, 1851–54.

Journal of R. I. Institute of Instruction, 1845–48, 3 vols. $3.75.

The American Journal of Education—from 1856 to 1873. 24 Volumes (over 20,000 octavo pages), with 800 wood cuts of structures for educational purposes, and 125 portraits of eminent educators and teachers. *Price*, $120 in cloth; $132 in half goat; Single Volume in cloth $5.00, in half goat $5.50; Current Volume in numbers (1875-6—*International Series*, Vol. I.), $4.00. Single number, $1.25.

The International Series will complete the publication as projected by the Editor in 1850 and will embrace the Treatises (1 and 2) in the Plan submitted by him to the American Association for the Advancement of Education in 1854 on the

History of Education: or the Progressive Development of Schools of different kinds and grades, and other Formal Agencies of Instruction for children, youths, and adults in different countries, with a General Survey of National Systems in 1876–7.

☞ *The following Treatises were originally published as separate chapters in the American Journal of Education, but were prepared with special reference to being ultimately issued in the form in which they now appear.* 1876.

National Education: General and Special. 10 Volumes.

1. *Elementary and Secondary Instruction* in the German States: Anhalt, Austria, Baden Bavaria, Brunswick, Hanover, Hesse-Cassel, Hesse-Darmstadt, Liechtenstein, Lippe-Detmold, Lippe-Schaumberg, Luxemburg and Limberg, Mecklenburg-Schwerin, Mecklenburg-Strelitz, Nassau, Oldenburg, Prussia, Reuss, Saxony, Saxe-Altenburg, Saxe-Coburg, Saxe-Meiningen, Saxe-Weimar, Waldeck, Wurtemberg, and the Free Cities, with a general summary of the Educational Systems and Statistics for the whole of Germany, 1871. 856 pages. Price $5.50.

2. *Elementary and Secondary Instruction* in Switzerland (each of the 23 Cantons), France, Belgium, Holland, Denmark, Norway and Sweden, Russia, Turkey, Greece, Italy, Portugal and Spain, 1872. 800 pages. Price $5.50. *Revised Edition.* 1876.

3. *Contributions to the History and Statistics of Common or Public Schools* (*Elementary and High*), *Academies, Colleges, and Professional Schools* in the United States, and other American States. 900 pages. Price, $5.50.

4. *Elementary, Secondary, and Superior Instruction* in England, Scotland, and Ireland, and the different dependencies of Great Britain. Two Parts—$3.50 each.

(1.) Elementary, Parochial, and National Schools, including Training Colleges, and Industrial and Reformatory Institutions, with the views of Practical Teachers on the Subjects and Methods of Primary Instruction.

(2.) Grammar, Burgh, and Endowed Schools, and the Universites of Oxford, Cambridge, London, Durham, St. Andrews, Aberdeen, Glasgow, Edinburgh, Dublin, and Queen's; with the views of eminent authorities on Higher Studies.

5. *Superior Instruction in Different Countries.*—Ancient Greece, Rome, and Alexandria; Early Christian Schools; Medieval Universities; and Systems and Institutions of Higher Education in European and American States, 1876. 960 pages. $5.50.

6. *Scientific and Industrial Education* in Austria, Baden, Bavaria, Brunswick, Free Cities, Hanover, Nassau, Prussia, Saxony, Saxon Principalities, Wurtemberg, France, Belgium, Holland, Denmark, Norway, Sweden, Russia, Switzerland, Italy. 800 pages. Price $5.50.

7. *Special Instruction in Science and the Arts in Great Britain.* 256 pages. $3.00.

8. *Schools and Colleges of Science, Agriculture, and the Mechanic Arts in the United States.* In press. $3.00. *Revised Edition.* 1876.

9. *Military and Naval Schools* in France, Prussia, Bavaria, Italy, Russia, Holland, England, and the United States. 960 pages. $6.00.

10. *Professional Training and Improvement* in (1.) Teaching; (2.) Theology; (3.) Law (4.) Medicine, &c., *in Different Countries.* 850 pages. $5.50. *Revised Edition.* 1876.

# BARNARD'S NATIONAL PEDAGOGY.

AND

## LIBRARY OF PRACTICAL EDUCATION.

BOOKS FOR PARENTS, TEACHERS, SCHOOL OFFICERS, AND STUDENTS.

---

National Pedagogy and Library of Practical Education:

1. Studies and Conduct: Letters, Essays, and Suggestions on the Relative Value of Studies, Books and the best Methods of Reading, Manners and the Art of Conversation, the Acquisition and True Uses of Wealth, and the Conduct of Life generally. 564 pages. $3.50. 1875.

The best evidence of the intrinsic value of these Letters, Suggestions, and Essays, is in the names of their authors—Addison, Aiken, Bacon, Barrow, Bodleigh, Brougham, Burleigh, Bulwer, Burns, Carlyle, Channing, Chatham, Chesterfield, Collingwood, De Quincey, Dupanloup, Everett, Faraday, Franklin, Froude, Gladstone, Grimke, Hall, Hamilton, Herschel, Humboldt, Huxley, Jameson, Jerome, Locke, Lowe, Macaulay, Mackintosh, Mill, Milton, More, Niebuhr, Newman, Pitt, Pope, Potter, Raumer, Sidney, Southey, South, Swift, Taylor, Temple, Tyndal, Whately, Wordsworth, and others.

2. Primary Schools and Elementary Instruction: Object Teaching and Oral Lessons on Social Science and Common Things, with the Principles and Practice of Elementary Instruction in the Primary, Model, and Training Schools of Great Britain. *Revised Edition.*—544 pp. $3.00.

Ashburton, Barnard (Sketch of Systems of Public Elementary Schools in England, Scotland, and Ireland), Bell, Brougham, Currie, Dunn, Ellis, Hay, Keenan, Knight, Lancaster, Macaulay, Mayo, Morrison, Ross, Shields, Stow, Sullivan, Tainsh, Wilderspin, Young.

3. English Pedagogy—Old and New: or, Treatises and Thoughts on Education, the School, and the Teacher. *First Series.* 480 pages. *Second Series.* 608 pages. $3.50 each. 1876.

*First Series.*—Ascham, Bacon, Cowley, Cowper, Crabbe, Coleridge, Fuller, Gray, Hartlib, Hood, Locke, Milton, Petty, Shenstone, Spencer, Whately, Wotton.

*Second Series.*—Arnold, Brinsly, Calderwood, Colet, Collis, Coote, Defoe, Donaldson, Duff, Elyot, Evelyn, Goldsmith, Hoole, Johnson, Jolly, Lyttleton, Macaulay, Mulcaster, Parker, Parr Payne, Pope, Quick, Smith, South, Southey, Steele, Strype, Todhunter, Wase, Webster, Wolsey.

4. American Pedagogy: Contributions to the Principles and Methods of Education, by Barnard, Burgess, Bushnell, Channing, Cowdery, Dickinson, Doane, Everett, Fairchild, Hart, Hopkins, Huntington, Mann, Page, Philbrick, Pierce, Potter, Sheldon, Wayland, and Wilbur, First Series. *Revised Ed.* 576 pages. $3.50.

5. German Pedagogy: Views of German Educators and Teachers on the Principles of Education, and Methods of Instruction for Schools of different Grades. *Revised Edition.* 640 pages. $3.50. 1876. Abbenrode, Benneke, Diesterweg, Fichte, Frœbel, Gœthe, Graser, Hentschel Hencomp, Herbart, Hentz, Jacobs, Meierotto, Raumer, Riecke, Rosenkranz, Ruthardt, Wichern.

6. Pestalozzi and Swiss Pedagogy: Memoir, and Educational Principles, Methods, and Influence of John Henry Pestalozzi, and Biograpical Sketches of several of his Assistants and Disciples: together with Selections from his Publications, and accounts of Schools and Teachers in Switzerland. *Revised Edition.* 656 pages. $3.50.

7. German Teachers and Educational Reformers: Memoirs of Eminent Teachers and Educators with contributions to the History of Education in Germany. 1876. 586 pages. $3.50.

Early Christian Teachers, Basedow, Comenius, Erasmus, Franke, Hieronymians, Luther, Melancthon, Ratich, Sturm, Trotzendorf, Felbiger, Kindermann, Frederic II., Maria Theresa, etc.

8. French Teachers, Schools, and Pedagogy—Old and New. 648 pages. $3.50.

Early Christian Teachers and Schools; Jesuits, Christian Brothers and other Teaching Orders; Rabelais, Ramus, Montaigne, Port Royalists, Fenelon, Rollin, Montesquieu, Rousseau; Talleyrand, Condorcet, Daunau, Napoleon; Oberlin, Cuvier, Cousin, Guizot, Ravaisson, Remaset, Marcel, Duruy, LeVerrier, Dupanloup, Mayer, Marbeau, Wilm, and others.

9. English Teachers, Educators, and Promoters of Education. 556 pages. $3.50.

10. American Teachers, Educators, and Benefactors of Education, with 130 Portraits. 5 vols. $3.50 per volume.

11. American Graded Public Schools, with Plans of School-houses and Equipment and Regulations for Schools in Cities. 556 pages. $3.50.

12. Aphorisms and Suggestions on Education and Methods of Instruction—Ancient and Modern. $3.00.

13. School Codes.—Constitutional Provisions respecting Education, State School Codes, and City School Regulations. $3.00.

14. School Architecture: Principles, Plans and Specifications for structures for educa t onal purposes *Revised Edition*—800 pages. $5.00.

# CLASSIFIED INDEX

TO

## BARNARD'S AMERICAN JOURNAL OF EDUCATION.

VOLUMES I. TO XVI.

### CLASSIFICATION OF SUBJECTS.

## CHAPTER I. GENERAL PRINCIPLES AND HISTORY OF EDUCATION.

## II. INDIVIDUAL VIEWS AND SPECIAL SYSTEMS OF EDUCATION.

## III. STUDIES AND METHODS; SCHOOL ORGANIZATION AND DISCIPLINE.

## IV. TEACHERS; NORMAL AND MODEL SCHOOLS; TEACHERS' INSTITUTES.

## V. STATE AND NATIONAL SYSTEMS.

## VI. SECONDARY, INTERMEDIATE AND ACADEMICAL SCHOOLS.

## VII. UNIVERSITY AND COLLEGE EDUCATION.



## VIII. SCHOOLS OF SCIENCE AND ARTS; MUSEUMS, &C.

## IX. MILITARY AND NAVAL EDUCATION.



## X. PREVENTIVE AND REFORMATORY EDUCATION.



## XI. EDUCATION FOR DEAF-MUTES, BLIND AND IDIOTS.



## XII. MORAL AND RELIGIOUS EDUCATION; DENOMINATIONAL SCHOOLS.

## XIII. EDUCATION AND SCHOOLS FOR FEMALES.



## XIV. PHYSICAL EDUCATION.



## XV. SUPPLEMENTARY, SELF AND HOME EDUCATION.



## XVI. EDUCATIONAL ASSOCIATIONS.

## XVII. PHILOLOGY AND BIBLIOGRAPHY.



## XVIII. SCHOOL ARCHITECTURE.

## XIX. EDUCATIONAL ENDOWMENTS AND BENEFACTORS.



## XX. MISCELLANEOUS.

## XXI. EDUCATIONAL BIOGRAPHY AND LIST OF PORTRAITS.

BIOGRAPHICAL SKETCHES.

PORTRAITS.

# GENERAL INDEX TO NATIONAL SERIES

OF

# BARNARD'S AMERICAN JOURNAL OF EDUCATION.

[VOLUME XVII—XXIV, ENTIRE SERIES.]

*With References to the Classified Index to Volumes I—XVI, and the General Index to Volumes I—V, including subjects which will be still further treated in the International Series (I. S.)*

---

Notice of any important omission, or error of reference, in this Index, will be thankfully received by the Editor. P. O. BOX U, HARTFORD, CONN.

ASCHAM, BACON, WOTTON, MILTON, LOCKE, AND SPENCER, ON EDUCATION. Edited by HENRY BARNARD, LL. D. 1862.

ENGLISH PEDAGOGY: or Education, the School, and the Teacher in English Literature—in a Series of Papers prepared for "*The American Journal of Education.*" Edited by HENRY BARNARD, LL. D.

# INDEX TO ENGLISH PEDAGOGY.

ENGLISH PEDAGOGY—OLD AND NEW: or, Treatises and Thoughts on Education, the School, and the Teacher in English Literature. *Second Series.* Republished from Barnard's American Journal of Education. 608 pages. $3.50. 1876.

# CONTENTS.

## ENGLISH PEDAGOGY—SECOND SERIES.

ENGLISH PEDAGOGY—OLD AND NEW: or, Treatises and Thoughts on Education, the School, and the Teacher in English Literature. *Second Series.* Republished from Barnard's American Journal of Education. 608 pages. Brown & Gross: Hartford. 1876. $3.50.

# INDEX

TO

## ENGLISH PEDAGOGY—OLD AND NEW.

www.ingramcontent.com/pod-product-compliance
Lightning Source LLC
LaVergne TN
LVHW021105110826
845150LV00001B/174